MICROCOMPUTER ARCHITECTURE AND PROGRAMMING

MICROCOMPUTER ARCHITECTURE AND PROGRAMMING

JOHN F. WAKERLY

Stanford University

JOHN WILEY & SONS, New York • Chichester • Brisbane • Toronto

Library of Congress Cataloging in Publication Data:

Wakerly, John F.
    Microcomputer architecture and programming.

    Includes bibliographical references and
index.
    1. Microcomputers—Programming.   2. Computer
architecture.   I. Title.
QA76.6.W325   001.64'2   80-29060
ISBN 0-471-05232-9

Printed in the United States of America

10 9 8 7 6

***To Regina Marie**
who was conceived at about
the same time as this book*

PREFACE

The "microcomputer revolution" is best understood by realizing that a microcomputer is just an inexpensive computer. The basic principles of computer organization and programming have changed very little as a result of this revolution. The major impact of the proliferation of microcomputers has been to heighten the need for programmers who understand basic computer principles and who know how to apply them.

The purpose of this book is to explain basic computer architecture and programming using microcomputers as examples. We emphasize basic principles rather than details of a particular microcomputer's instruction set. Still, we must use *some* specific computer organization for examples. Therefore, we explain basic principles using two "hypothetical" computer processors whose instructions and features are subsets of two real processors, the Motorola 6809 and the Zilog Z8000. After covering the basic principles, we present detailed case studies of seven contemporary microprocessors.

The book is organized into three parts. Part 1 contains four chapters of introductory material that each reader may or may not have studied before. The heart of the book is Part 2, eight chapters that describe basic principles of computer organization and assembly language programming, using the two hypothetical processors as examples. Using these basic principles, Part 3 gives reasonably detailed but concise descriptions of seven important contemporary microprocessor architectures: DEC PDP-11 and LSI-11, Motorola 68000, Zilog Z8000, Texas Instruments 9900, Motorola 6809, Intel 8086, and Intel MCS-48.

USES OF THIS BOOK

This book is suitable for an introductory course on (micro)computer organization and assembly language programming, typically the third programming course in a computer science or computer engineering curriculum.

(The first two courses usually cover programming principles in a high-level language such as Pascal or FORTRAN.) Such an introductory course would make use of the basic principles in Parts 1 and 2 of this book and would also refer to one of the detailed processor descriptions in Part 3. This book treats all of the topics recommended for course CS 3 and stresses techniques of good programming style as recommended in the ACM's Curriculum '78 [*Comm. ACM*, Vol. 22, No. 3, March 1979, pp. 147–166].

The development of concepts in Parts 1 and 2, and the consistent use of these concepts to describe different processors in Part 3, make this book also suitable for a course on "comparative computer architectures" or "micro-computer architectures." Such a course examines and compares the structure and features of several different computers.

A third use of this book is as a reference, both by students who have used it in a course and by practicing computer professionals. The book is organized into well-structured topic areas to facilitate reference use, and there is a comprehensive index as well.

CHAPTER DESCRIPTIONS

Chapters 1 through 4 comprise Part 1, introductory and remedial material that is used in the remainder of the book.

- Chapter 1 defines terms and discusses fundamental concepts, so that a serious student without a previous or recent programming course can understand the rest of the book.

- Chapter 2 describes Pascal, the most popular structured high-level language for microcomputers. The remainder of the book uses Pascal both for documenting algorithms and for defining the internal operations of a computer, and so a reading knowledge of simple Pascal programs is required. This chapter can serve either as a review of Pascal or as a quick introduction.

- Chapter 3 introduces data structures including arrays, stacks, and queues; these data structures are used later in descriptions of several aspects of computer organization and programming.

- Chapter 4 presents basic concepts of the number systems and arithmetic operations used in typical computers.

Part 2 describes basic principles that are applicable to all computers, using two "hypothetical" computer processors whose instructions and features are subsets of two real processors: the H6809, a subset of the Motorola 6809; and the H8000, a subset of the Zilog Z8000.

- Chapter 5 describes the basic instructions, organization, and assembly language of the two hypothetical processors. An optional section on a hypothetical stack machine is also included for completeness.

- Chapter 6 describes the concepts of assemblers and assembly language programming in more detail, including topics of relocation and linking, position-independent code, macros, and structured assembly languages.

- Chapter 7 is an encyclopedia of addressing modes, describing all of the popular modes that are used in different processors. Memory mapping and memory management are also covered.

- Chapter 8 explains the formats and effects of the most popular computer operation types.

- Chapter 9 begins with a discussion of procedures and functions in Pascal and then relates these high-level concepts to subroutine calling and parameter-passing conventions in assembly language programs. It also covers concepts of recursion and coroutines.

- Chapter 10 discusses input/output architecture and related software structures.

- Chapter 11 covers interrupts, traps, and DMA, and introduces the advanced concepts of processes, shared data structures, and reentrancy.

- Chapter 12 contains often-neglected introductory material on software engineering and the program development process.

Part 3 consists of Chapters 13 through 19. Each chapter describes the architecture of a specific microcomputer, drawing on basic principles that were presented in Part 2. It is quite appropriate that the first architecture covered is that of the PDP-11 and LSI-11, because all contemporary microcomputers have borrowed ideas from the PDP-11. Other processors that are covered in detail are Motorola 68000, Zilog Z8000, Texas Instruments 9900, Motorola 6809, Intel 8086, and Intel MCS-48. Each chapter in Part 3 consists of six sections that parallel material that was developed in Part 2:

- Basic Organization

- Assembly Language

- Addressing

- Operations

- Sample Programs

- Input/Output, Interrupts, and Traps

The processor descriptions in Part 3 are fairly detailed, so that readers can make intelligent judgments about the processors. For example, all of the addressing modes and instructions of each processor are explained. However, in the interest of brevity not all of the details of assembly language, instruction side-effects, and development system operation are included. Also, bus structures, timing, interfacing arrangements, and other hardware details are not included. A reader who wishes to write and run programs for one of Part 3 processors may wish to supplement the material in this book with documentation from the processor's manufacturer.

Three appendices appear at the end of the book. Appendix A describes the ASCII character code and special characters used in CRT terminals. Appendix B describes extensions to Pascal for bit manipulation; however, these extensions are also explained in Chapters 4, 5, and 8 where they are used. Appendix C describes the asynchronous serial communication protocol and interfaces commonly used with CRT terminals.

HOW THIS BOOK WAS PREPARED

The manuscript drafts for this book were prepared using word-processing programs on my own microcomputer system. The final manuscript stored in my microcomputer system was translated by a program into a form that could be entered directly into a commercial phototypesetter to produce typeset galleys, avoiding a separate, error-prone rekeying process. A similar approach using large computers has been used in the past by many computer science authors, including two who developed their own word processing tools: Donald E. Knuth [*TEX and Metafont*, Digital Press, 1979] and Brian W. Kernighan [*Software Tools*, Addison-Wesley, 1976; *The Elements of Programming Style*, Second Edition, McGraw-Hill, 1978; and *The C Programming Language*, Prentice-Hall, 1978]. However, I believe that this book is one of the first to be produced using a low-cost microcomputer system. Some readers may be interested in additional details of the book preparation process discussed below.

My microcomputer system is a Southwest Technical Products 6800-based system with 48K bytes of memory, a Smoke Signal Broadcasting BFD-68 triple minifloppy disk system and DOS68 operating system, an ADM-3A CRT terminal, a Diablo 1620 daisy-wheel printer, and an ancient papertape reader/punch. The complete system hardware cost was well under $10,000 in 1978.

The three most important programs that I have used in this project are a text editor, a text formatter, and a typesetting translator. In the last two years I have spent more time "talking to" the text editor program than any other program or person, and so I am lucky to have had a delightful screen-oriented text editor to work with. The editor is called 6800 PIE and was written by Tom Crosley. PIE stands for Programma International Editor; Tom has also written a version for the Apple II computer called "Apple PIE."

To write the book, I used the editor to produce text files that contain unformatted text and formatting commands such as "begin paragraph," "begin section heading," "change font," and so on. The unformatted text files were processed by a formatting program to produce the formatted text. The formatting program, based on the NROFF formatter on Bell Laboratories' UNIX system, was written by Technical Systems Consultants for the 6800 and enhanced by me to handle book formats and typesetting parameters.

The text formatter is macro-driven, so that the effects of each formatting command are defined by a macro file. I was able to create two macro files, one of which produced formatted manuscripts that could be printed on my Diablo printer, the other of which produced formatted text that could be massaged by my typesetting translator program and fed to a phototypesetter.

Thus, I was able to simulate the ultimate typeset text on printed draft manuscripts that were used by hundreds of students. Since the typeset text was produced from the the same unformatted text file as the draft manuscripts, all errors found in the draft manuscripts could be corrected in the unformatted text file with the assurance that (almost) no new errors would be introduced in the typesetting process. This has yielded a very accurate typeset book (welll, ass acurate as de authers orignal manuscrapt).

You may recall that my computer system hardware includes an (ugh!) papertape reader/punch. It turns out that the typesetting industry is fairly slow to change, and that the only standard input medium is paper tape with a bizarre 6-bit character coding called TTS. Thus, I had to write a program to translate from ASCII to TTS, and punch 6-level paper tapes to feed into the phototypesetter. The tapes turned out to be the weak link in the system; papertape errors seemed to occur at the rate of about one per 10–20 book pages. Because of the effectiveness of student proofreaders on the manuscript drafts, the typeset manuscript was near-perfect except for papertape errors. As a result, it was impractical to motivate a proofreader who is used to finding a couple of keying errors per page to look for one papertape error every 10–20 pages. Therefore I must apologize for the errors that remain, be they paper-tape errors or otherwise.

ERRORS

It has been said that there is no such thing as a completely debugged program, only a program with undiscovered bugs. The same thing is true of books. I am anxious to learn of errors in this book so that they may be fixed in future printings and editions. Therefore I will pay $3 to the first finder of each undiscovered error, be it technical, typographical, or otherwise. Please send your comments to me at Computer Systems Laboratory, Stanford University, Stanford CA 94305.

Any reader can request an up-to-date list of discovered errors by writing to me at the above address and enclosing a stamped self-addressed envelope. Only one ounce of first class postage will be needed, I hope.

ACKNOWLEDGEMENTS

Many people deserve thanks for making this book possible. My sponsoring editor at Wiley, Gene Davenport, gets the credit (or blame) for tricking me into writing this book in the first place. He tricked me by sending me other microcomputer book proposals to review, to which I would always respond, "No, they've got it all wrong; if they were smart, they'd do it *this* way." Eventually I had to back up my reviews by actually writing a book *this* way.

Now I suppose that some other authors will review *my* book and be motivated to write their own improved versions.

Harold Stone provided thorough reviews of the outline and preliminary manuscript that helped guide this book to its final form. Comments from Joel Boney, Dave Hodges, John Hennessy, Dennis Allison, Mike Mulder, Martha Sloan, Skip Stritter, John Zolnowsky, and several anonymous reviewers were also very helpful. Hamid Nabavi painstakingly read the entire manuscript for technical accuracy and consistency, and provided dozens of corrections and improvements. I am grateful to all of these reviewers for their contributions.

Over 500 students who took Stanford's introductory computer organization and assembly language programming course in the last two years used draft manuscripts during the book's preparation. In addition to suggesting or otherwise motivating many improvements, the students spotted over 200 typographical and technical errors whose fixes are incorporated in the typeset book. Richard Beigel was the clear winner, having spotted over 40 errors.

Recently I have been giving my students an incentive of $2 for each new error they find. I offered them the option of putting their names in the preface instead of giving them money, but I had no takers. Oh well.

Thanks go to all the students who used this book with me, and to my teaching assistants Glenn Hahn, Peter Van Sickel, Helen Hunziker, Susan Roberts, and David Lakritz. Thanks also go to Marie Noelle Lu for her fine offset printing of the class notes on tight schedules. Special thanks go to Motorola for providing 6809 EXORciser development systems that were used in the class, and to the National Science Foundation for an Instructional Scientific Equipment Grant that paid for terminals and other equipment.

Most authors get few glimpses of the production aspects of book publishing, but I have been actively involved in the production of this book. Therefore, I must thank all the people of Holmes Composition for their efforts and especially Bob Holmes for helping me learn to be a typesetter (uh, a typesetter can be a person as well as a machine). Thanks also go to Linda Marcetti for her fine job of book design and layout, and to Bob Ballinger of Wiley for coordinating the production efforts.

Special thanks go to my friend Tom Crosley for finding and developing the word processing tools that I used to produce the manuscript.

When I started writing this book in November 1978, I took a six-month leave of absence from my job at BNR INC. I was going to write this and a companion volume on microcomputer hardware, all in six months! To BNR I can only say, thanks for the leave, and sorry I never made it back!

Of course I must thank my wife Kate for putting up with the late hours and occasional pressures that come with a writing project such as this. My daughter Gina, born on this date two years ago, has said more new words in the last three months than I've written, so it must be time to finish up and get this book rolling off the presses.

Mountain View, California   John F. Wakerly
November 13, 1980

PREFACE TO INSTRUCTORS

The information in this preface is intended to help instructors weave their way through all the material in this book. Readers who are using the book as a reference should simply consult the appropriate section or the index to find what they're looking for.

From the Table of Contents you can see that this book has been organized into logical topic areas, striving for thorough coverage of each topic. As a result, the book is a comprehensive reference containing far more information than would ever be used in an introductory course on computer organization and assembly language programming. Typical courses might cover only half to two-thirds of the material in Parts 1 and 2, and only one processor from Part 3.

When I started writing this book, a number of reviewers suggested that the book be organized as a narrative that introduces small pieces of each topic as needed, so that the Table of Contents of the book would roughly follow a typical instructor's lecture outline. The problem with this approach in my view is that it requires *me* to decide what material should be covered and in what order. But why trust me to decide? Even in my own teaching I don't follow exactly the same outline from quarter to quarter!

Therefore, I chose an organization that allows you as an instructor to easily assemble topics into an optimal course outline for your own student population and time schedule. This requires you to do a little more work up front than simply "following the book," but there are two benefits. First, you can find almost all of the material that *you* want to cover in this book, without requiring a lot of supplementary reading material. Second, when the course is over, your students have a comprehensive reference in which they can find even the material that you didn't want to cover, including descriptions of several different microprocessors that they are likely to encounter in the future.

A POSSIBLE COURSE OUTLINE

On the chance it may make your job a little easier, I'll tell you about the course format I use at Stanford. The goal is to teach assembly language programming and basic computer organization from a programmer's point of view to students who have previously had one or two programming courses in a high-level language. The academic quarter is ten weeks long with thirty 50-minute lectures.

Table 1 gives an outline of the topics that I cover, the corresponding reading material, and the approximate number of lectures I spend on each topic. I cover topics in the first part of the table every time I teach the course, and I pick up topics from the second part of the table towards the end of the quarter according to time and interest.

USE OF PASCAL

In the first lecture or so, I handle administrative chores and describe the philosophy and a few salient features of Pascal, and then ask students unfamiliar with Pascal to skim Chapter 2. Although I use Pascal for explaining computer operations and as a documentation language for some assembly language programming examples, students need not be Pascal programmers to use this book. A reading knowledge of elementary Pascal programs is all that is required to understand the Pascal examples in this book.

PROGRAMMING ASSIGNMENTS

My course uses a real machine for all example programs, and I require students to write several programs for this machine and run and debug them in our programming lab. The same topics can be covered in the course regardless of which machine is used for examples and programming assignments. For example, I have taught essentially the same course on different occasions using the Motorola 6809 and the Hewlett-Packard 21MX.[1] Reading assignments such as "n.1" in Table 1 refer to the Part 3 chapter for a particular real machine (e.g., n=17 for the 6809).

The course outline requires careful planning to introduce topics and still leave enough time for corresponding programming assignments, especially in a 10-week quarter. In my Stanford course, there is a lab familiarization exer-

[1]I have available a draft chapter on the 21MX, written in the style of Part 3 chapters; instructors using this book with the 21MX may write to me for permission to use and reproduce the 21MX chapter.

TABLE 1 Computer Organization and Assembly Language Programming course outline.

Essential topics	Reading	Lectures
Introduction and course overview	Notes	0.5
Review of Pascal	2.1–2.9	1.0
Computer data types	1.6, 4.12	0.5
Positional number systems	4.1–4.4	1.0
Complement number systems	4.5–4.6	1.0
Basic computer organization	1.3, 5.1–5.2.5, n.1	1.5
Basic assembly language	5.2.6, n.2	0.5
Simple addressing modes	5.2.9, 7.1–7.2.4, n.3	0.8
Simple operations	8.1–8.5, n.4	0.8
Programming assignment #1	Notes	0.4
Assemblers and loaders	6.1–6.3	1.0
Condition codes, branches	8.6	0.5
Subroutines	5.2.10, 8.6	0.5
How to write programs and how to use the programming lab	Notes, 12.3, 12.5	1.0
Advanced addressing modes	7.2.4–7.3.4	1.0
Addressing-mode applications	3.1–3.4	2.0
Miscellaneous operations	8.7–8.8	0.5
Programming assignment #2	Notes	0.5
Subroutines and parameters	9.1–9.3.6	2.0
Input/Output	10.1–10.3, n.6	1.5
Terminals	A, C.3 or notes	0.5
Queues	3.4, 9.3.7	1.0
Interrupts	11.1–11.3	1.5
Programming assignment #3	Notes	0.5
Interrupt processes	11.5–11.6	2.0

Optional topics	Reading	Lectures
Program development techniques	12.1–12.6	1.0
Recursion	9.4	1.0
Coroutines	9.5	1.0
Relocation and linking	6.4	0.5
Macros	6.5	0.5
Linked lists	3.5–3.7	1.0
Multiplication and division	4.8–4.9, 8.10	1.0
Multiprecision arithmetic	8.9	0.5
Decimal arithmetic	4.10, 8.11	0.5
Floating-point arithmetic	4.11	1.0
Stack machines	5.4	1.0
Classification of computers	5.5	1.0
Architecture of a different CPU	13–19 (pick one)	3.0
DMA, block I/O devices	11.4, Notes	1.0
Serial I/O protocols and devices	C.1–C.3	1.0

cise at the very beginning of the course. Later, there are three nontrivial programming assignments.

The first programming assignment requires only knowledge of basic operations (load, store, add, branch) and addressing modes (register, immediate, absolute). I give the students a Pascal algorithm for a problem such as binary-to-ASCII conversion (Exercise 5.13) or prime factors (Exercise 8.12). Input/output, if any, is performed using utility programs in the computer's ROM monitor. The students learn how to use the assembler and other software tools, they learn how to use the basic features of the example processor, and they get their first taste of debugging.

The second programming assignment introduces advanced addressing modes, nontrivial data structures, and simple I/O programming. In a semester course these topics could be covered in at least two separate assignments. I have found Exercises 7.5 and 10.16 to be ideal for this purpose, since the resulting program is interesting and fun to use. Besides the information in the text, I give the students a program design that breaks down the assignment into several modules with well-defined interfaces and then let them design and code the internals of each module.

The third programming assignment builds on the second by using interrupts to make the I/O more efficient. Exercise 11.17 is quite appropriate. Once again, I give the students module specifications and let them design and code the internals.

PROGRAMMING ENVIRONMENT

Typical microprocessor development systems cannot support a horde of students doing text editing, assembling, and other program development work. For large classes, there are two ways around this problem. One way is to provide a horde of microprocessor development systems.

The other approach, used at Stanford and many other institutions, is to use an existing large campus computer facility to support text editing and cross assembly. Object files created by the cross assembler on the campus facility are downloaded to development systems for running and debugging. To simplify downloading, we use a printable ASCII format for object files and a serial link between the campus computer and the development system; however, floppy disks or cassette tapes could be used as well. For the serial link, either a direct or dial-up connection may be used. We have a small program in the development system's ROM that creates a virtual connection between the campus computer and the development system console so that students can log onto the campus facility and load their object files.

The use of a campus computing facility has many advantages in a large class. Individual development systems require no mass storage, only a CPU, memory, a few I/O cards, a system terminal, and another terminal or other simple I/O device for assignments, at a cost of only a few thousand dollars per system. Since most of the hardware is in the campus facility, most of the hardware maintenance problems occur and are handled there.

Instructors and teaching assistants can make use of centralized file storage and mail facilities on the campus system. For example, at Stanford we have a few "canned" source code modules that students can edit into their programs. When assignments are due, the students turn in an assembler listing of their program for grading, but they also mail the teaching assistant a copy of the object file which can be downloaded and checked for correctness.

Finally, the use of a large central computer for program development is typical of the way that large microprocessor programming projects are handled in industry. Universal microprocessor development systems such as the Hewlett-Packard 64000 and the Tektronix 8001 have been designed to support this approach.

ADDITIONAL MATERIALS

This book does not describe all of the idiosyncrasies of different processors, assembly languages, and development systems that must be understood to write working programs. Therefore, instructors and readers must refer to appropriate technical literature for their own needs. Up to four system-specific documents may be needed:

(1) Processor Reference Manual (published by the processor manufacturer). This manual completely describes the processor's instructions and all side effects.

(2) Assembly Language Reference Manual (published by the processor manufacturer or cross-assembler vendor). This manual describes the syntax of the assembly language and how to run the assembler program.

(3) Development System Reference Manual (published by the development system manufacturer). This manual describes the physical operation of the development system (e.g., how to turn it on), and the program facilities available (e.g., built-in I/O ports, utility programs in ROM, debugging procedures and commands).

(4) Lab Procedures and Configuration Guide (prepared by the instructor). These few pages give the students administrative information such as sign-up policy and lab hours, and describe the lab equipment and its configuration (e.g., memory map of I/O ports).

At Stanford we give students a Lab Manual that covers all four of the above areas: (1) A 6809 pocket reference card; (2) A 4-page specification of our cross assembler and how to use it; (3) An 8-page summary of useful debugging commands and built-in subroutines in our system's monitor ROM; (4) A 5-page description of our lab equipment. In addition, the Lab Manual contains a lab familiarization exercise and a short, system-specific tutorial on writing, running, and debugging programs. The tutorial is based on the recurring problems observed by my teaching assistant Peter Van Sickel, and much of it has been paraphrased in Section 12.5 of this book.

Instructors interested in more information on my particular way of organizing the computer organization and assembly language course using the Motorola 6809 can write to me (on letterhead) at Computer Systems Laboratory, Stanford University, Stanford CA 94305. Much of the information can be adapted for non-6809 courses as well. You will receive a fact sheet and course outline; sample programming assignments, exams, and solutions; complete exercise solutions for Chapters 2 and 4 and scattered solutions for others; excerpts from our Lab Manual; and a list of jokes to use at appropriate places in your lectures.

CONTENTS

*Denotes advanced topics that may be omitted on a first reading.

1

INTRODUCTION TO COMPUTERS AND PROGRAMMING

1.1 WHAT IS A COMPUTER?

A computer is a large room full of equipment, clicking and clanking, whirring and flashing, satisfying the data processing needs of a large organization. It monitors inventory, bills customers, pays creditors, edits and types reports, sends out personalized advertising notices, communicates with other computers, and, most important, prints payroll checks every second Wednesday. On some days it seems like the computer does everything but cook lunch.

A computer is a rack of equipment and a teleprinter in one corner of a scientist's laboratory. It controls an experiment by means of electrical impulses and mechanical actuators, and monitors its progress with temperature, pressure, and motion sensors. When the experiment is completed, the computer analyzes and graphs the results. Each morning when the scientist turns the computer on, it prints out, "Good morning, Susan!"

A computer is a small box that sits in the hobby room where the ham radio used to be. It has a keyboard, a video display, a speaker, a tiny printer, and a slot that gobbles "floppy disks" with information stored on them. The computer stores correspondence, recipes, and financial records, gives educational quizzes to the children, calculates the tax refund every April 14 (includ-

1

ing of course its own deduction as a tax-preparation expense), engages opponents in tournament-level chess, and plays the Star Wars theme in four-part harmony. The computer owner's old-fashioned friends warn, "Watch out — the computer can take over your mind!"

A computer is a miniature electronic circuit deep inside a home appliance. It *does* cook lunch, but that's about all.

All of the above answers are valid, roughly spanning (but not defining) four categories of computers: maxicomputers, minicomputers, microcomputers, and microcontrollers. Even though the computers described above have widely varying size, capabilities, and cost, they share a great many characteristics and operating principles. The goal of this text is to describe general principles of computer architecture and programming that apply to computers of any category. However, we draw most of our examples from computers that we now classify as "microcomputers," hence the title of the text.

Taken as a whole, a computer is an incredibly complex system, with many more levels of detail than, say, the non-computer part of an automobile. Fortunately, a computer system *is* structured into many levels, so that it is easy to understand if taken one level at a time.

The lowest level in a computer is its *hardware* — the electronic circuits from which it is built. The next level is its *architecture* — the interconnection of hardware elements and the structure and features perceived by someone using the machine (some people may refer to this area as hardware also). The highest (and most noble?) level is *software* — the sequences of instructions, or *programs*, that make the computer do useful work. Each of the above levels could be further decomposed into additional levels. In the next few sections we give a "bottom-up" description of the hardware, architecture, and software of modern computer systems.

1.2 DIGITAL COMPUTER HARDWARE

Most computers in use today are digital, as opposed to analog. An *analog computer* represents numbers by a continuously varying phenomenon such as pressure, position, or voltage. Slide rules and specialized calculating wheels are familiar examples of analog computers. An *electronic analog computer* performs a computation by means of an electrical circuit whose operating characteristics emulate the desired computation. For example, addition of two numbers can be emulated by a circuit whose output voltage is the sum of two input voltages; the value of e^{-t} can be obtained by timed observations of the voltage across a capacitor as it discharges through a resistor. Electronic analog computers have been used most often for simulation of physical systems modeled by complicated differential equations.

The distinguishing characteristic of a *digital computer* is that it stores and manipulates entities representing *digits*. Most of the physical phenomena that have been exploited in modern computer technology have one of two stable states, thereby representing one of two digits. Hence, digital computers process *binary digits*, or *bits*; a bit has the value 0 or 1.

Examples of the physical phenomena used to represent bits in some modern computer technologies are given in Table 1–1. With most phenomena, there is an undefined region between the 0 and 1 states (e.g., voltage = 1.5, dim light, capacitor slightly charged, etc.). This undefined region is necessary so that the 0 and 1 states can be unambiguously defined and reliably detected. Noise can more easily corrupt results if the boundaries separating the 0 and 1 states are too close.

Digital logic is used to manipulate bits inside a computer. The basic logic elements are *gates*, which take one or more bits as inputs and produce one bit of output. Figure 1–1 shows three basic gates, AND, OR, and NOT (or INVERTER), and their function tables. Any desired logic function can be developed from these basic gates. For example, a circuit that adds two 16-bit numbers could be designed using about 250 of these gates. Gates are *combinational* logic elements — they accept their inputs, combine them, and produce an output immediately, within 10 nanoseconds (10×10^{-9} seconds) in typical technologies.

Memory elements are used to retain logic values in a digital circuit. The basic memory element is the *S-R flip-flop* shown in Figure 1–2. Normally both inputs to the flip-flop are 0. If a logic 1 is momentarily applied to the S input, the Q output will go to the value 1. Because of the feedback of Q into the bottom OR gate, Q will remain at 1 even after the S input returns to 0. The

TABLE 1–1 Physical states representing bits in different computer logic and memory technologies.

Technology	State representing bit	
	0	1
Transistor-transistor logic	0–0.8 volts	2.0–5.0 volts
Fiber optics	Light off	Light on
Dynamic memory	Capacitor discharged	Capacitor charged
Nonvolatile, erasable memory	Electrons trapped	Electrons released
Bipolar read-only memory	Fuse blown	Fuse intact
Charge-coupled device memory	No charge	Charge present
Bubble memory	No magnetic bubble	Bubble present
Magnetic tape or disk	No flux reversal	Flux reversal
Polymer memory	Molecule in state 0	Molecule in state 1

Notes: A *positive logic* convention is assumed. In *negative logic*, the state correspondences are simply reversed.

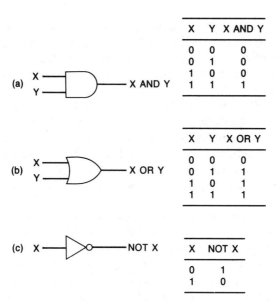

X	Y	X AND Y
0	0	0
0	1	0
1	0	0
1	1	1

(a) X, Y ── X AND Y

X	Y	X OR Y
0	0	0
0	1	1
1	0	1
1	1	1

(b) X, Y ── X OR Y

(c) X ── NOT X

X	NOT X
0	1
1	0

FIGURE 1–1   Logic gates: (a) AND; (b) OR (c) NOT.

Q output can be reset to 0 by momentarily applying a 1 to the R input. Hence the flip-flop can be used to store one bit of information.

The function table for a more complicated flip-flop is shown in Figure 1–3. This *positive edge-triggered D flip-flop* has two inputs, CLK (clock) and D (data). Each time the CLK input changes from 0 to 1, the value on the D input is sampled and transferred to the Q output. At all other times, the value of Q is held at its current value and the D input is ignored. D flip-flops are grouped together into *registers* to store multi-bit quantities in a computer. For example, 16 D flip-flops form a register that stores a 16-bit number. Although flip-flops are the most common storage element in a computer processor, other memory elements shown in Table 1–1 are typically used to store large quantities of information in the main memory or mass storage devices in a computer.

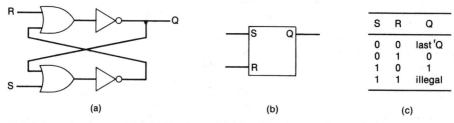

S	R	Q
0	0	last 'Q
0	1	0
1	0	1
1	1	illegal

(a)   (b)   (c)

FIGURE 1–2   A simple S-R flip-flop: (a) circuit; (b) symbol; (c) function table.

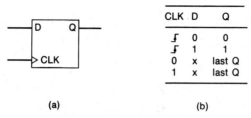

| | | |
CLK	D	Q
∫	0	0
∫	1	1
0	x	last Q
1	x	last Q

(a)   (b)

FIGURE 1–3   Positive edge-triggered D flip-flop: (a) symbol; (b) function table.

Computer logic elements are manufactured as *integrated circuits (ICs)*, tiny electronic circuits etched in rectangular chips of silicon no larger than a centimeter on a side. The smallest ICs contain only a small number of individual logic gates or flip-flops and are called *small scale integration (SSI)* circuits. SSI circuits in computer systems today are used mainly for miscellaneous, irregular control functions. Larger, more regular control and data manipulation functions are performed in *medium scale integration (MSI)* circuits. A typical MSI circuit contains 10 to 100 individual gates and flip-flops arranged to perform a well-structured and often-used function such as adding two 4-bit numbers, storing an 8-bit quantity, or selecting one output bit from 8 input bits.

High-level system functions requiring more than 100 gates are performed by *large scale integration (LSI)* and *very large scale integration (VLSI)* circuits. The dividing line between LSI and VLSI in terms of gate count is fuzzy. It is sometimes given as 100,000 devices (transistors or diodes); a logic gate may use five devices while a dynamic memory cell uses one. The smallest function that might be classified as LSI is a 4×4-bit register file; larger functions falling into the LSI category include memories storing up to 64K bits[1], 8-bit and 16-bit microprocessors, memory management units, serial communication circuits, and peripheral device controllers. VLSI parts include 128K-bit and larger memories, sophisticated 16-bit microprocessors and microcomputers, and 32-bit processors (which should no longer be called "micro"!).

Figure 1–4 gives an indication of the physical size and packaging of digital ICs. Larger circuits generally require larger packages, both to contain the larger silicon chip and to provide more input/output pins. However, some very large regular circuits such as 64K-bit memories can still be squeezed into a small package. A complete computer system may contain anywhere from 1 to 100,000 integrated circuit packages, and so system packaging techniques obviously can vary widely.

---

[1]In normal business jargon, the letters "K" and "M" refer to the quantities 1,000 and 1,000,000, respectively. However, in computer memory jargon, these letters are used to refer to the quantities 2^{10} (1,024) and 2^{20} (1,048,576), as recommended by the American National Standards Institute (ANSI). Warning: If you apply for a programming job and ask for a salary of $25K, don't expect $25,600!

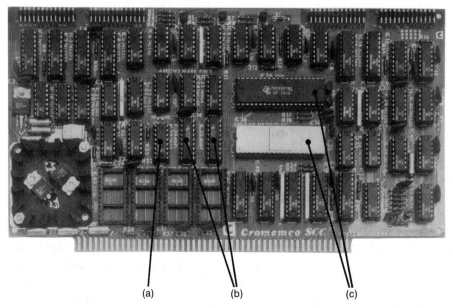

(a) (b) (c)

FIGURE 1–4 Printed-circuit card with integrated circuit packages: (a) 16-pin; (b) 18-pin: (c) 40-pin (photo courtesy of Cromemco).

1.3 BASIC COMPUTER ORGANIZATION

A computer system consists of three major subsystems: processor, memory, and input/output (I/O), as shown in Figure 1–5. The *processor* (or *central processing unit, CPU*) is the heart of the computer. As shown in Figure 1–6 a simple processor contains control circuits for fetching and executing instructions, an arithmetic logic unit for manipulating data, and registers for storing the processor status and a small amount of data. It also has interface circuits for controlling and communicating with the memory and I/O subsystems.

The block diagram in Figure 1–6 is a rather incomplete description of a processor. A *register-transfer level description* of a processor indicates the names and functions of registers and computation units, and describes the operations and interactions of these units for every instruction that the processor can execute. Beginning in Chapter 5, we shall use the programming language Pascal as a register-transfer language to describe various processors.

The *memory* (or *main memory*) of a computer contains storage for instructions and data, and is tied to the processor via the Memory Bus in Figure 1–5. A *bus* is simply a bundle of wires or any other physical medium for transferring information. A computer memory has some number of *locations*,

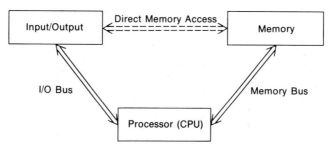

FIGURE 1-5 Block diagram of a typical computer.

each of which stores a b-bit quantity. Associated with each location in the memory is a unique binary number called the *address*. If there are n locations then the addresses range from 0 to $n-1$.

The key feature that distinguishes main memory from other forms of mass storage in a computer is *random access* — the processor has equally fast access to every location in memory. Random access memory is analogous to a wall of post office boxes; a postal clerk can deposit mail in any box with equal ease. Compare this with the *serial access* method of a letter carrier who visits locations sequentially, in the order of the route. Magnetic tapes provide serial-access memory in computer systems.

Figure 1-7 shows how the processor accesses main memory in a typical small computer system. The memory is an array of n locations of b bits each. To read the data stored at address X, the processor places the number X on the Address Bus, and activates a Read control signal; the memory responds by placing the contents of address X on the Data Bus. To write a value V at

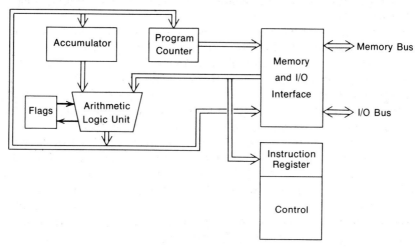

FIGURE 1-6 Block diagram of a simple processor.

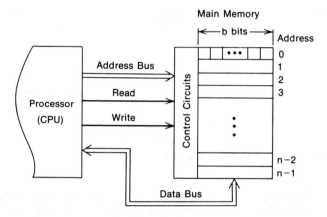

FIGURE 1-7   Main memory in a typical computer.

address X, the processor places X on the Address Bus and V on the Data Bus and activates Write; the memory immediately writes the value V in the specified location. Subsequent reading of address X will now return the value V.

The *input/output (I/O)* subsystem contains *peripheral devices* for communicating with, observing, and controlling the world outside the computer. Peripheral devices include terminals, printers, communication devices, and mechanical sensors and actuators. Also included in the I/O subsystem are *mass storage* devices such as magnetic tapes and disks. These devices are used to store information not needed in the main memory at all times, such as applications programs and text files. Not all computers have mass storage devices, but all useful computers have at least one peripheral device, since by definition a peripheral is the computer's only means of communicating with the outside world.

The processor writes and reads information to and from peripherals by means of I/O instructions that place commands and data on the I/O Bus. In many computers, both memory and peripherals share the same physical bus. Going one step further, some computers communicate with their peripherals using registers that behave as if they were memory locations. In such systems, the hardware makes no distinction between accessing main memory and accessing peripherals; examples will be seen in Chapter 10.

In simple computer systems, there is no direct path from peripherals to main memory; the only way to transfer data between a peripheral and memory is for the processor to read it from the peripheral and store it in memory, or vice versa. However, systems requiring a higher data transfer rate incorporate *direct memory access (DMA)*, a link between a special peripheral controller and memory that allows a peripheral to read and write memory without processor intervention; DMA will be explained in Chapter 11.

1.4 COMPUTER SYSTEM SOFTWARE

Computer *software* consists of the instructions and data that the computer hardware manipulates to perform useful work. A sequence of instructions for a computer is called a *program*. The data manipulated by a program is called a *data base*, a *file*, *input*, or simply *data*, depending on its nature and extent (and to some degree, the whims of the speaker!).

The most primitive instructions that can be given to a computer are those interpreted directly by hardware, in the *machine language* of the computer. Machine language instructions are encoded as strings of bits in the computer's memory, often one instruction per memory location. The processor fetches machine instructions from memory and executes them one by one. Machine instructions perform primitive operations such as "add 1 to register A," "store the contents of register A into memory location 15," "add the contents of memory location 35 to register B," or "jump to the instruction sequence starting at location 207 if register B is zero."

Since it is difficult for humans to read and recognize strings of bits, machine language programs are written in *assembly language* and translated into bit strings by an *assembler*. Assembly language represents machine instructions by mnemonic names and allows memory addresses and other constants to be represented by symbols rather than bit strings.

For example, the machine instruction that adds the contents of memory location 35 to register B might be encoded as the bit string 11011011 00100011, where 11011011 is the "opcode" for "Add Memory to B" and 00100011 is the 8-bit binary encoding of 35. In assembly language, the same instruction could be written as "ADDB VAR," where ADDB is the instruction "mnemonic" and VAR is a symbolic 8-bit constant whose value is defined elsewhere in the program to be 35. Memory location 35 contains the variable (named VAR) that is added to register B. The assembler translates the symbolic instruction ADDB VAR into the bit string 11011011 00100011.

Much computer software is written in assembly language. Assembly language is most often used for small computers and for frequently-invoked program modules in large computers. However, it takes a fairly large number of assembly language instructions to perform operations that can be stated in one line in English, such as "Set W equal to W plus X minus Y divided by Z," or "Repeat the next sequence of instructions until X is less than 0 or Y equals Z."

Studies have shown that both the time to write and debug a program and the difficulty of understanding and maintaining it are proportional to the number of instructions, with little dependency on the complexity of each instruction. Therefore, most programs are written in *high-level languages* that allow common operations such as expression evaluation, repetition, assignment, and conditional action to be invoked in a single high-level *statement*.

Furthermore, *structured* high-level languages such as Pascal impose a programming discipline that makes programs easier to design, understand, and maintain.

Few computers execute a high-level language directly. Therefore, a *compiler* is needed to translate a high-level language program into a sequence of machine instructions that performs the desired task. Since five to ten machine instructions might be required for each high-level statement, the savings in programming time and cost over an equivalent assembly language program should be obvious.

Still, there are some arguments to support programming in assembly language. Since assembly language allows explicit access to the machine language, it is always theoretically possible to write an assembly language program that is at least as compact and efficient as the machine language program emitted by any compiler. Depending on the compiler, the computer, and the application, a compiled program might be anywhere from 0% to 300% longer and slower than the *optimal* machine language program, but it may be substantially better than a machine language program written by a person with average skills.

The reduced development cost and enhanced maintainability of high-level language programs almost always outweigh their inefficiencies. In most development projects, the cost of more memory to store longer programs is less than the cost of hiring more programmers, especially since in a large project it may take four times as many programmers to write a program twice as long. This is not a criticism of programmers, rather it indicates the non-linear increase in the time spent communicating as the size of the project increases.

The speed of high-level language programs is usually not a problem. If a program is found to be too slow, it can often be improved without rewriting much of it. In a typical program, 10% of the written program accounts for 90% of its execution time. Critical subprograms, once identified, can be rewritten and optimized in either the original high-level language or assembly language.

Since machine instructions in a computer are en*coded*, the act of writing instructions in any language has come to be known as "coding," and the written instructions are called "code." Coding is just a small part of "programming," which is the overall process of designing, specifying, documenting, coding, and debugging programs.

Assemblers and compilers are not the only *software tools* that a programmer may encounter. Other useful tools related to program development are interpreters, simulators, and on-line debuggers. Like a compiler, an *interpreter* processes a high-level language program. Unlike a compiler, an interpreter actually executes the high-level language program one statement at a time, rather than translating each statement into a sequence of machine instructions to be run later. A *simulator* is a program that simulates individual machine instructions, usually on a machine other than the one being simulated. A typical use of a simulator is to test programs to be run on a processor before the processor hardware is available. An *on-line debugger* executes a program on a machine one or a few instructions at a time, allowing the programmer to see the effects of small pieces of the program and thereby isolate programming errors (*bugs*).

Text editors are used to enter and edit text in a general-purpose computer, whether the text is a letter, a report, or a computer program. *Text formatters* read text with imbedded formatting commands and produce pretty, formatted documents such as this book. Text editors and formatters belong to the area of computing known as *word processing*.

In a medium to large computer system, cooperating programs run under the control of an *operating system*. An operating system schedules programs for execution, controls the use of I/O devices, and provides utility functions for all of the programs that run on the computer. Programs and text stored on disks and other mass storage devices are managed by a *file system*, a collection of programs for reading, writing, and structuring such information in "files." The operating systems in most computers include file systems. Even a very small computer with no mass storage or file system has a simple operating system, at least to monitor inputs and accept commands from the outside world.

1.5 ALGORITHMS

"Computers are dumb, they won't do anything unless they're told; and once told, they'll perform *exactly* as specified, even if it's dumb." This is an often-heard and accurate description of the computational capability of computers. A computer requires a precise sequence of instructions to perform any task; such a sequence is called an *algorithm*.

To be an algorithm, a sequence of instructions must satisfy two important properties. First of all, each instruction must be taken from a basic set of "primitive operations" available in the machine carrying out the algorithm. Thus, the algorithm for multiplying 119 by 102 may be just one instruction in a machine with multiplication as a primitive; it may consist of a few additions and shifts in a machine with these operations as primitives; and it consists of 102 successive additions of 119 in a machine with only addition and counting as primitives.

Second, an algorithm must produce a result in a finite number of steps. Not only does this mean that the algorithm itself contains a limited number of instructions, but also that any instructions specifying enumeration, repetition, or trial and error will eventually terminate. For example, a sequence of instructions that tries to compute all of the prime numbers can't be an algorithm, since there are an infinite number of primes.

Even when a problem has a finite solution, a particular sequence of instructions to find the solution may never terminate. Consider the following sequence of instructions to divide a positive number X by 5:

(1) Set Q equal to 0.

(2) Set X equal to $X-5$ and set Q equal to $Q+1$.

(3) If X is between 0 and 4, then terminate; the quotient is Q and the remainder is X. Otherwise, return to step 2.

This sequence works fine if X is initially 5 or larger. However, it never terminates if X is initially between 0 and 4. The first time that the test in step 3 is encountered, X will be negative, and it will just keep getting more negative with successive repetitions of steps 2 and 3. This example is typical of a common error in computer "algorithms" — an instruction sequence that works most of the time, but fails because of unexpected test results in one or more special cases.

The example could be modified in step 3 above to test only for X less than or equal to 4. Then it will terminate, but still produce incorrect results for X between 0 and 4. The following algorithm terminates and produces correct results for all positive values of X:

(1) Set Q equal to 0.

(2) If X is between 0 and 4, then terminate; the quotient is Q and the remainder is X. Otherwise, set X equal to $X-5$ and set Q equal to $Q+1$.

(3) Return to step 2.

Even "correct" algorithms can be improved upon. The algorithm above relies on the user to supply a positive value of X; if X is initially negative, the sequence above never terminates. Robust algorithms always check that their inputs are within an allowed range. Formulating correct and robust algorithms is one of the most important aspects of programming.

1.6 COMPUTER DATA TYPES

Although we may sometimes think that computers manipulate only numbers, in reality they process many different types of data. In fact, it is fair to say that most of the input and output of computers today is non-numeric.

Recall that the basic unit of information storage in a digital computer is the *bit*, which has a value of either 0 or 1. Obviously a single-bit data type is not very useful for numeric computation, since it only allows us to count from 0 to 1! Nevertheless, the bit is a very useful data type if we interpret its values 1 and 0 to represent the two logic values TRUE and FALSE. The resulting data type is called *logical* or *boolean*, after George Boole who invented a mathematical system forming the basis for the two-valued *boolean algebra* used in digital logic design. The boolean type has many uses in a program, for example, to save the results of comparisons, to mark special cases, and in general to distinguish between two possible outcomes or conditions.

By assembling two or more bits into a string, we can represent more than two values or conditions. The bits in a string of n bits can take on 2^n different combinations of values. For example, a 4-bit string has 16 different values, and Table 1–2 shows several different ways of assigning meanings to the 16 combinations. In Chapter 4 we shall look at many different systems for assigning numeric values to bit strings. However, we can also assign non-numeric meanings as shown by the last two columns in the table. It is usual to associate a numeric name with each unique bit string even if the bit string represents a non-numeric value. For example, referring to the third column of Table 1–2 we might say, "The number 5 represents the color green."

Strings of eight bits are usually referred to as *bytes*. The name "byte" was invented at IBM in the early days of electronic computers. The name for a string of four bits is fancifully derived from the byte — the *nibble*.

A bit string manipulated by a computer in one operation is usually called a *word*. Some computers have a *word length* as short as 4 bits, others as long as 64 bits or more. Many minicomputers and microcomputers have standardized in using "word" to describe 16-bit strings, and using "double word" to describe 32-bit strings. Some large computers, such as the IBM 370, use "word" to describe a 32-bit string, and use "double word" and "half word" to describe 64-bit and 16-bit strings, respectively. We will adopt "standard"

TABLE 1–2   4-bit string values and meanings.

String	Unsigned Number	Signed Number	Color	City
0000	0	+0	Black	St. Louis
0001	1	+1	Brown	Miami
0010	2	+2	Red	Chicago
0011	3	+3	Orange	San Francisco
0100	4	+4	Yellow	Detroit
0101	5	+5	Green	New York
0110	6	+6	Blue	Boston
0111	7	+7	Violet	Houston
1000	8	−8	Gray	Denver
1001	9	−7	White	Memphis
1010	10	−6	Silver	Portland
1011	11	−5	Gold	Milwaukee
1100	12	−4	Tan	Seattle
1101	13	−3	Indigo	Juneau
1110	14	−2	Pink	Honolulu
1111	15	−1	Puce	Albuquerque

microcomputer usage in this text: nibble = 4 bits; byte = 8 bits; word = 16 bits; double or long word = 32 bits; quadruple word = 64 bits.

Bits, nibbles, bytes, and words are easy data types to classify because they require differing amounts of storage in the computer memory. There are other data types that are classified not by how much storage they take, but how they are interpreted and used by the computer hardware and software. For example, a microcomputer might define the following four data types, all using a 16-bit word:

- *Unsigned Integer.* The word represents an unsigned integer between 0 and 65,535.

- *Signed Integer.* The word represents a signed integer between $-32,768$ and $+32,767$.

- *Address.* The word represents an address in a memory with a maximum size of 65,536 bytes.

- *Logical Array.* The word contains 16 independent boolean flags.

Even though all four data types could be stored exactly the same way in the computer's memory, they may be manipulated by the hardware and software differently. For example, an arithmetic operation on an unsigned integer

while an operation on a signed integer overflows when the result is less than $-32,768$ or greater than 32,767.

The same computer might define three different data types employing a 32-bit double word:

- *Long Signed Integer.* The double word represents an integer in the range $-2,147,483,648$ to $+2,147,483,647$.

- *Floating-point.* The double word represents a number in the range $-1.7 \cdot 10^{38}$ to $+1.7 \cdot 10^{38}$.

- *Long Address.* The low-order 24 bits of the double word are used as an address in memory and the high-order 8 bits are not used.

A data type is said to be *supported* by a computer if the computer's instruction set contains operations that manipulate data and produce results according to the data type's interpretation of bit strings.

1.7 CLASSIFICATION OF COMPUTERS

Computers can be examined from several different viewpoints and classified according to many different criteria. We shall describe one classification here in order to clarify our own use of computer jargon.

Computers are classified as supercomputers, maxicomputers, midicomputers, minicomputers, and microcomputers according to system size. We'll give a rough definition of each category and then explain:

- *Supercomputer:* a very high performance computer for large scientific "number-crunching" applications, costing millions of dollars. Examples: CRAY–I, ILLIAC IV.

- *Maxicomputer:* a large, high-performance, general-purpose computer system costing over a million dollars. Examples: CYBER 76, IBM 3033.

- *Midicomputer:* a general-purpose computer lying between minis and maxis in performance and price. Example: VAX–11/780.

- *Minicomputer:* a general-purpose computer, often tailored for a specific, dedicated application, costing between $20,000 and $200,000. Examples: HP 300, PDP–11/70.

- *Microcomputer:* a computer whose CPU is a microprocessor, usually configured for a specific, dedicated application and costing well under $20,000. Examples: Apple II, TRS–80, PDP–11/23.

Before we continue, we should clarify the meanings of four other terms that use the prefix "micro":

- *Microprocessor:* a complete processor (CPU) contained in one or a few LSI circuits, used to build a microcomputer in the context above. Examples: MC68000, Z8000, M6809.

- *Microcomputer:* in another context, a processor, memory, and I/O system contained in one LSI circuit, often referred to as a *single-chip microcomputer* for clarity. Examples: Z8, MCS–48, M6801.

- *Microcontroller:* a processor, memory, and I/O system contained in one or a few LSI circuits, tailored to an application that hides the general-purpose data processing capabilities of the computer from the users. Examples: processors used in microwave ovens, automobiles, electronic games.

- *Microprogrammed processor:* a particular type of processor hardware that executes each machine instruction as a sequence of primitive *microinstructions*. "Microprogramming" refers to writing sequences of microinstructions, *not* the programming of microprocessors. Most programmers never see a microprogram. Examples of microprogrammed processors: MC68000, LSI–11/2, Z8.

The definitions of computer classes are vague for a number of reasons. Advances in technology tend to blur classifications based on hardware design or performance. For example, many contemporary minicomputers outperform the maxicomputers of 10 years ago.

A classification based on application is also imprecise, because computers of different sizes and costs are often used in the same application, simply depending on the size and requirements of the application. For example, an individual author may use a dedicated microcomputer for word processing, while in a large company many users may share word-processing facilities on a maxicomputer.

Cost is the best single characteristic for distinguishing the above computer classes. As time goes on, advances in technology make higher performance available for the same price, matching the demands of users of a particular computer class for better capabilities for the same price.

Because the definition of computer classes is fuzzy, different people sometimes place the same machine in different categories. However, most machines at any given time will clearly fall into one class or another. Rather than trying to be more precise, we close this section by noting that computer classification is really important only to authors who feel obliged to write about it. The general concepts of architecture and programming discussed in Part 2 are applicable to computers of all classes.

REFERENCES

Digital computer hardware, including gate-level design, MSI and LSI building blocks, memory systems, I/O devices and interfaces, and system design, is discussed in detail in several texts. Popular texts include *Digital Logic and Computer Design* by M. Morris Mano [Prentice-Hall, 1979], *Computer Organization* by V. C. Hamacher, Z. G. Vranesic, and S. G. Zaky [McGraw-Hill, 1978], and *Microcomputer-Based Design*, by John Peatman [McGraw-Hill, 1978].

There are many more dimensions to computer architecture than we can possibly cover or even mention in an introductory text. You can sample some advanced concepts in hardware and software organization in *Introduction to Computer Architecture*, edited by Harold Stone [SRA, 1980 (second edition)], and *Principles of Computer Structures* by D. P. Siewiorek, C. G. Bell, and A. Newell [McGraw-Hill, 1981]. A recent collection of papers on all the machines produced by Digital Equipment Corporation, *Computer Engineering* by C. G. Bell, J. C. Mudge, and J. E. McNamara [Digital Press, 1978], is especially recommended for hardware engineers; it contains a wealth of practical insight not found in ordinary textbooks. It also has a chapter on seven different ways to classify computers, for those of you who found the last section of this chapter unsatisfactory.

Computer software has dominated hardware in cost for some time now, and the importance of the field is probably best evidenced by your own interest in it. There are many software areas that merit your additional study; we'll mention them as they occur in later chapters.

One somewhat nebulous area not covered in this book is *how to program*. We introduce some rules and tools and give examples, but we do not describe the actual creative process of writing a program. We hope that most readers will have already experienced this creativity by writing programs in a high-level language. If not, there are some books that can help. *An Introduction to Programming and Problem Solving With Pascal* by Schneider, Weingart, and Perlman [Wiley, 1978] has an extended discussion of how to develop algorithms. Both this book and *Programming in PASCAL* by Peter Grogono [Addison-Wesley, 1978] show the step-by-step construction of many Pascal programs. *Software Tools* by Brian W. Kernighan and P. J. Plauger [Addison-Wesley, 1976] does the same using a variant of FORTRAN called RATFOR, and describes some very useful software tools in the process. Even if you think you already know how to write programs, read *The Elements of Programming Style* by Kernighan and Plauger [McGraw-Hill, 1978] to see if you know how to write *good* programs.

THE PROGRAMMING LANGUAGE PASCAL

Pascal is a "structured" high-level language that allows programs and data to be defined in a natural, hierarchical fashion. In addition to having widespread use on large computers in the academic, scientific, and business communities, Pascal has emerged as the most popular high-level language for microcomputers. Pascal compilers exist for all major microcomputers; several microcomputer chip manufacturers provide Pascal-based software; and there is even a microcomputer (the Pascal Microengine by Western Digital Corp.) that has primitive Pascal "P-code" as its machine language.

The language's designer, Niklaus Wirth, named Pascal after the French philosopher, but not because of Pascal's teachings. Wirth said in a letter to *Electronics*[1],

> Actually, I am neither capable of fully understanding his philosophy nor of appreciating his religious exaltations. Pascal, however, was (perhaps one of) the first to invent and construct a device that we now classify as a digital computer. He did so at the age of 16, when he was called upon by his father, who was a tax collector, to assist in the numerous and tedious calculations.

[1]Vol. 1, No. 26, December 21, 1978, p. 6.

This chapter gives a brief description of the programming language Pascal. It serves as an introduction for a reader with no previous exposure to Pascal, and as a review for a reader who has used it before.

The description of Pascal in this chapter is not complete. Some features of Pascal are described elsewhere in this book: arrays in Sections 3.1 and 3.2, and procedures and functions in Sections 9.1 and 9.2. Some Pascal features have been omitted completely: set types, file handling, records, pointers, dynamic data structures, formatted input/output, and implementation dependencies. (A Pascal "implementation" consists of the compiler and run-time environment for a particular computer system.)

Nevertheless, the subset of Pascal presented here is quite adequate for giving algorithmic descriptions of data structures, assembly language programs, and computer instruction sets in later chapters. In fact, it covers enough of the language to write rather powerful "real" Pascal programs. The reader who plans to write and run "real" Pascal programs should still consult the reference manual for the compiler being used, and possibly one of the Pascal books listed at the end of this chapter.

2.1 OVERVIEW

Three key elements contribute to making Pascal a "structured" language: declarations, block structure, and procedural code. *Declarations* require the programmer to give certain information to the compiler about the structure of the program — the name and types of all variables that will be used, and the names of all labels referenced by discontinuities in program flow (GOTO statements). They also allow a good programmer to give optional information to the compiler and to improve program readability in a number of ways: by defining identifiers that convey the meaning of program constants; by restricting the range of variables to allow automatic error-checking; and by explicitly defining data structures in a way that the compiler supports and a reader understands.

Figure 2–1 illustrates the *block structure* of Pascal programs. *Statements* specify the actions in a program; Pascal defines both simple and structured statements. A *simple statement* performs a single action; for example, the *assignment statement* "x := (3+y)/7" computes the value of the expression "(3+y)/7" and assigns it to the variable x. A *structured statement* contains one or more other statements and controls them by well-defined rules. The most important structured statement is the *compound statement*, a list of other statements bracketed by the words BEGIN and END. Another example is the FOR statement, which repeats a statement a predetermined number of times.

Now here's where block structure comes in: a structured statement can control *any* statement, including another structured statement. If we draw

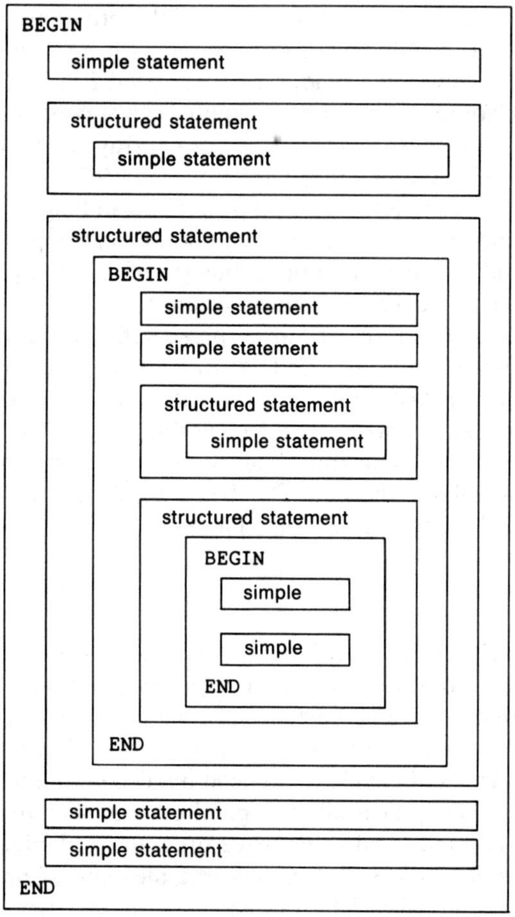

```
BEGIN
   ┌──────────────────────────────────────────────┐
   │ simple statement                               │
   └──────────────────────────────────────────────┘
   ┌──────────────────────────────────────────────┐
   │ structured statement                           │
   │   ┌──────────────────────────────────────┐     │
   │   │ simple statement                      │     │
   │   └──────────────────────────────────────┘     │
   └──────────────────────────────────────────────┘
   ┌──────────────────────────────────────────────┐
   │ structured statement                           │
   │   ┌──────────────────────────────────────┐     │
   │   │ BEGIN                                 │     │
   │   │   ┌──────────────────────────────┐    │     │
   │   │   │ simple statement              │    │     │
   │   │   └──────────────────────────────┘    │     │
   │   │   ┌──────────────────────────────┐    │     │
   │   │   │ simple statement              │    │     │
   │   │   └──────────────────────────────┘    │     │
   │   │   ┌──────────────────────────────┐    │     │
   │   │   │ structured statement          │    │     │
   │   │   │   ┌──────────────────────┐     │    │     │
   │   │   │   │ simple statement      │     │    │     │
   │   │   │   └──────────────────────┘     │    │     │
   │   │   └──────────────────────────────┘    │     │
   │   │   ┌──────────────────────────────┐    │     │
   │   │   │ structured statement          │    │     │
   │   │   │   ┌──────────────────────┐     │    │     │
   │   │   │   │ BEGIN                 │     │    │     │
   │   │   │   │   ┌──────────────┐     │     │    │     │
   │   │   │   │   │ simple        │     │     │    │     │
   │   │   │   │   └──────────────┘     │     │    │     │
   │   │   │   │   ┌──────────────┐     │     │    │     │
   │   │   │   │   │ simple        │     │     │    │     │
   │   │   │   │   └──────────────┘     │     │    │     │
   │   │   │   │ END                   │     │    │     │
   │   │   │   └──────────────────────┘     │    │     │
   │   │   └──────────────────────────────┘    │     │
   │   │ END                                   │     │
   │   └──────────────────────────────────────┘     │
   └──────────────────────────────────────────────┘
   ┌──────────────────────────────────────────────┐
   │ simple statement                               │
   └──────────────────────────────────────────────┘
   ┌──────────────────────────────────────────────┐
   │ simple statement                               │
   └──────────────────────────────────────────────┘
END
```

FIGURE 2–1   Block structure in Pascal.

each statement as a block, the program shown in Figure 2–1 looks like a "nested" set of blocks. Block structure lets Pascal programs reflect a natural method of problem-solving: repetitively and conditionally executing simple instruction sequences.

   Procedural code is the name used to describe a program that is decomposed into modules with well-defined interfaces and interactions. Procedural code results from a "top-down" program design approach, wherein a program is defined in terms of a few high-level modules (procedures and functions), each of which is defined in terms of lower-level modules.

   A *procedure* is a defined sequence of declarations and statements that can be invoked by a single statement. A *function* is defined similarly, but is invoked by writing the function name in an expression, as one would normally use a variable name. Besides including a number of predefined procedures and functions, Pascal allows each program to define its own procedures and functions. As shown in Figure 2–2, Pascal supports top-down design by using the same general structure for procedures and functions as it does for programs, and by allowing each procedure or function to define its own subservient procedures and functions.

The *scope* of an item defined within a program or procedure is the part of the program in which that definition is recognized. In Figure 2–2 the scope of an item defined in a given block is limited to that block and all the smaller blocks contained in it. Items defined in the outermost block are called *global*; items defined in an inner block are *local* to that block. Thus, the programmer may define local variables, data structures, and procedures within one block without concern about possible conflicts in other blocks at the same or higher levels.

To give you a preview of what an actual Pascal program looks like, a complete program is shown in Table 2–1. Like all good programs, the example is self-contained so that someone conversant in the language can readily

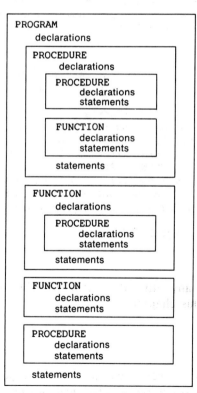

FIGURE 2–2 Program, procedure and function structure in Pascal.

TABLE 2-1 Pascal program to simulate a simple adding machine.

```
PROGRAM AddingMachine (input,output);
{ This program simulates a simple adding machine with 13 keys:
      0-9  Digits -- entered one digit at a time, left-to-right.
      C    Clear -- sets the accumulated sum to zero.
      +    Plus -- adds the current number to the accumulated sum.
      S    Stop -- stops the machine (and program).
  The keys are simulated by reading characters one-at-a-time from the
  input.  The current number and sum are printed after each C, +, or S
  operation.  Illegal characters clear the sum and current number. }
VAR
  sum, number : integer;   charIn : char;

PROCEDURE PrintNums;        {Print current number and sum so far.}
  BEGIN writeln (number,sum) END;

PROCEDURE InitNums;         {Clear current number and sum and print them.}
  BEGIN sum := 0;  number := 0;  PrintNums;  END;

FUNCTION DigitVal (c : char) : integer;   {Evaluate a digit from 0 to 9.}
  BEGIN
    {The value of a digit is the value of its numeric character
       code minus the value of zero's numeric character code.}
    DigitVal := ord(c) - ord('0');
  END;

BEGIN  {Main Program}
  InitNums;  read(charIn);  {Initialize variables; get first char.}
  WHILE charIn <> 'S' DO   {Read a character at a time.}
    BEGIN
      IF (charIn>='0') AND (charIn<='9') THEN  {If charIn is a digit...
            multiply current number by 10 and add charIn's digit value.}
        number := number*10 + DigitVal(charIn)
      ELSE IF charIn='C' THEN InitNums  {Clear sum on 'C'.}
      ELSE IF charIn='+' THEN    {Add on '+'}
        BEGIN sum := sum + number;  PrintNums;  number := 0  END
      ELSE InitNums;  {Clear sum and number on bad input characters.}
      read(charIn);   {Always get next character.}
    END;
  writeln('All done -- bye');   {Got an 'S' -- stop.}
END.
```

understand it without any other documentation. Details of Pascal are discussed in the rest of this chapter.

2.2 VOCABULARY

At the very lowest level, a Pascal program is just a series of letters, digits, and special symbols recognized by the compiler. A *special symbol* may be a single character or a pair of characters, as shown in Table 2–2. There are

TABLE 2–2 Special symbols in Pascal.

Special symbols

;	:	.	,	'	<	>	{	}	(	)	[	]	
^	=	+	-	*	/	:=	<=	>=	<>	..			

two symbols in this list that you don't see — space and "newline" (or carriage return). In addition, the language defines *reserved words* shown in Table 2–3. All other symbols in a program are groups of characters that form numbers, identifiers, or strings. Throughout this text we use Courier for all characters in Pascal and assembly language programs, and Pascal reserved words are printed in UPPER CASE.

Numbers are written in decimal in either *fixed-point notation* (17, -999, 123.456, 0.000000005168) or *scientific notation*, (17E0, -99.9E1, 123456E-3, 5.168E-9), where "E" means "times 10 to the power of." An *identifier* is a series of letters and digits beginning with a letter. A program may contain arbitrarily defined identifiers with length limited only by the input line, but the first eight characters of each distinct identifier must be unique. Also, some identifiers called *standard identifiers* are predefined in any Pascal implementation; they may be redefined by the programmer, but it's usually best not to. The standard identifiers included in every Pascal implementation are shown in Table 2–4; a particular implementation may define additional ones.

Good programmers choose identifier names that are descriptive of the identifiers' meaning or function. Different programmers use different conventions for separating the words in multi-word identifiers. For example, some Pascal compilers treat the underline character as a letter, which allows a programmer to use identifiers such as item_count, stack_size, and get_next_char. Pascal implementations accepting both upper and lower

TABLE 2–3 Pascal reserved words.

Reserved words

AND	END	NIL	SET
ARRAY	FILE	NOT	THEN
BEGIN	FOR	OF	TO
CASE	FUNCTION	OR	TYPE
CONST	GOTO	PACKED	UNTIL
DIV	IF	PROCEDURE	VAR
DO	IN	PROGRAM	WHILE
DOWNTO	LABEL	RECORD	WITH
ELSE	MOD	REPEAT	

TABLE 2–4 Standard identifiers in Pascal.

Files	Constants	Types	Procedures		Functions		
input	false	boolean	get	readln	abs	odd	arctan
output	true	integer	new	reset	chr	ord	succ
	maxint	real	pack	rewrite	cos	pred	trunc
		char	page	unpack	eof	sin	eoln
		text	put	write	exp	sqr	round
			read	writeln	ln	sqrt	

case characters support the convention used by many Pascal programmers and in this book:

- Reserved words are written in lower case for simplicity when typing real programs, in upper case for emphasis in printed text.

- The "body" of an identifier is written in lower case.

- User-defined program, procedure, and function names begin with an upper case letter; all other identifiers begin with a lower case letter.

- The first letter of the second and successive words in a multi-word identifier is capitalized.

Thus, head, itemCount, and stackSize may be variable names, while Sort, GetNextChar, and TicTacToe are user-defined program, procedure, or function names. In standard Pascal, matching upper and lower case letters appearing in identifiers and reserved words are equivalent. Forgetting to capitalize a letter doesn't bother the compiler, only a copy editor!

A *string* is a sequence of characters enclosed in single quotes, for example, 'string'. Capitalization in strings *is* significant. A quote is included in a string by writing it twice, 'Don''t think twice, it''s alright!'.

A sequence of characters other than curly brackets {}, enclosed by curly brackets, is called a *comment* and is ignored by the compiler. Comments, spaces, and newlines are used as *separators*. One or more separators *must* occur between consecutive Pascal reserved words and identifiers. No separators are *required* between a special symbol and any other character sequence, but one or more separators *may* occur. A program can be written with a minimum number of separators, but a look at the programming examples in this and other chapters should show the desirability of freely using separators to improve readability.

2.3 PROGRAM STRUCTURE

Viewed from the highest level, a Pascal program consists of declarations and statements. *Declarations* appear at the beginning of the program and specify such things as the program's name, its operating environment, the names and types of constants and variables it uses, and the definitions of functions and procedures it uses. *Statements* specify the actions performed by the program.

Formally, a *program* is defined to be a program heading and a block followed by a period. This format can be described by a *syntax diagram* as shown in Figure 2–3(a). In a syntax diagram, rectangular boxes surround the names of the program elements that are defined elsewhere, such as *"program heading"* and *"block"*. Circles or boxes with rounded corners surround special symbols and reserved words. Syntax diagrams give only the *syntax* of program elements — the format that they must follow. Their meaning or *semantics* must be described separately.

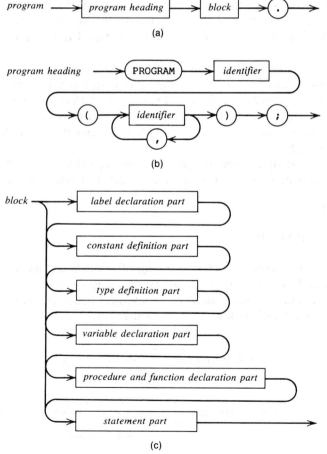

FIGURE 2–3 Syntax diagrams: (a) program; (b) program heading (c) block.

The description of a program is refined in Figure 2–3(b) and (c). A *program heading* consists of the reserved word PROGRAM, followed by an identifier, followed by a list of one or more identifiers enclosed in parentheses, followed by a semicolon. A *block* consists of six parts in a prescribed order; all parts except the statement part are optional.

The program heading is always the first line of a Pascal program and gives its name and the files that it accesses:

```
PROGRAM Example (input,output);
```

The program named Example reads from the standard file input, and sends its results to the standard file output. The identities of the files input and output are implementation-dependent. For example, in a batch system input might be a card reader and output a line printer; in a timesharing system both input and output might be named files in the user's directory; and in a personal computer input might be a keyboard and output a display screen. The program may access additional files by specifying them in the program heading, but general file handling in Pascal is beyond the scope of our discussion.

Figure 2–3 defined a block as five optional declaration parts and a statement part. Each of the declaration parts is described in subsequent sections; the statement part is defined in Figure 2–4. A *statement part* is simply a sequence of statements bracketed by the reserved words BEGIN and END (this is called a *compound statement*). Individual statements are defined in Sections 2.7 through 2.9.

An example of a simple program is given in Table 2–5. In this example, the label, constant, type, and function and procedure declarations are "empty."

2.4 DECLARATIONS

Declarations appear at the beginning of a block, as defined in the previous section. Every Pascal program contains at least one block; a procedure or function definition also contains a block, and hence declarations. Syntax diagrams for declarations are given in Figure 2–5.

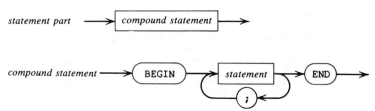

FIGURE 2–4 Syntax diagrams for statement part and compound statement.

TABLE 2–5 A simple Pascal program.

```
PROGRAM Example (input,output);
VAR x, square, recipr : real;
BEGIN
  read(x);
  square := x*x;
  recipr := 1/x;
  write('Square of', x, 'is', square, 'reciprocal is', recipr)
END.
```

The *label declaration part* of a block gives a list of labels used in the block, for example:

```
LABEL 17, 6851, 357;
```

A *label* in Pascal is an unsigned integer of up to four digits. Labels are used to mark statements referenced by GOTO statements, as described later; every label must be declared before it is used. If there are no labels in the program, the label declaration part is "empty" — it contains no characters.

The *constant definition part* contains a list of identifier/constant equations terminated by semicolons:

```
CONST pi = 3.14159265;
  first = 1;   last = 50;
  heading = 'Areas of circles';
```

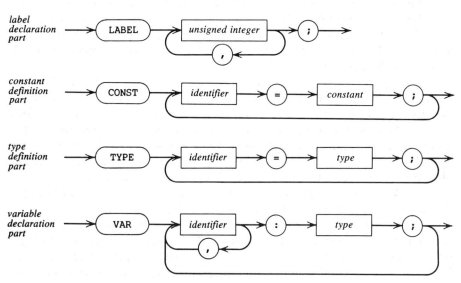

FIGURE 2–5 Syntax diagrams for declarations.

The type of each identifier is implied by the type of the constant with which it is equated; types are discussed in the next section. If no constants are to be defined, this declaration is omitted.

The constant definition part provides a nice facility present in assembly language but missing from most high-level languages — the ability to define an identifier as a synonym for a constant. Whenever the compiler encounters such an identifier, it replaces it with the constant itself. This aids program readability, since a well-chosen name has more meaning than a number. More significantly, it enhances program portability and maintainability, since the programmer can change important parameters such as input range or internal data structure size in a single declaration line without searching the entire program for occurrences of the changed parameters.

The *type definition part* contains a list of identifier/type equations. Section 2.6 will show two ways to create user-defined types in a Pascal program. If a program defines no new types, the type definition part is omitted.

Every variable used in a Pascal program must be declared in the *variable declaration part*, which contains a list of identifier/type associations. Each such association contains one or more identifiers and a type, and declares each identifier to be a variable of that type:

```
VAR
   count, id, nScores : integer;
   average, sigma : real;
   inputChar : char;
   greater, finished : boolean;
   stripe1, stripe2, stripe3 : colorCode;
```

The type may be a standard type or a type previously defined in the type definition part. Every nontrivial program has at least one variable, and so the variable declaration part always appears in a program block. However, it is possible to define a procedure or function with no local variables, in which case this part is omitted.

The syntax for the *procedure and function declaration part* is shown in Figure 2–6. Each procedure or function declaration is similar in structure to the program itself; "block" has the same definition given in the previous section. The *procedure heading* or *function heading* gives the name of a procedure or function and lists its parameters as described in detail in Chapter 9. If there are no parameters, then the parameter list is empty. Simple examples of procedure and function declarations were given in Table 2–1.

At this point, you should observe the "recursive" nature of a procedure or function declaration — since it contains a block, it may define its own procedures and functions. This allows top-down design, in which a procedure can define its own subservient procedures. Rather than cluttering up the high-level program description with a lot of little low-level procedures, the low-level procedures can be defined inside the high-level procedures that use them.

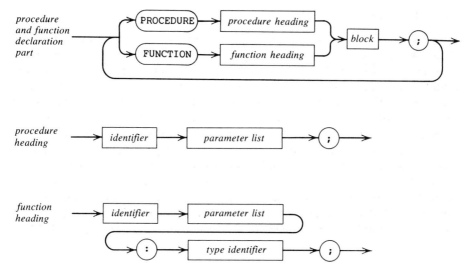

FIGURE 2–6　Procedure and function declaration part syntax diagram.

2.5 STANDARD DATA TYPES AND EXPRESSIONS

Data types in Pascal are classified into simple types and structured types. A *simple type* defines an ordered set of values, such as integers or characters. The standard simple types integer, real, char, and boolean are described in the next four subsections. A *structured type* is characterized by the type(s) of its components and a structuring method. The simplest structure is the array, discussed in Sections 3.1 and 3.2.

Data may be compared and combined in *expressions*. A *relational expression* compares two arguments of like type using one of the *relational operators*:

=	equal
<	less than
>	greater than
<=	less than or equal
>=	greater than or equal
<>	not equal

An *arithmetic expression* combines arguments of type real, integer, or subrange of integer, and produces results in one of these types according to rules given in the next two subsections. A *boolean expression* combines boolean arguments and produces a boolean result as discussed in the last subsection.

2.5.1 Integer

The value of an integer variable or constant is a whole number in the range -maxint to +maxint, where maxint is an implementation-dependent constant. As discussed in Section 4.5, most modern computers use two's-complement representation for integers, so that maxint = $2^{w-1}-1$, where w is the word length of the machine or a multiple thereof. For example, in a typical 16-bit microprocessor Pascal, maxint = 32,767. An integer constant is a sequence of decimal digits, possibly preceded by a plus or minus sign.

The arithmetic operators add (+), subtract (-), and multiply (*) in Pascal yield integer results when applied to integer operands. There are two "division" operators that yield integer results: DIV produces a truncated quotient, for example, 9 DIV 4 = 2; and MOD produces the remainder, for example, 9 MOD 4 = 1. The "normal" division operator (/) when applied to integer operands yields a result of type real, for example, 9/4 = 2.25.

2.5.2 Real

A real value is an element of an implementation-dependent subset of the real numbers, the floating-point numbers of the machine. Floating-point representations allow both positive and negative numbers, and typically allow absolute values as small as 10^{-38} and as large as 10^{38} (refer to Section 4.11). A real constant is a signed sequence of decimal digits possibly including a decimal point, or a number in scientific notation. The magnitude of a real constant must begin with a digit, so we write 0.005 or 5E-3, not .005 or .5E-2.

There are four operations that can be applied to real operands: addition (+), subtraction (-), multiplication (*), and division (/). Division always produces a real result; the other operations produce a real result whenever at least one of the operands is type real.

An expression that produces an integer result can be assigned to a real variable; the result will be automatically converted to real. However, a real result cannot be assigned to an integer variable. The standard functions trunc and round may be used to convert a real result to integer by truncation and rounding, respectively.

As in most other high-level languages, multiplication and division operations in Pascal have precedence over addition and subtraction in expressions, and parentheses may be used freely. Thus, the right-hand and left-hand sides of the equations below are equivalent:

```
a*b+c*d = (a*b) + (c*d)
a+b/c+d = a+ (b/c) +d
a*b/c = (a*b) /c
```

Although the precedence is well-defined, parentheses should be used whenever it isn't obvious. Parentheses can sometimes affect `integer` operations more than `real`:

```
5.0*3.0/2.0  =  (5.0*3.0)/2.0  =  5.0*(3.0/2.0)  =  7.5
5*3 DIV 2    =  (5*3) DIV 2    =  7  <>  5*(3 DIV 2)  =  5
```

2.5.3 Char

A value of the type `char` is an element of a set of characters used to communicate with the computer. Both the set of characters recognized (and printed) by a machine, and the internal bit strings used to represent those characters, are implementation-dependent. However, there exists a standard character set and bit-string encoding used by almost every computer manufacturer but IBM. This is the ASCII code, shown in Appendix A.

A character enclosed in single quotes (apostrophes) denotes a constant of type `char`. The set of characters is assumed to be ordered. In most implementations, the ordering will be the same as the numerical ordering of the corresponding bit strings. Thus, in ASCII, `'B'>'A'`, `'Q'<'q'`, and `'+'<'P'`.

2.5.4 Boolean

A `boolean` value is always either `true` or `false`. Pascal defines the logical negation operator, `NOT`, which returns the complement of a `boolean` operand `x`, as shown in Table 2–6. Negation is called a *unary operation* because it has only one operand; a *binary operation* has two operands. Pascal defines two binary operations on `boolean` operands, `AND` and `OR`, also shown in the table. `Boolean` operands can be combined by these logical operations to make complex program decisions.

When operands of other types are compared by relational operators, the result of the comparison is a value of type `boolean`. For example, if `j` is an integer, the expression "`j>1`" yields `true` only if the value of `j` is greater than 1, `false` otherwise; "`1=1`" always yields `true`; and "`5<2`" always yields

TABLE 2–6 Boolean operators in Pascal.

x	y	NOT x	x OR y	x AND y
false	false	true	false	false
false	true	true	true	false
true	false	false	true	false
true	true	false	true	true

false. More examples of boolean expressions are given below, assuming
cnt and limit are type integer, inChar is char, and testOK is boolean.

```
cnt <= 50
(cnt < limit) AND (inChar <> '.')
((cnt > limit-10) AND (inChar = '?')) OR NOT testOK
```

As with arithmetic expressions, Pascal has a well-defined operator precedence, but it's best for clarity and safety to use parentheses around all sub-
expressions where the precedence isn't obvious.

2.6   USER-DEFINED TYPES

Pascal provides several classes of user-defined types. This section describes the simplest of these — enumerated and subrange types. User-defined
types help make better programs in a number of ways. Enumerated types
allow a nonnumeric problem to be stated more clearly than the alternative of
writing a long series of constant declarations equating identifiers with numbers (e.g., "black=0; brown=1; red=2; . . ."). Subrange types restrict
the range of variables, thereby allowing a compiler to perform more thorough
error checking and possibly create more efficient programs.

Set types, not described here, provide a natural means of expression for
many combinatorial problems. And structured types, some of which will be
discussed in Chapter 3, allow explicit definition of complex data structures in
a manner understandable by both the compiler and a human reader.

2.6.1   Enumerated Types

In Section 1.6 we indicated that a bit string need not represent a number,
that it could represent an element of any set of related objects. Recognizing
that computers process much nonnumeric data, Pascal provides a formal
mechanism for defining nonnumeric *enumerated types* and allowing the program to refer to such data values by nonnumeric names. A program may
introduce a new enumerated type in the *type definition part*; three such types
are defined below:

```
TYPE
   color = (black,brown,red,orange,yellow,green,blue,violet,
      grey,white,silver,gold,tan,indigo,pink,puce);
   city = (stLouis,miami,chicago,sanFrancisco,detroit,
      newYork,boston,houston,denver,memphis,portland,
      milwaukee,seattle,juneau,honolulu,albuquerque);
   direction = (north,south,east,west);
```

Once a new type has been defined, variables of this type may be declared, for example:

```
VAR
   birthplace, origin, destination : city;
   route, alternate : direction;
   favorite : color;
```

Variables of enumerated types may also be declared without naming the type, for example:

```
VAR route, alternate :  (north,south,east,west);
```

The identifiers listed in a type definition become the constants of the defined type. A variable may be assigned the value of any variable or constant of the same type, but expressions and mixed assignments are not allowed. For example, the first four assignment statements below are valid; the last three are not.

```
{valid}
   origin := chicago;
   favorite := puce;
   alternate := route;
   route := north;
{invalid}
   destination := west;
   favorite := birthplace;
   birthplace := origin OR destination;
```

When they are listed in the type definition, the constants of an enumerated type acquire an ordering: they are assigned *ordinal numbers*, consecutive integers beginning with 0. The compiler uses the ordinal number to represent the constant in the computer's memory. The predefined function ord returns the ordinal number for a variable or constant of any enumerated type, for example,

```
ord(white) = 9
ord(sanFrancisco)  = 3
ord(north) = 0
```

The predefined functions pred and succ use this ordering to return the predecessor and successor of an argument.

```
pred(green)  = yellow
succ(east)  = west
pred(milwaukee)  = portland
succ(west)  = ?   {undefined}
pred(black)  = ?   {undefined}
```

Besides assignment, the only operation allowed on enumerated types is comparison by the relational operators. When two arguments are compared, the result is obtained by comparing their ordinal numbers. For example,

```
(chicago > sanFrancisco) = (2 > 3) = false
```

The predefined standard types integer, char, and boolean are also considered to be enumerated types to which the preceding discussion applies. Thus, we can make several useful statements.

```
pred(29) = 28
succ(-5) = -4
ord(false) = 0
ord(true) = 1
false < true
succ('i') = 'j'
pred('8') = '7'
ord('9') <> 9
ord('9') - ord('0') = 9
```

The statements about characters are guaranteed true only if characters have the ordinal values implied by the ASCII encoding (Appendix A). For example, succ('i')='j' is false in the EBCDIC encoding used in IBM computers. Therefore, statements that assume a contiguous ordering of the characters should be avoided. Still, the IEEE Pascal standard makes the following guarantees:

(1) The ordinal values of '0'-'9' are ordered and contiguous.

(2) The ordinal values of 'A'-'Z' are ordered but not necessarily contiguous.

(3) The ordinal values of 'a'-'z' are ordered but not necessarily contiguous.

2.6.2 Subrange Types

The values in a *subrange type* are a contiguous subset of a *host type*, which may be any enumerated type or simple type other than real. A subrange type is defined in the type definition part by giving constants (in the host type) for first and last values in the subrange. For example,

```
TYPE
  digit = 0..9;
  digitChar = '0'..'9';
  colorCode = black..white;
```

defines the three subranges `digit` of `integer`, `digitChar` of `char`, and `colorCode` of the enumerated type `color`. Subrange variables may be defined much like variables of an enumerated type, for example:

```
VAR
   units, tens, hundreds : digit;
   outChar : digitChar;
   band1, band2, band3 : colorCode;
   index : 1..100;
```

Subrange variables may be used in expressions and on the left-hand side of assignment statements anywhere that the associated scalar type would be allowed. However, an attempt to assign a subrange variable a value beyond its range causes an error when the program is run.

An `integer` variable, especially when used for counting, indexing, or enumeration, seldom takes on unpredictable values in a program. Subrange types let the programmer inform the compiler of the allowable range of such variables in normal operation, so that abnormal operation due to bad inputs or programming errors can be detected by simple range checks automatically inserted into the program by the compiler. Subrange types are also essential to the syntax of Pascal, for they are used in `CASE` statements and `ARRAY` declarations, as described in Sections 2.9 and 3.1, respectively.

2.7 SIMPLE STATEMENTS

Statements are the sequences of reserved words, identifiers, and symbols that specify the actions in a Pascal program. The statements in each block of a Pascal program are executed sequentially, in the order in which they were written. Pascal statements are classified into two types: simple and structured. A *simple statement* is a statement that contains no other statement. The three types of non-trivial simple statements will be described in this section. The *empty statement*, which consists of no characters and performs no action, is also a simple statement. The discussion of structured statements in the next section will show that there *are* good uses for the empty statement.

2.7.1 Assignment Statements

An *assignment statement* assigns the value of an expression on the right-hand side of the symbol ":=" to a variable on the left-hand side. The variable and the expression must have the same type, with two exceptions: (a) if the expression is `integer` or a subrange thereof, the variable may be `real`; (b) the expression type may be a subrange of the variable type, or vice-versa. Several examples of assignment statements have already been given; Table 2–7 gives some more.

TABLE 2–7   Examples of assignment statements.

```
VAR
    i, j, k : integer;
    a, b, c : real;
    outChar, inChar : char;
    done, valid : boolean;
BEGIN
    . . .
    i := j + k - 1;
    a := j + k - 1;
    k := j*i + 5;
    b := a*b/c;
    c := b*a/1E10;
    inChar := 'q';
    outChar := inChar;
    valid := (i<j) AND ((inChar<>outChar) OR (c>3.14));
    done := NOT valid;
    . . .
END.
```

2.7.2   The GOTO Statement

Any Pascal statement may be preceded by the construct "*label*: ", where *label* is a unique 1-to-4-digit unsigned integer that has been listed in the label declaration part. The GOTO statement has the form "GOTO *label*", and has the effect of transferring control to the labeled statement. That is, the next statement executed after the GOTO will be the labeled statement, and execution of the program will continue from this new point.

The use of the GOTO statement is generally discouraged, because the resulting "jumping around" of control is difficult to follow (and therefore, difficult to debug and verify its correctness). The "structured statements" in the next section give a much more regular and readable means of program control. Examples will demonstrate this by showing all the extra statements that are needed in the absence of structured statements.

The most frequent legitimate use of GOTO is to jump out of a structured statement on some abnormal termination condition. Jumping *into* a structured statement from outside yields unpredictable results.

2.7.3   Procedure Statements

A *procedure* is a defined sequence of declarations and statements (i.e., a block) that can be invoked by a single statement, called a *procedure statement*. Procedures will be discussed in detail in Chapter 9, but we shall briefly introduce them here.

Pascal has four built-in procedures that allow a program to read and write data. They may be invoked by the following procedure statements:

- read (*var1,var2,. . .,varn*) — reads values from the standard file named input and assigns them to listed variables. The types of the input values must match the corresponding variables.

- readln (*var1,var2,. . .,varn*) — same as read, except a new input line is started after the last variable has been read.

- write (*expr1,expr2,. . .,exprn*) — writes the values of the listed expressions to a standard file named output.

- writeln (*expr1,expr2,. . .,exprn*) — same as write, except a new output line is started after the last expression has been written.

These procedures can also read and write files other than the standard input and output, and take simple data formatting specifications. Pascal has several other built-in procedures dealing with input and output; their effects are somewhat implementation-dependent and in any case beyond the scope of our discussion.

Like any other high-level language, Pascal allows and encourages user-defined procedures. Consider the task of printing the reciprocal, square, and integer part of a real variable a, as accomplished by the program fragment below:

```
VAR a, recipr, square : real; int : integer;
  . . .
  recipr := 1/a;
  square := a*a;
  int := trunc(a);
  writeln(a,recipr,square,int);
  . . .
```

If we wanted to do the same with variables b, c, and d, we could write three similar sequences, changing a to b, c, and d in each one, but still using recipr, square, and int for temporary storage. Table 2–8 shows how a procedure can instead be declared and invoked to compute the desired functions on arbitrary real values. If the input values to this program are "4.5 1.7 0.5 6.8", then the output will be

```
4.5000   0.2222   20.2500    4
1.7000   0.5882    2.8900    1
0.5000   2.0000    0.2500    0
6.8000   0.1471   46.2400    6
```

The variable x in the procedure declaration in Table 2–8 is called a *formal parameter*; the variables a, b, c, and d in the PrintVal procedure

TABLE 2–8 Program using a procedure.

```
PROGRAM Print4Values (input,output);
{Declare variables used by the program}
VAR a, b, c, d : real;

{Declare the printing procedure}
PROCEDURE PrintVal (x : real);
  {declare local variables}
  VAR recipr, square : real; int : integer;
  BEGIN  {This is the statement part of the procedure}
    recipr := 1/x;
    square := x*x;
    int := trunc(x);
    writeln(x,recipr,square,int);
  END;

{Now comes the statement part of the main program}
BEGIN
  read(a,b,c,d);
  PrintVal(a);
  PrintVal(b);
  PrintVal(c);
  PrintVal(d);
END.
```

statements are called *actual parameters*. When a procedure statement is encountered, the actual parameters are substituted for the formal parameters in the body of the procedure before it is executed. In Pascal there are a number of possible ways that this substitution can take place, as discussed in Section 9.2.

By requiring only one copy of a commonly used sequence of instructions, a procedure can save time during program development and space during program execution. Procedures (and functions) are essential to the "structure" of Pascal or any other computer language, high-level or assembly. The use of procedures contributes to program modularity, readability, and testability by breaking down a problem into a structured group of smaller problems with well-defined interfaces.

2.8 STRUCTURED STATEMENTS I

A *structured statement* contains one or more additional statements as components. Pascal defines a set of structured statements that allow decision and repetition in a program, and together handle the most common program control situations. We shall describe all of Pascal's structured statements except WITH, which is used in conjunction with RECORD variables.

The decision and repetition statements in Pascal can be contrasted with the primitive capabilities of typical computer machine languages. A typical machine primitive tests a condition and, based on the outcome, either jumps to a different sequence of instructions or continues the current instruction sequence. This is roughly equivalent to the following Pascal statement:

```
IF condition THEN GOTO label
```

When we discuss the Pascal decision and repetition statements, we shall compare them with sequences using only the above primitive. Also, when we describe individual machine architectures in Part 3, we shall give equivalent assembly language sequences for the Pascal statements.

2.8.1 Compound Statements

A *compound statement* is a sequence of statements separated by semi-colons and bracketed by the reserved words BEGIN and END:

```
BEGIN
    statement1;
    statement2;
    . . .
    statementn−1;
    statementn
END
```

A syntax diagram was given in Figure 2–4. We have already seen many examples of compound statements, since the statement part of a program, procedure, or function must be a compound statement.

Each statement within a compound statement can be any simple or structured statement; the structured statements may include more compound statements. This "recursive" definition is essential to the structure of Pascal. It is responsible for the power of the rest of the structured statements — an IF, FOR, WHILE, REPEAT, or CASE statement can control a complex structured statement just as easily as it controls a simple assignment statement.

One thing to notice about the definition of a compound statement is that the semicolon is a statement *separator* rather than a statement *terminator*. Some block-structured languages, most notably C, PL/1, and PL/M, use the semicolon as a terminator — *every* statement must be followed by one. In Pascal, the last statement in a compound statement is *not* followed by a semicolon. Nevertheless, the following compound statement is still legal:

```
BEGIN
    temp := x;
    x := y;
    y := temp;
END
```

It contains *four* statements, the last being the empty statement. Even though the extra semicolon is shunned by purists, it is still a good idea to include it, to avoid the error of forgetting it when appending additional statements. However, semicolons cannot be used indiscriminately after every statement in Pascal — the next subsection will show why.

2.8.2 The IF Statement

The decision primitive in a Pascal program is the IF statement; its basic format is

    IF *condition* THEN *statement*

where *condition* may be any boolean expression and *statement* may be any statement, simple or structured. The *statement* is executed only if *condition* has the value true.

Quite often it is necessary to choose between two alternative actions, depending on a condition. This is accomplished in Pascal by appending an "ELSE clause" to an IF statement:

    IF *condition* THEN *statement1* ELSE *statement2*

If *condition* is true then *statement1* is executed, otherwise *statement2* is executed. In assembly language or in any language with only a primitive test and jump facility, an IF–THEN–ELSE statement would have to be implemented as follows:

```
IF condition THEN GOTO labelA;
statement2;
GOTO labelB;
labelA : statement1;
labelB : . . . ;
```

A syntax diagram for IF is shown in Figure 2–7 and an example program using IF statements is given in Table 2–9. It should be noted from the IF syntax and from the examples that a semicolon is *not* used to separate the ELSE clause from the IF clause. The examples also show how IF statements

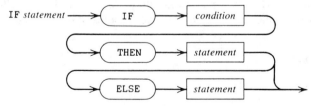

FIGURE 2–7 Syntax diagram for IF statement.

TABLE 2-9 Program using IF statements.

```
PROGRAM Iffy (input,output);

VAR radius, area, diameter : real;
    hour, minute, number : integer;
    inchar : char;

BEGIN

{Find the radius and diameter of a circle of a given area.}
  read(area);
  IF area >= 0 THEN
    BEGIN
      radius := sqrt(area/3.1416);
      diameter := 2*radius;
      writeln('For a circle with area', area, 'the radius is',
          radius, 'and the diameter is', diameter);
    END
  ELSE writeln('Negative area (', area, ') not allowed');

{Convert 24-hour time to 12-hour time.}
  read(hour,minute);
  IF (hour < 0) OR (hour > 23)
      OR (minute < 0) OR (minute > 59) THEN
    BEGIN {If input out of range, set to default.}
      hour := 0;  minute := 0;
    END;
  IF hour <= 11 THEN
    BEGIN
      IF hour = 0 THEN hour := 12;
      writeln('Time is', hour, ':', minute, 'AM');
    END
  ELSE
    BEGIN
      hour := hour - 12;
      IF hour = 0 THEN hour := 12;
      writeln('Time is', hour, ':', minute, 'PM');
    END;

{Read a hex-digit character and convert to an integer.}
{Assumes ASCII ordering of characters.}
  number := -1;
  read(inchar);
  IF (inchar >= '0') AND (inchar <= '9') THEN
    number := ord(inchar) - ord('0')
  ELSE IF (inchar >= 'a') AND (inchar <= 'f') THEN
    number := ord(inchar) - ord('a') + 10
  ELSE IF (inchar >= 'A') AND (inchar <= 'F') THEN
    number := ord(inchar) - ord('A') + 10
  ELSE writeln(inchar, ' -- not a hex character');
  writeln('The decimal value of ', inchar, ' is', number);
END.
```

may be nested. When an IF statement contains a compound statement, any of the components of the compound statement may of course be IF statements. The last part of the example shows a "compound IF" statement, where the ELSE clause of each succeeding IF statement is another IF statement. This is a useful and common structure. On the other hand, consider an IF statement wherein the THEN clause contains another IF clause:

```
IF condition1 THEN
    IF condition2 THEN statement1
ELSE statement2;
```

From the statement indentation, it appears that the ELSE clause belongs to the first IF. However, the language syntax attaches the ELSE clause to the nearest IF that doesn't have one, the opposite of the way we've formatted it. Even though the language is unambiguous, the "THEN IF" construct should be avoided because of the confusion it can introduce. The ambiguity can be resolved by negating *condition1* and reversing the order of the clauses if *statement2* isn't also an IF, or by simply using BEGIN–END to bracket the subordinate IF statement:

```
IF condition1 THEN
    BEGIN IF condition2 THEN statement1 END
ELSE statement2;
```

2.8.3   The FOR Statement

The FOR statement provides a means of repeating a statement a predetermined number of times; its general format is

```
FOR control := first TO last DO statement
```

Here *control* is a declared variable, and *first* and *last* are expressions, all of the same simple type (excluding real). The *first* and *last* expressions are evaluated at the beginning of the FOR statement execution, and the value of *first* is assigned to *control*. Then the value of *control* is compared to *last*; if (*control*>*last*) is false, then *statement* is executed once, *control* is bumped to its successor value, and the whole process is repeated. Otherwise the FOR statement terminates. An equivalent sequence can be written using only primitive tests and jumps as follows:

```
control := first;
temp := last;
labelA : IF (control > temp) THEN GOTO labelB;
statement;
control := succ (control) ;
GOTO labelA;
labelB :  . . . ;
```

Here temp is a variable of the same type as *first* and *last* that is not otherwise defined in the program. There is one slight exception to the equivalency — in standard Pascal the value of *control* is undefined after exiting the FOR statement, even when GOTO is used to exit.

The reserved word TO in a FOR statement may be replaced with the reserved word DOWNTO, resulting in a FOR statement that counts down instead of up. In this case, pred (*control*) produces the next value of *control* after each iteration, and (*control*<temp) is the termination criterion. Figure 2–8 gives a syntax diagram for both types of FOR statements.

Each execution of *statement* above is called an *iteration* of the FOR loop. Since *first* and *last* are expressions, the number of iterations may be different each time the FOR statement is executed, even though the number is fixed once a particular execution is begun. Also, because *control* is checked at the *beginning* of each iteration, it is possible for *statement* to be executed zero times. Table 2–10 gives examples of FOR statements.

2.9 STRUCTURED STATEMENTS II

There is no particular reason to split off the next three structured statements from the previous three, except that the previous section was getting a little too long!

2.9.1 The WHILE Statement

In contrast with the FOR statement, which produces a predetermined number of iterations each time it is executed, a WHILE statement repeats a number of times determined by computation within the WHILE statement itself. The format of a WHILE statement is shown in Figure 2–9 and below:

WHILE *condition* DO *statement*

Here *condition* is any boolean expression and *statement* is of course any statement. The WHILE statement evaluates *condition* and then executes *statement* if *condition* is true; this process repeats as long as *condition* continues to be true. Obviously, the variables affecting *condition* must be modified

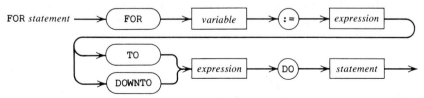

FIGURE 2–8 Syntax diagram for FOR statement.

TABLE 2–10 Program using FOR statements.

```
PROGRAM FourFORloops (input,output);
VAR
  i, power, n, m, nsum : integer;
  char1, char2, pchar : char;
  innum, sum : real;
BEGIN
{Print a table of integers and squares.}
  FOR i := 1 TO 10 DO writeln(i,i*i);

{Print a table of powers of 2.}
  power := 1;
  FOR i := 0 TO 10 DO
    BEGIN writeln(i,power); power := power*2 END;

{Read two characters and print all the ones between.}
  readln(char1,char2);
  IF char1 < char2 THEN
    FOR pchar := char1 TO char2 DO writeln(pchar)
  ELSE FOR pchar := char1 DOWNTO char2 DO writeln(pchar);

{Compute sums of n groups of input numbers.}
  read(n);   {Number of groups to be summed.}
  FOR nsum := 1 TO n DO
    BEGIN
      sum := 0;  read(m);   {Number of components in this group.}
      FOR i := 1 TO m DO
        BEGIN read(innum); write(innum); sum := sum+innum END;
      writeln(sum);
    END;
END.
```

within *statement* if the WHILE statement is ever to terminate. Some examples of WHILE statements are given in Table 2–11.

A primitive sequence equivalent to WHILE is shown below:

```
labelA : IF NOT condition THEN GOTO labelB;
statement;
GOTO labelA;
labelB :  . . . ;
```

It is clear from this sequence that the WHILE statement can have zero iterations if *condition* is already false when the WHILE statement is encountered.

FIGURE 2–9 Syntax diagram for WHILE statement.

TABLE 2–11   Program using WHILE statements.

```
PROGRAM Whilst (input,output);
VAR
  n, power, nnums, hour : integer;
  innum, sum : real;
BEGIN
{Print a table of powers of 2.}
  n := 0; power := 1;
  WHILE power < (maxint DIV 2) DO
    BEGIN writeln(n,power); n := n+1; power := power*2 END;
  writeln(n,power);    {Print last table entry.}

{Average a sequence of nonnegative numbers.}
  sum := 0; nnums := 0;
  write('Input sequence:'); read(innum);
  WHILE innum >= 0 DO {Any negative number terminates sequence.}
    BEGIN
      sum := sum + innum; nnums := nnums + 1;
      write(innum); read(innum);
    END;
  writeln; writeln(nnums, 'numbers, average is', sum/nnums);

{While away the hours.}
  read(hour); {Out-of-range hour terminates loop.}
  WHILE (hour >= 0) AND (hour <= 23) DO
    BEGIN
      IF hour = 0 THEN writeln('Hour 0 is midnight')
      ELSE IF hour < 12 THEN
          writeln('Hour', hour, 'is', hour, 'AM')
      ELSE IF hour = 12 THEN writeln('Hour 12 is noon')
      ELSE writeln('Hour', hour, 'is', hour-12, 'PM');
      read(hour);
    END;
END.
```

Also, you may notice a similarity to the FOR statement. A FOR statement can actually be simulated using the WHILE:

```
control := first;
temp := last;
WHILE control <= temp DO
  BEGIN
    statement;
    control := succ(control);
  END;
```

However, the FOR statement should still be used when appropriate because it is easier to read, and because as a restricted case it gives the compiler more opportunity for optimization.

2.9.2 The REPEAT Statement

The REPEAT statement is similar in effect to the WHILE, except that it tests a condition *after* each iteration; its syntax is shown in Figure 2–10. There are three major differences from the WHILE statement — the REPEAT statement always has at least one iteration; a false condition continues rather than terminates the iterations; and a sequence of statements, not just one, may be controlled. The last difference occurs because the compiler treats the reserved word REPEAT as if it were really "REPEAT BEGIN", and UNTIL as if it were really "END UNTIL".

Because the condition test is at the end of the loop, the primitive equivalent of a REPEAT statement is a little simpler than that of a WHILE:

labelA : *statement;*
IF NOT *condition* THEN GOTO *labelA;*

WHILE statements are used more commonly than REPEAT, because in most situations it is important to be able to execute a loop zero times. However, Table 2–12 shows two situations where the REPEAT statement is preferred. In the first sequence, a loop is executed for cases up to *and including* a termination case, saving complexity over the corresponding WHILE statement in Table 2–11. In the second sequence, REPEAT is needed because the termination condition is indeterminate until the loop is executed once.

With any of the repetitive statements (REPEAT, WHILE, and FOR), it is sometimes necessary to terminate the loop because of some unusual condition. Often it is impractical to include all of the unusual termination conditions in the basic termination clause, especially if the conditions do not arise until the middle of the loop. The simplest solution in this situation is to jump out of the repetitive statement with a GOTO for each unusual condition. Because GOTOs are "unstructured," some Pascal implementations provide an EXIT statement that terminates a repetitive statement from within.

2.9.3 The CASE Statement

The CASE statement can be viewed as a multivalued generalization of IF. While IF executes one of two statements according to a boolean value, a CASE statement selects among a number of statements according to a value belonging to an enumerated or subrange type. The syntax of a CASE statement

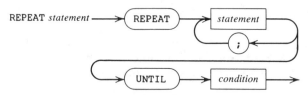

FIGURE 2–10 Syntax diagram for REPEAT statement.

TABLE 2–12 Program using REPEAT statements.

```
PROGRAM Repetitious (input,output);
VAR
  n, power  : integer;
  inchar : char;
BEGIN
{Print a table of powers of 2.}
  n := 0; power := 1;
  REPEAT
    n := n + 1; power := power * 2; writeln(n,power);
  UNTIL power > (maxint DIV 2);

{Read and print a sentence.}
  REPEAT
    read(inchar); write(inchar);
  UNTIL inchar = '.';
END.
```

is shown in Figure 2–11. Here *selector* is an expression whose value belongs to one of the types integer, boolean, or char, or to an enumerated or subrange type. The *case list* has one or more elements, each of which specifies one or more constants of the same type as *selector*, and a *statement* to be executed if *selector* has one of these values.

An example of a CASE statement with four selector values and three possible outcomes is shown below.

```
TYPE myCases = 1..4;
VAR which : myCases;
  . . .
  CASE which OF
    1 : write('This is case 1');
    2 : write('But this is case 2');
    3,4 : write('This could be either case 3 or case 4');
  END;
```

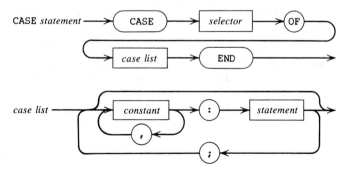

FIGURE 2–11 Syntax diagram for CASE statement.

The semicolon after the last case list element is optional. Each distinct value of *selector* may appear in only one case list element. It is advisable that every possible value of the scalar or subrange type of *selector* be specified in some case list element, since the behavior of the case statement may be undefined if *selector* takes on an unrepresented value (however, this event should cause a run-time error according to the proposed IEEE Pascal standard).

To write the equivalent of a CASE statement using only primitive test and jump instructions, a separate test and jump is needed for each case. However, the CASE statement can be implemented efficiently in most computers by means of a jump table, as shown for various machines in Part 3.

Many problems naturally break down into a few cases, and so the CASE statement is ideal. The CASE statement is also used quite often to decode commands and to classify objects. Table 2–13 is an example program using a CASE statement.

REFERENCES

The computing exploits of Blaise Pascal and many others are described in *The Computer from Pascal to von Neumann*, by Herman H. Goldstine [Princeton University Press, Princeton, NJ, 1972]. This book has a wealth of historical information and good references to original source material.

The original definition of the standard Pascal language is given in the *Pascal User Manual and Report* by K. Jensen and N. Wirth [Springer-Verlag, 1978 (second edition)]; this is a useful reference for the serious Pascal user. An international effort has been made to standardize the language; a draft standard by the IEEE Computer Society appears in the April 1979 issue of *Computer* magazine [Bruce W. Ravenel, "Toward a Pascal Standard," Vol. 12, No. 4, pp. 68–82]. Subsequent standardization efforts have been or will be publicized in *Computer*.

Many tutorial texts on Pascal are available. Two good books at the introductory level are *An Introduction to Programming and Problem Solving with Pascal* by G. M. Schneider, S. W. Weingart, and D. M. Perlman [Wiley, 1978] and *Programming in Pascal* by Peter Grogono [Addison-Wesley, 1978]; both are lucid and complete and have good bibliographies of their own. *Problem Solving Using Pascal* by Ken Bowles [Springer-Verlag, 1977] is also a popular text. Niklaus Wirth's *Algorithms + Data Structures = Programs* [Prentice-Hall, 1976] covers basic techniques of program and data structuring using Pascal.

TABLE 2–13 Program using a CASE statement.

```
PROGRAM ClassifyOrClassyIf (input,output);
{
   This program reads a lower case letter and classifies it
   according to certain characteristics.  The program assumes that
   inputs are in the ASCII character set so that the subrange
   'a'..'z' contains only the lower case letters.  The program
   may not work with other character sets.
}
TYPE letter = 'a'..'z';
VAR inchar : letter;
   vowel, hexdigit, dull, descender, multistroke : boolean;
BEGIN
   vowel := false; hexdigit := false; dull := false;
   descender := false; multistroke := false;
   read(inchar);
   CASE inchar OF
      'a','e' : BEGIN vowel := true; hexdigit := true END;
      'i' : BEGIN vowel := true; multistroke := true END;
      'o','u' : vowel := true;
      'y' : BEGIN vowel := true; descender := true END;
      'b','c','d','f' : hexdigit := true;
      'g','p','q' : descender := true;
      'j' : BEGIN descender := true; multistroke := true END;
      't','x' : multistroke := true;
      'h','k','l','m','n','r','s','v','w','z' : dull := true;
   END;
   writeln(inchar, ' has the following properties:');
   IF vowel THEN writeln('It is a vowel.')
   ELSE writeln('It is a consonant.');
   IF hexdigit THEN writeln('It is a hexadecimal digit.');
   IF descender THEN writeln('It has a descender.');
   IF multistroke THEN
       writeln('You must lift your pen to write it in script.');
   IF dull THEN writeln('It is a very boring character.');
END.
```

EXERCISES

2.1   What are the advantages of using a CONST declaration to declare constants, as opposed to defining variables with the same names and assigning constant values to them at the beginning of the program?

2.2 Assuming that the variable declarations in Table 2–7 have been made, explain whether or not each of the following assignment statements can be compiled without type-matching or other errors.

```
k := j * i + 5;
j := (i + k)/2;
b := a*c/1.1E10;
i := (j + m) MOD k;
k := ord(inChar);
done := (a = 2);
valid := valid OR (j=k) OR NOT done;
a := b * c - k + succ('a');
outChar := pred(inChar);
```

2.3 Replace the following compound IF statement with a less confusing IF that has the same effect.

```
IF x>=0 THEN
   BEGIN
      IF x<=10 THEN
         BEGIN
            IF x=0 THEN result := 0 ELSE result := x;
         END
      ELSE result := sqrt(x)
   END
ELSE IF x<-20 THEN result := sqrt(-x+10)
ELSE result := -x;
```

2.4 The program in Table 2–9 sets hour and minute to 0 if either is out of range. Modify the program so that it instead prints an error message for out-of-range inputs, and prints the time only if both inputs are in range.

2.5 Modify the program in Table 2–9 so that it writes number only if a valid hex character was received.

2.6 Find a simpler statement equivalent to the following IF statement.

```
IF x>y THEN greater := true ELSE greater := false;
```

2.7 The adding-machine program in Table 2–1 fails if the input ever causes sum or number to be greater than maxint. Modify the program so that it detects "overflow" and prints a message whenever it occurs.

2.8 Eliminate the GOTOs in the following program fragment.

```
IF x = 1 THEN GOTO 1;
IF x = 2 THEN GOTO 2;
IF x = 3 THEN GOTO 3;
IF x = 4 THEN GOTO 4;
5: statementa;
4: statementb;
3: statementc;
2: statementd;
1: statemente;
```

2.9   Are the following two statements equivalent? Why or why not?

```
FOR i := 1 TO n DO
  IF prod < (maxint DIV i) THEN prod := prod * i
  ELSE n := i;

BEGIN
  i := 1;
  WHILE i <= n DO
    BEGIN
      IF prod < (maxint DIV i) THEN prod := prod * i
      ELSE n := i;
      i := i + 1;
    END;
END;
```

2.10   Write the output values produced by the first two FOR-loops in Table 2–10.

2.11   Assuming that maxint $= 2^{15}-1$, write the table of powers of two produced in Table 2–11. Repeat for Table 2–12.

2.12   Are the following two statements equivalent? Why or why not?

```
WHILE condition1 DO
  WHILE condition2 DO
    statement;

WHILE condition1 AND condition2 DO
  statement;
```

2.13   Give a general format for replacing a REPEAT statement with an equivalent sequence using WHILE.

2.14   Give the general format of a CASE statement that replaces an IF statement.

2.15   Eliminate the read operation in Table 2–13 and instead provide a FOR statement to classify all of the lower case letters.

2.16   (Electrical engineers only) Write a sequence of Pascal statements that computes the resistance of a resistor, assuming that its color code is contained in three variables, stripe1, stripe2, stripe3, of the subrange type colorCode.

DATA STRUCTURES
IN PASCAL PROGRAMS

Niklaus Wirth, the designer of Pascal, has written a programming textbook called *Algorithms + Data Structures = Programs*. From the previous chapters, you should already have a good idea of what programs and algorithms are. To find out what data structures are, just subtract, and you don't have to read this chapter. . .

Seriously, Wirth's equation indicates the fundamental importance of data structures in programming. A *data structure* can be defined as a collection of related data and a set of rules for organizing and accessing it. A list of the members of a family is an example of a simple data structure; a family tree is a more complex example.

The choice of a data structure obviously affects what we can do with the data. With either a family list or a family tree we can sort the names alphabetically, determine whether or not a given name is in the family, find the persons with the longest and shortest names, and so on. But only with the family tree can we determine the relationships of people as siblings, cousins, parents, spouses, and children, and determine how many generations are represented.

Even when two data structures contain exactly the same information, the choice between the two may affect the efficiency of accessing the information, depending on the application. For example, the telephone company gives its customers a phone book sorted by last name. But it also sells the same data sorted by street address to the perpetrators of nuisance calls.

Another factor is the amount of storage needed to contain the data structure. Suppose we want to store all of the prime numbers between 1 and 1000. There are 168 such numbers, and so we could allocate 168 words of memory and store one number in each. In a computer with 16-bit memory words, this would require a total of 2688 bits of memory. Alternatively, we could allocate only 1000 bits of memory, one for each number in the range 1 to 1000. Each bit in this "bit map" would be set to 1 if the corresponding number were prime, 0 if not.

In this chapter we shall learn how data structures can be defined and manipulated in Pascal programs. When we discuss individual computer instruction sets in Part 3 we shall see how strongly the instruction set influences the way data structures are set up and manipulated in assembly language programs.

3.1 ONE-DIMENSIONAL ARRAYS

The simplest and most familiar type of data structure is the array. An *array* is an ordered list of data components of the same type. A *one-dimensional array* specifies each component by the array name and a single index value. Multidimensional arrays are discussed in the next section. A simple example of a one-dimensional array of 10 integers is shown in Table 3–1. As shown in this example, array components are customarily stored in sequential locations in memory. A one-dimensional array is sometimes called a *vector*.

The primary characteristics of an array are its name, the type of its components, and the indices of its first and last components. A high-level language program does not specify the actual addresses in memory used by an

TABLE 3–1 An array "ints" of 10 integers.

Array Element	Hex Address in Memory	Value
ints[1]	2300	119
ints[2]	2302	−17
ints[3]	2304	−88
ints[4]	2306	24
ints[5]	2308	0
ints[6]	230A	27
ints[7]	230C	−99
ints[8]	230E	32
ints[9]	2310	6
ints[10]	2312	−51

Notes: Address sequence assumes each integer occupies two bytes in a byte-addressable computer.

TABLE 3–2   Characteristics of arrays in different high-level languages.

Language	Index of First Element	Index of Last Element	Multidim'l Arrays?	Dynamic Arrays?
Algol	Declared	Declared	Yes	Yes
Basic	0 or 1	Decl. or default	Yes	No
Fortran	1	Declared	Yes	No
Pascal	Declared	Declared	Yes	No
PL/1	1	Declared	Yes	Yes
PL/M	0	Declared	No	No
PL/Z	0	Declared	Yes	No

array; each component of the array is referenced by the array name (e.g., ints) and an index value (e.g., [3]) giving the component's position in the array. Different high-level languages impose different restrictions on arrays, as shown in Table 3–2. Some languages fix the index number of the first array component, others allow an arbitrary first index. Some allow dynamic arrays, in which the starting and ending indices can be inputs to the program or even values computed by the program, rather than fixed when the program is written. Most languages allow multidimensional arrays.

To see the usefulness of being able to specify the first index of an array, consider a 100-component array containing the gross national product for each year in the 19th century. Pascal allows the starting and ending indices to be specified as follows:

VAR gnp : ARRAY [1801..1900] OF real;

In a language that forces the first index to be 1, we would have two less desirable alternatives. We could declare an array biggnp of 1900 components and waste the first 1800; or we could declare an array shfgnp of 100 components and compute index := year−1800 and access shfgnp[index] to get the GNP for year.

An array is the simplest of *structured types* in Pascal. You may notice that the range specification in the example above has the same format as a subrange type specification. The general format of an array variable declaration in Pascal is

VAR
    identifier : ARRAY [*index type*] OF *component type*;

where *index type* is any enumerated or subrange type (not integer or real), and *component type* is any type. The following variable declarations make use of example types that were defined in Section 2.6.

```
VAR
   population : ARRAY [city] OF integer;
   opposite : ARRAY [direction] OF direction;
   digitCount : ARRAY [digit] OF integer;
   paintSupply : ARRAY [color] OF real;
```

Going one step further, Pascal also allows user-defined types that are arrays. Array types may be defined in the type definition part of a program; array variables may then be declared by referring to the defined type, as shown in the following examples.

```
TYPE
   vector = ARRAY [1..50] OF real;
   cityNums = ARRAY [city] OF integer;
   mapLinks = ARRAY [direction] OF direction;
VAR
   a, b, c : vector;
   population, elevation : cityNums;
   opposite, clkwise, cclkwise : mapLinks;
```

Strings of characters are stored as arrays in Pascal. For example, a line of text to be displayed on a terminal could be declared as follows:

```
VAR
   line : ARRAY [1..80] OF char;
```

Pascal array declarations may use the reserved word PACKED to tell the compiler that array elements are to be packed as efficiently as possible into the computer's memory words, for example:

```
VAR
   line : PACKED ARRAY [1..80] OF char;
```

Theoretically, the use of PACKED should have no effect on the results of the program's execution, but it sometimes can in strange boundary cases. In any case, it definitely affects both the size and execution time of the program. Packing obviously reduces data storage requirements, but it usually increases program size and execution time because of extra instructions for packing and unpacking the data.

A Pascal program that averages and normalizes students' scores on an exam is given in Table 3–3. The scores must be stored in an array so that each score can be normalized after the highest score is determined. Since Pascal does not allow dynamic arrays, the program declares an array with size equal to the maximum number of students ever expected. Each time the program is run, it reads the number of scores to be handled on that particular run, followed by the scores themselves.

TABLE 3-3 Pascal program using an array.

```
PROGRAM Normalize (input,output);
{
   This program reads exam scores and places them in an array.
   It computes and prints the average score, normalizes all scores
   according to the highest, and prints the normalized scores.
}
CONST maxscores = 100;   {maximum number of scores}
TYPE idnum = 1..maxscores;
VAR id, nscores : idnum;
   score : ARRAY [idnum] OF real;
   sum, hiscore, avg : real;
BEGIN
   read(nscores);   {Read number of scores for this run.}
   writeln('Number of scores for this run: ',nscores);
   sum := 0; hiscore := 0;
   FOR id := 1 TO nscores DO
      BEGIN
         read(score[id]);   {Read score}
         sum := sum + score[id];   {Get sum for average.}
         IF score[id] > hiscore THEN
            hiscore := score[id];   {Get highest score for normalization.}
      END;
   writeln('Highest score is: ',hiscore);
   avg := sum/nscores;   {Compute average and print results.}
   writeln('Average score is: ',avg);
   writeln('Normalized average is: ',avg/hiscore);
   writeln('Input and normalized scores are: ');
   FOR id:=1 TO nscores DO   {Print normalized scores.}
      writeln(id,score[id],score[id]/hiscore);
END.
```

At this point, a few words should be said about validity checking of inputs to a program. It is standard programming practice to check the "reasonableness" of inputs to a program if inputs outside a specified range will cause abnormal program behavior or nonsensical results. The program in Table 3–3 fails if the number of scores (nscores) is greater than 100 or less than or equal to 0. For example, if nscores is greater than 100 the program will attempt to access array components beyond the declared range of the array. If id and nscores were of type integer, a good Pascal compiler would generate code that checks these values against the array boundaries each time the array is accessed. However, restricting these variables to be in the subrange 1..100 allows more efficient checks — a check is required only when a new value is assigned to id or nscores. In an assembly language program, it is always up to the programmer to provide such checks.

3.2 MULTIDIMENSIONAL ARRAYS

Although a computer's memory is one-dimensional, a program can define multidimensional arrays and map them into the one-dimensional memory. For example, consider a 3×2 matrix A,

$$A = \begin{vmatrix} 1 & 2 \\ 3 & 4 \\ 5 & 6 \end{vmatrix}.$$

There are two obvious ways of storing the components of A in memory. They could be stored one row at a time, forming the sequence 1, 2, 3, 4, 5, 6; this storage sequence is called *row-major order*. Or the components could be stored one column at a time, 1, 3, 5, 2, 4, 6, in *column-major order*.

Pascal allows a multidimensional array to be declared as a one-dimensional array whose components are arrays. This means that the 3×2 array above could be declared as a one-dimensional array of 3 components of type "row", each of which was itself an array of 2 components:

```
TYPE
  row = ARRAY [1..2] OF integer;
  a3by2array = ARRAY [1..3] OF row;
VAR a : a3by2array;
```

Storing each row sequentially in memory by normal array storage rules results in row-major storage order. A component of A in row i, column j, would be referenced as a[i][j].

The above declaration can be abbreviated so that the definition of row is incorporated in the definition of a3by2array:

```
TYPE a3by2array = ARRAY [1..3] OF ARRAY [1..2] OF integer;
```

Pascal syntax allows this form to be further abbreviated by simply indicating the name of the array and the range of each of its dimensions:

```
TYPE a3by2array = ARRAY [1..3, 1..2] OF integer;
```

The array type need not be named if it is only used once, so we may write:

```
VAR a : ARRAY [1..3, 1..2] OF integer;
```

The array references may also be abbreviated; a[i][j] becomes a[i,j]. Declarations of arrays with three or more dimensions extend this syntax in the obvious manner; a $5 \times 19 \times 6$ array is declared below.

```
VAR b : ARRAY [0..4, 2..20, 10..15] OF real;
```

TABLE 3–4 Pascal program using a multidimensional array.

```
PROGRAM Average (input,output);
{
  This program reads four exam scores for each student and places
  them in an array.  It computes and prints the average score of
  each student for four exams, the average for each exam over all
  students, and the average of all students over all exams.
}
CONST
  maxStudents = 100;   {Maximum number of students handled}
  nExams = 4;   {Number of exams}
TYPE
  idNum = 1..maxStudents;
  examNum = 1..nExams;
VAR
  id, nStudents : idNum;
  exam : examNum;
  score : ARRAY [idNum,examNum] OF real;
  sum, average : real;

BEGIN
  read(nStudents);   {Read number of students for this run.}
  FOR id := 1 TO nStudents DO
    FOR exam := 1 TO nExams DO
      read(score[id,exam]);   {Read all scores.}
  writeln('Average for each student: ');
  FOR id := 1 TO nStudents DO   {Get average for each student.}
    BEGIN
      sum := 0;
      FOR exam := 1 TO nExams DO
        sum := sum + score[id,exam];
      average := sum/nExams;
      writeln(id,average);
    END;
  writeln('Average for each exam: ');
  FOR exam := 1 TO nExams DO   {Get average for each exam.}
    BEGIN
      sum := 0;
      FOR id := 1 TO nStudents DO
        sum := sum + score[id,exam];
      average := sum/nStudents;
      writeln(exam,average);
    END;
  sum := 0;
  FOR exam := 1 TO nExams DO   {Get average for all exams.}
    FOR id := 1 TO nStudents DO
      sum := sum + score[id,exam];
  average := sum/(nExams*nStudents);
  writeln('Average for all exams: ',average);
END.
```

A useful application of a multidimensional array is shown in Table 3–4. This Pascal program reads four exam scores for each student in a class of up to 100 students and stores them in a two-dimensional array. It then computes the class average for each exam, each student's average for the four exams, and the overall class average for four exams.

3.3 STACKS

A *push-down stack* (or simply a *stack*) is a one-dimensional data structure in which values are entered and removed one item at a time at one end, called the *top of stack*. A stack operates on a last-in, first-out basis, and is therefore sometimes called a *LIFO*.

As illustrated in Figure 3–1, a stack consists of a block of memory and a variable called the *stack pointer* (sp). In this example, the stack pointer always points to the location just beyond the item stored at the top of stack. Later, we will show an example in which the stack pointer points directly at the top stack item.

In the stack of Figure 3–1, a datum is entered by a *push* operation that stores the datum at the top of stack and points the stack pointer at the next

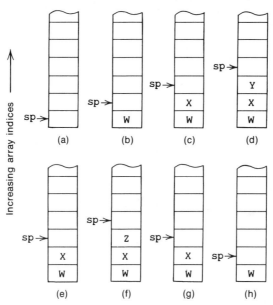

FIGURE 3–1 A push-down stack: (a) at initialization; after (b) pushing W; (c) pushing X; (d) pushing Y; (e) popping Y; (f) pushing Z; (g) popping Z; (h) popping X.

available memory location. Data is removed by a *pop* (or *pull*) operation that backs up the stack pointer by one memory location and removes the datum stored there.

A pushdown stack operates like the "IN" basket of a harried engineer. Each time a new task arrives, the current task is pushed down in the stack of work, and the new task is started. Once a task is completed, the engineer returns to the previous one.

If the harried engineer is given too many tasks, some of them will be lost or forgotten. The pushdown stack will likewise *overflow* if too many items are pushed onto it, as limited by the size of the memory block allocated for it. What happens at overflow depends on details of the stack's programming. A good program should either guarantee that stack overflow can never occur or provide a means of detecting it, since undetected overflow almost always causes program failure.

There is one situation that the pushdown stack encounters that a harried engineer never sees — trying to remove an item from an empty stack. This is called *underflow* and, left undetected, can be just as disastrous to a program as overflow.

One way to program a stack in Pascal is to declare an array stack and an integer variable sp to point into it. The elements of stack can be of any type; we use type char in our example:

```
CONST stackSize = 100;
VAR
  stack : ARRAY [1..stackSize] OF char;
  sp : integer;
  . . .
```

At the beginning of any program that uses a stack, the stack should be initialized to be empty:

```
BEGIN
  sp := 1;
  . . .
```

An item x can be pushed onto the stack by the following sequence:

```
{Push x}
  stack[sp] := x;
  sp := sp + 1;
```

and popped by the following sequence:

```
{Pop x}
  sp := sp - 1;
  x := stack[sp];
```

However, the first sequence fails if we try to put too many items in the stack. An explicit test for overflow should be included as shown below.

```
{Check and push x}
  IF sp <= stackSize THEN
    BEGIN stack[sp] := x; sp := sp + 1 END
  ELSE
    {Overflow, report error};
```

Likewise, the program should check that the stack is not empty before attempting to pop an item:

```
{Check and pop x}
  IF sp > 1 THEN
    BEGIN sp := sp - 1; x := stack[sp] END
  ELSE
    {Underflow, report error};
```

A simple program that makes use of a stack to reverse the order of a character string is shown in Table 3–5.

TABLE 3–5 Program to reverse character strings.

```
PROGRAM Reverse (input,output);
{
  This program reads and prints a line of text terminated by a
  period and saves it in a stack.  It then empties the stack,
  printing each character as it is removed.
}
CONST maxLen = 80;  {maximum length of a string}
  endChar = '.';  {string termination character}
VAR sp : integer;
  stack : ARRAY [1..maxLen] OF char;  inChar : char;
BEGIN
  sp := 1; read(inChar); write('Input string is: ');
  WHILE inChar <> endChar DO
    IF sp <= maxLen THEN
      BEGIN  {Stack not full.}
        stack[sp] := inchar; sp := sp + 1;  {Push the char.}
        write(inChar); read(inChar); {Print this char and read next.}
      END
    ELSE
      BEGIN  {Stack full.}
        write('!! String too long !!');  {Error message.}
        inChar := endChar;  {Force a terminator.}
      END;
  writeln; write('Reversed string is: ');
  WHILE sp > 1 DO  {Pop a char and print it.}
    BEGIN sp := sp - 1; write(stack[sp]) END;
END.
```

The stack pointers in the previous examples always point to the first free location in the stack, one past the top stack item. Reading the value stored at the top of stack without removing it requires an offset from the current value of the stack pointer:

```
{Read top of stack without popping}
  x := stack[sp-1];
```

In many applications it is desirable for the stack pointer to point directly at the top stack item, so that the top of stack can be read with less difficulty. Also, it is possible to make the stack grow in the opposite direction, so that the stack pointer is initialized to the *end* of the stack array, *decremented* for each push, and *incremented* for each pop. Table 3–6 is an example of such an application, a program that reads and sorts a sequence of numbers using two stacks.

Figure 3–2 illustrates the operation of the sorting program. One stack, stackL, stores numbers in ascending order, with the largest number at the top of stack. The other, stackH, stores numbers in descending order, with the smallest at the top of stack. Furthermore, the number at the top of stackL is always less than or equal to the number at the top of stackH. To enter a new number, we transfer data from stackL to stackH or from stackH to stackL so that the value of the new number lies between the values of the top of stackL and the top of stackH. Then we can push the new number onto either stack (stackL in the program) and maintain the sorted property of the stacks. When all input numbers have been processed in this manner, we move all of stackL into stackH, and then emptying stackH produces the sorted input numbers in ascending order.

Stacks are important data structures in several areas of systems programming. Algorithms for expression evaluation in compilers and interpreters depend on stacks to store intermediate results. Block-structured high-level languages such as Pascal keep local data and other information on a stack. Parameters of a procedure in a block-structured high-level language program are usually passed on a stack, and assembly language programs sometimes use this convention as well. And, as we shall see later, microprocessors universally provide hardware stacks to store return address and status information during subroutine calls and interrupt servicing. In assembly language programs, the stack pointer sp is usually stored as an absolute memory address, rather than as an index into an array.

3.4 QUEUES

A *queue* is a one-dimensional data structure in which data is entered at one end, called the *tail*, and removed at the other, called the *head*. As illustrated in Figure 3–3, a simple queue consists of a block of memory and two

TABLE 3–**6** Sorting program using stacks.

```
PROGRAM StackSort (input,output);
{
  This program reads a sequence of integers between -99 and +99,
  terminated by any number outside this range. As it reads the
  numbers, it sorts them using two stacks, stackL and stackH.
  After processing the last number, it prints the sorted series.
}
CONST
  maxLen = 200;   {Maximum length of a series.}
  stackSize = 201;   {Size needed in worst case.}
  minNum = -99;   maxNum = +99; {Allowable input range.}
VAR
  spL, spH, inNum, nNums : integer;
  stackL, stackH : ARRAY [1..stackSize] OF integer;

PROCEDURE PushH(v : integer); {Push v onto stackH.}
  BEGIN spH := spH - 1; stackH[spH] := v END;
FUNCTION PopH : integer; {Pop an integer from stackH.}
  BEGIN PopH := stackH[spH]; spH := spH + 1 END;
PROCEDURE PushL(v : integer); {Push v onto stackL.}
  BEGIN spL := spL - 1; stackL[spL] := v END;
FUNCTION PopL : integer; {Pop an integer from stackL.}
  BEGIN PopL := stackL[spL]; spL := spL + 1 END;

BEGIN
  spL := stackSize; stackL[spL] := minNum-1;   {Initialize stacks.}
  spH := stackSize; stackH[spH] := maxNum+1;
  read(inNum); nNums := 1;
  writeln('Input sequence: ');
  WHILE (inNum >= minNum) AND (inNum <= maxNum) DO   {Process inputs.}
    BEGIN
      {Make top of stackL <= inNum}
      WHILE stackL[spL] > inNum DO PushH(PopL);
      {Make top of stackH >= inNum}
      WHILE stackH[spH] < inNum DO PushL(PopH);
      PushL(inNum); {Now we have the right spot for inNum.}
      nNums := nNums + 1; {Keep track of how many inputs.}
      write(inNum);   {Print inNum.}
      IF nNums <= maxLen THEN   {If no overflow possible...}
        read(inNum)   {...get next inNum.}
      ELSE
        BEGIN   {Otherwise, print error message...}
          writeln('*** Too many inputs');
          inNum := minNum - 1;   {...and force termination.}
        END;
    END;
  {Finished all inputs, now move everything into stackH.}
  WHILE spL < stackSize DO PushH(PopL);
  writeln; write('Sorted sequence: '); {Print contents of stackH.}
  WHILE spH < stackSize DO write(PopH);
END.
```

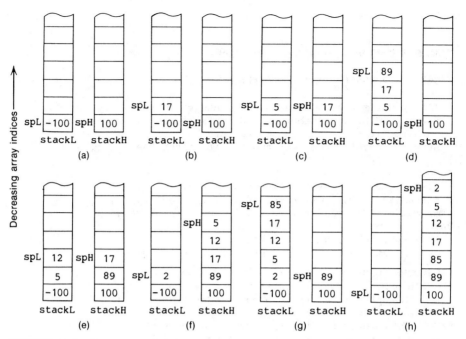

FIGURE 3–2 Contents of stacks used in sorting program: (a) at initialization; (b)–(h) after inputs 17, 5, 89, 12, 2, 85, −100.

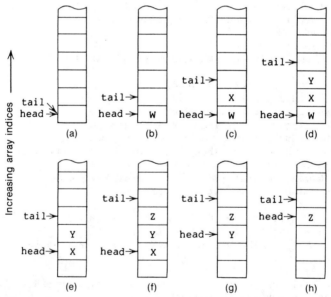

FIGURE 3–3 A simple queue: (a) at initialization; after (b) enqueueing W; (c) enqueueing X; (d) enqueueing Y; (e) dequeueing W; (f) enqueueing Z; (g) dequeueing X; (h) dequeueing Y.

variables to store pointers to the head and tail locations. Since a queue operates on a first-in, first-out basis, it is often called a *FIFO*.

In the queue of Figure 3–3, a datum is entered by an *enqueue* operation
that stores the datum at the location specified by `tail` and then advances
`tail` to the next available memory location. Data is removed by a *dequeue*
operation that reads the datum specified by `head` and then advances head to
point to the next item in the queue. The queue is empty whenever head
equals `tail`.

A queue could be declared and initialized in Pascal as follows:

```
CONST queueSize = 100;
VAR queue : ARRAY [1..queueSize] OF char;
  head, tail : integer;
BEGIN
  head := 1; tail := 1;
```

As in a stack, the elements in a queue can be of any type.

The queue as described so far has limited usefulness, since we exhaust
the storage space in an array of queueSize items as soon as queueSize items
have been enqueued, even if most of them have been subsequently removed.
What we need is a way to recover the space that is freed as items are dequeued, so that the queue overflows only if there are too many items actually
stored in the queue. This can be done quite simply by viewing the storage
array as a *circular buffer* as shown in Figure 3–4, wrapping around to the

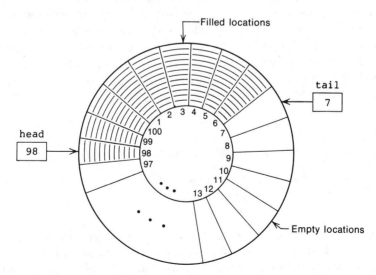

FIGURE 3–4 Circular buffer for queue.

beginning when the end is encountered. Then an item x can be enqueued and dequeued as follows:

```
{enqueue x}
  queue[tail] := x; tail := tail + 1;
  IF tail > queueSize THEN tail := 1;

{dequeue x}
  x := queue[head]; head := head + 1;
  IF head > queueSize THEN head := 1;
```

Like a stack, a queue can overflow if we try to put too many items in it. This condition can be detected by tail "catching up" with head and attempting to pass it. From Figure 3–3 it might appear that tail is always greater than or equal to head, so that overflow could be detected by the condition tail < head. However, due to the queue's circular nature tail < head can occur in normal operation, and so a strict equality check is needed before an item is enqueued:

```
{check and enqueue x}
  temp := tail + 1;
  IF temp > queueSize THEN temp := 1;
  IF temp = head THEN {overflow, report error}
  ELSE BEGIN queue[tail] := x; tail := temp END;
```

When tail is just one less than head, no more items can be stored in the queue, even though there is still one free memory location. Otherwise, we would have head=tail for a full queue, which is indistinguishable from the criterion for an empty queue. Therefore the queue can hold only queueSize-1 items. This makes sense if one considers that there are queueSize possible values of the (circular) distance from head to tail, corresponding to a range of 0 to queueSize-1 items stored in the queue.

A good program should also check for underflow before it dequeues an item:

```
{check and dequeue x}
  IF head = tail THEN {underflow, report error}
  ELSE BEGIN
    x := queue[head]; head := head + 1;
    IF head > queueSize THEN head := 1;
  END;
```

There is another, somewhat different way of designing a queue, wherein the head is fixed at the bottom of the memory buffer. Rather than move the head pointer when an item is removed, we can move all of the items in the queue down in memory. This is seldom done in programs, because of the large overhead of moving each item, one by one. However, hardware FIFO

chips quite commonly use this technique, because compact shift register circuits can be designed to do all the moving in parallel.

A contrived example of a text input/output program that makes use of a
queue is given in Table 3–7. The program reads a sequence of characters and
places them in a queue. Whenever the character "!" is received, the first
word in the queue is dequeued and printed, where a word is defined to be a
sequence of nonspace characters terminated by a space. Thus, the order of

TABLE 3–7 Word queue and output program.

```
PROGRAM WordQueue (input,output);
{
  This program enqueues a sequence of words, where each word is
  terminated by a space and the sequence is terminated by a
  period. Each time a '!' is received, it dequeues and prints
  one word. The '!' is not enqueued.
}
CONST qLen = 200;   {queue length}
  endChar = '.';   {input terminator}
  space = ' ';   {word separator}
  dumpChar = '!';   {command to print one word}
VAR inChar : char;
  queue : ARRAY [1..qLen] OF char;
  head, tail, temp : integer;
  wordFlag : boolean;
BEGIN
  head := 1; tail := 1; read(inChar); {Init queue and get first char.}
  WHILE inChar <> endChar DO {Process a character at a time.}
    BEGIN
      IF inChar <> dumpChar THEN
        BEGIN   {Enqueue the character.}
          temp := tail + 1;
          IF temp > qLen THEN temp := 1;
          IF temp <> head THEN
            BEGIN queue[tail] := inChar; tail := temp END;
        END {Lose characters on overflow.}
      ELSE
        BEGIN   {Dump one word to output.}
          wordFlag := true;
          WHILE (head<>tail) AND wordFlag DO
            BEGIN
              wordFlag := queue[head]<>space;
              write(queue[head]); head := head+1; {Dequeue, print char.}
              IF head > qLen THEN head := 1;
            END;
          writeln;   {Start a new line after each printed word.}
        END;
      read(inChar);   {Get next char.}
    END;
END.
```

the input characters is preserved, and the words are printed in the order in which they were received.

Queues are quite common in operating systems of large computers, where they are used to store requests for service in the order they are received, and then grant service on a first-come, first-served basis as the necessary resources become available. Queues are also a very natural data structure to use in the input/output software of any computer. When different devices and programs have varying speeds, a queue can be used to temporarily store data from a fast device or program and later transfer it to another device or program upon demand, without mixing up its order. A program that uses queues for input/output processing will be presented in Section 11.6.

In our Pascal examples, we have used arrays to store queue data, and so `head` and `tail` have been indices into the arrays. In an assembly language program, the array index computation can be avoided by storing absolute memory addresses in `head` and `tail`. A set of assembly language queue manipulation subroutines are presented in Section 9.3.

3.5 ONE-WAY LINKED LISTS

Stacks and queues allow data to be entered or removed at one end of the data structure, but not in the middle. A *linked list* is a one-dimensional data structure that allows data to be entered and removed at arbitrary locations. To get this flexibility, each item in the list has an associated *link* that points to the next item.

Figure 3–5 gives a conceptual view of a *one-way linked list*. (Two-way linked lists are discussed in the next section.) There is a variable called `head` that points to the first item in the list. Each item in the list has the same format: one cell (`link`) points to the next item, and a data block contains data in some format. The link and data block need not be contiguous in the computer's memory, but are drawn this way to indicate their close association.

The "next item" after an item X in the list is called the *successor* of X; the item before X is called the *predecessor* of X. If an item X has no successor, then its pointer is set to `null`, a special pointer value used only in this case.

To insert a new item Q in the list after an item P, we simply make Q's link point to the old successor of P, and make P's link point to Q. To delete the item Y after an item X, we make X's link point to Y's successor.

Pascal provides an efficient mechanism for using "pointer" and "record" data types to define linked lists and other dynamic data structures. But rather than get too deeply into Pascal, we'll show how to define linked lists using only the `array` type with which we're already familiar.

As an example, we will define a "class list" containing up to 100 names and an exam score for each. We can allocate storage for 100 names of 20

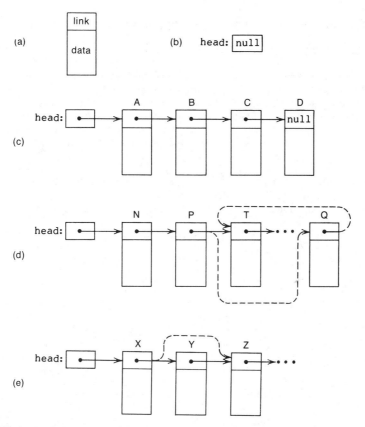

FIGURE 3-5 One-way linked lists: (a) general format of a list item; (b) an empty list; (c) a list with four items; (d) inserting an item Q after item P; (e) deleting the successor of X.

characters each as a 100×20 array of characters, the scores as an array of reals, and the corresponding links as an array of integers:

```
VAR name : ARRAY [1..100, 1..20] OF char;
    score : ARRAY [1..100] OF real;
    link : ARRAY [0..100] OF integer;
```

Each 20-character row of name and the like-numbered component of score comprise the data block for one list item; the like-numbered component of the link array stores the link. A link may be any valid index into the name, score, and link arrays, or the value null. We'll use null=−1 in our example; any value outside the range 1 to 100 could have been chosen. The link array has one extra component, link[0], used to store the head of the list.

TABLE 3–8 Name and exam score sorting program.

```
PROGRAM ClassList (input,output);
{
  This program reads a sequence of names and exam scores separated
  by spaces, with the entire sequence terminated by a period. As it
  reads each name/score pair, it enters it into a linked list that is
  kept sorted by name. After all name/score pairs have been read, all
  entries with scores less than the class average are ruthlessly
  deleted, and the names and scores of the survivors are printed.
}
CONST
  listLen = 100;  nameLen  = 20;   {List and name lengths}
  null = -1;  {End-of-list link value}
  endChar = '.'; space = ' '; {Terminator and separator}
VAR
  name : ARRAY [1..listLen, 1..nameLen] OF char;
  score: ARRAY [1..listLen] OF real;
  link : ARRAY [0..listLen] OF integer;   {link[0] = head}
  sum, avg : real;
  nNames, nChar, j, prev, next : integer;
  inChar : char;  greater : boolean;
BEGIN
  sum:=0; nNames:=0; link[0]:=null;  {Initialization}
  read(inChar);  {Get first char.}
  WHILE inChar <> endChar DO
    BEGIN  {Read all names and scores.}
      nNames := nNames + 1;  nChar := 1;
      WHILE (inChar<>space) AND (inChar<>endChar) DO
        BEGIN  {Read one name.}
          IF nChar <= nameLen THEN
            name[nNames,nChar] := inChar;
            read(inChar);  nChar := nChar + 1;
        END;
      FOR j:=nChar TO nameLen DO   {Pad end with spaces}
        name[nNames,j] := space;
      readln(score[nNames]);   {Get score and start new line}
      sum := sum + score[nNames];   {Add to sum for average.}
      prev := 0; next := link[0];  {Point to class list head.}
      greater := false;
      WHILE (next <> null) AND (NOT greater) DO
        BEGIN  {Chase down list until end or greater name found.}
          FOR j := nameLen DOWNTO 1 DO
            greater := (name[next,j] > name[nNames,j])
              OR ((name[next,j] = name[nNames,j]) AND greater);
          IF NOT greater THEN {Get next item}
            BEGIN prev := next; next := link[next] END;
        END;  {Then insert new item after prev.}
      link[nNames] := next;  link[prev] := nNames;
      IF nNames < listLen THEN read(inChar)
      ELSE inChar := endChar;  {Terminate if too many names.}
    END;
```

TABLE 3–8 (continued)

```
   avg := sum/nNames;  {Compute average.}
   writeln('Average score:', avg, 'Lower scores will be purged');
   prev := 0;  {Purge all scores lower than class average.}
   WHILE link[prev] <> null DO
      BEGIN
        IF score[link[prev]] < avg THEN
           link[prev] := link[link[prev]]
        ELSE prev := link[prev];
      END;
   next := link[0]; writeln; {Now print the remaining sorted list.}
   WHILE next <> null DO
      BEGIN
        FOR j := 1 TO nameLen DO write(name[next,j]);
        writeln(score[next]); next := link[next];
      END;
END.
```

The head could have been declared as a separate integer variable, but we shall see that some list operations are easier if the head is accessed the same as any other list item.

In the example above, suppose q is the index of an item we wish to insert after an item with index p. The insertion can be accomplished as follows, assuming that the data block of the new item has already been filled:

```
{insert item Q after item P}
   link[q] := link[p];
   link[p] := q;
```

Deleting an item is even simpler; the following statement deletes the successor of an item with index x:

```
{delete successor of item X}
   IF link[x] <> null THEN link[x] := link[link[x]]
   ELSE {error, item X has no successor};
```

Table 3–8 is a program that reads names and exam scores one at a time, entering each one into the class list, always keeping the list sorted by name. The program starts with the list head (link[0]) equal to null, and with empty name and score arrays. As each name/score pair is read, the program allocates the next sequential row of the name array and the next location in the score array to store it. Starting at the head, it then scans down the list until an alphabetically greater name or the end of the list is found. It enters the new name before the greater name, or at the end of the list if no name was greater. After all name/score pairs have been read, the program unsympathetically deletes the entries for all of the unfortunate students whose scores were less than the class average, and prints the remaining sorted list.

Notice that the use of link[0] to store the head of the list allows items to be inserted and deleted at the beginning of the list without tests for this special case. Use of a separate head variable would have complicated these operations considerably.

In our example we used arrays to store data and links in the list, and we used indices into the arrays as pointers. Using an array index as a pointer requires the compiled code to calculate a memory address in the array each time a list item is referenced. In an assembly language program, we can avoid this overhead by using absolute memory addresses as pointers; examples appear in Section 7.3.

3.6 TWO-WAY LINKED LISTS

The list insertion and deletion operations described so far operate on the *successor* of a list item (insert Q after P, delete successor of X). Suppose we are handed a pointer to a list item X and told, "Insert Y in front of X," or "Delete X." Both of these operations must change the link of X's *predecessor*. If all we have is a pointer to X, the only way to find X's predecessor is to start at the beginning of the list and search until X is found:

```
{insert item Y in front of item X}
{assume link[0] is the head}
  prev := 0;
  WHILE (link[prev] <> null) AND (link[prev] <> x) DO
    prev := link[prev];
  IF link[prev] = x THEN
    BEGIN link[prev] := y; link[y] := x END
  ELSE {error, item X not found};

{delete item X}
  prev := 0;
  WHILE (link[prev] <> null) AND (link[prev] <> x) DO
    prev := link[prev];
  IF link[prev] = x THEN link[prev] := link[link[prev]];
  ELSE {error, item X not found};
```

One operation that always requires searching through the entire list is deleting the last item in the list. Sometimes it may be worthwhile to avoid the overhead of searching by using a two-way linked list.

In a *two-way linked list*, each list item has two links; succlink points to the successor of the item and predlink points to the predecessor. Now we can always find an item's predecessor or successor in one step, but we have more links to update each time we insert or delete an item:

```
{insert item Y in front of item X}
  succlink[y] := x;
  predlink[y] := predlink[x];
  succlink[predlink[x]] := y;
  predlink[x] := y;
```

```
{insert item Y after item X}
  succlink[y] := succlink[x];
  predlink[y] := x;
  predlink[succlink[x]] := y;
  succlink[x] := y;

{delete item X}
  predlink[succlink[x]] := predlink[x];
  succlink[predlink[x]] := succlink[x];
```

These operations are illustrated in Figure 3–6. As with one-way linked lists, the operations are simplified by assuming that the head and tail of the list are accessed the same as other list items, for example, head = succlink[0] and tail = predlink[0]. At initialization, head and tail point to each other.

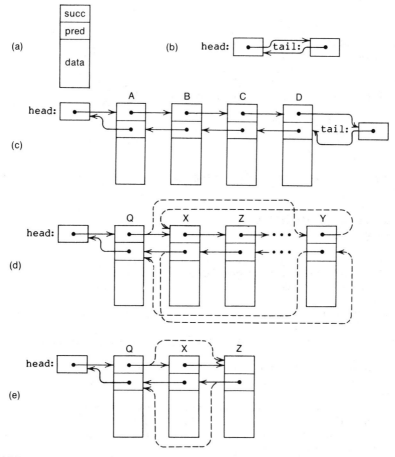

FIGURE 3–6 Two way linked lists: (a) general format of a list item; (b) an empty list; (c) a list with four items; (d) inserting item Y in front of item X; (e) deleting item X.

3.7 LIST STORAGE MANAGEMENT

So far, we have assumed that there is always enough storage available to create new list items when we need them, and we haven't worried about the storage that is lost when we delete a list item. However, in most applications that use lists, we need to manage the available storage so that none is wasted.

The easiest way to keep track of available list storage is by use of a *free list*, a list of all the unused blocks. At system initialization, we chain all of the available blocks together into the free list. When we want to add a new item to an active list, we remove the first block from the free list and use it to store the new item. When we delete an item from an active list, we return the block to the free list. Using the class list example from Section 3.5, a free list could be declared and initialized as follows:

```
VAR
  name : ARRAY [1..100, 1..20] OF char;
  score : ARRAY [1..100] OF real;
  link : ARRAY [0..100] OF integer;
  free, next, new, temp : integer;
BEGIN
  link[0] := null;  {init head of class list}
  free := 1;  {init free list}
  FOR next := 1 TO 99 DO
    link[next] := next + 1;
  link[100] := null;
```

To insert a new item after item x in the class list, we use the first item in the free list:

```
{insert new item after item x}
  IF free <> null THEN
    BEGIN
      new := free;  {get first item on free list}
      free := link[free];  {delete from free list}
      link[new] := link[x];  link[x] := new;  {insert}
    END;
  ELSE {error, out of free space};
```

To delete the successor of x, we return the deleted item to the free list:

```
{delete successor of item x}
  IF link[x] <> null THEN
    BEGIN
      temp := link[x];  {save pointer to deleted item}
      link[x] := link[link[x]];  {delete item}
      link[temp] := free;  {put at front of free list}
      free := temp;
    END;
  ELSE {error, x has no successor};
```

An alternative to systematically returning deleted items to a free list is a technique known as *garbage collection*. Whenever the free list becomes empty, an audit is made of all the active lists that share it. Any list item that does not appear in some active list is assumed to be garbage and is returned to the free list. This eliminates the overhead of updating the free list with each deletion in favor of a periodic, possibly more efficient garbage collection operation.

Garbage collection is essential in complicated list processing applications where several lists may contain the same item or sublist — when we delete an item from one list, we don't know if there are other lists still pointing to the same item and therefore we *can't* return it to the free list. Free list management and garbage collection are part of the run-time package of list processing languages such as LISP and are invisible to the programmer.

One interesting application uses lists to program queues. Consider a computer that distributes messages to 100 different destinations in a network. Assuming that we can sometimes generate messages for a particular destination faster than we can transmit them, we must provide a message queue for each destination to temporarily store pending messages. Suppose that in the worst case, we might have to queue 20 messages for a particularly busy destination. Therefore, providing a separate maximum-length queue for each destination using the structure in Section 3.4 would require storage for $100 \cdot 20 = 2000$ messages. If each message block is 100 characters long, we need 200,000 characters of memory!

On the other hand, we may know that there will never be more than 100 outstanding messages in the system, even if some destinations have 20. Therefore, we can allocate a free list with 100 message blocks, and program each queue to be a linked list that uses this free list. During normal operation most queues would be empty or near-empty, but there would be sufficient free space that a few queues could become very large if they needed to. By sharing one free list, we can do the job with only 10,000 characters of storage.

REFERENCES

Since 1968, the best reference on data structures has been Knuth's *Fundamental Algorithms* [Addison-Wesley, 1973 (second edition)]; it will continue to be the best reference for a long time to come. Knuth's treatment of data structures is especially applicable for assembly language programmers, since examples are given in the assembly language of a fairly general, hypothetical machine called MIX. Advanced data structures and techniques applicable to sorting and searching are covered in Knuth's *Sorting and Searching* [Addison-Wesley, 1973].

Wirth's *Algorithms + Data Structures = Programs* [Prentice-Hall, 1976] begins with a description of basic data structures in the context of Pascal programs, and continues with a study of some useful algorithms and data structures. Data structures are discussed in most basic programming texts, including *Introduction to Computer Organization and Data Structures* by H. S. Stone and D. P. Siewiorek [McGraw-Hill, 1975], *Minicomputer Systems* by Eckhouse and Morris [Prentice-Hall, 1979 (second edition)], and *Introduction to Computer Science* by C. W. Gear [SRA, 1973].

EXERCISES

3.1   Write a Pascal program that reads a series of input characters one at a time and places them in an array. Assume that there are three predefined constants of type char: backspace, endofline, and endoffile. Whenever a backspace is received, the previously stored character should be deleted from the array. When endofline is received, all valid characters in the array should be printed, and character collection should restart at the beginning of the array. When an endoffile is received, the array contents should likewise be printed, but the program should then terminate.

3.2   Write a Pascal program that reads a series of integers into an array and then sorts them as follows. Find the smallest number and exchange it with the first number in the array; find the second smallest number and exchange it with the second number in the array; continue in this manner until all numbers have been processed. The program should then print the sorted series of numbers. (*Hint:* After each iteration, the next smallest number can be found by starting the search one location deeper in the array. *Further note:* This isn't a very good sorting algorithm.)

3.3   Write a Pascal program that computes the prime numbers from 2 to 1000 using a boolean array prime [2..1000]. Initialize all the array elements to true. Starting with array element 2·2, mark all of the array elements corresponding to multiples of 2 as false. Continue with multiples of 3, 4, 5, and so on, until all nonprime numbers have been marked, and then print the primes.

3.4   Optimize the preceeding program by only marking multiples of known primes. That is, do not mark multiples of 4, 6, 8, 9, etc., since they are already marked when this step is reached.

3.5   Given an $m \times r$ matrix A and an $r \times n$ matrix B, the matrix product $A \cdot B$ is an $m \times n$ matrix C, where each element C_{ij} of C is given by the following equation:

$$C_{ij} = \sum_{1 \leq k \leq r} A_{ik} \cdot B_{kj}$$

Write a Pascal program that reads two matrices A and B and computes and prints their product. Assume that the maximum value of m, n, and r for any run of the program is 20, but read their actual values at the beginning of the program.

3.6   The programs in Tables 3–3 and 3–4 begin by reading the number of students to be handled on a particular run of the program. This requires the input file to contain this number, and is a source of error when the input file is modified. Suggest a way to modify the input format and the programs so that the student count is not needed.

3.7   Rewrite the Pascal program in Table 3–4 so that the first and last for-loops are eliminated.

3.8   Write declaration, initialization, "check and push," and "check and pop" sequences in Pascal for a stack in which sp always points directly at the top stack item.

3.9   Write declaration, initialization, "check and push," and "check and pop" sequences in Pascal for a stack that grows by *decrementing* rather than incrementing the stack pointer.

3.10   Rewrite the Pascal program in Table 3–6 so that the constants minNum–1 and maxNum+1 do not have to be stored as the first elements in the stack to force termination of the second and third WHILE loops. How does this affect the speed of the WHILE loops?

3.11   Rewrite the Pascal program in Table 3–6 so that both stacks share a single array. One stack starts at the first location of the array and grows by incrementing the stack pointer; the other starts at the last location and grows by decrementing the stack pointer. With this arrangement, how big an array is needed to sort a sequence of 200 integers?

3.12   Assuming that the high-level language does *not* perform bounds checking on stack access, suggest a method of detecting stack overflow that allows "post mortem" detection of stack overflow without requiring a check before every push operation. Indicate any assumptions required for the method to be effective.

3.13   Write declaration, initialization, "check and enqueue," and "check and dequeue" sequences in Pascal for a queue that can actually store queueSize items in an array of size queueSize. (*Hint:* In order to do this, an extra variable will be needed to distinguish between full and empty when head = tail.)

3.14   Write declaration, initialization, "check and enqueue," and "check and dequeue" sequences in Pascal for a queue that fixes the head at the bottom of a memory buffer and shifts down the entire contents of the queue when an item is deleted. Using this technique, how many items can be stored in a buffer of size queueSize?

3.15   Show how to eliminate the variable wordFlag in Table 3–7 by using a GOTO statement in the innermost WHILE-loop. Is this a reasonable use of GOTO? Suggest how an "EXIT" statement could be added to Pascal to provide a more structured way of terminating loops in situations like this.

3.16 Modify the program in Table 3–7 so that multiple spaces can be used to separate words. The output of the program should be the same whether a single space or multiple spaces are used.

3.17 Ask your favorite engineer if his or her "IN" basket is a stack or a queue. Ask the same question to a few experienced computer scientists and learn about all kinds of unusual and fascinating data structures.

3.18 A *double-ended queue* (sometimes called a *dequeue*) may have items added or removed at either end. The variables required for such a structure are the same as for a normal queue — head, tail, and a storage block. However, there are four ways to access the queue:

(a) Enqueue item x at the head.
(b) Enqueue item x at the tail.
(c) Dequeue item x at the head.
(d) Dequeue item x at the tail.

Write instruction sequences, including error checking, for these functions. Note that (b) and (c) are the access methods for a normal queue, while (a) and (c) [or (b) and (d)] give behavior analogous to a stack.

3.19 Why did we use the identifier prev instead of pred for predecessors in the linked-list examples in Section 3.6?

3.20 Write a Pascal program that reverses the order of a one-way linked list, using as little intermediate storage as possible.

3.21 Repeat the previous problem using a stack to store the links.

3.22 Show how to add a single tail pointer to a one-way linked list in order to allow efficient appending to the end of the list. Write instruction sequences that perform each of the following functions, correctly updating tail as well as the other pointers: (a) append item q at the end of the list; (b) insert item q after item p; (c) delete the successor of item x.

3.23 Convince yourself that the instruction sequences given for inserting and deleting items in a two-way linked list are correct for the following special cases by working them out by hand: (a) inserting after the head in an empty list; (b) inserting in front of the tail in an empty list; (c) deleting the item in a list with only one item.

3.24 Write a Pascal program that reverses the order of a two-way linked list.

3.25 Explain why the value 0 could be used for null in the one-way linked list in Table 3–8, even though 0 is also the index of the list head. Then explain why 0 *cannot* be used as the value of null in the two-way linked list examples in Section 3–7.

3.26 Suppose elements of a two-way linked list are always accessed by scanning the list in one direction or the other, so that we always know either the predecessor or the successor of the current list item. Then instead of storing both predecessor and successor links with each list item, we can store a function of the two links such that, given the value of one link, we can derive the other from the stored function value. Describe two functions that have this property and require no more storage for the function value than for one link.

3.27 Add free-list maintenance to the program in Table 3–8. Define procedures GetFree and PutFree to get items from the free list and return surplus items to the free list. Provide appropriate error checks to determine if the free list is empty.

3.28 Describe potential advantages of using an element of the link array (e.g., link[-1]) to store the free list head, instead of using a separate variable free.

4

NUMBER SYSTEMS
AND ARITHMETIC

The study of computer number systems and arithmetic is essential for under-standing how computers process numeric data. And like all mathematics, number systems can be put to good use in everyday affairs too, if you just look hard enough. Here are some examples from my own experience:

- Correctly decorating the cake for my wife's 31st birthday with only five candles.

- Making my checkbook look like it had a large positive balance when it was really in the red.

- Finding HFC in the phone book after my efforts to hide the negative balance failed.

In the first crisis above, a binary number system saved the day. In the second, a system called ten's complement came in handy. And in the last case, re-membering how characters are represented by numbers in a computer helped me understand why HFC isn't listed between Heywood and Hiatt in the white pages. After reading this chapter, you too will be able to apply different number systems to your personal affairs, and you'll understand computer arithmetic as well.

4.1 POSITIONAL NUMBER SYSTEMS

Positional number systems are used in all computers and almost all day-to-day business of people. In a *positional number system*, a number is represented by a string of digits where each digit position has an associated weight. For example, the value D of a 4-digit decimal number $d_3 d_2 d_1 d_0$ is

$$D = d_3 \cdot 10^3 + d_2 \cdot 10^2 + d_1 \cdot 10^1 + d_0 \cdot 10^0$$

Each digit d_i has a weight of 10^i. Thus, the value of 6851 is computed as follows:

$$6851 = 6 \cdot 1000 + 8 \cdot 100 + 5 \cdot 10 + 1 \cdot 1$$

A decimal point is used to allow negative as well as positive powers of 10 in a decimal number representation. Thus, $d_1 d_0 . d_{-1} d_{-2}$ has the value

$$D = d_1 \cdot 10^1 + d_0 \cdot 10^0 + d_{-1} \cdot 10^{-1} + d_{-2} \cdot 10^{-2}$$

For example, the value of 34.85 is computed as:

$$34.85 = 3 \cdot 10 + 4 \cdot 1 + 8 \cdot 0.1 + 5 \cdot 0.01$$

In a general positional number system, each digit position has an associated weight of b^i, where b is called the *base* or *radix* of the number system. The general form of a number in such a system is

$$d_{p-1} d_{p-2} \cdots d_1 d_0 . d_{-1} d_{-2} \cdots d_{-n},$$

where there are p digits to the left of the point and n digits to the right of the point, called the *radix point*. The value of the number is

$$D = \sum_{p-1 \geqslant i \geqslant -n} d_i \cdot b^i,$$

the summation of each digit times the corresponding power of the radix. If the radix point is missing, it is assumed to be to the right of the rightmost digit.

Except for possible leading and trailing zeroes, the representation of a number in a positional number system is unique. (Obviously, 34.85 equals 034.85000, and so on.) The leftmost digit in such a number is called the *high-order* or *most significant digit*; the rightmost is the *low-order* or *least significant digit*.

The *binary radix* is used in almost all computers. The allowable digits, 0 and 1, are called *bits*, and each bit d_i has weight 2^i. Using subscripts to indicate the radix of a number, we show examples of binary numbers and their decimal equivalents below.

$$10001_2 = 1 \cdot 16 + 0 \cdot 8 + 0 \cdot 4 + 0 \cdot 2 + 1 \cdot 1 = 17_{10}$$

$$101010_2 = 1 \cdot 32 + 0 \cdot 16 + 1 \cdot 8 + 0 \cdot 4 + 1 \cdot 2 + 0 \cdot 1 = 42_{10}$$

$$110.011_2 = 1 \cdot 4 + 1 \cdot 2 + 0 \cdot 1 + 0 \cdot 0.5 + 1 \cdot 0.25 + 1 \cdot 0.125 = 6.375_{10}$$

The leftmost bit of a binary number is called the *high-order* or *most significant bit (MSB)*; the rightmost is the *low-order* or *least significant bit (LSB)*.

4.2 OCTAL AND HEXADECIMAL NUMBERS

Other radices besides 2 and 10 are important for computer users. In particular, the radices 8 and 16 provide convenient representations for numbers in a computer. The *octal number system* uses radix 8, while the *hexadecimal number system* uses radix 16. Table 4–1 shows the binary numbers from 0 through 1111 and their octal, decimal, and hexadecimal equivalents. The octal system requires 8 digits, and so the digits 0–7 of the decimal system are used. The hexadecimal system requires 16 digits, so the letters A–F are used in addition to digits 0–9 of the decimal system.

The octal and hexadecimal number systems are useful for representing binary numbers because their radices are powers of two. Since a string of three bits can take on eight different combinations, it follows that each 3-bit

TABLE 4–1   Binary, decimal, octal, and hexadecimal numbers.

Binary	Decimal	Octal	3-Bit String	Hexadecimal	4-Bit String
0	0	0	000	0	0000
1	1	1	001	1	0001
10	2	2	010	2	0010
11	3	3	011	3	0011
100	4	4	100	4	0100
101	5	5	101	5	0101
110	6	6	110	6	0110
111	7	7	111	7	0111
1000	8	10	—	8	1000
1001	9	11	—	9	1001
1010	10	12	—	A	1010
1011	11	13	—	B	1011
1100	12	14	—	C	1100
1101	13	15	—	D	1101
1110	14	16	—	E	1110
1111	15	17	—	F	1111

string is uniquely represented by one octal digit, according to the third and fourth columns of Table 4–1. Likewise, a 4-bit string is represented by one hexadecimal digit according to the fifth and sixth columns of the table.

Thus, it is very easy to convert a binary integer to octal (or hexadecimal). Starting at the binary point and working left, we simply separate the bits into groups of three (or four) and replace each group with the corresponding octal (or hexadecimal) digit. Two examples are shown below.

$$101011000110_2 = 101\ 011\ 000\ 110_2 = 5306_8$$
$$= 1010\ 1100\ 0110_2 = AC6_{16}$$

$$1101100111010101001_2 = 011\ 011\ 001\ 110\ 101\ 001_2 = 331651_8$$
$$= 0001\ 1011\ 0011\ 1010\ 1001_2 = 1B3A9_{16}$$

Notice in the examples that zeroes can be freely added on the left to make the total number of bits a multiple of three or four as required.

If a binary number contains digits to the right of the binary point, we can convert them by starting at the binary point and working right. As before, zeroes can be freely added as required (this time on the right), as shown in the example below.

$$11.1010011011_2 = 011\ .\ 101\ 001\ 101\ 100_2 = 3.5154_8$$
$$= 0011\ .\ 1010\ 0110\ 1100_2 = 3.A6C_{16}$$

Conversion from octal or hexadecimal to binary is easy too. We simply replace each octal or hexadecimal digit with the corresponding 3- or 4-bit string. The examples below also show that we can convert from octal to hexadecimal or vice versa by converting first to binary.

$$1573_8 = 001\ 101\ 111\ 011_2 = 0011\ 0111\ 1011_2 = 37B_{16}$$

$$A748_{16} = 1010\ 0111\ 0100\ 1000_2 = 001\ 010\ 011\ 101\ 001\ 000_2 = 123510_8$$

$$3.145_8 = 011\ .\ 001\ 100\ 101\ _2 = 0011\ .\ 0011\ 0010\ 1000_2 = 3.328_{16}$$

Most computer software uses either octal or hexadecimal numbers to describe binary numbers in the machine. For example, the PDP-11 uses octal, while all of the other computers in this book use hexadecimal. A 16-bit word takes on 65,536 values, a range of 0 to 177777 in octal, or 0 to FFFF in hexadecimal.

The choice between octal and hexadecimal representations is almost entirely a documentation convention. The only hardware impact of the choice is whether the computer's front panel lights and switches (if any) are arranged in groups of three or four!

4.3 GENERAL POSITIONAL NUMBER SYSTEM CONVERSIONS

In general, conversion between two bases cannot be done by simple substitutions; arithmetic operations are required. In this section we will show how to convert a number in any base to base-10 and vice versa, using base-10 arithmetic.

In Section 4.1 we indicated that the value of a number in any base is given by the formula,

$$D = \sum_{p-1 \geq i \geq -n} d_i \cdot b^i,$$

where b is the base of the number and there are p digits to the left of the radix point and n to the right. Thus, the value of the number can be found by converting each digit of the number to its base-10 equivalent and expanding the formula using base-10 arithmetic. Some examples are given below:

$$1BE8_{16} = 1 \cdot 16^3 + 11 \cdot 16^2 + 14 \cdot 16^1 + 8 \cdot 16^0 = 7144_{10}$$

$$F1AC_{16} = 15 \cdot 16^3 + 1 \cdot 16^2 + 10 \cdot 16^1 + 12 \cdot 16^0 = 61868_{10}$$

$$437.5_8 = 4 \cdot 8^2 + 3 \cdot 8^1 + 7 \cdot 8^0 + 5 \cdot 8^{-1} = 287.625_{10}$$

$$122.1_3 = 1 \cdot 3^2 + 2 \cdot 3^1 + 2 \cdot 3^0 + 1 \cdot 3^{-1} = 17.\overline{3}_{10}$$

The overbar in the last example indicates a repeated decimal.

A shortcut for converting whole numbers to base 10 is obtained by rewriting the expansion formula as follows:

$$D = ((\cdots((d_{p-1}) \cdot b + d_{p-2}) \cdot b + \cdots) \cdot b + d_1) \cdot b + d_0$$

That is, we start with a sum of 0; beginning with the leftmost digit, we multiply the sum by b and add the next digit to the sum, repeating until all digits have been processed. For example, we can write

$$F1AC_{16} = (((15) \cdot 16 + 1) \cdot 16 + 10) \cdot 16 + 12.$$

Although the formula above is not too exciting in itself, it forms the basis for a very convenient method of converting a decimal number D to a base b. Consider what happens if we divide the formula by b. Since the parenthesized part of the formula is evenly divisible by b, the quotient will be

$$Q = (\cdots((d_{p-1}) \cdot b + d_{p-2}) \cdot b + \cdots) \cdot b + d_1$$

and the remainder will be d_0. Thus, d_0 can be computed as the remainder of the long division of D by b. Furthermore, the quotient Q has the same form as the original formula. Therefore, successive divisions by b will yield successive digits of D from right to left, until all the digits of D have been derived. Examples are given below.

$$179 \div 2 = 89 \text{ remainder } 1 \quad \text{(LSB)}$$
$$\div 2 = 44 \text{ remainder } 1$$
$$\div 2 = 22 \text{ remainder } 0$$
$$\div 2 = 11 \text{ remainder } 0$$
$$\div 2 = 5 \text{ remainder } 1$$
$$\div 2 = 2 \text{ remainder } 1$$
$$\div 2 = 1 \text{ remainder } 0$$
$$\div 2 = 0 \text{ remainder } 1$$
$$\text{(MSB)}$$

$$179_{10} = 10110011_2$$

$$467 \div 8 = 58 \text{ remainder } 3 \quad \text{(least significant digit)}$$
$$\div 8 = 7 \text{ remainder } 2$$
$$\div 8 = 0 \text{ remainder } 7 \quad \text{(most significant digit)}$$
$$467_{10} = 723_8$$

$$3417 \div 16 = 213 \text{ remainder } 9 \quad \text{(least significant digit)}$$
$$\div 16 = 13 \text{ remainder } 5$$
$$\div 16 = 0 \text{ remainder } 13 \quad \text{(most significant digit)}$$
$$3417_{10} = D59_{16}$$

4.4 ADDITION AND SUBTRACTION OF NONDECIMAL NUMBERS

Addition and subtraction of nondecimal numbers by hand uses the same technique that we learned in grammar school for decimal numbers; the only catch is that the addition and subtraction tables are different. Table 4–2 is the

TABLE 4–2 Binary addition and subtraction table.

c_{in}, b_{in}	x	y	$x + y + c_{in}$	c_{out}	$x - y - b_{in}$	b_{out}
0	0	0	0	0	0	0
0	0	1	1	0	1	1
0	1	0	1	0	1	0
0	1	1	0	1	0	0
1	0	0	1	0	1	1
1	0	1	0	1	0	1
1	1	0	0	1	0	0
1	1	1	1	1	1	1

addition and subtraction table for binary numbers. To add two binary numbers X and Y, we add together the least significant bits with an initial carry (c_{in}) of 0, producing sum ($x+y+c_{in}$) and carry (c_{out}) bits according to the table. We continue processing bits from right to left, including the carry out of each column in the next column's sum. Two examples of decimal additions and the corresponding binary additions are shown below, with the carries shown as a bit string C.

C		101111000
X	190	10111110
Y	+ 141	+ 10001101
$X+Y$	331	101001011

C		001011000
X	173	10101101
Y	+ 44	+ 00101100
$X+Y$	217	11011001

Subtraction is performed similarly, using borrows (b_{in} and b_{out}) instead of carries:

B		001111100
X	229	11100101
Y	− 46	− 00101110
$X-Y$	183	10110111

A very common use of subtraction in computers is to compare two numbers. For example, if the operation $X-Y$ produces a borrow out of the most significant bit position, then X is less than Y; otherwise X is greater than or equal to Y. The use of subtraction for comparing numbers will be explored in detail in Sections 8.4 and 8.6.

Addition and subtraction tables can be developed for octal and hexadecimal numbers, or any other desired base. However, few computer scientists bother to memorize these tables, for a number of reasons. Subtraction tables are never needed, since subtraction can always be performed using complement number systems and addition as shown in the next section. Even addition is seldom done by hand, especially in high-level language programming. Hard-core assembly language programmers can purchase a hex calculator from Texas Instruments to facilitate calculations in binary, octal, or hexadecimal.

If the calculator's battery wears out, some mental shortcuts can be used to facilitate nondecimal arithmetic. In general, each column addition (or subtraction) can be done by converting the column digits to decimal, adding in decimal, and converting the result to corresponding sum and carry digits in the nondecimal base. (A carry is produced whenever the column sum equals or exceeds the base.) Since the addition is done in decimal, we rely on our knowledge of the decimal addition table; the only new thing we need to learn is the conversion from decimal to nondecimal digits and vice versa. The sequence of steps for mentally adding two hexadecimal numbers is shown below.

C	1 1 0 0		1	1	0	0
X	1 9 B 9$_{16}$		1	9	11	9
Y	+ C 7 E 6$_{16}$	+	12	7	14	6
$X+Y$	E 1 9 F$_{16}$		14	17	25	15
			14	16+1	16+9	15
			E	1	9	F

4.5 REPRESENTATION OF NEGATIVE NUMBERS

So far, we have dealt only with positive numbers, but there are many ways to represent negative numbers. In everyday business we use the signed-magnitude system, but most computers use a complement number system. All of the important systems are covered below.

4.5.1 Signed-Magnitude Representation

The representation of decimal numbers used in everyday business is called the *signed-magnitude system*. In this system, a number consists of a magnitude and a symbol indicating whether the magnitude is positive or negative. Thus we interpret decimal numbers $+98$, -57, $+123.5$, and -13 in the usual manner. In the decimal number system we make the convention that the sign is interpreted as "$+$" if no sign symbol is present. There are two possible representations of zero, "$+0$" and "-0", but both have the same value.

The signed-magnitude system can be applied to binary numbers quite easily by using an extra bit position to represent the sign. Traditionally, the most significant bit (MSB) is used to represent the sign (0=plus, 1=minus), and the lower bits contain the magnitude. Thus, we can write several 8-bit signed-magnitude numbers and their decimal equivalents:

$00101011_2 = +43_{10}$ $10101011_2 = -43_{10}$

$01111111_2 = +127_{10}$ $11111111_2 = -127_{10}$

$00000000_2 = +0_{10}$ $10000000_2 = -0_{10}$

The signed-magnitude system contains an equal number of positive and negative numbers. An n-bit signed-magnitude number falls in the range $-(2^{n-1}-1)$ through $+(2^{n-1}-1)$, with two possible representations of zero.

To add two signed-magnitude numbers, we follow the rules that we learned in grammar school. If the signs are the same, we add the magnitudes and give the result the same sign. If the signs are different, we subtract the smaller magnitude from the larger and give the result the sign of the larger. To subtract signed-magnitude numbers, we change the sign of the subtrahend and proceed as in addition.

4.5.2 Complement Number Systems

Negative numbers in a computer are usually represented by *complement number systems*. While the signed-magnitude system negates a number by changing its sign, a complement number system negates a number by taking its complement as defined by the system. Taking the complement is more difficult than changing the sign, but two numbers in a complement number system can be added or subtracted directly without the sign and magnitude checks required by the signed-magnitude system. We shall describe two complement number systems, called the *radix complement* and the *diminished radix-complement*.

In any complement number system, we always deal with a fixed number of digits, say n. We shall further assume that the base or radix is b, and that numbers have the form

$$D = d_{n-1}d_{n-2} \cdots d_1 d_0.,$$

so that the radix point is on the right and the number is an integer. If any operation produces a result that requires more than n digits, we throw away the extra high-order digit(s). If a number D is complemented twice, the result is always D.

4.5.3 Radix-Complement Representation

In the decimal number system, the radix complement is called the *10's complement*. In this system, the complement of an n-digit number is obtained by subtracting it from 10^n. Some examples using 4-digit numbers (and subtraction from 10,000) are shown below.

Number	10's complement
1849	8151
2067	7933
5374	4626
100	9900
8151	1849

In general in the radix-complement system, the complement of an n-digit number D is obtained by subtracting it from b^n. If D is between 1 and b^n-1, this subtraction will result in another number between 1 and b^n-1. If D is 0, the result of the subtraction is b^n; this has the form $100\cdots00$, where there are a total of $n+1$ digits. We throw away the extra high-order digit and get the result 0. Thus there is only one representation of zero in a radix-complement system.

From the above discussion it would seem that a subtraction operation is needed to form the radix complement of a number. However, this subtraction is avoided by rewriting b^n as $(b^n-1)+1$ and b^n-D as $((b^n-1)-D)+1$. The number b^n-1 has the form $mm\cdots mm$, where $m=b-1$ and there are n m's. For example, 10,000 equals 9,999 + 1. If we define the complement of a digit d as $b-1-d$, then $(b^n-1)-D$ is obtained by complementing the digits of D. Therefore, the radix complement of a number D is obtained by complementing the individual digits of D and adding 1. You should mentally confirm that this trick works for the 10's-complement examples above. Table 4–3 gives digit complements for binary, octal, decimal, and hexadecimal numbers.

4.5.4 Two's-Complement Representation

For binary numbers, the radix complement is called the *two's complement*. In this system, a number is positive if the most significant bit is 0, negative if it is 1. The decimal equivalent of a two's-complement binary

TABLE 4–3 Digit Complements.

	Complement			
Digit	Binary	Octal	Decimal	Hexadecimal
0	1	7	9	F
1	0	6	8	E
2	–	5	7	D
3	–	4	6	C
4	–	3	5	B
5	–	2	4	A
6	–	1	3	9
7	–	0	2	8
8	–	–	1	7
9	–	–	0	6
A	–	–	–	5
B	–	–	–	4
C	–	–	–	3
D	–	–	–	2
E	–	–	–	1
F	–	–	–	0

number is computed the same as for an unsigned number, except that the weight of the most significant bit is -2^{n-1} instead of $+2^{n-1}$. The range of representable numbers is $-(2^{n-1})$ through $+(2^{n-1}-1)$. Some examples of 8-bit numbers and their two's complements are shown below.

$$17_{10} = 00010001_2$$
$$11101110 \quad \text{(compl. bits)}$$
$$\underline{+1}$$
$$11101111_2 = -17_{10}$$

$$-99_{10} = 10011101_2$$
$$01100010 \quad \text{(compl. bits)}$$
$$\underline{+1}$$
$$01100011_2 = 99_{10}$$

$$119_{10} = 01110111_2$$
$$10001000 \quad \text{(compl. bits)}$$
$$\underline{+1}$$
$$10001001_2 = -119_{10}$$

$$-127_{10} = 10000001_2$$
$$01111110 \quad \text{(compl. bits)}$$
$$\underline{+1}$$
$$01111111_2 = 127_{10}$$

$$0_{10} = 00000000_2$$
$$11111111 \quad \text{(compl. bits)}$$
$$\underline{+1}$$
$$1|00000000_2 = 0_{10}$$

$$-128_{10} = 10000000_2$$
$$01111111 \quad \text{(compl. bits)}$$
$$\underline{+1}$$
$$10000000_2 = -128_{10}$$

In the two's-complement number system, zero is considered positive because its sign bit is 0. This convention is compatible with number theory and all programming languages. Since the two's-complement system has only one representation of zero, we end up with one extra negative number, -2^{n-1}, that doesn't have a positive counterpart. As shown in the example above, an attempt to negate this number gives us back the number itself. However, arithmetic operations can still give correct results when this number appears as an intermediate result, as long as we never attempt to negate it.

The two's-complement system is used in all minicomputers and micro-computers, and almost all large computers in operation today.

4.5.5 Diminished Radix-Complement Representation

In a *diminished radix-complement system*, the complement of an n-digit number D is obtained by subtracting it from $b^n - 1$. This can be accomplished by complementing the individual digits of D, *without* adding 1 as in the radix-complement system. In decimal, this is called the *9s' complement*; some examples are given below.[1]

---

[1]The apparent inconsistency in naming 10's and 9s' complements can be explained. If the radix point is considered to be just to the right of the leftmost digit, then the largest number is $9.99\cdots99$ and the 10's complement of D is obtained by subtracting it from 10 (singular possessive). Regardless of the position of the radix point, the 9s' complement is obtained by subtracting D from the largest number, which has all 9s (plural).

Number	9s' complement
1849	8150
2067	7932
5374	4625
7100	2899
8150	1849

4.5.6 Ones'-Complement Representation

The diminished radix-complement for binary numbers is called the *ones' complement*. As in two's complement, the most significant bit is the sign, 0 if positive, 1 if negative. Thus there are two representations of zero, positive zero $(00 \cdots 00)$ and negative zero $(11 \cdots 11)$. Positive number representations are the same for both ones' and two's complements. However, negative number representations differ by 1. A weight of $-(2^{n-1}-1)$, rather than -2^{n-1}, is given to the most significant bit when computing the decimal equivalent of a ones'-complement number. The range of representable numbers is $-(2^{n-1}-1)$ through $+(2^{n-1}-1)$. Some examples of 8-bit numbers and their ones' complements are given below.

$$17_{10} = 00010001_2$$
$$11101110_2 = -17_{10}$$

$$119_{10} = 01110111_2$$
$$10001000_2 = -119_{10}$$

$$0_{10} = 00000000_2 \text{ (positive zero)}$$
$$11111111_2 = 0_{10} \text{ (negative zero)}$$

$$-99_{10} = 10011100_2$$
$$01100011_2 = 99_{10}$$

$$-127_{10} = 10000000_2$$
$$01111111_2 = 127_{10}$$

The main advantages of the ones'-complement system are its symmetry and the ease of complementation. However, addition of ones'-complement numbers is somewhat more difficult than for two's-complement numbers. Also, number-testing hardware in a ones'-complement machine must always check for both representations of zero, or always convert $11 \cdots 11$ to $00 \cdots 00$. The ones'-complement system is used in some Control Data Corporation computers, but is seldom considered for new computer designs. It is still a useful system for certain software checksum applications (see Section 6.3).

4.5.7 Excess-2^{m-1} Representation

The *excess-2^{m-1}* system represents a number X in the range -2^{m-1} through $+2^{m-1}-1$ by the m-bit binary representation of $X+2^{m-1}$ (which is always nonnegative and less than 2^m). The range of this representation is exactly the same as m-bit two's-complement numbers. In fact, the representations of any number in the two systems are identical except for the sign bits, which are always opposite. We'll see the major use of excess-2^{m-1} representation when we discuss floating-point number systems in Section 4.11.

4.6 TWO'S-COMPLEMENT ADDITION AND SUBTRACTION

4.6.1 Addition Rules

A table of decimal numbers and their equivalents in different number systems, Table 4–4, reveals why the two's complement is preferred for arithmetic operations. If we start with 1000_2 (-8_{10}) and count up, we see that each successive two's-complement number all the way to 0111_2 ($+7_{10}$) can be obtained by adding 1 to the previous one, ignoring any carries beyond the fourth bit position. The same cannot be said of signed-magnitude and ones'-complement numbers. Because ordinary addition is just an extension of counting, two's-complement numbers can thus be added by ordinary binary addition, ignoring any carries beyond the MSB. The result will always be the

TABLE 4–4 Decimal and 4-bit numbers.

Decimal	Two's-Complement	One's-Complement	Signed-Magnitude	Excess-2^{m-1}
−8	1000	—	—	0000
−7	1001	1000	1111	0001
−6	1010	1001	1110	0010
−5	1011	1010	1101	0011
−4	1100	1011	1100	0100
−3	1101	1100	1011	0101
−2	1110	1101	1010	0110
−1	1111	1110	1001	0111
0	0000	1111 or 0000	1000 or 0000	1000
1	0001	0001	0001	1001
2	0010	0010	0010	1010
3	0011	0011	0011	1011
4	0100	0100	0100	1100
5	0101	0101	0101	1101
6	0110	0110	0110	1110
7	0111	0111	0111	1111

correct sum as long as the range of the number system is not exceeded. Some examples of decimal addition and the corresponding 4-bit two's-complement additions confirm this.

+3	0011		−2	1110
+ +4	+ 0100		+ −6	+ 1010
+7	0111		−8	1| 1000

+6	0110		+4	0100
+ −3	+ 1101		+ −7	+ 1001
+3	1| 0011		−3	1101

4.6.2 A Graphical View

Another way to view the two's-complement system uses the 4-bit "counter" shown in Figure 4–1. Here we have shown the numbers in a circular or "modular" representation. Starting with the arrow pointing to any number, we can add $+n$ to that number by moving the arrow n positions clockwise, where n is between 0 and 7. It is also evident that we can subtract n from a number by moving the arrow n positions counterclockwise.

What is most interesting is that we can also subtract n (or add $-n$) by moving the arrow $16-n$ positions clockwise. Notice that the quantity $16-n$ is what we defined to be the 4-bit two's complement of n, that is, the two's-complement representation of $-n$. This graphically supports our earlier claim that a negative number in two's-complement representation may be added to another number by simply adding the 4-bit representations using ordinary binary addition. Adding a number in Figure 4–1 is equivalent to moving the arrow a corresponding number of positions clockwise.

4.6.3 Overflow

If an addition operation produces a result that exceeds the range of the number system, *overflow* is said to occur. Addition of two numbers with different signs can never produce overflow, but addition of two numbers of like sign can, as shown by the following examples.

−3	1101		+5	0101
+ −6	+ 1010		+ +6	+ 0110
−9	1| 0111 = +7		+11	1011 = −5

−8	1000		+7	0111
+ −8	+ 1000		+ +7	+ 0111
−16	1| 0000 = +0		+14	1110 = −2

Fortunately, there is a simple rule for detecting overflow in addition: an addition overflows if the signs of the addends are the same and the sign of the sum is different. The overflow rule is sometimes stated in terms of carries generated during the addition operation: an addition overflows if the carry bits into and out of the sign position are different. Close examination of Table 4–2 shows that the two rules are equivalent.

An overflow rule may also be stated in terms of Figure 4–1. Starting with the arrow pointing at any number, adding a positive number causes overflow if the arrow is advanced through the +7 to −8 transition.

Most computers have built-in hardware for detecting overflow.

4.6.4 Subtraction Rules

Two's-complement numbers may be subtracted as if they were ordinary unsigned binary numbers, and appropriate rules for detecting overflow may be formulated. However, two's-complement subtraction is seldom performed directly. Rather, the subtrahend is negated by taking its two's complement and then the minuend and subtrahend are added, following the normal rules for addition. Negating the subtrahend and adding the minuend can be accomplished with only one addition operation as follows: perform a bit-by-bit complement of the subtrahend and add the complemented subtrahend to the minuend with an initial carry of 1 instead of 0. Examples are given below.

$$
\begin{array}{rrl}
        &   & 1 \text{ — initial carry} \\
   +4   &   0100   & 0100 \\
 -\ +3 & -\ 0011   & +\ 1100 \\ \hline
   +1   &   & 1\,|\,0001
\end{array}
$$

$$
\begin{array}{rrl}
        &   & 1 \text{ — initial carry} \\
   +3   &   0011   & 0011 \\
 -\ +4 & -\ 0100   & +\ 1011 \\ \hline
   -1   &   & 1111
\end{array}
$$

$$
\begin{array}{rrl}
        &   & 1 \text{ — initial carry} \\
   +3   &   0011   & 0011 \\
 -\ -4 & -\ 1100   & +\ 0011 \\ \hline
   +7   &   & 0111
\end{array}
$$

Overflow in subtraction can be detected by examining the signs of the minuend and the *complemented* subtrahend, using the same rule as in addition. Or, using the technique in the examples above, the carries into and out of the sign position can be observed and overflow detected irrespective of the signs of inputs and output, again using the same rule as in addition.

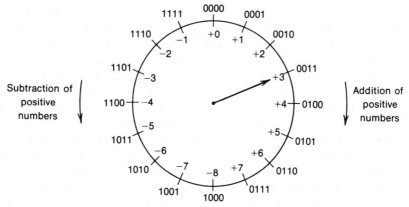

FIGURE 4-1 A modular counting representation of 4-bit two's-complement numbers.

An attempt to negate the "extra" negative number results in overflow according to the rules above, when we add 1 in the complementation process:

$$-(-8) = -1000 = \begin{array}{r} 0111 \\ +\ 0001 \\ \hline 1000 = -8 \end{array}$$

However, this number can still be used in additions and subtractions as long as the final result does not exceed the number range:

$$\begin{array}{rr} +4 & 0100 \\ +\ -8 & +\ 1000 \\ \hline -4 & 1100 \end{array}$$

$$\begin{array}{rrr} & & 1 \text{ — initial carry} \\ -3 & 1101 & 1101 \\ -\ -8 & -\ 1000 & +\ 0111 \\ \hline +5 & & 1|0101 \end{array}$$

4.6.5 Two's-Complement and Unsigned Binary Numbers

Since two's-complement numbers are added and subtracted by the same basic binary addition and subtraction algorithms as unsigned numbers of the same length, a computer needs only one type of addition or subtraction instruction to handle numbers of both types. However, a program must interpret the results of such an addition or subtraction instruction differently depending on whether it thinks it is dealing with signed numbers (e.g., -8 through $+7$) or unsigned numbers (e.g., 0 through 15).

We have already shown a graphical representation of the 4-bit two's-complement system in Figure 4–1. We can relabel this figure as shown in Figure 4–2 to obtain a representation of the 4-bit unsigned numbers. The binary combinations occupy the same positions on the wheel, and a number is still added by moving the arrow a corresponding number of positions clockwise, subtracted by moving the arrow counterclockwise.

An addition operation exceeds the range of the 4-bit unsigned number system in Figure 4–2 if the arrow moves clockwise through the 15 to 0 transition. In this case a "carry" is said to occur; in a paper-and-pencil addition this carry would be indicated by a carry out of the most significant bit position.

Likewise a subtraction operation exceeds the range of the number system if the arrow moves counterclockwise through the 0 to 15 transition. In this case a "borrow" is said to occur; in a paper-and-pencil subtraction this borrow would be indicated by a borrow in the most significant bit position.

From Figure 4–2 it is also evident that we may subtract an unsigned number n by counting *clockwise* $16-n$ positions. This is equivalent to *adding* the 4-bit two's-complement of n. The subtraction produces a borrow if the corresponding addition of the two's complement *does not* produce a carry.

In summary, in unsigned addition the carry or borrow in the most significant bit position indicates an out-of-range result. In signed, two's-complement addition the *overflow* condition defined earlier indicates an out-of-range result. The carry from the most significant bit position is irrelevant in signed addition in the sense that overflow may or may not occur independently of whether or not a carry occurs.

4.7 ONES'-COMPLEMENT ADDITION AND SUBTRACTION

Another look at Table 4–4 helps to explain the rule for adding ones'-complement numbers. Starting at 1000_2 (-7_{10}) and counting up, successive

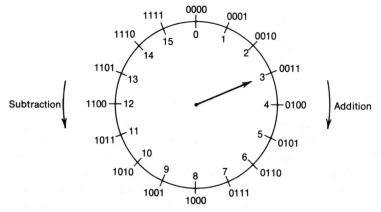

FIGURE 4–2 A modular counting representation of 4-bit unsigned numbers.

ones'-complement numbers are obtained by adding 1 to the previous one, *except* at the transition from 1111_2 (minus 0) to 0001_2 ($+1_{10}$). To maintain the proper count, we must add 2 instead of 1 whenever we count past 1111_2. This suggests a technique for adding ones'-complement numbers: perform a standard binary addition, but add an extra 1 whenever we count past 1111_2.

Counting past 1111_2 during an addition can be detected by observing the carry out of the sign position. Thus the rule for adding ones'-complement numbers can be stated quite simply. Perform a standard binary addition; if there is a carry out of the sign position, add 1 to the result. This rule is often called *end-around carry*. Examples of ones'-complement addition are given below.

$+3$	0011	$+4$	0100	$+5$	0101
$+ \ +4$	$+ \ \ 0100$	$+ \ -7$	$+ \ \ 1000$	$+ \ -5$	$+ \ \ 1010$
$+7$	0111	-3	1100	-0	1111

-2	1101	$+6$	0110	-0	1111
$+ \ -5$	$+ \ \ 1010$	$+ \ -3$	$+ \ \ 1100$	$+ \ -0$	$+ \ \ 1111$
-7	1|0111	$+3$	1|0010	-0	1|1110
	1		1		1
	1000		0011		1111

Following the two-step addition rule above, the addition of a number and its ones' complement produces negative 0. In fact, an addition operation using this rule can never produce positive 0 unless both of the addends are positive 0.

Some hardware adder circuits perform ones'-complement addition in one step by connecting carry output from the MSB directly to the LSB carry input. Unless the carry output is forced to 0 before the addition is begun, this can actually cause an ambiguity or even an oscillation when a number and its complement are added, and the result can be either positive or negative 0.[2] Except for this case, end-around carry causes no ambiguity.

As with two's-complement, the easiest way to do ones'-complement subtraction is to complement the subtrahend and add. Overflow rules for ones'-complement addition and subtraction are the same as for two's-complement. Ones'-complement operations can be performed on two's-complement machines by using "Add with carry" and "Subtract with carry" instructions.

---

[2]"One's Complement Adder Eliminates Unwanted Zero," by J. Wakerly, *Electronics*, Vol. 49, No. 9, February 5, 1976, pp. 103–105. An *Electronics* editor introduced the punctuation error in the article's title.

4.8   BINARY MULTIPLICATION

In this section we shall describe algorithms for signed and unsigned binary multiplication. Many computers implement these or similar algorithms in machine instructions. However, small computers omit these instructions to save hardware, and so the algorithms must be implemented in software using addition and shifting as primitives.

The algorithms in this and the next section are described in an extended Pascal that allows access to individual bits of a word; refer to Appendix B for a complete summary of the extensions. The algorithms can be easily translated into the assembly language of most computers.

4.8.1   Unsigned Multiplication

In grammar school we learned to multiply by adding a list of shifted multiplicands computed according to the digits of the multiplier. The same technique can be used to obtain the product of two unsigned binary numbers as shown below.

$$
\begin{array}{r}
11 \\
\times\ 13 \\
\hline
33 \\
11 \\
\hline
143
\end{array}
\qquad
\begin{array}{rl}
1011 & \text{multiplicand} \\
\times\ 1101 & \text{multiplier} \\
\hline
1011 & \\
0000 & \\
1011 & \text{shifted multiplicands} \\
1011 & \\
\hline
10001111 & \text{product}
\end{array}
$$

Forming the shifted multiplicands is trivial in binary multiplication, since the only possible values of the multiplier digits are 0 and 1.

Instead of listing all the shifted multiplicands and then adding, in a computer it is more convenient to add each shifted multiplicand as it is created to a *partial product*. The previous example is repeated in Table 4–5 using this technique.

When we multiply an n-bit word and an m-bit word in a computer, the resulting product will take at most $n+m$ bits to express. Therefore, a typical multiplication algorithm multiplies two n-bit words and produces a $2n$-bit double word product. Table 4–6 shows an algorithm that multiplies two positive integers mpy and mcnd, and produces a positive integer product stored in hiProd and loProd.

Table 4–6 uses extended Pascal to describe operations on bits. The extended Pascal operations are straightforward. Variables of type bit can have the values 0 and 1. A word is defined as an array of bits, numbered left to right from wlen to 0. The function Bshr(x,c) shifts the bit-array x one

TABLE 4–5 Multiplication with partial products.

1011	multiplicand
× 1101	multiplier
00000000	partial product
1011	shifted multiplicand
00001011	partial product
0000	shifted multiplicand
00001011	partial product
1011	shifted multiplicand
00110111	partial product
1011	shifted multiplicand
10001111	product

position as shown in Figure 4–3(a). The vacated MSB is filled with the bit value c; the value of the lost LSB is placed in the global bit variable BC. As shown in Figure 4–3(c), the function Badd(x,y,c) adds two bit-arrays x and y with an initial carry of c, using unsigned binary addition as in Section 4.4; BC is set to 1 if the operation produces a carry from the MSB, to 0 otherwise.

Figure 4–4 illustrates the operation of the multiplication program. Like the example in Table 4–5, it processes the low-order bits of the multiplier

TABLE 4–6 Program to multiply two 16-bit unsigned integers.

```
PROGRAM UnsignedMultiply (input,output);
CONST wlen = 15;
TYPE word = ARRAY [wlen::0] OF bit;
VAR cnt : integer;  mpy, mcnd, hiProd, loProd : word;
BEGIN
  read(mpy,mcnd);  loProd := 0;  hiProd := 0;  {Initialization}
  FOR cnt := 0 TO wlen DO
    BEGIN  {Process the multiplier one bit at a time.}
      {If multiplier LSB is 1, add multiplicand to high-order
          product, setting BC according to carry from MSB.}
      IF mpy[0] = 1 THEN hiProd := Badd(hiProd,mcnd,0) ELSE BC := 0;
      {Shift hiProd right, put BC into MSB, and put lost LSB into BC.}
      hiProd := Bshr(hiProd,BC);
      {Shift loProd right, picking up LSB that was lost from hiProd.}
      loProd := Bshr(loProd,BC);
      {Now move the next bit of multiplier to the LSB position.}
      mpy := Bshr(mpy,0);
    END;
  writeln(hiProd,loProd);
END.
```

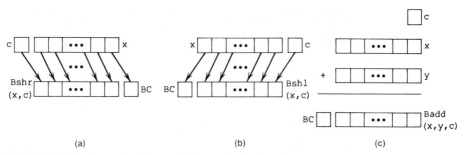

FIGURE 4–3 Extended-Pascal bit manipulation functions:
(a) Bshr(x : bitarray; c : bit); (b) Bshl(x : bitarray; c : bit);
(c) Badd(x,y : bitarray; c: bit).

first. However, instead of shifting the multiplicand left, it "positions" the multiplicand under the high-order word of the partial product, and shifts the partial product right.

The number of iterations of the loop in Table 4–6 equals the number of bits in the multiplier. In each iteration, if the LSB of mpy is 1, then mcnd is added to hiProd. This addition may result in a carry that sets BC; if the addition is not performed, BC is cleared. In this way, the resulting high-order partial product (hiProd and BC) may be shifted right one position, and the LSB is shifted into loProd. After being shifted into loProd, a product bit never changes.

At the beginning of the multiplication, loProd has no information in it, while mpy is full of multiplier bits to be processed. At the end, loProd is filled with the low-order product bits, while mpy has been emptied. Close examination of the program leads us to conclude that both mpy and loProd may be

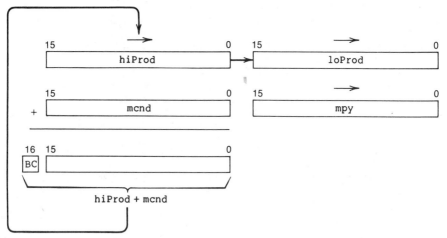

FIGURE 4–4 Variables used by multiplication algorithm.

combined into one variable. In fact, this trick is used in most hardware multi-pliers to save circuitry.

4.8.2 Signed Multiplication

Multiplication of signed numbers can be accomplished using unsigned multiplication and the usual grammar school rules: perform an unsigned multiplication of the magnitudes and make the product positive if the operands had the same sign, negative if they had different signs. This is very convenient in signed-magnitude systems.

In the two's-complement system, a complement operation is required to get the magnitude of a negative number, and the unsigned product must be complemented if a negative result is required. This overhead leads us to seek a more efficient way of performing two's-complement multiplication.

Conceptually, unsigned multiplication is accomplished by a sequence of unsigned additions of the shifted multiplicands; at each step the shift of the multiplicand corresponds to the weight of the multiplier bit. The bits in a two's-complement multiplier have the same weights as an unsigned multiplier, except for the MSB, which has a negative weight. It follows that we can perform two's-complement multiplication by a sequence of two's-complement additions of shifted multiplicands, except for the last step, which is a subtraction. This leads us to the two's-complement multiplication algorithm shown in Table 4–7.

In extended Pascal, the global `bit` variable `BV` is set after each `Badd` operation according to whether or not two's-complement overflow occurred. The function `Bxor(c,d)` returns the Exclusive OR of two bit-values c and d; that is, it returns c if d is 0, the complement of c if d is 1. Since `BV` is set to 1 if and only if the result of `Badd` has the incorrect sign, the expression `Bxor(hiProd[wlen],BV)` always returns the correct sign of the result.

The function `Bcom(x)` returns the bit-by-bit complement of a bit array x. Thus, `Badd(hiProd,Bcom(mcnd),1)` performs the two's-complement subtraction hiProd–mcnd in the last part of the program.

You are encouraged to explore the subtleties of the algorithm in Table 4–7 by working several examples with 4-bit two's-complement numbers. Like the unsigned algorithm, the signed algorithm can be modified to use the same variable for `mpy` and `loProd`.

4.9 BINARY DIVISION

4.9.1 Unsigned Division

The simplest binary division algorithm is also based on the technique we learned in grammar school, as shown in Table 4–8. In both the decimal and binary cases, we mentally compare the reduced dividend with multiples of the

TABLE 4–7 Program to multiply two 16-bit two's-complement integers.

```
PROGRAM SignedMultiply (input,output);
CONST wlen = 15;
TYPE word = ARRAY [wlen::0] OF bit;
VAR cnt : integer; mpy, mcnd, hiProd, loProd : word;
BEGIN
   read(mpy,mcnd); loProd := 0; hiProd := 0; {Initialization}
   FOR cnt := 0 TO wlen-1 DO
     BEGIN {Process all mpy bits except MSB.}
       {If multiplier LSB is 1, add multiplicand to high-order
           product, set BV to 1 on two's-complement overflow.}
       IF mpy[0] = 1 THEN hiProd := Badd(hiProd,mcnd,0) ELSE BV := 0;
       {Shift hiProd right, replicate the correct sign of
           the result, and put the lost LSB into BC.}
       hiProd := Bshr(hiProd,Bxor(hiProd[wlen],BV));
       {Shift loProd right, picking up LSB that was lost from hiProd.}
       loProd := Bshr(loProd,BC);
       {Move the next bit of mpy to the LSB position.}
       mpy := Bshr(mpy,0);
     END;
   {Process the sign bit of mpy.}
   {If mpy's LSB is 1, subtract multiplicand from high-order
       product, setting BV to 1 on two's-complement overflow.}
   IF mpy[0] = 1 THEN hiProd := Badd(hiProd,Bcom(mcnd),1) ELSE BV := 0;
   {Shift hiProd right, give it the correct sign, and put LSB into BC.}
   hiProd := Bshr(hiProd,Bxor(hiProd[wlen],BV));
   {Shift loProd right, picking up the LSB that was lost from hiProd.}
   loProd := Bshr(loProd,BC);
   writeln(hiProd,loProd);
END.
```

divisor to determine which multiple of the shifted divisor to subtract. In the decimal case, we first pick 11 as the smallest multiple of 11 less than 21, and then pick 99 as the smallest multiple less than 107. In the binary case, the choice is somewhat simpler, since the only two choices are zero and the divisor itself. Still, a comparison operation *is* needed to pick the proper shifted divisor.

Unsigned division in a computer processor is complementary to multiplication. A typical division algorithm accepts a double-word dividend and a single-word divisor, and produces single-word quotient and remainder. Such a division *overflows* if the divisor is zero or the quotient would take more than one word to express. The second situation occurs only if the divisor is less than or equal to the high-order word of the dividend.

Table 4–9 gives a division algorithm that can be easily converted into an assembly language program for most microprocessors. It divides a double-word unsigned integer hiDvnd,loDvnd by a single-word divisor dvsr, and

TABLE 4-8 Example of long division.

19	10011	quotient
11) 217	1011) 11011001	dividend
11	1011	shifted divisor
107	0101	reduced dividend
99	0000	shifted divisor
8	1010	reduced dividend
	0000	shifted divisor
	10100	reduced dividend
	1011	shifted divisor
	10011	reduced dividend
	1011	shifted divisor
	1000	remainder

TABLE 4-9 Program to divide two unsigned integers.

```
PROGRAM UnsignedDivide (input,output);
CONST wlen = 15;
TYPE word = ARRAY [wlen::0] OF bit;
VAR hiDvnd, loDvnd, dvsr, quot, rmdr : word;
  cnt : integer; flag : boolean;
BEGIN
  read(hiDvnd,loDvnd,dvsr);
  IF Beq(dvsr,0) THEN writeln('Error, division by 0 not allowed')
  ELSE IF Bls(dvsr,hiDvnd) THEN writeln('Error, quotient too big')
  ELSE
    BEGIN
      quot := 0;
      FOR cnt := 0 TO wlen DO
        BEGIN
          quot := Bshl(quot,0); {Make room for next quotient bit.}
          loDvnd := Bshl(loDvnd,0); hiDvnd := Bshl(hiDvnd,BC);
          {Shift double-word dividend left one bit,
              old MSB ends up in BC.}
          flag := BC=1; {Set flag if shifted dividend
             definitely greater than divisor.}
          hiDvnd := Badd(hiDvnd,Bcom(dvsr),1); {Do trial subtraction,
              set BC if the result is positive.}
          IF flag OR (BC=1) THEN
             quot[0] := 1  {Positive result, set quotient bit.}
          ELSE hiDvnd := Badd(hiDvnd,dvsr,0); {Negative result, }
        END;                                  { restore hiDvnd. }
      rmdr := hiDvnd;
      writeln(quot,rmdr);
    END;
END.
```

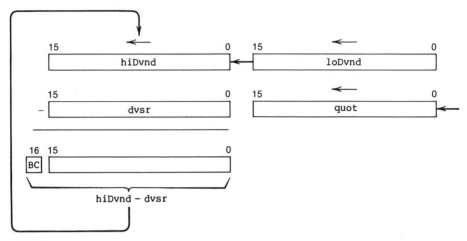

FIGURE 4–5   Variables used by unsigned division algorithm.

produces single-word quotient and remainder quot and rmdr. The relationships of these variables are shown in Figure 4–5.

The algorithm begins by checking for the two overflow conditions, using two extended-Pascal functions Beq and Bls. Beq(x,y) returns true if its two bit-array arguments are equal, false otherwise; Bls(x,y) returns true if x is lower than or the same as y when both are interpreted as unsigned numbers.

If there is no overflow, the quotient is initialized to zero and the division loop is executed once for each quotient bit (i.e., 16 times for a 16-bit quotient). Each time the loop is entered, it is known that hiDvnd is strictly less than dvsr. Therefore, shifting the double-word dividend left one bit makes the 17-bit word consisting of BC and hiDvnd still less than 2·dvsr. If this quantity is greater than or equal to dvsr, then a 1 is placed in the quotient and dvsr is subtracted, once again leaving hiDvnd less than dvsr. The extended-Pascal shifting function Bshl was shown in Figure 4–3(b).

The comparison of BC,hiDvnd and dvsr is somewhat involved. First, flag is set true if BC=1; if flag is true then BC,hiDvnd is a full 17-bit number and definitely greater than dvsr, a 16-bit number. In any case, dvsr is subtracted from hiDvnd in a "trial subtraction" by the operation Badd(hiDvnd,Bcom(dvsr),1). Since a borrow is the complement of a carry, this operation sets BC to 1 if there was no borrow out of the MSB, to 0 otherwise. If flag is true or no borrow was produced, then BC,hiDvnd was greater than dvsr and a 1 bit is placed in the quotient. Otherwise, the value of hiDvnd before the operation must be restored by adding dvsr to it.

At each iteration, quot is shifted left one bit to make room for the next quotient bit. At the end of 16 iterations, the quantity left in hiDvnd is the remainder.

As in the multiplication algorithms, we have one variable being filled with result bits while another is being emptied. Thus, quot and loDvnd may share the same variable. Again, this trick is often implemented in hardware. Also like the multiplication algorithms, the division algorithm is best understood by working several examples and special cases with 4-bit numbers.

This division algorithm is usually called *restoring division*. There is also a *nonrestoring division* algorithm that avoids the restoring addition step in the divide loop; most hardware dividers use it for its speed. However, in assembly language programs, nonrestoring division gives at best only marginally faster performance than restoring division, and so we don't cover it here.

4.9.2 Signed Division

As in multiplication, there are special techniques for performing division directly on two's-complement numbers; these techniques are often implemented in hardware dividers. However, in assembly language programs the easiest way to divide two's-complement numbers is to convert them to positive numbers, perform restoring division, and convert the results back to the appropriate sign.

The restoring division algorithm is somewhat simplified in this case because negative numbers produced by trial subtractions are now representable within the word length of the operands. Adapting the previous program, the divisor, remainder, and quotient are now 15 bits plus sign, and the dividend is 31 bits plus sign. The new program is shown in Table 4–10. The signs of the divisor and dividend are tested at the outset, and both operands are made positive for the division algorithm. The results are converted to the proper signs at the end. The conversions are done so that the remainder has the same sign as the dividend, so that the remainder plus the divisor times quotient equals the original dividend.

4.10 BINARY-CODED DECIMAL REPRESENTATION

The *binary-coded decimal (BCD)* number system encodes the digits 0 through 9 by their 4-bit unsigned binary representations, 0000 through 1001. The codes 1010 through 1111 are not used. Conversions between BCD and decimal representations are trivial, a direct substitution of four bits for each decimal digit. Two BCD digits may be packed into one byte; thus one byte may represent the values from 0 to 99 as opposed to 0 to 255 for a normal unsigned 8-bit binary number. BCD numbers with any desired number of digits may be obtained by using one byte for each two digits.

As with binary numbers, there are many possible representations of negative BCD numbers. Signed BCD numbers have one extra digit position for the sign. Both the signed-magnitude and 10's-complement representations

TABLE 4-10 Program to divide two's-complement integers.

```
PROGRAM SignedDivide (input,output);
CONST wlen = 15;
TYPE word = ARRAY [wlen::0] OF bit;
VAR hiDvnd, loDvnd, dvsr, quot, rmdr : word;
   cnt : integer; negDvsr, negDvnd : boolean;
BEGIN
   read(hiDvnd,loDvnd,dvsr);
   negDvsr := dvsr[wlen]=1;  negDvnd := hiDvnd[wlen]=1;
   IF negDvsr THEN dvsr := Badd(0,Bcom(dvsr),1); {Make dvsr positive.}
   IF negDvnd THEN  {Make dvnd positive.}
     BEGIN  {A 'double precision' negate.}
       loDvnd := Badd(0,Bcom(loDvnd),1);
       hiDvnd := Badd(0,Bcom(hiDvnd),BC);
     END;
   IF Beq(dvsr,0) THEN writeln('Error, divide by 0 not allowed')
   ELSE IF Bls(dvsr,hiDvnd) THEN writeln('Error, quotient too big')
   ELSE
     BEGIN {Compute quotient and remainder.}
       quot := 0;
       FOR cnt := 0 TO wlen-1 DO
         BEGIN
           quot := Bshl(quot,0); {Make room for next quotient bit.}
           {Shift double-word dvnd left one bit.}
           loDvnd := Bshl(loDvnd,0); hiDvnd := Bshl(hiDvnd,BC);
           hiDvnd := Badd(hiDvnd,Bcom(dvsr),1); {Do trial subtraction.}
           IF hiDvnd[wlen]=0 THEN
              quot[0] := 1; {Positive result, set quotient bit.}
           ELSE hiDvnd := hiDvnd + dvsr; {Negative -- restore hiDvnd.}
         END;
       IF negDvnd THEN rmdr := Badd(0,Bcom(hiDvnd),1)
       ELSE rmdr := hiDvnd;  {Remainder gets sign of dividend.}
       IF (negDvsr AND (NOT negDvnd)) OR
         ((NOT negDvsr) AND negDvnd) THEN quot := Badd(0,Bcom(quot),1);
       writeln(quot,rmdr);
     END;
END.
```

are popular. In signed-magnitude BCD, the encoding of the sign bit is arbitrary; in 10's-complement, 0000 indicates plus, 1001 indicates minus.

Addition of BCD digits is similar to adding 4-bit unsigned binary numbers, except that a correction must be made if a result exceeds 1001. The result is corrected by adding 6; examples are shown below:

4	0100		5	0101
+ 5	+ 0101		+ 9	+ 1001
9	1001		14	1110
				+ 0110 — correction
			10+4	1|0100

```
    5         0101                    9          1001
 + 11      +  1011                 +  9       +  1001
 ─────     ──────                  ─────      ──────
   16       1│0000                   18        1│0010
           + 0110 — correction                + 0110 — correction
           ──────                             ──────
10 + 6      1│0110                 10 + 8       1│1000
```

Notice that the addition of two BCD digits produces a carry into the next digit position if either the initial binary addition or the correction factor addition produces a carry.

Although the BCD encoding's utilization of memory is less efficient than binary, BCD is still a useful encoding in applications with much I/O of decimal data, such as point-of-sale terminals, since it avoids conversions to and from binary at each I/O operation. Many computers have a full set of instructions for processing BCD data, including addition, subtraction, and conversions to and from binary. Other computers at least have a "Decimal adjust" instruction that allows the binary operations to be adapted to decimal data. Examples of signed and unsigned BCD operations using typical microcomputer instructions will be given in Section 8.11.

4.11 FIXED-POINT AND FLOATING-POINT REPRESENTATIONS

4.11.1 Fixed-Point Representation

All of the number systems that we've discussed so far fix the binary point to the right of the rightmost bit. Thus, a 16-bit unsigned number lies in the range 0 through +65,535:

$$0000000000000000._2 = 0_{10}$$
$$1100000000000000._2 = 49142_{10}$$
$$0010000000000000._2 = 8192_{10}$$
$$1000000000000000._2 = 32768_{10}$$
$$1111111111111111._2 = 65535_{10}$$
$$0000000000000001._2 = 1_{10}$$

This type of number system is most appropriate for programs that count objects or otherwise deal with integer quantities.

On the other hand, many programs must deal with fractional quantities. For example, in a scientific program that computes a table of positive sines it might be convenient to fix the binary point to the right of the *leftmost* bit of a 16-bit number, as shown on the following page:

$$0.000000000000000_2 = 0_{10}$$
$$1.100000000000000_2 = 1.5_{10}$$
$$0.010000000000000_2 = 0.25_{10}$$
$$1.000000000000000_2 = 1.0_{10}$$
$$1.111111111111111_2 = 1.999\ 969\ 482\ 421\ 875_{10}$$
$$0.000000000000001_2 = 0.000\ 030\ 517\ 578\ 125_{10}$$

The weights of the bits to the right of the binary point are negative powers of two, as previously explained in Section 4.1. This example provides as many bits as possible to the right of the binary point for accurate representation of sine values less than one, while still allowing the largest sine value (1.0) to be represented.

The numbers in the two examples above are related — if X is a number in the first example and x is the corresponding number in the second example, then $x = X \cdot 2^{-15}$, where 2^{-15} is an *implicit scale factor*. Conceptually, a number system could use any scale factor — 2^{+15}, 2^{-25}, 3.14159, 10^9, and $186000 \cdot 60 \cdot 60 \cdot 24 \cdot 365$ might all be reasonable for different applications. However, powers of two are preferred because multiplication or division by the scale factor is then accomplished by shifting the binary point.

Addition and subtraction of numbers with implicit scale factors can be performed directly with normal binary addition and subtraction rules:

$$
\begin{array}{cc}
x & X \cdot 2^{-15} \\
\underline{+\quad y} & \underline{+\quad Y \cdot 2^{-15}} \\
x+y & (X+Y) \cdot 2^{-15}
\end{array}
$$

However, some adjustment for scale factors is needed when numbers are multiplied or divided:

$$
\begin{array}{cc}
x & X \cdot 2^{-15} \\
\underline{\times\quad y} & \underline{\times\quad Y \cdot 2^{-15}} \\
x \cdot y & (X \cdot Y \cdot 2^{-15}) \cdot 2^{-15}
\end{array}
$$

Number systems that fix the position of the binary point and require the programmer to keep track of implicit scale factors are called *fixed-point representations*. Because of the extra bookkeeping associated with implicit scale factors other than 1, virtually all computer hardware and software for fixed-point numbers uses an implicit scale factor of 1, so that the binary point is on the right as we have been assuming all along.

Regardless of the value of the scale factor, the "dynamic range" of a fixed-point number system is fairly limited. For example, the ratio between the largest and smallest nonzero numbers in a 16-bit fixed-point number system is about 2^{16}, even if the largest number is 2^{100}.

4.11.2 Basic Floating-Point Representation

To avoid error-prone bookkeeping and to represent a large dynamic range of numbers with relatively few bits, a *floating-point representation* can be used to explicitly encode a scale factor in each number. For example, we could break up a 16-bit word into two fields as shown in Figure 4–6. The value of a number X in this format is $M \cdot 2^E$, where both M and E are encoded as unsigned binary numbers. The value M is called the *mantissa* of the number, and the explicit scale factor is 2^E, where E is called the *exponent* of the number. This is simply the binary equivalent of decimal scientific nota-tion, which specifies numbers such as $34 \cdot 10^{29}$ and $186 \cdot 10^3$.

Some binary numbers and their decimal equivalents in the above floating-point system are shown below:

$$
\begin{array}{ll}
E \qquad\quad M & \\
000000\ \ 0000000000_2 & = \ 0 \cdot 2^0 \ = \ 0_{10} \\
000000\ \ 1000000101_2 & = \ 517 \cdot 2^0 \ = \ 517_{10} \\
001000\ \ 0100101101_2 & = \ 301 \cdot 2^8 \ = \ 77\ 056_{10} \\
111111\ \ 1111111111_2 & = \ 1023 \cdot 2^{63} \ = \ 9\ 423\ 991\ 637\ 655\ 520\ 332\ 924_{10}
\end{array}
$$

With only sixteen bits we can now represent very large numbers, the largest being over nine *sex*tillion. However, we haven't gotten something for nothing. By stealing six bits for the exponent field, we have reduced the resolution or *precision* of the number system to only 10 bits instead of 16. Given any real number between 0 and nine sextillion, we are very unlikely to be able to represent it exactly, and we'll typically encounter an error of one part in 2^{11} by picking the representable integer nearest to it. Compare this with the 16-bit integer fixed-point system — given any real number between 0 and $2^{16}-1$, we can pick an integer within 0.5 of it, an error of one part in 2^{17} for the largest number. Also, the 16-bit floating-point system can represent fewer than 2^{16} distinct numbers. For example, there are 64 different representations of zero (any exponent will do), and other numbers may have up to nine different representations (e.g., $1536_{10} = 3 \cdot 2^9 = 6 \cdot 2^8 = \ldots = 768 \cdot 2^1$). Still, a floating-point system is useful if we embellish it as described in the next subsection:

- To obtain adequate precision we increase the number of mantissa bits.

- To represent both positive and negative numbers, we allocate one bit for the sign of the mantissa.

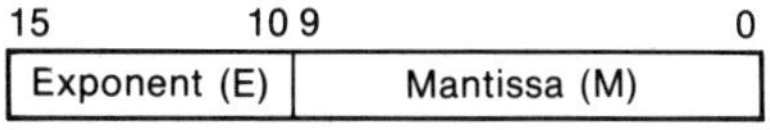

FIGURE 4–6 16-bit floating-point representation.

- To increase the dynamic range we increase the number of exponent bits.

- To represent fractions, we allow both positive and negative exponents.

4.11.3   Floating-Point Representation in a Typical Computer

A variety of floating-point formats are used in different computers because of the many different choices for mantissa length, exponent length, positioning of the radix point in the mantissa, encoding of negative numbers, and use of a "hidden bit." The format that was adopted by the designers of the PDP-11 is shown in Figure 4–7. Here the mantissa M is a 24-bit unsigned number with the binary point just to the left of bit position HB. (The "hidden bit" HB will be explained shortly.) Thus the smallest mantissa is .00. . .00=0, and the largest mantissa is .11. . .11, a number just 2^{-24} less than 1. The MS bit gives the sign of the mantissa, 0 for positive and 1 for negative. Thus MS and M together form a conventional 25-bit signed-magnitude number.

The exponent E is an 8-bit excess-128 number (Section 4.5.7); thus the bit strings 00000000 through 11111111 represent the exponents -128_{10} through $+127_{10}$ respectively. The choice of excess-128 representation is appropriate for the ordering of numbers, as we'll see shortly.

There appear to be many different representations for some numbers in PDP-11 format, for example,

$$
\begin{array}{lll}
& MS\quad E & M \\
+1 = & 0\ \ 10000001 & 100000000000000000000000 \\
& \quad (+1) & \quad\quad (0.5) \\
= & 0\ \ 10000010 & 010000000000000000000000 \\
& \quad (+2) & \quad\quad (0.25) \\
= & 0\ \ 10000011 & 001000000000000000000000 \\
& \quad (+3) & \quad\quad (0.125)
\end{array}
$$

However, most computers follow a convention that yields a unique, preferred, *normalized* representation for each number. A nonzero floating-point number is normalized if the leftmost bit of the mantissa is nonzero. Thus, the first representation of +1 above is the preferred one. The normalized representation of zero is all zeroes.

By convention, the PDP-11 processes only normalized numbers. Therefore, the leading mantissa bit of a nonzero number is always 1. Instead of

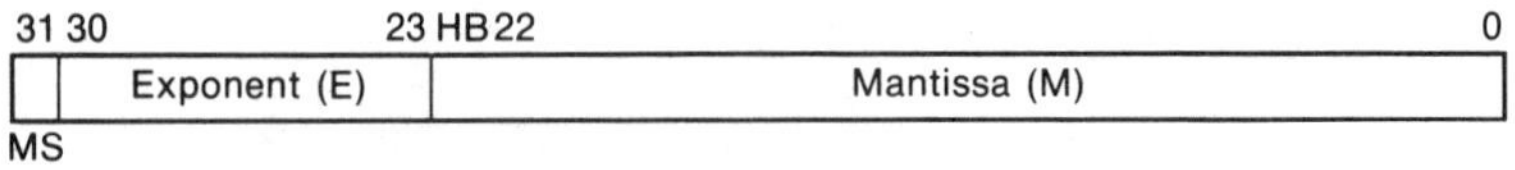

31	30	23 HB 22	0
	Exponent (E)	Mantissa (M)	

MS

FIGURE 4–7   PDP-11 floating-point representation.

explicitly storing this bit (labeled *HB* in Figure 4–7), the PDP-11 discards it when storing a floating-point number into a register or memory location. All operations on nonzero floating-point numbers assume that the "hidden bit" is 1. Thus, all 33 bits in the format of Figure 4–7 are packed into 32 bits of memory.

With normalized numbers, the smallest mantissa is 0.5 instead of 0, while the largest mantissa is still $1-2^{-24}$. In order to represent zero, the PDP-11 assumes that the hidden bit is zero if the exponent is 00000000 (-128). Some decimal numbers and normalized equivalents are shown below.

```
           MS    E       HB              M
 +3.000 =  0  10000010   1  1000000000000000000000000
               (+2)                 (0.75)
-17.375 =  1  10000101   1  0001011000000000000000000
               (+5)                (0.54296875)
 +0.125 =  0  01111110   1  0000000000000000000000000
               (-2)                 (0.5)
 +0.000 =  0  00000000   0  0000000000000000000000000
              (-128)                (0.0)
```

If two numbers X and Y are normalized, then we can guarantee that X is greater than Y if the exponent of X is numerically greater than exponent of Y (see Exercise 4.31). Only if the exponents are equal does the relationship between X and Y depend on the values of the mantissas. Thus, the positioning of the *MS*, *E*, and *M* fields in Figure 4–7 makes it possible to compare 32-bit normalized floating-point numbers as if they were 32-bit signed-magnitude numbers; no unusual operations are needed.

Floating-point formats in other computers typically use 32 bits or more for the combined mantissa, exponent, and sign fields. A 32-bit floating-point format is usually called "single precision."

The IEEE Standards Committee has proposed a 32-bit floating-point format similar to the PDP-11's. In the proposed standard, the binary point lies to the *right* of the hidden bit; thus mantissas are between 1 and 2. The exponent uses excess-127 notation for normalized numbers, with the range of valid exponents being -126 (00000001_2) through $+127$ (11111110_2). The maximum and minimum exponents (00000000_2 and 11111111_2) are used to indicate exceptional conditions. The standard also specifies a 64-bit ("double precision") format and gives guidelines for extended formats (e.g., 128-bit "quad precision" format).

Many IBM computers use a 32-bit floating-point format with a major difference from the formats we've seen so far: the exponent specifies a power of 16 instead of 2! The format contains a 7-bit exponent in excess-64 representation, a mantissa sign bit, and a 24-bit mantissa magnitude with radix point on the left (no hidden bit). The mantissa can be viewed as six 4-bit hexadecimal digits; the leading hexadecimal digit must be nonzero for a normalized number.

4.11.4   Floating-Point Operations

Now that we've studied some formats, it would be nice to be able to do some useful computation on floating-point numbers. A minimum set of floating-point operations includes addition, subtraction, multiplication, division, and comparison of floating-point numbers, and conversion to and from integer fixed-point format.

The exact rules for any of the above operations of course depend on the floating-point format, but there are some basic steps that are used universally. First, we note that a left shift of the binary point in the mantissa corresponds to a division by 2, and therefore can be compensated by increasing the exponent by 1. Likewise, a right shift of the binary point is compensated by decreasing the exponent by 1. Thus,

$$1101.001 \cdot 2^0 \ = \ .1101001 \cdot 2^4 \ = \ 1101001. \cdot 2^{-3}$$

A number can be converted from a fixed-point to a floating-point format as follows:

(1) Convert the number to the system used to represent the mantissa (e.g., signed-magnitude).

(2) Starting with an exponent of 0, shift the mantissa's binary point to the left or right, adjusting the exponent accordingly, until the mantissa is normalized.

(3) Convert the resulting exponent into the appropriate representation (e.g., excess-127).

(4) Pack the mantissa sign, normalized mantissa, and exponent into the floating-point format.

To convert a number from floating-point to fixed-point format, we can simply expand the formula that defines the floating-point format, performing any necessary number system conversions along the way. Sometimes we will detect an "overflow" condition, a floating-point number too large for the fixed-point format. At other times we may encounter floating-point numbers that don't have an exact representation in the prescribed fixed-point format, in which case we must use approximate values obtained by truncating digits or rounding.

The algorithm for addition and subtraction of floating-point numbers has three steps:

(1) The radix points of the numbers are "aligned" so that both numbers have the same exponent. This is accomplished by "unnormalizing" the smaller operand so that the exponents of both operands are equal.

(2) The mantissas are added or subtracted.

(3) The result is normalized. Normalization is necessary because addition of mantissas may produce a result greater than 1 and subtraction may produce a result much less than 0.5 (assuming PDP-11 format).

Multiplication and division of floating-point numbers do not require the radix points to be aligned, since multiplication or division of scale factors corresponds to addition or subtraction of exponents. Multiplication and division are accomplished as follows:

(1) The exponents are added (in multiplication) or subtracted (in division).

(2) The mantissas are multiplied or divided.

(3) The result is normalized.

Two approaches are possible for performing floating-point operations on a computer. Some computer systems have built-in hardware and instructions to process floating-point numbers in a prescribed format. With or without floating-point hardware, it is always possible to write programs that process numbers in any desired format. However, hardware generally performs floating-point operations 10 to 100 times faster than software on the same machine, and so the hardware approach is preferred for applications that make frequent use of floating-point operations.

4.12 CHARACTER CODES

In Chapter 1 we pointed out that a bit string need not represent a number, and that in fact most input and output of contemporary computers is nonnumeric. The most common type of nonnumeric data is *text*, strings of characters from some character set. Each character is represented in the computer by a bit string according to an established convention.

The most commonly-used character code is ASCII, the American Standard Code for Information Interchange. ASCII represents each character by a 7-bit string, a total of 128 different characters as shown in Appendix A. Thus, the text string "Yeccch!" is represented by a rather innocent looking list of seven 7-bit numbers:

    1011001   1100101   1100011   1100011   1100011   1101000   0100001

Some of the 7-bit strings in ASCII denote device control functions instead of "printing" characters. For example, CR (0001101) returns the print head or cursor on a printer or display to the first column, and LF (0001010) advances to the next line. Most of the other control characters are intended for use by data communication links, but different computer systems may use these characters for different functions.

Most computers manipulate an 8-bit quantity as a single unit, a byte, and store one character in each byte. The disposition of the extra bit when 7-bit ASCII is used depends on the system or program. Sometimes this bit is set to a particular value, sometimes it is ignored, and sometimes it is used to encode an additional 128 non-ASCII characters.

An important feature of ASCII is that the bit strings for letters and digits form a reasonable numerical sequence, so that text strings can be sorted by computer instructions that compare numerical values. The ASCII code chart also explains why HFC, NCR, and TWA come before Haag, Naar, and Taaffe respectively in the phone book.

REFERENCES

Precise, thorough, and entertaining discussions of all of the topics in this chapter can be found in Knuth's *Seminumerical Algorithms* [Addison-Wesley, 1969]. Mathematically inclined readers will find Knuth's analysis of the properties of number systems and arithmetic to be excellent, and all readers should enjoy the insights and history sprinkled throughout the text.

Descriptions of arithmetic hardware as well as properties of various number systems appear in *Computer Arithmetic* by K. Hwang [Wiley, 1979]. *Decimal Arithmetic* by H. Schmid [Wiley, 1974] contains a thorough description of techniques for BCD arithmetic.

EXERCISES

4.1   How does one decorate a 31-year-old's birthday cake with only five candles?

4.2   Justify lighting only three candles on your birthday cake at the following ages: 3, 7, 13, 21, 31, 43, 57, 73.

4.3   Perform the following number system conversions:

(a) $1101011_2 = ?_{10}$ (b) $174003_8 = ?_{10}$
(c) $10110111_2 = ?_{10}$ (d) $67.24_8 = ?_{10}$
(e) $10100.1101_2 = ?_{10}$ (f) $F3A5_{16} = ?_{10}$
(g) $12010_3 = ?_{10}$ (h) $AB3D_{16} = ?_{10}$
(i) $7156_8 = ?_{10}$ (j) $15C.38_{16} = ?_{10}$

4.4   Perform the following number system conversions:

(a) $1101011_2 = ?_{16}$ (b) $174003_8 = ?_2$
(c) $10110111_2 = ?_{16}$ (d) $67.24_8 = ?_2$
(e) $10100.1101_2 = ?_{16}$ (f) $F3A5_{16} = ?_2$
(g) $11011001_2 = ?_8$ (h) $AB3D_{16} = ?_2$
(i) $101111.0111_2 = ?_8$ (j) $15C.38_{16} = ?_2$

4.5   Perform the following number system conversions:

(a) $125_{10} = ?_2$ (b) $3489_{10} = ?_8$
(c) $209_{10} = ?_2$ (d) $9714_{10} = ?_8$
(e) $132_{10} = ?_2$ (f) $23851_{10} = ?_{16}$
(g) $727_{10} = ?_5$ (h) $57190_{10} = ?_{16}$
(i) $1435_{10} = ?_8$ (j) $65113_{10} = ?_{16}$

4.6   Add the following pairs of binary numbers, showing all carries:

(a)   110101   (b)   101110   (c)   11011101   (d)   1110010
       + 11001   + 100101   + 1100011   + 1101101

4.7   Repeat the previous problem using subtraction instead of addition, and showing borrows instead of carries.

4.8   Add the following pairs of octal numbers:

(a)   1372   (b)   47135   (c)   175214   (d)   110321
       + 4631   + 5125   + 152405   + 56573

4.9   Add the following pairs of hexadecimal numbers:

(a)   1372   (b)   4F1A5   (c)   F35B   (d)   1B90F
       + 4631   + B8D5   + 27E6   + C44E

4.10   Give the 8-bit signed-magnitude, two's-complement, and ones'-complement representations for each of the following decimal numbers: $+18$, $+115$, $+79$, -49, -3, -100.

4.11   Suppose a $4n$-bit number B is represented by an n-digit hexadecimal number H. Prove that the two's complement of B is represented by the 16's complement of H. Make a similar statement that is true for the octal representation of a binary number.

4.12   Repeat the preceding problem using the ones' complement of B and the 15s' complement of H.

4.13 Indicate the most likely real balances in my checking account if the following balances appear: \$9871.23, \$9905.74, \$123.46. For each of these balances, what should the new balance be if I deposit \$102.99?

4.14 Given an integer x where $-2^{n-1} \leqslant x \leqslant 2^{n-1}-1$, we define $[x]$ to be the two's-complement representation of x, expressed as a positive number: $[x]=x$ if $x \geqslant 0$ and $[x]=2^n-|x|$ if $x<0$, where $|x|$ is the absolute value of x. Let y be another integer in the same range. Prove that the rules for two's-complement addition as defined in Section 4.6 are correct by verifying that the following equation is always true:

$$[x+y] = [x] + [y] \text{ modulo } 2^n$$

(*Hints:* Consider four cases based on the signs of x and y. Without loss of generality, you may assume $|x| \geqslant |y|$.)

4.15 Repeat the previous problem using the appropriate expressions and rules for ones'-complement addition.

4.16 Indicate whether or not overflow occurs when adding the following 8-bit two's-complement numbers:

(a)	11010100	(b)	10111001	(c)	01011101	(d)	00100110
	+ 10101011		+ 11010110		+ 00100001		+ 01011010

4.17 Given an m-bit two's-complement number X, prove that the n-bit two's complement representation of X, where $n>m$, can be obtained by appending $n-m$ copies of X's sign bit to the left of the m-bit representation of X.

4.18 Show how to implement the extended-Pascal function Bls using Badd and Bcom as primitives.

4.19 Let X and Y be n-bit numbers, and let $\overline{Y}$ represent the bit-by-bit complement of Y. Prove that the operation $X-Y$ produces a borrow out of the MSB position if and only if the operation $X+\overline{Y}+1$ *does not* produce a carry out of the MSB position.

4.20 Prove that a two's-complement number can be multiplied by two by shifting it one bit position to the left, with a carry of 0 into the least significant bit position and disregarding any carry out of the most significant bit position, assuming no overflow. State the rule for detecting overflow.

4.21 State and prove correct a technique similar to the above, for multiplying a ones'-complement number by two.

4.22 Describe a rule for dividing a two's-complement number by two by means of a right shift operation. Give a Pascal statement that precisely defines the integer quotient obtained when the dividend is not a multiple of two. Use only positive arguments with DIV and MOD, since standard Pascal allows their results with negative arguments to vary in different implementations.

4.23 Repeat the preceding exercise for ones'-complement numbers.

4.24 Rewrite the unsigned multiplication program in Table 4–6 so that mpy and loProd are the same variable.

4.25 Using extended Pascal, write a multiplication program that processes the multiplier bits from left to right, instead of right to left as in Table 4–6. State the advantages and disadvantages of this approach.

4.26 Rewrite the unsigned division program in Table 4–9 so that quot and loDvnd are the same variable.

4.27 Show how to subtract BCD numbers, by stating the rules for generating borrows and applying a correction factor. Show how your rules apply to each of the following subtractions: $9-3$, $5-7$, $4-9$, $1-8$.

4.28 How many different unnormalized (hidden bit $= 0$) representations does $+1.0$ have in PDP-11 floating-point format?

4.29 What is the smallest nonzero positive normalized number in PDP-11 floating-point format? What is the largest?

4.30 Show how the following numbers would be stored in a computer's memory in PDP-11 floating-point format: 17, 40, 9.25, 15/64, 7/1024.

4.31 Prove that if two numbers X and Y in PDP-11 floating-point format are normalized, then X must be greater than Y if the exponent of X is greater than the exponent of Y. (*Hint:* Consider the worst-case values of the exponents and mantissas.)

4.32 Why do HFC, NCR, and TWA come before Haag, Naar, and Taaffe respectively in the phone book?

5

BASIC COMPUTER ORGANIZATION

A typical computer consists of a processor, memory, and input/output. All three of these subsystems have had major technological improvements since the first electronic digital computers were constructed in the 1940s. The improvements in processor and memory cost and performance due to integrated circuit technology in the last decade have been breathtaking — for the price of a good stereo system today, you can buy a personal computer as powerful as a computer that cost more than a four-bedroom house in 1970.

Despite the technological advances, the basic organization and operating principles of computers haven't changed too much. For example, in a 1946 description of the design of the first proposed electronic stored program computer, Burks, Goldstine, and von Neumann said[1],

> Conceptually we have . . . two different forms of memory: storage of numbers and storage of orders. If, however, the orders to the machine are reduced to a numerical code and if the machine can in some fashion distinguish a number from an order, the memory organ can be used to store both numbers and orders.

To this day, almost all computers use the same memory for storing both data (numbers) and instructions (orders). The MCS-48 single-chip microcomputer

[1]"Preliminary discussion of the logical design of an electronic computing instrument," in *Computer Structures: Readings and Examples*, by C. G. Bell and A. Newell, McGraw-Hill, 1971.

described in Chapter 19 is one of the rare exceptions. The early machines contain many other similarities to contemporary computers and precursors of their features.

In this chapter we describe the basic organization and features of computer processors and memory. Three representative types of processor organizations are described: accumulator-based processors, general-register processors, and stack machines. The description of processors is given in terms of hypothetical machines that have a subset of the features and instructions of real ones. Detailed, generic descriptions of processor addressing modes and operation types are presented in Chapters 7 and 8. Specific, real processor organizations are described in Part 3.

We should point out that our discussion does not include every possible computer architecture or feature. Architectures quite different from the traditional have been proposed, and many have even been built: machines whose data memory is a stack rather than an array; machines that process streams of data rather than streams of instructions; machines in which the processor sends instructions to memory instead of reading operands from it; machines in which algorithms are defined by functional relations rather than by explicit steps to compute a result. Also, there are a very large number of computer systems that have more than one processor. However, the traditional concepts discussed here apply to the vast majority of computers in production and in use today.

5.1 MEMORY

A computer *memory* is simply an array of randomly accessible bit strings, each of which is identified by a unique *address*. If the smallest addressable bit string in the memory is a byte, then the memory is *byte-addressable*; if it is a word, then the memory is *word-addressable*. Most contemporary computers have byte-addressable memories.

5.1.1 Memory Organizations

Figure 5–1(a) gives a conceptual view of a memory with 2^{16} bytes; a 16-bit address uniquely specifies any byte in this memory. We shall always draw computer memories with the lowest-numbered address on top. By convention, the bits in a word or byte will be numbered from right to left starting with 0, so that the bit numbers correspond to the exponents of their unsigned numerical weights written as powers of two (e.g., bit 5 has a weight of $2^5 = 32$). Almost all minicomputers and microcomputers, and all computers in this book except the 9900, follow this convention. Perversely, the IBM 370 family uses the opposite ordering (that's OK — it was there first).

Even if a computer has 16-bit or wider data paths, it can still have a byte-addressable memory. For example, Figure 5–1(b) shows the memory

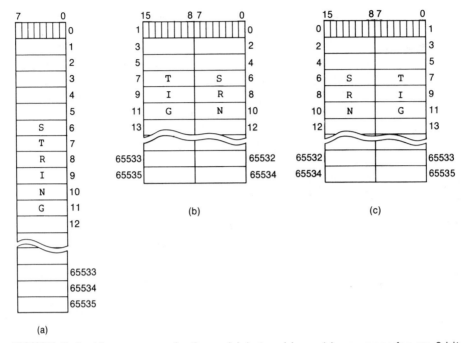

(a)

(b)

(c)

FIGURE 5–1   Memory organizations: (a) byte-addressable memory for an 8-bit processor; (b) byte-addressable memory for a 16-bit processor; (c) alternative byte-addressable memory for a 16-bit processor.

organization of a PDP-11. Each 16-bit word consists of two consecutive bytes starting on an even address (a *word boundary*). For example, bytes 2 and 3 form a word but bytes 3 and 4 do not. Instructions that manipulate words must specify even addresses; instructions that manipulate bytes may specify any address.

   From the point of view of number theory, the arrangement of bytes in a word as shown in Figure 5–1(b) is the natural one, since the least significant bits are contained in the lower-numbered byte. Figure 5–1(c) shows an alternative method of addressing bytes in a 16-bit machine, with the lower-numbered byte on the left. Although the equations relating bit and byte numbers are less elegant with this arrangement, some more practical problems of storing 8-bit characters in successive bytes are easier to deal with. In both Figure 5–1(b) and (c), the character string "STRING" is stored in sequential bytes beginning at byte address 6; Figure 5–1(c) is obviously easier to read. More importantly, the arrangement of Figure 5–1(c) has very tangible benefits when we use word instructions to do lexicographic sorting of strings (see Exercise 5.3). All of the computers in this book except the 8086 and the PDP-11 use the byte addressing arrangement shown in Figure 5–1(c).

5.1.2 Pascal Simulation of Processors and Memories

We can simulate the operation of a computer's processor and memory on another, larger computer by means of a Pascal program. Since the main memory of the simulated machine is just an array of bit strings, it can be defined by extended-Pascal declarations as shown below for the memory of Figure 5–1(a).

```
TYPE
  byte = ARRAY [7::0] OF bit;
  address = 0..65535;
VAR
  MEM : ARRAY [address] OF byte;
```

The extensions to Pascal for describing computer organizations are defined in Appendix B. In most cases, the extensions do exactly what someone familiar with standard Pascal would guess they do. The second line above defines a byte to be an array of 8 bits, numbered left to right from 7 to 0, where bit is a predefined type with values 0 and 1. The next line states that a valid address is a number in the range 0 through 65535. The last line defines the memory itself, an array of bytes, one byte per valid address. Since the total number of memory bytes is 2^{16}, an address may be specified by a 16-bit unsigned integer.

5.1.3 Memory Types

Several types of memories are commonly used in computer main memory systems. With a *read/write memory (RWM)*, we can store data at any address and read it back at any time. With a *read-only memory (ROM)*, we can read the contents of any address at any time, but data can be stored only once, when the ROM is manufactured.

A *programmable read-only memory (PROM)* is similar to a ROM, except that the customer may store the data (i.e., "program the PROM") using a *PROM programmer*. A PROM chip is manufactured with all its bits at a particular value, say 1. The PROM programmer can be used to set desired bits to 0, typically by blowing tiny fuses inside the PROM corresponding to each bit.

An *erasable programmable read-only memory (EPROM)* is similar to a PROM, except that the EPROM can be "erased" to the all-1s state by exposing it to ultraviolet light. No, the light does not cause fuses to grow back! Rather, EPROMs use a different technology. The EPROM programmer forces electrons into tiny wells corresponding to each 0 bit, where they remain trapped unless excited by ultraviolet light.

Every computer has RWM for storing variable data. Depending on the computer and the application, the programs may also be stored in RWM, or they may be stored in ROM, PROM, or EPROM.

All of the memories described above are *random-access memories*, because all locations have equally fast access. However, computer jargon has developed so that the acronym "RAM" most commonly refers to read/write memory only. To be correct, use "RWM" when writing about read/write memory, but pronounce it "ram" to keep your tongue intact!

5.2   ACCUMULATOR-BASED PROCESSORS

The simplest processor organization has only one or two registers, called *accumulators*, in which arithmetic and logical operations and data transfers take place. The Intel MCS-48 is a single-accumulator processor; the Motorola 6809 is a two-accumulator processor. Processors with more than two registers for arithmetic and logical operations are classified as general-register processors and are discussed in the next section.

5.2.1   Organization of a Single-Accumulator Processor

Figure 5–2 shows the internal organization of a single-accumulator processor. This hypothetical processor has only one accumulator and a subset of the other registers and of the instructions of the Motorola 6809 (Chapter 17), so we'll call it the H6809.

The H6809 accesses a memory of up to 2^{16} (65,536) bytes, arranged as shown in Figure 5–1(a); addresses are two bytes long. Most instructions manipulate 1-byte quantities; a few process 2-byte quantities. An H6809 instruction occupies one, two, or three bytes in memory. The processor has several registers and functional units, briefly described on the following page:

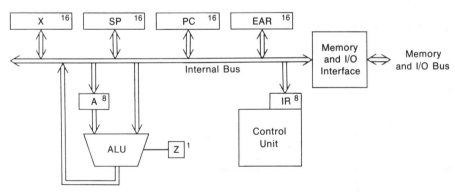

FIGURE 5–2   Single-accumulator processor organization, the H6809.

- *Instruction Register (IR):* an 8-bit register that holds the first byte of the currently executing instruction.

- *Effective Address Register (EAR):* a 16-bit register that holds an address at which the processor reads or writes memory during the execution of an instruction.

- *Program Counter (PC):* a 16-bit register that holds the memory address of the next instruction to be executed.

- *Accumulator (A):* an 8-bit register containing data to be processed.

- *Index Register (X):* a 16-bit register containing an address or 16-bit data used by a program.

- *Stack Pointer (SP):* a 16-bit register containing the address of the top of a return-address stack in memory.

- *Zero Bit (Z):* a 1-bit register that the processor sets during the execution of each data manipulation instruction, to 1 if the instruction produces a zero result, to 0 if the instruction produces a nonzero result.

- *Arithmetic and Logic Unit (ALU):* combines two 8-bit quantities to produce an 8-bit result.

- *Control Unit:* decodes instructions and controls the other blocks to fetch and execute instructions.

- *Memory and I/O Interface:* reads and writes memory and communicates with I/O devices according to commands from the Control Unit.

Although all of the blocks above are essential to the internal operation of the H6809, only the registers PC, A, X, SP, and Z are explicitly manipulated by instructions and have values that are meaningful after each instruction's execution. Such registers comprise the *processor state*, and may be shown in a *programming model* for the processor, as in Figure 5–3. Only these registers are of concern to a programmer.

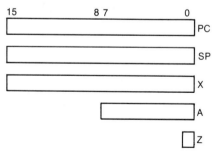

FIGURE 5–3 Programming model for H6809.

5.2.2 Basic Instruction Cycle

The operation of the H6809 (or almost any other computer processor) consists of endless repetition of two steps: read the next instruction from memory (the *fetch cycle*), and perform the actions it requires (the *execution cycle*). This basic instruction cycle may be defined by the Pascal simulation in Table 5–1. The fetch cycle simply reads the first byte of the instruction that PC points to, and increments PC to point to the next byte in memory. The operations performed during the execution cycle depend on the instruction, and may include reading additional instruction bytes and updating PC accordingly. The use of a counter for PC is no accident. As observed by von Neumann,

> It is clear that one must be able to get numbers from any part of the memory at any time. The treatment in the case of orders can, however, be more methodical since one can at least partially arrange the control instructions in a linear sequence. Consequently the control will be so constructed that it will normally proceed from place n in the memory to place $(n+1)$ for its next instruction.

5.2.3 Machine Instructions

The "machine instructions" of the hypothetical H6809 are one to three bytes long. The first byte of each instruction is called the *opcode*; it uniquely

TABLE 5–1 Basic instruction cycle of the H6809 processor.

```
PROGRAM H6809 (input,output);
TYPE byte = ARRAY [7::0] OF bit;
  word = ARRAY [15::0] OF bit;
VAR MEM : ARRAY [0..65535] OF byte;
  EAR, PC, X, SP : word;
  IR, A : byte; Z : bit;
PROCEDURE Fetch;
  BEGIN
    IR := MEM[PC];   {Read next instruction.}
    PC := PC + 1;   {Bump PC to next instruction.}
  END;

PROCEDURE Execute;
  BEGIN  {Will be defined later.}  END;

BEGIN
  PC := 0;  {Start at PC=0 on cold start.}
  WHILE true DO
    BEGIN
      Fetch;
      Execute;
    END;
END.
```

specifies the operation to be performed. Additional bytes specify an *operand*, giving an 8-bit data value or a 16-bit memory address to use when executing the instruction.

Table 5–2 lists the 29 machine instructions of the H6809. With an 8-bit opcode, we could have defined up to 256 instructions, and in fact the real 6809

TABLE 5–2 Machine instructions of the H6809.

Mnem.	Operand	Length (bytes)	Opcode (hex.)	Description
NOP		1	12	No operation
CLRA		1	4F	Clear A
COMA		1	43	Ones' complement bits of A
NEGA		1	40	Negate A (two's complement)
LDA	#data	2	86	Load A with data
LDA	@X	1	A6	Load A with MEM[X]
LDA	addr	3	B6	Load A with MEM[addr]
STA	@X	1	A7	Store A into MEM[X]
STA	addr	3	B7	Store A into MEM[addr]
ADDA	#data	2	8B	Add data to A
ADDA	addr	3	BB	Add MEM[addr] to A
ANDA	#data	2	84	Logical AND data to A
ANDA	addr	3	B4	Logical AND MEM[addr] to A
CMPA	#data	2	81	Set Z according to A−data
CMPA	addr	3	B1	Set Z according to A−MEM[addr]
LDX	#addr	3	8E	Load X with addr
LDX	addr	3	BE	Load X with MEMW[addr]
STX	addr	3	BF	Store X into MEMW[addr]
CMPX	#addr	3	8C	Set Z according to X−addr
CMPX	addr	3	BC	Set Z according to X−MEMW[addr]
ADDX	#addr	3	30	Add addr to X
ADDX	addr	3	31	Add MEMW[addr] to X
LDS	#addr	3	8F	Load SP with addr
BNE	offset	2	26	Branch if result is nonzero (Z=0)
BEQ	offset	2	27	Branch if result is zero (Z=1)
BRA	offset	2	20	Branch unconditionally
JMP	addr	3	7E	Jump to addr
JSR	addr	3	BD	Jump to subroutine at addr
RTS		1	39	Return from subroutine

Notes: Mnem. = mnemonic; hex. = hexadecimal; data = 8-bit data value; addr = 16-bit memory address (two bytes); offset = 8-bit signed integer added to PC if branch is taken.

MEM[i] denotes the memory byte stored at address i.

MEMW[i] denotes the memory word beginning at address i, that is, the concatenation of MEM[i] and MEM[i+1].

Opcodes are the same as in the Motorola 6809, except for ADDX, LDS, LDA @X, and STA @X, which are two bytes long in the real 6809.

The ADDX mnemonic and some assembler notations differ from those used in Motorola's 6809 assembly language. See Chapter 17 for details.

defines instructions for 223 8-bit opcodes. Associated with each 8-bit opcode is an alphabetic *mnemonic* that we can use to conveniently name and recognize the instruction. In some cases two or three opcodes have the same mnemonic (e.g., three opcodes have "LDA"); we symbolically distinguish them by placing a special symbol (# or @) before the operand.

It is impossible to distinguish between instructions and data just by looking at the contents of memory. For example, the byte $4F_{16}$ may represent either the opcode CLRA or the number 79_{10}. Only the processor distinguishes between the two. During the fetch cycle, the processor interprets memory bytes as instructions. During the execution cycle, it interprets them as data. There are no other checks. If an error causes PC to point into a data area, the processor will blindly forge ahead, trying to interpret the data as a sequence of instructions. Likewise, if a program stores data bytes into the memory locations occupied by its own instructions, it will destroy itself.

5.2.4 Instruction Groups

Instructions in the first group in Table 5–2 involve the accumulator A. The load and store instructions (LDA, STA) are by far the most commonly used, since data must be placed in the accumulator in order to be manipulated. ADDA adds an 8-bit quantity to A, while ANDA performs the bit-by-bit logical AND of A with another 8-bit value. CMPA compares A with another value without modifying either one. CLRA, COMA, and NEGA clear, complement, and negate A. NOP does nothing; it is used in program debugging to fill holes left by deleted instructions.

The second group contains instructions that manipulate X and SP. In most programs, X is used to hold a 16-bit address or other 16-bit data. The value of X can be loaded, stored, incremented, decremented, or compared with another 16-bit value. SP always points to the top of a push-down stack of return addresses, used by subroutine call and return instructions as explained later. The LDS instruction may be used to initialize SP at the beginning of a program.

Instructions in the last group can conditionally or unconditionally alter the program flow by forcing a new value into PC. The 3-byte instructions JMP and JSR can jump to any address in memory, while the shorter BNE, BEQ, and BRA branch to addresses nearby the current instruction.[2] A branch instruction interprets its offset byte as a signed, two's-complement number in the range −128 through +127. If the branch is taken, this number is added to PC, otherwise control passes to the instruction at the next address. Thus, the branch target address is within −128 to +127 bytes of the next address.

---

[2]"Branch" and "Jump" mean the same thing. However, the words are sometimes used to distinguish between absolute jumps and relative branches as explained in Section 8.6.

The instructions may also be grouped according to how they "address" their operands:

- *Inherent addressing.* The identity of the operand is inherent in the op-code itself (NOP, CLRA, COMA, NEGA, RTS).

- *Immediate addressing.* An 8-bit operand is contained in the byte follow-ing the opcode (LDA #data, ADDA #data, ANDA #data, CMPA #data), or a 16-bit operand is contained in the two bytes following opcode (LDX #addr, CMPX #addr, ADDX #addr, LDS #addr).

- *Absolute addressing.* The address of the operand is given in the two bytes following the opcode, high-order byte first (LDA addr, STA addr, ADDA addr, ANDA addr, CMPA addr, LDX addr, STX addr, CMPX addr, ADDX addr, JMP addr, JSR addr).

- *Register indirect addressing.* The address of the operand is contained in the index register X (LDA @X, STA @X).

- *Relative addressing.* The address of the operand is computed as the sum of the PC and an 8-bit two's-complement number in the byte following the opcode (BNE offset, BEQ offset, BRA offset).

A precise description of each instruction will be given later by means of a Pascal simulation.

5.2.5   A Machine Language Program

Table 5–3 shows the values stored in memory for a sequence of instruc-tions and data that forms a program for multiplying 23 by 5. The sequence of addresses, opcodes, and data in the two left-hand columns of the table is called a *machine language program*. This sequence completely specifies the operations to be performed by the computer. We shall explain the operation of the program shortly.

5.2.6   Assembly Language

Obviously, the two left-hand columns of Table 5–3 don't mean much to a human reader. Fortunately, the Label, Opcode, and Operand columns specify the machine language program in symbolic form, using mnemonics for opcodes and alphanumeric labels for addresses and data values. The Com-ments column gives an English explanation of what the program does. These four columns form an *assembly language program* that can be translated into machine language by a program called an *assembler*. The assembler produces, among other things, a listing of the equivalent machine language program as in the two left-hand columns of the table. In addition to machine instructions,

TABLE 5–3 Memory contents for a sequence of instructions and data.

Machine Language		Assembly Language			
Addr (hex)	Contents (hex)	Label (sym)	Opcode (mnem)	Operand (sym)	Comments
...			ORG	2A40H	Multiply MCND by MPY.
2A40	4F	START	CLRA		Set PROD to 0.
2A41	B7		STA	PROD	
2A42	2C				
2A43	00				
2A44	B6		LDA	MPY	Set CNT equal to MPY
2A45	2C				
2A46	02				
2A47	B7		STA	CNT	and do loop MPY times.
2A48	2C				
2A49	01				
2A4A	B6	LOOP	LDA	CNT	Done if CNT = 0.
2A4B	2C				
2A4C	01				
2A4D	27		BEQ	OUT	
2A4E	10				
2A4F	8B		ADDA	#-1	Else decrement CNT.
2A50	FF				
2A51	B7		STA	CNT	
2A52	2C				
2A53	01				
2A54	B6		LDA	PROD	Add MCND to PROD.
2A55	2C				
2A56	00				
2A57	BB		ADDA	MCND	
2A58	2C				
2A59	03				
2A5A	B7		STA	PROD	
2A5B	2C				
2A5C	00				
2A5D	20		BRA	LOOP	Repeat the loop again.
2A5E	EB				
2A5F	B6	OUT	LDA	PROD	Put PROD in A when done.
2A60	2C				
2A61	00				
2A62	7E		JMP	1000H	Return to operating system.
2A63	10				
2A64	00				
...			ORG	2C00H	
2C00	??	PROD	RMB	1	Storage for PROD.
2C01	??	CNT	RMB	1	Storage for CNT.
2C02	05	MPY	FCB	5	Multiplier value.
2C03	17	MCND	FCB	23	Mutliplicand value.
...			END	START	

Notes: Addr=Address; hex=hexadecimal; sym=symbolic; mnem=mnemonic.

the assembly language program contains *pseudo-operations* that tell the assembler how to store the machine language program. The four pseudo-operations used in Table 5–3 are described below:

- ORG (Origin). The operand specifies the address at which the next instruction is to be deposited when the program is loaded into memory. Subsequent instructions are deposited in successive memory addresses.

- RMB (Reserve Memory Bytes). The operand specifies a number of memory bytes to be skipped without storing any instructions or data, thereby reserving space to be used by variables in a program.

- FCB (Form Constant Byte). The specified byte value is stored into memory when the program is first loaded into memory, thereby establishing a constant value that may be accessed when the program is run.

- END (End Assembly). This instruction denotes the end of the text to be assembled and gives the address of the first executable instruction of the program.

In all of the assembly language statements, numeric arguments are assumed to be given in decimal notation unless they are followed by an H for hexadecimal. When an identifier appears in the Label field, it is assigned the value of the Address field. For example, the values of START and CNT are 2A40H and 2C01H, respectively. When an identifier appears in the Operand field, the assembler substitutes the value that has been assigned to it. Therefore, the instruction "STA CNT" is equivalent to "STA 2C01H".

All of the above operations occur at *assembly time*; an identifier such as CNT refers to the memory address of a variable. At *run time*, when the program is executed, values stored in memory will be manipulated. Strictly speaking, we should refer to such a value as MEM[CNT]. However, when we discuss run-time operations, it is customary to use the identifier to refer to the value in memory itself. Thus, the comment "Set CNT equal to MPY" means "MEM[2C01H] := MEM[2C02H]."

The difference between assembly-time and run-time operations is probably the greatest single source of confusion to novice assembly language programmers, and so we'll explain it again. The assembler is a system program that translates lines of text into a sequence of instruction and data bytes that can be stored in the computer's memory; the assembler "goes away" before the machine language program that it produced is executed. As far as the assembler is concerned, an identifier such as PROD stands for the address that was assigned to it (2C00H); the assembler is unconcerned with what may happen to the contents of the memory address 2C00H when the program is run. Using an identifier frees the programmer from keeping track of the exact address at which an instruction or datum is located. Even though the identifier refers to an address, the programmer is usually more interested in the *contents* of the memory address at run time. Therefore the programmer informally uses the *name* of the address (PROD) to refer to its contents (MEM[2C00H]), just to save typing.

Most instructions in the H6809 are more than one byte long. It is therefore convenient to compress the program listing, showing all bytes associated with the same instruction on one line as in Table 5–4.

5.2.7   Operation of a Simple Program

Now we can explain how the program in Table 5–4 works. It multiplies MCND by MPY by intializing PROD to 0 and then adding MCND to it MPY times. The program's execution is traced by Table 5–5, which shows the contents of registers and memory *after* each instruction is executed, and by the steps below.

(1) CLRA sets A to zero.

(2) STA PROD is a "memory reference" instruction. The two bytes following the opcode B7H refer to memory location 2C00H, the address where the contents of A (00H) are to be stored.

TABLE 5–4   Compressed program listing.

Addr	Contents	Label	Opcode	Operand	Comments
...			ORG	2A40H	Multiply MCND by MPY.
2A40	4F	START	CLRA		Set PROD to 0.
2A41	B7 2C00		STA	PROD	
2A44	B6 2C02		LDA	MPY	Set CNT equal to MPY
2A47	B7 2C01		STA	CNT	and do loop MPY times.
2A4A	B6 2C01	LOOP	LDA	CNT	Done if CNT = 0.
2A4D	27 10		BEQ	OUT	
2A4F	8B FF		ADDA	#−1	Else decrement CNT.
2A51	B7 2C01		STA	CNT	
2A54	B6 2C00		LDA	PROD	Add MCND to PROD.
2A57	BB 2C03		ADDA	MCND	
2A5A	B7 2C00		STA	PROD	
2A5D	20 EB		BRA	LOOP	Repeat the loop again.
2A5F	B6 2C00	OUT	LDA	PROD	Put PROD in A when done.
2A62	7E 1000		JMP	1000H	Return to operating system.
...			ORG	2C00H	
2C00	??	PROD	RMB	1	Storage for PROD.
2C01	??	CNT	RMB	1	Storage for CNT.
2C02	05	MPY	FCB	5	Multiplier value.
2C03	17	MCND	FCB	23	Multiplicand value.
...			END	START	

TABLE 5-5 Register and memory contents after executing instructions in multiplication program.

Step	Instruction	PC	A	Z	MEM[2C00] (PROD)	MEM[2C01] (CNT)
0	...	2A40	??	?	??	??
1	CLRA	2A41	00	1	??	??
2	STA PROD	2A44	00	1	00	??
3	LDA MPY	2A47	05	0	00	??
4	STA CNT	2A4A	05	0	00	05
5	LDA CNT	2A4D	05	0	00	05
6	BEQ OUT	2A4F	05	0	00	05
7	ADDA #-1	2A51	04	0	00	05
8	STA CNT	2A54	04	0	00	04
9	LDA PROD	2A57	00	1	00	04
10	ADDA MCND	2A5A	17	0	00	04
11	STA PROD	2A5D	17	0	17	04
12	BRA LOOP	2A4A	17	0	17	04
5	LDA CNT	2A4D	04	0	17	04
6	BEQ OUT	2A4F	04	0	17	04
	...					
5	LDA CNT	2A4D	03	0	2E	03
6	BEQ OUT	2A4F	03	0	2E	03
	...					
5	LDA CNT	2A4D	02	0	45	02
6	BEQ OUT	2A4F	02	0	45	02
	...					
5	LDA CNT	2A4D	01	0	5C	01
6	BEQ OUT	2A4F	01	0	5C	01
	...					
5	LDA CNT	2A4D	00	1	73	00
6	BEQ OUT	2A5F	00	1	73	00
13	LDA PROD	2A62	73	0	73	00
14	JMP 1000H	1000	73	0	73	00

(3) LDA MPY is another memory reference instruction. It specifies that A is to be loaded with the contents of memory location 2C02H.

(4) STA CNT stores the multiplier into memory location 2C01H to keep track of how many more times the loop must be executed.

(5) LDA CNT puts the value of location 2C01H into A again. Since data manipulation instructions set Z according to their results, this instruction sets Z to 1 if CNT=0, and to 0 otherwise.

(6) BEQ OUT causes PC to be set to 2A5FH if Z=1, that is, it branches to step 13 if CNT=0. Instead of giving the actual target address (2A5FH), the second byte of the machine instruction contains an offset: if the condi-

tion is true then the next instruction to be executed is 10_{16} bytes past the instruction that would normally be next. In other words, the offset is added to the updated PC if the branch is taken. However, notice that the assembly language statement specifies the actual target address; the assembler figures out the proper offset value for the machine instruction and gives an error message if an out-of-range target is specified.

(7) ADDA #-1 subtracts 1 from A (if the program hasn't just branched to OUT). This instruction uses an "immediate" operand. When the control unit decodes opcode 8BH (ADDA#), it reads the next byte from the instruction stream (FFH) and adds it to A.

(8) STA CNT stores A as before.

(9) LDA PROD puts the value of location 2C00H into A.

(10) ADDA MCND adds the value of location 2C03H to A.

(11) STA PROD stores the new value of A back into location 2C00H.

(12) BRA LOOP unconditionally loads the value 2A4AH into PC, returning control to step 5. The target address 2A4AH is obtained by extending the sign of the offset EBH to make a 16-bit two's-complement integer, FFEBH, and adding to the updated PC (2A5FH).

(13) LDA PROD puts the value of location 2C00H into A again.

(14) JMP 1000H unconditionally loads the value 1000H into PC when the program is done. We've assumed that this is the starting address of an operating system program that controls the machine when the user's program has finished executing.

5.2.8 Pascal Simulation of Instruction Execution

Before discussing the rest of the H6809 instruction set, we present an extended-Pascal simulation that precisely defines the operation of each instruction. Table 5–6 is the Execute procedure that goes with the simulation given in Table 5–1. We've taken some liberty with Pascal by allowing "#" and "@" to appear in identifiers. The body of the procedure is a CASE statement, one case for each valid opcode. You should study Table 5–6 to verify that each of the instructions that we've introduced so far does what you think it does, and also to get a preview of the instructions yet to come.

Notice that the standard fetch cycle in Table 5–1 leaves the PC pointing to the byte after the opcode, regardless of whether this byte is the next opcode or part of the current instruction. The execution cycle reads one or two additional bytes and bumps PC past them only for opcodes that require them, so that at the end of the execution cycle PC always points to the first byte of the next instruction.

5.2.9 Indirect Addressing

The program in Table 5–4 manipulated only simple variables and constants. More complicated data structures such as arrays, stacks, and queues are used in almost all programs. Consider the problem of initializing the five components of an array Q[0..4] to zero, using only the instructions that we've introduced so far. An assembly language solution is shown in Table 5–7. Note that the operand expressions "Q+1," "Q+2," and so on are evaluated at assembly time. Also, the second ORG statement affects the next line to be assembled, but does not affect the Address column on its own line.

The choice of a 5-component array above was very judicious — the corresponding program for a 100-component array would not fit on one page. A problem with the direct addressing mode used by most H6809 instructions is that addresses must be known at assembly time, resulting in programs like Table 5–7. *Indirect addressing* avoids this problem by computing addresses at run time. The H6809 has one indirect addressing mode, in which the address of the operand is taken from the X register when the instruction is executed. The accumulator may be loaded from or stored into memory using this mode. Thus we can write a loop to initialize an array, in which the X register contains a new address in the array on each iteration of the loop. Before showing such a loop, we must introduce some instructions for manipulating the X register itself.

TABLE 5–6 Instruction execution procedure for the H6809.

```
PROCEDURE Execute;
  CONST  {Mnemonic-opcode correspondences}
    NOP=12H; CLRA=4FH; COMA=43H; NEGA=40H; LDA#=86H; LDA@X=0A6H;
    LDA=0B6H; STA@X=0A7H; STA=0B7H; ADDA#=8BH; ADDA=0BBH;
    ANDA#=84H; ANDA=0B4H; CMPA#=81H; CMPA=0B1H; LDX#=8EH;
    LDX=0BEH; STX=0BFH; CMPX#=8CH; CMPX=0BCH; ADDX#=30H; ADDX=31H;
    LDS#=8FH; BNE=26H; BEQ=27H; BRA=20H; JMP=7EH; JSR=0BDH; RTS=39H;
  VAR opnum : integer;

  FUNCTION NextByte : byte;  {Get next byte in instruction stream.}
    BEGIN NextByte := MEM[PC]; PC := PC + 1 END;

  PROCEDURE FetchAddr;  {Get 2-byte address from instruction stream.}
    BEGIN EAR[15::8] := NextByte; EAR[7::0] := NextByte END;

  PROCEDURE TestByte (b : byte);  {Set Z according to byte value.}
    BEGIN IF b=0 THEN Z:=1 ELSE Z:=0 END;

  PROCEDURE TestWord (w : word);  {Set Z according to word value.}
    BEGIN IF w=0 THEN Z:=1 ELSE Z:=0 END;

  PROCEDURE Branch;
    BEGIN  {Sign-extend offset in EAR[7::0] and add to PC.}
      IF EAR[7]=0 THEN EAR[15::8] := 0 ELSE EAR[15::8] := 0FFH;
      PC := PC + EAR;
    END;
```

TABLE 5–6 (continued)

```
BEGIN  {Statement part of Execute}
  opnum := IR;
  CASE opnum OF
    NOP:   ;
    CLRA:  BEGIN A := 0; TestByte(A) END;
    COMA:  BEGIN A := Bcom(A); TestByte(A) END;
    NEGA:  BEGIN A := -A; TestByte(A) END;
    LDA#:  BEGIN A := NextByte; TestByte(A) END;
    LDA@X: BEGIN A := MEM[X]; TestByte(A) END;
    LDA:   BEGIN FetchAddr; A := MEM[EAR]; TestByte(A) END;
    STA:   BEGIN FetchAddr; MEM[EAR] := A; TestByte(A) END;
    STA@X: BEGIN MEM[X] := A; TestByte(A) END;
    ADDA#: BEGIN A := A + Nextbyte; TestByte(A) END;
    ADDA:  BEGIN FetchAddr; A := A + MEM[EAR]; TestByte(A) END;
    ANDA#: BEGIN A := Band(A,Nextbyte); TestByte(A) END;
    ANDA:  BEGIN FetchAddr; A := Band(A,MEM[EAR]); TestByte(A) END;
    CMPA#: BEGIN TestByte(A-Nextbyte) END;
    CMPA:  BEGIN FetchAddr; TestByte(A-MEM[EAR]) END;
    LDX#:  BEGIN FetchAddr; X := EAR; TestWord(X) END;
    LDX:   BEGIN FetchAddr; X[15::8] := MEM[EAR];
              X[7::0] := MEM[EAR+1]; TestWord(X) END;
    STX:   BEGIN FetchAddr; MEM[EAR] := X[15::8];
              MEM[EAR+1] := X[7::0]; TestWord(X) END;
    CMPX#: BEGIN FetchAddr; TestWord(X-EAR) END;
    CMPX:  BEGIN FetchAddr; TestWord(X-(MEM[EAR]|MEM[EAR+1])) END;
    ADDX#: BEGIN FetchAddr; X := X + EAR; TestWord(X) END;
    ADDX:  BEGIN FetchAddr; X := X + (MEM[EAR]|MEM[EAR+1]);
              TestWord(X) END; {"|" denotes concatenation of bytes}
    LDS#:  BEGIN FetchAddr; SP := EAR; TestWord(SP) END;
    BNE:   BEGIN EAR[7::0] := NextByte; IF Z=0 THEN Branch END;
    BEQ:   BEGIN EAR[7::0] := NextByte; IF Z=1 THEN Branch END;
    BRA:   BEGIN EAR[7::0] := NextByte; Branch END;
    JMP:   BEGIN FetchAddr; PC := EAR END;
    JSR:   BEGIN
              FetchAddr; SP := SP - 2;  {Reserve 2 bytes on stack.}
              MEM[SP] := PC[15::8]; MEM[SP+1] := PC[7::0]; {Save PC}
              PC := EAR;  {...and jump to subroutine.}        END;
    RTS:   BEGIN {Restore PC from top of stack.}
              PC[15::8] := MEM[SP]; PC[7::0] := MEM[SP+1];
              SP := SP + 2;  {Pop stack.}                     END;
    END; {End CASE}
  END; {End Execute}
```

As shown in the second part of Table 5–2, X may be loaded with an immediate value (LDX #addr), in which case the immediate value is two bytes long and is contained in the second and third bytes of the instruction. If X is loaded from a memory address (LDX addr), the instruction specifies the address of the first byte of a word. The high-order byte of X is loaded with

TABLE 5-7 Initializing an array the hard way.

Addr	Contents	Label	Opcode	Operand	Comments
			ORG	3000H	
3000	4F	INIT	CLRA		Set components of Q to zero.
3001	B7 3100		STA	Q	First component.
3004	B7 3101		STA	Q+1	Second component.
3007	B7 3102		STA	Q+2	Third component.
300A	B7 3103		STA	Q+3	Fourth component.
300D	B7 3104		STA	Q+4	Fifth component.
3010	7E 1000		JMP	1000H	Return to operating system.
3013			ORG	3100H	
3100	??	Q	RMB	5	Reserve 5 bytes for array.
3105			END	INIT	

MEM[addr], and the low-order byte of X is loaded with MEM[addr+1]. The X register may also be stored into memory, compared with an immediate or memory operand, or have an immediate or memory operand added to it.

The program in Table 5–8 solves the array initialization problem using indirect addressing. As shown in Figure 5–4, it initializes X to point to the first component of Q, and then executes a loop that clears successive components of Q, incrementing X once per iteration of the loop. The CMPX instruction compares the contents of X with an immediate value, the address just past the last array component; it sets Z to 1 if they're equal. Because X is used to access array components with different indices, it is called an *index register*.

Not only does the program in Table 5–8 occupy fewer bytes than the one in Table 5–7, but it also stays the same length for an array of any size. The program is easily modified to work on a different length array by changing the occurrences of the length "5" to the desired length.

TABLE 5-8 Initializing an array using indirect addressing.

Addr	Contents	Label	Opcode	Operand	Comments
			ORG	3000H	
3000	4F	INIT	CLRA		Set components of Q to zero.
3001	8E 3100		LDX	#Q	Address of first component.
3004	A7	ILOOP	STA	@X	Set MEM[X] to zero.
3005	30 0001		ADDX	#1	Point to next component.
3008	8C 3105		CMPX	#Q+5	Past last component?
300B	26 F7		BNE	ILOOP	If not, go do some more.
300D	7E 1000		JMP	1000H	Return to operating system.
3010			ORG	3100H	
3100	??	Q	RMB	5	Reserve 5 bytes for array.
3105			END	INIT	

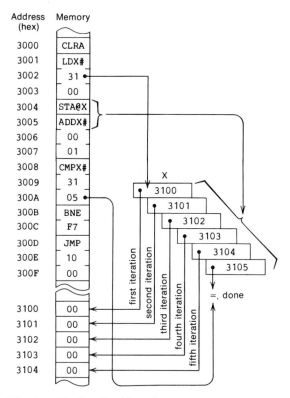

FIGURE 5–4 Effects of indirect addressing.

Many variations on indirect addressing are found in the real 6809 and most other computers. These addressing modes are explored in Chapter 7.

5.2.10 Subroutines

A *subroutine* is the machine language equivalent of a procedure or function in Pascal: a sequence of instructions, defined and stored only once, that may be invoked (or *called*) from many places. In order to write subroutines in machine language, we need instructions to save the current value of the PC each time the subroutine is called, and restore it when the subroutine is finished.

In the H6809, the JSR and RTS instructions provide for subroutine calls and returns in conjunction with the stack pointer register SP. Any program that uses subroutines is required to reserve a small area of memory for a push-down stack for return addresses. At the beginning of such a program SP must be initialized to point at this area using the LDS #addr instruction. As shown in Figure 5–5, SP points to the top item in the stack, or just past the stack area if the stack is empty. SP is decremented once before storing each

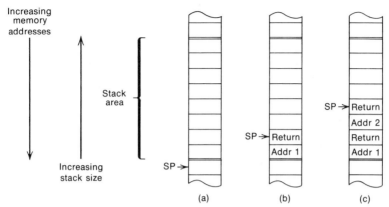

FIGURE 5–5 H6809 return-address stack: (a) empty; (b) after one subroutine call; (c) after second (nested) subroutine call.

byte on the stack, and incremented once after popping each byte. A return address occupies two bytes.

Table 5–9 outlines a Pascal program with two nested subroutines and the corresponding assembly language statements. The JSR addr instruction saves

TABLE 5–9 Program with two nested subroutines.

Addr	Contents	Label	Opcode	Operand	Comments
			ORG	3000H	PROGRAM Subrs (input,output);
3000	...	SUBR2	...		PROCEDURE P2;
...	...		...		BEGIN
...	...		...		...
3055	39		RTS		END;
3056	...	SUBR1	...		PROCEDURE P1;
...	...		...		BEGIN
...	...		...		...
30A2	BD 3000		JSR	SUBR2	P2; {Call P2}
30A5	...	RET2	...		...
...	...		...		...
30C2	39		RTS		END;
30C5	8F 3FF8	MAIN	LDS	#STK+8	BEGIN {Main program}
...	...		...		...
312F	BD 3056		JSR	SUBR1	P1; {Call P1}
3132	...	RET1	...		...
...	...		...		...
31A7	7E 1000		JMP	1000H	END.
...			ORG	3FF0H	
3FF0	...	STK	RMB	8	
...			END	MAIN	

the address of the next instruction by pushing it onto the stack and then jumps to the instruction at location addr, the first instruction of the subroutine. At the end of the subroutine, RTS pops an address from the stack into PC, effecting a return to the original program sequence.

A stack is the most appropriate data structure for saving return addresses, because it can store more than one return address when subroutines are nested. The number of levels of nesting is limited only by the size of the memory area reserved by the programmer for the stack.

A detailed example program using subroutines is given in Table 5–10. Before describing it, we should point out a few additional assembly language pseudo-operations and features that it uses:

- FCW (Form Constant Word). The specified 16-bit value is stored into two successive memory bytes, high-order byte first. Both FCW and FCB can take multiple operands, separated by commas.

- RMW (Reserve Memory Words). If the value of the operand is n, then $2n$ memory bytes are skipped without storing any instructions or data in them.

- EQU (Equate). The identifier in the Label field is assigned the value in the Operand field, instead of the value in the Address field. This makes the identifier a synonym for a constant value for the duration of the assembly process.

- * (Comment Lines). Any line beginning with an asterisk is completely ignored by the assembler.

- * (Program Location Counter). When used in an expression, the symbol "*" denotes the current address at which assembly is taking place.

The program in Table 5–10 contains a main program and two subroutines. The main program initializes SP to point to a 7-word stack. A stack of 2 words would have been sufficient for this program, but it is a good practice to provide "headroom" in case programming errors, modifications, or interrupts (Chapter 11) increase the space required.

The main program loads a 16-bit word into X and calls a subroutine WCNT1S that counts the number of "1" bits in X. WCNT1S splits X into two bytes and calls a subroutine BCNT1S to count 1s in each byte. The power of subroutines is evidenced by the fact that BCNT1S can be called more than once and with a different byte to be converted each time.

Figure 5–6 shows the state of the stack after each instruction that affects it. When WCNT1S returns to the main program, the stack is again empty and A contains the 1s count. The main program terminates by jumping to the operating system.

The individual subroutines in Table 5–10 are worth discussing. On entry, WCNT1S expects the input word to be in X. This is the first case we've seen

TABLE 5–10 Program that uses subroutines to count the number of "1" bits in a word.

Addr	Contents	Label	Opcode	Operand	Comments
			ORG	2000H	
2000	8F 201A	MAIN	LDS	#STKE	Initialize SP.
2003	BE 201A		LDX	TWORD	Get test word.
2006	BD 201C		JSR	WCNT1S	Count number of 1s in it.
2009	7E 1000		JMP	SYSRET	Return to operating system.
200C		SYSRET	EQU	1000H	Operating system address.
200C	??	STK	RMW	7	Space for 7 return addresses.
201A		STKE	EQU	*	Initialization address for SP.
201A	5B29	TWORD	FCW	5B29H	Test-word to count 1s.
201C		*			
201C		*		Count the number of '1' bits in a word.	
201C		*		Enter with word in X, exit with count in A.	
201C	BF 2032	WCNT1S	STX	CWORD	Save input word.
201F	B6 2032		LDA	CWORD	Get high-order byte.
2022	BD 2035		JSR	BCNT1S	Count 1s.
2025	B7 2034		STA	W1CNT	Save '1' count.
2028	B6 2033		LDA	CWORD+1	Get low-order byte.
202B	BD 2035		JSR	BCNT1S	Count 1s.
202E	BB 2034		ADDA	W1CNT	Add high-order count.
2031	39		RTS		Done, return.
2032	??	CWORD	RMW	1	Save word being counted.
2034	??	W1CNT	RMB	1	Save number of 1s.
2035		*			
2035		*		Count number of '1' bits in a byte.	
2035		*		Enter with byte in A, exit with count in A.	
2035	B7 2061	BCNT1S	STA	CBYTE	Save input byte.
2038	4F		CLRA		Initialize '1' count.
2039	B7 2062		STA	B1CNT	
203C	8E 2059		LDX	#MASKS	Point to 1-bit masks.
203F	A6	BLOOP	LDA	@X	Get next bit mask.
2040	B4 2061		ANDA	CBYTE	Is there a '1' there?
2043	27 08		BEQ	BNO1	Skip if not.
2045	B6 2062		LDA	B1CNT	Otherwise increment
2048	8B 01		ADDA	#1	'1' count.
204A	B7 2062		STA	B1CNT	
204D	30 0001	BNO1	ADDX	#1	Point to next mask.
2050	8C 2061		CMPX	#MASKE	Past last mask?
2053	26 EA		BNE	BLOOP	Continue if not.
2055	B6 2062		LDA	B1CNT	Put total count in A.
2058	39		RTS		Return.
2059		*		Define 1-bit masks to test bits of byte.	
2059	80402010	MASKS	FCB	80H,40H,20H,10H,8H,4H,2H,1H	
205D	08040201				
2061		MASKE	EQU	*	Address just after table.
2061	??	CBYTE	RMB	1	Save byte being counted.
2062	??	B1CNT	RMB	1	Save '1' count.
2063			END	MAIN	

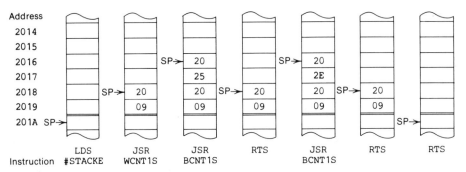

FIGURE 5–6 Stack contents after the execution of instructions in Table 5–10.

where X is used as a convenient place to hold arbitrary 16-bit data, not an address. Using STX CWORD, the subroutine saves X in two memory bytes that are individually read by LDA CWORD and LDA CWORD+1 and passed to BCNT1S.

When BCNT1S is entered, it expects the input byte to be in A and saves it in CBYTE. The subroutine then checks each bit position for a "1" and maintains a count in B1CNT accordingly. It uses a table of eight "mask bytes," each having a "1" in a different bit position. X contains the address of a mask byte, and CBYTE is combined with each mask byte using the ANDA CBYTE instruction. At each iteration of the loop, ANDA produces a nonzero result if and only if the tested bit of CBYTE is 1.

Like procedures and functions in Pascal, subroutines are the key to the structure of assembly language programs. A typical program is divided into many "modules," each of which is a subroutine with inputs, outputs, and local data. Subroutines will be discussed in detail in Chapter 9.

5.3 GENERAL-REGISTER PROCESSORS

A general-register processor (or machine) has a set of *general registers* in which arithmetic and logical operations and data transfers take place. The registers are "general" because they are all treated identically (or almost identically). Any register may contain data to be used by an instruction, or may be used to specify an address. Typical general-register processors have 8 or 16 registers of 16 to 36 bits each. The PDP-11, Z8000, and 68000 are the best examples of general-register processors in this book.

5.3.1 Organization of a General-Register Processor

The internal organization of a hypothetical general-register processor is shown in Figure 5–7. This processor contains a subset of the registers and features of the Zilog Z8000, so we'll call it the H8000. Comparing the H8000

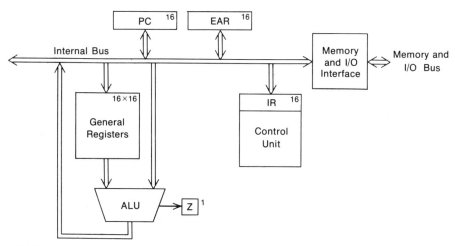

FIGURE 5–7 General-register processor organization, the H8000.

with the H6809, we see that IR has been expanded to 16 bits, SP and X have been eliminated, and A has been replaced by a bank of sixteen 16-bit general registers, R0–R15. The function of SP in the H6809 is performed by R15 in the H8000, and the function of X may be performed by any register except R0. As before, the Z bit is set according to the result of each data manipulation instruction.

The programming model for the H8000 is shown in Figure 5–8. Since addresses are 16 bits long, the memory address space is 64K bytes, arranged as shown in Figure 5–1(c). Arithmetic and logical operations and data transfers can be performed on words (in a 16-bit register) and on bytes (in half of a register). For byte operations, the first eight 16-bit registers are treated as sixteen 8-bit registers, and the last eight 16-bit registers are not used.

5.3.2 Instruction Formats

Instructions in the H8000 are one or two words long. Like most real processors, the H8000 has many different instruction formats due to the varying number and type of operands for different instructions. The first word of each H8000 instruction contains an opcode and other information such as a register number and addressing mode. The second word, if present, contains an immediate operand or a memory address. Figure 5–9 shows six different formats used for the first word of H8000 instructions.

Most H8000 instructions can operate on either words or bytes, depending on the contents of the W/B bit (word=1). Most instructions specify an operand using the mode and reg1 fields as explained in the next subsection. The second operand of a double-operand instruction is a register specified by the reg2 field.

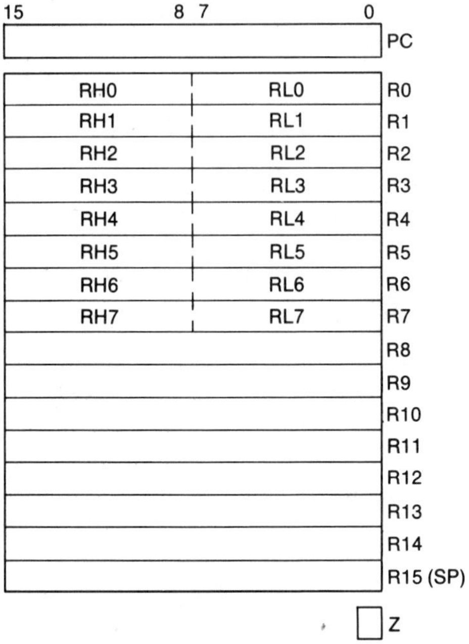

```
15              8 7              0
┌─────────────────────────────┐
│                             │ PC
└─────────────────────────────┘

┌──────────────┬──────────────┐
│     RH0      │     RL0      │ R0
├──────────────┼──────────────┤
│     RH1      │     RL1      │ R1
├──────────────┼──────────────┤
│     RH2      │     RL2      │ R2
├──────────────┼──────────────┤
│     RH3      │     RL3      │ R3
├──────────────┼──────────────┤
│     RH4      │     RL4      │ R4
├──────────────┼──────────────┤
│     RH5      │     RL5      │ R5
├──────────────┼──────────────┤
│     RH6      │     RL6      │ R6
├──────────────┼──────────────┤
│     RH7      │     RL7      │ R7
├──────────────┴──────────────┤
│                             │ R8
├─────────────────────────────┤
│                             │ R9
├─────────────────────────────┤
│                             │ R10
├─────────────────────────────┤
│                             │ R11
├─────────────────────────────┤
│                             │ R12
├─────────────────────────────┤
│                             │ R13
├─────────────────────────────┤
│                             │ R14
├─────────────────────────────┤
│                             │ R15 (SP)
└─────────────────────────────┘

                        □ Z
```

FIGURE 5–8 Programming model for H8000.

5.3.3 Addressing Modes

The mode and reg1 fields of an instruction specify an operand as shown in Table 5–11. Instructions that specify register and register indirect addressing are one word long; the other modes require a second word. With the two-word modes, the programmer may write any expression (expr) in the

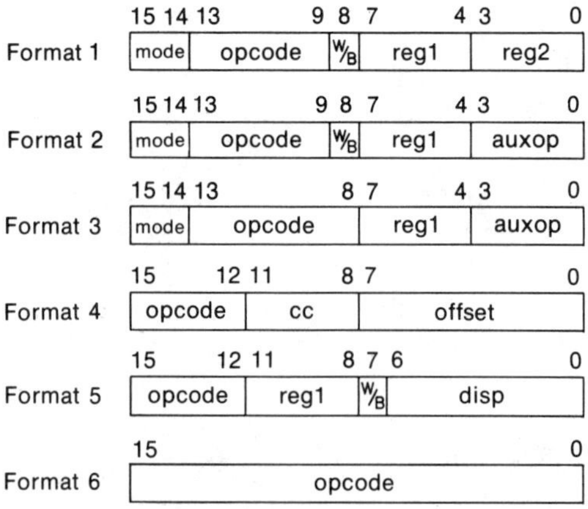

```
          15 14 13      9 8 7      4 3      0
         ┌────┬────────┬───┬──────┬────────┐
Format 1 │mode│ opcode │W/B│ reg1 │  reg2  │
         └────┴────────┴───┴──────┴────────┘

          15 14 13      9 8 7      4 3      0
         ┌────┬────────┬───┬──────┬────────┐
Format 2 │mode│ opcode │W/B│ reg1 │ auxop  │
         └────┴────────┴───┴──────┴────────┘

          15 14 13        8 7      4 3      0
         ┌────┬───────────┬──────┬────────┐
Format 3 │mode│  opcode   │ reg1 │ auxop  │
         └────┴───────────┴──────┴────────┘

          15     12 11     8 7             0
         ┌────────┬────────┬───────────────┐
Format 4 │ opcode │   cc   │    offset     │
         └────────┴────────┴───────────────┘

          15     12 11     8 7 6           0
         ┌────────┬────────┬───┬───────────┐
Format 5 │ opcode │  reg1  │W/B│   disp    │
         └────────┴────────┴───┴───────────┘

          15                               0
         ┌─────────────────────────────────┐
Format 6 │             opcode              │
         └─────────────────────────────────┘
```

FIGURE 5–9 H8000 instruction formats.

TABLE 5-11 Addressing modes of the H8000.

mode	reg1	Assembler Notation	Name	Operand
00	R0	`#expr`	Immediate	`expr`
00	R1–R15	`@reg1`	Register Indirect	`MEM[reg1]`
01	R0	`expr`	Absolute	`MEM[expr]`
01	R1–R15	`expr(reg1)`	Indexed	`MEM[expr+reg1]`
10	R0–R15	`reg1`	Register	`reg1`
11	R0–R15		(Illegal)	

assembly language statement; the assembler evaluates `expr` and places its value in the second word.

The first three addressing modes in Table 5–11 have counterparts in the H6809. The Indexed mode computes an effective address by combining a register with the second word of the instruction; this mode is discussed in Section 7.3.2. The Register mode allows instructions to work on registers without accessing operands in memory. By keeping frequently-used variables in registers, a program can run much faster than a similar program on an accumulator-based processor.

5.3.4 Instruction Set

Table 5–12 lists the instructions of the H8000. In the table, "op1" is determined by the reg1 and mode fields of the instruction. There are five double-operand instructions; each instruction has a counterpart in the H6809.[3] Not all addressing modes can be used with all instructions. For example, immediate mode makes no sense with ST(B), because it would store a register value into the instruction stream.

Three single-operand instructions, CLR(B), COM(B), and NEG(B), specify their operand just like op1 in double-operand instructions. These instructions can clear, complement, and negate memory locations as well as registers.

Each of the first eight instructions operates on words or bytes as dictated by the W/B bit (word=1). In the H8000 assembly language, a "B" is appended to the mnemonic to indicate a byte operation. For example, the instruction "CLR R5" clears both bytes of R5, while "CLRB RH5" clears only the high-order byte of R5.

The JP and CALL instructions specify a single operand that must be a word in memory, not an immediate operand or register. Presuming that the word is an instruction, JP jumps to it, that is, it sets PC equal to the word's address. "CALL" is just another name for "JSR", a subroutine calling instruc-

---

[3]As in the H6809, all of these H8000 instructions affect condition bit Z. However, in the real Z8000, loads and stores don't affect any of the condition bits, an inconvenience.

TABLE 5-12   Instruction set of the H8000.

Mnem.	Operands	Format	Opcode (hex)	Auxop (hex)	Description
LD(B)	reg2,op1	1	10		Load reg2 with op1
ST(B)	reg2,op1	1	17		Store reg2 into op1
CMP(B)	reg2,op1	1	05		Set Z by reg2 minus op1
ADD(B)	reg2,op1	1	00		Add op1 to reg2
AND(B)	reg2,op1	1	03		Logical AND op1 to reg2
CLR(B)	op1	2	06	8	Clear op1
COM(B)	op1	2	06	0	Complement bits of op1
NEG(B)	op1	2	06	2	Negate op1
JP	op1	3	1E	8	Jump to address of op1
CALL	op1	3	1F	0	Call subroutine at address of op1
JR	cc,offset	4	E		Jump if condition cc is true
D(B)JNZ	reg1,disp	5	F		Decrement reg1, jump if not zero
RET		6	9E08		Return from subroutine
NOP		6	8D07		No operation

Notes: The notation (B) indicates an instruction that exists for both bytes and words. For example LD loads a word, LDB a byte.

reg1 and reg2 may be any register.

op1 indicates an operand using one of the addressing modes from Table 5-11. However, register and immediate modes are not allowed with ST(B), JP, CALL; and immediate mode is not allowed with CLR(B), COM(B), NEG(B).

cc is one of the conditions from Table 5-13; offset is an 8-bit signed integer that is doubled and added to PC if cc is true; disp is a 7-bit nonnegative number that is doubled and subtracted from PC if reg is not zero.

Opcodes are the same as in Zilog Z8000; mnemonics and assembly language notations are different from those used by various Z8000 assembly languages in some cases.

tion that pushes the return address onto a stack and then jumps. The H8000 always uses register R15 as the stack pointer for CALL and handles R15 the same as the H6809 handles SP. It is up to the programmer to initialize R15 at the beginning of a program. The RET instruction returns from a subroutine by popping the stack into PC, just like RTS in the H6809.

A conditional branch instruction JR cc,offset contains an 8-bit signed offset field and a 4-bit cc field that specifies a condition to be tested as summarized in Table 5-13. All H8000 instructions are required to start on a word boundary. Therefore, a target of a branch must always be an even number of bytes away. The H8000 uses this fact to increase the range of branches — it multiplies the signed offset value by two before adding it to PC. Thus, if offset=+5, a branch skips ahead five *words* if taken. In assembly language programs, the operand field of a JR instruction specifies the actual 16-bit target address and the assembler figures out the proper 8-bit offset for the machine instruction, giving an error if the target address is not in range.

As we'll soon see, D(B)JNZ is a useful loop control primitive. It decrements a register and then jumps backwards if the register is not yet zero. Its

TABLE 5–13 Branch conditions in the H8000.

Assembler Notation	cc (hex)	Meaning
JR offset	8	Branch always
JR EQ,offset	6	Branch if Z=1 (result=0)
JR NE,offset	E	Branch if Z=0 (result<>0)

7-bit disp value is interpreted as a positive number which is multiplied by two and *subtracted* from the PC if the register is not zero. Like JR, an assembly language DJNZ instruction specifies the actual 16-bit target address and the assembler figures out the proper 7-bit offset for the machine instruction.

5.3.5 Sample Programs

The multiplication program for the H6809 (Table 5–4) has been rewritten for the H8000 in Table 5–14. The program processes byte data but can be easily modified for words instead. Note that the B in CLRB, ADDB, and so on indicates a byte instruction, not a B register.

Even though individual H8000 instructions are longer, the program as a whole is shorter. The savings can be attributed to the general registers that store the iteration count and product, avoiding the need to shuttle them between a single accumulator and memory as in the H6809. The DBJNZ (Decrement Byte, Jump if Not Zero) instruction also makes for a very short, efficient inner loop.

An H8000 version of the array initialization program of Table 5–8 is shown in Table 5–15. Just for variety, Q has been declared this time as an array of words, but the program is easily modified to handle a byte array. R1 is used as an index register to point to the components of Q. Any general

TABLE 5–14 Multiplication by repeated addition in the H8000.

Addr	Contents		Label	Opcode	Operand	Comments
				ORG	2A40H	Multiply MCND by MPY.
2A40	8C18		START	CLRB	RH1	Keep product in RH1.
2A42	6000	2A52		LDB	RH0,MPY	Keep iteration count in RH0.
2A46	E603			JR	EQ,OUT	Done if multiplier zero.
2A48	4001	2A53	LOOP	ADDB	RH1,MCND	Add MCND to product.
2A4C	F003			DBJNZ	RH0,LOOP	Multiplier zero yet?
2A4E	5E08	1000	OUT	JP	1000H	Return with product in RH1.
2A52	05		MPY	FCB	5	Multiplier value.
2A53	17		MCND	FCB	23	Multiplicand value.
2A54				END	START	

TABLE 5–15 H8000 program to initialize an array.

Addr	Contents		Label	Opcode	Operand	Comments
				ORG	3000H	Initialize an array to 0.
3000	2101	3100	INIT	LD	R1,#Q	Address of first component.
3004	0D18		ILOOP	CLR	@R1	Clear a word.
3006	0101	0002		ADD	R1,#2	Point to next word.
300A	0B01	310A		CMP	R1,#Q+10	Past the end?
300E	EEFA			JR	NE,ILOOP	Continue if not.
3010	5E08	1000		JP	1000H	
3014				ORG	3100H	
3100	??		Q	RMB	10	Reserve 5 words.
310A				END	INIT	

register except R0 or R15 could have been chosen for this purpose (why?). This H8000 program actually turned out five bytes longer than the corresponding H6809 program. In a very small problem, an accumulator-based processor can have a shorter program because all of the variables can be accessed by short instructions.

Finally, the bit-counting program of Table 5–10 is rewritten in Table 5–16. This program has an interesting mix of byte instructions to manipulate the data bytes whose bits are being counted, and word instructions to manipulate data words (TWORD and bit counts) and addresses (pointers into the mask table). Notice that WCNT1S splits the input word into bytes by simply referencing the high and low bytes of R0 using LDB instructions.

The program in Table 5–16 is fairly involved, and so it's not surprising that it occupies fewer bytes than the corresponding H6809 program. More significantly, it has fewer executable instructions (21 vs. 27). Since programmers tend to produce a constant number of instructions per day independent of language, this indicates that programmers may be more productive when writing programs for a general-register processor than for an accumulator-based processor.

5.4 STACK MACHINES

A *stack machine* has neither general registers nor accumulators, only a stack pointer SP that points to a pushdown stack in memory; all operations are performed on the stack. Many of Hewlett-Packard's desktop and hand-held calculators (and many imitators) are stack machines. The HP 300 and HP 3000 minicomputers are also stack machines. (Perhaps HP is trying to make up for the lack of stack in its first minicomputer, the 2116.) Also, most accumulator-based and general register processors have at least a few stack-oriented instructions.

TABLE 5-16 Program to count the number of "1" bits in a word.

Addr	Contents	Label	Opcode	Operand	Comments
			ORG	2000H	
2000	210F 201E	MAIN	LD	R15,#STKE	Initialize SP.
2004	6100 201E		LD	R0,TWORD	Get test word.
2008	5F00 2020		CALL	WCNT1S	Count number of 1s in it.
200C	5E08 1000		JP	SYSRET	Return to operating system.
2010		SYSRET	EQU	1000H	Operating system address.
2010	??	STACK	RMW	7	Space for 7 return addresses.
201E		STKE	EQU	*	Stack initialization address.
201E	5B29	TWORD	FCW	5B29H	Test word to count 1s.
2020		*			
2020		*		Count the number of '1' bits in a word.
2020		*		R0 = input word on entry
2020		*		R1 = bit count on exit
2020	A002	WCNT1S	LDB	RH2,RH0	Count 1s in high byte.
2022	5F00 2032		CALL	BCNT1S	
2026	A131		LD	R1,R3	Put high byte count in R1.
2028	A082		LDB	RH2,RL0	Count 1s in low byte.
202A	5F00 2032		CALL	BCNT1S	
202E	8131		ADD	R1,R3	Add low byte count to R1.
2030	9E08		RET		Done, return.
2032		*			
2032		*		Count the number of '1' bits in a byte.
2032		*		RH2 = input byte on entry
2032		*		RL2 = temporary byte value for ANDing
2032		*		R3 = bit count on exit
2032		*		R4 = pointer to bit masks
2032	8D38	BCNT1S	CLR	R3	Clear count.
2034	2104 204E		LD	R4,#MASKS	Point to 1-bit masks.
2038	204A	BLOOP	LDB	RL2,@R4	Get next bit mask.
203A	862A		ANDB	RL2,RH2	Is there a '1' there?
203C	E602		JR	EQ,BNO1	Skip if not.
203E	0103 0001		ADD	R3,#1	Otherwise increment count.
2042	0104 0001	BNO1	ADD	R4,#1	Point to next mask.
2046	0B04 2056		CMP	R4,#MASKE	Past last mask?
204A	EEF6		JR	NE,BLOOP	Continue if not.
204C	9E08		RET		Else return.
204E		*		Define 1-bit masks to test bits of byte.
204E	80402010	MASKS	FCB	80H,40H,20H,10H,8H,4H,2H,1H
2052	08040201				
2056		MASKE	EQU	*	End of mask table.
2056			END	MAIN	

   None of the processors discussed in Part 3 are pure stack machines. However, the Digital Equipment Corporation PDP-11, a general-register processor, has instructions that easily simulate those of a pure stack machine. It is instructive to study the architecture of a simple, hypothetical stack machine based on these PDP-11 instructions.

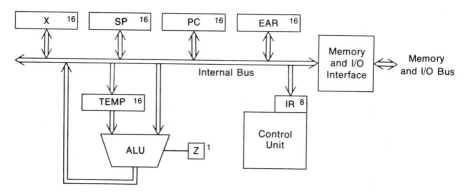

FIGURE 5–10 Organization of a hypothetical stack machine, the H11.

5.4.1 Organization of a Stack Machine

Figure 5–10 shows the internal organization of a hypothetical stack machine. In Chapter 13 we'll show how the PDP-11 can easily simulate this machine; for now we'll call the hypothetical machine the H11.

The H11's organization is similar to that of the H6809, except that the H6809's 8-bit accumulator A has been changed to a 16-bit register TEMP. As shown in the H11's programming model, Figure 5–11, TEMP is not accessible to the programmer; it is only used during the execution of each instruction to temporarily hold an operand.

The H11 has a byte-addressable memory of 64K bytes, organized as shown in Figure 5-1(b). Thus, addresses are two bytes long. Data manipulated by an H11 program is stored in a pushdown stack in memory. The instructions that we describe here manipulate only 16-bit (2-byte) data. As shown in Figure 5–12, high memory is used for the stack, which grows downward, and low memory is used for instructions and "global" data. Register SP points to the top of the stack, using the same conventions as SP in the H6809. Index register X normally contains the address of a location somewhere inside the

FIGURE 5–11 Programming model for the H11.

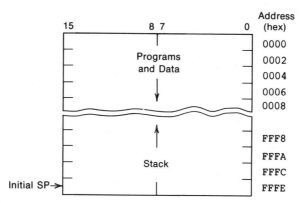

FIGURE 5–12 Memory organization of the H11.

stack. The region of memory near this address is called a *stack frame*, and therefore X may be called a *stack frame pointer* (FP).

5.4.2 Instruction Set

The instruction set of the H11 is given in Table 5–17. Instructions in the first group are used to push and pop arbitrary data on the stack. Any word in memory may be pushed onto the stack by a PUSH addr instruction, which specifies a 16-bit absolute address in two bytes following the opcode. Likewise, the word at the top of the stack (TOS) may be popped into any memory location by means of a POP addr instruction. When a word is pushed, SP is decremented by two; then the word is stored at the memory address indicated by the new value of SP (which must be even). A word is popped by storing the TOS into the specified memory address and then incrementing SP by two. Figure 5–13 illustrates the contents of memory for a sequence of several pushes and pops.

Several other PUSH and POP instructions are provided. PUSH #data pushes an immediate data value; PUSHX pushes a copy of register X; PUSHT and PUSHS push a copy of the top and second from the top items in the stack, respectively. PUSH offset(X) and POP offset(X) push and pop memory words "near" the word pointed to by register X. Here offset is an 8-bit two's-complement number (−128 through +127) that is added to X to obtain the effective address of the operand.[4] Figure 5–14 shows several operations using X.

---

[4]In general, offset must be even, a result of using the PDP-11 to simulate the stack machine. If we were designing the machine from scratch, we would either allow odd offsets to access individual bytes, or we would multiply the offset by two to increase the number of words accessible by indexed instructions.

The second group of instructions in Table 5–17 performs arithmetic and logical operations on data at the top of the stack. As shown in Figure 5–15, single-operand instructions modify the value stored at the top of the stack. Double-operand instructions combine two operands at the top of the stack, replacing them with the result of the operation. These are called "zero-

TABLE 5–17 Machine instructions of the H11.

Mnem.	Operand	Length (bytes)	Opcode (hex.)	Description
PUSH	addr	3	01	Push MEMW[addr] onto stack
PUSH	#data	3	02	Push data onto stack
PUSH	offset(X)	2	03	Push MEMW[X+offset] onto stack
PUSHT		1	04	Push TOS onto stack
PUSHS		1	05	Push SOS onto stack
PUSHX		1	06	Push X onto stack
POP	addr	3	07	Pop TOS, store into MEMW[addr]
POP	offset(X)	2	08	Pop TOS, store into MEMW[X+offset]
CLR		1	10	Clear TOS
COM		1	11	Ones' complement bits of TOS
NEG		1	12	Negate TOS (two's complement)
SWAB		1	13	Swap bytes of TOS
ADD		1	14	Pop TOS, add to new TOS
AND		1	15	Pop TOS, logical AND to new TOS
CMP		1	16	Pop TOS, compare with new TOS
MUL		1	17	Pop TOS, SOS, and push TOS·SOS (one-word result, overflow ignored)
LD	r,#data	3	20+r	Load r with data
LD	r,addr	3	22+r	Load r with MEMW[addr]
LDXS		1	24	Load X with a copy of SP
ST	r,addr	3	26+r	Store r into MEMW[addr]
ADD	r,#offset	2	28+r	Add offset to r
VAL		1	30	Replace TOS with MEMW[TOS]
STOW		1	31	Store TOS into MEMW[SOS], pop both
BNE	offset	2	40	Branch if Z=0
BEQ	offset	2	41	Branch if Z=1
BRA	offset	2	42	Branch always
JMP	addr	3	50	Jump to addr
JSR	addr	3	51	Jump to subroutine at addr
RTS		1	52	Return from subroutine
NOP		1	00	No operation

Notes: data = 16-bit data value; addr = 16-bit memory address; offset = 8-bit signed integer.
  r = X or SP; add 1 to opcode if r = SP.
  MEMW[n] = memory word at address n; n must be even.
  TOS = word at top of stack; SOS = second word on stack.
  Opcodes, mnemonics, and instruction lengths are different from the corresponding PDP-11 instructions given in Chapter 13.

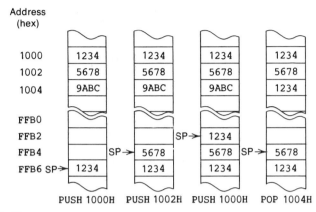

FIGURE 5–13 Memory contents after various stack pushes and pops.

address" instructions, because they contain no address specifications; they implicitly manipulate the top one or two stack items.

The third group contains "housekeeping" instructions for SP and X. The fourth group provides a method of indirect addressing for accessing array elements and other data by means of pointers computed at run time. If the address of a variable is stored on the top of the stack, VAL replaces the address with the value of the variable itself. STOW performs the inverse operation, storing the data word from the top of the stack at an address contained in the second word on the stack (one below the top).

All of the instructions in the first four groups set Z to 1 if they produce a zero result, to 0 otherwise. BEQ and BNE test Z and branch as in the H6809. The other instructions in the fifth group also operate the same as in the H6809.

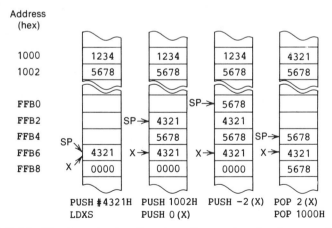

FIGURE 5–14 Stack contents after operations using the frame pointer.

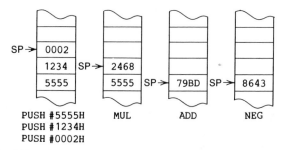

PUSH #5555H   MUL   ADD   NEG
PUSH #1234H
PUSH #0002H

FIGURE 5–15 Effects of single- and double-operand instructions.

5.4.3 Sample Programs

Our standard algorithm for multiplying two numbers by repeated addition is coded for the H11 in Table 5–18. The state of the stack at various points in the program is shown in Figure 5–16. There are at most five items on the stack at any time. Although SP changes as the stack expands and shrinks

TABLE 5–18 Multiplication by repeated addition on the H11.

Addr	Contents	Label	Opcode	Operand	Comments
			ORG	2A40H	Multiply MCND by MPY.
2A40		SPROD	EQU	-2	Offset to PROD in stack frame.
2A40		SCNT	EQU	-4	Offset to CNT.
2A40		SMCND	EQU	-6	Offset to MCND.
2A40		*	Assume	SP has	already been loaded on entry.
2A40	24	START	LDXS		Set up frame pointer.
2A41	04		PUSHT		Push a word onto the stack.
2A42	10		CLR		Clear it (initial PROD).
2A43	01 2C00		PUSH	MPY	Set CNT equal to MPY.
2A46	01 2C02		PUSH	MCND	Make a copy of MCND in stack.
2A49	50 2A58		JMP	IN	Do the loop MPY times.
2A4C	02 FFFF	LOOP	PUSH	#-1	Decrement CNT.
2A4F	14		ADD		
2A50	08 FC		POP	SCNT(X)	
2A52	04		PUSHT		Make a copy of MCND.
2A53	03 FE		PUSH	SPROD(X)	
2A55	14		ADD		
2A56	08 FE		POP	SPROD(X)	
2A58	03 FC	IN	PUSH	SCNT(X)	Push a copy of CNT.
2A5A	40 F0		BNE	LOOP	Continue if not yet zero.
2A5C	29 06	DONE	ADD	SP,#6	Else clean up stack.
2A5E	50 1000		JMP	1000H	Return to operating system,
2A61		*			PROD is at top of stack.
2A61			ORG	2C00H	
2C00	05	MPY	FCW	5	Multiplier value.
2C02	17	MCND	FCW	23	Multiplicand value.
2C04			END	START	

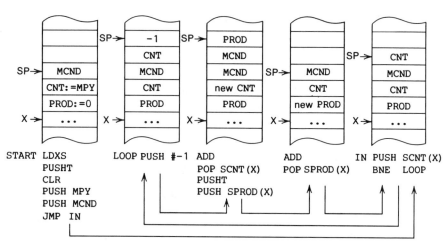

FIGURE 5–16 Stack contents after execution of instructions in multiplication program.

during each iteration of the loop, the frame pointer X always provides a fixed reference address for accessing CNT and PROD.

In spite of some gross inefficiencies, such as using five instructions to decrement and test CNT, the H11 program is still slightly shorter than the corresponding program for the H6809. The decrease in length may be attributed to efficient access of local variables on the stack using the frame pointer, and the use of short 1-byte instructions. However, when compared with the corresponding H8000 program, the H11 program is still much longer. The H8000 can access local variables much more efficiently by simply keeping them in registers.

An array initialization program for the H11 is shown in Table 5–19. This program also illustrates the use of the STOW and CMP instructions. As an exercise, you should sketch the contents of the stack during the execution of the program.

5.4.4 Strengths and Weaknesses of Stack Machines

Stack machines show their greatest strength in evaluating complicated expressions. To show this, we'll look at some expressions involving multiplication and addition. The H11 MUL instruction multiplies the top two words on the stack and replaces them with a one-word product. If the product requires more than one word to express, then the high-order bits are lost. Now suppose we augment the H8000 with a similar instruction, MUL reg2,op1, that multiplies a register by an operand, leaving a 1-word product in the register. Some Pascal assignment statements using addition and multiplication are coded for the H8000 and H11 in Table 5–20.

TABLE 5–19   Initializing an array on the H11.

Addr	Contents	Label	Opcode	Operand	Comments
			ORG	3000H	Initialize an array to 0.
3000		*	Assume SP has		already been loaded on entry.
3000	02 3100	INIT	PUSH	#Q	Base address of array.
3003	04	ILOOP	PUSHT		Get a copy of array address.
3004	04		PUSHT		Push 0 (initial value).
3005	10		CLR		
3006	31		STOW		Initialize an array location.
3007	02 0002		PUSH	#2	Update array address.
300A	14		ADD		
300B	02 310A		PUSH	#Q+10	Past end?
300E	16		CMP		
300F	40 F2		BNE	ILOOP	Continue if not.
3011	29 02		ADD	SP,#2	Else clean up stack.
3013	50 1000		JMP	1000H	Go to operating system.
3016			ORG	3100H	
3100	??	Q	RMW	5	Reserve 5 words.
310A			END	INIT	

Although the H11 requires more instructions than the H8000 to evaluate each expression, its individual instructions are shorter, making the overall H11 program slightly shorter. A stack machine can have shorter instructions than a general-register machine because it does not need any bits to encode register numbers. Compare the 3-byte PUSH and POP instructions in the H11 with the 4-byte LD and ST in the H8000. Both specify a 16-bit memory address, but the H8000 instructions "waste" an extra byte to select two registers out of the sixteen.

Although stack machines may have slightly shorter programs, they are not necessarily faster than general-register machines. Because execution of a typical instruction can be overlapped with fetching the next instruction, the speed of a modern computer processor tends to be limited by the speed of the memory system. Therefore, a good approximation of the relative execution speed of a program can be obtained by simply counting the number of times it accesses memory (i.e., reads or writes it) while fetching and executing its instructions.

In Table 5–20, we have counted the number of bytes of memory that are accessed during the H8000 and H11 expression evaluation programs. The H11 programs, although slightly shorter in bytes, take much more execution time than the H8000 programs. This is directly attributable to the fact that the only "working register," where arithmetic operations take place, is the top of the stack. And the top of stack is stored in memory, which we claim is the bottleneck in the system!

In order to get around the memory bottleneck, many real stack machines are designed to keep the top few items of the stack in "scratchpad" processor registers, in a way transparent to the programmer. When the top of stack is accessed by a program, the hardware accesses memory only if the processor stack registers have become full or empty because of too many more pushes

TABLE 5-20 Assignment statements in general-register and stack machines.

Statement	H8000 Instructions		H11 Instructions		Stack Contents
P:=Q*R+S+T	LD R0,Q	(4,6)	PUSH Q	(3,5)	Q
	MUL R0,R	(4,6)	PUSH R	(3,5)	Q, R
	ADD R0,S	(4,6)	MUL	(1,7)	Q*R
	ADD R0,T	(4,6)	PUSH S	(3,5)	Q*R, S
	ST R0,P	(4,6)	ADD	(1,7)	Q*R+S
	-------		PUSH T	(3,5)	Q*R+S, T
		(20,30)	ADD	(1,7)	Q*R+S+T
			POP P	(3,5)	empty

				(18,46)	
P:= (Q+R)	LD R0,Q	(4,6)	PUSH Q	(3,5)	Q
* (S+T)	ADD R0,R	(4,6)	PUSH R	(3,5)	Q, R
	LD R1,S	(4,6)	ADD	(1,7)	Q+R
	ADD R1,T	(4,6)	PUSH S	(3,5)	Q+R, S
	MUL R0,R1	(2,2)	PUSH T	(3,5)	Q+R, S, T
	ST R0,P	(4,6)	ADD	(1,7)	Q+R, S+T
	-------		MUL	(1,7)	(Q+R) * (S+T)
		(22,32)	POP P	(3,5)	empty

				(18,46)	
P:= (Q*R+S*T)	LD R0,Q	(4,6)	PUSH Q	(3,5)	Q
* (U+V)	MUL R0,R	(4,6)	PUSH R	(3,5)	Q, R
	LD R1,S	(4,6)	MUL	(1,7)	Q*R
	ADD R1,T	(4,6)	PUSH S	(3,5)	Q*R, S
	ADD R0,R1	(2,2)	PUSH T	(3,5)	Q*R, S, T
	LD R1,U	(4,6)	MUL	(1,7)	Q*R, S*T
	ADD R1,V	(4,6)	ADD	(1,7)	Q*R+S*T
	MUL R0,R1	(2,2)	PUSH U	(3,5)	Q*R+S*T, U
	ST R0,P	(4,6)	PUSH V	(3,5)	Q*R+S*T, U, V
	-------		ADD	(1,7)	Q*R+S*T, U+V
		(32,44)	MUL	(1,7)	(Q*R+S*T) * (U+V)
			POP P	(3,5)	empty

				(26,70)	

Notes: Parentheses indicate instruction length in bytes and number of memory bytes accessed during instruction fetching and execution.
Commas separate entries in Stack Contents column; rightmost entry is top of stack.

than pops or vice versa. Even after going through all this trouble, computer architects still debate whether a stack machine can be made to run as fast as a general-register machine designed with an equal amount of circuitry and engineering effort.

The main advantage of stacks is not in expression evaluation anyway. Rather, stacks are the most natural data structure for saving return addresses and other information during subroutine calls. And as we'll see in Chapter 9, they can also be used to store subroutine parameters and local variables in both assembly and high-level language programs.

Luckily, we don't need a pure stack machine to get the benefits of stacks for calling subroutines. Because stacks are so useful in this situation, almost all modern processors have registers and instructions that can be used to manipulate data and addresses in stacks.

5.5 OTHER PROCESSOR ORGANIZATIONS AND CLASSIFICATIONS

Few real processors fall precisely into the categories of accumulator, general-register, and stack machines. For example, the 8086 has eight 16-bit registers that Intel calls "general registers" because they are treated the same in many operations. However, multiplication, division, and decimal operations can be performed on only one register (the "accumulator"), and each register is used differently in address calculations. Luckily, our purpose for classifying different machines is not to create a strict taxonomy, rather it is to provide a framework for discussing and understanding diverse processor architectures.

Another classification criterion to study is the number of memory addresses given in a typical instruction. Consider the general form of a double-operand instruction:

```
OP3 := F(OP2,OP1);
```

Here F is a function like addition or multiplication. In an accumulator-based processor, this general form is simplified to:

```
A := F(A,MEM1);
```

Here A is the accumulator and MEM1 is an operand in memory. The instruction specifies only one memory address, that of MEM1, so it is called a *one-address instruction*.

In a general-register processor, the effect of a double-operand instruction is:

```
REG := F(REG,MEM1);
```

A full memory address is again given for MEM1, but a short register number is given for REG, hence the name *one-and-a-half-address instruction*. All general-register processors have one-and-a-half-address instructions. Their instructions are further classified as *memory-to-register*, as above, and *register-to-memory*, as below:

        MEM1 := F(MEM1,REG);

Some processors also have *two-address instructions*, in which both operands are specified by memory addresses:

        MEM2 := F(MEM2,MEM1);

In a stack instruction, both operands are in memory, but their addresses are implied to be at the top of the stack:

        PUSH(F(POP,POP));

Since the instruction doesn't contain any memory addresses, it is called a *zero-address instruction*.

Processors that have predominantly one type of instruction format are named accordingly, for example, the H6809 is a "one-address machine." However, some processors have many different instruction formats. For example, the PDP-11 can easily simulate any of the above instruction formats, plus some that we haven't classified:

        ADD   MEM1,REG   REG := REG + MEM1;
        ADD   REG,MEM1   MEM1 := MEM1 + REG;
        ADD   MEM1,MEM2   MEM2 := MEM2 + MEM1;
        ADD   (SP)+,(SP)   PUSH(POP+POP);
        ADD   (SP)+,REG   REG := REG + POP;
        ADD   (SP)+,MEM1   MEM1 := MEM1 + POP;
        ADD   REG,(SP)   PUSH(POP+REG);
        ADD   MEM1,(SP)   PUSH(POP+MEM1);

Many "non-traditional" features have appeared in recent microprocessor architectures. One feature we usually take for granted is that instructions and data are stored in the same memory. In most systems this is necessary, since instructions and data are interchanged by some program development tools. For example, a *loader* loads a saved program into memory and must treat it as data to do so. However, in dedicated applications such as point-of-sale terminals or automobile ignitions there are no resident program development tools, and programs and data never mix. Therefore, some microcontrollers such as the MCS-48 store their instructions and data in different memories; their instructions do not allow program memory locations to be read and written as data.

Another interesting concept is that of a working-register set. Instead of having just one set of general registers, some processors have many sets, using a "working-register pointer" to specify which set is currently in use. For example, the MCS-48 has two register sets, and the 9900 can use a block of 16 words anywhere in its 32K-word address space as its register set.

Processors are also classified by the size of the data that they process. Most contemporary processors can address and process data as small as a byte; some can even address individual bits in registers or memory. Except for character strings, the largest data type handled by a processor is usually four or eight bytes for floating-point operations.

A particular processor is called an n-bit machine if the largest operand handled by the majority of its data operations is n bits. This is a characteristic of the processor registers and operations, not of the processor hardware design, the memory organization, or the memory bus. Thus, the 6809 is an 8-bit processor even though it has some 16-bit index registers and operations; the 8086 is a 16-bit processor even though its instructions are strings of 1 to 7 bytes; and the 68000 is a 32-bit processor even though the MC68000 chip introduced in 1979 has a 16-bit memory data bus and 16-bit internal data paths.

Processors are also classified by their size and cost, as discussed in Section 1.7. They can also be classified by their addressing modes and by the size of the memory they can access, as discussed in Chapter 7.

REFERENCES

The best way to study computer organization is to examine the architectures of real machines. Of the processors in this book, the 6809 is the best example of an accumulator-based machine. The PDP-11, Z8000, and 68000 are all good examples of general-register machines, and each has architectural features that make it interesting. Although we don't cover any pure stack machines, the PDP-11 (Chapter 13) can be used as one. The HP3000 and HP300 are popular midi/minicomputers with a pure stack architecture.

Several textbooks discuss general computer organization from the hardware viewpoint, including *Digital Systems: Hardware Organization and Design* by Hill and Peterson [Wiley, 1980 (third edition)], *Computer Organization* by Hamacher, Vranesic, and Zaky [McGraw-Hill, 1978], and *Computer Architecture and Organization* by John Hayes [McGraw-Hill, 1978]. Probably the best overall efforts on classification and taxonomy of computer organizations appear in *Computer Structures: Readings and Examples* by Bell and Newell [McGraw-Hill, 1971] and *Principles of Computer Structures* by Siewiorek, Bell, and Newell [McGraw-Hill, 1981].

Discussions of the design decisions that went into several DEC computer organizations including the PDP-11 may be found in *Computer Engineer-*

ing by Bell, Mudge, and McNamara [Digital Press, 1978]. The designers of several recent microprocessors have also explained their processors' organizations and some of the technical and marketing decisions that produced them. The Z8000 is described in "Architecture of a New Microprocessor" by Bernard Peuto and the 68000 in "A Microprocessor Architecture for a Changing World" by Skip Stritter and Tom Gunter; both articles appear in the February 1979 issue of *Computer* [Vol. 12, No. 2]. Terry Ritter and Joel Boney describe "the best 8-bit machine so far made by human" in a three-part series in *Byte*, "A Microprocessor for the Revolution: The 6809" [Jan., Feb., Mar. 1979 (Vol. 4, No. 1,2,3)]. Morse, Pohlman, and Ravenel explain the source of the 8086's quirks in the title of their June 1978 *Computer* article [Vol. 11, No. 6]: "The Intel 8086 Microprocessor: A 16-bit Evolution of the 8080."

EXERCISES

5.1   What is the relationship, if any, between the length of an instruction and the length of the data that it processes?

5.2   How many address bits are needed in a byte-addressable machine with 131,072 words of memory? What if it is a word-addressable machine? (Remember, one word contains two bytes.)

5.3   Two values may be arithmetically compared by subtracting them and determining whether the result is less than, greater than, or equal to zero. A typical processor has instructions for comparing bytes and for comparing words. Lexicographical sorting of a pair of ASCII character strings can be accomplished by comparing them a byte at a time, starting with the leftmost bytes, until an unequal byte is found. Discuss whether word-comparing instructions can be used to speed up the sorting, depending on whether the memory is organized as shown in Figure 5–1(b) or 5–1(c).

5.4   A *decimal instruction* processes strings of decimal digits. Describe how the data for such an instruction could be stored in a binary memory, assuming that the desired memory organization could be described in Pascal as follows:

```
TYPE
  digit = 0..9;
  word = PACKED ARRAY [0..8] OF digit;
  address = 0..9999;
VAR
  MEM : ARRAY [address] OF word;
```

5.5   In Table 5–3, why does the assembly language pseudo-operation "FCB 23" store the value 17 into memory instead of 23?

5.6 The speed of a typical processor is limited by the speed of the memory. Therefore the execution time of each instruction depends mainly on the number of times that memory must be accessed to fetch and execute the instruction. As a first approximation, the total time to execute an instruction equals the number of memory bytes the instruction accesses (reads or writes) times the length of time for one access. Assuming that each access takes one microsecond, construct a table that shows the execution times for all of the H6809 instructions. Example: STX addr — 3 instruction bytes fetched, 2 bytes stored, total execution time is 5 microseconds. Note: Assume that the offset byte of a branch instruction is fetched even if the branch is not taken.

5.7 Using the table developed in Exercise 5.6 (or using real M6809 times), calculate the execution time of one iteration of the inner loop of the program in Table 5–4.

5.8 Using the table developed in Exercise 5.6 (or using real M6809 times), compare the execution times of the programs in Tables 5–7 and 5–8. Develop formulas that give the execution times of both programs as a function of the size of the array being initialized.

5.9 Suppose that the H6809's index register X and all instructions related to it are eliminated. Show how to rewrite the array initialization program in Table 5–8 using an instruction that modifies the addr part of another instruction. The new program should still be capable of initializing an array of any size with no increase in program length. Why is it a bad idea to write such "self-modifying" code in practice?

5.10 Suppose that the last instruction an H6809 subroutine executes before returning, is to call another subroutine. Show that the two-instruction sequence JSR addr; RTS can always be replaced by the single instruction JMP addr. Why is it a bad practice to actually do this?

5.11 If an H6809 "operating system" calls the main program in Table 5–10 using a JSR instruction, can the main program return to the operating system using an RTS instead of JMP SYSRET? Explain.

5.12 Assemble the following H6809 subroutine by hand, producing a listing in the format of Table 5–4. While you're at it, add comments that explain what the subroutine does (it's too bad that real assembler programs can't do this!).

```
            ORG    3000H
START       LDX    #V
            CLRA
            STA    Z
LOOP        LDA    @X
            ADDA   Z
            STA    Z
            ADDX   #1
            CMPX   #V+LEN
            BNE    LOOP
            LDA    Z
```

```
          RTS
Z         RMB    1
LEN       EQU    10
V         RMB    LEN
          END    START
```

5.13 Write an H6809 subroutine that converts an 8-bit number DECNUM into a sequence of three ASCII characters, the digits of the corresponding unsigned decimal number. When the subroutine is entered, the input number is assumed to be contained in the A register, and on exit, the result should be contained in three memory bytes, ASC2 (most significant), ASC1, ASC0. Use the following algorithm:

```
ASC2 := 30H; ASC1 := 30H; ASC0 := 30H; {ASCII '0'}
WHILE DECNUM <> 0 DO
  BEGIN
    ASC0 := ASC0 + 1;
    IF ASC0 = 30H + 10 THEN BEGIN
      ASC0 := 30H;   ASC1 := ASC1 + 1;
      IF ASC1 = 30H + 10 THEN BEGIN
        ASC1 := 30H;   ASC2 := ASC2 + 1
        END;
      END;
    DECNUM := DECNUM - 1;
  END;
```

5.14 Why can't the H8000 allow a value of 11_2 in the mode field of an instruction in Format 1, 2, or 3?

5.15 Why is register mode illegal for the H8000 ST instruction? What about JMP and CALL?

5.16 Rewrite the H8000 program in Table 5–14 so that it multiplies words instead of bytes.

5.17 The approximate execution times of H8000 instructions can be calculated using the same ideas presented in in Exercise 5.6 for the H6809. However, a 16-bit processor such as the H8000 typically has a 16-bit wide data path to memory, so that it can access a whole word at a time. Assuming that each *word* takes one microsecond to access, construct a table that shows the execution times for all H8000 instructions as a function of opcode and addressing mode. Examples: LD reg2, op1 takes one cycle to fetch the instruction, plus addressing mode time; Register mode takes no additional cycles; Direct mode takes two additional cycles, one to fetch address and one to access operand.

5.18 Using the H6809 instruction execution times developed in Exercise 5.6 and the H8000 execution times developed above, compare the execution times of the inner loops of the programs in Tables 5–4 and 5–14. Alternative: Use real execution times for the M6809 or Z8000 or both.

5.19 Repeat the previous exercise, assuming that the H8000 has only an 8-bit data path to memory, so that it takes two microseconds to access a word in memory.

5.20 Show how to reduce the execution time of the program in Table 5–14 by keeping M2 in a register, and calculate the speeds of the old and new inner loops.

5.21 Rewrite the array initialization program in Table 5–15 so that it uses DJNZ instead of CMP to control the number of iterations. Compare the program size and execution speed with the original version.

5.22 The H8000 program in Table 5–16 may have fewer executable instructions than the corresponding H6809 program in Table 5–10, but it takes more comment lines to explain it. How did this happen?

5.23 Assemble the following H8000 subroutine by hand, producing a listing in the format of Table 5–14. Also, add comments that explain what the subroutine does.

```
          ORG     3000H
START     LD      R1,#V
          CLR     R0
LOOP      ADD     R0,@R1
          ADD     R1,#2
          CMP     R1,#V+LEN
          BR      NE,LOOP
          RET
LEN       EQU     20
V         RMB     LEN
          END     START
```

5.24 Do Exercise 5–13 for the H8000, using a 16-bit input number and a 5-digit output.

5.25 Write a Pascal simulation of the H8000.

5.26 Using the same structure as the programs in Tables 5–10 and 5–16, write a main program and bit-counting subroutines for the H11. Values passed to and from the subroutines should be contained in the stack, not fixed memory locations. Use the SWAB instruction to allow you to process the high and low bytes of a word separately. You need not assemble the program.

5.27 Assemble the following H11 subroutine by hand, producing a listing in the format of Table 5–18. Also, add comments that explain what the subroutine does.

```
          ORG     3000H
VSUM      LDXS
          PUSH    #V
          PUSHT
          CLR
          PUSH    VADDR(X)
LOOP      VAL
          ADD
          PUSH    VADDR(X)
          PUSH    #2
          ADD
```

```
            PUSHT
            POP      VADDR (X)
            PUSH     #V+LEN
            CMP
            BNE      LOOP
            PUSH     RADDR (X)
            POP      VADDR (X)
            PUSH     SUM (X)
            POP      RADDR (X)
            ADD      SP,#4
            RTS
RADDR       EQU      0
VADDR       EQU      -2
SUM         EQU      -4
LEN         EQU      20
V           RMB      LEN
            END      VSUM
```

5.28 Write a Pascal simulation of the H11.

5.29 Classify each of the processors in Sections 5.2,3,4 according to two criteria: basic operation size (8, 16, or 32 bits) and number of addresses per instruction (0, 1, 1.5, or 2).

6

ASSEMBLY LANGUAGE PROGRAMMING

Machine language and assembly language are not the same thing. The *machine language* of a computer is the set of bit strings recognized as instructions; the actions performed by each machine instruction are defined by the computer's hardware. *Assembly language* is a software tool, a symbolic language that can be directly translated into machine language by a system program called an *assembler*. The output of an assembler is an *object module* containing the bit strings that comprise the machine language program, and information that tells a *loader* program where to place these bit strings in the computer's memory.

The program development process using assembly language is illustrated in Figure 6–1. A typical programmer uses a *text editor* to create a text file containing an assembly language program. The names *source file* and *source program* are often used for assembly language and high-level language text files. The assembler accepts a source program as input, checks for format errors, and produces an object module containing the machine language program. A loader then loads the object module into the memory of the target machine. There the machine language program is run, possibly with the aid of a *debugger*.

The loader, debugger, and machine language program described above *must* run on the target machine; the text editor and assembler may run there

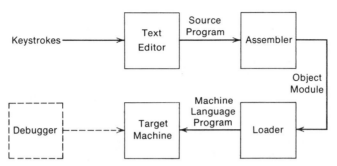

FIGURE 6-1 Assembly language program development.

or on a different machine. An assembler that runs on one machine and produces object modules for another is called a *cross assembler*. For example, it is possible to generate an assembly language program using an intelligent terminal with a tape unit, carry the source file on tape to a large computer that runs a cross assembler, and "download" the object module to a loader in a local microcomputer using a serial data link.

6.1 ASSEMBLY LANGUAGE

Although every computer manufacturer defines a standard assembly language for a new machine when it is introduced, other users may define different assembly languages for the same machine. While the effect of each machine language instruction is fixed in hardware, the person who defines an assembly language is free to specify:

- a mnemonic for each machine language instruction;

- a standard format for the lines of an assembly language program;

- formats for specifying different addressing modes and other instruction variations;

- formats for specifying character constants and integer constants in different bases;

- mechanisms for associating symbolic names with addresses and other numeric values;

- mechanisms for defining data to be stored in memory along with the instructions when the program is loaded;

- directives that specify how the program is to be assembled.

Normally, all assembly languages for a given machine agree on instruction mnemonics and addressing mode designators, but may differ on details like line formats, maximum identifier lengths, constant formats, and assembler directives. Although conceptually there can be dozens of different assembly languages for a given machine, in practice there are only a few — the manufacturer's standard and perhaps one or two different versions from independent software suppliers.

Even though there is a standard assembly language for every computer, there is no standard that is used by all computers, or even by a reasonable fraction of all computers. In this chapter we'll define a simple assembly language for the H6809. Like the H6809 itself, the H6809 assembly language is hypothetical. In Part 3 we'll describe the manufacturers' standard assembly languages for real machines.

6.1.1 Assembly Language Formats

Examples of simple assembly language statements and programs were given in Chapter 5. Unlike Pascal programs, assembly language programs are usually line-oriented, so that each assembly language statement is contained in a single line with a prescribed format. Each line has four fields arranged as shown below:

```
LABEL    OPCODE    OPERAND        COMMENTS
```

The LABEL field is optional. A *label* is simply an identifier (or *symbol* in assembler parlance), that is, a sequence of letters and digits beginning with a letter. The maximum symbol length varies with different assemblers; most allow symbols at least six characters long. Like some Pascal compilers, many assemblers allow symbols of arbitrary length, but only recognize the first six or eight characters.

Every symbol in an assembly language program is assigned a value at the time that it is defined; the assembler program keeps track of labels and their values by an internal *symbol table*. For example, in the statement below,

```
START    LDA    XX        Load A with contents of memory location XX.
```

the value of the symbol "START" equals the memory address at which the LDA instruction is stored. In general, the value of a symbol is the memory address at which the corresponding instruction or data is stored. (An exception occurs for the EQU pseudo-operation discussed later.) Each symbol may be defined only once, but may be referenced as often as needed.

The OPCODE field contains the mnemonic of either a machine instruction or a pseudo-operation. Depending on the contents of the OPCODE field, the OPERAND field specifies zero or more operands separated by commas. An operand is an expression consisting of symbols, constants, and operators such as + and −. The simplest expression consists of a single symbol or constant.

In H6809 assembly language, we use a sequence of digits to denote a decimal constant, and a sequence of hexadecimal digits followed by H to denote a hexadecimal constant. Constants such as 0F123H use a leading zero to distinguish them from symbols. Character constants are surrounded by single quotes (e.g., 'A'), and have the corresponding ASCII value. Other assembly languages may use prefixes or other suffixes to denote constants.

Hexadecimal is the most convenient notation for data and address values in 8-, 16-, and 32-bit machines. Byte values are conveniently expressed in two characters, and 16- and 32-bit quantities are easily split into bytes. Compare with the difficulties encountered with decimal or even octal notation; for example, what word value is obtained by concatenating the bytes $235_8, 312_8$?

The COMMENTS field is ignored by the assembler, but it is essential to good programming. This field should contain a high-level description of the algorithms and data structures used in the program. All assembly language programs in this book are commented either by English sentences and phrases or by corresponding Pascal statements.

Many assembly languages, including the H6809's, require *fixed-format* lines with the following restrictions:

- Fields are separated by one or more spaces.

- A label, if present, begins in the first column of the line. If the LABEL field is empty, the line must begin with at least one space.

- Multiple operands are separated by commas (or other punctuation marks in some cases); no spaces may appear in the operand field.

- The comment field is assumed to start with a space after the last operand.

- A line beginning with an asterisk (*) is a full line comment.

Free-format assembly languages, while still being line-oriented, allow a more flexible format within each line:

- A label consists of an identifier followed by a colon; zero, one, or more labels may appear at the beginning of each line.

- Spaces may be used to separate fields and operands according to the programmer's taste, as in Pascal.

- Fields need not be separated by spaces, except between the OPCODE and OPERAND fields to keep identifiers from running together.

- Comments start with a special character such as "; ".

An example of a free-format assembly language is shown below:

```
START: FIRST: MOV@R0,Y; These two lines are really tight.
SUB QQ,ZEB
;        The rest of these lines are more typical.
NEXT:    ADD     ZEB, Y       ;It's nice to make fields line up...
         MOV     @R1, ZEB     ;Where to put the semicolon is a
         BEQ     FIRST;           matter of taste, but be consistent!
```

6.1.2 Pseudo-operations and the PLC

The program in Table 6–1 contains both machine instructions and pseudo-operations. *Pseudo-operations* (or *assembler directives*) give the assembler instructions on how to assemble the program, and may or may not cause instructions or data to be generated. Table 6–2 describes the effects of each pseudo-operation; we'll explain them shortly.

An assembler that processes the text in Table 6–1 produces a listing such as the one shown in Table 6–3. The assembler automatically numbers the lines of the text file to facilitate references and corrections to them. To keep track of where assembled instructions and data are to be loaded in memory, the assembler uses an internal variable called the *program location counter* (PLC). The second column in Table 6–3 shows the value of the PLC before each line of code is assembled.

The PLC is initialized by means of the ORG pseudo-operation. It is updated after each line of assembly code is processed, normally by adding the length of the instruction or data just assembled. The current value of the PLC may be referenced in expressions by a special symbol such as *.

TABLE 6–1 Assembly language program for H6809.

```
*                          Add the first 15 integers.
         ORG     2000H     Start assembly at location 2000 hex.
START    CLRA              Clear SUM.
         STA     SUM
         LDA     ICNT      Get initial value for CNT.
ALOOP    STA     CNT       Save value of CNT.
         ADDA    SUM       Add to SUM.
         STA     SUM
         LDA     CNT       Update CNT.
         ADDA    #-1
         BNE     ALOOP     Continue if CNT not zero yet.
         JMP     SYSA      Return to operating system when done.
SYSA     EQU     1000H     Operating system return address.
CNT      RMB     1         Reserve storage for CNT.
SUM      RMB     1         Reserve storage for SUM.
IVAL     EQU     15        Initial value is 15.
ICNT     FCB     IVAL      Store intial value.
         END     START
```

TABLE 6–2 Assembly language pseudo-operations.

Name	Format	Description
Origin	label ORG expr	Enter(label,PLC); PLC := expr;
Equate	label EQU expr	Enter(label,expr);
Form Constant Byte	label FCB expr	Enter(label,PLC); MEM[PLC] := expr MOD 256; PLC := PLC + 1;
Form Constant Word	label FCW expr	Enter(label,PLC); MEM[PLC] := expr DIV 256; MEM[PLC+1] := expr MOD 256; PLC := PLC + 2;
Reserve Memory Bytes	label RMB expr	Enter(label,PLC); PLC := PLC + expr;
Reserve Memory Words	label RMW expr	Enter(label,PLC); PLC := PLC + 2*expr;
End Assembly	label END expr	Enter(label,PLC); StartingAddr := expr; EndAssembly;

Notes: expr is any allowed expression.
        MEM[x] is loaded at load time.
        Enter(label,expr) enters label into the symbol table with value expr.

During the assembly of instructions, the PLC corresponds to the value that the hardware program counter (PC) has when the program runs. However, the PLC is not always the same as the run-time PC. For example, during the assembly of data constants the PLC takes on values that the PC never has unless the program tries to execute its data as instructions!

The assembler keeps track of user-defined symbols by means of a *symbol table*. Normally, when an identifier appears in the LABEL field, it is entered into the symbol table with the current value of the PLC. Notice that many of the symbols are used before they are defined; this is called a *forward reference*. The assembler resolves forward references by making two passes over the program, building the symbol table in the first pass and assembling the instructions in the second pass, as described in detail in the next section. (If this isn't clear, you may need a two-pass reading!)

The EQU pseudo-operation is the only operation that does not assign the current PLC value to its label; the value of the EQU's operand is used instead. Thus, EQU can be used to assign a constant value to a symbol, much like a CONST definition in Pascal. It is possible to write a program without using EQU

TABLE 6–3 Assembler listing for a program.

LN#	PLC	CONTENTS	LABEL	OPCODE	OPERAND	COMMENTS
001	0000		*			Add the first 15 integers.
002	0000			ORG	2000H	Start at location 2000 hex.
003	2000	4F	START	CLRA		Clear SUM.
004	2001	B7 201B		STA	SUM	
005	2004	B6 201C		LDA	ICNT	Get initial value for CNT.
006	2007	B7 201A	ALOOP	STA	CNT	Save value of CNT.
007	200A	BB 201B		ADDA	SUM	Add to SUM.
008	200D	B7 201B		STA	SUM	
009	2010	B6 201A		LDA	CNT	Update CNT.
010	2013	8B FF		ADDA	#-1	
011	2015	26 F0		BNE	ALOOP	Continue if CNT not zero yet.
012	2017	7E 1000		JMP	SYSA	Return to system when done.
013	201A		SYSA	EQU	1000H	System return address.
014	201A		CNT	RMB	1	Reserve storage for CNT.
015	201B		SUM	RMB	1	Reserve storage for SUM.
016	201C		IVAL	EQU	15	Initial value is 15.
017	201C	0F	ICNT	FCB	IVAL	Store intial value.
018	201D			END	START	

SYMBOL TABLE:

SYMBOL	VALUE	SYMBOL	VALUE	SYMBOL	VALUE	SYMBOL	VALUE
START	2000	ALOOP	2007	SYSA	1000	CNT	201A
SUM	201B	IVAL	000F	ICNT	201C		

at all, but using EQU can make programs more readable and easier to update. The program in Table 6–3 shows two different uses of EQU. In line 13 EQU is used to define an address, while in line 16 it is used to define a constant data value.

It is important to note that EQU directly affects only the symbol table generated during the assembly process; it does not cause any values to be stored in memory when the program is loaded. Therefore, the PLC is not changed by the EQU statements in Table 6–3.

Constant values are stored in memory by the FCB and FCW pseudo-operations, which evaluate their operands at assembly time and store the resulting byte or word values in memory when the program is loaded. FCB and FCW may have multiple operands separated by commas; the values are stored into successive memory locations.

The distinction between EQU and FCB/FCW pseudo-operations has been known to escape some students, yet it is an extremely important distinction to understand. An EQU statement defines an *assembly-time constant*, making an association between a symbol and a number that is valid only during the assembly process. Any time that the assembler encounters the EQU'ed symbol, it substitutes the corresponding numeric value as if the number itself has been typed. Thus, the statement

```
IVAL    EQU    15
```

allows a programmer to write the statement

```
        LDA    #IVAL
```

instead of

```
        LDA    #15
```

If the programmer wants to change the initial value (IVAL), only the EQU statement defining IVAL must be changed; the programmer need not search the entire program for all LDA #15 instructions. Indeed, the latter procedure requires extraordinary care if the number 15 is also used in other contexts unrelated to its use as "IVAL".

An FCB or FCW statement defines one or more *run-time constants*, numbers that are actually stored into the computer's memory when the program is loaded, numbers that are available for the processor to read while executing the program. Thus, the statement

```
ICNT    FCB    15
```

sets aside a memory location in which the number 15 is stored when the program is loaded. In the assembler's symbol table, the value of the symbol ICNT is not 15 but *the address at which the number 15 is stored*. Hence a program could load the number 15 into A with the statement

```
        LDA    ICNT
```

We continue with a few more pseudo-operations. RMB advances the PLC to reserve one or more memory bytes for storing variables, without causing the bytes to be initialized when the program is loaded. This is analogous to a variable declaration in Pascal, where the values of variables in a program or procedure block are undefined when the block is entered. RMW is similar to RMB; it reserves a specified number of words.

Unlike Pascal CONST and VAR declarations, the EQU, FCB, FCW, RMB, and RMW pseudo-operations may appear in the middle or at the end of an assembly language program. However, pseudo-operations that store constants or reserve memory must not be used in the middle of a sequence of executable instructions. For example, consider the following program fragment:

```
        LDA    SUM
SUM     RMB    1
        ADDA   NEXT
```

After executing the LDA instruction, the computer will interpret whatever value happens to be stored in location SUM as an instruction, creating havoc by performing an unpredictable operation.

The END pseudo-operation indicates the end of the assembly language program, and may be optionally followed by the address of the first executable instruction, the "starting-execution address" of the program. This information may be used by the loader to automatically start execution of the program after it is loaded.

6.1.3 Expressions

The operand field of an assembly language statement may contain an expression; the allowable expressions depend on the assembler. The following are valid expressions in any assembly language:

- A constant value.

- The current value of the PLC (e.g., *).

- A previously-defined symbol.

- Two or more items above combined by arithmetic operators "+" and "−".

Some assemblers also support multiplication, division, logical, and shift operators. Even so, assemblers usually don't allow parenthesization or recognize operator precedence as a high level language does. Expression evaluation is usually strictly left-to-right, so that "P+Q*R" is evaluated as (P+Q)*R, not P+(Q*R) as we would expect in Pascal. For clarity and safety, it's best to write "Q*R+P" in this situation so that we get the same result in any case.

There is another very important distinction between expressions in assembly language and in high-level languages. An operand expression in a high-level assignment statement is evaluated at *run time*, while the operand expression in an assembly language statement is evaluated at *assembly time*. Compare the following two statements:

```
A := XX;       {Assign the value of variable XX to A.}
LDA     XX     Load A with the contents of memory location XX.
```

Apparently, the effect of both statements is the same, if we say that the address of a variable is equivalent to its name. However, consider what happens if the operand is not a simple variable:

```
A := XX+1;     {Assign the value of 1 plus variable XX to A.}
LDA     XX+1   Load A with contents of memory location XX+1.
```

In the high-level language statement, the value of variable XX is read when the program is run, and then 1 is added. In assembly language, the operand expression is evaluated when the program is assembled, *not* when the program is run. The effect of LDA XX+1 is to load A with the contents of memory location XX+1, which has nothing to do with the contents of location XX.

6.1.4 Assembly-Time, Load-Time, and Run-Time Operations

Probably the most important concept for novice assembly language programmers to learn is the distinction between assembly-time, load-time, and run-time operations, so we'll discuss them one more time:

- *Assembly-time operations* are performed by the assembler program, only once, when the assembly language program is assembled. Operand expressions are always evaluated at assembly time. When you see the operators + and −, remember that the additions and subtractions are performed by the assembler, not when the program is run.

- *Load-time operations* are performed by the loader program, only once, when the object program is loaded into the target machine's memory. All instructions, and data constants generated by FCB and FCW, are deposited in memory at load time.

- *Run-time operations* are performed by the machine language program on the target machine, each time the corresponding instructions are executed. For example, an "ADD" instruction performs a run-time addition.

Sometimes the jargon used by assembly language programmers blurs the distinction between assembly-time and run-time operations. For example, as far as an assembler is concerned, a symbol such as CNT in Table 6–3 is equivalent to its value in the symbol table, 201A. However, when programmers talk about run-time operations, they often use a symbol to refer to the contents of the corresponding memory address. Thus, a program might contain the comment "CNT:=15" or "Address(CNT)=201A" when what it should really say is "MEM[CNT]:=15" or "CNT=201A." The meaning of such comments is generally clear from the context.

Like instructions, all of the data values generated by FCB and FCW statements are loaded into memory by the loader only once, at *load time*. It is customary to initialize run-time constants at load time, such as ICNT in Table 6–3. However, a good programmer must resist the temptation to initialize *variables* at load time. For example, changing line 15 of Table 6–3 to

```
SUM      FCB      0
```

apparently eliminates the need for the instructions on lines 3 and 4 that set SUM to zero. This would be true if the program were executed only once. However, if the program were restarted at address 2000H a second time without reloading it, SUM would still have the value produced by the program's previous execution, not zero. Therefore, all variables must be initialized at *run time*.

A program that can be terminated at an arbitrary point and immediately restarted from the beginning without error is called *serially reusable*. Assuming that a program is usable to begin with, adherence to one simple rule guarantees that the program is serially reusable:

- No instruction may modify another instruction or any other memory location that was initialized at load time.

In particular, locations initialized by FCB or similar pseudo-operations must not be modified by the program.

Programs that modify their own instructions are called *self-modifying*. Self-modifying code was necessary in early machines that did not have indirect addressing; the only way to reference a memory location whose address was computed at run time was to "plug" the address into an instruction. However, the use of self-modifying code in modern machines is completely unnecessary, highly unstructured, difficult to debug, and likely to lead to the programmer's dismissal, especially when someone tries to run the program in read-only memory!

6.2 THE TWO-PASS ASSEMBLER

Assembly language allows forward references whereby a symbol may be referenced before it is defined, as shown below:

```
INITN   RMB     1
        ...
        LDA     INITN           Get initial value.
        BNE     NEXT            OK if nonzero.
        LDA     #10             If zero use default.
NEXT    STA     CNT             Initialize count.
        ...
CNT     RMB     1
```

Here, the machine instruction for "LDA INITN" can be generated immediately, because the address INITN has already been defined. However, "STA CNT" and "BNE NEXT" contain forward references; their operands are not defined until later in the program. By moving the definition of CNT to the beginning of the program we could eliminate one forward reference, but this trick isn't applicable to the other one.

A *two-pass assembler* program resolves forward references by reading the source file twice. On the first pass, each line is scanned and the symbol definitions that are encountered are used to build the symbol table. On the second pass, the lines are scanned again, and this time the appropriate machine language instructions and data values are generated and placed in the object module (and a listing is made if requested). Since all symbols are defined in the symbol table by the end of the first pass, symbolic references can be resolved in the second pass by searching the symbol table.[1]

To build the symbol table, a two-pass assembler must be able to properly update the PLC after reading each line of the source program on the first pass. If a source line contains a machine instruction, the assembler must determine the length of the instruction, even though the value of its operand(s) may not yet be known. Fortunately, the length of an instruction usually can be determined from the opcode mnemonic alone; in some cases, an addressing mode designator must be examined also. For example, in the H6809 CLRA is one byte long, while LDA addr is always three bytes long regardless of the value of addr. In the H8000, LD reg2,op1 is two bytes long if op1 specifies register or register indirect addressing; it is four bytes long otherwise.

If a source line contains a pseudo-operation that affects the PLC, the assembler must determine the effect on the PLC the first time the line is encountered. For example, on FCB the PLC should be incremented by the number of operands, that is, the number of memory byte values being formed. In Pass 1 the number of operands is known even if their values aren't. On the other hand, an operand of ORG, RMB, or RMW must be already defined when the pseudo-operation is first encountered in Pass 1, because the effect on the PLC depends on the operand's value.

Although EQU doesn't affect the PLC, its operands generally should not contain forward references. "Smart" assemblers may tolerate one level of forward referencing as shown in Table 6–4. Others may produce an error message if any symbols are still undefined at the end of Pass 1.

A simple two-pass assembler for the H6809 is outlined in Table 6–5. During Pass 1, each line is scanned and labels are entered into the symbol table. Each line is classified according to the type of pseudo-operation or machine instruction specified by the opcode field. The machine instructions are classified by their length in bytes. Branches are a special case because the assembler must calculate an offset from the specified target address in the operand field. After each line is scanned, the PLC is updated by an appropriate amount according to the instruction type, and in the case of pseudo-operations, according to the number or value of operands. During Pass 2, the PLC is maintained in the same way, and the object module is generated.

The details of most of the procedures in Table 6–5 are beyond the scope of this text. For example, a discussion of efficient methods for structuring and managing symbol tables would easily fill a chapter. Also, Table 6–5 does not

---

[1] A *one-pass assembler* avoids the second pass by clever programming techniques that "fix up" forward references as the necessary symbol definitions are encountered.

TABLE 6–4 Forward references using EQU.

```
*       One level of forward referencing with EQU.
*       This is acceptable to some assemblers.
START   ...
        ...
LEN     EQU    LAST-START      LAST is undefined at this point in
*                              Pass 1, and therefore so is LEN.
LENGTH  FCW    LEN             However, LEN is properly defined in
*                              Pass 2, in time to be used here.
        ...
        JMP    START           Last instruction in program.
LAST    EQU    *               Address just past program end.
        END

*       Two levels of forward referencing with EQU -- unacceptable.
START   ...
        ...
LENGTH  FCW    LEN             LEN is undefined at this point in both
*                              Pass 1 and Pass 2 -- error.
LEN     EQU    LAST-START      LAST is undefined at this point in
*                              Pass 1, and therefore so is LEN.
*                              LEN is defined here in Pass 2,
*                              but too late to use above.
        ...
        JMP    START           Last instruction in program.
LAST    EQU    *               Address just past program end.
        END
```

show how a typical assembler checks for errors. The most commonly detected errors in assembly language programs are listed below:

- Multiple Symbol Definition. In Pass 1, a symbol already in the symbol table was defined again.

- Illegal Opcode. In Pass 1 or 2, an unrecognizable mnemonic was encountered in the opcode field.

- Undefined Symbol. In Pass 2, the operand field contained a symbol not in the symbol table.

- Addressing Error. In Pass 2, an instruction specified an inaccessible address (e.g., a relative branch more than 127 bytes away).

- Syntax Error. In Pass 1 or 2, an illegal character or ill-formed expression was encountered (e.g., X+:Y).

Of course, the assembler detects only errors in assembly language format; the message "NO ERRORS DETECTED" is no guarantee that the program will run properly when loaded!

TABLE 6–5 Two-pass assembler program.

```
PROGRAM Assembler (input,output);
TYPE
  charCol = 1..128; {Column numbers in input line}
  byteVal = 0..255; wordVal = 0..65535; {Bytes and words}
  string8 = ARRAY [1..8] OF char; {Up to 8-char labels}
  mnemonicType = (null,comment,org,equ,fcb,fcw,rmb,rmw,aend,
                  length1Instr,length2Instr,length3Instr,branchInstr);
VAR
  mnemonic : mnemonicType;  opcode : byteVal;  PLC : wordVal;
  label8 : string8;  inputLine : ARRAY [charCol] OF char;
  opExpr : charCol; {Points to start of operand expr. in inputLine}
  gotOperand, gotLabel : boolean;
  symbols : ARRAY [1..200] OF string8; {Symbol Table: 8-char symbols}
  symVals : ARRAY [1..200] OF wordVal; {Symbol Table: 16-bit values}

PROCEDURE Enter (symbol : string8; symVal : wordVal);
  { Enter a symbol and its value into the symbol table.}

FUNCTION SymbolValue (symbol : string8) : wordVal;
  { Find a symbol in the symbol table and return its value.}

PROCEDURE GetLine;
  { Get next line of text from input file and put in inputLine.}

PROCEDURE ScanLine;
  { Scan inputLine and perform the following functions:
    1. Set gotOperand := false; gotLabel := false.
    2. If the line begins with a *, set mnemonic := comment and exit.
    3. If there is a label, set gotLabel:=true; label8:=(the label).
    4. If a valid mnemonic is present, set mnemonic := (the
       corresponding mnemonicType constant); if it is a machine
       instruction, set opcode := (the proper opcode byte value).
    5. If an operand is present, set gotOperand := true and set
       opExpr := (the starting column number of the operand).}

PROCEDURE GetNextOperand;
  { Look at global variable opExpr, and update it to point to the
    start of the next operand expression in inputLine. If there are
    no more operands then set gotOperand:=false.}

FUNCTION OperandValue : wordVal;
  { Evaluate an operand expression in inputLine and return its value.
    The expression is assumed to begin in column opExpr in inputLine.
    The values of symbols that are encountered are looked up in the
    symbol table by calling SymbolValue.}

PROCEDURE RewindSourceFile;
  { Rewind the source file so that the next call of GetLine will
    fetch the first line of text again.}

PROCEDURE PutObject(addr : wordVal; objectByte : byteVal);
  { Enter the value of objectByte into the object file so it will be
    placed at memory address addr when the object module is loaded.}
```

TABLE 6–5 (continued)

```
BEGIN
  {PASS1}
  PLC := 0;  mnemonic := null;
  WHILE mnemonic <> aend DO
    BEGIN
      GetLine; ScanLine;
      IF gotLabel AND (mnemonic<>equ) THEN Enter(label8,PLC);
      CASE mnemonic OF
        null, comment, aend: ; {Do nothing}
        org: PLC := OperandValue;
        equ: Enter(label8,OperandValue);
        fcb: WHILE gotOperand DO BEGIN PLC:=PLC+1; GetNextOperand END;
        fcw: WHILE gotOperand DO BEGIN PLC:=PLC+2; GetNextOperand END;
        rmb: PLC := PLC + OperandValue;
        rmw: PLC := PLC + 2*OperandValue;
        length1Instr: PLC := PLC + 1;
        length2Instr, branchInstr: PLC := PLC + 2;
        length3Instr: PLC := PLC + 3;
      END;
    END;
  {PASS2}
  RewindSourceFile; PLC := 0; mnemonic := null;
  WHILE mnemonic <> aend DO
    BEGIN
      GetLine; ScanLine;
      CASE mnemonic OF
        null,comment,equ,aend: ; {Do nothing}
        org: PLC := OperandValue;
        fcb: WHILE gotOperand DO BEGIN
            PutObject(PLC, OperandValue MOD 256); {8-bit value}
            PLC := PLC + 1; GetNextOperand;  END;
        fcw: WHILE gotOperand DO BEGIN
            PutObject(PLC, OperandValue DIV 256); {High-order byte}
            PutObject(PLC+1, OperandValue MOD 256); {Low-order byte}
            PLC := PLC + 2; GetNextOperand;  END;
        rmb: PLC := PLC + OperandValue;
        rmw: PLC := PLC + 2*OperandValue;
        length1Instr: BEGIN PutObject(PLC,opcode); PLC := PLC+1 END;
        length2Instr: BEGIN PutObject(PLC,opcode);
            PutObject(PLC+1,OperandValue MOD 256); PLC := PLC+2 END;
        length3Instr: BEGIN PutObject(PLC,opcode);
            PutObject(PLC+1,OperandValue DIV 256); {High-order byte}
            PutObject(PLC+2,OperandValue MOD 256); {Low-order byte}
            PLC := PLC + 3;  END;
        branchInstr: BEGIN PutObject(PLC,opcode); {Compute offset}
            PutObject(PLC+1, (OperandValue-(PLC+2)+256) MOD 256);
            PLC := PLC + 2;  END;
      END;
    END;
END.
```

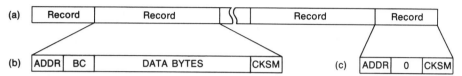

FIGURE 6–2 Object module format: (a) total program; (b) typical record; (c) starting-execution-address record.

6.3 OBJECT MODULES AND LOADERS

An *object module* (or program or file) specifies bit strings to be placed into the computer's memory by a loader program. Symbolic information that was present in the assembly language source program is no longer necessary, and so a simple, terse format may be used.

A typical object module format is shown in Figure 6–2(a); an object module consists of a series of "records". Each record has the format shown in Figure 6–2(b), and contains instruction and data bytes to be loaded into sequential locations in memory. The ADDR field tells the loader the address at which to deposit the first data byte, and the BC (byte count) field indicates how many bytes follow. If a record has a byte count of 0 as in Figure 6–2(c), its ADDR field is interpreted to be the starting-execution address of the program, the address to which the loader may jump after processing the last record.

The CKSM (checksum) field at the end of a record is the two's-complement sum of all the bytes in the record (including the 2-byte ADDR and the 1-byte BC).[2] This field may be checked by the loader to verify the integrity of the record. If any errors (tape dropouts, noise, etc.) occur when the record is written or read, the chances are 255/256 that the record's checksum will not match the one computed for the corrupted data.

Table 6–6 shows the object module for the source program given in Section 6.1. The bytes to be loaded in addresses 2000H through 2019H could have been put into one long record. However, a maximum record length of 16 was imposed for a more readable printed format.

Notice in Table 6–6 that a new record is started for the byte at address 201CH, so that nothing is loaded at addresses 201AH and 201BH. This is done because the corresponding RMB pseudo-operations in the source program merely reserve space; they do not cause any values to be stored in memory.

At this point, you should be wondering how object modules are actually stored as files on disk or tape. A common technique is to simply store a sequence of 8-bit bytes. For example, the object program in Table 6–6 would

---

[2]A ones'-complement sum actually provides better detection of certain types of errors. See "Detection of Unidirectional Multiple Errors Using Low-Cost Arithmetic Codes," by J. Wakerly, in *IEEE Trans. Comput.*, Vol. C–24, No. 2, pp. 210–212, February 1975.

TABLE 6–6 Object program for the source program in Tables 6–1 and 6–3.

ADDR	BC	DATA BYTES	CKSM
2000	10	4F B7 20 1B B6 20 1C B7 20 1A BB 20 1B B7 20 1B	3C
2010	0A	B6 20 1A 8B FF 26 F0 7E 10 00	58
201C	01	0F	4C
2000	00		20

Notes: Each line in the table represents one record; all values are hexadecimal.

require a total of 43 bytes on the disk or tape: 8 for addresses, 4 for byte counts, 4 for checksums, and 27 for actual bytes to be loaded into memory.

With the above technique it is not possible to print an object file directly, since the 8-bit bytes have no relation to ASCII printing characters. An alternative often used in microcomputer systems is to store object modules as text files containing the actual printing characters that appear in Table 6–6. This format allows object modules to be printed directly, but also requires twice as much storage space since two characters are needed to represent one byte in hexadecimal. This format also makes the loader slightly more complicated, because each character pair must be converted into a byte value as it is read.

Object modules may be concatenated, for example, when several independently assembled program modules are joined to create a large program. It is possible for two or more records in an object module to store bytes at the same address. In this case, the record closest to the end of the module is the last to be processed and therefore has precedence. The last value loaded at a particular address overwrites previous ones. Likewise, if there are two or more starting-execution-address records, the last one takes precedence. For example, suppose the two records in Table 6–7 are appended to the object program in Table 6–6. If this were done, the program would start execution at location 2004 without initializing SUM, and CNT would be initialized to 13_{10} instead of 15_{10}. Such perturbations are known as "patches."

6.4 RELOCATING ASSEMBLERS AND LOADERS

6.4.1 Relocation

The *load address* of a program is the first address that it occupies in memory. Until now we have assumed that the load address is fixed by an ORG pseudo-operation and is therefore known at assembly time. This allows the assembler to use absolute memory addresses when constructing address constants and machine instructions that have addresses as operands.

TABLE 6-7 Additional records to "patch" object program.

ADDR	BC	DATA BYTES	CKSM
201C	01	0D	4A
2004	00		24

In a large programming project, several different modules of the program may be written by different people and at different times, and the length of each module is not known until it is completed. Furthermore, as the program is debugged and maintained, the sizes of different modules can shrink and expand. How then should load addresses be assigned?

One approach is to make a worst-case estimate of the length of each module and allow enough memory for it; then each module contains a corresponding ORG statement. This method has two drawbacks. First, the extra memory at the end of each module is wasted. Second, it is still possible to underestimate the amount of memory needed by a module. This error is not always obvious to the programmer, in which case the loader will place part of one module on top of another, perhaps without even giving an error message. Once the error is detected, more space must be allocated for the long module and the load addresses of other modules must be adjusted accordingly.

Relocating assemblers and *relocating loaders* avoid these problems by allowing load addresses to be specified at load time. In order to do this, relocating assemblers and loaders distinguish between absolute and relocatable quantities:

- The value of an *absolute* quantity (or symbol or expression) is independent of where the program is loaded.

- The value of a *relocatable* quantity (or symbol or expression) depends on where the program is loaded.

A relocating assembler has a set of rules for distinguishing between absolute and relocatable quantities. A fairly standard set of rules is given below:

- A numeric constant is absolute.

- The PLC is relocatable.

- A symbol appearing in the label field of a non-EQU statement is relocatable.

- A symbol appearing in the label field of an EQU statement has the same type as the value in the operand field.

- An expression involving only absolute constants and symbols yields an absolute value.

- If REL is a relocatable symbol and ABS is an absolute constant, symbol, or expression, then the following expression forms yield relocatable values: REL, REL+ABS, ABS+REL, REL−ABS.

- The difference of two relocatable symbols (REL−REL) is absolute. (The offset between two addresses stays constant when the program is moved.)

- The following expression forms are not allowed: REL+REL, ABS−REL, REL*REL, REL*ABS, ABS*REL. Here * is any operator but + or −.

Table 6–8 shows a relocatable assembly language program for the M6809 (some of the machine instructions in this program are not introduced until Chapters 7 and 8). The pseudo-operation "RORG addr" indicates that the load address is *relocatable* address addr. The assembler then generates subsequent instructions and data as if the program will be loaded at memory address addr. However, it also appends to the object module a list of all the locations containing relocatable quantities, values that must be adjusted if the program is loaded elsewhere. At load time, the programmer specifies a constant called the *load displacement*, which the loader adds to the load address of the relocatable object module and to all relocatable quantities as they are loaded.

All of the 16-bit quantities marked with an "R" in Table 6–8 are relocatable. The load module for this program has a list of nine addresses (000B, 000E, 0011, 0014, 0020, 0026, 0029, 002E, 0031) that contain 2-byte relocatable quantities. If a load displacement of 2000 is specified at load time, then the load address is 2000, the starting address is 2008, and the loader adds 2000 to all relocatable quantities (e.g., locations 200B, 200C store the value 2005).

Three symbols in Table 6–8 show typical uses of absolute quantities:

- A symbol equated with a numeric constant used for counting or similar purposes is absolute (NBITS).

- The difference between two addresses is absolute (LENGTH).

- A fixed address outside the program is independent of the load address and hence absolute (SYSOVF).

6.4.2 Linking

The program in Table 6–8 communicates with another program using a known absolute address (1800H); however this technique is usually impractical in the development of large programs. Just as one does not know the final load address of a module at assembly time, one also does not know the addresses of global variables and subroutines. Therefore, a relocating assem-

TABLE 6–8 Relocatable subroutine to divide unsigned numbers on the 6809 using the algorithm in Table 4–10.

```
LN# PLC   CONTENTS LABEL    OPCODE OPERAND   COMMENTS

001 0000                    RORG   0         Start at relocatable addr 0.
002 0000           NBITS    EQU    8         8-bit division.
003 0000           DVND     RMB    2         2-byte dividend placed here.
004 0002           DVSR     RMB    1         Divisor placed here.
005 0003           QUOT     RMB    1         Reserve byte for quotient.
006 0004           REM      RMB    1         Reserve byte for remainder.
007 0005           CNT      RMB    1         Counter storage.
008 0006 002B      PRGLEN   FCW    LENGTH    Length of program.
009 0008 86 08     DIVIDE   LDA    #NBITS    Initialize count.
010 000A B7 0005R           STA    CNT
011 000D B6 0000R           LDA    DVND      Put dividend in A,B.
012 0010 F6 0001R           LDB    DVND+1
013 0013 B1 0002R           CMPA   DVSR      Will quotient fit in 1 byte?
014 0016 25 03             BLO    DIVLUP    Branch if it will.
015 0018 7E 1800           JMP    SYSOVF    Else report overflow.
016 001B 58        DIVLUP   ASLB             Left shift A,B with LSB:=0.
017 001C 49                 ROLA             A carry here from MSB means
018 001D 25 05             BCS    QUOT1       high DVND surely > DVSR.
019 001F B1 0002R           CMPA   DVSR      Compare high DVND with DVSR.
020 0022 25 04             BLO    QUOTOK    Quotient bit = 0 if lower.
021 0024 5C        QUOT1    INCB             Else set quotient bit to 1.
022 0025 B0 0002R           SUBA   DVSR      And update high DVND.
023 0028 7A 0005R QUOTOK   DEC    CNT       Decrement iteration count.
024 002B 2E EE             BGT    DIVLUP    Continue until done.
025 002D B7 0004R           STA    REM       Store remainder.
026 0030 F7 0003R           STB    QUOT      Store quotient.
027 0033 39                 RTS              Return.
028 0034           SYSOVF   EQU    1800H     System overflow report addr.
029 0034           ENDADR   EQU    *
030 0034           LENGTH   EQU    ENDADR-DIVIDE
031 0034                    END    DIVIDE
```

SYMBOL TABLE:

SYMBOL	VALUE	SYMBOL	VALUE	SYMBOL	VALUE	SYMBOL	VALUE
NBITS	0008	DVND	0000R	DVSR	0002R	QUOT	0003R
REM	0004R	CNT	0005R	PRGLEN	0006R	DIVIDE	0008R
DIVLUP	001BR	QUOT1	0024R	QUOTOK	0028R	SYSOVF	1800
ENDADR	0033R	LENGTH	002B				

bler provides one more facility — the ability to define symbolic entry points and external references that are resolved at load time.

The EXT (External) pseudo-operation gives a list of symbols whose definitions are outside the current assembly language program module. The ENT (Entry) pseudo-operation gives a list of symbols that are defined in the

TABLE 6-9 Program with an external reference.

```
        EXT    PTIME              PTIME subroutine is defined elsewhere.
MAIN    . . .
        JSR    PTIME              Print current time of day.
        . . .
```

current module but whose definitions are also required by other program modules. A set of modules that make use of ENT and EXT are shown in Table 6-9, Table 6-10, and Table 6-11. Notice that ENT and EXT may refer to either global data addresses (HOUR, MINUTE) or instruction addresses (PTIME).

Like absolute and relocatable expressions, external expressions must conform to a specific format. The following expression forms yield external values, where EXT is an external symbol: EXT, EXT+ABS, ABS+EXT, EXT−ABS. All other forms involving EXT yield undefined values.

Since external symbol references are not resolved until load time, the relocating assembler must append still more information to the object module: (1) a table of all external symbols and the object module locations whose values depend on the external symbols; (2) a table of all entry symbols and their values. The relocating loader then processes all of the object modules of a large program together, building its own table of external and entry symbols. Since the lengths of the object modules are now known, they can be optimally packed into memory without wasting space. Errors such as undefined and doubly defined external symbols may be detected. The loader may automatically search a library of standard functions (such as mathematics, input/output, general utilities) when undefined symbols are detected. In any case, all of the locations that depend on external symbols are adjusted by adding the value of the external symbol.

A loader that resolves external references, relocates object modules, and loads them is called a *linking loader*. In some systems a separate program called a *link editor* resolves external references and concatenates object modules into one contiguous relocatable object module, without loading it. The new, large object module can then be loaded anywhere in memory by a simple relocating loader that performs no linking.

TABLE 6-10 Program with external references and entry points.

```
*       This routine prints the current time of day on a terminal.
        EXT    HOUR,MINUTE    HOUR and MINUTE are defined elsewhere.
        ENT    PTIME          PTIME may be called by other programs.
PTIME   LDA    HOUR
        . . .
        LDA    MINUTE
        . . .
        RTS                   Return to calling program.
```

TABLE 6–11 Program with entry points.

```
*        The operating system runs this subroutine once per minute
*           to update the time of day.
         ENT    HOUR,MINUTE   Global variables.
TIMER    LDA    MINUTE
         INCA
         ...
         LDA    HOUR
         ...
         RTS                  Return.
HOUR     RMB    1
MINUTE   RMB    1
```

6.5 MACROS

It is sometimes necessary to use a particular sequence of instructions in many different places in a program. For example, suppose we want to transfer an 8-bit value in accumulator A of the H6809 to the low-order byte of index register X, setting the high-order byte of X to zero. The following instruction sequence does this, assuming that a 2-byte temporary variable TEMPX has been reserved by the statement "TEMPX RMW 1" elsewhere in the program.

```
         STA    TEMPX+1    Save A in low-order byte of TEMPX.
         CLRA              Clear high-order byte of TEMPX.
         STA    TEMPX
         LDX    TEMPX      Load 16-bit value TEMPX into X.
```

Although space must be allocated for TEMPX only once, the above instruction sequence must be replicated each time that A is to be transferred to X. A *macro assembler* eliminates this tedium by allowing the programmer to define *macro instructions (macros)* that are equivalent to longer sequences. A macro assembler performs all the functions of a standard assembler, plus some more. Exact macro formats and features vary widely, but all macro assemblers perform the basic functions described below.

Two new pseudo-operations, MACRO and ENDM, allow the programmer to define a new mnemonic that takes the place of an entire instruction sequence. In the example above, the programmer may place the following *macro definition* at the beginning of the program:

```
TFRAX    MACRO
         STA    TEMPX+1    Save A in low-order byte of TEMPX.
         CLRA              Clear high-order byte of TEMPX.
         STA    TEMPX
         LDX    TEMPX      Load 16-bit value TEMPX into X.
         ENDM
```

Without actually generating any machine instructions, this defines the mnemonic TFRAX to stand for the 4-instruction sequence that transfers A to X. Later in the program, the statements

```
LDA     J
TFRAX
```

may be used to transfer the 8-bit variable J to X. The macro assembler *textually* replaces the TFRAX line with the predefined 4-line sequence. The TFRAX line is a *macro call* and the textual replacement is a *macro expansion*.

The usefulness of macros is further enhanced by the use of *parameters*. A macro definition may contain *formal parameters*; in the example below, VAR is a formal parameter:

```
TFRVX   MACRO   VAR
        LDA     VAR             Put variable into A.
        STA     TEMPX+1         Save A in low-order byte of TEMPX.
        CLRA                    Clear high-order byte of TEMPX.
        STA     TEMPX
        LDX     TEMPX           Load 16-bit value TEMPX into X.
        ENDM
```

A call of the TFRVX macro specifies *actual parameters* that are substituted for the formal parameters when the macro is expanded. Thus, the line

```
TFRVX   J
```

generates instructions to transfer J to X; in fact, it generates exactly the same machine instructions as the previous 2-line sequence using TFRAX.

The general form of a macro definition with parameters is

```
NAME    MACRO   FP1,FP2,...,FPN
        ...
        ...                     Macro body
        ...
        ENDM
```

Such a macro is called by the statement

```
NAME    AP1,AP2,...,APN
```

When the macro is expanded, each appearance of a formal parameter FP*i* in the macro body is textually replaced by the corresponding actual parameter AP*i*.

Macro calls may be *nested*, that is, the body of a macro definition may contain a call to another macro. For example, we could have defined TFRVX as follows:

```
TFRVX   MACRO   VAR
        LDA     VAR              Load VAR into A,B
        TFRAX                    Transfer A to X
        ENDM
```

A number of extra pseudo-instructions are provided in macro assemblers. One such instruction is SET, which is the same as EQU except that it allows a symbol to be redefined without causing an error message. To see how this might be used, consider the following problem. A programmer wishes to reserve one contiguous block of memory for all variables; however, the variable definitions are to appear throughout the program, near the routines that use them. To accomplish this, the programmer reserves the memory and defines a macro at the beginning of the program as follows:

```
VARBLK  RMB     100              Allocate 100 bytes for variables.
VAREND  EQU     *
NEXTV   SET     VARBLK
*
RESERV  MACRO   VAR,SIZE         Reserve SIZE bytes for variable VAR.
VAR     EQU     NEXTV            Enter VAR into symbol table.
NEXTV   SET     NEXTV+SIZE       Bump NEXTV to next available address.
        ENDM
```

Later in the program, three 1-byte variables and one 2-byte variable may be declared as follows:

```
        RESERV HOUR,1
        RESERV MINUTE,1
        RESERV SECOND,1
        RESERV DATE,2
```

Macro assemblers also contain *conditional assembly* pseudo-operations that cause subsequent statements to be assembled only if a specified condition is true. The condition is tested at *assembly time*, not run time. For example, the following version of RESERV generates an "error message" if the available data area has been exceeded.

```
RESERV  MACRO   VAR,SIZE
        IFGT    NEXTV+SIZE-VAREND
** WARNING!! OUT OF VARIABLE SPACE! **
        ENDIF
        IFLE    NEXTV+SIZE-VAREND
VAR     EQU     NEXTV
NEXTV   SET     NEXTV+SIZE
        ENDIF
        ENDM
```

Here, IFGT expr causes subsequent statements until ENDIF to be processed if expr>0, and skips them otherwise. Likewise, IFLE expr processes the statements if expr<=0.

Sometimes it is necessary to use a label within a macro body, as in the example below:

```
TST32Z  MACRO  VAR          Test a 32-bit variable for zero.
        LDX    VAR          Test high-order word.
        BNE    .L1          Word not zero if high-order not zero.
        LDX    VAR+2        Test low-order word.
.L1     EQU    *            Addr just past end of TST32Z expansion.
*                           Z is now 1 if 32-bit word was 0.
        ENDM
```

The same label (.L1) is used every time the macro is invoked, which would normally cause a multiple symbol definition error on the second invocation of the macro. However, we solved the problem by using another feature — any label preceded by a period is assumed to be local to the current macro expansion. When the assembler enters .L1 into the symbol table, it appends additional information to distinguish .L1 from other instances of the same label.[3]

Different macro assemblers handle label definition problems in different ways. Some allow the programmer to declare symbols within a macro as either local or global. Some have a facility for automatically generating unique symbols (e.g., L00001, L00002, etc.). The most primitive simply require the programmer to make up and pass a unique label as a parameter on each macro invocation.

A macro assembler is a very powerful software tool. In fact, in principle it is possible to write a set of macros for a macro assembler for one machine so that it will recognize the mnemonics of a completely different machine and generate object code for it. The most powerful macro assemblers allow operations such as defining new macros within a macro call and concatenating strings to create unique symbols.

6.6 STRUCTURED ASSEMBLY LANGUAGE

Block-structured high-level languages such as Pascal derive their power and convenience from many features not found in "unstructured" assembly languages:

- The compiler translates each high-level statement into a sequence of machine instructions to perform a desired action, including run-time evaluation of arithmetic and logical expressions.

---

[3]Of course, a clever programmer would have avoided the problem altogether by changing the branch instruction to "BNE *+2+3," knowing that the branch skips over a 3-byte instruction. Or does it? In the real 6809 the instruction LDX VAR+2 is only two bytes long if address VAR+2 is in the "direct page" of memory. Thus, the "clever" programmer has introduced an insidious bug.

- The language allows programs and statements to be partitioned into a natural, hierarchical block structure.

- Using block structure, the compiler applies scope rules to variable names and other identifiers so that naming conventions are simplified.

- The language provides high-level statements such as WHILE, REPEAT, and FOR to simplify the control of loops.

- The language provides a facility for user-defined structured data types.

- The user may write the source program in a free format using separators and comments to improve readability.

A *structured assembly language* provides all of these features except for the first — it still translates each assembly language statement into only one machine instruction.

Table 6–12 recodes the DIVIDE program from Table 6–8 into a hypothetical structured assembly language for the 6809, which we'll call SCAL (Structured-Coding Assembly Language). The SCAL program looks like Pas-

TABLE 6–12   Structured assembly language version of DIVIDE program.

```
LABEL divaddr, endaddr;
VAR dvnd : word; dvsr, quot, rem : byte;
proglength : DATAWORD endaddr-divaddr;
PROCEDURE Divide;
  CONST nbits = 8; sysovfl = 1800H;
  VAR cnt : byte;
  BEGIN
    divaddr: {Define starting address of procedure code.}
    lda #nbits;  sta cnt;  {cnt := # of bits/byte}
    lda dvnd;  ldb dvnd+1; {a,b := dvnd}
    cmpa dvsr;  {Will quotient fit in one byte?}
    IF HS THEN jmp sysovf;  {Report overflow if not.}
    REPEAT
      aslb; rola;  {Double-prec. arithmetic shift a,b}
      IF CS THEN  {High dvnd > dvsr,  set quotient bit}
        BEGIN incb; suba dvsr END {and update dividend.}
      ELSE {Trial subtraction needed.}
        BEGIN
          cmpa dvsr;
          IF HS THEN  {High dvnd >= dvsr,  set quotient bit}
            BEGIN incb; suba dvsr END {and update dividend.}
        END;
      dec cnt;
    UNTIL LE; {Repeat for all bits.}
    sta rem; stb quot; {Save results.}
    rts; {Return.}
    endaddr: {Define last address of procedure code.}
  END;
```

cal, but it generates almost the same machine instructions as the unstructured assembly language version.

SCAL programs use spaces, newlines, colons, semicolons, and curly brackets just as Pascal does to format and comment programs. The meanings of reserved words are similar to those in Pascal:

- PROCEDURE: indicates the beginning of a procedure block, beginning a new scope for variable names and other identifiers. Parameters are not shown, but could be supported in a fancier version of SCAL using a stack-oriented passing convention.

- VAR: reserves storage for variables of indicated types; SCAL knows the length of standard types such as byte and word. Variables have scope limited to the block in which they are declared. VAR replaces RMB and RMW from unstructured assembly language.

- DATAWORD: at load time, stores a sequence of words with the specified values, replacing FCW from unstructured assembly language.

- DATABYTE: at load time, stores a sequence of bytes with the specified values, replacing FCB from unstructured assembly language.

- CONST: at assembly time, equates an identifier with a specified constant or constant expression, replacing EQU from unstructured assembly language. Constants have scope limited to the block in which they are defined.

- LABEL: declares an identifier to be a legal statement or data label in the current scope. If a label is not declared by LABEL, then its scope is limited to the procedure in which it is defined. For example, the DATAWORD statement in Table 6–12 would contain undefined identifiers if endaddr and divaddr were not declared, because they are defined inside the procedure, a lower-level block.

- BEGIN,END: delimit compound statements, including procedure bodies, as in Pascal.

Like Pascal, SCAL contains both simple and structured statements. Standard assembly language statements such as "lda #nbits" are the simple statements in SCAL. Structured statements include compound statements, IF, REPEAT, and WHILE. Table 6–13 shows the unstructured equivalents of SCAL's conditional and repetitive statements. While Pascal statements can test conditions that are arbitrary boolean expressions, SCAL requires *condition* to be one that is tested by a 6809 conditional branch instruction. The condition is specified by the last two letters in the branch mnemonic (Table 8–3). A condition test must be preceded by a machine instruction that sets the condition bits for the test. Thus, in Table 6–12 the SCAL statements

TABLE 6–13 Comparison of SCAL structured statements and unstructured assembly language equivalents.

SCAL Structured Statement	Assembly Language Equivalent
IF *condition* THEN *statement*	B (NOT *condition*) *labelA* *statement* *labelA*: •••

IF *condition*
    THEN *statement1*
    ELSE *statement2*
	B (NOT *condition*) *labelA*
	statement1
	BRA *labelB*
	labelA: *statement2*
	labelB: •••

REPEAT *statement list* UNTIL *condition*	*labelA*: *statement list* B (NOT *condition*) *labelA*
WHILE *condition* DO *statement*	BRA *labelB* *labelA*: *statement* *labelB*: B (*condition*) *labelA*

```
cmpa dvsr;  {Will quotient fit in one byte?}
IF HS THEN jmp sysovf;  {Report overflow if not.}
```

generate machine instructions corresponding to the assembly language instructions that were shown in Table 6–8:

```
        CMPA   DVSR
        BLO    DIVLUP         NOT HS (Higher or Same) = LO (Lower)
        JMP    SYSOVF
DIVLUP  ...
```

In a program with complicated loops, the structured statements allow the flow of control to be expressed much more clearly than by a maze of conditional branches. Occasionally the structured statements may produce code that is slightly longer than code with intertwined branches. For example, the program in Table 6–12 replicates two instructions (incb, suba dvsr) that appeared only once in the unstructured assembly language version. However, the improvement in readability is worth the slight increase in length using SCAL.[4]

---

[4]For skeptics, here's justification. If the code is short it doesn't hurt to replicate it. If the code is long, it should probably be defined as a separate procedure anyway, and the replicated segments should be replaced by procedure calls. In any case, in super-critical areas it is always possible to forget about structured statements and use explicit branches.

This section has given only a brief introduction to structured assembly language. Like their unstructured counterparts, structured assembly languages have instructions and features that vary widely. Many machines have only an *un*structured assembly language available. An exception in this book is the Z8000, for which Zilog provides a structured assembly language called PLZ/ASM.

REFERENCES

Although there is no universally accepted standard assembly language, the IEEE Standards Committee has made an effort to establish one. The first draft of the standard appeared in *Computer* magazine [Wayne P. Fischer, "Microprocessor Assembly Language Draft Standard," Vol. 12, No. 12, December 1979].

The most accurate description of the assembly language for a particular computer can usually be found in the software supplier's documentation. More general treatments of assemblers, loaders, and macro processors can be found in J. J. Donovan's *Systems Programming* [McGraw-Hill, 1972] and in D. W. Barron's little book *Assemblers and Loaders* [MacDonald/Elsevier, 1969]. Jim Peterson has written sample assembler and loader programs in the MIX assembly language in his *Computer Organization and Assembly Language Programming* [Academic Press, 1978].

Structured assembly languages have existed for some time. Niklaus Wirth described such a language for the IBM System/360 family in "PL/360, A Programming Language for the 360 Computers" [*Journal of the ACM*, January 1968]. Zilog introduced PLZ/ASM in "PLZ: A Family of System Programming Languages for Microprocessors" by Charlie Bass [*Computer*, March 1978].

EXERCISES

6.1   Delete line 010 of Table 6–3 and reassemble the program by hand, showing the effects on the LN#, PLC, and CONTENT columns and on the symbol table.

6.2   Find all the syntax errors in the H6809 assembly language program below.

```
        ORG     2000H
INIT    CLRA                    Initialize variables.
        STA     V1
        STA     L1
                                Now do some computation.
LOOP    LDA     V3              Get value of V3.
        STA     V2              Save it.
        ADD     V1
```

```
          BEQ    L1
          STA    V3
L1        STA    V1
          BMI    LOOP          Continue until positive.
          BEQ    SYSOVF
          RET                  Done, return.
V1        RMB    1
V3        RMB    1
L1        FCB    0D
SYSOVF    EQU    1990
          END    INIT
```

6.3   If an operand expression has the value -12_{10}, what value should be returned by the function OperandValue in Table 6–5?

6.4   An "FCC" (Form Character Constant) pseudo-operation has one operand, a string of characters surrounded by a pair of delimiters such as single quotes, for example,

```
          FCC    'A 17-byte string.'
```

The FCC pseudo-operation stores the ASCII values of the characters in successive bytes of memory. Enhance the assembler in Table 6–5 to process FCC.

6.5   Explain how the branchInstr case in Pass 2 of Table 6–5 computes the two's-complement offset value for a branch instruction.

6.6   Suppose that both RORG and ORG statements can appear in a (partially) relocatable program. Modify the second and third rules for distinguishing absolute and relocatable quantities so that labels and the PLC are handled correctly.

6.7   Suppose that the object module produced by an H6809 relocatable assembler is stored as a sequence of ASCII printing characters, as suggested in Section 6.3. Give a complete specification for the object module format, including the list of addresses containing relocatable quantities and the list of external and entry symbols.

6.8   Can IF pseudo-operations be nested? How can the assembler match up ENDIFs with the appropriate IFs?

6.9   Define an ELSEIF pseudo-operation that allows an IF pseudo-operation to assemble one set of statements or another. How can the assembler match up ELSEIFs and ENDIFs with the appropriate IFs? How does this affect nesting of IFs?

6.10 Using the instruction execution times that were derived in Exercise 5.6, write a macro DELAY with a single parameter T, such that the expanded code delays exactly T microseconds. (Since few instructions are needed, you can derive their execution times now even if you didn't work Exercise 5.6.) Assume that T is interpreted as a 16-bit two's-complement number, and generate no delay if T is zero or negative. The expanded code should have less than 20 instructions for any value of T. Define all new pseudo-operations (e.g., IFEQ) and operators (e.g., DIV) that you find necessary to write the macro.

6.11 Rewrite the multiplication program in Table 5–4 using SCAL. Your version need not generate exactly the same machine instructions.

6.12 Rewrite the 1's-counting program in Table 5–10 using SCAL. Your version need not generate exactly the same machine instructions.

6.13 In a structured assembly language like SCAL, the WHILE statement may have a pitfall not shared by REPEAT. Find the bug in the following SCAL version of the 1's-counting subroutine from Table 5–10 and explain.

```
PROCEDURE Bcnt1s;
  BEGIN
    sta cbyte; ldx #masks; clra; sta b1cnt; {Initialization}
    WHILE NE DO {Do while X not pointing past last mask.}
      BEGIN
        lda @x; anda cbyte; {Check for a 1.}
        IF NE THEN {Update count.}
          BEGIN lda b1cnt; adda #1; sta b1cnt END;
        addx #1; cmpx #maske; {Bump X to next mask.}
      END;
    lda b1cnt; rts;
  END;
```

6.14 A different format for the WHILE statement may be used to eliminate the problem raised above. Explain the format below, by showing the equivalent assembly language statements that it should generate, and applying the new WHILE to the Bcnt1s procedure above.

WHILE *statement-list condition* DO *statement*

6.15 Write a SCAL version of the REPEAT loop in Table 6–12 that generates no more machine instructions than the unstructured assembly language version and uses no explicit conditional branch instructions. Is saving machine instructions worth the time and trouble?

6.16 The assembly language equivalents of SCAL structured statements in Table 6–13 may not work if they are to control very long statements. Explain why and write equivalents that are guaranteed to work with controlled statements of any length.

7

ADDRESSING

In order to do useful work, a computer must process data stored in memory. Data-processing instructions contain or imply *addresses* that locate the desired data. The length in bits of an address implies the maximum amount of memory that can be accessed by the processor, for example, a 16-bit address implies a 64K-byte memory. According to the designers of the PDP-11 family[1],

> The biggest (and most common) mistake that can be made in a computer design is that of not providing enough address bits for memory addressing and management. It is clear that another address bit is required every two or three years, since memory prices decline about 30 percent yearly, and users tend to buy constant price successor systems.

Of the computers in this book, only a few provide enough address bits to gracefully evolve in their intended applications. The 68000 and Z8000 architectures allow for 32 and 31 address bits, specifying over 2 billion bytes of memory. Other computers can use memory mapping to increase the amount

[1]C. G. Bell and J. C. Mudge, "The Evolution of the PDP-11", in *Computer Engineeering: A DEC View of Hardware Systems Design*, by C. G. Bell, J. C. Mudge, and J. E. McNamara, Bedford, MA: Digital Press, 1978, pp. 381-382.

of physical memory in the system, as discussed in the last section of this chapter.

Although the simplest way to specify an address is to store it as part of the instruction, the address manipulations required in typical applications suggest additional addressing modes that are more efficient or appropriate. The purposes of some of these addressing modes are to:

- Allow an instruction to access a memory location whose address is computed at run time, allowing efficient access of arrays, lists, and all kinds of data structures.

- Manipulate addresses in a way appropriate for the most commonly used data structures, such as stacks and one-dimensional arrays.

- Specify a full memory address with a smaller number of bits, thereby making instructions shorter.

- Compute addresses relative to instruction position so that a program may be loaded anywhere in memory without changing it.

No processor has all addressing modes, but all of the important modes are covered in this chapter.

7.1 GENERAL CONCEPTS

The number of bits in an address and in a typical register or datum in a processor are not necessarily equal, but they are related. Table 7–1 summarizes the address space and register sizes of the processors in Part 3. The address size is usually one or two times the register size. Thus, addresses can be stored in registers or register pairs, and the same registers and instructions can be used for manipulating data and addresses.

TABLE 7–1 Address characteristics of Part 3 processors.

Processor	Address Size (bits)	Register Size (bits)
PDP-11	16	16
68000	32^1	32
Z8000	31^1	16
9900	16	16
6809	16	8&16
8086	16^2	16
MCS-48	8&12	8

Notes: 1. Only 24 bits used in initial chip design.
2. On-chip memory management extends this to 20 bits.

Most of the addressing modes described in the next two sections are available in the Motorola 6809 processor. Therefore we'll give examples using 6809 instructions. For details on how different addressing modes are encoded in instructions for the 6809 and other processors, refer to the corresponding chapters in Part 3.

The assembly language notation for addressing modes used by different computers varies widely. Some of the addressing modes of the 6809 and our assembly language notation for them are shown in Table 7–2. Here expr is an expression that is evaluated at assembly time and placed in the instruction. In the hypothetical H6809, reg would have to be X, while in the real 6809, reg may be any of several index registers. Similar addressing modes exist in most general-register processors, where reg may be any general register. In the rest of this chapter we'll use the term *address register* to mean any register that can hold an address.

The purpose of addressing modes is to provide an *effective address* for an instruction. In a data manipulation instruction, the effective address is the address of the data being manipulated. In a jump instruction, it is the address of the instruction being jumped to.

Addressing modes may be classified as direct and indirect. In a *direct* addressing mode, the effective address is taken directly from the instruction, or computed by combining a value in the instruction with a value in a register. In an *indirect* (or *deferred*) addressing mode, the address calculation yields an *indirect address*, the address of a memory location that contains the ultimate effective address. In some computers, such as the 6809 and the PDP-11, each direct addressing mode has a corresponding indirect counterpart. Other com-

TABLE 7–2 Some addressing modes of 6809.

Name	Assembler Notation	Operand
Register	reg	reg
Register Indirect	@reg or (reg)	MEM[reg]
Absolute	expr	MEM[expr]
Absolute Indirect	@expr	MEM[MEM[expr]]
Immediate	#expr	expr
Auto-Increment	(reg)+	MEM[reg], then reg:=reg+1
Auto-Decrement	-(reg)	reg:=reg-1, then MEM[reg]
PC Relative	expr(PCR)	MEM [(expr-PLC) + PC]
Based (or Indexed)	expr(reg)	MEM[expr+reg]
Based Indexed	reg1(reg2)	MEM[reg1+reg2]

Notes: expr is any allowed expression.
In PC-relative mode, the assembler computes the proper offset between the given expr and the current PLC such that MEM[expr] is accessed at run time.
Notation used by Motorola's assembly language for the 6809 is different in some cases. Refer to Chapter 17 for details.

puters, such as the Z8000 and the 8086, have only one indirect addressing mode (register indirect).

7.2 SINGLE-COMPONENT ADDRESSING MODES

The simplest addressing modes specify an effective address by a single value in the instruction or in a register. Multi-component addressing modes, described later, combine a value in the instruction with the contents of one or more registers to obtain the effective address.

7.2.1 Register

In *register mode*, an operand is contained in one of the processor's registers. Figure 7–1 shows the encoding of a typical register mode instruction. In this and other figures in this chapter, "OPCODE" denotes the instruction fields that contain the opcode and other information such as addressing mode and word/byte selection. For generality, the figures in this chapter do not show the width of the data, addresses, or other fields.

The Zilog Z8000 uses a 4-bit field in its instructions to select among 16 general registers. The Motorola 6809 has two accumulators and four index registers; therefore it also has register-select fields in many instructions. The H6809 has only one accumulator and one index register; which register to use is implied by the opcode, and the addressing mode is called *inherent*.

All processors must have register mode in some form, otherwise it would be impossible to do anything with the registers! However, some operations make no sense with register mode, for example JMP reg — a program can't jump to a register.

In assembly language programs, registers are usually identified by reserved identifiers (A, X, R0, etc.). Some assemblers allow any identifier to represent a register, requiring a special prefix to distinguish register numbers from memory addresses (e.g., R0=%0, SP=%6 in the PDP-11 assembler).

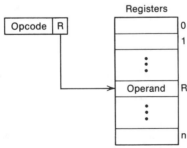

FIGURE 7–1 Register addressing.

7.2.2 Absolute

The simplest way to specify a full memory address is to include it as part of the instruction using *absolute* mode, as shown in Figure 7–2. We used this mode for most memory reference instructions in the H6809 and H8000 examples in Chapter 5. Absolute mode gives the flexibility of specifying any location in the address space of the computer.

Absolute mode takes many instruction bits in a computer with a large address space — 32 in the 68000. In order to reduce this number, some computers provide a *short absolute* addressing mode that gives direct access to a limited part of the entire address space. For example, the 68000 provides a mode in which the instruction gives a 16-bit address, and the remaining high-order address bits are set equal to the sign of the 16-bit part. This mode can thus specify any location in the top or bottom 32K bytes of the address space. When an assembly-language instruction specifies absolute addressing, the assembler automatically selects short absolute mode if the address can be expressed in 16 bits using the sign-extension rule. Otherwise, long absolute mode is used.

Because of its simplicity and flexibility, an absolute addressing mode is provided in almost all computers. Of the computers discussed in this book, only the MCS-48 does not have long absolute addressing.

An *absolute indirect* mode is provided in a few processors, including the 6809. As shown in Figure 7–2(c), this mode simply uses the contents of the specified absolute address as the effective address.

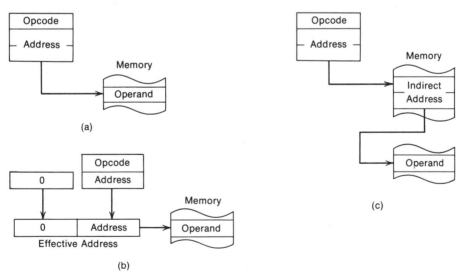

FIGURE 7–2   Absolute addressing modes: (a) long absolute; (b) short absolute; (c) absolute indirect.

7.2.3 Immediate

Immediate addressing allows a constant (or *literal*) to be specified as part of the instruction. As shown in Figure 7–3(a,b), an immediate operand is fetched from the location(s) in memory immediately following the instruction opcode. For example, PDP-11, 8086, and 6809 instructions may contain 1-byte or 2-byte immediate operands; the Z8000 and 68000 may have immediate operands up to 4 bytes long. The programs in the previous chapter illustrated some of the many uses of immediate operands (refer to Table 5–10):

- Constants to initialize variables.

- Constants to combine with variables by arithmetic or logical operations (ADDA #1).

- Data or address constants to compare against variables for list and string terminations, branching conditions, and so on (CMPX #MASKE).

- Address constants to put in registers for later use by other addressing modes (LDS #STKE, LDX #MASKS).

Except for address constants, most immediate operands tend to be small signed integers, often requiring 8 bits or less to represent. Therefore, some processors provide 8-bit immediate values that are sign-extended to 16 or 32 bits as required. The Z8000 and 68000 also provide a very short immediate mode for some instructions as shown in Figure 7–3(c). For example, "Increment by n" includes a 4-bit value for n as part of a 1-word instruction, avoiding an extra immediate word altogether. Some instructions make no sense with immediate mode, such as JUMP and STORE.

Immediate addressing is not really a necessary architectural feature, since constants can always be stored in arbitrary memory locations and accessed like other data using absolute addressing. For example, instead of "ADDA #1" we could write

```
        ADDA   ONE
        • • •
ONE     FCB    1
```

However, immediate addressing reduces program size and speeds up program execution by eliminating out-of-sequence addresses for constants. Just as im-

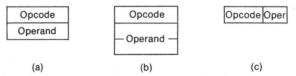

FIGURE 7–3 Immediate addressing formats: (a) immediate operand same length as opcode part; (b) double-length immediate; (c) short immediate.

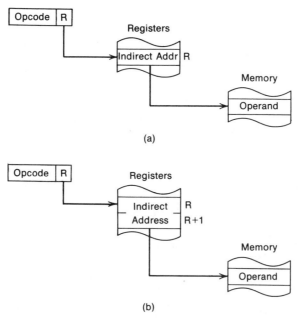

(a)

(b)

FIGURE 7–4 Register indirect mode: (a) address size equals register size; (b) address size twice the register size.

portant, it gives the programmer one less set of bookkeeping details to worry about, such as thinking up unique names for all those constants!

7.2.4 Register Indirect

In *register indirect mode*, a register or register pair contains the effective address of an operand. The PDP-11, 9900 and H8000 have 16-bit general registers and 16-bit addresses; the 6809 and H6809 have 16-bit index registers and 16-bit addresses; the 68000 has 32-bit registers and 32-bit addresses. In all these processors, one register may be used to specify any address in memory, as shown in Figure 7–4(a).

The Z8000 has 16-bit registers and can have 31-bit addresses. In this case, a register pair is used to form a full effective address in register indirect mode as shown in Figure 7–4(b).

All contemporary computers have register indirect mode in some form. This allows memory addresses to be computed during program execution rather than being fixed when the program is assembled. For example, compare the program in Table 5–7 with the one in Table 5–8. Execution-time address computation is required for many common operations, such as passing certain types of parameters to subroutines and accessing arbitrary data in arrays, stacks, queues, linked lists, and other data structures.

7.2.5   Auto-Increment and Auto-Decrement

Register indirect mode is often used to step through tables and lists of data, successively accessing each data item and bumping the register to point to the next one, as in the array initialization program in Table 5–8. An *auto-increment* addressing mode computes an effective address the same as register indirect mode and then automatically increments the register by the operand size as shown in Figure 7–5. Thus, in Table 5–8, the sequence

```
ILOOP   STA    @X              Set component to zero.
        ADDX   #1              Point to next component.
```

can be replaced by

```
ILOOP   STA    (X)+            Clear component and bump X to next.
```

As another example, in Table 5–10 the instruction LDA @X at BLOOP becomes LDA (X)+, and the ADDX #1 instruction at BNO1 is eliminated.

The amount added to the register on auto-increment depends on the operand size. In a byte-addressable machine, the register must be incremented by 1 to point to the next byte, by 2 to point to the next word, or by 4 to point to the next double word. The operand size can be deduced from the instruction opcode. For example, Load byte auto-increment should add 1, while Load word auto-increment should add 2.

Not all processors have an auto-increment addressing mode, and not all operand sizes are supported in the processors that do. The 68000 is the most flexible, allowing auto-increment addressing of bytes, words, and double words. The PDP-11, 6809, and 9900 support auto-increment addressing of bytes and words only.

Auto-decrement mode is similar to auto-increment, subtracting the operand size from the address register as shown in Figure 7–6. However, it performs the subtraction *before* using the register contents as the effective

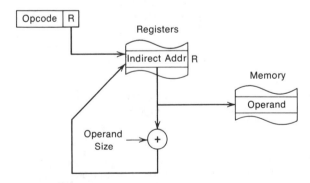

FIGURE 7–5 Auto-increment addressing.

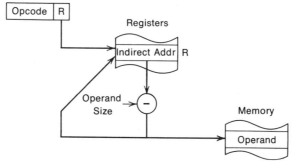

FIGURE 7–6 Auto-decrement addressing.

address, not after. In combination with auto-increment mode, this allows any address register to be efficiently used as the stack pointer for a stack with the following characteristics:

• The stack pointer always points directly at the top stack item.

• The stack grows by decrementing the stack pointer.

With these conventions, auto-decrement mode in the 6809 can be used to push the contents of A onto a stack using X as a stack pointer as follows:

```
STA     - (X)
```

The item at the top of the stack can be referenced by register indirect mode. For example,

```
LDA     @X
```

copies the item at the top of the stack into A. Finally, an item may be popped by auto-increment mode. For example,

```
ADDA    (X) +
```

pops the item at the top of the stack and adds it to A. Notice how the assembly language notation emphasizes auto-*pre*-decrement and auto-*post*-increment. The 68000, 6809, and PDP-11 all have auto-decrement addressing; the 9900 does not.

The 6809 and the PDP-11 have *auto-increment indirect* and *auto-decrement indirect* modes, which add one level of indirection to the above modes. As shown in Chapter 13, auto-increment indirect applied to the program counter (which is one of the general registers in the PDP-11) yields absolute mode! However, auto-decrement indirect found little use and was dropped from DEC's successor to the PDP-11, the VAX-11.

Table 7–3 gives an example of a program using auto-increment and auto-decrement addressing. This is a 6809 assembly language version of the

TABLE 7-3 Sorting program using stacks.

*			PROCEDURE StackSort; {Based on Table 3-6}
MAXLEN	EQU	200	CONST maxLen=200;
SIZE	EQU	201	stackSize=201;
MINNUM	EQU	-99	minNum=-99;
MAXNUM	EQU	99	maxNum=99;
NNUMS	RMB	1	VAR nNums,inNum : byte; spL,spH : address;
*			{Register usage: A=inNum; X=spL; Y=spH;}
STACKL	RMB	SIZE	stackL, stackH :
STKEL	EQU	STACKL+SIZE-1	ARRAY [1..stackSize] OF byte;
STACKH	RMB	SIZE	
STKEH	EQU	STACKH+SIZE-1	
*			BEGIN
SORT	LDX	#STKEL	spL := MemAddress(stackL[stackSize]);
	LDY	#STKEH	spH := MemAddress(stackH[stackSize]);
	LDA	#MINNUM-1	MEM[spL] := minNum-1;
	STA	@X	
	LDA	#MAXNUM+1	MEM[spH] := maxNum+1;
	STA	@Y	
	LDA	#1	nNums := 1;
	STA	NNUMS	
	JSR	WRMSG1	writeln('Input sequence: ');
	JSR	READ	read(inNum);
WHILE1	CMPA	#MINNUM	WHILE inNum>=minNum
	BLT	WHILE4	
	CMPA	#MAXNUM	AND inNum<=maxNum DO
	BGT	WHILE4	BEGIN
WHILE2	CMPA	@X	WHILE inNum < MEM[spL] DO
	BGE	WHILE3	{Top of stackL --> stackH.}
	LDB	(X)+	PushH(PopL);
	STB	-(Y)	
	BRA	WHILE2	
WHILE3	CMPA	@Y	WHILE inNum > MEM[spH] DO
	BLE	OUT3	{Top of stackH --> stackL.}
	LDB	(Y)+	PushL(PopH);
	STB	-(X)	
	BRA	WHILE3	
OUT3	STA	-(X)	PushL(inNum);
	JSR	WRNUM	write(inNum);
	LDA	NNUMS	nNums := nNums + 1;
	ADDA	#1	
	STA	NNUMS	
IF1	CMPA	#MAXLEN	IF nNums <= maxLen THEN
	BGT	ELSE1	
THEN1	JSR	READ	read(inNum)
	BRA	IFEND1	ELSE BEGIN
ELSE1	JSR	WRMSG2	writeln('** Too many inputs');
	LDA	#MINNUM-1	inNum := minNum - 1;
IFEND1	BRA	WHILE1	END;
*			END; {Inputs are now sorted.}

TABLE 7–3 (continued)

```
WHILE4   CMPX   #STKEL          WHILE spL <>
         BEQ    OUT4                MemAddress(stackL[stackSize]) DO
         LDB    (X)+              {Move everything into stackH.}
         STB    -(Y)             PushH(PopL);
         BRA    WHILE4
OUT4     JSR    WRMSG3          writeln; write('Sorted sequence: ');
WHILE5   CMPY   #STKEH          WHILE spH <>
         BEQ    OUT5                MemAddress(stackH[stackSize]) DO
         LDA    (Y)+              {Print contents of stackH.}
         JSR    WRNUM               write(PopH);
         BRA    WHILE5
OUT5     RTS                    {Return to caller.}
         END    SORT           END;
```

Pascal sorting program in Table 3–6. It uses a few features of the 6809 that don't exist in the H6809:

- There is a second accumulator, B, used in the same way as A.

- There is a second index register, Y, used in the same way as X.

- There are additional condition bits that are set after each data manipulation operation, allowing the relations <, <=, >, and >= on two's-complement integers to be tested by branch instructions BLT, BLE, BGT, and BGE, respectively.

The program in Table 7–3 uses X and Y as pointers into two stacks that contain numbers sorted in ascending and descending order. Auto-increment and auto-decrement addressing are used to manipulate the stacks. The program calls five subroutines for input/output: READ reads an input number and leaves its value in A; WRNUM prints the value of the integer in A; and WRMSG1, WRMSG2, and WRMSG3 print messages.

Because stacks are so important in programming, most processors without auto-increment and auto-decrement addressing modes at least have PUSH and POP instructions. In the Z8000, PUSH and POP may use any register as a stack pointer, while PUSH and POP in the 8086 uses a dedicated register, SP. The MCS-48 does not have any addressing modes or instructions for pushing or popping an item in one step; the 9900 has auto-increment addressing (POP) but no PUSH.

While auto-increment and auto-decrement can be used with any memory reference instruction, including arithmetic operations, PUSH and POP only allow data to be moved to and from the stack. Letting R0=A and R1=X, the Z8000 counterpart of the 6809 instruction ADDA (X)+ is

```
         POP    R2,@R1
         ADD    R0,R2
```

7.3 MULTICOMPONENT ADDRESSING MODES

7.3.1 Paged

As shown in Figure 7–7(a) for a 64K-byte memory, *paged addressing* partitions memory into a number of equal-length *pages*. A 16-bit absolute address can now be split into two components as shown in Figure 7–7(b). In this example an 8-bit *page number* indicates which of 256 pages a byte belongs to. An 8-bit *page address* gives the location of the byte within a 256-byte page.

Paged addressing has nothing to do with the physical organization or packaging of the memory system. It is simply used to specify an address in a smaller number of bits than the single-component addressing modes in the

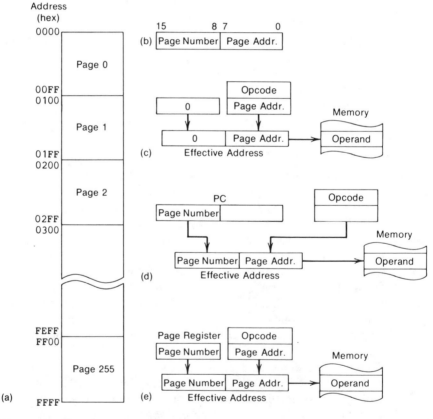

FIGURE 7–7 Paged addressing scheme: (a) address space partitioning; (b) address values; (c) base-page addressing; (d) current-page addressing; (e) page-register addressing.

previous section. In paged addressing, an instruction contains only a page address as shown in Figure 7–7(c,d,e); the page number is obtained in some way implied by the instruction to create a long absolute address:

- *Base-page addressing.* The page number is set to zero, yielding absolute addresses in page 0 (the *base page*) of memory.

- *Current-page addressing.* The page number is set equal to the high-order bits of the program counter (PC), yielding an address in the same page as the instruction itself (the *current page*).

- *Page-register addressing.* The page number is found in a *page register* that the program has previously loaded with the desired page number.

Only a few computers in this book have paged addressing, as summarized in Table 7–4. Although paging reduces the address size for many instructions, it is still necessary at times to specify a full address. Therefore, machines with paging always have other addressing modes such as absolute and register indirect.

7.3.2 Indexed

An *indexed* addressing mode combines two components by adding, and is the appropriate addressing mode for accessing arrays and tables. As shown in Figure 7–8, a fixed *base address* is specified as part of the instruction, as in absolute addressing. Then an *offset* (or *index*) in a specified address register is added to the base address to form an effective address. When indexed mode is used to access an array, the base address in the instruction corresponds to the

TABLE 7–4 Paged addressing modes.

Computer	Memory Address Bits	Page Address Bits	Page Number Bits	Addressing Mode
6809	16	8	8	8-bit page register DPR implied by instruction
MCS-48 (data mem.)	8	3	5	1-bit page register selects page 0 or page 3
MCS-48 (prog. mem.)	12	8	4	Conditional jumps go to target in current page

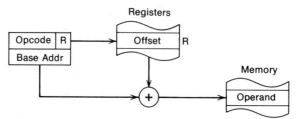

FIGURE 7–8 Indexed addressing computation.

base address of the array, while the value in the register corresponds to the index of the array component.

Suppose a Pascal program defines an array as follows:

```
VAR aname : ARRAY [first..last] OF baseType;
```

The corresponding assembly language program must reserve a total of (last-first+1) ·n bytes of storage for the array, where n is the size in bytes of baseType. In typical Pascal implementations, the values of n are 1, 2, and 4 for types char, integer, and real, respectively. A 4-byte array for the 6809 is declared below:

```
        ORG    1700H
FIRST   EQU    1              CONST first=1;
LAST    EQU    4                    last=4;
SCORE   RMB    LAST-FIRST+1   VAR score: ARRAY [first..last] OF byte;
```

In the assembly language program, the symbol SCORE is equated with the address of the first component of the array. Memory locations are used as shown in Figure 7–9. Thus, the symbol SCORE is equivalent to the number 1700H.

The address of component j in an array is given by a formula called the *address polynomial*. For the array score[1..4] the address polynomial is

```
Address(score[j]) = SCORE + j - 1.
```

Address (hex)	Memory
1700	score[1]
1701	score[2]
1702	score[3]
1703	score[4]

FIGURE 7–9 Storage allocation for array SCORE[1..4].

The address polynomial must take into account the index of the first component (first) and the length of each component (n) of an array. As shown in Figure 7–10, if the address of component aname[first] is ANAME, then the address of aname[first+x] is ANAME+x·n, where n is still the length of each component. Letting j=first+x we get the general address polynomial:

```
Address(aname[j])  = ANAME + (j-first)·n
                   = (ANAME - first·n) + j·n
                   = EffectiveBaseAddress(aname) + j·n
```

The *effective base address* of a one-dimensional array is the address assigned to component 0 if there is one. As shown by the parenthesization above, the effective base address is the constant part of the address polynomial.

For the score array, the general address polynomial yields:

```
Address(score[j])  = EffectiveBaseAddress(score) + j·1
                   = (SCORE - 1) + j
```

Thus, component j of the score array can be read into the A register of the 6809 by the following instruction sequence, assuming that J is a 16-bit variable in memory:

```
        LDX     J               Read j
        LDA     SCORE-1(X)      Read score[j]
```

The expression SCORE–1 is the effective base address of the array, so the value 16FFH is stored as the base address in the indexed instruction. Figure 7–11 shows the operation of the instruction sequence, assuming that it starts at address 2000H and J is stored at 2100H.

The multiplication of j by n in the address polynomial must always be done at run time, since j isn't known until then. However, n is usually a simple power of two, so the multiplication can be done by simple addition or

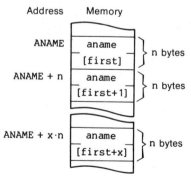

FIGURE 7–10 Addressing a one-dimensional array.

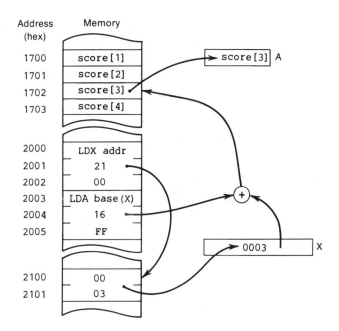

FIGURE 7–11 Indexed instruction execution.

shifts. For example, we could declare a 10-word array for the 6809 and access component j as follows:

```
FRST    EQU   1                     CONST first=1;
LST     EQU   10                    last=10;
WORDS   RMB   (LST-FRST+1)*2        VAR words: ARRAY [first..last] OF word;
EWORDS  EQU   WORDS-(2*FRST)          {Define effective base address}
        ...
        LDX   J                     Read j.
        ADDX  J                     Multiply by 2 to get word offset.
        LDX   EWORDS(X)             X := words[j].
```

A subroutine that uses indexed addressing to access an array is shown in Table 7–5. The program finds prime numbers without performing multiplication or division, by tabulating the multiples of known primes in an array. It introduces another new instruction of the 6809, ABX, which adds the 8-bit unsigned number in accumulator B to X.

Address polynomials can be developed for multi-dimensional arrays as well. Figure 7–12 shows the row-major storage allocation for a 3×4 array of bytes. The address polynomial is

```
Address(matrix[j,k]) = MATRIX + (j-1)·4 + (k-1)
```

TABLE 7-5 Subroutine to find primes using an array and indexed addressing.

```
*           This subroutine finds and prints all prime numbers between
*       2 and NPRIME using the 'Sieve of Eratosthenes.' It declares
*       a boolean array PRIME[2..NPRIME], whose components indicate
*       whether or not each number between 2 and NPRIME is prime.
*       For simplicity, one byte is used for each component, with
*       0=false, 1=true.
*           The program begins by setting all components true; every
*       integer is potentially a prime. Then it marks the multiples
*       of the first prime (2) as being nonprimes. Then it looks for
*       the next prime and marks off its multiples. This continues
*       until we've marked the multiples of all primes less than
*       PLIMIT, approximately the square root of NPRIME. Now only
*       primes are left marked true, and they are printed.
*
*                                   PROCEDURE FindPrimes;
NPRIME  EQU     1000                CONST nPrime = 1000;
PLIMIT  EQU     32                      pLimit = 32;
PRIME   RMB     NPRIME-1            VAR prime: ARRAY [2..nPrime] OF boolean;
*                                       {reg} X : word; {reg} B : byte;
FNDPRM  LDB     #1                  BEGIN
        LDX     #2                  FOR X := 2 TO nPrime DO
SETEM   STB     PRIME-2(X)              prime[X] := true;
        ADDX    #1                      {Set the entire array true.}
        CMPX    #NPRIME
        BLE     SETEM
        LDB     #2                  B := 2; {First known prime.}
MARKEM  LDX     #0                  REPEAT {Check integers...}
        ABX                             X := B; {...from 2 to pLimit.}
        LDA     PRIME-2(X)              IF prime[X] THEN
        BEQ     NOTPRM                     BEGIN
        ABX                                  X := X+B; {Mark multiples...}
CLRLUP  CLR     PRIME-2(X)                   REPEAT  {...of B as not prime.}
        ABX                                     prime[X] := false; X := X+B;
        CMPX    #NPRIME                      UNTIL X > nPrime;
        BLE     CLRLUP                     END;
NOTPRM  INCB                            B := B+1;
        CMPB    #PLIMIT             UNTIL B > pLimit;
        BLE     MARKEM
        JSR     WRMSG1              write('Here are primes from 2 to ');
        LDX     #NPRIME             X := nPrime;
        JSR     PRINTX              writeln(X); {Print the number in X.}
        LDX     #2                  FOR X := 2 TO nPrime DO
PRTLUP  LDB     PRIME-2(X)              {Print all the primes.}
        BEQ     NEXTP                   IF prime[X] THEN
        JSR     PRINTX                     writeln(X);
NEXTP   ADDX    #1
        CMPX    #NPRIME
        BLE     PRTLUP
        RTS                             {All done, return to caller}
        END     FNDPRM              END;
```

Column

Row	1	2	3	4
1	1700	1701	1702	1703
2	1704	1705	1706	1707
3	1708	1709	170A	170B

Legend: | Addr. |

FIGURE 7-12 Row-major storage of matrix[1..3,1..4].

Given a general two-dimensional array declaration,

```
VAR aname [jf..jl,kf..kl] OF baseType;
```

the address polynomial takes into account the effective base address of the array (the address of component [0,0]), the length of each row ((kl-kf+1)*n), and the size of each component (n):

$$
\begin{aligned}
\text{Address}(\text{aname}[j,k]) &= \text{ANAME} + ((j-jf) \cdot (kl-kf+1) + (k-kf)) \cdot n \\
&= (\text{ANAME} - (jf \cdot (kl-kf+1) + kf) \cdot n) + (j \cdot (kl-kf+1) + k) \cdot n \\
&= \text{EffectiveBaseAddress}(\text{aname}) + (j \cdot (kl-kf+1) + k) \cdot n
\end{aligned}
$$

The quantity $(\text{ANAME} - (jf \cdot (kl-kf+1) + kf) \cdot n)$ is the effective base address of the array; this quantity is stored in the indexed instruction and the remaining quantity is computed at run time as shown below for an 8×4 array of words on the 6809:

```
BOXES    RMB    4*8*2           VAR boxes: ARRAY [1..8,1..4] OF word;
EBOXES   EQU    BOXES-(4+1)*2     {Define effective base address}
J        RMW    1               j, k : integer;
K        RMW    1
TEMPX    RMW    1
         ...
         LDX    J               Read j.
         ADDX   J               Multiply by length of row (4).
         STX    TEMPX
         ADDX   TEMPX
         ADDX   K               Add column number.
         STX    TEMPX           Multiply by 2 to get word offset.
         ADDX   TEMPX
         LDX    EBOXES(X)        X := boxes[j,k].
```

In general, multiplication is needed to compute addresses in a multidimensional array, because the length of a row usually isn't a simple power of two. However, multiplication can be avoided by a technique called *addressing by indirection*, which uses an auxiliary table of row addresses. Instead of computing the starting address of a row as the effective base address plus $j \cdot (kl-kf+1) \cdot n$, we simply look it up by using the row number as an index into the row address table. The column number is then added to the row address to

obtain the address of desired component. This technique is illustrated in Table
7–6 for a 5 × 10 array in the 6809.

Most contemporary machines have at least one indexed addressing
mode; of the machines described in Part 3, only the MCS-48 does not. Some
machines have an indexed indirect mode; there are two varieties of this mode:

- *Pre-indexed indirect*. The offset is added to the base address to form an
  indirect address; the contents of the indirect address is the effective
  address.

- *Post-indexed indirect*. The base address is used as an indirect address;
  the offset is added to the contents of the indirect address to obtain the
  effective address.

Two machines in Part 3 have a pre-indexed indirect mode: the PDP-11 and the
6809. The MOS Technology 6502, a processor related to the Motorola 6809
family, has both pre-indexed and post-indexed indirect.

7.3.3 Based

Based addressing is similar to indexed addressing, and therefore often
confused with it. A *base address* is always a full-length address, while *offsets*
may be short or long. In indexed addressing, the instruction contains a base
address and an index register contains an offset. *Based addressing* is just the
opposite — the instruction contains an offset and an address register (or *base
register*) contains a base address. If offsets and base addresses are the same
length, the two modes are indistinguishable. The difference is apparent when
short offsets are used.

Figure 7–13 shows a based addressing calculation in the 6809. The instruction contains an 8-bit signed offset and an address register contains a

TABLE 7–6 Multidimensional array addressing by indirection.

```
J        RMW    1                     VAR j, k : integer;
K        RMW    1
ROW1     RMB    10                        cell : ARRAY [1..5,1..10] OF byte;
ROW2     RMB    10
ROW3     RMB    10
ROW4     RMB    10
ROW5     RMB    10
ROWTB    FCW    ROW1,ROW2,ROW3,ROW4,ROW5
         ...
         LDX    J                     Read j and multiply
         ADDX   J                       by size of ROWTB components (2).
         LDX    ROWTB-2(X)            Get base address of row.
         ADDX   K                     Add column number.
         LDA    -1(X)                 A := cell[j,k].
```

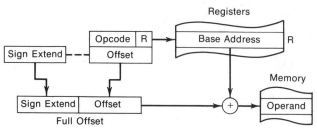

FIGURE 7–13 Based addressing in the 6809.

16-bit base address. Before the addition, the offset is made into a 16-bit signed number by sign extension.

Machines with based addressing include the 68000, Z8000, and 6809. In a general-register machine, any register may be used as a base register, with the possible exception of R0. In an accumulator-based machine, the index registers are often used as base registers. In fact, the "index registers" in the 6809 should really be called base registers, since they hold 16-bit addresses while instructions may specify 5-, 8-, or 16-bit offsets.

Indexed addressing is used when the base address of a data structure is known at assembly time, but an arbitrary component must be accessed when the program is run, as in most array manipulation problems. Based addressing is used when the relative position of an item in a data structure is known at assembly time, but the starting address of the structure is not. Typical applications of based addressing include:

- Accessing data in a parameter area whose base address is passed to a subroutine (see Section 9.3).

- Accessing items in a stack frame; the base register becomes a stack frame pointer (see Sections 5.4 and 9.3).

- Accessing data and jumping to addresses in a position-independent program, when the base register is loaded with the starting address of the program (see Section 7.4).

- Accessing a particular field of a block in a linked list, by loading the base register with the starting address of the block.

For an example of the last application, suppose we maintained a list of student names and exam scores, where each list item has the format shown in Figure 7–14. Now suppose that a number of such items have been chained together in a linked list, so that a variable HEAD contains the address of the first item, the LINK field of each item contains the address of the next one, and a LINK of 0 indicates the end of the list. Then the 6809 subroutine in Table 7–7 may be used to set the score fields of all list items to zero. At each

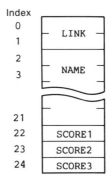

FIGURE 7–14 Student information table format.

iteration of the loop, X contains the base address of an item and the offsets SCORE1, SCORE2, and SCORE3 are used to access the score fields.

7.3.4 Based Indexed

The address calculation for *based indexed addressing* is shown in Figure 7–15 for the 6809; this mode adds a base register and an index register together to form the effective address. The 6809 uses one of the 16-bit "index" registers as the base register, and allows either an 8-bit accumulator (A or B) or a 16-bit accumulator pair (A,B) to specify the index value. The Z8000 and the 68000 also have based indexed addressing.

Based indexed addressing allows run-time computation of both the base address of a data structure and the offset to an item in it. For example, after a

TABLE 7–7 List initialization subroutine.

```
NULL     EQU    0            End-of-list value.
LINK     EQU    0            Define format of list items.
NAME     EQU    2
SCORE1   EQU    22
SCORE2   EQU    23
SCORE3   EQU    24
*
SCOREI   LDX    HEAD         Point to first list item.
SCLOOP   CMPX   #NULL        End of list?
         BEQ    OUT          If so, done.
         CLRA                Else clear the three exam scores.
         STA    SCORE1 (X)
         STA    SCORE2 (X)
         STA    SCORE3 (X)
         LDX    LINK (X)     Get address of next item.
         BRA    SCLOOP       Go check it.
OUT      RTS                 Done, return.
```

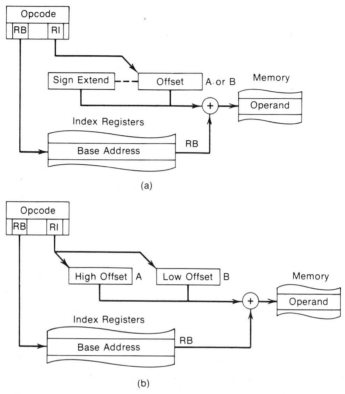

FIGURE 7–15 Based indexed addressing in the 6809: (a) 1-byte offset; (b) 2-byte offset.

program computes the base address of a table or array, it may load it into a base register and then access arbitrary components whose indices are also computed at run time.

We can augment the SCOREI subroutine in the previous subsection so that it also initializes the entire NAME field of a list item to contain spaces. Since there are 20 characters in the NAME field, this could be accomplished just before the LDX LINK(X) instruction by loading A with the ASCII code for space and then executing 20 instructions of the form "STA NAME+i(X)". However, a sequence using based indexed addressing takes a lot fewer instructions, as shown in Table 7–8.

7.3.5 Relative

Modes that compute an effective address as the sum of a fixed displacement in the instruction and the current value of the program counter fall into the category of *(PC) relative addressing*. A *short relative* addressing mode uses a small displacement to specify addresses nearby the current instruction,

TABLE 7–8 List initialization including name field.

```
SCOREI  LDX    HEAD          Point to first list item.
SCLOOP  CMPX   #NULL         End of list?
        BEQ    OUT           If so, done.
        CLRA                 Else clear the three exam scores.
        STA    SCORE1(X)
        STA    SCORE2(X)
        STA    SCORE3(X)
        LDA    #20H          ASCII space.
        LDB    #NAME         Starting index of NAME field.
NLOOP   STA    B(X)          Store a space.
        ADDB   #1            Bump index to next NAME byte.
        CMPB   #SCORE1       Finished entire field?
        BNE    NLOOP         Continue until all processed.
        LDX    LINK(X)       Get address of next item.
        BRA    SCLOOP        Go check it.
OUT     RTS                  Done, return.
```

avoiding extra bits needed for a full absolute address. Figure 7–16(a) shows the technique used in the 6809 and 8086. The instruction contains an 8-bit displacement that is sign-extended to 16 bits and then added to the PC to obtain the effective address. (When PC is added, it is already pointing to the next instruction.)

Assembly language instructions using relative addressing usually specify the desired absolute address, rather than the displacement. The assembler computes the required displacement from the current value of the PLC, and gives an error message if the absolute address is outside of the range accessible by the relative addressing mode.

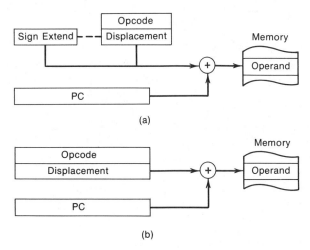

FIGURE 7–16 Address calculations: (a) short relative on 6809 and 8086; (b) long relative on PDP-11.

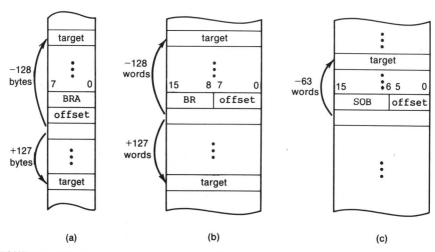

FIGURE 7–17 Address ranges accessible by relative branches: (a), 6809 and 8086 branches; (b) PDP-11 branches; (c) PDP-11 SOB.

The most common use of short relative addressing is in Branch (or Jump) instructions. Although the GOTO statement does not appear too often in good Pascal programs, the corresponding Branch primitive is essential for creating control structures in the corresponding machine language programs. The statements controlled by high-level structured statements in Pascal programs are usually short. It follows that the branch instructions in the corresponding machine language programs usually jump to "nearby" addresses. For example, the targets of over 80% of all branch instructions were within 127 bytes of the instruction itself in one study of Intel 8080 programs. Therefore, short relative addressing allows most branch instructions to be specified in a smaller number of bits. Figure 7–17(a) shows the range of addresses accessible by the 6809 and 8086 Branch instructions.

Besides the 6809 and 8086, other machines with short relative branch instructions include the PDP-11, Z8000, 68000, and 9900. Since these machines require instructions to start on even addresses, they extend the range of the relative branches as shown in Figure 7–17(b) by multiplying the displacement by two before adding to the PC.[2] Another trick is used by branch instructions that control REPEAT-type loops, such as Decrement and Jump if Not Zero (DJNZ) in the Z8000 and Subtract One and Branch (SOB) in the PDP-11. Since this control structure normally requires a backwards branch, the displacement is always interpreted as a positive number and *subtracted* from the PC. In the PDP-11, this gives a branch range of 0 to −63 words as shown in Figure 7–17(c).

[2]Except for the 68000, which still gives offsets in bytes. This inefficiency was probably allowed so that instruction lengths in future extensions of the 68000 architecture would not be limited to even numbers.

The 68000, PDP-11, 8086, and 6809 also provide a *long relative* addressing mode with 16-bit displacements, as shown in Figure 7–16(b) for the PDP-11. This mode can be used in both jumps and general data manipulation instructions. In the 68000, long relative mode gives a savings over the alternative of specifying a 32-bit absolute address. In the other machines, the 16-bit displacement gives no memory savings over specifying a 16-bit absolute address. However, long relative mode is still preferred because it helps to create position-independent programs, as discussed in the next section.

7.4 POSITION-INDEPENDENT CODE

The *load address* of a program is the first address that it occupies in memory. As we discussed in Section 6.4, it is difficult to determine load addresses at the outset of a large programming project. Relocating assemblers and linking loaders allow the load address to be specified later, at load time. In almost all applications these two tools are sufficient. However, they may not help when software modules are placed in read-only memory (ROM) chips.

When a program is "burned" into a ROM chip, it is committed forever; we can make no adjustments of data or instructions, even if we know what adjustments are needed. For example, suppose we're selling a 4K-byte ROM containing a set of floating-point subroutines for the 6809. The "load address" of such a ROM is fixed when our customer plugs the ROM into the computer's memory circuit board — different sockets correspond to different load addresses. The problem is that different customers will almost certainly want to plug the ROM into different sockets, due to varying system configurations. We need a program that works correctly with *any* load address. Such a program is called *(statically) position independent*.

In a few applications, it is also useful to be able to move a program in memory after its execution has already begun. No, this doesn't mean that programmers are unplugging and rearranging ROMs while their programs are running. More likely, this occurs when programs run under the control of a multi-user operating system that dynamically swaps jobs in and out of available read/write memory as needed. After a program is temporarily suspended, it may be reloaded into an area of memory different from where it started. A program that can be moved around in this way is called *dynamically relocatable* (or *dynamically position independent*).

The key characteristic of position-independent code is that it does not contain any absolute addresses. Two addressing modes can provide position independence: relative and based.

In relative addressing modes, a displacement gives the *difference* between the instruction address and the effective address. Therefore, the instruction and operand can be picked up as a unit and moved to a different part of memory without changing the displacement value stored in the instruction. The effective address is recomputed as a function of the current PC each time the instruction is executed, so instructions that use this mode are dynamically position independent.

Based addressing can also be used to achieve position independence. The program somehow computes its own load address when it starts running and places this value in a base register.[3] Once the load address is in a base register, all references to addresses within the program may be specified by based addressing with offsets from the beginning of the program, as if the program were loaded at address 0. Since the load address is computed only once, at load time, instructions that use this mode are only statically position independent.

Adherence to the following rules will create programs that are statically position independent:

- The values of all address constants must be computed relative to the load address or the PC when the program is executed, rather than being specified using immediate addressing. Non-address constant values, like those used for initializing counters, making comparisons, and so on, may be accessed by immediate addressing.

- Other local data accesses must use based addressing referenced to the load address of the program or use PC-relative addressing. Absolute addressing is not allowed.

- All local jumps and subroutine calls must use based addressing referenced to the load address of the program or PC-relative addressing.

- Absolute addresses may be used to refer to absolute locations outside the position-independent program (for example, in a call to an operating system utility).

The static position independence rules are easier to follow in some machines (68000) than in others (6809, PDP-11).[4] In fact, statically position-independent code is difficult to write for machines without PC-relative addressing or a straightforward way to load the PC into a base register (Z8000, 9900, MCS-48). In summary, the ability to write statically position-

---

[3]The 68000 and 6809 have a Load Effective Address (LEA) instruction that computes an effective address according to a specified mode and places it in an address register. For example, the instruction LEAX START(PCR) in the 6809 computes the address of label START as a function of the current PC and places it in base register X. In the PDP-11, the desired effect can be achieved by copying PC into a register using a MOV instruction and then adding a small offset. In other machines, programming "tricks" may be needed to copy the PC into an address register.

[4]All three of these machines have PC-relative and based addressing. The 68000 and 6809 also have based indexed addressing. But the 68000 is most flexible, having an addressing mode that the others lack: PC-relative with index and offset (effective address equals PC plus specified index register plus 8-bit signed offset in the instruction).

independent code is a useful processor feature for some applications, but most processors seem to get by without it.

Dynamic position independence can be achieved in simple programs by means of PC-relative addressing alone. However, in a program that manipulates address values such as pointers, dynamic position independence requires extensive use of based addressing. Each time the program is moved, a new base address must be placed in a base register, and all data references must be made relative to the base register, using based or based indexed addressing. Still, dynamic position independence rules are difficult to enforce manually; for example, see Exercise 7.10. Therefore, dynamic position independence usually appears only in processors that have a special base register that the processor implicitly uses for *all* memory references (e.g., the 8086), and in processors that use memory mapping and management.

7.5 MEMORY MAPPING AND MANAGEMENT

Memory mapping and management units (MMUs) are added to computer systems for one or both of the following reasons:

(1) To increase the amount of main memory in the system beyond that provided by the basic CPU architecture.

(2) To partition a large amount of main memory in a way that allows several programs to share the memory without accidently or maliciously interfering with each other.

It is convenient to think of *memory mapping* as performing the first function above, and *memory management* as performing the second; we'll introduce the two topics separately. However, as the discussion develops we'll see that there is actually a fair amount of overlap between the two areas in practice.

7.5.1 Memory Mapping

As we indicated at the beginning of this chapter, one of the most common "mistakes" in computer processor design is the failure to provide enough address bits for a large memory. The software investment of users of a small-address-space CPU makes it desirable to find ways to increase the usable address space of the existing machine, rather than rewrite all the software for a different, large-address-space machine. Therefore, memory-mapping units have been designed and built to increase the amount of main memory that can be attached to CPUs with relatively small address spaces, such as the PDP-11 and the 6809 (64K bytes each).

The typical placement of an MMU in a computer system is shown in Figure 7–18. The MMU intercepts each m-bit address from the CPU and

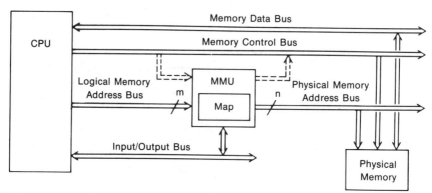

FIGURE 7–18 Placement of an MMU in a computer system.

translates it into an n-bit address for the memory, where $n \geqslant m$. The m-bit address from the CPU is called the *logical address*, while the n-bit address is called the *physical address*. The logical-to-physical translation is controlled by a "map" in the MMU as explained shortly.

The MMU is also connected to the CPU's input/output (I/O) bus. The CPU can read and write entries in the MMU's translation map using ordinary I/O instructions, as if the map consisted of a set of I/O ports. The interface is a little trickier if the computer uses memory-mapped I/O, in which case a special default mapping may be needed to access the MMU's "I/O ports." See Sections 10.1 and 10.2 and the references for discussions of relevant I/O concepts. In any case, the CPU controls the translation process since it can change the map from time to time as required.

With memory mapping, a program can still only access as much physical memory at one time as the basic CPU architecture allows, for example, 64K bytes in a PDP-11 or 6809. However, by changing the map a program can access different "chunks" of the physical memory at different times. Thus, a program that manipulates a very large data structure could partition the data structure into chunks of 64K bytes or less, and explicitly change the map in order to access different chunks of the data structure.

Another common use of memory mapping is in multi-user operating systems. Each user's program may use the entire logical address space of the machine (say 64K bytes), yet the operating system may allocate a different chunk of physical memory for each user. In this case, it is the operating system's responsibility to set up the map appropriately as each user's program is run. In this kind of application, the memory management function discussed in the next subsection is also very important; it provides "protection" to keep different users' programs from interfering with each other.

An example of a simple MMU map is shown in Figure 7–19, which assumes that $m = 16$ and $n = 20$. The MMU maps the 64K-byte logical address space of the CPU into one megabyte of physical address space. The 13 low-

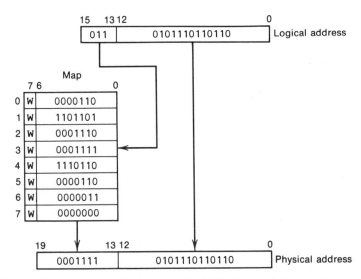

FIGURE 7–19 Simple logical-to-physical MMU translation map.

order bits of the logical address are passed through (or around) the MMU without modification. The three high-order bits are used as an index into the map, which has eight rows. A 7-bit number in the selected row is prefixed to the 13 low-order logical address bits to form a 20-bit physical address.

As shown in Figure 7–20, the MMU has the effect of dividing both the logical and the physical address spaces into 8K-byte "pages." At any time, addresses in each logical page are mapped into corresponding addresses in a physical page designated by a map entry. Conceptually, there is nothing to prevent two or more logical pages from being mapped into the same physical page, but usually different logical pages are mapped into different physical pages. In any case, a program can access only a fraction of the entire physical memory at any time. To access a physical page that no logical page currently maps into, the program must change the map.

More sophisticated MMUs may allow a logical page to use less than a full page of physical memory and may also offer a finer choice of boundaries for physical pages. In this way, a program need not use a maximum-size physical page if it doesn't need it, improving the memory utilization in the computer.

7.5.2 Memory Management

Memory management allows several different programs (or "tasks" or "processes") to use the same physical memory without interfering with each other. For example, consider the MMU that we described in the previous subsection. One megabyte of physical memory could store a 64K-byte operat-

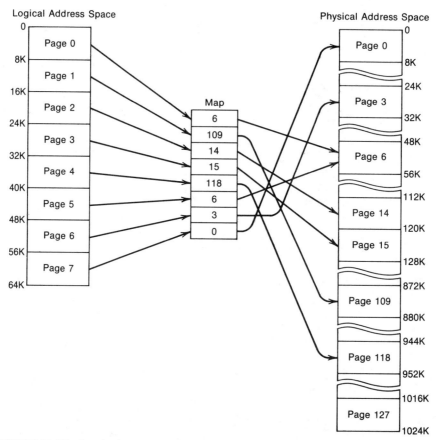

FIGURE 7–20 Logical-to-physical page mapping created by MMU.

ing system and fifteen independent user programs of 64K bytes each. Before running a particular program, the CPU could set up the MMU to map the 64K-byte logical address space of the CPU into 64K bytes of physical memory reserved for that program. Programs could not interfere with each other because each could access only its own 64K-byte portion of the physical memory, as determined by the map.

In fact, a program could even be protected from interfering with itself. For example, Figure 7–19 shows an extra bit called "W" that is available in each map entry. With appropriate circuitry inside the MMU and interconnections to the control portion of the Memory Bus, this bit could be used to "write-protect" selected pages. When this bit was set for a particular logical page, the CPU could be prevented from inadvertently overwriting instructions or data in the page. A more sophisticated MMU could provide other forms of access control, such as "execute only" pages containing instructions that the

CPU could execute but not read as data. In a multi-user system, this would allow one user to execute another user's proprietary program with no possibility of copying it.

At this point, readers who enjoy thwarting operating systems will have said to themselves, "Why can't my program simply change the map to gain access to another program's physical pages?" Indeed, this is a very real possibility unless precautions are taken in the system's hardware and software design. Several different approaches have been used in practice, but most rely on the idea of having at least two separate maps in the MMU, one for the operating system and one or more for user programs. In addition, the CPU hardware may be designed to have two modes of operation, user mode and supervisor mode.

In *supervisor mode*, the MMU's supervisor map is selected and the CPU may execute any instruction in its instruction set. In *user mode*, a user map is selected and the CPU may not execute any instruction from a predefined set of "privileged" instructions. These are instructions whose execution might compromise the integrity of the operating system.

The set of privileged instructions typically includes all I/O instructions. The operating system always changes the CPU to be in user mode before transferring control to a user program. Therefore, if the MMU maps are accessed by I/O instructions, a user program cannot access the maps. Of course, all other I/O must also be done by the operating system, since only it can execute I/O instructions.

In a system that uses memory-mapped I/O (Section 10.2), there are no I/O instructions to privilege, and the MMU "I/O ports" reside in the same physical address space as the rest of the memory. In this case, all that is needed is to ensure that the MMU I/O port addresses are never accessible through a page in the user map. A user program may be given access to other I/O ports, but never to the MMU's.

Several problems must still be overcome to make memory management useful:

- How should the memory management hardware and software be initialized?

When power is first applied to a computer, the MMU maps are blank or contain garbage. Therefore, the hardware must ensure that the CPU "comes up" in supervisor mode and that some default logical-to-physical mapping is in effect. In this way, the CPU can run a "bootstrap" program from read-only memory in the default page(s) to set up the maps.

- If user programs don't have access to the operating system's pages and they can't change the CPU operating mode or the map, then how can they transfer control to the operating system?

Once again, a hardware solution is required. The CPU must provide special instructions, such as software interrupts or system calls (Section 11.3.2), that automatically invoke supervisor mode and jump to a subroutine in the operating system's address space, as determined by the supervisor map.

- What happens with interrupts?

The hardware should automatically switch to the supervisor mode and use the supervisor map when an interrupt takes place. Thus, all interrupts are handled (at least initially) by service routines in the operating system's address space.

- Memory management imposes many restrictions for memory access, privileged instructions, and so on. What happens when a program violates one of the rules?

The CPU and MMU hardware should detect all such "protection" violations. When a violation occurs, a high-priority interrupt or trap should be created. Like other interrupt service routines, the handler for this interrupt or trap should be in the operating system's address space.

- What happens if the stack pointer is not pointing into a valid stack area when an interrupt or trap occurs? At best, wouldn't the return address and processor status be lost? At worst, wouldn't the processor generate "protection violation" traps forever as it tries to push into nonexistent or protected memory?

The operating system can't do much to force users to write correct programs, and so a hardware solution is required. The CPU should have *two* stack pointers, one for the user and the other for the operating system. In user mode, the CPU always uses the user stack pointer, and the user has no way of messing up the supervisor stack pointer. In supervisor mode, the CPU always uses the supervisor stack pointer; interrupt and trap information is pushed onto the supervisor stack. Therefore, the operating system need only ensure that it leaves its own stack pointer in a valid state each time it returns control to a user program.

- How can data be moved between different programs' logical address spaces in applications that require data sharing?

The operating system can always set up its own map to read and write data in any physical pages that it wants to. Therefore, user programs can call the operating system to do inter-program transfers under operating system control.

- What about direct-memory access (DMA) transfers?

In one approach, the hardware is arranged to bypass the MMU during DMA transfers, so that DMA interfaces must deal with physical addresses. In another approach, there is at least one additional map in the MMU for DMA transfers, which the hardware selects automatically; in this case the DMA interfaces deal with logical addresses only.

The solutions offered above are not unique. Also, many other issues must be considered in the design and use of memory management units and operating systems. Since a complete discussion is beyond the scope of this text, you should consult the references if you wish to pursue this topic further.

REFERENCES

Bell and Mudge's view that a large address space is essential for an extensible, long-lived computer architecture is widely supported. For example, see the papers by the architects of the Zilog Z8000 and the Motorola 68000 which appear in the February 1979 issue of *Computer* [Vol. 12, No. 2].

On the other hand, different architects disagree on the importance of different addressing modes. For example, the architects of the 68000 felt that providing auto-increment and auto-decrement modes was the best way to manipulate stacks and also to provide primitives for moving and searching contiguous blocks of data. The architects of the Z8000, on the other hand, decided to omit the extra addressing modes and instead provide specialized PUSH, POP, and block move and compare instructions. (See the papers cited above.)

In another instance of disagreement, addressing modes that support position-independent code were "one of the highest priority design goals" for the architects of the Motorola 6809 [Ritter and Boney, "A Microprocessor for the Revolution: The 6809," *Byte*, Jan. 1979, Vol. 4, No. 1, p. 34]. Other architects have downplayed the importance of 6809-type static position-independent code in favor of memory mapping and management schemes that allow dynamic position independence [Bernard Peuto and Harold Stone, private communications]. The difference of opinion occurs mainly because the different architects are focusing on different applications; 6809-type static position-independent code is very useful for "canned" software in ROMs, whereas the dynamic position independence provided by memory mapping and management is needed in large multiprogramming systems that may run a program in different parts of physical memory at different times.

We have barely touched on the issues of memory mapping and management and their relationship to operating systems. A discussion of memory mapping and management schemes from the overall system architecture point of view may be found in *Introduction to Computer Architecture*, edited by Harold Stone [SRA, 2nd edition, 1980]. A very good discussion of protection at several levels, including logical and physical memory, CPU mode, and higher-level objects, may be found in *Timesharing System Design Concepts* by Richard W. Watson [McGraw-Hill, 1970].

EXERCISES

7.1 Rewrite the program in Table 7–5 without indexed addressing, using auto-increment addressing instead.

7.2 Many assemblers do not allow parentheses in operand expressions, and give all operators equal precedence (i.e., an expression is evaluated strictly from left to right). Rewrite the declaration of the WORDS array in Section 7.3.2 for such an assembler.

7.3 The effective base address of a two-dimensional array as defined in Section 7.3.2 is not really the address of component [0,0]. Explain.

7.4 What factors limit the maximum value of NPRIME that may be declared in Table 7–5?

7.5 Write an assembly language program that simulates Conway's "Life." The simulation takes place on a rectangular array of cells, each of which may contain an organism. Except for borders each cell has eight cells immediately adjacent to it, and so each organism may have up to eight neighbors. The survival and reproduction of organisms from generation to generation depends on the number of neighbors according to four simple rules:

(1) If an organism has no neighbors or only one neighbor, it dies of loneliness.

(2) If an organism has two or three neighbors, it survives to the next generation.

(3) If an organism has four or more neighbors, it dies of overcrowding.

(4) An organism is born in any empty cell that has exactly three neighbors.

All changes occur simultaneously; the fate of an organism depends on the current generation irrespective of what may happen to its neighbors in the next generation. Therefore, the game may be simulated in the program using two $m \times n$ arrays of bytes, CURG and TEMPG. Each array component contains the ASCII code for the letter "O" if the cell contains an organism, an ASCII space otherwise.

For each cell in CURG, the program examines the neighbors and puts the next generation outcome in the corresponding cell in TEMPG. (Border processing may be simplified by using an $m+2 \times n+2$ array in which the borders have been initialized to always contain spaces.) After processing all cells in CURG, the program can copy TEMPG into CURG, or simply swap the roles of CURG and TEMPG.

The array size $m \times n$ may correspond to the size of a CRT screen (e.g., 24×80). In Chapter 10 we shall continue the assignment by specifying a means of displaying the generations of Life on a CRT screen.

7.6 Rewrite the 1s-counting subroutine of Table 5–10 for the 6809 or some other processor. The new version should contain a 256-byte table, N1S[0..255], initialized at load time, where N1S[i] contains the number of 1s in the binary representation of i. The BCNT1S subroutine should simply look up the number of 1s in its input number, using indexed addressing.

7.7 Modify the binary-to-ASCII conversion subroutine of Exercise 5.13 so that the result characters are not stored in fixed memory locations. Instead, when the subroutine is called, the X register is assumed to contain the base address of a three-byte array ASC[0..2] in which the result characters are to be stored.

7.8 In many CPUs it is very difficult to write position-independent code because it is difficult for a program to read the current value of the PC; in fact, in the H6809 it is impossible. We could have defined an H6809 instruction TFR PC,X to transfer PC into X. However, to make things difficult suppose we defined only an instruction TFR S,X that transfers the current value of SP into X. Write a subroutine TFRPCX that computes and puts into X the address of the instruction following a JSR TFRPCX instruction.

7.9 Explain why the code below is statically position independent.

```
FOP     RMB    20              Storage for FOP[1..20] of bytes.
I       RMB    1               Storage for an index into FOP.
        ...
        TFR    PC,X            (Or JSR TFRPCX from previous exercise.)
HERE    ADDX   #FOP-1-HERE
        LDB    I(PCR)
        LDA    B(X)            A := FOP[I].
```

7.10 Explain why the above code is not dynamically position independent.

8

OPERATIONS

As we saw in Chapter 5, every processor organization defines its own formats for instructions; even more variations appear in the processors in Part 3. Despite the variations, there are many similarities among the operations performed by different processors, sometimes for historical reasons, but just as often for practical ones. In a paper[1] describing trade-offs in the design of the Z8000, Bernard Peuto said,

> A large number of opcodes is very important: having a given instruction implemented in hardware saves bytes and improves speed. But usually one needs to concentrate more on the completeness of the operations available on a particular data type than on adding more and more esoteric instructions.

This chapter discusses the operations available in typical computer processors, except for input/output, which is covered in Chapter 10. Although a "complete set" of operation types is covered, the "esoteric" operations of particular processors are omitted; the manufacturers' literature is the best source for that level of detail.

[1]B. L. Peuto, "Architecture of a New Microprocessor," *Computer*, Vol. 12, No. 2, pp. 10–21, February, 1979.

A representative mnemonic is given for each operation in this chapter. However, you are cautioned that different manufacturers use quite different mnemonics for the same operations, and identical mnemonics may have different meanings in different computers. The descriptions of real computers in Part 3 give manufacturers' mnemonics for each one; still, the users' manuals published by the manufacturers are the best source for details not covered in this book.

Each operation in this chapter is described by an extended-Pascal statement. As reviewed below, several features of extended Pascal are important to these descriptions:

- If X is a bit-array variable, then X[bnum] denotes bit bnum of X.

- The standard function Badd(x,y : bitarray; c : bit) adds n-bit arrays x and y with an initial carry of c, producing an n-bit result and setting global variables BC and BV according to the carry from the MSB and two's-complement overflow, respectively.

- The standard function Bcom(x : bitarray) computes the bit-by-bit complement of an n-bit array x.

- The standard functions Band(x,y : bitarray), Bor(x,y : bitarray), and Bxor(x,y : bitarray) compute the logical AND, OR, and Exclusive OR of two n-bit arrays x and y, returning an n-bit result.

8.1 INSTRUCTION FORMATS

The data manipulation operations in the next few sections can be classified by the number of operands; the most common are single-operand and double-operand instructions. *Single-operand instructions* have the following format:

```
Opcode  Operand        Description

OP      dst            dst := F(dst);
```

Such instructions generally read the value of a *destination operand* dst, perform some function on it, and store the result back into dst. Depending on the processor and the instruction, dst may be either a register or a memory location specified by one of the allowed addressing modes.

Double-operand instructions in most processors have the following format:

```
OP      dst,src        dst := F(src,dst);
```

Such instructions generally read the values of dst and a *source operand* src, combine them in some way, and store the result back into dst. Data movement instructions are a special case, simply copying the value of src into dst.

As a documentation convention, all PDP-11 and 68000 instructions and some 9900 instructions have the order of src and dst reversed in assembly language programs:

        OP   src,dst   dst := F(src,dst);

The allowed identities of src and dst in a double-operand instruction depend on the processor architecture. In a one-address (accumulator-based) processor such as the 6809 or MCS-48, dst is usually an accumulator and src is a register or memory location specified by an addressing mode:

        OP   accum,src   accum := F(src,accum);

Likewise, in the one-and-a-half-address instructions found in general-register processors such as the Z8000, 68000, 9900, or 8086, dst is usually one of the registers while src may be any register or memory location specified by an allowed addressing mode:

        OP   reg,src   reg := F(src,reg);

Some instructions may also have a "reverse" form in which src is in a register and dst is in a register or memory:

        OP   dst,reg   dst := F(reg,dst);

In two-address instructions in the PDP-11, 68000, and 9900, both src and dst may be registers or memory locations specified by addressing modes; only in this case are memory-to-memory operations possible.

Most 16-bit and 32-bit processors also support operations on bytes. Thus, typical data movement and manipulation instructions specify the length of the operand(s) as well as the operation. Both src and dst in double-operand instructions must have the same length. In assembly language, the operand length is usually indicated by a suffix on the instruction mnemonic. For example, ADD, ADDL, and ADDB refer to addition of words, long words, and bytes in the Z8000.

8.2 CONDITION BITS

In some accumulator-based processors, such as the MCS-48, a conditional branch (or jump) instruction tests the value of the accumulator, and jumps according to a specified condition (e.g., zero/nonzero, positive/

negative). In a general-register processor, this scheme would require each branch instruction to specify not only the condition and target address, but also which register to test. In typical computer programs, a high percentage of all instructions (up to 20%) are conditional branches, and so it's very important to optimize their length and execution efficiency. Luckily, conditional branches most often test an operand that has just been operated on. Processors with condition bits take advantage of this characteristic.

Condition bits (or *condition codes* or *flags*) are a collection of individual status bits that a processor automatically sets according to the result of each instruction. For example, the Z bit in each processor in Chapter 5 is set to 1 whenever an operation produces a zero result.

A *conditional branch instruction* tests the value of one or more condition bits and branches to a new location if they have a specified value. The only conditional branch instructions in the Chapter 5 processors are Branch if equal and Branch if not equal, because the only condition bit is Z. However, in the sorting program in Table 7–3 we saw that there are other interesting conditions to test, such as greater than or less than zero. Additional condition bits are needed to indicate such relations.

The number, naming, and meaning of condition bits vary on different processors, but the most popular set is the one found in the PDP-11, 6809, 68000, Z8000, and 8086:

- N (Negative). Equals the most significant (sign) bit of the result.

- Z (Zero). Set to 1 if all the bits of a result are zero, to 0 otherwise.

- V (Overflow). Set to 1 on arithmetic operations that cause two's-complement overflow; set to 0 if no overflow occurs. When a program adds or subtracts n-bit *signed* numbers, V=1 indicates that the true result is greater than $2^{n-1}-1$ or less than -2^{n-1}. The expression N XOR V always gives the correct sign of a two's-complement result, since V=1 indicates that N is wrong.

- C (Carry): During addition operations, set equal to the carry out of the most significant bit (MSB) position. When a program adds n-bit *unsigned* numbers, C=1 indicates that the true result is greater than 2^n-1. During subtraction operations, C is set to the *borrow* out of the MSB. When unsigned numbers are subtracted, C=1 indicates that the true result is less than zero.

The condition bit settings are consistent with operand size. For example, the N bit equals bit 7 of the result after a byte operation, bit 15 after a word operation. However, the exact rules for setting the condition bits still can vary for different instructions and different processors. Where there is a clear interpretation, all processors use the same rules; for example, all set V to 1 if ADD produces two's-complement overflow, to 0 otherwise. However, the rules are somewhat arbitrary for many instructions.

For example, how should the condition bits be set after a "Load" operation? Clearly, N and Z should be set according to the value just loaded. But what about C and V? In most processors, V is set to 0 and C is not affected. The reasons for this rule are subtle — clearing V assures that certain signed conditional branches will work properly, while preserving C is important in multiprecision operations. Then what should the rules be for a "Store" operation? Shouldn't they be the same as for Load? Perhaps, but some computer architects believe that Store should not affect the condition bits at all! In general, one must carefully examine the user's manual for a processor to find the exact rules for condition bit setting.

The Z8000 uses S instead of N to denote the sign; the 8086 calls the condition flags CF, OF, SF, and ZF. The 9900 has a slightly different set of flags that give the same information. The MCS-48 does not have a full set of condition bits and conditional branches. However, some processors have additional condition bits that aid in special operations:

- P (Parity). Indicates that the result has even parity, that is, an even number of 1 bits.

- H (Half-carry). Equals the carry between bits 3 and 4 of a byte during addition; used in binary-coded decimal (BCD) operations.

- D (Decimal adjust). Indicates whether an addition or a subtraction occurred most recently; used in conjunction with H in BCD operations.

- X (Extend). An extra carry bit, set in the same way as C but not by all operations; used in the 68000 for multiprecision arithmetic.

Although the condition bits are affected by almost every data movement and manipulation instruction, sometimes it is necessary to test an operand that doesn't need to be moved or manipulated. The TEST instruction is provided just for this purpose — TEST dst reads its operand dst and sets the condition bits according to its value, and does nothing else.

Occasionally it is necessary to set a condition bit to a particular, known value. Most processors have convenient instructions for doing this, such as the ones below:

CLRC	C := 0;
SETC	C := 1;
CLRV	V := 0;
SETV	V := 1;
CLRN	N := 0;
SETN	N := 1;
CLRZ	Z := 0;
SETZ	Z := 1;

The condition bits are part of the "processor state" that we defined in Chapter 5. In the programming model of a processor they are often grouped

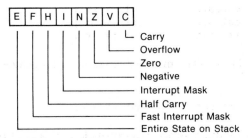

FIGURE 8-1 Condition Code (CC) register in the 6809.

together with other processor state information into a single *n*-bit register with a name such as *Processor Status Word (PSW)*. The 6809 uses a register called CC (Condition Codes), as shown in Figure 8-1. The instruction PSHS CC pushes all the condition bits onto the stack as a unit, so they can later be popped and restored by PULS CC.

In subsequent sections we'll point out how the condition bits are affected when appropriate. Conditional branches that test the condition bits will be described fully in Section 8.6.

8.3 DATA MOVES

By far the most frequently used instructions in typical computer processors are *data moves* — operations that move data from one place to another in the registers and memory. In processors that support different lengths of data, such as bytes, words, and double words, there are separate data movement instructions for each length. Data moves usually set the condition codes according to the value of the datum just moved.

The two most important data movement instructions are Load (LD) and Store (ST). Traditionally, LD and similar mnemonics denote operations that move data from memory to a processor register; ST denotes movement from a register to memory. However, there are many variations.

In the Z8000, the assembly language mnemonic LD is used for both directions of transfer, even though the instructions are encoded with different opcodes. The assembler deduces the intended transfer direction from the order of the operands. Similarly, the MCS-48 and 8086 use MOV for both directions. In these computers, memory-to-memory moves are not allowed.

The PDP-11, 68000, and 9900 legitimately use the mnemonic MOV for both directions, since MOV is a full two-address instruction where both source and destination can be registers or memory locations. Therefore, memory-to-memory moves are possible.

Data movement instructions transfer data from source to destination. However, not all computers use the same convention for the direction of transfer in assembly language programs. Most have the following format:

```
MOV   dst,src      dst := src;
LD    dst,src      dst := src;
ST    src,dst      dst := src;
```

However, PDP-11, 68000, and 9900 assembly languages have the opposite format:

```
MOV   src,dst      dst := src;
```

Most contemporary processors provide a means of pushing and popping data on a stack in one instruction. Processors such as the PDP-11, 68000, and 6809 have auto-increment and auto-decrement as standard addressing modes, so that PUSH and POP are just special cases of the regular data movement instructions, ST – (SP) and LD (SP) +, respectively. The Z8000 provides PUSH and POP as separate instructions. In these processors, any address register may be used as a stack pointer. The 8086 also provides PUSH and POP as specialized instructions that can only use the system stack pointer register for pushing and popping.

The 6809 has two instructions, PSHS and PULS, that can push or pull (pop) one or more processor registers on the system stack in a single instruction. The 68000 has two similar instructions, STM and LDM, that can do the same using any address register as a stack pointer.

There are a number of other specialized data movement instructions in different processors. Most have instructions for moving the contents of the PSW and other processor control and status registers to and from the accumulators, general registers, or stack. The 6809 has a Transfer (TFR) instruction that copies the contents of any CPU register into any like-sized register. Some processors have an Exchange (XCH) instruction that swaps the contents of two registers or a register and a memory location; a SWAP instruction swaps halves of an operand (e.g., swaps bytes in a single-word operand). Some processors have Load multiple (LDM) and Store multiple (STM) instructions that allow a group of registers to be saved in memory or restored from memory in one instruction, useful in subroutines and interrupt routines. And some have instructions that can move entire blocks of data from one part of memory to another.

8.4 ADDITION AND SUBTRACTION

The basic arithmetic operation in any computer is binary addition. A typical ADD instruction has the following format:

```
ADD   dst,src      dst := Badd(dst,src,0);
```

The ADD instruction adds two n-bit operands using n-bit binary addition with an initial carry of 0, stores an n-bit sum in dst, and sets the condition bits

TABLE 8-1 Condition bit settings for addition.

Operation	N Z V C	Signed Interpretation	Unsigned Interpretation
0100		+4	4
+ 0010		+ +2	+ 2
0110	0 0 0 0	+6	6
0101		+5	5
+ 0111		+ +7	+ 7
1100	1 0 1 0	−4, overflow	12
1101		−3	13
+ 0011		+ +3	+ 3
0000	0 1 0 1	0	0, carry 1
1001		−7	9
+ 1100		+ −4	+ 12
0101	0 0 1 1	+5, overflow	5, carry 1

accordingly. Some examples of the condition bit settings are given in Table 8–1 using 4-bit numbers. The arithmetic weight of the carry bit is +16.

Most processors also have a subtraction operation that subtracts the source operand from the destination using two's-complement subtraction:

```
SUB     dst,src         dst := Badd(dst,Bcom(src),1);
                        { = dst - src}
```

That is, the individual bits of src are complemented and then added to dst with an initial carry of 1. However, there is one important difference from the equivalent addition in most processors. In all the computers in this book except the 9900, the condition bit C is set to 1 if SUB produces a *borrow*. The borrow bit is the *complement* of the carry bit produced in the corresponding addition, as shown below in examples using 4-bit unsigned numbers:

```
                                    1  —  initial carry
        9        1001            1001
      − 5      − 0101          + 1010
        4        0100, no borrow  1|0100  carry = 1, so borrow = 0


                                    1  —  initial carry
        2        0010            0010
      −13      − 1101          + 0010
      5−16      0101, borrow 1   0|0101  carry = 0, so borrow = 1
```

```
                                   1 — initial carry
    7       0111              0111
  − 7     − 0111            + 1000
  ─────   ──────            ──────
    0       0000, no borrow  1|0000   carry = 1, so borrow = 0
```

In 4-bit subtraction, the weight of borrow is −16. Complete examples of the condition bit settings are given in Table 8–2.

Subtraction is a useful operation for comparing the values of two numbers. For example, X is less than Y if and only if X−Y is less than zero. Thus, if SUB X,Y produces a negative result, then X is less than Y.

It usually isn't necessary to store the difference when comparing two numbers. The Compare (CMP) instruction subtracts two operands and sets the condition bits *without* storing the difference. CMP is used with conditional branch instructions as explained in Section 8.6. Like SUB, CMP sets C if the subtraction produces a borrow, not a carry. The format of the CMP instruction in a typical processor is

```
    CMP    dst,src       Set condition bits according to dst-src
```

As always, the PDP-11 and 9900 reverse src and dst:

```
    CMP    src,dst       Set condition bits according to src-dst
```

However, notice that they also reverse the order of the subtraction operation, with the happy result that CMP P,Q performs the same operation (P−Q) in almost every processor in this book.[2]

8.5 SOME SINGLE-OPERAND INSTRUCTIONS

Because adding or subtracting 1 is such a common operation for maintaining counters and stepping through tables, most processors have short instructions that do this:

```
    INC    dst       dst := dst + 1;
    DEC    dst       dst := dst - 1;
```

Any register may be the dst in these instructions; many processors can also increment and decrement memory locations.

---

[2]In the 68000, "CMP src,dst" performs the operation dst-src, which is backwards. Therefore, "CMP P,Q; BGT OUT" branches if Q>P. The src and dst fields in the CMP machine instruction and the operation dst-src are committed in the 68000 hardware. It is possible for a 68000 assembler to eliminate the problem by reversing the order in which it picks up src and dst in the operand field of a CMP instruction, reading "CMP dst,src". However, Motorola's standard 68000 assembly language leaves the problem for the programmer to deal with.

TABLE 8–2 Condition bit settings for subtraction.

Operation	N Z V C	Signed Interpretation	Unsigned Interpretation
0100		+4	4
− 0010		− +2	− 2
0010	0 0 0 0	+2	2
0101		+5	5
− 0111		− +7	− 7
1110	1 0 0 1	−2	14, borrow 1
1101		−3	13
− 1101		− −3	− 13
0000	0 1 0 0	0	0
1001		−7	9
− 0100		− +4	− 4
0101	0 0 1 0	+5, overflow	5

In some processors INC dst is not quite equivalent to ADD dst,#1 for a subtle reason — ADD affects the C bit whereas INC does not. The same relationship holds between DEC and SUB. This means that conditional branches that test C will work properly after ADD and SUB but not after INC and DEC. Historically, this anomaly originated in the PDP-11/20, in which loops are typically controlled as follows:

```
LOOP:   ...                 REPEAT
        ...                     ...
        DEC   CNT               cnt := cnt − 1;
        BNE   LOOP          UNTIL cnt = 0;
```

The problem arose when such loops were used for multiplication, division, and multiprecision arithmetic. In these loops it is desirable to preserve the value of C from the end of one iteration to the beginning of the next; hence INC and DEC were designed to preserve C. The PDP-11/45 later introduced the Subtract one and branch (SOB) instruction that combines DEC and BNE into one instruction, solving the problem by not affecting the condition bits at all. The 68000 solves the problem by having an extra condition bit X that is set the same as C for multiprecision operations, but is not affected by data movement and loop control instructions.

Three other single-operand instructions are Clear (CLR), Complement (COM), and Negate (NEG), defined in extended Pascal as follows:

```
CLR   dst        dst := 0;
COM   dst        dst := Bcom(dst);
NEG   dst        dst := Badd(0,Bcom(dst),1);
```

COM complements the individual bits of dst, that is, it takes the ones' complement. NEG negates dst by taking its two's complement — it complements the bits and then adds 1. The condition bits are set according to the result, but the rules for C and V vary widely among different processors. For the NEG instruction, a consistent rule is to set C if there would be a borrow in the implied subtraction from 0 (i.e., if dst is anything but 0), and to set V only if dst is the "extra" negative number 10. . .0.

8.6 PROGRAM CONTROL

Program control instructions have fundamental importance, since they are the primitives that allow conditional action and repetition in machine language programs. The simplest program control instruction is the Unconditional jump (JMP). The JMP instruction in most processors allows an effective address to be specified by any of a variety of addressing modes. Unlike other instructions, which read or write an operand at the effective address, the JMP instruction simply loads the program counter (PC) with the effective address, thereby transferring control to the instruction stored there:

```
JMP     dst              PC := effectiveAddress(dst);
```

Addressing modes such as register and immediate don't make any sense with the JMP instruction, and are never allowed. However, other addressing modes make JMP instruction very flexible. For example, absolute and relative modes can be used to perform jumps to fixed memory locations, while register indirect and indexed modes allow CASE-type statements to be coded by dynamically computing a target address using a register (see Exercise 8.6).

The CALL (or Jump to subroutine) instruction provides the means of calling a subroutine, the machine-language equivalent of a Pascal procedure or function. Most contemporary processors dedicate one register as a stack pointer, and the CALL instruction saves a return address in the stack before jumping to the subroutine:

```
CALL    dst              Push(PC); PC := effectiveAddress(dst);
```

When the subroutine's execution is completed, control is given back to the calling program by a Return (RET) instruction which pops the value off the top of the stack and loads it into the PC:

```
RET                      PC := Pop;
```

In processors that don't have a stack, CALL deposits the return address in a specified register, and the return can be accomplished by a JMP instruction with register indirect addressing. Subroutines will be discussed in detail in Chapter 9.

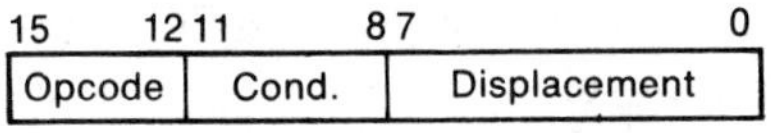

```
15      12 11      8 7                    0
   Opcode | Cond. |   Displacement
```

FIGURE 8–2 Format of short conditional branches.

Conditional jump instructions test a specified condition and jump only if the condition is true. In processors without condition codes, typical conditions are "Accumulator zero" and "Accumulator negative". In processors with condition codes, the values of one or more condition bits are tested.

Jumps that specify a target using PC-relative addressing are usually called *branch* instructions. As discussed in Section 7.3, typical branch instructions contain a short displacement to a target address "nearby" the current instruction. This reduces the size of the branch instruction and produces position independence. Because of their usefulness, conditional branches with short (1-byte) displacements are provided in most processors; their typical instruction format is shown in Figure 8–2. The displacement is interpreted as a signed, two's-complement integer and added to the PC if the branch is taken. The 6809 and 68000 also have conditional branches with long (1-word) displacements.

There are 15 standard branch conditions provided in most processors with condition codes, as shown in Table 8–3. There are 17 rows in the table because the pairs BCC,BHS and BCS,BLO are alternate mnemonics for the

TABLE 8–3 Typical conditional branch instructions.

Type	Mnemonic	Branch If	Condition
Single Bit			
	BRA offset	Always	true
	BCS offset	Carry set	$C = 1$
	BCC offset	Carry clear	$C = 0$
	BVS offset	Overflow set	$V = 1$
	BVC offset	Overflow clear	$V = 0$
	BMI offset	Minus	$N = 1$
	BPL offset	Plus	$N = 0$
	BEQ offset	Equal (to zero)	$Z = 1$
	BNE offset	Not equal (to zero)	$Z = 0$
Signed			
	BLT offset	Less than (zero)	N XOR V $= 1$
	BGE offset	Greater than or equal (to zero)	N XOR V $= 0$
	BLE offset	Less than or equal (to zero)	(N XOR V) OR Z $= 1$
	BGT offset	Greater than (zero)	(N XOR V) OR Z $= 0$
Unsigned			
	BLO offset	Lower	$C = 1$
	BHS offset	Higher or the same	$C = 0$
	BLS offset	Lower or the same	C OR Z $= 1$
	BHI offset	Higher	C OR Z $= 0$

same machine instructions. Branches in the first part of the table test the states of individual condition bits.

The second part of the table describes branches that test the value of a *signed* integer. If rr is one of the relations LT, GE, LE, GT, NE, EQ, then X rr Y if and only if X-Y rr 0. Since the CMP X,Y instruction sets the condition bits according to X-Y, the following instruction sequence branches if and only if X rr Y:

```
CMP     X,Y
Brr     LABEL
```

Note that the expression N XOR V gives the sign of the true result, since V is 1 only if the subtraction overflowed, producing the wrong sign. The signed conditional branches also work correctly after data movement and TEST instructions, branching if the just-accessed operand has the specified relationship with 0.[3] This explains why data movement instructions should clear V.

Branches in the last part of the table are used after comparisons of *unsigned* integers. Since they test the value of C, they should only be used after CMP instructions; data movement instructions usually don't affect C. A CMP X,Y instruction subtracts Y from X and sets C to 1 only if a borrow occurs, that is, only if X is less than Y when interpreted as an unsigned number. This observation produces the combinations of C and Z tested by the unsigned conditional branches in the last four rows of the table.

The BNE and BEQ instructions work on both signed and unsigned numbers. In fact, they test for bit-by-bit equality regardless of what a byte or word represents.

The program in Table 7-3 used *signed* conditional branches to sort numbers in the range -99 through +99. The program in Table 8-4, adapted from Table 3-7, uses *unsigned* conditional branches (BLS) to check the head and tail pointers of a queue against a buffer limit. Unsigned conditional branches are appropriate because head and tail contain absolute memory addresses, which are unsigned integers. A very common programming error is to use signed conditional branches in this situation. When this is done, the program fails if numbers of opposite sign are compared, quite a mysterious bug to track down (in this example, it occurs only if the queue buffer includes the boundary between the top and bottom 32K halves of the memory address space).

The program in Table 8-4 also shows the correspondence between Pascal statements and assembly language instructions, and it illustrates many of the instructions that have been covered so far in this chapter. Notice that in the main program there is an assembly language construct that cannot be

---

[3]Except in the Z8000, whose designers also goofed. The data movement instructions don't affect the condition bits, an inconvenience. Instead, TEST is supposed to be used after a load when needed. However, TEST fails to clear the V bit, and so the signed conditional branches may fail unless V is explicitly cleared by a RESFLG V instruction after TEST. The best solution is to not use TEST VAR at all, and use CMP VAR,#0 instead.

modeled in standard Pascal without using GOTO. This is a good example of a situation where a Pascal "EXIT" statement would have been handy.

A frequently-used construct in program loops is

```
LOOP    ...                    REPEAT
        ...                      ...
        DEC    CNT               cnt := cnt - 1;
        BNE    LOOP             UNTIL cnt = 0;
```

TABLE 8–4 Word queueing program for the 6809.

```
*           This program enqueues a sequence of words. Each word is a
*           sequence of characters terminated by a space. The sequence
*           is terminated by a period. Each time a '!' is received, the
*           program dequeues and prints a word. The '!' is not printed.
*                              PROGRAM WordQueue;
QLEN    EQU    200             CONST qlen = 200;
ENDCHR  EQU    2EH               endChar = '.';
SPACE   EQU    20H               space = ' ';
DMPCHR  EQU    21H               dumpChar = '!';
*                              VAR inChar : char; {Uses accumulator A}
QUEUE   RMB    QLEN               queue : ARRAY [1..qlen] OF char;
QENDA   EQU    QUEUE+QLEN-1       {Define address of last queue item.}
HEAD    RMB    2                  head, tail, X, Y : address;
TAIL    RMB    2                  {X,Y = index registers}
STACK   RMB    20                 {Space for return address stack.}
STACKE  EQU    *
*                              PROCEDURE Enqueue(A : char);
ENQ     LDX    TAIL              BEGIN
        ADDX   #1                  X := tail + 1;
        CMPX   #QENDA              IF X > Addr(queue[qlen]) {Last addr}
        BLS    ENQ2                  THEN
        LDX    #QUEUE                  X := Addr(queue[1]); {First addr}
ENQ2    CMPX   HEAD                IF X <> head THEN
        BEQ    ENQOUT                BEGIN
        STA    @TAIL                   MEM[tail] := A;
        STX    TAIL                    tail := X;
ENQOUT  RTS                         END; {Lose chars on overflow.}
*                              END; {Enqueue}
*                              FUNCTION Dequeue : char; {Result in A,}
DEQ     LDX    HEAD              BEGIN {... Z-bit = 1 if queue empty.}
        CMPX   TAIL                X := head;
        BEQ    DEQOUT              IF X <> tail THEN
        LDA    @X                    BEGIN  A := MEM[X];
        ADDX   #1                      X := X + 1;
        CMPX   #QENDA                  IF X > Addr(queue[qlen]) THEN
        BLS    DEQ2
        LDX    #QUEUE                    X := Addr(queue[1]);
DEQ2    STX    HEAD                    head := X;
        CLRZ                          Z := 0;
*                                   END;
*                                 ELSE Z := 1; {Z-bit = 1 from BEQ}
DEQOUT  RTS                      END; {Dequeue}
```

TABLE 8–4 (continued)

```
WORDQ   LDS    #STACKE      BEGIN {Main Program}
        LDX    #QUEUE
        STX    HEAD             head := Addr(queue[1]);
        STX    TAIL             tail := Addr(queue[1]);
        JSR    READ             read(A);  {Get a char, returned in A.}
WHILE1  CMPA   #ENDCHR      WHILE inChar <> endChar DO
        BEQ    ENDW1            BEGIN
IF1     CMPA   #DMPCHR          IF inChar <> dumpChar THEN
        BEQ    ELSE1
        JSR    ENQ                 Enqueue(inChar)
        BRA    ENDIF1           ELSE BEGIN
*                                  WHILE true DO {GOTOs needed.}
ELSE1   JSR    DEQ                 BEGIN  A := Dequeue;
        BEQ    L10                   IF Z = 1 {queue empty}
        CMPA   #SPACE                  THEN GOTO 10;
        BEQ    L10                   IF A = space THEN GOTO 10;
        JSR    WRCHAR                write(A);  {Print char in A.}
        BRA    ELSE1               END;
L10     JSR    WRITELN          10: writeln;  {Start new line.}
*                                END;
ENDIF1  JSR    READ             read(inChar);  {Get next char.}
        BRA    WHILE1           END;
ENDW1   JMP    1000H        {Return to operating system.}
        END    WORDQ     END. {Main Program}
```

The last two machine instructions in such a loop are combined in the Decre-ment and jump if not zero (DJNZ) machine instruction, producing a slightly shorter loop:

```
LOOP    ...                  REPEAT
        ...                     ...
        DJNZ   CNT,LOOP        cnt := cnt - 1;
*                            UNTIL cnt = 0;
```

Besides shortening the loop and speeding execution, this instruction has the advantage of not disturbing the condition codes, important in multiprecision arithmetic loops that pass a value in C from the end of one iteration to the beginning of the next. The PDP-11's version of DJNZ is called Subtract one and branch if not zero (SOB).

8.7 LOGICAL OPERATIONS

Logical operations treat a data word as an array of bits, and handle each bit independently. An operation that we've already covered, COM, can be considered a logical operation because it complements the bits in a word, bit

TABLE 8–5 Function table for logical operations.

X	Y	NOT X	X AND Y	X OR Y	X XOR Y	X BIC Y
0	0	1	0	0	0	0
0	1	1	0	1	1	1
1	0	0	0	1	1	0
1	1	0	1	1	0	0

by bit. In fact, the operation should really be named NOT in this context. Logical operations on two operands include AND, OR, and XOR:

```
AND     dst,src        dst := Band(dst,src);
OR      dst,src        dst := Bor(dst,src);
XOR     dst,src        dst := Bxor(dst,src);
```

The function tables for various logical operations are given in Table 8–5. Most computers have AND, OR, and Exclusive OR (XOR) instructions. Instead of AND, the PDP-11 has an asymmetric AND function called Bit clear (BIC):

```
BIC     src,dst        dst := Band(Bcom(src),dst)
```

This function clears the bits of dst corresponding to 1s in src, as shown in the function table; X BIC Y is equivalent to (NOT X) AND Y.

The logical operations are most often used for extracting and combining fields that are packed into different data words. For example, suppose that the 4-bit field F1 appears in bits 11-8 of a data word P, and the 7-bit field F2 appears in the low-order bits of Q, as shown in Figure 8–3. The other bits of each word contain unknown values, not zeroes. The fields can be combined into one word T by the following Z8000 instruction sequence:

```
LD      R0,P
AND     R0,#0F00H        Clear all but bits 11-8.
LD      R1,Q
AND     R1,#007FH        Clear all but bits 6-0.
OR      R0,R1            Combine words.
ST      R0,T
```

The hexadecimal constants 0F00H and 007FH are called *masks*; they have ones in the fields to be extracted and zeroes elsewhere. The AND instructions

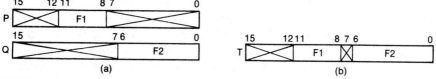

FIGURE 8–3 Packed data fields: (a) P and Q; (b) desired result T.

set the unused bits in P and Q to zero so that the desired fields can be combined by OR. General operations on packed data fields also require shifting fields left or right in a word; this will be covered in Section 8.8.

The logical operations in most processors set N and Z according to the result, clear V, and leave C at its previous value. Sometimes it's desirable to test a field of a word using a mask and the AND operation, setting the condition codes but not storing the result anywhere. The Bit test (BIT) instruction in the PDP-11 and 6809 accomplishes this.

In programs that pack many boolean flags into a data word, it is desirable to address individual bits of a word. The standard logical instructions can do this using masks with a single 1 or 0 bit. For example, the instructions

```
AND    dst,#7FFFH
OR     dst,#8000H
XOR    dst,#8000H
BIT    dst,#8000H
```

respectively clear, set, complement, and test the most significant bit of a 16-bit word dst. The *bit manipulation instructions* provided in some processors perform these functions more efficiently:

```
BCLR    dst,bnum     dst[bnum] := 0;
BSET    dst,bnum     dst[bnum] := 1;
BCHG    dst,bnum     dst[bnum] := Bcom(dst[bnum]);
BTST    dst,bnum     Z := Bcom(dst[bnum]);
```

These instructions manipulate a specified bit bnum in the dst word. Bit manipulation instructions are classified as *static* or *dynamic* depending on whether the instruction specifies bnum or a register that contains bnum. The Z8000 and 68000 have both kinds of bit manipulation instructions.

8.8   ROTATES AND SHIFTS

Rotate and shift operations manipulate the contents of one data word (or byte or long word), moving the bits of the word one or more positions to the right or left. All processors can shift and rotate the contents of registers, and many can also perform these operations on memory locations. Extended Pascal defines two shift functions, Bshl and Bshr, that operate as shown in Figure 8–4. They shift the contents of a bit array x left or right one position, fill the vacated position with the value c, and place the lost bit in the global bit variable BC. All of the rotates and shifts in real processors can be defined in terms of these primitives. We describe many different shifts and rotates in this section, but not all of them are available in every processor.

The name *rotation* is generally used if no bits are lost in the operation. Rotation operations are sometimes called *circular shifts* or *cyclical shifts*.

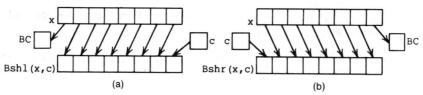

FIGURE 8–4 Extended Pascal shift functions: (a) Bshl (x : bitarray; c : bit); (b) Bshr (x : bitarray; c : bit).

Typical 1-bit rotation instructions are described in extended Pascal as follows, assuming 16-bit operands:

```
RL     dst          {rotate left} dst := Bshl(dst,dst[15]);
RR     dst          {rotate right} dst := Bshr(dst,dst[0]);
RLC    dst          {rotate left with C}
                    dst := Bshl(dst,C); C := BC;
RRC    dst          {rotate right with C}
                    dst := Bshr(dst,C); C := BC;
```

Figure 8–5 shows the effect of these operations. Simple left and right rotations move each bit of dst one position, filling the vacated position with the bit that "falls off" the other end. Rotations with carry employ the C condition bit; the vacated position is loaded with the value of C, and C is loaded with the bit that falls off the other end. In some processors, the simple rotations without C still set C, even though C is not used in the actual rotation:

```
RL     dst          {rotate left} C := dst[15];
                    dst := Bshl(dst,dst[15]);
RR     dst          {rotate right} C := dst[0];
                    dst := Bshr(dst,dst[0]);
```

The N and Z condition bits are set in the obvious manner; the setting of V varies in different processors and is not obvious.

Multiprecision rotations can be programmed using C as a link. For example, suppose that R0,R1 are a pair of 16-bit registers containing a 32-bit operand, high-order word in R0, in a processor such as the Z8000. The equiva-

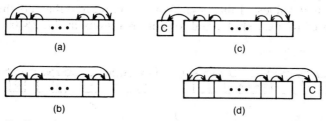

FIGURE 8–5 Rotation operations: (a) left; (b) right; (c) left with carry; (d) right with carry.

lent of a "rotate left with carry" can be performed on the 32-bit operand by two 16-bit rotates:

```
RLC    R1        R1 := Bshl(R1,C); C := BC {old R1[15]};
RLC    R0        R0 := Bshl(R0,C); C := BC {old R0[15]};
```

A rotation of R0,R1 *without* carry is a little trickier, as we'll soon see.

The name *logical shift* is normally applied to shift operations that force a 0 into the vacated position. The value of the bit shifted off the end is usually saved in C, and the old value of C is lost. The other condition bits are set in much the same way as rotations. One-bit logical left and right shifts are illustrated in Figure 8–6 and are defined below for 16-bit operands:

```
SLL    dst       {shift left logical} C := dst[15];
                 dst := Bshl(dst,0);
SRL    dst       {shift right logical} C := dst[0];
                 dst := Bshr(dst,0);
```

Now we return to the problem of performing a rotation without carry on a 32-bit operand in R0,R1. In the following instruction sequence, SLL is used to shift R1 left and force a 0 into its LSB; then if the left rotation of R0 produces a carry, the LSB of R1 is set to 1.

```
       SLL    R1        R1 := Bshl(R1,0); C := BC {old R1[15]};
       RLC    R0        R0 := Bshl(R0,C); C := BC {old R0[15]};
       BCC    LSB0      IF C=1 THEN R1[0] := 1;
       INC    R1        {Remember, INC doesn't affect C.}
LSB0   . . .            {Now C equals LSB of new R0,R1.}
```

Rotations and logical shifts are useful for manipulating *packed data*, that is, data words that have two or more independent values stored in different fields. To illustrate this concept, Figure 8–7(a) shows a 16-bit data word P with four fields F1, F2, F3, and F4. This format is good for a program that must store many data records. It takes a lot less storage to pack each record into one word than to use four full words in the *unpacked* format of Figure 8–7(b). However, when a particular record is processed, it may be necessary to copy the packed values into an unpacked format, process them, and then repack the new values. Table 8–6 shows subroutines that do this using a combination of rotates, shifts, and logical operations in the Z8000.

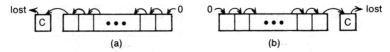

(a) (b)

FIGURE 8–6 Logical shifts: (a) left; (b) right.

TABLE 8–6 Data packing and unpacking subroutines for the Z8000.

```
*          This subroutine unpacks four values in a packed word P,
*          placing them in registers R1, R2, R3, R4.
*          Notation: Vi = contents of field Fi.
*
UNPACK  LD     R0,P           Get packed word.
        CLR    R1             Prepare R1 to accept V1.
        SLL    R0             Put MSB of V1 in C.
        RLC    R1             Rotate into R1.
        SLL    R0             Repeat for one more bit.
        RLC    R1
        CLR    R2             Prepare R2 to accept V2.
        SLL    R0             Put MSB of V2 in C.
        RLC    R2             Rotate into R2.
        SLL    R0             Repeat for two more bits.
        RLC    R2
        SLL    R0
        RLC    R2
        CLR    R3             Prepare R3 to accept V3.
        SLL    R0             Put MSB of V3 in C.
        RLC    R3             Rotate into R3.
        SLL    R0             Repeat for one more bit.
        RLC    R3
        LD     R4,P           Get another copy of packed word.
        AND    R4,#01FFH      Get rid of V1,V2,V3, leaving V4.
        RET                   Unpacked values are now in R1-R4.
*
*          This subroutine packs the four values in registers
*          R1, R2, R3, R4 into a packed word P.
*
PACK    CLR    R0             Prepare R0 to receive packed values.
        SRL    R3             Put LSB of V3 into C.
        RRC    R0             Shift into R0.
        SRL    R3             Repeat for another bit.
        RRC    R0
        SRL    R2             Put LSB of V2 into C.
        RRC    R0             Shift into R0.
        SRL    R2             Repeat for two more bits.
        RRC    R0
        SRL    R2
        RRC    R0
        SRL    R1             Put LSB of V1 into C.
        RRC    R0             Shift into R0.
        SRL    R1             Repeat for another bit.
        RRC    R0
        AND    R4,#01FFH      Make sure no garbage with V4.
        OR     R0,R4          Merge with V1,V2,V3.
        ST     R0,P           Store packed word.
        RET                   Done, return.
```

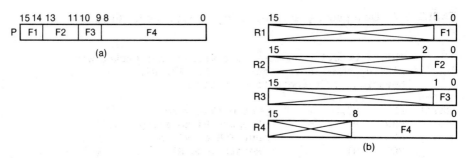

FIGURE 8–7 Four fields: (a) packed format; (b) unpacked format.

Arithmetic shifts treat their operands as signed, two's-complement numbers. They operate in such a way that a 1-bit left shift is equivalent to multiplication by two and a 1-bit right shift is equivalent to division by two. One-bit arithmetic left and right shifts are illustrated in Figure 8–8 and are defined below for 16-bit operands:

```
SLA     dst            {shift left arithmetic} C := dst[15];
                       dst := Bshl(dst,0);
SRA     dst            {shift right arithmetic} C := dst[0];
                       dst := Bshr(dst,dst[15]);
```

Notice that the SLL and SLA instructions appear to be equivalent. The only possible difference is in the setting of the condition bits; we did not specify the setting of V for SLL. In SLA, the V bit is always set according to an interpretation of arithmetic overflow: it is set to 1 if the operation caused the sign bit of dst to change, to 0 otherwise.

In the SRA operation, arithmetic overflow is impossible. However, instead of clearing V after this instruction, some processors set V to a strange value, an anomaly first introduced in the PDP-11. Another problem with SRA is that it truncates in the "wrong" direction when its operand is negative, so that $-1 \div 2$ equals -1, not 0.

Multiprecision arithmetic shifts can be obtained by combining single-precision arithmetic shifts with rotates or logical shifts, using C as a link. For example, the following instruction sequence arithmetically right shifts a register pair R0,R1:

```
SRA     R0             R0:=Bshr(R0,R0[15]); C:=BC {old R0[0]};
RRC     R1             R1:=Bshr(R1,C); C:=BC {old R1[0]};
```

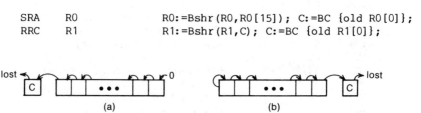

FIGURE 8–8 Arithmetic shifts: (a) left; (b) right.

Many processors have multiprecision shift and rotate instructions built in. Many also have instructions that shift or rotate an operand by more than one bit position at a time, for example,

```
SLL     dst,nbits      FOR i:=1 TO nbits DO dst := bshl(dst,0);
```

Depending on whether the length of the shift nbits is given by a field in the instruction or by a register specified by the instruction, multibit shift instructions are classified as *static* or *dynamic*. Unfortunately, multibit shifts cannot generally be used to efficiently code multibit multiprecision operations needed in floating-point and other algorithms, since there is only a 1-bit link (C) between words.

8.9 MULTIPLE PRECISION ADDITION AND SUBTRACTION

In multiple-precision arithmetic, the carry (or borrow) bit must be propagated from the least significant words or digits to the most significant. The Add with carry (ADC) and Subtract with carry (SBC) instructions in many processors facilitate such operations. For example, suppose on a 16-bit processor such as the Z8000 we have two 32-bit operands P and Q of type long unsigned integer, stored in memory words PH,PL and QH,QL. Then their 32-bit sum SH,SL can be computed as follows:

```
LD      R0,PL          SL := PL + QL;
ADD     R0,QL
ST      R0,SL
LD      R0,PH          SH := PH + QH + C;
ADC     R0,QH
ST      R0,SH
```

The ADC instruction adds the two operands, plus 1 if C is 1 at the beginning of the instruction. The above sequence shows why data movement instructions should not modify C; when the ADC instruction is encountered, C still has the value produced by the previous ADD. The above sequence is also correct if the 32-bit operands are interpreted as signed integers. After the last ST, the N bit gives the sign and the V bit indicates two's-complement overflow. However, in either case the Z bit reflects only the status of the high-order word, not a 32-bit zero result.

The SBC instruction is similar, subtracting src from dst, minus an additional 1 if C is 1. A double-length difference P–Q is computed as follows:

```
LD      R0,PL          SL := PL - QL;
SUB     R0,QL
ST      R0,SL
LD      R0,PH          SH := PH - QH - C;
SBC     R0,QH
ST      R0,SH
```

The sequence is correct for both signed and unsigned long integers, and the same remarks apply to the condition bit settings as in addition.

Sometimes signed integers of unequal lengths must be combined; in this case, the shorter operand must be extended to match the length of the longer one. The length of a two's-complement number may be extended to any number of bits simply by replicating the sign bit to the left. For positive numbers, this rule is obvious; proving that the rule is correct for negative numbers is left as an exercise for the reader. Two examples are given below:

$$+5_{10} = 0101_2 = 00000101_2 = 0000000000000101_2$$
$$-5_{10} = 1011_2 = 11111011_2 = 1111111111111011_2$$

Most processors provide a Sign extend (SXT) instruction that extends the sign of the least significant half of a register, register pair, or memory word into the most significant half.

8.10 MULTIPLICATION AND DIVISION

Most processors have instructions for performing either signed or unsigned multiplication or both. Multiplication generally uses one of the algorithms given in Section 4.8, so that multiplying two words gives a double-word product. Overflow is impossible since the result must be representable in two words.

A typical multiplication instruction has the format

```
MUL    Rn,src        Rn,Rn+1 := Rn * src;
```

where Rn is a single-word register and src is a single-word operand in a register or memory. Since a double-word product is produced, two consecutive registers are used to store it, high-order word in Rn and low-order word in Rn+1.

In processors with only unsigned multiplication, signed multiplication can be performed by testing the signs of the operands, negating the negative operands, performing an unsigned multiplication, and finally negating the product if the signs were opposite.

Multiprecision unsigned multiplication can be performed by using short unsigned multiplication as a primitive. For example, consider multiplying two 2-byte operands XH,XL and YH,YL to produce a 4-byte product. The operation may be written as follows:

$$X \cdot Y = (XL + 2^8 \cdot XH) \cdot (YL + 2^8 \cdot YH)$$
$$= XL \cdot YL + 2^8 \cdot (XL \cdot YH + YL \cdot XH) + 2^{16} \cdot XH \cdot YH$$

The equation above has been translated into a 6809 program in Table 8–7, in which the four bytes P3,P2,P1,P0 represent the product, and MUL performs unsigned multiplication. In contrast with this program, performing multiprecision signed or unsigned multiplication using *signed* multiplication as a primitive is more difficult.

A division instruction is also provided in most processors. Again, either signed or unsigned division or both may be provided. As in the algorithms in Section 4.9, a division instruction divides a double-word dividend by a single-word divisor, producing single-word quotient and remainder. The overflow bit is set if the divisor is zero or if the quotient requires more than one word to represent. Signed division is usually performed so that the remainder has the same sign as the dividend. A typical division instruction has the format

```
DIV     Rn,src          Rn+1 := Rn,Rn+1 DIV src;
                        Rn := Rn,Rn+1 MOD src;
```

TABLE 8–7 Multiprecision unsigned multiplication subroutine for 6809.

```
*       Multiply XH,XL by YH,YL and store product in P3,P2,P1,P0.
*       All variables are one byte long, stored in memory.
*
DBLMUL  LDA     XL          P1,P0 := XL*YL;
        LDB     YL
        MUL                 {Multiply A by B, leave product in A,B.}
        STB     P0          {High-order prod in A, low-order in B.}
        STA     P1
        LDA     XL          P2,P1 := 0,P1 + XL*YH;
        LDB     YH
        MUL
        ADDB    P1
        STB     P1
        ADCA    #0          {This operation can't produce a carry.}
        STA     P2
        LDA     YL          P3,P2,P1 := 0,P2,P1 + 0,YL*XH;
        LDB     XH
        MUL
        ADDB    P1
        STB     P1
        ADCA    P2          {This operation can produce a carry.}
        STA     P2
        LDA     #0          {CLRA no good -- it would also clear C.}
        ADCA    #0          {Add in carry.}
        STA     P3          {Previous operation can't carry.}
        LDA     XH          P3,P2 := P3,P2 + XH*YH;
        LDB     YH
        MUL
        ADDB    P2
        STB     P2
        ADCA    P3          {Carry is impossible here too.}
        STA     P3
        RTS                 {Done, return.}
```

where Rn,Rn+1 is a register pair and src is a single-word divisor in a register or memory.

Like multiplication, signed division can be performed using unsigned division as a primitive. However, there is no obvious way to perform multi-precision division using a shorter division instruction as a primitive.

8.11 DECIMAL ARITHMETIC

Two binary-coded decimal (BCD) digits may be packed into a byte, with the high-order digit on the left; decimal numbers with any desired number of digits may then be represented by strings of bytes. Although few microprocessors have instructions that directly add packed-BCD numbers, most have a Decimal adjust (DAA) instruction that can be used in conjunction with normal binary addition of bytes. For example, suppose two 2-digit numbers PH,PL and QH,QL are stored in bytes P and Q. Then P and Q may be combined by normal binary addition to produce a sum A as shown in Figure 8–9. During the addition the C bit is set to the carry out of bit 7 and the H (half carry) bit is set to the carry between bits 3 and 4. The DAA instruction examines the states of C and H and restores A to valid packed BCD, so that the packed BCD numbers P and Q may be added by the 6809 instructions below:

```
LDA     P              Get P byte.
ADDA    Q              Add Q byte.
DAA                    Decimal adjust sum byte in A.
```

The DAA instruction adjusts the contents of A to be a proper packed-BCD sum AH,AL as follows:

(1) If the half-carry bit H is 1, then PL plus QL exceeded 15_{10}; AL is a valid BCD digit but it is off by 6. This error is corrected by adding 6 to AL; no correction of AH is required since a carry has already occurred.

(2) If AL is between 10_{10} and 15_{10}, it is not a valid BCD digit. This error is corrected by adding 6 to AL, setting H to 1, and adding 1 to AH to reflect

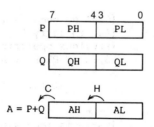

FIGURE 8–9 BCD interpretation of a sum of two bytes.

TABLE 8–8 Examples of decimal addition using binary addition and DAA.

	Example 1		Example 2		Example 3		Example 4	
P	0100 0110	46	0011 1001	39	0101 1000	58	1001 0111	97
Q	0101 0010	52	0100 0101	45	0111 1001	79	0110 1000	68
A=P+Q	1001 1000	98	0111 1110	7E	1101 0001	D1	1111 1111	FF
C,H	0 0		0 0		0 1		0 0	
DAA	1001 1000	98	1000 0100	84	0011 0111	137	0110 0101	165
C,H	0 0		0 1		1 1		1 1	

the carry that should have occurred; this operation sets the C bit if AH was 15_{10} before 1 was added.

(3) If C is now 1, then PH plus QH exceeded 15_{10}; AH is a valid BCD digit but it is off by 6. This error is corrected by adding 6 to AH.

(4) If AH is between 10_{10} and 15_{10}, it is corrected by adding 6 to AH and setting C to 1 to reflect the carry that should have occurred.

Table 8–8 gives some examples of how DAA works. Notice that if the sum of the two 2-digit numbers exceeds 99_{10}, then the C bit will be set, so that multiprecision BCD addition can be accomplished with ADDC instructions. For example, suppose that two 6-digit BCD numbers P and Q are stored as 3-byte quantities P2,P1,P0 and Q2,Q1,Q0. Then a 6-digit sum S2,S1,S0 may be computed by the subroutine in Table 8–9.

Packed-BCD numbers may also be subtracted, but the correction rules are different from those for addition (and left as an exercise for the reader). In the Z8000, an extra condition bit D indicates whether an addition or subtrac-

TABLE 8–9 Subroutine to add 6-digit numbers on the 6809.

```
*       P is a 6-digit BCD number in P2,P1,P0.
*       Likewise Q is a 6-digit BCD number in Q2,Q1,Q0.
*       Sum S = P+Q is stored in S2,S1,S0.
*
ADD6D   LDA     P0
        ADDA    Q0              Add rightmost digits of P and Q.
        DAA                     Adjust.
        STB     S0              Save rightmost digits of S.
        LDA     P1
        ADCA    Q1              Add middle digits, including carry.
        DAA                     Adjust.
        STA     S1              Save middle digits.
        LDA     P2
        ADCA    Q2              Add leftmost digits, including carry.
        DAA                     Adjust.
        STA     S2              Save leftmost digits.
        RTS                     Done, C=1 if result exceeded 6 digits.
```

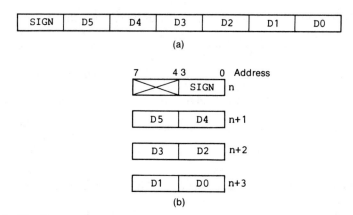

FIGURE 8–10 Representation of a signed BCD number, six digits plus sign: (a) conventional representation; (b) memory addresses.

tion occurred most recently, so that the DAA instruction can operate according to the appropriate rules. The 8086 simply has two DAA-type instructions, one that performs the correction steps for addition, the other for subtraction.

Signed BCD numbers may be represented in the signed-magnitude system. Figure 8–10 shows one way that signed-magnitude BCD numbers may be stored in memory. In order to carry out the rules for signed-magnitude addition and subtraction, the operands' signs must be checked first. When P and Q are added, there are four separate cases (and instruction sequences) implied by the signs of P and Q.

Signed BCD numbers can be added directly by the subroutine in Table 8–9 if they are represented in the 10's-complement number system. Subtraction may be performed by complementing the subtrahend and then adding. The 10's complement of a 6-digit number stored in bytes P2,P1,P0 can be obtained as shown in Table 8–10, where the leftmost digit is the sign — 0000 if positive, 1001 if negative. The program first computes the 9s' complement of P2,P1,P0 and then adds 1 to obtain the 10's complement.

REFERENCES

Information on computer operation types is widely scattered; most computer engineers and architects learn about different operation types through their experience on different computers. The purpose of this chapter has been to bring some of this information together in a reasonable, structured format.

A considerable amount of study has been devoted to the design of compact, efficient, and well-structured computer instruction sets. In "A Design Philosophy for Microcomputer Architectures" [*Computer*, Vol. 10, No. 2, February 1977], Dennis Allison makes the case (as have many others) for language-directed machine design — fitting the machine instructions and fea-

TABLE 8-10   Subroutine to compute the 10's complement of P on the 6809.

```
*          P is a 10's-complement BCD number, 5 digits plus sign,
*          stored in P2,P1,P0. This subroutine computes its
*          10's complement and leaves the result in P2,P1,P0.
*

NEG6D   LDA    #99H        P2 := 99H - P2; {9s' complement}
        SUBA   P2
        STA    P2
        LDA    #99H        P1 := 99H - P1; {9s' complement}
        SUBA   P1
        STA    P1
        LDA    #99H        A := 99H - P0; {9s' complement}
        SUBA   P0
        ADDA   #1          P0 := A + 1; {10's complement}
        DAA                {Adjust}
        STA    P0
        LDA    P1          P1 := P1 + C; {Propagate carries}
        ADCA   #0
        DAA                {Adjust}
        STA    P1
        LDA    P2          P2 := P2 + C; {Propagate carries}
        ADCA   #0
        DAA                {Adjust}
        STA    P2
        RTS                {Done, result in P2,P1,P0}
*                          {Overflow if A = 10H;  Why?}
```

tures to the high-level language (or languages) that will most frequently run on it. Microprocessor architects have also received guidance from instruction-frequency studies such as Leonard J. Shustek's "Analysis and Performance of Computer Instruction Sets" [Ph.D. thesis, Stanford University, 1978, available from University Microfilms, Ann Arbor, MI].

The detailed specification of condition bit settings is still more of an art than a science. Most contemporary microprocessors base their condition bits on the PDP-11, but the PDP-11 has problems of its own, as described in "The PDP-11: A Case Study of How *Not* to Design Condition Codes," by Robert Russell [*Proc. 5th Annual Symp. on Computer Architecture*, IEEE Publ. No. 78CH1284-9C, April 1978]. A discussion of the considerations that influenced the design of the 68000 condition bits appears in Appendix A of the *MC68000 16-bit Microprocessor User's Manual* by Motorola.

EXERCISES

8.1   The Z8000 has a combined condition bit P/V that is set according to parity by some operations, and two's-complement overflow by others. The TESTB instruction sets P/V according to parity. Why is this undesirable in the vast majority of programs?

8.2   The Z8000 P/V bit traces its origin to Zilog's Z80, an enhanced version of the
      Intel 8080. The 8080 had a P bit but not V, making signed conditional branches
      very difficult to program. The Z80 "fixed" the problem by using the existing P bit
      to indicate overflow after arithmetic instructions, hence the name P/V. For com-
      patibility with the Z80, the Z8000 kept P/V instead of having separate P and V
      bits, leading to the problem with the TESTB instruction. Now the question: How
      did Intel's successor to the 8080, the 8086, solve the P/V problem? Is it a good
      solution?

8.3   What is the arithmetic weight of the C bit after a 16-bit unsigned addition? After a
      16-bit unsigned subtraction?

8.4   The instruction CMP src TO dst in the Motorola 68000 performs the same opera-
      tion as SUB src FROM dst. Why should it do just the opposite?

8.5   Modify the SORT program in Table 7–3 so that it sorts unsigned numbers in the
      range 1 through 255, terminating on a 0 input.

8.6   Show how to translate the following Pascal CASE statement into assembly lan-
      guage by using a jump instruction with indirect addressing:

```
CASE select OF
  1: statementA;
  2,3,8: statementB;
  4,7: statementC;
  5: statementD;
  6: statementE;
END;
```

8.7   In *threaded code*, a contiguous sequence of subroutine calls is replaced by a
      table of subroutine starting addresses, for example:

```
*       NON-THREADED              THREADED
*
*       Subroutine calls:         A "thread":
FIRST   JSR    SUBR1       FIRST  FCW    SUBR1
        JSR    SUBR2              FCW    SUBR2
        JSR    SUBR3              FCW    SUBR3
        JSR    SUBR1              FCW    SUBR1
        JSR    SUBR3              FCW    SUBR3
        ...                       ...
        JSR    SUBR27             FCW    SUBR27
END     JMP    1000H              FCW    1000H    Return to op. sys.
*
*       Typical subroutine format:
SUBR1   LDA    VAR         SUBR1  LDA    VAR      First instruction.
        ...                       ...
        RTS                       JMP    @(X)+    Auto-increment
*                                                 indirect addressing.
*       To get started:
MAIN    JMP    FIRST       MAIN   LDX    #FIRST   Start of thread.
                                  JMP    @(X)+
```

Explain what's going on here, and then comment on the speed and size of threaded code compared to non-threaded code.

8.8   Optimize the H8000 BCNT1S subroutine in Table 5–16 by using the Z8000 Bit Test (BIT) instruction.

8.9   Rewrite the H6809 BCNT1S subroutine in Table 5–10 so that it counts ones by a series of eight rotations and tests.

8.10   Write an assembly language program that initializes a table N1S[0..255] of bytes, where N1S[i] contains the number of ones in the binary representation of i. Use a series of eight rotations and tests to compute the number of ones for each entry.

8.11   Modify the FNDPRM program in Table 7–5 so that it finds all primes between 2 and 8000 still using only a 1000-byte PRIME array, by packing eight boolean array components per byte.

8.12   Write an assembly language subroutine that computes all the prime factors of an unsigned integer N. Use the algorithm below.

```
PROCEDURE Factors (N : integer);
  VAR rem, quot, I : integer;
  BEGIN
     WHILE N>=2 DO
       BEGIN
          I := 1
          REPEAT {Try dividing by integers from 2 to N.}
            I:=I+1;
            {The next three lines divide N by I, yielding
             a quotient quot and a remainder rem.}
            quot := 0; rem := N;
            WHILE rem>=I DO
               BEGIN rem := rem-I; quot := quot+1 END;
            {Try values of I until we find one that divides N evenly.}
          UNTIL rem = 0;
          {The above statement will terminate when I=N, worst case.}
          writeln(I); {Output a prime factor.}
          N := quot;   {Set N to be the quotient last found.}
       END;
  END;
```

8.13   Write a sequence of 6809 instructions that divides an 8-bit signed integer in A by two, and truncates both positive and negative numbers towards zero, so that $-1 \div 2 = 0$.

8.14   Translate the algorithm in Table 4–6, 7, 9, or 10 into an assembly language program for the 6809, Z8000, or any other processor.

8.15   Does the following 6809 instruction sequence correctly negate a 2-byte two's-complement integer XH, XL? Justify your answer.

```
                  COM    XH
                  NEG    XL
                  BNE    SKIP
                  INC    XH
          SKIP    ...
```

8.16 The following 6809 subroutine for adding two 3-byte integers P2,P1,P0 and
     Q2,Q1,Q0 fails for some values of P and Q. Explain why and fix it.

```
MY3SUMS LDA    P0                    Add low-order bytes.
        ADDA   Q0
        STA    S0                    Save low-order sum.
        LDA    P1                    Add middle bytes.
        BCC    SKIP1
        INCA                         Add 1 to A if C=1.
SKIP1   ADDA   Q1
        STA    S1                    Save middle byte of sum.
        LDA    P2                    Add high-order bytes.
        BCC    SKIP2
        INCA                         Add 1 to A if C=1.
SKIP2   ADDA   Q2
        STA    S2                    Save high-order byte of sum.
        RTS                          Done, return.
```

8.17 Explain why C, V, and N indicate the true status of the 24-bit result when the
     (corrected) subroutine above returns to the calling program, but Z does not.

8.18 Fix the 6809 subroutine in the exercise above so that it works correctly, and so
     that when the subroutine returns, Z indicates the correct status of the 24-bit
     result. (C, V, and N must still be correct also.)

8.19 Write a subroutine to negate a 24-bit two's-complement integer P on the 6809,
     storing the result back into P. The variable P should be stored in three succesive
     bytes of memory.

8.20 The following two instruction sequences subtract unsigned integers and test the
     result. Do they have the same effect?

```
        LDA    UNS1                  LDA    UNS2
        SUBA   UNS2                  NEGA
        BHS    LABEL                 ADDA   UNS1
                                     BHS    LABEL
```

8.21 Rewrite the H6809 multiplication program in Table 5–4 so that it produces a
     2-byte result PRODH,PRODL. You may use any 6809 instruction except MUL, and
     the new program should still perform multiplication by repeated addition.

8.22 Rewrite the H8000 multiplication program in Table 5–14 so that it produces a
     2-byte result in RH2,RL2. You may use any Z8000 instruction except MULT, and
     the new program should still perform multiplication by repeated addition.

8.23 Write a binary-to-ASCII conversion algorithm along the lines of Exercise 5.13 that uses division by 10 to form the decimal digits (see also Section 4.3). Use this algorithm to develop an assembly language binary-to-ASCII conversion routine for the Z8000 or any other processor with a divide instruction.

8.24 Do Exercise 8.12 on a machine that has a division instruction instead of using successive subtraction.

8.25 State the rule for detecting overflow when 10's-complement packed-BCD numbers are added.

9

SUBROUTINES
AND PARAMETERS

Subroutines are the key to the structure of programs in any language, high or low level. A *subroutine* is a sequence of instructions that is defined and stored only once in a program, but which may be invoked (or *called*) from one or more places in the program. Two examples of frequently-used subroutines in a typical computer are the instruction sequences that write a character to and read a character from a terminal.

One advantage of using subroutines should be obvious: program size is reduced by storing a commonly-used sequence only once. Instead of repeating the entire sequence each time it is needed, only a single instruction or short sequence of instructions is needed to call the subroutine. Another advantage is crucial in the development of large programs: individual tasks can be defined and processed by subroutines with well-defined interfaces and interactions with the rest of the program. In this way, different programmers can work on different subroutines (i.e., tasks), and individual subroutines can be written, debugged, optimized, and modified, more or less independently from the rest of the program. Indeed, the development of a large program would be virtually impossible without a subroutine mechanism to decompose large tasks into a collection of smaller ones.

All of the advantages of subroutines are amplified by the use of parameters. A *parameter* is a "dummy variable" in the subroutine definition, simply a place-holder whose identity is bound to a real variable or value each time the subroutine is called. The dummy variable in the subroutine definition is called a *formal parameter*, while the variable or value used on a particular call is called an *actual parameter*. Since different actual parameters may be specified on each call of a subroutine, the same subroutine may be used to perform identical processing on many different sets of data. For example, the subroutine PrintAvg(x,y) could be defined to print the average of two formal parameters x and y. Calling PrintAvg with three different sets of actual parameters would print three different results: PrintAvg(1,5) prints 3; PrintAvg(17,100) prints 58.5; and if a=26 and b=58, PrintAvg(a,b) prints 42.

Early in Chapter 2 we showed Pascal programs with ''subroutines'' called procedures and functions. We have been using Pascal procedures and functions informally ever since. In the first part of this chapter we discuss Pascal procedures and functions in more depth, both to obtain a better understanding of Pascal and to see how procedures and functions relate to assembly language subroutines. We emphasize both areas for a number of reasons:

- Familiarity with the structure of Pascal procedures and functions can help a programmer improve the structure of corresponding assembly language subroutines.

- Pascal procedures and functions can be useful documentation aids for assembly language programs.

- Assembly language parameter-passing conventions can explain some of the mysteries of the run-time environment of a high-level language. For example, why do the values of local variables in a Pascal procedure become undefined each time the procedure is exited? We'll find out in Section 9.3.6.

- A good understanding of both high-level and assembly language parameter-passing conventions is required when a programmer links together high-level and assembly language program modules to perform a task.

9.1 PROCEDURES AND FUNCTIONS IN PASCAL

9.1.1 Procedures

A Pascal *procedure* is a program-defined sequence of statements that can be invoked by a single statement, called a *procedure statement*. A procedure is defined in the *procedure and function declaration part* of a program block as shown in Figure 9–1. The *block* in a procedure declaration consists of declarations and a statement part, the same as a program block. The *identifier* names the procedure, while the *parameter list* gives the names and types of zero or more formal parameters, as described in the next section. The

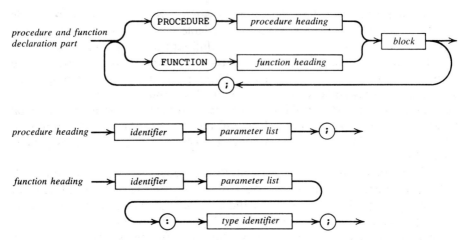

FIGURE 9-1 Procedure and function declaration part syntax diagram.

procedure may be invoked (called) by a *procedure statement* which simply gives its name and any actual parameters to be substituted for the formal parameters, as shown in Figure 9–2. In general, a procedure (or function) must be defined before being invoked.[1]

The declarations in a procedure block define constants, variables, types, and additional procedures and functions that are all *local* to the current procedure. Such local items may not be referenced outside the scope of the current procedure; if items with the same names already exist outside, then they are redefined within the procedure without affecting their external definitions. If a procedure definition references an item not defined within the procedure, the item must have been defined outside.

Table 9–1 shows some examples of the scope rules. The global variables common and maxi are used within the scope of procedure ProcA. However, the global variable maxi is redefined within the scope of ProcB. The variable temp, which is local to ProcA, is erroneously used in ProcB and in the main program. Although the scope rules allow multiple uses of the same identifier, it is still best for clarity and correctness to use unique identifier names in different procedures.

The statement part of a procedure block indicates the actions performed each time the procedure is invoked. The values of all local variables are undefined each time the statement part is entered; they are not preserved between successive calls of the procedure.

---

[1]Unlike assembly language, the syntax of Pascal was defined so that a program can be compiled by a one-pass algorithm. Since labels, constants, types, variables, and procedures and functions must all be defined before they are used, there are no forward references. However, if two procedures call each other, then neither can be defined before being invoked. Pascal gets around this problem as described in Section 9.4.

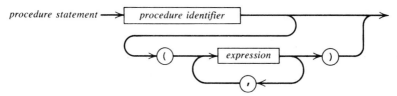

FIGURE 9–2 Procedure statement syntax.

Table 9–2 contains a program that removes spaces from input text. The program is rewritten in Table 9–3 using a procedure SkipSpaces to replace the innermost REPEAT statement. In the program body, the line "SkipSpaces" is the procedure statement; when it is encountered, the programmer-defined sequence (i.e., the REPEAT statement) is executed. The program actually became longer by using a procedure in this example, but there are still several advantages to using procedures in general:

- A well-chosen procedure name contributes to program readability by concisely describing the operation being performed.

- Partitioning a program into a hierarchical structure of procedures with well-defined interfaces and interactions makes the program easier to design, debug, maintain, and modify.

TABLE 9–1 Examples of scope rules for procedures.

```
PROGRAM ScopeRules (input,output);
VAR common, maxi : integer;

PROCEDURE ProcA;
VAR temp, x : integer;
  BEGIN
    ...
    x := maxi;            {uses global 'maxi'}
    common := temp + x;   {global 'common', local 'temp', 'x'}
  END;

PROCEDURE ProcB;
VAR maxi, mini : integer; {'maxi' redefined locally}
  BEGIN
    ...
    mini := maxi;    {OK – 'mini' and 'maxi' both local}
    temp := 0; {error – 'temp' undefined in current scope}
    ...
  END;

BEGIN
  read(common,maxi);   {OK – initialize globals}
  temp := 10; {error – 'temp' undefined in current scope}
  ...
END.
```

TABLE 9–2 Pascal program to remove spaces from input text.

```
PROGRAM RemSpace (input,output);
{Remove spaces from input text terminated by a period.}
VAR inChar : char;
BEGIN
  REPEAT
    REPEAT read(inChar) UNTIL inChar <> ' ';
    write(inChar);
  UNTIL inChar = '.';
END.
```

- If a procedure is invoked more than once, program size is reduced compared to the alternative of repeating the procedure body for each invocation.

To illustrate the above ideas, Table 9–4 shows a more complex program for processing spaces. Instead of being discarded, strings of spaces are converted to the character "#" followed by a letter corresponding to the number of spaces in the string. Also, the main program uses a WHILE instead of a REPEAT statement, so that the terminating period is not printed. This example illustrates a number of concepts:

- The procedure has no parameters, but it communicates with the main program via the global variable inChar.

- The procedure has one local variable scnt, whose value it reinitializes each time it is called.

- The procedure is called from two different places in the main program, the first place to "prime" the WHILE-loop.

TABLE 9–3 Removing spaces with a procedure.

```
PROGRAM RemSpaceProc (input,output);
{Remove spaces from input text terminated by a period.}
VAR inChar : char;

PROCEDURE SkipSpaces;
  BEGIN
    REPEAT read(inChar) UNTIL inChar <> ' ';
  END;

BEGIN
  REPEAT
    SkipSpaces;
    write(inChar);
  UNTIL inChar = '.';
END.
```

TABLE 9–4 Program to compress strings of spaces.

```
PROGRAM Compress (input,output);
{Compress a series of spaces in input text terminated by a period.}
VAR inChar : char;

PROCEDURE SkipSpaces;
   {A series of 1 to 26 spaces is translated into '#' followed by a
   character 'A' to 'Z'. Longer series are truncated to 26 spaces.}
   VAR scnt : integer;
   BEGIN
     scnt := -1;
     REPEAT
       read(inChar); scnt := scnt + 1;
     UNTIL inChar <> ' ';
     IF scnt > 26 THEN scnt := 26;
     IF scnt > 0 THEN write('#',chr(ord('A')-1+scnt));
   END;

BEGIN
  SkipSpaces;
  WHILE inChar <> '.' DO
    BEGIN
      write(inChar);
      SkipSpaces;
    END;
END.
```

• The procedure may be modified to do a better job of space compression
  without changing the main program (see Exercise 9.1).

9.1.2 Functions

A *function* is a programmer-defined sequence of statements that assigns
a value to the function name (i.e., *returns* a value). A function is defined much
like a procedure, as shown in Figure 9–1. The *function heading* is like a
procedure heading, but it also must specify the *type* of the value returned by
the function. The function name (*identifier*) must be assigned a value of this
type within the function block. Like a procedure block, a function block may
have its own local constants, types, variables, and subservient procedures and
functions.

The main difference between procedures and functions is in the way
they are invoked. Whenever the function name and actual-parameter list appear in an expression in the calling program, the function statement part is
executed, and the last value assigned to the function name in the function
statement part is returned to the expression evaluation.

Table 9–5 shows a program that uses a function to read the next
nonspace character of input text. The variable inChar is needed since the

TABLE 9–5 Removing spaces with a function.

```
PROGRAM RemSpaceFunc (input,output);
{Remove spaces from input text terminated by a period.}
VAR inChar : char;

FUNCTION NextNonspace : char;
  VAR tempChar : char;
  BEGIN
    REPEAT read(tempChar) UNTIL tempChar <> ' ';
    NextNonspace := tempChar;
  END;
BEGIN
  REPEAT
    inChar := NextNonspace;
    write(inChar);
  UNTIL inChar = '.';
END.
```

function is invoked *every* time the function name appears in an expression. The following main program, although syntactically correct, would read two nonspace characters per iteration but write only one of them:

```
BEGIN
  REPEAT write(NextNonspace) UNTIL NextNonspace = '.';
END.
```

The local variable tempChar and the assignment statement in the function statement part in Table 9–5 are also necessary. The alternative function statement part,

```
  BEGIN
    REPEAT read(NextNonspace) UNTIL NextNonspace <> ' ';
  END;
```

would not use the value just assigned to NextNonSpace in the comparison. Instead, it would cause a recursive call of the function to itself (see Section 9.4). Unless recursive calls are desired, the function name must not appear in expressions in the function statement part.

9.2 PARAMETERS IN HIGH-LEVEL LANGUAGE PROGRAMS

9.2.1 Pascal Parameters

Both procedures and functions in Pascal handle parameters in the same way. A procedure or function declaration indicates formal parameters in a *parameter list*, as shown by the syntax diagram in Figure 9–3. If there are no

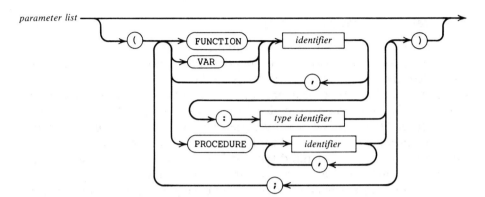

FIGURE 9-3 Parameter list syntax diagram.

parameters, then the parameter list is empty, as in the examples in the previous section. If there are one or more parameters, then each formal parameter is listed with its type as shown in the examples below:

```
PROCEDURE PrintAvg (x : real; y : real);
PROCEDURE FindChar (target : char; terminator : char; max : integer);
FUNCTION Xor (p : boolean; q : boolean) : boolean;
FUNCTION Power (x : real; n : integer) : real;
FUNCTION Prime (num : integer) : boolean;
```

If two or more formal parameters of the same type appear successively, the list may be abbreviated:

```
PROCEDURE PrintAvg (x,y : real);
PROCEDURE FindChar (target,terminator : char; max : integer);
FUNCTION Xor (p,q : boolean) : boolean;
```

Formal parameters may appear in any order and parameters of the same type need not be grouped together. However, when a procedure or function is called, the actual parameters must be listed in parentheses in the same order as in the definition:

```
VAR
  a,b : real; i,j,len : integer; f1,f2,f3 : boolean;
BEGIN
  ...
  PrintAvg(a,b);
  FindChar('t','.',len);
  f3 := Xor(f1,f2);
  a := Power(a*b,i+j);
  f1 := Prime(j+1);
  ...
```

9.2.2 Value Parameters

Pascal supports four kinds of parameters, listed in Table 9–6. The examples above have shown only *value parameters*. When a value parameter is specified, the actual parameter in the procedure call may be any expression whose result is the same type as the formal parameter. A constant or variable of this type is the simplest example of such an expression. When the procedure is called, the expression is evaluated and the resulting value is *copied* into a parameter area and passed to the procedure. Copying takes place even if the result is a large structured type such as an array. The procedure may modify the formal parameter via assignment statements, but this affects only the copy stored in the parameter area. For example, the program shown in Table 9–7 computes the value of n^2 for each n. When Fact is executed, the value of n is not disturbed even though the copy of n in the parameter area is eventually decremented to 1.

9.2.3 Variable Parameters

Value parameters are the appropriate choice for passing inputs to a procedure or function. However, it is often necessary for a procedure to pass output results to the caller by using one or more parameters. A classical example of this requirement is the swapping procedure shown in Table 9–8. The Swap procedure declares *variable parameters* x and y. When a variable parameter is specified in a Pascal procedure or function, the actual parameter used in calls must be a *variable* of the corresponding type. The *address* of the variable, not a copy of its value, is passed to the procedure, and all statements in the procedure manipulate the variable directly. Thus, the program in Table 9–8 does actually swap the values of a and b and prints "2 1". If value parameters were used in the procedure definition, the program would print "1 2".

TABLE 9–6   Kinds of parameters in Pascal.

Kind of Formal Parameter	Syntax	Required Actual Parameter	Effect of Assignment in Procedure
value	`identifier : type`	expression	local
variable	`VAR identifier : type`	variable	variable changed
procedure	`PROCEDURE identifier`	procedure name	not allowed
function	`FUNCTION identifier : type`	function name	not allowed

TABLE 9–7 Factorial and square program.

```
PROGRAM FactorialsAndSquares (input,output);
VAR n : integer;

FUNCTION Fact (i : integer) : real;
  VAR prod : real;
  BEGIN
    prod := 1;
    WHILE i>1 DO
      BEGIN prod:=prod*i; i:=i-1 END;
    Fact := prod;
  END;

BEGIN
  read(n);
  WHILE n>0 DO      {Pass a copy of n to Fact}
    BEGIN writeln(n,Fact(n),n*n); read(n) END;
END.
```

9.2.4 Procedure and Function Parameters

Pascal also allows procedure and function names to be passed as parameters. Table 9–9 gives a contrived example of a "using-procedure" that accepts the name of a "passed-procedure" as a parameter. Procedures and functions are seldom used as parameters in Pascal, but when they are, several precautions must be observed:

- If a passed-procedure has parameters, they may only be value parameters.

TABLE 9–8 Program using a swapping procedure.

```
PROGRAM Swapping (input,output);
VAR a,b : integer;
PROCEDURE Swap (VAR x,y : integer);
  VAR t : integer;
  BEGIN
    t := x;
    x := y;
    y := t;
  END;

BEGIN
  a := 1;  b := 2;
  Swap(a,b);     {Pass the addresses of a,b to Swap}
  write(a,b);
END.
```

TABLE 9-9 Program with procedures passed as parameters.

```
PROGRAM ArrayProcs (input,output);
CONST len = 80;
VAR charBuffer : ARRAY [1..len] OF char;

PROCEDURE DoBuff (PROCEDURE proc); {'using-procedure'}
  VAR i : integer;
  BEGIN
    FOR i := 1 TO len DO proc(i);
  END;

PROCEDURE Init (i : integer); {'passed-procedure'}
  BEGIN
    charBuffer[i] := ' ';
  END;

PROCEDURE Readc (i : integer); {'passed-procedure'}
  BEGIN
    read(charBuffer[i]);
  END;

PROCEDURE Printc (i : integer); {'passed-procedure'}
  BEGIN
    write(charBuffer[i]);
  END;

BEGIN
  DoBuff(Init);
  DoBuff(Printc); {Print a blank line.}
  writeln;
  DoBuff(Readc); {Read and print a line.}
  DoBuff(Printc);
END.
```

- Only a procedure or function name is passed, not its parameters; therefore the parameters must be "filled in" by the using-procedure.

- The compiler does not necessarily check that the number of parameters required by passed-procedure equals the number of parameters assumed in the definition of the using-procedure.

9.2.5 Parameters in Other High-Level Languages

Parameter-passing conventions in other high-level languages may be similar to or different from Pascal's. For example, Algol has two methods. The *Algol Call by Value* method handles parameters just as Pascal handles value parameters. The *Algol Call by Name* method has no equivalent in Pascal. It is defined to have the same effect as a textual substitution of the actual parameters for the corresponding formal parameters in the subroutine;

this is called the *Replacement Rule*. Although this method allows procedures like Swap to be written in the same way that Pascal would use variable parameters, it is still somewhat different. For example, consider the effect of the replacement rule on the procedure body of Swap if next is an array of integers and we call Swap(i,next[i]):

```
BEGIN
  t := i;
  i := next[i];
  next[i] := t;
END;
```

The apparent intent of the call is to swap the values of i and next[i]. However, suppose that i=5, next[5]=4, and next[4]=0. Then calling Swap(i,next[i]) sets i to 4 (OK) while setting next[4] to 5 (wrong — we wanted to set next[5] to 5).

The *Fortran Call by Value* method is similar to Pascal and Algol Call by Value, except that the (possibly modified) value in the parameter area is copied back into the original actual parameter when the subroutine is completed. PL/1 has a method called *Call by Reference* which is similar in effect to the use of a Pascal variable parameter, except that it also allows an expression to be used as the actual parameter, temporarily allocating variable storage for the value of the expression.

The moral of the foregoing discussion is that a programmer must thoroughly understand the parameter-passing convention of a particular high-level language before writing any procedures that assign values to parameters. Fortunately for our purposes, Pascal variable and value parameters correspond nicely to the parameters most frequently used in assembly language subroutines. Value parameters correspond to numbers, characters, or other values passed to a subroutine, while variable parameters correspond to pointers or addresses. In the next section we shall discuss how parameters are passed in assembly language subroutines.

9.3 ASSEMBLY LANGUAGE SUBROUTINES AND PARAMETERS

9.3.1 Subroutine Calling Methods

In order to execute subroutines, a processor must have a means for a program to save a return address when the subroutine is called, and a way for the subroutine to jump to the return address when the subroutine is finished. Theoretically, subroutine return addresses could be handled by ordinary instructions, as shown in Table 9–10 for the 6809. Here the programmer has set up a convention for subroutine calling programs to save a return address in two reserved bytes at the beginning of the subroutine.

TABLE 9–10 How to call subroutines in the 6809 without using JSR and RTS.

```
*          By convention, a subroutine return address is deposited in
*          the first two bytes of the subroutine.  The first executable
*          instruction begins in the third byte of the subroutine.
*
MAIN       ...                        Main program.
           LDX     #RET1             Save return address.
           STX     SUBR
           JMP     SUBR+2            Jump to subroutine.
RET1       ...                        Return here when subroutine finishes.
           ...
           LDX     #RET2             Save return address again.
           STX     SUBR
           JMP     SUBR+2            Jump to subroutine.
RET2       ...                        Return here when subroutine finishes.
           ...
*
SUBR       RMB     2                 Save two bytes for return address.
           STA     P1                First executable instruction.
           ...
           LDX     SUBR              Get return address from loc. SUBR.
           JMP     @X                Jump to address contained in X.
```

Because subroutines are used so often, all modern processors have special built-in instructions for calling subroutines and returning from them. As we showed in Section 5.2.10, a pushdown stack is the natural data structure for saving subroutine return addresses. Most processors have a dedicated register (SP) that points into a stack of subroutine return addresses. The subroutine calling instructions (JSR or CALL) push return addresses onto the stack, and subroutine return instructions (RTS or RET) pop return addresses off the stack.

Processors that don't have a hardware stack pointer, such as the 9900, have subroutine calling instructions that save the return address in a specified processor register. When subroutine calls are nested, it is up to the programmer to save the contents of this register in dedicated memory locations or in a stack.

9.3.2 Subroutine Parameters

In the previous section we discussed several types of parameters used in Pascal procedures and functions. Table 9–11 shows the corresponding parameter types in assembly language subroutines.

The parameter types specified in Pascal procedure and function definitions should be called *input parameters*, because they are passed from a calling program to a subroutine. However, subroutines can also pass results to a calling program. For example, a Pascal function returns one value to the

TABLE 9-11 Parameters in Pascal and assembly language programs.

Pascal Parameter Type	Assembly Language Parameter Type
Value	Data value
Variable	Address of variable
Procedure or function	Address of procedure or function

calling program, while an assembly language subroutine can return many values. We'll call these values *output parameters*, *outputs*, or *results*.

To see the difference between variable parameters and value parameters, compare the swapping procedures in Table 9–12 and Table 9–13. In the first example, the main program passes the subroutine the addresses of the two variables; the subroutine accesses the variables by indirect addressing. In the second example, the main program passes copies of the variables to the subroutine, which the subroutine manipulates directly; the subroutine has no way to get at the original variables themselves.

The "Load Effective Address (LEA)" instruction found in many processors is very useful for passing variable parameters. For example, suppose that a programmer wanted to swap VARP and SCORE[J], where SCORE[1..100] is an array of bytes. Then the following main program statements in Table 9–12 would do the trick:

```
LDX    #VARP        X now has address of VARP.
LDY    J            Get index of array item J.
LEAY   SCORE-1(Y)   Y now has address of SCORE[J].
JSR    SWAP
```

Here the LEAY instruction loads Y with the address of SCORE[J] as computed at run time — the sum of J and the effective base address SCORE-1.

From these examples, it is apparent that all parameters in assembly language programs are really "values." With "variable" parameters, the "value" that is passed just happens to be the address of a variable. How parameters are classified doesn't make much difference, as long as the subroutine and calling program agree on how the parameters will be used.

9.3.3 Passing Parameters in Registers and Memory Locations

The simplest way for a program to pass parameters to a subroutine is to place them in the processor's registers. Likewise, the subroutine can return results to the calling program in the same way. This technique was used in the

TABLE 9–12 Swapping subroutine using variable parameters.

```
*         Swap two 8-bit variables x and y whose addresses
*         are passed in index registers X and Y.
SWAP      LDA    @X              Put x and y into A and B.
          LDB    @Y
          STA    @Y              Save A and B into y and x.
          STB    @X
          RTS
*
*         Main program -- swap the values of VARP and VARQ.
MAIN      ...
          LDX    #VARP           Address of VARP.
          LDY    #VARQ           Address of VARQ.
          JSR    SWAP
*         Values of VARP and VARQ are now swapped.
          ...
VARP      RMB    1               Reserve storage for VARP and VARQ.
VARQ      RMB    1
```

subroutines in the previous subsection and in Tables 5–10 and 5–16. Of course, the programmer must ensure that the calling program and the subroutine agree on which register contains each parameter. The register allocation for parameters is usually stated in a comment at the beginning of the subroutine. For example, subroutine WCNT1S in Table 5–10 states that the input parameter is passed in register X and the result in register A.

If a processor does not have enough registers to hold all of the input or output parameters of a subroutine, then dedicated memory locations may be used instead. These memory locations are associated with the subroutine

TABLE 9–13 Swapping subroutine using value parameters.

```
*         Swap two 8-bit values passed in registers A and B.
SWAP      STA    TEMP            Save value of A.
          TFR    B,A             Transfer B to A.
          LDB    TEMP            Put saved value of A into B.
          RTS
TEMP      RMB    1               Local variable.
*
*         Main program -- swap copies of the values of VARP and VARQ.
MAIN      ...
          LDA    VARP            Value of VARP.
          LDB    VARQ            Value of VARQ.
          JSR    SWAP
*         Copies of VARP and VARQ in A and B are
*         swapped, original VARP and VARQ untouched.
          ...
VARP      RMB    1               Reserve storage for VARP and VARQ.
VARQ      RMB    1
```

itself, not the calling program, so that each calling program places inputs and retrieves outputs in the same pre-arranged locations. For example, the 6809 DIVIDE subroutine in Table 6–8 expects the caller to place input parameters in locations DVND and DVSR, and it places outputs in locations QUOT and REM.

9.3.4 Parameter Areas

It is also possible to associate a parameter area with the calling program instead of the subroutine. In this case, the calling program places parameters in the parameter area and passes the subroutine the base address of the parameter area. For example, Table 9–14 shows a new version of the DIVIDE subroutine in which the calling program uses register X to pass the base address of the parameter area. Table 9–15 shows a program that calls this DIVIDE subroutine. Notice how the parameter area is associated with the calling program, not the DIVIDE subroutine. The calling program may use the

TABLE 9-14 6809 DIVIDE subroutine that uses a parameter area.

```
*            Input and output parameters are passed in a 5-byte parameter
*            area.  The base address of the parameter area is passed to
*            the subroutine in register X.  The offsets below define the
*            positions of each parameter in the parameter area.
*
DVND    EQU     0               2-byte dividend.
DVSR    EQU     2               1-byte divisor.
QUOT    EQU     3               1-byte quotient.
REM     EQU     4               1-byte remainder.
*
DIVIDE  LDA     #8              Initialize count.
        STA     CNT
        LDA     DVND(X)         Put dividend in A,B.
        LDB     DVND+1(X)
        CMPA    DVSR(X)         Will quotient fit in 1 byte?
        BLO     DIVLUP          Branch if it will.
        JMP     SYSOVF          Else report overflow to oper. sys.
DIVLUP  ASLB                    Left shift A,B with LSB:=0.
        ROLA                    A carry here from MSB means
        BCS     QUOT1             high DVND definitely > DVSR.
        CMPA    DVSR(X)         Compare high DVND with DVSR.
        BLO     QUOTOK          Quotient bit = 0 if lower.
QUOT1   INCB                    Else set quotient bit to 1.
        SUBA    DVSR(X)         And update high DVND.
QUOTOK  DEC     CNT             Decrement iteration count.
        BGT     DIVLUP          Continue until done.
        STA     REM(X)          Store remainder.
        STB     QUOT(X)         Store quotient.
        RTS                     Return.
SYSOVF  EQU     1800H           System overflow report address.
CNT     RMB     1               Local storage for counter.
```

TABLE 9–15 Program that calls DIVIDE.

```
*           Compute PDIVQ := P DIV Q; PMODQ := P MOD Q;
*              where all are 1-byte variables in memory.
DIVPQ   LDX     #PARMS          X points to parameter area.
        CLR     DVND(X)         Clear high-order dividend.
        LDA     P               Store low-order dividend.
        STA     DVND+1(X)
        LDA     Q               Store divisor.
        STA     DVSR(X)
        JSR     DIVIDE          Do the division.
        LDA     QUOT(X)         Save the quotient.
        STA     PDIVQ
        LDA     REM(X)          Save the remainder.
        STA     PMODQ
        ...
P       RMB     1               Storage for P, Q, PDIVQ, PMODQ
Q       RMB     1                  (all 1-byte variables).
PDIVQ   RMB     1
PMODQ   RMB     1
        ...
PARMS   RMB     5               Storage for parameter area.
```

same parameter area for other subroutines. If a main program calls many different subroutines, using a single parameter area saves memory compared with the alternative of allocating separate parameter variables for each subroutine. Of course, the parameter area must be big enough to hold the largest number of parameters used in any one subroutine.

Parameter areas are sometimes useful for subroutines that are stored in read-only memory (ROM). Since parameter values can't be stored into a ROM, it is more convenient to allocate storage for them with their calling programs in read/write memory (RWM).

One special form of parameter area is called an *in-line parameter area*. Here the parameters are stored in the calling program immediately following the subroutine calling instruction (JSR). The "return address" stored by JSR is really the address of the first parameter. Before returning, the subroutine must bump this return address value past the parameter area; presumably, the subroutine knows exactly how many memory bytes to skip over. In-line parameter areas should only be used if the actual parameters for any given subroutine call are always constant. If the actual parameters are variables, then the in-line parameter area must be modified each time the subroutine is called, impossible in ROM and undesirable even in RWM (some memory management systems enforce write protection on program areas).

9.3.5 Static and Dynamic Allocation

Storage allocation methods for subroutine parameters can be classified as static and dynamic. With *static allocation*, memory locations are reserved for the parameters of a particular subroutine or caller, and are unused at other times. Both versions of the DIVIDE subroutine above use static allocation. With *dynamic allocation*, parameters are stored in the designated area during subroutine execution, but the storage is available for other uses the rest of the time. Passing parameters in registers as in Tables 5–10 and 5–16 is the simplest form of dynamic allocation.

9.3.6 Stack-Oriented Parameter Passing Conventions

Placing parameters in a pushdown stack is a form of dynamic allocation used both by assembly language programmers and by compilers for block-structured high-level languages such as Algol and Pascal. Parameters can generally use the same pushdown stack as return addresses, since most processors have instructions to push, pop, and access arbitrary data in the return-address stack.

Figure 9–4 shows a typical use of a return-address stack for passing parameters. The calling program reserves space on the stack for any output parameters and then pushes input parameters onto the stack. After the subroutine is called, the stack has the state shown in Figure 9–4(a). An address register FP is now used as a *stack frame pointer* (or *frame pointer*). The

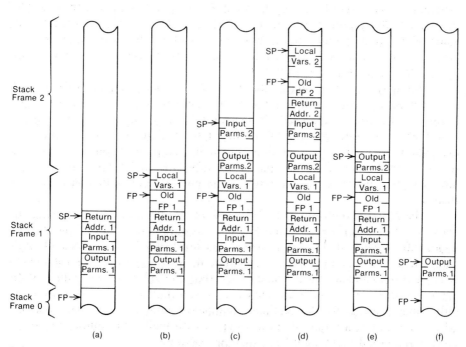

FIGURE 9–4 A pushdown stack with return address, parameters, and local variables: (a) just after calling SUBR1; (b) during execution of SUBR1; (c) just before a call to SUBR2; (d) during execution of SUBR2; (e) just after return from SUBR2; (f) just after return from SUBR1.

subroutine saves the old value of FP by pushing it onto the stack and then copies the value of SP into FP. The frame pointer provides a fixed reference for accessing parameters that does not change with SP as more items are pushed onto the stack. The region of the stack accessed during a subroutine's execution is called a *stack frame*.

As shown in Figure 9–4(b), local variables can also be pushed onto the stack during a subroutine's execution and accessed by offsets from FP. If a second (nested) subroutine is called, parameters are again pushed onto the stack and a new stack frame is created, as shown in Figure 9–4(c,d). As each subroutine returns, it "cleans up" the stack by

(1) Removing its local data by setting SP equal to FP.

(2) Restoring the old value of FP by popping it from the stack.

(3) Removing the input parameters from the stack and jumping to the return address, leaving only the output parameters on the stack.

The stack-oriented subroutine calling convention is illustrated by the DIVIDE subroutine in Table 9–16. Register X is used as the frame pointer. A program that calls DIVIDE is shown in Table 9–17. The state of the stack before the DIVIDE subroutine is called is shown in Figure 9–5(a). The calling program reserves two bytes on the stack for REM and QUOT and then pushes DVND and DVSR (Figure 9–5(b)) and calls DIVIDE. Then DIVIDE pushes the old value of the frame pointer and CNT onto the stack as shown in Figure 9–5(c). Upon return, the stack is cleaned up, leaving only the output parameters REM and QUOT as shown in Figure 9–5(d).

You may have noticed that the use of X as a frame pointer in Table 9–16 is somewhat superfluous since SP doesn't change throughout the subroutine's execution; we could have used SP instead of X by adding 1 to all the offsets. However, in a more general subroutine, intermediate results of expression evaluations and other computations might be temporarily pushed onto and popped from the stack, so that parameter offsets from SP would be continually changing. In this case, the fixed frame pointer (X) is much easier to use than SP.

The DIVIDE subroutines in Tables 9–14 and 9–16 both access parameters in a "parameter area," using based addressing with offsets from X. The major difference is that the parameter area for Table 9–14 is allocated statically when the program is assembled, while the parameter area for Table 9–16 is created dynamically on the stack each time the subroutine is called. With static parameter areas we need one for each subroutine; with a stack we need only enough storage for the maximum number of parameters that are "active" when subroutines are nested. In a program with many subroutines the stack convention could yield significant memory savings.

Procedures and functions in Pascal pass parameters using a stack-oriented convention similar to the one described above. Local variables are

TABLE 9–16 DIVIDE subroutine that passes parameters on a stack.

```
*          The offsets below define positions of parameters and local
*          variables in the stack relative to a frame pointer (reg. X).
CNT        EQU    -1
OLDFP      EQU    0            Old value of frame pointer.
RETADR     EQU    2            Return address.
DVSR       EQU    4            1-byte divisor (input).
DVND       EQU    5            2-byte dividend (input).
REM        EQU    7            1-byte remainder (output).
QUOT       EQU    8            1-byte quotient (output).
*
DIVIDE     PSHS   X            Push old frame pointer onto stack.
           TFR    S,X          Copy SP into X for new frame pointer.
           LDA    #8           Push initial count.
           PSHS   A
           LDA    DVND(X)      Put dividend in A,B.
           LDB    DVND+1(X)
           CMPA   DVSR(X)      Will quotient fit in 1 byte?
           BLO    DIVLUP       Branch if it will.
           JMP    SYSOVF       Else report overflow to oper. sys.
DIVLUP     ASLB                Left shift A,B with LSB:=0.
           ROLA                A carry here from MSB means
           BCS    QUOT1          high DVND definitely > DVSR.
           CMPA   DVSR(X)      Compare high DVND with DVSR.
           BLO    QUOTOK       Quotient bit = 0 if lower.
QUOT1      INCB                Else set quotient bit to 1.
           SUBA   DVSR(X)      And update high DVND.
QUOTOK     DEC    CNT(X)       Decrement iteration count.
           BGT    DIVLUP       Continue until done.
           STA    REM(X)       Store remainder.
           STB    QUOT(X)      Store quotient.
           TFR    X,S          Remove local variables.
           PULS   X            Restore frame pointer.
           PULS   Y            Get return address, save in Y.
           ADDS   #3           Remove input parms (add 3 to SP).
           JMP    @Y           Return to address contained in Y.
SYSOVF     EQU    1800H        System overflow report address.
```

also stored on the stack. This explains why the values of local variables are not preserved between successive invocations of the same procedure — the stack pointer may start at a different position on each invocation, so that the variables could actually be stored in different memory locations on different invocations.

9.3.7 Another Example: Queue Manipulation Subroutines

To conclude this section, we give a set of 6809 subroutines that manipulate queues, including "prologues" that explain how the subroutines work. A

TABLE 9–17 Program that calls stack-oriented DIVIDE.

```
*          Compute PDIVQ := P DIV Q; PMODQ := P MOD Q;
*             where all are 1-byte variables in memory.
DIVPQ      ADDS    #-2             Make room for output parms (SP:=SP-2).
           LDA     P               Push low-order dividend.
           PSHS    A
           CLRA                    Push high-order dividend = 0.
           PSHS    A
           LDA     Q               Push divisor.
           PSHS    A
           JSR     DIVIDE          Do the division.
           PULS    A               Pop remainder and store.
           STA     PMODQ
           PULS    A               Pop quotient and store.
           STA     PDIVQ
           ...
P          RMB     1               Storage for P, Q, PDIVQ, PMODQ
Q          RMB     1                  (all 1-byte variables).
PDIVQ      RMB     1
PMODQ      RMB     1
```

program that uses these subroutines will be presented in Section 11.6.3. In keeping with the philosophy that programs should be self-documenting, we leave you to read Table 9–18. Also see Section 12.3 for a discussion of the documentation conventions used here.

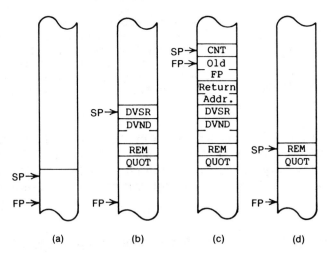

FIGURE 9–5 Stack contents during DIVPQ program: (a) at start; (b) just before calling DIVIDE; (c) after first four instructions of DIVIDE; (d) on return.

TABLE 9–18 Queue manipulation subroutines for the 6809.

```
* QUEUE MODULE
*
* This module contains three subroutines for manipulating queues
* of 8-bit bytes. A queue is defined by a queue descriptor table
* and a block of storage, as shown below.
*
```

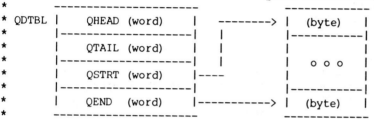

```
*
* Offsets in descriptor table:
*
QHEAD    EQU     0
QTAIL    EQU     2
QSTRT    EQU     4
QEND     EQU     6
*
* In this table, the last two words are constants, initialized at
* load time, that give the starting and ending addresses of the block
* of storage (buffer) reserved for the queue itself. The first and
* second words are reserved to store the queue head and tail (absolute
* memory addresses), and are manipulated by the subroutines.
*
* If a program defines several queues, it allocates a separate queue
* descriptor table and storage block for each one.  For example, the
* statements below define a 5-byte queue Q1 and a 100-byte queue Q2:
*
*Q1BLK   RMB     5              Storage block for Q1.
*Q1END   EQU     *-1            Last location in Q1 storage block.
*Q1DT    RMB     4              Q1 descriptor table -- QHEAD and QTAIL.
*        FCW     Q1BLK,Q1END                         QSTRT and QEND.
*Q2BLK   RMB     100            Storage block for Q2.
*Q2END   EQU     *-1            Last location in Q2 storage block.
*Q2DT    RMB     4              Q2 descriptor table -- QHEAD and QTAIL.
*        FCW     Q2BLK,Q2END                         QSTRT and QEND.
*
* Subroutines are provided to initialize a queue (QINIT), enqueue
* a byte (QENQ), and dequeue a byte (QDEQ).  Each subroutine must
* be passed the address of the descriptor table for the queue
* to be manipulated.
*
```

TABLE 9-18 (continued)

```
* SUBROUTINE QINIT -- Initialize a queue to be empty.
*
* INPUTS
*    #QDTBL -- The address of the queue descriptor table for the
*              queue to be initialized, passed in register X.
* OUTPUTS, GLOBAL DATA, LOCAL DATA -- None
* FUNCTIONS
*    (1) Initialize the queue to empty by setting QHEAD and QTAIL
*        in QDTBL equal to the first address in the queue buffer.
* REGISTERS AFFECTED -- Y, CC
* TYPICAL CALLING SEQUENCE
*        LDX    #Q1DT
*        JSR    QINIT
*
QINIT  LDY    QSTRT(X)       Load buffer starting address into Y.
       STY    QHEAD(X)       Store into QHEAD and QTAIL.
       STY    QTAIL(X)
       RTS                   Done, return.
*
* SUBROUTINE QENQ -- Enqueue one byte into a queue.
*
* INPUTS
*    #QDTBL -- The address of the queue descriptor table for the
*              queue to be manipulated, passed in register X.
*    QDATA  -- The byte to be enqueued, passed in register A.
* OUTPUTS
*    QFULL  -- 1 if the queue is already full, else 0;
*              passed in condition bit Z.
* GLOBAL DATA, LOCAL DATA -- None.
* FUNCTIONS
*    (1) If the queue described by QDTBL is full, set QFULL to 1.
*    (2) If the queue described by QDTBL is not full, enqueue QDATA
*        and set QFULL to 0.
* REGISTERS AFFECTED -- Y, CC
* TYPICAL CALLING SEQUENCE
*        LDX    #Q1DT          Enqueue byte ABYTE.
*        LDA    ABYTE
*        JSR    QENQ
*        BEQ    OVFL           Branch if queue is full.
*
QENQ   LDY    QTAIL(X)       Get queue tail.
       ADDY   #1             Bump to next free location.
       CMPY   QEND(X)        Wrap-around?
       BLS    QENQ1
       LDY    QSTRT(X)       Reinitialize on wrap-around.
QENQ1  CMPY   QHEAD(X)       Queue already full?
       BEQ    QENQ2          Return with Z=1 if full.
       STA    @QTAIL(X)      Else store QDATA.
       STY    QTAIL(X)       Update tail.
       CLRZ                  Set Z:=0 since not full.
QENQ2  RTS                   Return.
```

TABLE 9–18   (continued)

```
* SUBROUTINE QDEQ -- Dequeue one byte from a queue.
*
* INPUTS
*    #QDTBL -- The address of the queue descriptor table for the
*              queue to be manipulated, passed in register X.
* OUTPUTS
*    QEMPTY -- 1 if the queue is empty, else 0; passed in
*              condition bit Z.
*    QDATA  -- The byte dequeued, passed in register A.
* GLOBAL DATA, LOCAL DATA -- None.
* FUNCTIONS
*    (1) If the queue described by QDTBL is empty, set QEMPTY to 1.
*    (2) If the queue described by QDTBL is not empty, dequeue
*        QDATA and set QEMPTY to 0.
* REGISTERS AFFECTED -- A, Y, CC
* TYPICAL CALLING SEQUENCE
*         LDX    #Q1DT          Dequeue a byte into ABYTE.
*         JSR    QDEQ
*         BEQ    UNDFL          Branch if queue is empty.
*         STA    ABYTE
*
QDEQ      LDY    QHEAD(X)       Get queue head.
          CMPY   QTAIL(X)       Queue empty?
          BEQ    QDEQ2          Return with Z=1 if empty.
          LDA    @Y             Read QDATA byte from queue.
          ADDY   #1             Bump to next item in queue.
          CMPY   QEND(X)        Wrap-around?
          BLS    QDEQ1
          LDY    QSTRT(X)       Reinitialize on wrap-around.
QDEQ1     STY    QHEAD(X)       Save new value of head.
          CLRZ                  Set Z:=0 since not empty.
QDEQ2     RTS                   Return.
          END
```

9.4 RECURSION

9.4.1 Recursive Procedures and Functions

A procedure or function that calls itself is said to be *recursive*. The Pascal factorial function from Table 9–7 is redefined below as a recursive function:

```
FUNCTION Fact (i : integer) : real;
  BEGIN
    IF i <= 1 THEN Fact := 1 ELSE Fact := i * Fact(i-1);
  END;
```

Essential to this definition is a *basis part* that defines Fact(i) to be 1 for any i<=1. For larger i, Fact(i) is defined to be the product of i and Fact(i-1).

For example, to compute Fact(5) we must first compute Fact(4), which depends on Fact(3), which depends on Fact(2), which depends on Fact(1). The basis part ensures that we eventually reach a value of i for which Fact(i) does not depend on Fact(i-1), so that we can eventually terminate the recursive calls of Fact.

The example above illustrates *simple recursion*, using a procedure that calls itself directly. It is also possible for a procedure to call one or more intermediate procedures that eventually call it. This is called *indirect recursion* and is illustrated below.

```
PROCEDURE ProcA(x, y : integer);
   BEGIN
   ...
   ProcB(a);  {Call ProcB}
   ...
   END;

PROCEDURE ProcB(z : integer);
   BEGIN
   ...
   ProcA(b,c);  {Call ProcA}
   ...
   END;
```

Since Pascal requires a procedure to be defined before it is called, the above program fragment is syntactically incorrect as it stands. The programmer must inform the compiler of the forward reference by placing the following declaration before the definition of ProcA:

```
PROCEDURE ProcB(z : integer); forward;
```

The directive "forward" takes the place of the block that is normally required in the syntax of Figure 9–1. It alerts the compiler that the block defining ProcB is coming later. The parameter list is included in the forward declaration so that statements that refer to ProcB can be checked and compiled. Later, body of ProcB may be defined in the normal way, except that the parameter list is not repeated.

Block-structured languages such as Algol and Pascal allow all procedures and functions to be called recursively. Unstructured languages like Fortran usually do not permit recursion.

The recursive function definition above may be clever, but the iterative solution in Table 9–7 may be more efficient. In general, problems that have easily-stated iterative solutions are best solved iteratively. Recursion should be reserved for problems that are most clearly stated recursively or that have no obvious iterative solution. An example of such a problem is given in the next subsection.

9.4.2 Recursive Subroutines

Recursion can be utilized in assembly language subroutines, but it places constraints on the subroutine calling and parameter passing conventions that may be used. Return addresses, parameters, and local variables may *not* be stored in dedicated, static locations, because they would be wiped out the first time that the subroutine recursively called itself. Instead, a new area for the return address, parameters, and local variables must be allocated on each recursive call, and deallocated on each return. Hence, a pushdown stack is the appropriate data structure for storing these items.

A subroutine that stores its return address and all parameters and local variables using a stack convention such as the one in Section 9.3.6 can be called recursively without error. This explains why Pascal procedures can call each other recursively, and Fortran subprograms cannot; Fortran normally uses static memory allocation for parameters.

A pair of recursive subroutines can be used to analyze the game of NIM, a two-person game that begins with a heap of sticks. The players alternately remove sticks from the heap; the player who removes the last stick loses. The game is fully characterized by two parameters: NHEAP is the number of sticks initially in the heap, and NTAKE is the maximum number of sticks a player may take on each turn, the minimum being 1.

We would like to write a program that determines, given NHEAP and NTAKE, whether or not an intelligent first player (P1) can always win by making optimal moves. In order to formulate a recursive algorithm to make this determination, we first define a *winning position* for P1:

(1) If it is P1's turn and there are no sticks left, then the second player (P2) has just taken the last stick. This is a winning position for P1.

(2) If it is P1's turn and there is at least one winner among the new positions obtained by taking 1 to minimum(NTAKE,STICKSLEFT) sticks, then P1 can take the appropriate number of sticks and eventually win. This is a winning position for P1.

(3) If it is P2's turn and there are no sticks left, then P1 has just taken the last stick. This is *not* a winning position for P1.

(4) If it is P2's turn and at least one of the new positions obtained by taking 1 to minimum(NTAKE,STICKSLEFT) sticks is not a winner, P2 can take the appropriate number of sticks to keep P1 from winning. This is *not* a winning position for P1.

Steps 1 and 3 above form the basis parts of two recursive subroutines, P1TURN and P2TURN, that call each other. Each subroutine determines, given NTAKE and STICKSLEFT, whether or not the current position is a winning position for P1, assuming it is P*i*'s turn to move. The subroutines are coded in

6809 assembly language in Table 9–19. Input and output parameters are passed in registers, and local variables are saved in the stack at the beginning of each subroutine and restored on exit. A program can initialize NTAKE to any desired value and call P1TURN with the initial heap size in register A to determine whether or not the game is a guaranteed win for an intelligent first player, as in the example below.

```
              LDA    #5           Take 5 sticks maximum at a time.
              STA    NTAKE
              LDA    #30          Can I win if I start with 30 sticks?
              JSR    P1TURN
              BEQ    IWIN
ILOSE    ...
IWIN     ...
```

Recursive programs often perform a tremendous amount of useful computation with relatively little memory. For example, the NIM subroutines are short, they have only one global variable (NTAKE), and they never have more than about 4·NHEAP bytes on the stack. Yet called with NHEAP=30 and NTAKE=5, the two subroutines are executed a total of 1,687,501 times. Try to figure out whether P1 won or lost that game yourself!

9.5 COROUTINES

9.5.1 General Structure

So far we have discussed subroutines in the context of a master/slave relationship — a calling program (master) calls the subroutine (slave), which executes from beginning to end and returns to the calling program. In Pascal, subroutines (procedures and functions) are so subservient that they aren't even allowed to remember their own local data between successive calls. *Coroutines* replace this master/slave structure with a set of cooperating program modules with no identifiable master. Consider the following problem statement by R. W. Floyd:[3]

> Read lines of text, until a completely blank line is found. Eliminate redundant blanks between the words. Print the text, thirty characters to a line, without breaking words between lines.

According to Floyd, novice programmers take an unreasonably long time to solve this problem using typical programming languages. Even though both input and output are naturally expressed using levels of iteration, the input and output iterations do not mesh, which can make controlling the input and output an "undisciplined mess."

---

[3]"The Paradigms of Programming," *Comm. ACM*, Vol. 22, No. 8, August 1979, pp. 455-460.

TABLE 9-19 Recursive subroutines to analyze the game of NIM.

```
* Subroutine P1TURN determines if the current position
* is a winner, given NTAKE (global variable) and
* STICKSLEFT (passed in register A), assuming that it's
* P1's turn to move.  P1TURN saves registers A and B on
* entry and restores them on exit.  The result is returned
* in condition bit Z: 1 if a winning position, 0 otherwise.
*
P1TURN   PSHS   A,B          Save registers B and A on stack.
         TST    A            Any sticks left?
         BEQ    WIN          Return with Z=1 if none (we just won).
         LDB    NTAKE        B := maximum # of sticks to take.
         BRA    P1L2         Jump into loop.
P1LOOP   JSR    P2TURN       Do we have a winning position?
         BEQ    WIN          Found one, mark this a winner.
         DECB                Otherwise, try taking another stick.
         BEQ    LOSE         Lose if we've tried up to NTAKE sticks.
P1L2     DECA                Also lose if there are no more sticks.
         BGE    P1LOOP
*
LOSE     PULS   A,B          Restore A and B from stack.
         CLRZ                Return with Z=0 (not a winner).
         RTS
WIN      PULS   A,B          Restore A and B from stack.
         SETZ                Return with Z=1 (a winner).
         RTS
*
*
* Subroutine P2TURN determines if the current position
* is a winner, given NTAKE (global variable) and
* STICKSLEFT (passed in register A), assuming that it's
* P2's turn to move.  P2TURN saves registers A and B on
* entry and restores them on exit.  The result is returned
* in condition bit Z: 1 if a winning position, 0 otherwise.
* Exit code is shared with P1TURN.
*
P2TURN   PSHS   A,B          Save registers B and A on stack.
         TST    A            Any sticks left?
         BEQ    LOSE         Return with Z=0 if none (we just lost).
         LDB    NTAKE        B := maximum # of sticks to take.
         BRA    P2L2         Jump into loop.
P2LOOP   JSR    P1TURN       Do we have a losing position?
         BNE    LOSE         Found one, mark this a loser.
         DECB                Otherwise, try taking another stick.
         BEQ    WIN          Win if we've tried up to NTAKE sticks.
P2L2     DECA                Also win if there are no more sticks.
         BGE    P2LOOP
         BRA    WIN
*
NTAKE    RMB    1            Global var -- max # of sticks to take.
```

FIGURE 9–6 Three coroutines for text formatting.

The problem can be solved naturally by decomposing it into three communicating coroutines for reading input characters, assembling them into words, and printing words, as shown in Figure 9–6. The GetChar coroutine reads input characters and detects blank lines. GetWord assembles words and discards spaces, getting individual characters from GetChar and passing complete words to PrintWord. The PrintWord coroutine formats words onto lines according to the line length limit.

9.5.2 Extended-Pascal Coroutines

In order to study coroutines in more detail, we shall use a new reserved word "COROUTINE" to define coroutines in extended Pascal, and a reserved word "RESUME" to call a coroutine. When a coroutine is "resumed" for the first time, execution is started at its first statement. Once entered, a coroutine Cor1 may be temporarily suspended by the statement "RESUME Cor2", which transfers control to Cor2, another coroutine. Now the statement "RESUME Cor1" will leave Cor2 and continue execution of Cor1 at the point just after Cor1 called Cor2, not back at the beginning. Table 9–20 illustrates.

Table 9–21 defines the coroutines GetChar, GetWord, and PrintWord for formatting text.[4] An important difference between coroutines and standard Pascal procedures is that coroutines must preserve the values of their local variables between successive calls. Thus column in PrintWord "remembers" the current output column number to properly handle the next word.

Each of the coroutines in Table 9–21 has been written independently as if the other coroutines were its subroutines. For example, GetChar reads characters and passes them to GetWord; it also translates an end-of-line condition into a space character for GetWord. Looking from another point of view, GetWord calls GetChar from two different places to get a character, totally unaware that GetChar may be resumed in either of two different places.

Coroutines GetChar and GetWord contain endless loops. However, a blankLine flag is passed up from GetChar to PrintWord, which returns control to the main program when all the lines have been processed.

---

[4]Since standard Pascal doesn't really support coroutines, we ignore a syntax error: these coroutine definitions contain forward references to each other.

TABLE 9–20 Two coroutines.

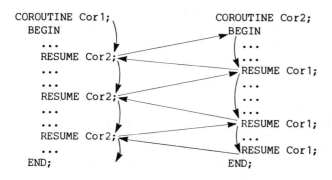

```
COROUTINE Cor1;              COROUTINE Cor2;
  BEGIN                        BEGIN
    ...                          ...
    RESUME Cor2;                 ...
    ...                          RESUME Cor1;
    RESUME Cor2;                 ...
    ...                          ...
    ...                          RESUME Cor1;
    RESUME Cor2;                 ...
    ...                          RESUME Cor1;
  END;                         END;
```

9.5.3 Assembly Language Coroutines

In order to program coroutines in assembly language, we need to save a "resumption address" for each coroutine. When Cor1 resumes Cor2, it should save the current value of the program counter in a memory location RES1 and jump to the address contained in a memory location RES2. Now Cor1 may be resumed by jumping to the address that was saved in RES1.

If a coroutine Cor1 in the 6809 calls Cor2 by JSR COR2 and vice versa, then the following statements may be used to link the two coroutines:

```
COR1    PULS    Y            Save Cor2's resumption address in RES2.
        STY     RES2
        JMP     @RES1        Jump to Cor1's resumption address.
COR2    PULS    Y            Save Cor1's resumption address in RES1.
        STY     RES1
        JMP     @RES2        Jump to Cor2's resumption address.
RES1    RMB     2            Storage for Cor1's resumption address.
RES2    RMB     2            Storage for Cor2's resumption address.
```

Notice the use of indirect addressing in the JMP instructions. All that remains is for the values stored in RES1 and RES2 to be initialized when the program is started, to the address of the first executable instruction of each coroutine.

The line-formatting coroutines in Table 9–21 have been coded for the 6809 in Table 9–22. A macro COLINK is defined at the end of the program to generate coroutine linkages. In general, the coroutine linkage instructions must take into account both the coroutine that is being suspended and the one that is being resumed. For example, GetWord can be resumed from both GetChar and PrintWord and so two different linkages are needed. However, notice that there is still only one resumption address for each coroutine.

9.5.4 Coroutine Applications

Coroutines find their most common application in programs that read inputs, perform some transformation, and produce outputs, as shown in Figure 9–7(a). Because of the analogy with electronics, such programs are often

TABLE 9–21 Line-formatting program using coroutines.

```
PROGRAM Format (input,output);
{ This program reads lines of input text until a completely
  blank line is found. It eliminates extra spaces between words
  and then packs them on output lines with a maximum line
  length of 30 characters, never breaking a word in the middle.
  Words longer than 30 characters are truncated.
}
CONST lineLen = 30;
VAR inChar : char; {Passes characters from GetChar to GetWord.}
    wordBuf : ARRAY [1..lineLen] OF char; {Buffer for accumulating
                words and passing them from GetWord to PrintWord.}
    wordPnt : integer; {Index of last valid character in wordBuf.}
    blankLine : boolean; {Set true when a blank line is read.}
COROUTINE GetChar;
  BEGIN
    REPEAT {forever}
      blankLine := true; read(inChar); {'read' sets eoln true...}
      WHILE NOT eoln DO                {...at the end of a line.}
        BEGIN
          blankLine := false; RESUME GetWord;   read(inChar);
        END;
      {A space is needed to flush the last word on a line.}
      inChar := ' '; RESUME GetWord;
    UNTIL false;
  END;

COROUTINE GetWord;
  BEGIN
    REPEAT {forever}
      wordPnt := 0;
      REPEAT {Skip spaces.}
        RESUME GetChar; IF blankLine THEN RESUME PrintWord;
      UNTIL inChar <> ' ';
      REPEAT
        IF wordPnt < lineLength THEN
          BEGIN
            wordPnt := wordPnt + 1;
            wordBuf[wordPnt] := inChar;
          END;
        RESUME GetChar;
      UNTIL inChar = ' ';
      RESUME PrintWord; {Got a word, go print it.}
    UNTIL false;
  END;
```

TABLE 9–21 (continued)

```
COROUTINE PrintWord;
  VAR column, i : integer;
  BEGIN
    column := 0;
    RESUME GetWord; {Get first word.}
    WHILE NOT blankLine DO
      BEGIN {Read and print a word.}
        {Will the word fit, including a separating space?}
        IF column = 0 THEN {Do nothing.}
        ELSE IF column + wordPnt + 1 <= lineLength THEN
          BEGIN write(' '); column := column+1 END
        {Start a new line if word doesn't fit.}
        ELSE BEGIN writeln; column := 0 END;
        FOR i:=1 TO wordPnt DO {Print the current word.}
          BEGIN write(wordBuf[i]); column := column+1 END;
        RESUME GetWord; {Get next word.}
      END;
    writeln; {Finish last line and return to Main.}
  END;

BEGIN {Main Program}
  Printword;
END.
```

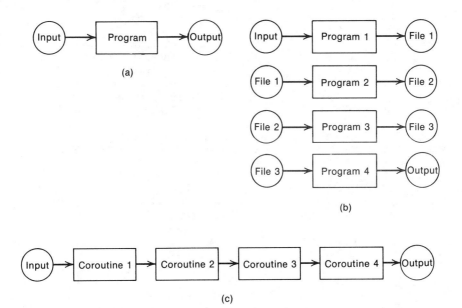

(a)

(b)

(c)

FIGURE 9–7 Filters and coroutines: (a) a simple filter; (b) a cascade of filters using intermediate files; (c) an equivalent coroutine structure.

called *filters*; sometimes filters are cascaded. For example, the following filters might be applied to a text file to find spelling errors:

(1) Remove all punctuation and reformat the text so that each line contains only one word.

(2) Remove all words that consist of only upper case letters (assuming that they are acronyms or mnemonics).

TABLE 9–22 6809 version of line-formatting program.

```
        ORG     2000H
SPC     EQU     20H             ASCII space.
CR      EQU     0DH             ASCII carriage return.
LINELN  EQU     30              Maximum output line length.
WRDBUF  RMB     LINELN          Word buffer.
BLANK   RMB     1               Blank-line flag.
COLUMN  RMB     1               Output column number.
XTEMP   RMB     2               Temporary storage for X.
STACK   RMB     20              Stack area.
STACKE  EQU     *               Stack initialization address.
*
*       COROUTINE GetChar -- returns a character in A.
GCHRIN  LDA     #0FFH           Assume we have a blank line unless
        STA     BLANK              we get a nonspace.
GCHR1   JSR     READ            Read a character.
        CMPA    #CR             Is it the end of line?
        BEQ     GCHR5
        CLR     BLANK           No, not a blank line.
GCHR2   JSR     GETWRDG         Give the character to GETWRD...
        BRA     GCHR1           ...and do some more.
GCHR5   LDA     #SPC            At end of line, force a space...
        JSR     GETWRDG         ...and give it to GETWRD.
        BRA     GCHRIN          Go read more lines.
*
*       COROUTINE GetWord -- puts a word in WRDBUF[1..X].
GWRDIN  LDX     #0              Set index before start of WRDBUF.
GWRD1   JSR     GETCHR          Get a character.
        TST     BLANK           Hit a blank line?
        BEQ     GWRD2           No, continue.
        JSR     PRTWRD          Yes, resume PRTWRD.
GWRD2   CMPA    #SPC            Skip over spaces.
        BEQ     GWRD1
GWRD3   CMPX    #LINELN         Is there room left in WRDBUF?
        BHS     GWRD4           No, ignore character.
        ADDX    #1              Yes, put the character in WRDBUF.
        STA     WRDBUF-1(X)
GWRD4   JSR     GETCHR          Get another character...
        CMPA    #SPC            ...and continue processing until a
        BNE     GWRD3              space character is found.
        JSR     PRTWRD          Now we have a word, go print it...
        BRA     GWRDIN          ...and then get some more words.
```

TABLE 9–22   (continued)

```
*          COROUTINE PrintWord -- prints the word in WRDBUF[1..X].
PWRDIN CLR     COLUMN         Set output column to zero.
PWRD1  JSR     GETWRDP        Get a word.
       TST     BLANK          Hit a blank line?
       BNE     PWRD9          Yep, exit.
       TST     COLUMN         Nope, are we in the middle of a line?
       BEQ     PRTBUF         Print word now if we're at column zero.
       STX     XTEMP          Otherwise, will the word fit?
       LDB     XTEMP+1        Get the word length (low-order X)...
       ADDB    COLUMN         ...plus number of characters so far.
       CMPB    #LINELN-1      Will word fit, including a space?
       BHI     PWRD5          Start a new line if it won't fit.
       LDA     #SPC           Otherwise output a space...
       JSR     WRITE
       INC     COLUMN
       BRA     PRTBUF         ...and print the word.
PWRD5  JSR     WRITELN        Print CR and LF for a new line.
       CLR     COLUMN
PRTBUF STX     XTEMP          Print the word in WRDBUF.
       LDY     #1
PRTB1  CMPY    XTEMP
       BHI     PWRD1          Go process more words when done.
       LDA     WRDBUF-1(Y)    Else print another character...
       JSR     WRITE
       ADDY    #1
       INC     COLUMN         ...and update column # accordingly.
       BRA     PRTB1
PWRD9  JSR     WRITELN        Print CR and LF for a new line.
       RTS                    Return to main program.
*
MAIN   LDS     #STACKE        Initialize SP.
       LDX     #GWRDIN        Initialize coroutine linkage.
       STX     GWRDRES
       LDX     #GCHRIN
       STX     GCHRRES
       JSR     PWRDIN         Print words until blank line found.
       JMP     1000H          Return to operating system.
*
COLINK MACRO   FROM,TO        Coroutine linkages.
       PULS    Y
       STY     FROM
       JMP     @TO
       ENDM
*
GETCHR COLINK GWRDRES,GCHRRES
GETWRDG COLINK GCHRRES,GWRDRES
GETWRDP COLINK PWRDRES,GWRDRES
PRTWRD COLINK GWRDRES,PWRDRES
*
GCHRRES RMB    2              Resumption address for GetChar.
GWRDRES RMB    2              Resumption address for GetWord.
PWRDRES RMB    2              Resumption address for PrintWord.
```

(3) Translate each upper case letter into the corresponding lower case letter.

(4) Look up each word in a dictionary and output all words that are not found.

A program could be devised to perform these tasks one at a time, producing three temporary files that pass the results of one filter to the next, as shown in Figure 9–7(b). Alternatively, the program could be organized as four coroutines as shown in Figure 9–7(c). In the first case, the individual filters can be executed at different times and therefore can be fit individually into a small memory. In the second case, the coroutine structure avoids the extra file space and processing time associated with reading and writing temporary files, at the possible expense of requiring a larger program memory.

REFERENCES

The history of subroutines, coroutines, and related concepts has been traced by Donald E. Knuth in *Fundamental Algorithms* [Addison-Wesley, 1973 (second edition), pp. 225–227]. Instructions for calling subroutines were included in all of the early digital computers, although it was not until the 1960s that a pushdown stack was used to store return addresses (in the B 5000 [Lonergan and King, "Design of the B 5000 system," *Datamation*, Vol. 5, No. 7, May 1961, pp. 28–32; also in Bell and Newell's *Computer Structures*, McGraw-Hill, 1971]).

Techniques for passing parameters in high-level languages are thoroughly discussed in *Programming Language Structures* by Organick, Forsythe, and Plummer [Academic Press, 1978]. The correspondence between parameter-passing conventions and run-time storage allocation and operations is explained in *Compiler Construction for Digital Computers* by David Gries [Wiley, 1971].

The architecture of the B 5000 supported parameter passing on a stack; Algol and other related high-level languages have popularized the use of the stack. More recently, special instructions have been provided in new computer architectures to facilitate parameter passing on a stack (RET n in the 8086 and LINK and UNLK in the 68000).

Recursive algorithms are discussed in *Recursive Programming Techniques* by D. W. Barron [American Elsevier, 1968]. *Programming Language Structures* also contains an extensive discussion of recursion.

Coroutines and their relationship to multipass algorithms are discussed in *Programming Language Structures* and in *Fundamental Algorithms*. The word "coroutine" was coined by M. E. Conway and appears in his paper, "Design of a Separable Transition-Diagram Compiler" [*Comm. ACM*, Vol. 6, No. 7, July 1963, pp. 396-408]. However, Knuth has found the concept mentioned as early as 1954 in a UNIVAC "programming tip."

Many examples of filter programs are given in Kernighan and Plauger's *Software Tools* [Addison-Wesley, 1976]. The idea of cascading filters appears prominently in the UNIX operating system for the PDP-11 and other computers, where such a cascade is called a *pipe*. UNIX's pipes effectively allow a user to link together cooperating programs (coroutines) at run time.

EXERCISES

9.1   Fix the space-compressing program in Table 9–4 so that strings of one or two spaces are not translated, and strings of more than 26 spaces are translated into two or more "#x" codes.

9.2   What kind of parameters (value or variable) are used by the standard Pascal procedures read and write?

9.3   Explain what happens during the procedure call Swap(i,next[i]) if Pascal variable parameters are used and if Fortran value parameters are used.

9.4   List the name, type, and passing convention for each input and output parameter of the subroutines in Tables 5–10, 5–16, 7–7, 8–4, 8–6, 8–7, 6–8, 9–12, and 9–13.

9.5   In tabular form, list the advantages and disadvantages of each parameter-passing convention discussed in Section 9.3.

9.6   Suppose that all subroutines in a program share a common parameter area. What problems does this create when subroutines are nested?

9.7   Describe how the number of different subroutines versus the number of different callers affects the choice of static parameter passing methods (dedicated memory locations for each subroutine versus a parameter area for each caller).

9.8   Modify the DIVIDE subroutine in Table 9–14 so that it can be stored in a read-only memory. (Hint: CNT.) Modify the calling program in Table 9–15 to work with the new subroutine.

9.9   Modify the DIVIDE subroutine in Table 9–14 to use an in-line parameter area. Modify the calling program in Table 9–15 to work with the new subroutine.

9.10 Suppose we change the last three machine instructions in Table 9–16 to just one new instruction, "RTS 1". Define the required operation of the new 2-byte instruction RTS n, where n is an 8-bit unsigned integer.

9.11 How would you classify the parameters used in the queue manipulation subroutines in Table 9–18?

9.12 Explain why the two CLRZ instructions in Table 9–18 could be eliminated without affecting the operation of the program.

9.13   Add a subroutine QROOM (and prologue) to the queue manipulation subroutines in Table 9–18 whose input parameters are a 16-bit unsigned integer N and the address of a queue descriptor table, and whose output is a single bit indicating whether or not the specified queue has room for N more bytes in it.

9.14   Show that it is not necessary to push and pop A in the NIM subroutines in Table 9–19, if A is decremented at appropriate places instead.

9.15   Write a Pascal version of the NIM subroutines in Table 9–19.

9.16   Translate the NIM subroutines in Table 9–19 into assembly language for your favorite computer. Also write and run a main program that calls the subroutines for all values of NTAKE from 2 to 6 and NHEAP from 1 to 30 and prints the results (win or lose) for each possible starting configuration.

9.17   Study the results of the previous exercise and propose a simple formula that determines whether or not a starting position is a guaranteed winner for an intelligent first player, given NTAKE and NHEAP. Try to prove informally that your formula is correct (or use mathematical induction if you are so inclined).

9.18   The *eight queens problem* is a classic in computer science and mathematics. Its object is to place eight chess queens on an empty 8×8 chessboard so that no queen can capture any of the others. A queen can capture any piece in the same row, column, or diagonal. Therefore any solution must position each queen on a different row, column, and diagonal. There exist 92 different solutions (including symmetrical ones), which can be found by trial and error.

   Your assignment is to write a program in Pascal or assembly language to generate all of the solutions to the problem. The main data structure in the program is an 8×8 boolean array that represents the chessboard. The heart of the program is a recursive procedure try(col: integer) that tries to place $9 - col$ queens in columns col through 8 of the chessboard, printing solutions as they are found. It does this by finding all squares in column col that are not yet under attack. For each such square, it places a queen on the board and calls try(col+1), unless col=8, in which case it prints out a solution. The main program simply initializes the board array to contain no queens and calls try(1).

9.19   The 1s-counting program in Exercise 7.6 requires a table N1S[0..255] of 256 integers where N1S[i] contains the number of 1s in the 8-bit binary representation of i. The Pascal program below uses a recursive procedure to initialize such an array. Translate this program into assembly language for your favorite computer.

```
PROGRAM CountOnesInNonnegativeNumbers (input,output);
VAR inNum, tmp, cnt : integer; N1S : ARRAY [0..255] OF integer;
PROCEDURE CntInit (weight, index, ones : integer);
  BEGIN
    IF weight=256 THEN N1S[index] := ones
      ELSE BEGIN CntInit(weight*2,index,ones);
                 CntInit(weight*2,index+weight,ones+1) END;
  END;
```

```
BEGIN {Main program}
  CntInit(1,0,0); {Initialize N1S array.}
  read(inNum);
  WHILE inNum>=0 DO   {Process nonnegative input numbers.}
    BEGIN
      cnt := 0; tmp := inNum;
      WHILE tmp>0 DO
        BEGIN cnt := cnt + N1S[tmp MOD 256];
              tmp := tmp DIV 256                END;
        writeln('The number of ones in ',inNum,' is ',cnt);
        read(inNum);
    END;
END.  {All done, bye.}
```

9.20 A *recursive macro* is a macro that invokes itself. In a macro assembler that allows recursion, it is possible to write a recursive macro to initialize the N1S table from the previous exercise at load time. An example of such a macro and its invocation is shown below:

```
CINIT    MACRO  WT,CNT
         IFNE   WT,256
         CINIT  WT*2,CNT
         CINIT  WT*2,CNT+1
         ENDIF
         IFEQ   WT,256
         FCB    CNT
         ENDIF
         ENDM
*
N1S      CINIT  1,0              Initialize table of 256 bytes.
```

Although the above code creates a table of 256 bytes, it does not have the property that N1S[I] equals the number of ones in the binary representation of I. Explain why, and write a recursive macro that initializes N1S properly.

9.21 Rewrite the program in Table 9–21 in standard Pascal as a main program that does the work of GetWord, and two procedures GetChar and PrintWord. Describe the changes required in the absence of coroutines.

9.22 Getting coroutines started from a main program and later terminated is often tricky. Explain why the main program in Table 9–21 calls PrintWord with a standard Pascal procedure statement instead of using RESUME. Explain why the assembly language main program in Table 9–22 calls PWRDIN directly instead of going through the coroutine linkage.

9.23 Insert a Translate coroutine between GetChar and GetWord in Table 9–21 that processes "escape" sequences of the form '!x'. The processing for escape sequences depends on the character x:

1-9   Insert 1 to 9 "unpaddable" spaces into output stream.
      These spaces are treated like normal printing characters.

  !   Insert the character "!" into the output stream.

<   Convert upper case letters to lower case until further notice.

>   Suspend conversion of upper case letters until further notice.

u   Convert the next character to lower case if it is a letter.

If x is not one of the above characters, ignore the '!x' sequence.

9.24 Translate the Translate coroutine above into 6809 assembly language.

9.25 Why isn't PWRDRES initialized by the main program in Table 9–22?

9.26 Another way to initialize the coroutine linkages in Table 9–22 is via statements like GWRDRES FCW GWRDIN. What's wrong with this approach?

9.27 Show how a resumption address stored at the top of the stack can be used to link two coroutines on the 6809. Explain why this technique breaks down when there are three or more coroutines.

9.28 Devise a coroutine linkage structure for the 6809 that allows each coroutine to have an independent stack accessed by SP, such that the resumption address of each suspended coroutine is always at the top of its own stack.

10

INPUT/OUTPUT

In previous chapters we've indicated that basic computer organization hasn't changed drastically during the entire history of electronic computers, although technology improvements have certainly made computers faster, cheaper, more powerful, and smaller. Of the three major subsystems of a computer, input/output has experienced the biggest evolution, because of the explosion of computer applications and the hundreds of different devices that are now part of computer systems. Back in the 1950s, few computer architects would have predicted that some day more computers would be used in automobiles than in any other application, and that one of the most common output devices would be a fuel-injected carburetor!

Despite the proliferation of devices, fairly standard techniques are still used to connect typical devices to a computer system. For a programmer who understands the basic principles of input/output interfacing and programming, it is a relatively simple matter to learn the characteristics of any new device and program the computer to "talk to" it. This chapter describes these basic principles. The examples that we give in this chapter are somewhat stylized—the characteristics of input/output devices and interfaces for different computers vary widely.

10.1 I/O ORGANIZATION

10.1.1 Buses

In Section 1.3, we showed the basic organization of a computer as consisting of processor, memory, and input/output (I/O). The processor communicated with the I/O subsystem by means of an I/O bus. In Figure 10–1 we expand our view. Like a memory bus, the I/O bus in Figure 10–1 contains data, address, and control lines. The address lines allow a program to select among different I/O devices connected to the system, while the data lines carry the actual data being transferred.

The size of the I/O bus need not match the size of the memory bus. For example, the Z8000 memory bus has 23 address lines and 16 data lines, while its I/O bus has 16 address lines and either 8 or 16 data lines (system-dependent). Even if the I/O bus and the memory bus happen to share some lines (e.g., address), they are still logically independent. Numerically equal addresses on the two buses still refer to different entities, because a control signal from the processor distinguishes between memory and I/O operations. For example, I/O address 5 is totally independent from memory location 5.

10.1.2 Devices and Interfaces

The I/O subsystem in Figure 10–1 contains both devices and interfaces. A *peripheral device* (or *I/O device*) performs some function for the computer. An *I/O interface* (or *device interface*) controls the operation of a peripheral device according to commands from the computer processor; it also converts computer data into whatever format is required by the device and vice versa.

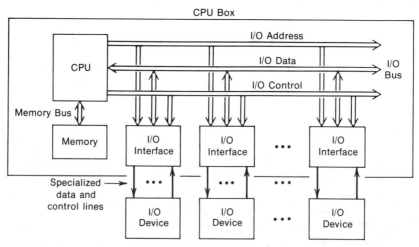

FIGURE 10–1 Input/output (I/O) subsystem.

Also as shown in the figure, a peripheral device is often housed separate from the processor, while the interface is almost always packaged together with the processor and memory in one "CPU box."

There are many different peripheral devices that convert computer data into forms that are useful in the world outside the computer; such devices include displays, printers, plotters, digital-to-analog converters, mechanical relays, and fuel-injected carburetors. Many other devices convert data from the outside world into forms usable by the computer; examples include keyboards, text scanners, joysticks, analog-to-digital converters, mechanical switches, and crash detectors. The sole purpose of some devices is simply to store data for later retrieval; these are called *mass storage devices* and include magnetic disks and tapes.

Sometimes the dividing line between an interface and the device it controls is fuzzy. For example, Figure 10–2 shows the circuitry associated with a simple mechanical keyboard. The encoder circuit converts a mechanical switch depression into a 7-bit number in the ASCII code (Appendix A). The bus interface can place this number on the I/O bus on demand by the processor. So it seems that the device interface consists of the Encoder and Bus Interface blocks. However, in a typical system the encoder is packaged with the keyboard; then only a small number of wires are needed between the encoder (in the keyboard package) and the bus interface (in the CPU box). Most computer designers would say that the Encoder block is part of the keyboard, and the device interface consists of the Bus Interface block alone. Fortunately, the dividing line is unimportant to I/O programs that deal with the keyboard. More important is the "I/O programming model" that an I/O program sees, as discussed in the next subsection.

10.1.3 Ports

An *I/O port* (or *I/O register*) is a part of a device interface, a group of bits accessed by the processor during I/O operations. The "I/O programming

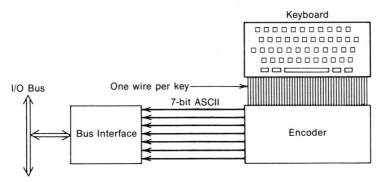

FIGURE 10–2 Keyboard and interface.

```
    7 6                  0
   ┌─┬──────────────────┐
   │0│ Key code (ASCII) │ KBDATA
   └─┴──────────────────┘ (read-only)
```

FIGURE 10–3 Programming model for a keyboard.

model" of the keyboard in Figure 10–2 contains one 8-bit I/O port named
KBDATA, as shown in Figure 10–3. The high-order bit of KBDATA is always 0.
The low-order bits of KBDATA contain the output of the Encoder block in
Figure 10–2, that is, the 7-bit ASCII code for the key that is currently being
depressed, or 0000000 if no key is depressed.

In order to read data from the keyboard in Figure 10–2, a program must
execute an instruction that transfers the contents of KBDATA into one of the
processor registers. Once the data is in the processor, it can be manipulated
like any other data. Although the interface "writes" keyboard data into
KBDATA, the port is read-only from the point of view of the processor; any
attempt by the processor to write data into KBDATA has no effect. Therefore,
we can call KBDATA an "input port."

Figure 10–4(a) shows a very simple output device that interprets an 8-bit
byte as two 4-bit BCD digits and displays the digits on two seven-segment
displays. The I/O programming model consists of one 8-bit port DIGOUT,
shown in Figure 10–4(b). In order to display two digits, the processor must
transfer an 8-bit value into DIGOUT. In this case, DIGOUT is an "output port"
and is write-only from the point of view of the processor; an attempt to read it
produces an undefined value.

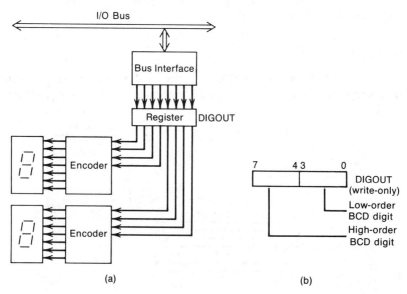

(a)   (b)

FIGURE 10–4 Seven-segment display: (a) device and interface; (b)
programming model.

There is an important distinction between the input and output ports described above. In the case of the input port, KBDATA contains the instantaneous value of the encoder output; when a key is depressed or released, KBDATA changes immediately. KBDATA is not really a "register," since it has no memory; it simply "buffers" the output of the encoder onto the I/O data bus. On the other hand, the output port DIGOUT *is* a storage register. After the processor writes a value into DIGOUT, it does not change until the next write operation. The interface hardware is purposely designed this way. Otherwise the processor would have to continuously write the same value into DIGOUT to maintain the display.

The keyboard and display above are very simple examples of I/O interfaces and ports. Later on we'll describe I/O interfaces with more complex ways of controlling I/O devices.

10.2 I/O PROGRAMMING

So far, we haven't said how I/O port data is transferred to and from processor registers. This section discusses two techniques that are used in different processors to perform I/O transfers.

10.2.1 Isolated I/O

In *isolated I/O* the ports are accessed by special I/O instructions. For example, the Z8000 has two instructions for transferring the contents of an 8-bit port to and from registers:

```
INB    rn,pn        REG[rn] := IPORT[pn];
OUTB   pn,rn        OPORT[pn] := REG[rn];
```

Here IPORT is an array of 2^{16} 8-bit input ports, OPORT is an array of 2^{16} 8-bit output ports, and REG is an array of sixteen 8-bit registers in the processor; rn is a 4-bit register number and pn is a 16-bit port number, both contained in the instruction. Thus the INB and OUTB instructions are both two words long; as shown in Figure 10–5, the first word contains the opcode and rn, and the second word contains pn.

The INB and OUTB instructions perform simple data transfers, like load and store instructions, except that they access an array of I/O ports instead of an array of memory bytes. Since the main memory and the I/O ports are on different buses, the "address spaces" accessed by memory reference and I/O

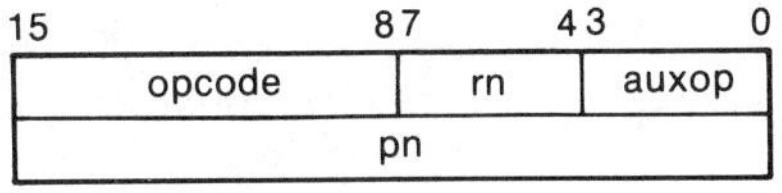

FIGURE 10-5 Format of Z8000 INB and OUTB instructions.

instructions are different, even though they both may happen to use 16-bit addresses.

Like memory banks, I/O ports need not be installed at every address that is available for them. In fact, a typical small computer has far less than 2^{16} or even 2^8 I/O ports; ten to fifty is a more typical range.

A simple Z8000 program using isolated I/O is shown in Table 10–1. When reading this program, you should recall that a "B" suffix in Z8000 instructions refers to byte operations, not a B register. The program reads a pair of decimal digits from the keyboard and displays them on the seven-segment displays until the next pair is typed.

The RDDIG subroutine reads characters from the keyboard, looking for decimal digits, characters in the range '0'..'9'. When it finds a valid decimal digit it converts it to a 4-bit number that is returned in RL0. The only way that RDDIG can determine when a key is typed is to continuously read the KBDATA port and wait for it to become nonzero. Once a key is pressed, the subroutine then waits for it to be released before continuing. Otherwise, the

TABLE 10–1 Keyboard input and display output for the Z8000.

```
*          Read two decimal digits from the keyboard and display them
*          on the seven-segment display. Ignore illegal characters.
*
KBDATA  EQU    5              Keyboard input port number.
DIGOUT  EQU    7              Seven-segment display port number.
*
*          First, a subroutine to read one decimal digit, convert
*          it to 4-bit BCD, and return the result in RL0.
RDDIG   INB    RL0,KBDATA     Read current character.
        TESTB  RL0            Set condition bits (INB doesn't).
        JR     EQ,RDDIG       Wait for a key to be pressed.
WAITUP  INB    RH0,KBDATA     Now the good character is in RL0,
        TESTB  RH0               keep reading keyboard data into RH0
        JR     NE,WAITUP         and wait for the key to be released.
        CMPB   RL0,#30H       Now, was it a valid decimal digit?
        JR     LT,RDDIG       Not if it's less than ASCII '0' ...
        CMPB   RL0,#39H
        JR     GT,RDDIG       ... or greater than ASCII '9'.
        SUBB   RL0,#30H       OK, convert ASCII '0'-'9' to 0-9.
        RET                   Done, return.
*
*          Now, the main program.
DIGDSP  CALL   RDDIG          Read high-order decimal digit into RL0.
        SLLB   RL0,#4         Shift left 4 bits
        LDB    RL1,RL0           and save in RL1.
        CALL   RDDIG          Read low-order decimal digit.
        ORB    RL1,RL0        Merge with high-order digit.
        OUTB   RL1,DIGOUT     Send to seven-segment display.
        JR     DIGDSP         Do another pair of digits.
        END    DIGDSP
```

next time the subroutine was entered, it would mistake the first key depression for a new one.

The main program merges pairs of BCD digits from RDDIG and sends them to the 2-digit seven-segment display. Notice that only one OUTB instruction is needed to load an 8-bit value into DIGOUT. Once the processor loads DIGOUT with a value, that value is displayed until the processor loads DIGOUT again.

We should say something now about I/O timing, since I/O devices usually exist in an environment where time is significant. In the example above, the processor spends almost all of its time executing the first three instructions of the RDDIG subroutine, waiting for some human (or maybe a monkey) to press a key. It spends only a small amount of time in the next three instructions waiting for the key to be released, unless someone is leaning on the keyboard. Even less time is spent in the remainder of the subroutine and in the main program, since each instruction takes only about 1 microsecond (10^{-6} second) to execute, while keys are depressed at a maximum rate of about five per second. Because of this great disparity in speed, it is extremely unlikely that the program would "miss" any key depressions. In more time-critical applications, however, the programmer must analyze the I/O requirements and the program to determine whether the program can keep up with the I/O.

Also, you may be concerned about the computer wasting its time waiting for a key to be pressed by a human (or worse, a monkey), when it could be doing some useful task like computing pi to one million digits. In Chapter 11 we'll see how interrupts avoid this waste of computer time, so that I/O programs are activated only when an I/O event is known to have occurred.

10.2.2 Memory-Mapped I/O

In the previous subsection we pointed out that I/O buses are very similar to memory buses, and that I/O instructions are similar to load and store instructions on memory. *Memory-mapped I/O* takes advantage of the similarity by eliminating the I/O bus and I/O instructions.

Figure 10–6 shows the hardware organization of a computer with memory-mapped I/O. Both the main memory and all I/O ports communicate with the processor using a shared Memory and I/O Bus. Each I/O port has an address in the main memory address space of the processor. An input port responds to any instruction that reads at its address; an output port responds to any instruction that writes at its address. Typically, the system designer reserves a portion of the total address space for I/O ports, for example, the top 4 Kbytes. However, theoretically a hardware designer can locate an I/O port at any address, as long as there is no memory at that address too.

Any processor can use memory-mapped I/O if the system hardware designer attaches I/O ports to the main memory bus. For example, if a Z8000

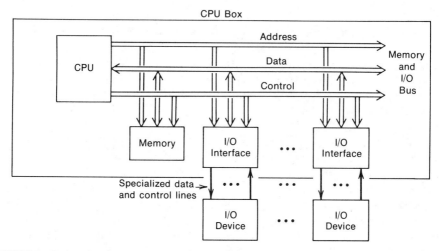

FIGURE 10-6 Memory-mapped I/O structure.

system designer decided to use memory-mapped I/O, then the I/O ports could be designed to connect to the memory bus, and the INB and OUTB instructions would be replaced by the following ones:

```
LDB    rn,pn        REG[rn] := MEM[pn]; {INB}
STB    rn,pn        MEM[pn] := REG[rn]; {OUTB}
```

Here pn is a memory address in the range reserved for I/O ports, and the system designer has simply fooled the processor into accessing I/O ports when it thinks that it is accessing memory bytes in that range.

Memory-mapped I/O is a necessity in processors that have no special I/O instructions. The PDP-11 was the first minicomputer to require memory-mapped I/O; the 68000, 6809, and 9900 processors in Part 3 also require it. Memory-mapped I/O has a number of advantages:

- No opcodes or processor circuits are used up for I/O instructions.

- All memory reference instructions, not just loads and stores, may be used to manipulate I/O ports.

- The number of available I/O port addresses is virtually unlimited.

- The hardware bus structure is simplified.

Of course, there are disadvantages too:

- Part of the memory address space is used up.

- Interfaces may need more circuitry to recognize longer addresses.

- Memory reference instructions may be longer or slower than optimized I/O instructions.

- In future systems, combining memory and I/O may make it difficult to achieve certain performance gains (see Bernard Peuto's Z8000 article, "Architecture of a New Microprocessor," in *Computer*, Feb. 1979).

The keyboard and display I/O program from the previous section has been rewritten in Table 10–2 for the 6809, which must use memory-mapped I/O. The program uses LDA and STA instead of the isolated-I/O INB and OUTB instructions. There is only one "improvement" in the 6809 version: in the RDDIG subroutine, a TST instruction tests the value of the KBDATA port without storing it in an accumulator; the Z8000 program had to load the value into a register in order to test it.

An observation that applies to both isolated I/O and memory-mapped I/O organizations is that the assignment of port numbers is determined strictly by the whims of the hardware designer. Read and write operations on a particular port number are totally independent, unlike normal memory where

TABLE 10–2 Keyboard input and display output for the 6809.

```
*        Read two decimal digits from the keyboard and display them
*        on the seven-segment display. Ignore illegal characters.
*
KBDATA   EQU    0F005H           Keyboard input port address.
DIGOUT   EQU    0F007H           Seven-segment display port address.
*
*        First, a subroutine to read one decimal digit, convert
*        it to 4-bit BCD, and return the result in accumulator A.
RDDIG    LDA    KBDATA           Read current character.
         BEQ    RDDIG            Wait for a key to be pressed.
WAITUP   TST    KBDATA           Now the character is in A,
         BNE    WAITUP             wait for the key to be released.
         CMPA   #30H             Now, was it a valid decimal digit?
         BLT    RDDIG            Not if it's less than ASCII '0' ...
         CMPA   #39H
         BGT    RDDIG            ... or greater than ASCII '9'.
         SUBA   #30H             OK, convert ASCII '0'-'9' to 0-9.
         RTS                     Done, return.
*
*        Now, the main program.
DIGDSP   JSR    RDDIG            Read high-order decimal digit into A.
         ASLA                    Shift left 4 bits ...
         ASLA
         ASLA
         ASLA
         STA    HIDIG              ... and save in HIDIG.
         JSR    RDDIG            Read low-order decimal digit.
         ORA    HIDIG            Merge with high-order digit.
         STA    DIGOUT           Send to seven-segment display.
         BRA    DIGDSP           Do another pair of digits.
HIDIG    RMB    1                Storage for high-order digit.
         END    DIGDSP
```

a read returns the last value written. In particular, a hardware designer who likes to confuse novice programmers could have assigned the KBDATA input port and the DIGOUT output port exactly the same port number (e.g., 5). As long as the programmer doesn't get too upset over this apparent conflict, everything still works fine.

However, it is more traditional to assign identical port numbers only when the functions or meanings of input and output ports are related. In fact, when designing an output port, a good hardware designer will provide an input port at the same address whose sole function is to read the data stored in the output port, as shown in Figure 10–7 for an improved seven-segment display port. Notice that in this case, we use the same name for the input port and the output port. The combined input/output port behaves more like a memory location, so that a program can read the input port to verify the contents of the output port. This is especially important if one wants to write a program that tests the hardware, as well as being useful in some application programs.

10.3 I/O PROTOCOLS

The keyboard and display in the previous section are very simple devices to control. More typical I/O devices require some kind of "handshake" protocol for proper operation.

10.3.1 Input Operations

The handshake protocol for a typical input device is shown in Figure 10–8. When the processor wants to read data, it sends a pulse on the START I/O control line. The device interface responds by initiating the input

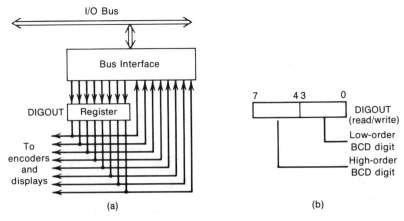

FIGURE 10-7 Input/output port with loopback.

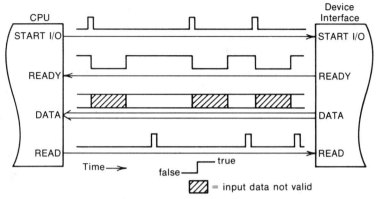

FIGURE 10-8 Handshake protocol for an input device.

operation (an action that is device-dependent), and by placing the logic value false on the READY line. When the operation is completed, the interface stores the input data in its DATA register, which really is a register with memory, unlike KBDATA in the previous section. At the same time it sets READY to true. Therefore, the processor can test the value of READY and read the input data as soon as READY becomes true. The input data remains valid until the next operation is begun.

Some processors with isolated I/O have special instructions for sending the START I/O control pulse and testing READY. For example, the Hewlett-Packard 21MX uses the instructions STC pn and SFS pn for these two functions, where pn is the port number. However, most microcomputers and many minicomputers provide special *control and status ports* that accomplish these functions using normal input and output instructions, independent of whether memory-mapped or isolated I/O is used.

For example, Figure 10-9 shows the I/O programming model for a keyboard with a control and status port KBCS (no, not the radio station KCBS). This is actually both an input port and an output port; each bit has one of the following behaviors:

- *Read-only (R)*. The value of the bit is set by the interface and can be read by the processor; writing a value into it has no effect.

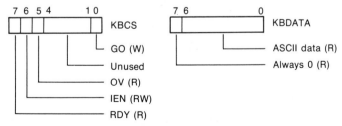

FIGURE 10-9 Programming model for a keyboard with control and status port.

- *Write-only (W)*. The value of the bit can be written by the processor; reading returns an unpredictable value.

- *Read/write (RW)*. The value of the bit can be read and written by the processor; reading generally returns the value last written.

- *Unused*. Writing this bit has no effect, and reading returns an unpredictable value.

Each bit in Figure 10–9 has a unique control and status function. Writing a 1 into the GO bit is equivalent to sending a START I/O pulse to the interface in Figure 10–8. This clears RDY (READY) and initiates the device operation. For a keyboard, initiating an operation simply consists of clearing KBDATA and waiting for someone to press a key. When a key is depressed, the interface cheers it up . . . no, it places the ASCII code for the key in KBDATA and sets RDY to 1. Thus, the following 6809 subroutine reads one character from the keyboard into A, assuming that the symbols KBCS and KBDATA have been equated with the addresses of the KBCS and KBDATA ports:

```
KBDIN   LDA    #1            Set GO to 1, starting an operation.
        STA    KBCS
KBDWT   TST    KBCS          Wait for RDY=1.
        BPL    KBDWT
        LDA    KBDATA        Get key data.
        ANDA   #7FH          Clear MSB.
        RTS                  Return with 7-bit ASCII in A.
```

The instructions that wait for RDY to become 1 above are called a *busy-wait loop*. When the processor is busy-waiting for an I/O operation to be completed, no useful computation takes place. Busy-waiting can be minimized by overlapping I/O as discussed in the next subsection, or by using interrupts as described in the next chapter.

Two other bits are provided in KBCS. When set to 1, the IEN bit enables the keyboard to interrupt the processor as described in the next chapter. It is a read/write bit so that a program can easily determine whether or not the keyboard interrupt is currently enabled (useful in interrupt polling programs, see Table 11–4). The OV bit indicates an "overrun" condition; the interface sets it to 1 whenever the keyboard receives two characters in a row without an intervening read of KBDATA by the processor. It is automatically cleared when GO is set. Table 10–3 shows a program that makes use of the OV bit to detect overrun.

10.3.2 Overlapped I/O

Suppose that we are reading characters from a mechanical input device such as a papertape reader. Because of mechanical motion there is fixed delay from the time each input byte is requested until it is available. The three basic

TABLE 10–3 Reading a keyboard with overrun detection.

```
*                                 Keyboard input subroutine.
KBDIN    LDA    KBCS              Check for overrun.
         ANDA   #20H
         BNE    KBOUT             Exit with Z=0 on overrun.
         LDA    #1                Else set GO to 1 to request a key.
         STA    KBCS
KBDWT    TST    KBCS              Wait for RDY=1.
         BPL    KBDWT
         LDA    KBDATA            Get key data.
         ANDA   #7FH              Clear MSB.
         SETZ                     Set Z:=1 for succesful return.
KBOUT    RTS                      Return with 7-bit ASCII in A.
*
MAIN     ...                      Initialization.
         ...
LOOP     ...                      Main processing loop.
         JSR    KBDIN             Get the next character.
         BNE    MISSIT            Bomb out if we missed it.
         ...                      Otherwise process the character...
         JMP    LOOP              ...and go do some more.
MISSIT   ...                      Handle the error.
         ...
         END    MAIN
```

steps we used for performing an input operation in the previous subsection
were (1) request a byte; (2) wait for the byte; (3) read the byte. These steps
yield a papertape input subroutine such as the following:

```
PTRIN    LDA    #1                Set GO to 1, starting the tape motion.
         STA    PTRCS
PTRWT    TST    PTRCS             Wait for the tape to stop on
         BPL    PTRWT                the next byte (RDY=1).
         LDA    PTRDATA           Read the input byte.
         RTS                      Return with 8-bit value in A.
```

Figure 10–10(a) shows the time behavior of a main program that calls this
subroutine. Each time the main program calls PTRIN, the next byte is requested and the subroutine busy-waits for the whole time the tape is moving.

If we allow our program to think ahead, we can overlap I/O with computation to reduce or even eliminate busy-waiting. The papertape input subroutine below simply rearranges the basic steps into (1) wait for the current
byte; (2) read the current byte; (3) request the next byte:

```
PTRIN    TST    PTRCS             Wait for the tape to stop on
         BPL    PTRIN                the current byte (RDY=1).
         LDA    PTRDATA           Read the input byte.
         LDB    #1                Set GO to 1, starting the tape moving
         STB    PTRCS                for the next byte.
         RTS                      Return with 8-bit value in A.
```

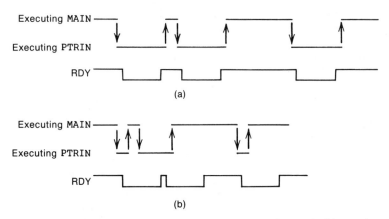

FIGURE 10-10   Input/output operations: (a) non-overlapped; (b) overlapped.

Figure 10–10(b) shows the time behavior of the new subroutine. The first time PTRIN is called, the tape is already stopped over the first byte; the byte is read immediately and the tape movement is started for the second byte. By the time PTRIN is called the second time, the tape has moved almost halfway to the second character, and so the amount of busy-waiting is reduced. In fact, the main program performs so much computation between the second and third characters that there is no busy-waiting on the third call of PTRIN at all. Thus, the I/O operation (reading the next character) is always overlapped with computation that must take place before the main program can process the next character.

Overlapped I/O is useful for devices for which the processor must request a mechanical action for each I/O operation. Depending on the nature of the device and interface, it may be necessary to request the first I/O operation from the main program in order to "prime" the I/O subroutine.

10.3.3   Output Operations

The handshake protocol for a typical output device is shown in Figure 10–11. First the processor sends output data to the interface using the DATA bus and the WRITE control signal; the interface stores the data in an internal register. Then the processor issues a START I/O pulse. The interface immediately sets READY to false and sends its data to the device. Later it sets READY to true, when more data can be accepted.

The I/O programming model for a character output device such as a printer or CRT display is shown in Figure 10–12. The RDY bit indicates that the device can accept another character, while GO indicates that the character currently in DSPDATA should be displayed.[1] IEN allows interrupts as described in the next chapter, and ERR indicates that an error occurred while displaying

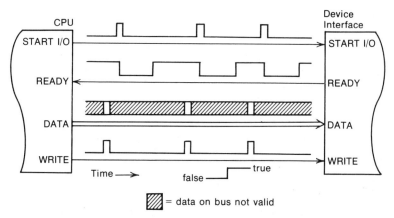

FIGURE 10-11   Handshake protocol for an output device.

the previous character (e.g., the printer ran out of paper). The ERR bit is automatically cleared when GO is set.

Output operations are almost always overlapped with computation. For example, once a character has been sent to a display, there is no reason for the program to wait for it to actually be displayed. The program needs to wait only if it is so fast that it tries to output a second character before the interface has displayed the previous one. Thus, the following 6809 subroutine can be used to perform overlapped output of characters using the interface defined in Figure 10–12:

```
*         Display a character passed in A.
CHROUT    TST    DSPCS         Has previous character been displayed?
          BPL    CHROUT        Wait until done.
          STA    DSPDATA       Send new character to the interface...
          LDA    #1            ...and display it.
          STA    DSPCS
          RTS                  Done, return.
```

10.4 I/O DRIVERS

Most computer operating systems provide a set of subroutines for performing input and output operations using standard I/O devices. These subroutines are called *I/O drivers*. An I/O driver hides the details of a device and its hardware interface from the programmer and provides a clean software interface instead. In this section we describe some simple I/O drivers, both to demonstrate the actual coding of the driver subroutines and to show typical software interfaces that I/O drivers present to application programs.

---

[1]In some interfaces the GO bit is eliminated. Each time the processor writes a character into DSPDATA, the interface automatically issues a "GO" command.

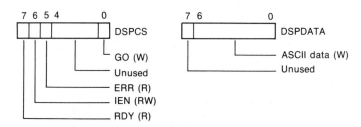

FIGURE 10–12 Programming model for a character output device.

10.4.1 Terminal I/O

Input and output drivers for the keyboard and display of the previous section are coded in Table 10–4. There are two subroutines for reading characters from the keyboard: CHRIN reads a single character and returns it in the A register, while LINEIN reads a line of text terminated by a carriage return, storing the line in a buffer supplied by the calling program. There are also two subroutines for printing characters on the display: CHROUT prints a single character passed in A, while LINEOUT prints the contents of a buffer supplied by the calling program.

The keyboard and display are logically independent devices, even if they happen to be physically packaged together, as in a CRT terminal. Therefore, characters that are typed on the keyboard do not automatically appear on the display unless they are "echoed" by a program, as in the CHRIN subroutine.

Most displays move their cursor or printing mechanism to the beginning of the current line when they receive a carriage return (CR) character, but they do not start a new line. To save the user the trouble of typing a line feed character (LF) after each carriage return, the LINEIN subroutine automatically sends LF to the display after CR is received. Also, LINEOUT appends LF to each CR it displays. The LF characters are not appended in CHRIN and CHROUT so that a user who so wishes can send or receive CR without echoing LF.

A main program that makes use of the LINEIN and LINEOUT drivers is shown in Table 10–5. The program reads an input line, reverses its order, and displays it. The assembler directive FCC (Form Constant Characters) takes a character string as its operand, and stores the ASCII values of the characters in successive bytes of memory. Notice that the formats of input buffers and output buffers are similar, so that the contents of an input buffer filled by LINEIN can be printed if LINEOUT is passed the address of the *second* word in the buffer. Also observe carefully which buffer pointers are initialized at load time by FCW pseudo-operations, and which are loaded at run time.

10.4.2 Shared I/O Drivers

Quite often a computer has several identical devices connected to it, for example several CRT terminals. Typically each device has its own interface;

TABLE 10–4 Keyboard and display I/O drivers.

```
* KEYBOARD/DISPLAY INPUT/OUTPUT MODULE
*
* This module contains two subroutines, CHRIN and LINEIN, to
* read a single character or a line of text from a keyboard.
* It also contains two subroutines, CHROUT and LINEOUT, to
* print a single character or a line of text on a display.
*
* Control characters and I/O port addresses are defined below.
LF       EQU     0AH             Line feed character.
CR       EQU     0DH             Carriage return character.
KBCS     EQU     0FF00H          Keyboard control and status.
KBDATA   EQU     0FF01H          Keyboard data.
DSPCS    EQU     0FF02H          Display control and status.
DSPDATA  EQU     0FF03H          Display data.
*
* SUBROUTINE CHRIN -- Read one input character from a keyboard
*                     and echo it on the display.
*
* INPUTS, GLOBAL VARIABLES, LOCAL VARIABLES -- None.
*
* OUTPUTS
*      INCHAR -- The character just read, passed in A.
*
* REGISTERS AFFECTED -- A
*
CHRIN    LDA     #1              Request one character.
         STA     KBCS
WTIN     TST     KBCS            Is it ready?
         BPL     WTIN            Wait for it.
         LDA     KBDATA          Get the character.
         ANDA    #7FH            Clear MSB.
         JSR     CHROUT          Echo the character on the display.
         RTS                     Done, return.
*
* SUBROUTINE CHROUT -- Print one character on a display.
*
* INPUTS
*      OUTCHAR -- The character to be displayed, passed in A.
*
* OUTPUTS, GLOBAL VARIABLES, LOCAL VARIABLES -- None.
*
* REGISTERS AFFECTED -- None.
*
CHROUT   TST     DSPCS           Has previous character been displayed?
         BPL     CHROUT          Wait for completion.
         STA     DSPDATA         Send the new character to interface.
         PSHS    A               Save the character.
         LDA     #1              Display the character.
         STA     DSPCS
         PULS    A               Restore the character.
         RTS                     Done, return.
```

TABLE 10-4 (continued)

```
* SUBROUTINE LINEIN -- Read a line of text into a buffer.
*
* This subroutine reads a line of text from a terminal into a
* buffer with the format shown below.  The input line is ter-
* minated by a carriage return.  The first two bytes of the
* buffer are initialized by the calling program to contain the
* address of the last byte of the buffer.  This is used to
* prevent the subroutine from overwriting memory if the user
* types in too long a line.  The next two bytes of the buffer
* are reserved for the subroutine to store a variable BUFPNT
* that points to the last input character in the filled buffer.
* The remainder of the buffer is used to store input characters.
*
* BUFFER FORMAT               ------------------
*                TXTBUF   |       o-------+---------
*                         |--           --|         |
*                         |               |         |
*                         ------------------         |
* BUFPNT (TXTBUF+2) |       o-------+------ |
*                         |--           --|   |   |
*                         |               |   |   |
*                         ------------------   |   |
*                TXTBUF+4 |               |   |   |
*                         |       o       |   |   |
*                         |       o       |<----- |
*                         |       o       |         |
*                         |               |<--------
*                         ------------------
*
* INPUTS   -- #TXTBUF -- a pointer to TXTBUF, passed in X.
* OUTPUTS -- TXTBUF+2,TXTBUF+3 -- points to last character.
*            TXTBUF+4,... -- input characters.
* GLOBAL VARIABLES, LOCAL VARIABLES -- None.
* REGISTERS AFFECTED -- A, Y
* NOTES    -- TXTBUF,TXTBUF+1 are not disturbed by LINEIN and
*             therefore may be initialized at load time.
*
LINEIN TFR    X,Y          Put address of first byte of
       ADDY   #4              character buffer into Y.
GETCHR JSR    CHRIN        Read one character.
       STA    @Y           Store it.
       CMPA   #CR          Done if carriage return.
       BEQ    LINDUN
       CMPY   @X           Else is it OK to bump pointer?
       BHS    GETCHR       Not if at end of buffer.
       ADDY   #1           Else bump pointer to next character.
       BRA    GETCHR       Get another character.
LINDUN STY    2(X)         Save pointer to last character.
       LDA    #LF          Give the typist a new line
       JSR    CHROUT          (CHRIN has already echoed CR).
       RTS                 Done, return.
```

TABLE 10–4 (continued)

```
* SUBROUTINE LINEOUT -- Display text from a buffer.
*
* This subroutine displays text on a terminal from a buffer
* with the format shown below.  The first two bytes of the
* buffer contain the address of the last character to be
* displayed, and are followed by the characters themselves.
* The buffer may contain any number of characters and lines.
*
* BUFFER FORMAT             ------------------
*                TXTBUF   |        o-------+------
*                         |--          --|     |
*                         |              |     |
*                         ------------------    |
*                TXTBUF+2 |              |     |
*                         |     o        |     |
*                         |     o        |     |
*                         |     o        |     |
*                         |              |<-----
*                         ------------------
*
* INPUTS   -- #TXTBUF -- a pointer to TXTBUF, passed in register X
* OUTPUTS, GLOBAL VARIABLES, LOCAL VARIABLES -- None.
* REGISTERS AFFECTED -- A, Y
* NOTES    -- Entire text buffer is not disturbed by LINEOUT
*             and therefore may be initialized at load time.
*
LINEOUT TFR    X,Y          Put address of first byte of
        ADDY   #1              character buffer into Y.
PUTCHR  ADDY   #1           Point to next character.
        LDA    @Y           Get it.
        JSR    CHROUT       Display it.
        CMPA   #CR          Character still in A --
        BNE    NOTCR           was it a carriage return?
        LDA    #LF          Always follow CR by a line feed.
        JSR    CHROUT
NOTCR   CMPY   @X           At the end?
        BLO    PUTCHR       Continue if not.
        RTS                 Else done, return.
```

the interfaces are identical except that each one has a different set of port numbers. Instead of writing separate drivers for each device, it is possible to write an I/O driver that can be shared by all devices. All this requires is that the base address of the set of port numbers of the device be passed to the driver as a parameter. For example, Table 10–6 adapts the CHRIN and CHROUT subroutines from the previous example to work with any keyboard and display whose I/O ports have the same functions and relative numbering order.

The address of the keyboard control and status register (KBCSADR) is passed to the subroutines in register Y, and the other ports are accessed using based addressing with fixed offsets from Y.

The shared drivers in Table 10–6 are more general than the "dedicated" drivers given previously. In fact, a dedicated driver subroutine can be coded by calling CHROUTY with a particular value of Y:

TABLE 10–5 Main program that calls LINEIN and LINEOUT.

```
*           Read input lines and display them in reverse order.
*
INBUF   FCW     INBUFE          Address of last byte in buffer.
INBUFP  RMB     2               Reserve space for buffer pointer...
INBUFT  RMB     100             ...and 100 characters of text.
INBUFE  EQU     *-1             Define address of last byte.
YTEMP   RMB     2
STACK   RMB     20              Reserve space for return-address stack.
STACKE  EQU     *
*
MSG1    FCW     MSG1E           Address of last byte in message.
        FCC     'Please type an input line:'
MSG1E   FCB     CR              Last byte is carriage return.
*
MSG2    FCW     MSG2E           Address of last byte in message.
        FCC     'Your line in reverse is as follows:'
MSG2E   FCB     CR              Last byte is carriage return.
*
REVERSE LDS     #STACKE         Set up return-address stack.
        LDX     #MSG1           Prompt user for an input line.
        JSR     LINEOUT
        LDX     #INBUF          Pass the address of input buffer.
        JSR     LINEIN          Get a line of input.
        LDX     #INBUFT         Address of first input character.
        LDY     INBUFP          Address of last input character.
        ADDY    #-1             Bump to char before carriage return.
SWAPEM  STY     YTEMP           Swap bytes until X >= Y.
        CMPX    YTEMP
        BHS     REVDUN
        LDA     @X              Swap the bytes pointed to by X and Y.
        LDB     @Y
        STA     @Y
        STB     @X
        ADDX    #1              Bump X forward and Y backward.
        ADDY    #-1
        BRA     SWAPEM          Repeat.
REVDUN  LDX     #MSG2           Display the second message.
        JSR     LINEOUT
        LDX     #INBUFP         Display the reversed input line.
        JSR     LINEOUT
        JMP     REVERSE         Run the program forever.
        END     REVERSE
```

```
*          Character output driver for terminal number 0.
CHROUT0 PSHS   Y               Save Y.
        LDY    #0FF00H          Address of KBCS for terminal 0.
        JSR    CHROUTY          Output the character in A.
        PULS   Y                Restore Y.
        RTS                     Done, return.
```

Shared drivers are easy to write in computers that use memory-mapped I/O, because all of the usual indirect and based addressing modes are available

TABLE 10–6 Shared keyboard input and display output drivers.

```
* SUBROUTINE CHRINY -- Read one input character from a selected
*                      keyboard and echo it on the display.
*
* INPUTS -- KBCSADR -- Address of the keyboard control and status
*                      port, passed in register Y.
* GLOBAL VARIABLES, LOCAL VARIABLES  -- None.
* OUTPUTS -- INCHAR -- The character just read, passed in A.
* REGISTERS AFFECTED -- A
*
* Port addresses are defined relative to the address of KBCS.
KBCS    EQU    0               Keyboard control and status.
KBDATA  EQU    1               Keyboard data.
DSPCS   EQU    2               Display control and status.
DSPDATA EQU    3               Display data.
*
CHRINY  LDA    #1              Request one character.
        STA    KBCS(Y)
WTIN    TST    KBCS(Y)         Is it ready?
        BPL    WTIN            Wait for it.
        LDA    KBDATA(Y)       Get the character.
        ANDA   #7FH            Clear MSB.
        JSR    CHROUTY         Echo the character on the display.
        RTS                    Done, return.
*
* SUBROUTINE CHROUTY -- Print one character on a selected display.
*
* INPUTS -- KBCSADR  -- Address of the keyboard control and status
*                       port, passed in register Y.
*           OUTCHAR  -- The character to be displayed, passed in A.
* OUTPUTS, GLOBAL VARIABLES, LOCAL VARIABLES -- None.
* REGISTERS AFFECTED -- None.
*
CHROUTY TST    DSPCS(Y)        Has previous character been displayed?
        BPL    CHROUTY         Wait for completion.
        STA    DSPDATA(Y)      Send the new character to interface.
        PSHS   A               Save the character.
        LDA    #1              Display the character.
        STA    DSPCS(Y)
        PULS   A               Restore the character.
        RTS                    Done, return.
```

for dynamically computing a port address at run time. On the other hand, in some computers with isolated I/O, shared drivers are impossible to write without using self-modifying code. For example, in the Intel 8080 and MCS-48, the I/O port number is always specified as part of the instruction; there are no instructions that take the port number from a register. The Z8000 solves the problem by providing two "flavors" of I/O instructions — one that specifies the port number as part of the instruction and one that takes the port number from a register.

REFERENCES

Detailed discussion of I/O system architecture from a hardware designer's point of view can be found in textbooks such as *Digital Systems: Hardware Organization and Design* by Hill and Peterson [Wiley, 1978 (second edition)] and *Microcomputer-Based Design* by John Peatman [McGraw-Hill, 1977]. An introduction to basic microcomputer I/O hardware can be found in J. Wakerly's article "Microprocessor Input/Output Architecture" [*Computer*, Vol. 10, No. 2, February 1977, pp. 26-33].

This chapter has only touched the surface of possible I/O driver organizations and I/O buffering schemes. A section in Jim Peterson's *Computer Organization and Assembly Language Programming* [Academic Press, 1978] shows how to perform overlapped I/O on blocks of data. A good discussion of several possible buffering schemes can be found in Knuth's *Fundamental Algorithms* [Addison-Wesley, 1973 (second edition)]. Both of the above books use Knuth's hypothetical MIX computer for assembly language program examples.

EXERCISES

10.1 Devise a programming model for a one-digit seven-segment display, where the interface does not have an ENCODER block like the one in Figure 10–4(a). Instead, there is a single output port SEGS with a bit corresponding to each of the seven segments; a 1 lights the segment and a 0 extinguishes it. Draw a figure that shows the correspondence between bits of SEGS and segments. Then write a 6809 or Z8000 subroutine that uses SEGS to display a single BCD digit passed in A or R0.

10.2 Suppose you are in charge of the design of a microcomputer system that is to contain an input device whose sole function is to keep track of the current date, day, and time of day to the nearest millisecond. You are to specify a programming model for the device interface so that your hardware engineers can start building it and your programmers can start writing I/O drivers for it. All numbers are to be stored as unsigned binary integers. The I/O ports associated with the device must provide the capability of both initializing and reading the time information.

10.3   Repeat the previous exercise, using BCD representation for numbers where appropriate.

10.4   The keyboard input and display programs in Tables 10–1 and 10–2 use signed conditional branches to determine whether or not each input character is in range. Although these particular programs work, unsigned branches are a better choice for comparing characters in general. Explain why.

10.5   Show how to eliminate one CMP instruction in the RDDIG subroutine in Table 10–1 or 10–2 by performing the subtraction first.

10.6   Explain why there is a slight chance that overrun may go undetected in the KBDIN subroutine in Table 10–3.

10.7   Rewrite the KBDIN subroutine in Table 10–3 to use overlapped I/O. Show how it is now possible to ensure that overrun never goes undetected. Is overrun now more or less likely to occur than in the original program?

10.8   Rewrite the RDDIG subroutine in Table 10–1 or 10–2 to reduce the amount of busy-waiting by waiting for key release at the beginning of RDDIG. Explain the differences in the two versions when keys are typed very quickly.

10.9   Modify the CHROUT subroutine in Table 10–4 so that it detects errors using the ERR bit, in much the same way as KBDIN in Table 10–3.

10.10   Modify the CHROUT subroutine in Table 10–4 to work with an interface that eliminates the GO bit as described in footnote 1.

10.11   Most of the ASCII control characters (columns 0 and 1 in Appendix A) have no effect when displayed or printed. Write a CHROUT driver that converts control characters other than CR, LF, and BS into a two character sequence, "^" followed by the corresponding character in column 4 or 5 of the ASCII code chart. This is reasonable because the control characters are generated on most keyboards by holding down the control (CTRL) key and typing the corresponding column 4 or 5 character.

10.12   Write a LINEIN driver that allows simple editing of input lines typed on a CRT terminal. Typing a backspace (CTRL-H) should remove the previous character from the input buffer and echo a backspace, space, and another backspace, thereby erasing the previous character and properly adjusting the display's cursor. Typing a CTRL-C should remove all characters from the input buffer and start a new line on the display. (Hints: Characters need not be physically removed from the input buffer; it is sufficient to update the buffer point appropriately.) Be sure that your program doesn't allow backspacing beyond the beginning of the input buffer.

10.13   Write a LINEIN driver that allows simple editing of input lines typed on a teleprinter. CTRL-C should operate the same as in the previous exercise. Typing a delete character (DEL or RUB key) should echo a backslash (\) and the previous character in the input buffer, and remove the character from the buffer. Successive delete characters should echo and delete additional characters in the input buffer, *without* echoing a backslash. After echoing the last deleted character in a sequence of deletions, the driver should echo another backslash. (Note that the program doen't know that it has received the last delete character until it receives a non-delete character.) Since partial input lines with many deletions are difficult to read, also provide a CTRL-R command that starts a new line on the printer, prints the current (edited) input buffer contents, and allows the user to resume typing at the next character position.

10.14   Write a program that combines the keyboard and display I/O drivers from this chapter with the queue module from Chapter 9. Define four queues UCQ, LCQ, DQ, and OQ that can be manipulated by the queue module. Provide a main program that continuously reads characters from the keyboard using CHRIN. As each character is received, it should be enqueued in UCQ, LCQ, DQ, or OQ according to whether it is an upper case letter, a lower case letter, a decimal digit, or any other character. If the queue is full, the character should be discarded; each queue should hold 10 characters when full. If the character is a carriage return, it should not be enqueued; instead a maximum of six characters from each queue should be dequeued and displayed. The contents of each queue should be displayed on a separate line.

10.15   Write a set of I/O drivers for the timing device defined in Exercise 10.2. You will have to define a buffer format and write two subroutines for initializing the time from a buffer and loading a buffer with the current time information. Be sure to consider the problem of correctly reading the current time just as the second is changing from $m.999$ to $n.000$. It may be possible to get the answer $m.000$ or $n.999$ depending on the order in which the ports are read. At what other transitions can this kind of anomaly occur? How could the person who specified the hardware interface have avoided this?

10.16   Write a program to play Life as described in Exercise 7.5, where the Life array size corresponds to the size of a CRT screen. Write a subroutine DISPLAY that displays the current generation of Life in the CURG array by calling another subroutine COUT to display each character in the Life array. If the CRT terminal does not have automatic wraparound at the end of a line, DISPLAY must send CR and LF characters after each line except the last. On the other hand, with automatic wraparound, DISPLAY must not send the last character on the last line in order to keep the display from "rolling." Write a main program that initializes the Life array to a random population and computes and displays Life one generation at a time.

11

INTERRUPTS,
DIRECT MEMORY ACCESS,
AND PROCESSES

"We interrupt this program for a special announcement..."

This familiar phrase describes the basic function of an *interrupt system* — to notify a program each time an I/O operation has been completed. Instead of busy-waiting for operation completion, the processor runs an I/O program only when an I/O event is known to have occurred.

In the first two sections of this chapter we describe typical interrupt system structures and programming. Some processors use interrupt-like structures to signal other events — these are described in the third section.

With devices that generate a large number of low-level I/O events, *direct memory access (DMA) channels* can be used to reduce processor loading. A DMA channel allows the processor to issue a single high-level command (e.g., "read block of data from tape") to initiate a whole sequence of low-level I/O events (e.g., reading individual bytes). As described in the fourth section of this chapter, DMA does this by transferring data directly between an I/O device and memory without processor intervention.

The last two sections of this chapter introduce the concept of I/O processes and describe some of the pitfalls that must be avoided to keep programs safe and sane in an interrupt environment.

11.1   BASIC INTERRUPT SYSTEM STRUCTURE AND PROGRAMMING

With a simple I/O system, the only way that the processor can determine that a device has completed an operation is to continuously test the READY flag in the device interface. However, in a computer with many I/O devices, such as terminals, printers, and disks, all devices must be kept running concurrently for maximum efficiency. The processor cannot afford to waste time busy-waiting for one device to complete an operation while other devices may already be ready for service. An interrupt system solves this problem by allowing any I/O device to initiate a service routine in the processor when it completes an I/O operation, freeing the processor to do other things when the I/O devices are busy.

Using an interrupt system, each device can send an *interrupt request* signal to the processor when it completes an operation. The processor accepts an interrupt request by temporarily suspending the operation of the current program. It then executes an *interrupt service routine* for the I/O operation that was just completed, perhaps initiating still another I/O operation. After "servicing the interrupt," the processor returns control to the interrupted program. Except for an increase in execution time, the fact that an interrupt occurred is transparent to the interrupted program. (Don't you sometimes wish that interruptions of your favorite TV program were just as transparent?)

There are at least as many variations in interrupt system structure as there are processor organizations[1]. In this section we discuss some general ideas and describe a fairly simple interrupt system structure, the one used by the Motorola 6809.

11.1.1   General Considerations

Interrupts are usually allowed to take place only between, not during, the execution of individual instructions. For example, interrupting the instruction LDA (X)+ after loading A but before auto-incrementing X is not allowed. In the Pascal simulation of the H6809 in Table 5–1, the presence of an interrupt would be tested by a procedure CheckForInterrupt called right after Execute in the main loop of the simulation program:

```
WHILE true DO {H6809 instruction interpretation cycle}
  BEGIN
    Fetch;
    Execute;
    CheckForInterrupt;
  END;
```

---

[1]Perhaps more, because modern LSI interrupt control circuits give computer system designers many choices among different interrupt structures, independent of the processor.

The actions that take place in CheckForInterrupt "fool" the processor into executing the interrupt service routine, so that the next instruction fetched will be the first instruction of the interrupt service routine; we'll give details later.

The processor normally has a means of disabling interrupts completely, typically by setting or clearing one of the processor status bits. When interrupts are allowed and one does occur, the processor takes the following actions:

(1) All or part of the current processor state is saved and the interrupt service routine is entered.

(2) The identity of the interrupting device interface is determined.

(3) The condition that caused the interface to request an interrupt is identified and serviced.

(4) The saved processor state is restored and the program that was interrupted is resumed.

In the first step above, "processor state" refers to the program counter (PC) and all of the registers in the programming model of the processor. When an interrupt takes place, the current value of the PC must be saved so that the interrupted program can later be resumed. The saved PC points to the instruction that would have been executed next if the interrupt hadn't occurred. All registers whose values might be disturbed must also be saved at the beginning and restored at the end of the interrupt service routine. As a minimum, the condition bits should be saved; typically all of the registers must be saved (an interrupt service routine can't do too much useful work without using registers).

The process of saving PC, registers, and condition bits after an interrupt, or restoring them later, is called *context switching*. In systems with frequent interrupts, the speed of context switching can have a significant impact on system performance. Therefore, many processors have features to speed up context switching, such as instructions that load and store multiple registers. In fact, some processors even save and restore the registers automatically on interrupt calls and returns.

The second step above, identifying the interrupting interface, can be accomplished in a number of different ways as described later. For the moment, we will assume that there is only one interrupting interface so that the second step is not needed.

The third step, servicing the condition that caused the interrupt, is accomplished by normal instructions on I/O ports. The last step, resuming the interrupted program, is another context switch. This is often accomplished by a special instruction that restores the saved processor state; restoring the PC in effect jumps back to the interrupted program.

11.1.2 A Simple Interrupt System

The Motorola 6809 processor has an interrupt request line called IRQ; a device interface can interrupt the processor by placing an appropriate logic signal on this line (or by "tugging" the line, as some hardware designers say). The processor will accept an interrupt request on this line only if the I (Interrupt mask) bit in the CC (Condition Code) register is 0 (bit 4, see Figure 8–1). Thus, a program can disable or "mask" interrupts by setting I to 1.

In practice, more than one device interface may be capable of tugging IRQ, in which case the processor must somehow determine which one is doing it. This is discussed later; for the moment we assume that only one interface is connected to IRQ.

If the processor accepts an interrupt request on IRQ, it performs a whole sequence of actions automatically. As shown in Figure 11–1, the processor saves its entire state by pushing PC and all registers except S onto the stack, using S as the stack pointer (S is called SP in the H6809). Then it sets the I bit in the CC register to 1, which prevents IRQ from causing further interrupts. There is also a change in CC bit 7, explained in Sections 11.1.4 and 11.1.5. Finally, the processor loads the PC with the 16-bit value contained in an "interrupt vector" stored at locations FFF8H and FFF9H. This value is the starting address of an interrupt service routine that has been written by a programmer. Even though the address of the vector (FFF8H, FFF9H) is fixed in the processor's hardware design, the interrupt service routine may be located anywhere in memory; the value of the interrupt vector determines the starting address.

After accepting an interrupt as described above, the processor returns to its normal instruction fetching and execution process. Since the PC has been loaded with the starting address of the interrupt service routine, the next instruction executed will be the first instruction of the interrupt service routine. The interrupt routine services whatever condition caused the interrupt, and causes the interface to remove its request from the IRQ line. Before IRQ is cleared, the request is still ignored because I=1.

The service routine returns to the interrupted program by executing an RTI (Return from interrupt) instruction. RTI restores the original values of all of the registers (including the PC and CC) by popping them off the stack. Therefore, just after RTI is executed the program will once again have exactly the state shown in Figure 11–1(a), as if the interrupt had never occurred (except for CC bit 7). Since the value of the I bit is restored to 0 when the saved CC register is popped from the stack, further interrupts may now be accepted when requested on the IRQ line.

11.1.3 An I/O Program Using Interrupts

A 6809 program that uses interrupts to print text strings using the display interface that was defined in Figure 10–12 is given in Table 11–1. The display interface places an interrupt request on IRQ whenever IEN=1 and RDY=1.

Thus a request is made on IRQ each time a character printing operation is completed. The request on IRQ is removed each time STRINT sends another character to the display (by setting GO, which clears RDY), or when STRINT finds that it has no more characters to send (and clears IEN).

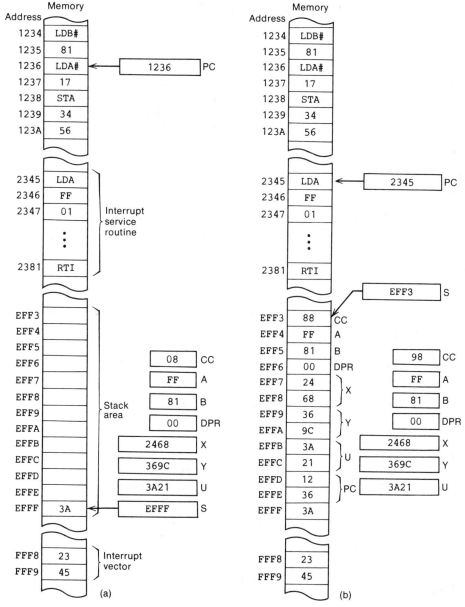

FIGURE 11–1 Program state during interrupt processing: (a) just before interrupt is accepted; (b) just after interrupt is accepted.

TABLE 11-1 Display output program using interrupts.

```
*           Subroutines STROUT and STRINT are used to print text
*      strings on the display.  A text string is defined to be a
*      sequence of non-NUL ASCII characters terminated by NUL (0).
*           To print a string, a program should call STROUT with X
*      containing the address of the first character of the string.
*      STROUT enables the display interrupt, prints the first char-
*      acter, and returns to the calling program.  Subsequent char-
*      acters are printed by the interrupt service routine STRINT.
*           The global variable SBUSY, when nonzero, indicates that
*      a string is currently being printed.  The main program must
*      initialize SBUSY to 0 so that STROUT doesn't hang the first
*      time it is called. When STROUT is entered, it will not start
*      printing a new string until it finds that the previous string
*      has been completely printed. STRINT clears SBUSY after
*      printing the last character.
*

        ORG    0FFF8H          IRQ interrupt vector address.
        FCW    STRINT          Address of interrupt service routine.
*
        ORG    1000H
*      Define display interface registers.
DSPCS   EQU    0FF02H          Display control and status port.
DSPDATA EQU    0FF03H          Display data port.
*      Local and global variables.
BUFPNT  RMW    1               Pointer to character being displayed.
SBUSY   RMB    1               Nonzero when string is being displayed.
*
STROUT  TST    SBUSY           Is a previous string being displayed?
        BNE    STROUT          Wait for it.
        STX    BUFPNT          Save buffer pointer.
        LDA    #0FFH           Set SBUSY flag.
        STA    SBUSY
        LDA    @X              Get first character.
        STA    DSPDATA         Display it.
        LDA    #41H            Set IEN and GO.
        STA    DSPCS
        RTS                    Done, return.
*
*      Registers are already saved on entry to STRINT.
STRINT  LDX    BUFPNT          Get buffer pointer.
        ADDX   #1              Bump pointer to next character.
        STX    BUFPNT
        LDA    @X              Get next character.
        BEQ    STRDUN          Quit if it's a zero.
        STA    DSPDATA         Otherwise display it.
        LDA    #41H            Set IEN and GO.
        STA    DSPCS
        RTI                    Return to interrupted program.
STRDUN  CLRA                   Redundant, since A=0 already.
        STA    DSPCS           Clear IEN.
        STA    SBUSY           Clear SBUSY flag.
        RTI                    Return to interrupted program.
```

TABLE 11–1   (continued)

```
*         Main program.
MAIN      ...                    Initialization.
          CLRA
          STA     SBUSY          Clear SBUSY flag.
LOOP      ...                    Do some processing.
          LDX     #MSG1          Print the first message.
          JSR     STROUT
          ...                    Do some more processing.
          LDX     #MSG2          Print the second message.
          JSR     STROUT
          ...                    Do some more processing.
          JMP     LOOP
*
MSG1      FCC     'The quick brown fox jumps over the lazy dog.'
          FCB     0
MSG2      FCC     'That was a pretty unimaginative message!'
          FCB     0
*
          END     MAIN
```

The main program can display a string by calling STROUT with the string's address in X. STROUT enables the display interrupt, prints the first character, and then returns control to the main program, which may continue to perform useful computation. The remainder of the string is displayed by the interrupt service routine STRINT, which uses the variable BUFPNT to keep track of which character is being displayed.

The time behavior of the interrupt program is shown in Figure 11–2. The global variable SBUSY indicates whether or not the current string has been completely printed, so that STROUT can automatically busy-wait for completion when a second string is requested too soon, as in Figure 11–2(b). Note that the RDY bit in the display control and status register is a hardware flag that indicates completion of a single character output operation, while SBUSY is a software flag that indicates completion of a higher level software process, the printing of an entire string.

11.1.4   Other Interrupt Lines

Besides IRQ, the 6809 has two other interrupt request lines, called NMI (Non-Maskable Interrupt) and FIRQ (Fast Interrupt Request). As summarized in Table 11–2, these lines differ from IRQ in their interrupt vector addresses, how they are masked, and the registers pushed onto the stack when the interrupt is accepted. The processor also responds to hardware resets and software interrupt instructions in a manner similar to hardware interrupts, as explained in Section 11.3.2.

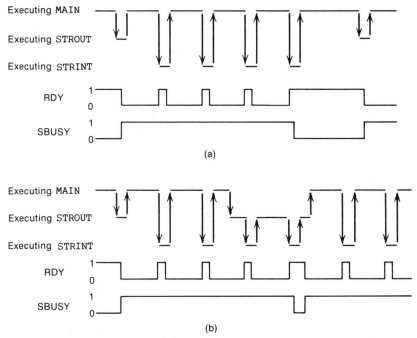

FIGURE 11–2 Time behavior of interrupt program: (a) first string printed before second is requested; (b) second string requested before first is printed.

Interrupts on FIRQ cause only the PC and condition bits (CC) to be stacked, saving execution time in interrupt service routines that don't use many or any registers. The E (Entire State on Stack) bit in the saved CC keeps track of whether or not all the registers were pushed; the RTI instruction looks at this to determine which registers to pop. Like FIRQ, most other processors only stack the PC and condition bits when an interrupt is accepted. Any other registers that might be disturbed must be saved by an explicit PUSH instruction at the beginning of the interrupt service routine and restored by a POP at the end.

A program cannot ignore interrupt requests on NMI, even if it wants to. NMI is especially useful for "watchdog timer" applications, where a timer is set to interrupt the program periodically. Even if a program goes berserk and permanently disables the other interrupts, it cannot prevent the NMI interrupt from being serviced. Another common use of NMI is in power-down applications. A typical power supply can provide a logic signal that indicates that the AC source voltage has been removed and that its DC output voltage will fall below acceptable levels within a few milliseconds. If this signal is connected to NMI, a program can perform crucial operations such as shutting down I/O devices before power is completely gone.

TABLE 11–2 Interrupt requests and vectors in the 6809.

Input Line	Vector Address	Mask Bit	Registers Pushed
IRQ	FFF8H	I	PC, U, Y, X, DPR, B, A, CC
FIRQ	FFF6H	F	PC, CC
NMI	FFFCH	none	PC, U, Y, X, DPR, B, A, CC
RESET	FFFEH	none	none

Instruction	Vector Address	Mask Bit	Registers Pushed
SWI	FFFAH	none	PC, U, Y, X, DPR, B, A, CC
SWI2	FFF4H	none	PC, U, Y, X, DPR, B, A, CC
SWI3	FFF2H	none	PC, U, Y, X, DPR, B, A, CC

11.1.5 Pascal Simulation of an Interrupt System

Table 11–3 gives an extended-Pascal simulation of how the 6809 checks for and handles interrupt requests. The procedure CheckForInterrupt shows how interrupt requests are checked after the execution of each instruction. The procedure ReturnFromInterrupt shows the actions performed by the 6809 RTI instruction. Notice how the E bit saved in the copy of CC on the stack is used to determine which registers RTI must pop from the stack.

11.2 VARIATIONS IN INTERRUPT SYSTEMS AND PROGRAMS

In this section we classify and discuss some of the many variations in interrupt system structures and programs.

11.2.1 Interrupt Levels and Enabling

A processor has a *multi-level* interrupt system if it has multiple lines (or levels) on which external devices can request interrupts, and if interrupt service routines on one level can be interrupted by requests on another level. If an interrupt system has *n* levels, then up to *n* interrupt service routines could be in progress at any time. For example, the 6809 has three interrupt levels (NMI, FIRQ, and IRQ), while the PDP-11 has four (BR4, BR5, BR6, and BR7). The MCS-48 has a *single-level* interrupt system — only one interrupt service routine can be in progress at any time.

Multi-level interrupt systems are useful for grouping devices of similar characteristics or priority into the same level. For example, all the disks and tapes in a system could be placed on one level, and all the terminals on

TABLE 11–3 Pascal simulation of 6809 interrupt handling.

```
PROGRAM M6809 (input,output);
  ...
VAR MEM : ARRAY [0..65535] OF byte; {Main memory.}
  EAR, PC, X, Y, S, U : word; {Processor registers.}
  A, B, DPR : byte;
  E, F, H, I, N, Z, V, C : bit;  {CC register.}
  IRQ, FIRQ, NMI : boolean;  {External interrupt requests.}
  ...
PROCEDURE PushByte(b : byte);
  BEGIN S := S - 1; MEM[S] := b END;

PROCEDURE PushWord(w : word);
  BEGIN PushByte(w[7::0]); PushByte(w[15::8]) END;

FUNCTION PopByte : byte;
  BEGIN PopByte := MEM[S]; S := S + 1 END;

FUNCTION PopWord : word; {Pop two bytes to make a word.}
  BEGIN PopWord := PopByte | PopByte END;

PROCEDURE AcceptInterrupt(vectorAddr : word);
  BEGIN
    PushWord(PC);
    IF E = 1 THEN
      BEGIN
        PushWord(U);  PushWord(Y);  PushWord(X);
        PushByte(DPR);  PushByte(B);  PushByte(A);
      END;
    PushByte(E|F|H|I|N|Z|V|C);
    PC[15::8] := MEM[vectorAddr]; PC[7::0] := MEM[vectorAddr+1];
  END;

PROCEDURE CheckForInterrupt;
  BEGIN
    IF NMI THEN
      BEGIN E := 1; AcceptInterrupt(0FFFCH); F := 1; I := 1 END
    ELSE IF FIRQ AND (F=0) THEN
      BEGIN E := 0; AcceptInterrupt(0FFF6H); F := 1; I := 1 END
    ELSE IF IRQ AND (I=0) THEN
      BEGIN E := 1; AcceptInterrupt(0FFF8H); I := 1 END;
  END;

PROCEDURE ReturnFromInterrupt;
  VAR CC : byte;
  BEGIN
    CC := PopByte;
    E := CC[7]; F := CC[6]; H := CC[5]; I := CC[4];
    N := CC[3]; Z := CC[2]; V := CC[1]; C := CC[0];
    IF E = 1 THEN
      BEGIN A:=PopByte; B:=PopByte; DPR:=PopByte;
            X:=PopWord; Y:=PopWord; U:=PopWord END;
    PC := PopWord;
  END;
```

another level. Then it is possible for a terminal interrupt service routine to be interrupted by a tape drive needing service.

By setting or clearing appropriate mask bits in the processor state, a processor can accept interrupt requests on some levels while ignoring others. Thus a program can quickly disable all interrupts on a "low priority" level (e.g., terminals) while still allowing interrupts from a "high priority" level (e.g., disks and tapes).

Regardless of the number of interrupt levels, it may still be possible for the processor to disable interrupts from a specific device by manipulating the "interrupt enable" (IEN) bit in the device interface control and status register. Figure 11–3 illustrates this for the 6809 (AND and OR gates were introduced in Section 1.2). Three interfaces have interrupt request outputs connected to IRQ. However, only two of the interfaces (1 and 3) have their IEN bits set to 1 and can request an interrupt when RDY is 1; and as shown only interface 3 is actually requesting an interrupt at this time. If the processor masks interrupt requests on IRQ by setting I to 1, then even this request will be ignored (and remain pending) until the processor sets I to 0 again.

Generally when a processor accepts an interrupt on a particular level, it disables interrupts on that level until the current interrupt has been fully serviced. However, reenabling the level after partial service may be permissible any time after the current interrupt request signal is removed.

11.2.2 Interrupt Priority

In a multi-level interrupt system, *interrupt priority* determines whether an interrupt service routine for one level can be interrupted by a request on another level. In a typical system, each interrupt line has a fixed priority. For

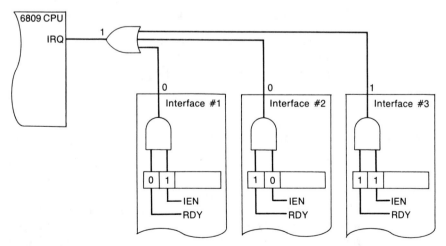

FIGURE 11–3 Interrupt enabling.

example, the 6809 NMI line has the highest priority, followed by FIRQ and IRQ; this priority is fixed in hardware by the way that the I and F mask bits are handled.

It is also possible for two or more devices to request interrupt service at exactly the same time. An unlikely way for this to happen is for two devices to actually complete their operations within one processor instruction cycle (about one microsecond) of each other. A more likely way is for two or more devices to request interrupts during a longer period of time in which the processor has masked interrupts. When the processor finally reenables interrupts, multiple requests will be pending. Interrupt priority also governs the order in which these multiple requests are serviced. Once again, the 6809 has priority NMI, FIRQ, IRQ, fixed in hardware by the order in which the lines are examined after each instruction interpretation cycle (see Table 11–2).

When multiple interfaces request interrupts on the same line, the processor must select one of the interfaces to service. The way in which the selection is made determines the interfaces' priority. One of two different techniques is generally used:

- *Fixed priority*. The interfaces are examined in fixed priority order; the first one found to be requesting an interrupt is serviced.

- *Round robin*. The interfaces are ordered, but the search for an interface needing service is started with the interface *after* the last one that was serviced; the search returns to the first one in the list when the end of the list is reached.

Round-robin priority is more "fair" than fixed priority because it keeps fast devices from monopolizing interrupt service at the expense of slower devices. It is also more "reliable" because it prevents a faulty high-priority device from locking out low priority devices by interrupting continuously. As we'll see in the next subsection, round-robin priority is easy to provide in software by polling.

When priority is resolved by hardware rather than software, fixed priority is most often used because the circuits are less complex. For example, the interrupt system of the PDP-11 imposes a fixed priority on each device according to its physical proximity on the I/O bus to the CPU.

11.2.3   Interrupt Identification and Polling

When a program knows that some device has interrupted, but it doesn't know which one, it can simply "go out and ask"! This is called *polling*.

The control and status registers of most device interfaces contain a bit or a group of bits that indicates whether or not an interrupt has been requested. For example, the keyboard and display interfaces in Figures 10–9 and 10–12 request an interrupt whenever both RDY and IEN are 1. If both devices request interrupts using IRQ, a program can determine which device has requested an interrupt at any time by checking the RDY and IEN bits on both interfaces.

If multiple interrupt requests are made simultaneously, the order in which the interfaces are polled determines their priority. Table 11-4 shows a 6809 program with routines for both fixed-priority and round-robin polling. A "polling table" specifies the address of the control and status register and the starting address of the interrupt service routine for each device that can request interrupts on IRQ. This example assumes there are only three devices, but an arbitrary number of devices could be serviced using additional table entries.

The polling routine FPOLL checks the control and status registers for interrupt requests in a fixed order, yielding fixed priority. RPOLL uses the variable LASTP to remember which interface was polled last, yielding round-robin priority. Depending on the address value that the programmer uses to initialize the IRQ vector, IRQ interrupts are serviced by either FPOLL or RPOLL (FPOLL in this example).

11.2.4 Vectored Interrupts

Polling programs take time to execute, and in a system with many devices and frequent interrupts, the time spent polling can be significant. Therefore many computers have built-in hardware that automatically selects a different interrupt service routine for each different device. An interrupt system with this capability is said to have *vectored interrupts*.

Vectored interrupt systems require a priority scheme (fixed or round robin) to be provided in hardware. In this way, when the processor accepts an interrupt, it can give a positive acknowledgement to the interrupting device interface with highest priority. When the interface receives this acknowledgement, it identifies itself by sending a unique "interrupt vector" to the processor.

Interrupt vectoring strategies vary widely among different computers. The 6809 processor could be said to have vectored interrupts for up to three devices, each connected to one of its three interrupt request lines. However, the term "vectored interrupts" is usually only applied to processors with a larger number of interrupt vectors.

Using additional hardware, we could provide interrupt vectors for many devices connected to one 6809 interrupt request line, say IRQ. This hardware would have to provide priority selection among the devices, and also the capability of responding to read operations on the Memory and I/O Bus at addresses FFF8H and FFF9H. These "pseudo-memory" locations would contain the address of the interrupt service routine for the highest priority device currently requesting an interrupt. Instead of the programmer providing the address of the service routine at load time, the hardware provides it dynamically at run time according to which device needs service.

TABLE 11-4   Interrupt polling programs for 6809.

```
*               Subroutines FPOLL and RPOLL identify an interrupting
*          device by polling and transfer control to its interrupt
*          service routine.  FPOLL uses fixed priority polling,
*          while RPOLL uses round-robin polling.  A device is assumed
*          to be interrupting if the RDY and IEN bits (bits 7 and 6)
*          in its control and status register are both 1.
*               One or more interrupting devices are listed in a
*          polling table.  Each table entry contains four bytes (two
*          words) -- the address of the control and status register
*          for the device and the starting address of its interrupt
*          service routine.  The table is terminated by a zero word.
*
         ORG    0FFF8H          IRQ interrupt vector address.
         FCW    FPOLL           Fixed priority polling
*                                 (or use RPOLL for round-robin).
         ORG    1000H
*          Polling table.  Addresses of control and status registers
*          and service routines are assumed to be defined elsewhere.
POLLTB   FCW    KBDCS,KBDINT    Keyboard.
         FCW    DSPCS,DSPINT    Display.
         FCW    PTRCS,PTRINT    Papertape reader.
         FCW    0               End of table.
LASTP    RMW    1               Last polled (used by RPOLL only) ...
*                               ...initialize to #POLLTB at run time.
*          Fixed priority polling routine.
FPOLL    LDX    #POLLTB-4       Start at beginning of POLLTB.
FNEXT    ADDX   #4              Address of next item in POLLTB.
         LDY    @X              Get address of C&S reg for next device.
         BEQ    ERROR           False interrupt if at end of table.
         LDA    @Y              Check C&S reg -- bits 7 and 6 = 1?
         ANDA   #0C0H           Clear 6 low-order bits.
         CMPA   #0C0H           A is 11000000 if device is interrupting.
         BNE    FNEXT           Try next device if not.
         LDX    2(X)            Else get address of service routine...
         JMP    @X              ...and jump to it.
*          Round-robin polling routine.
RPOLL    LDX    LASTP           Start after last device polled.
RNEXT    ADDX   #4              Address of next item in POLLTB.
         LDY    @X              Get address of C&S reg for next device.
         BNE    RCHK            Skip if nonzero.
         LDX    #POLLTB         Else wrap around to start of table.
         LDY    @X              Get address of C&S reg for first device.
RCHK     LDA    @Y              Check C&S reg -- bits 7 and 6 = 1?
         ANDA   #0C0H           Clear 6 low-order bits.
         CMPA   #0C0H           A is 11000000 if device is interrupting.
         BNE    CHKLST          Try next device if not.
         STX    LASTP           Else save pointer to last polled...
         LDX    2(X)            ...get address of service routine...
         JMP    @X              ...and jump to it.
CHKLST   CMPX   LASTP           Checked all devices?
         BNE    RNEXT           No, try another.
ERROR    RTI                    False interrupt, return.
```

The PDP-11 processor architecture has a sophisticated interrupt vectoring mechanism built into it. It reserves the first 128 words of memory for a table of 64 2-word interrupt vectors. An interrupting interface identifies itself by sending the processor a pointer into this table. The selected table entry contains new values for the PC and PSW, which the processor uses after saving the old values in the stack. As usual, the programmer is responsible for initializing the table entries with the starting PC and PSW for each interrupt service routine. The 68000, Z8000, 9900, and 8086 have similar vectoring mechanisms.

11.3 TRAPS AND SOFTWARE INTERRUPTS

11.3.1 Traps

Some processors can create hardware interrupt requests on the occurrence of certain internal processor events. Such interrupts are often called *traps* to distinguish them from I/O interrupts, and may occur on events such as the following:

(1) Exceptional conditions, such as overflow or underflow on floating-point operations.

(2) Program faults, such as attempts to execute illegal or undefined instructions or attempts to access nonexistent or protected memory.

(3) Hardware faults, such as power failures and memory parity errors.

When a trap event occurs, the processor pushes the PC and processor status onto the stack just as it does for an interrupt, and then jumps to a service routine whose starting address is contained in a predetermined "trap vector" location in memory. A typical processor provides different trap vectors for different conditions or groups of conditions. The Z8000 also pushes a 16-bit identifier onto the stack that gives the "reason" for the trap.

11.3.2 Software Interrupts

Many processors have explicit instructions that affect the processor state in much the same way as a hardware interrupt. These instructions are called *software interrupts* or *system calls*.

For example, the 6809 has three such instructions, SWI, SWI2, and SWI3. When one of these instructions is executed, the processor registers are pushed onto the stack in the same way as during an IRQ or NMI hardware interrupt. Then control is transferred to a corresponding interrupt service routine whose 16-bit starting address is found at the interrupt vector address shown in Table 11-2. For example, the starting address for the SWI service routine is contained in memory bytes FFFAH and FFFBH. The service routine does some processing and then returns control to the calling program by executing an RTI instruction.

Software interrupt instructions are often used as a convenient and efficient way to call operating system utilities. They are efficient because they are generally shorter than subroutine jumps, and they are convenient because they do not require the calling program to know the operating system's address in memory at assembly time, load time, or even run time.

In systems with memory mapping and management, a software interrupt is normally the only way for a program to call the operating system, since a direct subroutine call to an address in the region reserved for the operating system would normally be trapped as a protection violation.

Even though there are only a few software interrupt instructions in the 6809, a program can call a larger number of different operating system utility routines by placing a 1-byte code after the SWI instruction. When the service routine is entered, the value of the PC saved on the stack will point to this byte. The service routine can use this byte as an index into its own internal table of utility routine addresses, and it can increment the saved PC on the stack so that the 1-byte code is skipped on the return.

In the Z8000, the system call (SC) instruction is 16 bits long, containing an 8-bit opcode and an 8-bit "operand" field in which the user can place an arbitrary value. When a program executes SC, the processor pushes the return address, processor status, *and* the SC instruction itself onto the stack, and jumps to a service routine whose starting address is specified by an interrupt vector in memory, as in the 6809. The service routine may read the second byte of the SC instruction stored on the stack, and use it as an index into a table of utility routine addresses.

11.4 DIRECT MEMORY ACCESS

11.4.1 Motivation

It is reasonable for relatively slow devices such as terminals and printers to interrupt a program once for each datum that is transferred. For example, suppose that about 100 instructions, or 100 microseconds, are required to service a device interrupt, including register saving and restoring, device service, and I/O buffer manipulations. Then a rate of 100 I/O transfers (interrupts) per second uses only 1% of the total instruction execution time available to the CPU. This leaves plenty of time for the CPU to do other things.

Now consider the operation of a mass storage device such as a disk or tape. Information is stored in blocks of 128 to 2048 bytes or more, depending on the particular device format, and the basic unit of transfer is one block. For a program to transfer a single block of data between a typical mass storage device and memory, it must first initiate a mechanical operation (such as moving the tape) to bring the selected block under a read/write head. The time spent waiting for this operation to be completed is called *access latency*. Average access latency for a disk ranges from about 8 to 250 milliseconds; a long tape can have an access latency of minutes. In any case, it seems reasonable to use an interrupt to signal the appearance of the selected block under the read/write head, to avoid a long period of busy waiting.

Once the selected block appears under the read/write head, interrupts lose their usefulness. For example, in a single-density, 5" minifloppy disk, data passes under the read/write head at the rate of one byte per 64 microseconds. It is unlikely that an interrupt service routine could do all of the required operations in 64 microseconds and return to the interrupted program before the next byte appeared. More likely, a very tight, efficient busy-wait loop would be required to perform the transfer.

With a double-density minifloppy disk, the programming problem becomes even more difficult, with a byte appearing every 32 microseconds. And with a typical "hard" disk, a programmed transfer is impossible on most CPUs, since a byte appears every 8 microseconds or less. At this point we must look for another approach.

A *direct memory access (DMA) channel* is a special hardware arrangement that allows a device interface to quickly transfer data directly to or from main memory without processor intervention. Ordinarily, the CPU is the "master" of the Memory Bus — it provides the address and control signals for each transfer that takes place. However, a DMA channel can temporarily become bus master as required to control the transfer of I/O data directly between a device and main memory.

For example, suppose a hard disk has a transfer rate of one byte per 8 microseconds and the main memory cycle time is 1 microsecond. Then a DMA channel can "steal" 1 memory cycle out of every 8 to transfer disk data, still leaving available 7 out of every 8 memory cycles for the CPU's use.

Because a DMA channel transfers data directly between a device and memory, it has no effect on the processor state (assuming that the DMA transfer is not writing new information over the current program or its data!). The only effect on program operation is that instructions occasionally take a little longer to execute, because they must wait for a "slow" memory access. In the disk example above, the CPU is slowed down by a maximum of 12.5%. The actual slowdown may be less, because sometimes DMA may steal cycles that the CPU didn't need anyway. For example, the DMA channel might transfer I/O data while the CPU is executing a multiply, divide, or other instruction whose speed is not limited by memory speed.

11.4.2 DMA Channel Programming

As with other I/O interfaces, the programming models for DMA channels vary by device and computer. However, we can point out some common requirements of all DMA channels for mass storage devices such as disks. In

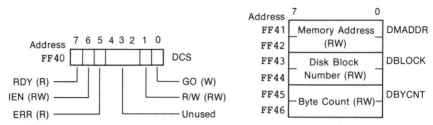

FIGURE 11–4   Programming model for a disk DMA channel.

order to perform a transfer, the channel must be told where to get or put the data on the disk, where to put or get it in main memory, and how many bytes to transfer. In addition, since the disk is a read/write device, the DMA channel must be told the direction of transfer: disk to memory (read) or memory to disk (write).

A stylized programming model for a disk DMA channel for the 6809 is shown in Figure 11–4. The control and status register (DCS) contains the RDY, IEN, ERR, and GO bits typical of other device interfaces. In addition, it contains a bit R/W for selecting the direction of transfer (1=read, 0=write). When IEN is 1, the DMA channel interrupts when an entire block transfer has been completed, not once per byte.

A 16-bit register DMADDR gives the starting address in main memory for the transfer. Another 16-bit register DBLOCK gives the starting block number on the disk for the transfer. Depending on the type of disk, DBLOCK may be subdivided into fields with information such as drive number, surface number, track number, and sector number. For large disks, multiple registers might be required. In any case, DBLOCK addresses only full blocks on the disk, not individual bytes. The size of a block depends on the disk; we'll use a size of 256 bytes in this example.

Register DBYCNT indicates the number of bytes to be transferred between the disk and main memory. Typically DBYCNT is set equal to the block size, so that exactly one block is transferred at a time. If DBYCNT specifies a larger number of bytes, then the DMA channel will automatically increment the block number in DBLOCK to access the next sequential block(s). A disk or tape physically can only read or write a full block at a time; if DBYCNT is not a multiple of the block size, then the DMA channel must compensate. For example, on read operations the channel still reads the entire last block from the device, but only stores in main memory the bytes actually required by DBYCNT. On write operations, it pads the end of the last block with zeroes to reach a multiple of the block size.

A program that uses DMA to read blocks of data from a disk is shown in Table 11–5. It reads one block at a time from the disk, using DMA to dump each block into a 256-byte memory buffer DSKBUF. After requesting a block, the program continues with other computation; when it is ready to process the

TABLE 11–5 Disk input program using DMA.

```
BLKSIZ  EQU    256              Disk block size.
*                               Addresses of disk interface registers.
DCS     EQU    0FF40H           Control and status.
DMADDR  EQU    0FF41H           Main memory address.
DBLOCK  EQU    0FF43H           Block number.
DBYCNT  EQU    0FF45H           Number of bytes to transfer.
*
BLOCKN  RMW    1                Program variable -- disk block #.
DSKBUF  RMB    BLKSIZ           Buffer for one disk block.
*
DISKIO  ...                     Begin program.
        ...
LOOP    ...                     Process one block per iteration.
*                               Determine block number, put in BLOCKN.
        ...
*                               Now ready to get a block from the disk.
        LDX    #DSKBUF          Address of memory buffer for transfer.
        STX    DMADDR           Store in disk memory address register.
        LDX    BLOCKN           Disk block number.
        STX    DBLOCK           Store in disk block number register.
        LDX    #BLKSIZ          Block and buffer size.
        STX    DBYCNT           Store in disk byte count register.
        LDA    #03H             Set disk for read and go.
        STA    DCS              Now the operation has begun.
*       If possible, do other work while waiting.
        ...
*       Now we need the buffer contents -- has the reading finished?
WTDSK   LDA    DCS
        BPL    WTDSK            Wait until ready.
        ANDA   #20H             Check error bit.
        BNE    DERROR           Handle errors if set.
*                               Now process the buffer...
        ..
        JMP    LOOP             ...and go do some more.
DERROR  ...                     Handle disk errors.
```

block, it must busy-wait on the RDY bit in DCS. After processing the block, the program decides which block to process next and repeats.

As the program stands, it can't begin reading a second block from the disk while still processing a first, because the DMA transfer could overwrite the contents of DSKBUF with the second block before the program has finished processing the first. However, a technique called *double buffering* allows this kind of overlap to take place. We provide two buffers: the DMA fills an I/O buffer while the program accesses data in a work buffer. After each program iteration and DMA transfer are completed, the program copies the contents of the I/O buffer into the work buffer for the next iteration and initiates another transfer. Alternatively, the copying operation could be eliminated by simply swapping the roles of the two buffers after each iteration. Either way, the I/O device can be kept busy continuously if computation is faster than I/O.

Interrupts are often used instead of busy-waiting for DMA completion in multi-block transfers. An interrupt indicates the completion of each DMA block transfer, and the interrupt service routine initiates the next DMA block transfer. After the last block has been transferred, the service routine signals completion to the main program using a software flag. Operation is similar to that of the string printing module in Table 11–1, except that interrupts occur once per block instead of once per character.

11.4.3 Memory-Mapped Screens

An important application of DMA in many computers is the *memory-mapped screen*. In this arrangement, a DMA channel is designed to access a block of memory in which each byte corresponds to a character position on a CRT display screen. In order to send a character to a particular position on the screen, a program simply writes the ASCII value of the character into the corresponding location in the memory buffer. The DMA channel automatically accesses each byte in the buffer sixty times per second, sending each character to video circuits that refresh the CRT screen, typically a high-resolution video monitor. In applications that do not require high resolution, an ordinary television can often be used instead of a monitor.

Memory-mapped screens are also used in computer graphics. In this case, each bit in each byte in the screen buffer corresponds to a dot on the screen that can be either on or off (bright or dark). A program creates an image on the screen by setting up appropriate bits in the screen buffer. Note that higher resolution displays require larger screen buffers than low-resolution displays. For example, a 512×512 display requires 2^{18} bits or 32K bytes of memory. Additional features, such as grey scale and color, require more than one bit of information for each dot (or picture element, "pixel"), and multiply the memory requirements by a corresponding factor.

Memory mapped screens in different computers have varying degrees of sophistication. For example, the address of the screen buffer may be fixed by the hardware, or it may be possible for the user to select among two or more buffers by issuing appropriate I/O commands to the DMA interface. In another example, scrolling a character display may require a program to move up all the data in the buffer to make room for a new line at the end, or it may only require a pointer and one line in the buffer to be updated. In the second case, the DMA starts the display in the middle of the buffer at a location designated by a "top-of-screen" pointer, and wraps back to the beginning when it hits the end of the buffer.

Small computers with memory-mapped screens include the Apple II and III and the TRS-80. In conjunction with a built-in keyboard, the memory-mapped screen takes the place of the separate CRT terminal that would otherwise be used to communicate with the machine. In fact, many "smart" CRT terminals such as the Heath/Zenith H19 actually contain a microcomputer with a memory-mapped screen interface.

11.5 INTERRUPT PROCESSES

The abstract concept of a "process" is a convenient aid to understanding and discussing the behavior of programs in an interrupt environment.

11.5.1 Processes

A *process* may be loosely defined as a program in execution. The state of a process includes the processor (CPU) state and the values of the program's variables stored in memory. Thus we can say that a process is a discrete progression in time of discernible changing states. The minimum grain of time is the processor's instruction interpretation cycle.

In an interrupt environment, it is convenient to think of a program as containing a set of processes that are activated, suspended, resumed, and terminated during the program's execution. A process is *active* if one or more of its instructions have been executed, and one or more instructions have yet to be executed; otherwise it is *inactive* (or *terminated*). An active process is *awake* if its instructions are currently being executed by the processor; otherwise it is *asleep*. An inactive process can be considered to be always asleep. Table 11–6 summarizes the possible conditions of processes.

For example, consider the display output program that was shown in Table 11–1. It contains two processes, the main program (MPP) and the string printing process (SPP). Periodically MPP activates SPP by calling STROUT. After sending one character to the display, STROUT suspends (or "puts to sleep") SPP and returns control to MPP. Thereafter, SPP is periodically resumed (or "awakened") by display interrupts, which are serviced by STRINT.

TABLE 11–6 Legal conditions of a process P.

Activity	Wakefulness	Description
Active	Awake	CPU is executing P's instructions.
Active	Asleep	CPU is executing instructions for some other process; but P may still be awakened by an interrupt or other event.
Inactive	Asleep	CPU is executing instructions for some other process and interrupts for P cannot occur; P may be awakened only by another process explicitly reactivating it.

SPP is put to sleep when STRINT returns to the interrupted program, and terminated when the last character of a line has been printed.

In Figure 11–2, the state of variable SBUSY corresponds to the active (1) or inactive (0) state of SPP, whereas MPP is always active. The asleep and awake states of the processes can be derived from the execution trace. SPP is awake when the processor is executing STROUT or STRINT, and asleep at other times; MPP is awake whenever SPP is asleep, and vice versa.

Because interrupts can occur at arbitrary times, it may be possible at any time for an awake process to be put to sleep and a sleeping process to be awakened. Within a given process, instructions will be executed in the order in which they were written, but instructions from other processes may intervene. At the very lowest level, this behavior imposes the requirement that all registers in the processor state be saved and restored by interrupt service routines. But there may also be effects at higher levels, in particular when two or more processes share instructions or data. Some of these effects and how they are handled are discussed later in this section and in Section 11.6.

11.5.2 A Simplifying Restriction

Multiple processes usually operate under the control of an operating system or executive. Some operating systems allow processes to be dynamically created and destroyed as suggested above, while others require all processes to be created at system initialization. In the latter case, processes are always active; they can only be awakened and put to sleep, not activated or terminated. We can use this idea in the MPP/SPP example by saying SPP never really terminates itself; even after printing the last character of a line, SPP simply puts itself to sleep. But now we must recognize that there are two distinct ways in which SPP could be reawakened after putting itself to sleep: by an interrupt or by an explicit command from another process.

We shall use the above ideas to simplify the discussions in the remainder of this chapter. We shall consider a process to be always active, but progressing through times of wakefulness and sleep. There are three basic situations in which a process can wake up or go to sleep:

(1) A process goes to sleep when an arbitrary device interrupt occurs, and is awakened when the interrupt service routine returns control to it.

(2) A process is awakened by its own device interrupt, and it executes its interrupt service routine. The process goes to sleep when it returns control to the interrupted program. Before going to sleep, it may or may not arrange to be reawakened later by its device interrupt.

(3) A process may be awakened by an explicit command from another process, (e.g., a command to begin printing a line of text). It goes to sleep by returning control to the calling process, but before doing so it usually arranges to be reawakened later by its device interrupt.

11.5.3   Concurrency and Multiple Interrupt Processes

For the most efficient use of computer resources, computation and I/O should be overlapped whenever possible. The display output program in Table 11–1 made good use of concurrency by using an interrupt process to complete output operations initiated by the main program.

In a typical program there may be an input process as well as an output process. The general outline for such a program is as follows:

(1) Read a set of inputs.

(2) Compute with the inputs to produce a set of outputs.

(3) Write the set of outputs.

(4) If there are more inputs, return to step 1, else terminate.

Without interrupts, a program would be forced to execute each step separately, with no time overlap, as shown in Figure 11–5(a). The circled numbers identify each set of data as it is read from the input device, processed by the CPU, and written to the output device.

A more desirable behavior, achieved by using interrupts, is illustrated in Figure 11–5(b). The main program must still wait for the first set of inputs. However, the input process can begin to read the second set of inputs as soon as the computation process has received the first set. When the computation process is ready for the second set of inputs, they are already waiting. From this point on, most of the computation is overlapped with input and output. Occasionally the computation process must wait for a slow input operation (third set) or output operation (third set also) to complete. After finding that the last (seventh) set of inputs is empty, the computation process must wait

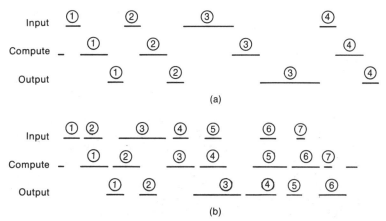

(a)

(b)

FIGURE 11–5 Input/output concurrency: (a) no interrupts and no overlap; (b) interrupts and overlap.

TABLE 11-7 Program to reverse lines of input text.

```
PROGRAM ReverseLines (input, output);
VAR inputBuffer, outputBuffer : ARRAY [1..100] OF char;
  inputAvailable, outputPrinted, working : boolean;

PROCESS LineIn;
  VAR kbdData : char;  kbdIEN, kbdReady, kbdGo : boolean;
  BEGIN
    WHILE true DO {forever}
      BEGIN
        inputAvailable := false;  ClearInputBuffer;
        REPEAT  {Enable interrupt, request keystroke, clear ready.}
          kbdIEN := true; kbdGo := true; kbdReady := false;
          SLEEP UNTIL kbdReady = true; {Wait for keyboard interrupt.}
          PutInInputBuffer(kbdData);
        UNTIL kbdData=terminator;
        kbdIEN := false; inputAvailable := true; SLEEP;
      END; {WHILE}
  END; {LineIn}

PROCESS LineOut;
  VAR dspData : char;  dspIEN, dspReady, dspGo : boolean;
  BEGIN
    WHILE true DO {forever}
      BEGIN
        outputPrinted := false;
        WHILE CharsLeftToBePrinted DO {If there's an output char...}
          BEGIN    {...send char to display data register,...}
            dspData := GetNextOutputChar;
            {...enable interrupt, start display, and clear ready.}
            dspIEN := true; dspGo := true; dspReady := false;
            SLEEP UNTIL dspReady = true; {Wait for display interrupt.}
          END;
        dspIEN := false; outputPrinted := true; SLEEP;
      END; {WHILE}
  END; {LineOut}

PROCESS MainLoop;
  LABEL 10; VAR workBuffer : ARRAY [1..100] OF char;
  BEGIN
    WAKEUP LineIn;   {Request LineIn to read the first line...}
    WHILE true DO                  {...and put it in inputBuffer.}
      BEGIN
        SLEEP UNTIL inputAvailable;  {Wait for an input line.}
        IF InputBufferEmpty THEN GOTO 10;  {Exit on blank line.}
        workBuffer := inputBuffer;   {Copy input line...}
        WAKEUP LineIn;  {...and start reading next line.}
        ReverseWorkBuffer; {Reverse characters in work buffer.}
        SLEEP UNTIL outputPrinted; {Wait for a chance to print.};
        outputBuffer := workBuffer; {Copy line...}
        WAKEUP LineOut;  {...and start printing it.}
      END;
  10: SLEEP UNTIL outputPrinted; {Wait for last line to be printed.}
    working := false;  SLEEP {forever};
  END;
```

TABLE 11–7 (continued)

```
BEGIN  {Main program.}
  working := true; outputPrinted := true;  {Initialization.}
  WAKEUP MainLoop; WHILE working DO ; {Wait for MainLoop to finish.}
END.
```

for the current output operation to complete before returning control to the operating system.

A program that achieves the behavior in Figure 11–5(b) is outlined in Table 11–7 in pseudo-Pascal. The program defines three processes to read lines of input text, reverse the order of the characters in each line, and print the reversed lines. The new reserved word PROCESS begins the definition of a process, and SLEEP and WAKEUP explicitly suspend and resume processes. A process can "SLEEP" until explicitly awakened by another process via WAKEUP, or it can "SLEEP UNTIL" a specified condition becomes true (e.g., an interrupt request).

The program simulates the bits in the control and status registers of a keyboard and display by boolean variables, and the data registers by char variables. The device interfaces can magically change the values of these variables (e.g., the keyboard interface sets kbdReady to true when a character is received). The definitions of several procedures and functions have been left to the reader's imagination.

The "main program" simply wakes up process MainLoop and busy-waits for MainLoop to finish all of its operations. MainLoop performs the three step loop (input, compute, output) and goes to sleep whenever the input process or output process has not completed its operation by the time that MainLoop is ready to initiate the next input or output operation.

11.5.4 Implementation Details

The processes in Table 11–7 are closely related to coroutines. When a process is resumed after sleeping, its computation should proceed where it left off, just like a coroutine that is resumed after calling another coroutine. In an assembly language version of the program, we could provide a variable that stores the resumption (or "wake-up") address for each process.

Another alternative is to simulate the more general coroutine structure using subroutines. For example, Table 11–8 shows how the LineOut process can be coded using two procedures. Instead of using a WAKEUP LineOut statement to print a line, a main program would simply invoke the procedure StartLineOut. The interrupt system then calls the procedure DspIntr each time a display interrupt occurs. These two pseudo-Pascal procedures have precisely the same structure as the 6809 subroutines STROUT and STRINT in Table 11–1.

TABLE 11-8 Procedure version of LineOut process.

```
PROCEDURE StartLineOut; {Display interrupt initialization routine.}
  BEGIN
    outputPrinted := false;  dspData := GetNextOutputChar;
    {Enable interrupt, start display, and clear ready.}
    dspIEN := true; dspGo := true; dspReady := false;
  END;

PROCEDURE DspIntr;  {Called by interrupt system when
                (dspIEN=true) AND (dspReady=true) }
  BEGIN   {Display interrupt service routine.}
    IF CharsLeftToBePrinted THEN
      BEGIN {Send character to display data register,...}
        dspData := GetNextOutputChar;
        {...enable interrupt, start display, and clear ready.}
        dspIEN := true; dspGo := true; dspReady := false;
      END;
    ELSE BEGIN dspIEN := false; outputPrinted := true END;
  END;
```

11.5.5 Waking and Sleeping

Regardless of whether coroutines or subroutines are used to code processes, we need ways to wake up processes and put them to sleep. We presume that the entire program is operating under the control of an operating system or executive, so that the main program is awakened for the first time when the executive runs it, and put to its final rest when control is finally returned to the executive.

In Table 11-7, MainLoop can wake up the interrupt process LineIn or LineOut by calling a subroutine that enables the device interrupt, requests the first I/O operation, and returns control to MainLoop. Subsequently LineIn and LineOut are reawakened periodically by interrupts; each puts itself to sleep by requesting another I/O operation and returning control to the interrupted program. When LineIn or LineOut eventually returns control to the interrupted program *without* requesting another I/O operation, it can only be reawakened explicitly, by another process.

That leaves us with the question of how MainLoop can put itself to sleep, since it has no interrupts of its own. If there is an operating system, MainLoop can temporarily return control to it, allowing the operating system to schedule other useful work while MainLoop is asleep. In the absence of such an executive, MainLoop can simply enter a busy-waiting loop. In either case, MainLoop must rely on some other process to wake it up. For example, suppose MainLoop uses a global boolean variable mainWaitingForInput to indicate that it has gone to sleep waiting for input. Then each time LineIn finishes reading a line, it can inspect mainWaitingForInput to determine if

`MainLoop` should be reawakened. A typical sequence of events might be as follows, assuming that computation for a line proceeds much faster than input:

(1) `MainLoop` finds that `inputAvailable` is `false`. Therefore it sets `mainWaitingForInput` to `true` and puts itself to sleep.

(2) `LineIn` wakes up, reads a character, and goes back to sleep; this step is repeated zero or more times.

(3) `LineIn` wakes up, reads the last character of a line, and then sets `inputAvailable` to `true`. Then it checks `mainWaitingForInput` and finds the value true; it wakes up `MainLoop` and puts itself to sleep.

(4) `MainLoop` wakes up, copies the new input line, and wakes up `LineIn`.

(5) `MainLoop` continues and eventually returns to step 1.

11.5.6 Timing-Dependent Errors and Critical Sections

The method suggested above for suspending and resuming `MainLoop` seems reasonable, but it contains a timing-dependent error. Consider the following sequence of operations that could occur if computation and input for one line take about the same length of time:

(1) `MainLoop` finds that `inputAvailable` is `false`. Therefore it sets `mainWaitingForInput` to `true` and is about to put itself to sleep when . . .

(2) `LineIn` wakes up, reads the last character of a line, and then sets `inputAvailable` to `true`. Then it checks `mainWaitingForInput`, finds the value `true`, "wakes up" `MainLoop`, and puts itself to sleep.

(3) `MainLoop` wakes up and immediately puts itself to sleep as planned.

(4) Both `MainLoop` and `LineIn` are now asleep, waiting to be reawakened by each other, and both sleep peacefully forever.

This situation is called a "deadlock;" two processes are *deadlocked* if neither can continue until the other continues. A similar deadlock can occur between `MainLoop` and `LineOut`.

The instructions in `MainLoop` that test `inputAvailable` and update `mainWaitingForInput` are called a "critical section." A *critical section* of a process is a set of instructions that access variables shared with one or more additional processes, such that the results of execution may vary unpredictably if the variables are accessed by another process during the critical section's execution.

In order to avoid deadlocks and other timing-dependent errors, a critical section, once entered, must be allowed to execute to completion without any instructions from other processes intervening. This is sometimes called *mutual exclusion*. We can provide mutual exclusion in a critical section in an assembly language program by disabling the processor interrupt system at the beginning of the critical section, and reenabling it at the end.

11.5.7 Detecting Critical Sections

We have defined critical sections but we have not given any rules on how to detect them. In general, finding critical sections requires a careful analysis of a program and its environment. For example, the last two instructions of LineIn might appear to be a critical section according to the following scenario:

(1) LineIn is awakened, reads the last character of an input line, sets inputAvailable to true, and is about to put itself to sleep when . . .

(2) MainLoop wakes up, finds that inputAvailable is true, copies the input line, and wakes up LineIn.

(3) LineIn wakes up and immediately puts itself to sleep as planned, without reading another line.

However, in most environments this can't happen, because LineIn is awakened by an interrupt and MainLoop can be resumed only after the LineIn interrupt service routine has run to completion. In other environments the scenario could be possible, for example, if LineIn and MainLoop actually run simultaneously on two different processors that share variables in a common main memory.

It might appear that the best course of action is to disable interrupts whenever a critical section possibly exists. However, this must be done with discretion for two reasons:

(1) Disabling interrupts for a long period of time can have an adverse effect on I/O system performance, resulting in lost inputs and delayed outputs.

(2) Disabling interrupts at the wrong place can lead to deadlocks.

Disabling interrupts for a short period of time usually does not cause inputs to be lost, since most device interfaces keep an interrupt request pending until it is serviced. However, if a second input appears while the interrupt for a first input is still pending, then a typical interface will lose one of the inputs and fail to issue a second interrupt request after the first has been serviced.

To illustrate the deadlock problem, suppose we disabled the interrupt system in MainLoop in Table 11–7 before the first SLEEP statement and reenabled it after checking InputBufferEmpty. Then if MainLoop ever goes to sleep waiting for input, it will do so with interrupts disabled. It can never be reawakened, because input interrupts are required to do so.

Thus, we must reiterate that correct structuring and coding of a program with multiple processes requires a careful analysis of the program and its environment.

11.5.8 Locking and Semaphores

Another way to guard critical sections is by *locking* shared resources so that only one process at a time may access them. This can be done by providing a flag or *semaphore* for each resource that indicates when the resource is in use. A process that wishes to access a shared resource uses the semaphore as follows:

(1) The process checks the current value of the semaphore. If the semaphore is zero, the process may proceed to the next step. A non-zero value indicates that some other process is accessing the shared resource. In this case, the current process should go to sleep until the other process sets the semaphore to zero.

(2) The process now may take control of the resource, excluding other processes by setting the semaphore to a non-zero value.

(3) The process accesses the resource and then releases it by setting the semaphore to zero.

A process that goes to sleep waiting for a semaphore must have some confidence that it will eventually be awakened, either by an interrupt or by an operating system that keeps track of semaphores and waiting processes. If a process "sleeps" by simply busy-waiting and if the interrupt system is off, then we've created not only mutual exclusion but also a deadlock!

A problem occurs in coding the above semaphore operations in assembly language. Consider the following Z8000 code:

```
CHECK   TEST   SEMAPH      Want MSB=0 ==> resource available.
        JR     MI,CHECK    Busy-wait for it.
        DEC    SEMAPH      Set semaphore to all 1s.
        ...                Use resource.
        CLR    SEMAPH      Release resource for others.
```

Now suppose that each of two different processes has a copy of this code for accessing a shared resource using the semaphore SEMAPH. An unfortunate sequence of events is depicted below:

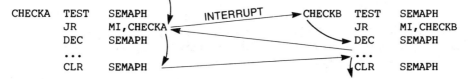

```
CHECKA  TEST   SEMAPH              INTERRUPT          CHECKB  TEST   SEMAPH
        JR     MI,CHECKA                                      JR     MI,CHECKB
        DEC    SEMAPH                                         DEC    SEMAPH
        ...                                                   ...
        CLR    SEMAPH                                         CLR    SEMAPH
```

Process A finds SEMAPH=0, but before decrementing it, an interrupt occurs and process B gains access to the resource, since it finds that SEMAPH is still zero. Now if control gets back to process A before process B releases the shared resource, then both processes will have simultaneous access to the resource. One way this could happen is if process B gives up control while waiting for an I/O event. Similar problems occur if the two processes actually run on different processors, and access SEMAPH in a shared memory.

The solution to the problem is to make testing and setting the semaphore an indivisible operation. To do this, many processors provide a Test and Set (TSET) instruction which reads the value of an operand in memory, sets the condition bits accordingly, and sets the memory value to all 1s, all in one instruction. In the Z8000, we can recode our shared resource check as follows:

```
CHECK   TSET    SEMAPH      Want MSB=0 ==> resource available.
        JR      NE,CHECK    Busy-wait for it.
        ...                 Resource available, got it, use it.
        CLR     SEMAPH      Release it for others.
```

In this code, the TSET instruction always sets SEMAPH to all 1s, even if SEMAPH already contains all 1s. Therefore, the shared resource always either becomes or remains locked during the execution of TSET. Control falls through the conditional branch instruction and a new process gains control of the resource only if the MSB of SEMAPH was 0 before it was set.

As you probably have gathered by now, there is a lot more to process management than meets the eye. A complete discussion of process communication and synchronization is beyond the scope of this text, but a large body of literature exists on the subject (see References). An example of an assembly language program with three processes will be presented in Section 11.6.3.

11.6 SHARED DATA AND INSTRUCTIONS

In a multiple process (interrupt) environment it is possible for two or more processes to share the same data or variables. Special precautions must be taken in programs with this behavior.

11.6.1 Shared Variables and Data Structures

In the previous section we studied a program with three processes that used variables in memory to synchronize their operations. Critical sections appeared when both processes could access a shared variable simultaneously, leading to the possibility of deadlocks.

Critical sections can also appear in more innocent-looking applications of shared data than process synchronization, and although the results may not be as severe as a deadlock, errors can nonetheless occur. For example, consider the Pascal outline of the interrupt service routine for a time-of-day clock, shown in Table 11–9. Suppose a main program reads the current time of day by a statement sequence such as the following:

```
sec1 := second;
min1 := minute;
hour1 := hour;
```

An error can occur if a timer interrupt takes place in the middle of this sequence. For example, suppose that the current time is 7:05:59, we have just executed the first statement above, and the timer interrupt occurs. Then when the processor has finished the above sequence it will have recorded the time as being 7:06:59. Even larger errors can occur at times like 7:59:59. In order to prevent such errors, timer interrupts must be disabled whenever a program reads the time.

The time variables above form a simple data structure. Turning off interrupts or otherwise preventing multiple processes from accessing a data structure is called *locking* the data structure. There are three basic ways in which

TABLE 11–9 Interrupt service routine for time-of-day clock.

```
{ The time-of-day clock is driven from the 60 Hz AC power line,
  producing an interrupt every 1/60th second if its IEN bit is 1.
  The interrupt service routine uses these 'ticks' to keep track
  of the current time of day to the nearest 1/60th second, using
  global variables tick, second, minute, and hour.
}
PROCEDURE TimerIntr; {Called by interrupt system if
                      (timerIEN=true) AND (timerReady=true)}
  BEGIN {Timer interrupt service routine.}
    tick := tick + 1;
    IF tick=60 THEN
      BEGIN tick := 0; second := second + 1;
        IF second = 60 THEN
          BEGIN second := 0; minute := minute + 1;
            IF minute = 60 THEN
              BEGIN minute := 0; hour := hour + 1;
                IF hour = 24 THEN
                  BEGIN hour := 0; IncrementDayAndDate END;
              END;
          END;
      END;  {Now request next timer tick.}
    timerIEN := true; timerGo := true; timerReady := false;
  END;
```

errors can occur when two or more processes simultaneously access an un-locked data structure:

(1) If the data structure is not locked for reading, then one process could interrupt and update the data structure while another process is reading it. The reading process could see inconsistent information.

(2) If the data structure is not locked for updating, then one process could interrupt and read the data structure while another process is updating it. Again the reading process could see inconsistent information.

(3) If the data structure is not locked for updating, then two processes could try to update the data structure at the same time, possibly destroying the data structure's integrity.

Note that no errors occur if two processes simply *read* a data structure simultaneously. We've already seen one way that case 1 above can occur. An example of case 2 is for the timer interrupt service routine itself to be inter-rupted by another process that reads the time, possibly yielding the time 7:05:00 during the transition from 7:05:59 to 7:06:00. Although some process reads the wrong time in either case 1 or 2, at least the integrity of the data structure is not affected.

To illustrate case 3 above, suppose a main program initializes the cur-rent time of day by the following instruction sequence:

```
read(hour1,min1,sec1);
hour := hour1;
minute := min1;
second := sec1;
```

Now suppose the current time of day as indicated by hour, minute, second is 1:59:59 and a user tries to reinitialize the time to 3:00:00 (e.g., to go onto daylight saving time). If a timer interrupt occurs between the second and third lines above, then the time will be incorrectly initialized to 4:00:00.

Worse errors can occur with more complicated data structures. For example, it is usually disastrous to interrupt a process that updates a linked list in order to perform another updating operation on the same list. This can often produce unwanted circular lists, dismembered sublists with no pointers to them, and all sorts of other horrors.

In a few rare instances it may be possible for two processes to update the same data structure simultaneously without error. For example, consider the case of two processes that access a queue, where one puts data into the queue and the other removes it. If the queue is implemented with head and tail pointers as suggested in Section 3.4, then you can convince yourself that the integrity of the queue will be preserved, since one process can only update the head and the other only the tail.[2] However, to be safe, one should always lock data structures that might be accessed by multiple processes.

11.6.2 Shared Instructions (Reentrant Programs)

Consider a subroutine that is invoked from two or more different processes. After being invoked from one process it might be "re-entered" from a second process before the first has finished executing it. A subroutine that still produces correct results when re-entered in this way is called *reentrant*.

For example, suppose a main program and one or more interrupt routines make use of a DIVIDE subroutine in the 6809. Suppose that the main program has called DIVIDE, and in the middle of its execution an interrupt from an output device occurs. And suppose that the interrupt service routine makes use of a binary-to-ASCII conversion algorithm that computes digits by successive divisions by 10. Then the interrupt routine will re-enter DIVIDE and execute it to completion before resuming DIVIDE in the main program process.

There is nothing inherently harmful about a sequence of instructions being executed "simultaneously" by two different processes. Since instructions in a non-self-modifying program are "read-only," the instruction sequence is the same for both processes. Each process may create a different set of values in the processor registers as instructions are executed, but this is no problem if the interrupting process follows the usual practice of pushing the registers onto a stack and popping them on exit. The problems occur when instructions refer to variables in fixed locations in memory.

For example, consider the 6809 DIVIDE program that was shown in Table 6–8. Four parameters are passed to the subroutine in fixed memory locations (DVND, DVSR, REM, QUOT), and another location is used to store a local variable (CNT). If the subroutine is suspended by an interrupt, the values of the registers and the return address will be preserved on the stack and properly restored on return. However, if DIVIDE is called again from the interrupt service routine the old values of the parameters and local variable will be lost forever. Figure 11–6 shows what happens. The computation remaining to be done in the first call of DIVIDE will be resumed with incorrect data, and the results will be wrong. In general, whenever a subroutine uses fixed memory locations for parameters or local variables, it is doomed to fail if it is ever re-entered.

---

[2]The worst that can happen is for the dequeueing process to think that the queue is empty just as the enqueueing process is putting data into it, or vice versa. However, the integrity of the queue is preserved, so that the dequeueing process will discover the newly-enqueued data the next time it checks the queue, as if the enqueueing process had operated just a little while later in the first place.

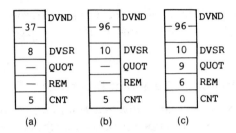

FIGURE 11-6 Effects on parameters when non-reentrant DIVIDE subroutine is re-entered: (a) dividing 37 by 8 just before interrupt; (b) dividing 96 by 10 on second entry of DIVIDE; (c) on return from interrupt.

Table 9-16 showed a DIVIDE subroutine that works properly when re-entered; it *is* reentrant. Since all parameters and local variables are placed on the stack, a new set is allocated for each invocation of the subroutine. Figure 11-7 traces the stack contents during the execution of a program using this version of DIVIDE. The values of the parameters and the local variable for the first invocation of DIVIDE are preserved on the stack during the interrupt service routine and again during the second, reentrant invocation of DIVIDE.

The DIVIDE program shown in Table 9-14 passes parameters in a parameter area. It is *almost* reentrant if each calling process uses a different parameter area. The local variable CNT still is a problem, because it is shared by all callers. The problem can be solved by storing CNT in a spare processor register (Y) or on the stack, or by requiring the calling program to allocate a byte in the parameter area for it.

The queue manipulation subroutines in Table 9-18 are reentrant because there are no local variables and the parameters are all passed in registers.

Using only registers and a stack for all parameters and local variables is the best way to create reentrant subroutines. In this way, space for parameters and local variables is allocated dynamically, only as much as needed at any time. Subroutines that use the stack convention described in Section 9.3.6 are reentrant if each invocation of the subroutine always runs to completion before any higher-level invocations are resumed. This is usually the case in a single-user interrupt environment. In some environments, such as multi-user systems, programs can be suspended and resumed at arbitrary points in their execution. In this case, a separate stack area must be provided for each process.

Reentrant programs are important in systems programming, especially in multiple-user environments where a process is associated with each user; typical applications include the following:

- Utility programs such as binary-to-ASCII conversion must be reentrant because they can be called by different users (processes) at the same time.

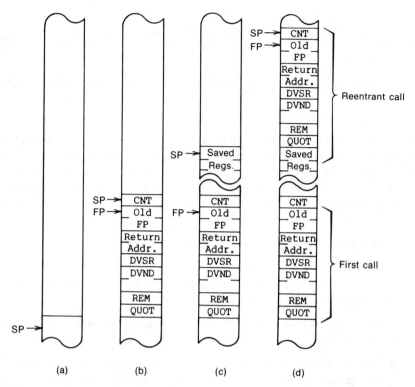

FIGURE 11-7 Stack contents using reentrant DIVIDE while: (a) executing MAIN; (b) executing DIVIDE from MAIN; (c) executing INTSVC; (d) executing DIVIDE from INTSVC.

- If a large, commonly-used program such as a compiler or text editor is reentrant, it may be stored in memory only once; different users may use it simultaneously, each with a separate data area.

- A group of identical I/O devices (say, CRT terminals) can share a reentrant interrupt service routine, using a separate buffer area and configuration table for each copy of the device.

11.6.3 Assembly Language Program Example

Figure 11-8 shows the general structure of a program that brings together many of the concepts of multiple processes, critical sections, and shared instructions and data. The program has three processes that perform the three steps of input, computation, and output.

Input and output are performed one character at a time, and the main program reads and writes one character at a time. In order to smooth input,

FIGURE 11–8 Structure of a program that uses queues to buffer input and output.

output, and processing time variations, queues are used to buffer the input and output characters. In this way, the input device can stay busy by "looking ahead" and filling up the input queue when the main program is slow, and likewise during bursts of speed the main program can dump lots of characters into the output queue without waiting for them to be printed. Thus, the three processes could be outlined as follows:

(1) Input process: gets characters from the input device and puts them in the input queue.

(2) Main process: gets characters from the input queue, processes them, and places results in the output queue.

(3) Output process: gets characters from the output queue and sends them to the output device.

A 6809 assembly language version of the program is shown in Table 11–10. Two queues (IQ and OQ) are declared according to the specifications of the queue module in Table 9–18; the queue module's subroutines QINIT, QENQ, and QDEQ are utilized accordingly. The main program initializes the two queues, marks the output process as waiting for data to appear in OQ, and wakes up the input process to request the first character. Then it enters a computation loop that reads and writes characters as necessary.

The input process is awakened for the first time by the subroutine IWAKE, which requests one character from the input device. Subsequently the input process is awakened by input device interrupts. The interrupt service routine ISVC puts each input character into IQ.

If the input device is very fast or MAIN is very slow, then ISVC may eventually find that IQ has become full. In this case, the input process saves the current input character in a variable SAVEIN, sets variable WAITIQ to 1 to show that it is waiting for space in IQ, and goes to sleep *without* requesting another input. Later, when MAIN removes a character from IQ, it puts the saved character SAVEIN into IQ and reawakens the input process by calling IWAKE again.

A similar situation occurs in the output process. OUTCHR calls OWAKE to print the first character from OQ. Subsequent characters are removed from OQ and printed by the output interrupt service routine OSVC. If OQ is empty, then OSVC sets WAITOQ to 1 and goes to sleep without printing another character.

Later, when MAIN puts another character into OQ, it reawakens the output process by calling OWAKE again.

MAIN calls two subroutines, INCHR and OUTCHR, to handle the details of reading and writing each character by manipulating the queues and waking up sleeping processes. For example, INCHR attempts to dequeue a character from IQ. If it is unsuccessful, it simply busy-waits for a character to appear. In any

TABLE 11–10 Assembly language program that uses queues to buffer input and output.

```
OQ       RMB    10              Output queue.
OQDT     RMW    2               Output queue descriptor table.
         FCW    OQ,OQ+9
IQ       RMB    10              Input queue.
IQDT     RMW    2               Input queue descriptor table.
         FCW    IQ,IQ+9
WAITOQ   RMB    1               Nonzero when output process is waiting
*                                 for a character to appear in OQ.
WAITIQ   RMB    1               Nonzero when input process is waiting
*                                 for space in IQ.
SAVEIN   RMB    1               Save input character when waiting
STACK    RMB    20                for room in IQ.
STACKE   EQU    *               Return address stack.
*
MAIN     LDS    #STACKE         Initialize return-address stack.
         LDX    #OQDT           Initialize output queue...
         JSR    QINIT
         LDX    #IQDT           ...and input queue.
         JSR    QINIT
         LDA    #1              Mark output processing waiting for a
         STA    WAITOQ            character to print.
         JSR    IWAKE           Wake up input and request first char.
LOOP     JSR    INCHR           Main processing loop.
         ...
         JSR    INCHR           Read and write as many characters
         ...                      as desired.
         JSR    OUTCHR
         ...
         JSR    INCHR
         ...
         JSR    OUTCHR
         ...
         JMP    LOOP            Repeat the processing loop.
*
*                               Come here when all done processing.
EXIT     JSR    INOFF           Turn off input interrupts.
WTOUT    TST    WAITOQ          Busy-wait until last char printed.
         BEQ    WTOUT
         JMP    1000H           Return to operating system.
```

TABLE 11-10 (continued)

```
*          Subroutine to get one input character from input queue.
INCHR  LDX   #IQDT      Get a character from the input queue.
       SETI             *** Critical section -- interrupts off.
       JSR   QDEQ
       PSHS  A,CC       Save char and queue status (Z-bit).
       TST   WAITIQ     Input queue must have room for
       BEQ   INCH4        at least one more character now,
       LDA   SAVEIN       so if input process was waiting on
       LDX   #IQDT        queue full, then
       JSR   QENQ         enqueue the saved character...
       BEQ   WHAAAT       (impossible error if queue full)
       JSR   IWAKE        ...and wake up the input process.
INCH4  PULS  CC,A       Restore input char and old queue status.
       CLRI             *** End critical sec. -- interrupts on.
       BEQ   INCHR      Check Z -- did we really get character?
       RTS              Return if we did, else try again.
WHAAAT JMP   1800H      Impossible error, return to oper. sys.
*
*          Subroutine to put one output character into output queue.
OUTCHR PSHS  A          Save output character.
       LDX   #OQDT      Try to enqueue it.
       SETI             *** Critical section -- interrupts off.
       JSR   QENQ
       PSHS  CC         Save queue status.
       TST   WAITOQ     Output queue must have...
       BEQ   OUTCH4       ...at least one character in it now...
       JSR   OWAKE        ...so wake up output if it was waiting.
OUTCH4 PULS  CC,A       Restore character and queue status.
       CLRI             *** End critical sec. -- interrupts on.
       BEQ   OUTCHR     Check Z -- did we really enqueue char?
       RTS              Return if we did, else try again.
```

case, after INCHR calls QDEQ there must be at least one free byte in IQ, so that the input process can now be awakened if it was waiting for space in IQ.

Most of the instructions in INCHR are in a critical section. The instructions SETI and CLRI manipulate the I interrupt mask bit to disable and enable interrupts for the critical section. Consider the following sequence of events that could occur if interrupts were not disabled:

(1) IQ is full and MAIN calls INCHR.

(2) INCHR calls QDEQ, leaving space in IQ for one more character.

(3) An input device interrupt occurs and makes IQ full again.

(4) Another input device interrupt occurs; since IQ is full, the input character is saved in SAVEIN, input interrupts are disabled, and WAITIQ is set to 1.

TABLE 11–10   (continued)

```
*          Device-dependent declarations and subroutines.
ICS      EQU    0F000H              Input device control and status reg.
IDATA    EQU    0F001H              Input device data register.
OCS      EQU    0F010H              Output device control and status reg.
ODATA    EQU    0F011H              Output device data register.

* Wake up input process and request one character.
IWAKE    CLR    WAITIQ              Mark the input process not waiting.
         LDA    #41H                Set IEN and GO...
         STA    ICS                 ...thereby requesting a character.
         RTS

* Interrupt service routine for input device.
ISVC     LDA    IDATA               Get character.
         STA    SAVEIN              Save it for possible later use.
         LDX    #IQDT               Put into input queue.
         JSR    QENQ
         BEQ    IQFUL               Queue full?
         LDA    #41H                No, set IEN and GO...
         STA    ICS                 ...thereby requesting next character.
         RTI                        Return to interrupted program.
IQFUL    JSR    INOFF               Disable interrupts from input device.
         LDA    #1                  Put the input process to sleep...
         STA    WAITIQ              ...until there's room in IQ.
         RTI                        Return to interrupted program.

INOFF    CLRA               Subroutine to turn off input device.
         STA    ICS
         RTS

* Wake up output process and print one character.
OWAKE    CLR    WAITOQ              Mark the output process not waiting.
         LDX    #OQDT               Get a character from the output queue.
         JSR    QDEQ
         BEQ    WHAAAT              Queue empty?? Impossible!
         STA    ODATA               Output the character.
         LDA    #41H                Set IEN and GO.
         STA    OCS
         RTS

* Interrupt service routine for output device.
OSVC     LDX    #OQDT               Get another character to print.
         JSR    QDEQ
         BEQ    OQMT                Go to sleep if none left.
         STA    ODATA               Else output the character.
         LDA    #41H                Set IEN and GO.
         STA    OCS
         RTI                        Return to interrupted program.
OQMT     CLRA                       Turn off output device.
         STA    OCS
         LDA    #1                  Put the output process to sleep...
         STA    WAITOQ              ...until there's a character in OQ.
         RTI                        Return to interrupted program.
```

(5) INCHR is finally resumed, and finds that WAITIQ is 1.

(6) Thinking that there must now be room in IQ, INCHR tries to enqueue the saved character and the "impossible" error occurs.[3]

Another reason for a critical section in INCHR is that it shares a data structure, IQ, with another process, the input process. If an input interrupt occurs while INCHR is executing QDEQ, then both processes will be manipulating the data structure simultaneously. Whether or not a timing-dependent error occurs in this situation depends on the internal workings of the QDEQ and QENQ subroutines, as we've explained before. Disabling interrupts in INCHR ensures that each process gets exclusive access to IQ.

With all the potential timing-dependent errors, one may be tempted to disable interrupts for most of the time. But this can cause problems too. For example, if we moved the CLRI instruction in INCHR down just one line, then interrupts will be disabled for the entire INCHR subroutine, even if INCHR is busy-waiting for a character to appear in IQ. In this case, it will busy-wait forever, because the input interrupt can't put a character into the queue.

The OUTCHR procedure has a structure similar to INCHR's, and it also contains a critical section.

Notice the order in which software flags are set and cleared in the wake-up and interrupt service routines. Two useful rules-of-thumb apply here:

- Any software action indicating that interrupts are being *enabled* (e.g., clearing WAITIQ) should be taken *before* the corresponding hardware action (e.g., ICS:=41H), lest an interrupt take place before the software has been "told" that such an event is possible.

- Conversely, any software action indicating that interrupts are being *disabled* (e.g., setting WAITIQ) should be taken *after* the corresponding hardware action (e.g., ICS:=0), lest one last interrupt slip in with the software "thinking" that interrupts are off.

Another potential pitfall is the way in which the interrupt system is disabled and re-enabled in subroutines like INCHR and OUTCHR. For example, suppose the main program performs some time-critical operation during which it must disable interrupts. If during that time the main program calls INCHR or OUTCHR, it will suddenly find that the interrupt system is back on again. The problem is that INCHR and OUTCHR turn off the interrupt system and then unconditionally turn it back on without checking whether it was on to begin with. This problem can be solved by replacing the SETI and CLRI instructions with calls to two subroutines, INTSOFF and INTSON, coded in Table 11–11.

---

[3] In this situation one might propose that the critical section could be eliminated by modifying the program's attitude — instead of giving up, let it try again! If we replace the instruction BEQ WHAAAT with BEQ INCH4, then if the queue is full, no harm is done and the wake-up operation is tried again later. However, this is not a general solution.

TABLE 11–11 Subroutines for nested disabling and enabling of interrupts.

```
INTCNT  RMB    1                      Counts number of times interrupts have
*                                        been turned off; init to 1 in MAIN.
*
INTSON  DEC    INTCNT                 Turn on interrupts
        BGT    LVOFF                     if turn-off count is <=0.
        CLR    INTCNT                 Clamp count at 0 just in case.
        CLRI                          Allow interrupts.
LVOFF   RTS
*
INTSOFF SETI                          Turn off interrupts.
        INC    INTCNT                 Remember how many times.
        RTS
```

These subroutines use a counter to keep track of how many times interrupts have been "disabled," so that nested critical sections will not enable interrupts until the outermost call to INTSON is reached.

As a final note, we should point out again that the implementations of the queue manipulation subroutines in Table 9–18 are fully reentrant. This means that the main computation loop in Table 11–11 could declare additional queues and manipulate them using QENQ and QDEQ. No errors will occur, even if QENQ and QDEQ are reentered by the interrupt service routines that use them.

The timing-dependent errors that can occur in multiple processes may seem rather obscure, which may encourage naive programmers to treat them lightly. Unfortunately, such errors are often difficult to predict before they are observed, and once observed they are difficult to reproduce for the purposes of analysis and correction. As discussed in the references, modern operating systems and high-level languages for concurrent processing provide facilities and impose restrictions that make it possible to write concurrent programs with predictable behavior.

REFERENCES

The possibility of overlapping computation with input/output was recognized in early computer designs, but was not immediately pursued. As explained in the classic Burks, Goldstine, and von Neumann paper (in C. G. Bell and A. Newell's *Computer Structures: Readings and Examples* [McGraw-Hill, 1971], pp. 117–118), "Simultaneous operation of the computer and the input–output organ requires additional temporary storage and introduces a synchronizing problem, and hence it is not being considered for the first model."

Interrupt systems provided the needed synchronization mechanism in machines such as the Univac 1103 (circa 1953), Lincoln Laboratory's TX-2 (circa 1957), and Manchester University's Atlas (circa 1960) [*Computer Structures*, pp. 45, 274, 277]. DMA channels were provided in the Atlas and in the IBM 7094 computer (circa 1960) [*Computer Structures*, pp. 523-524]. The Atlas computer also introduced the idea of "extracodes" upon which modern software interrupt and system call instructions are based [*Computer Structures*, pp. 274–277].

General discussions of the hardware structure of modern interrupt systems and DMA channels can be found in several texts, including *Computer Architecture and Organization* by John Hayes [McGraw-Hill, 1978], *Computer Organization* by Hamacher, Vranesic, and Zaky [McGraw-Hill, 1978], and *Digital Systems: Hardware Organization and Design* by Hill and Peterson [Wiley, 1978 (second edition)]. The best source of information on interrupt systems and DMA channels for specific processors is of course the manufacturers' literature.

Most systems programming books discuss issues of process management. Two good references are *Software System Principles* by Peter Freeman [SRA, 1975] and *Systems Programming* by John J. Donovan [McGraw-Hill, 1972].

The concepts of processes and concurrency and the methods for process management are crucial to modern operating system design. A detailed and enlightening discussion of processes and concurrency can be found in Per Brinch Hansen's book *Operating System Principles* [Prentice-Hall, 1973]. Brinch Hansen has also devised an extension of Pascal for "structured programming of computer operating systems" ["The Programming Language Concurrent Pascal," *IEEE Trans. Software Engr.*, Vol. SE–1, No. 2, June 1975, pp. 199–207].

Probably the most widely used language that supports concurrent processes is PL/I [D. Beech, "A Structural View of PL/I," *Computing Surveys*, Vol. 2, No. 1, pp. 33-64]. In PL/I the reserved word TASK declares that a procedure may be executed concurrently with the calling program, and EVENT variables are used as completion flags to synchronize processes. A process may use a WAIT statement to relinquish control to the operating system until a specified EVENT variable has been set to 1.

Burroughs Extended Algol is another language that supports multiple processes; it has been in use for well over a decade on Burroughs B6700-type computers. A very good chapter on "multisequence algorithms," including coroutines and asynchronous processes using Extended Algol, can be found in *Programming Language Structures* by E. I. Organick, A. I. Forsythe, and R. P. Plummer [Academic Press, 1978].

EXERCISES

11.1 A programmer noticed some common instructions in the STROUT and STRINT subroutines in Table 11–1 and decided to streamline STROUT by rewriting it as follows:

```
STROUT   TST    SBUSY        Is a previous string being
         BNE    STROUT          displayed?  Wait for it.
         LDA    #0FFH        Set SBUSY flag.
         STA    SBUSY
         BRA    STRINT1      Go output first character.
     *
STRINT   LDX    BUFPNT       Get buffer pointer.
         INCX                Bump pointer to next character.
STRINT1  STX    BUFPNT       Entry point for first character.
         ...
```

Explain why this code won't work properly as written. Insert a sequence of instructions between STA SBUSY and BRA STRINT1 to correct the problem.

11.2   Write a program that uses interrupts to measure and print the time between successive hits on a pushbutton. Three I/O devices are needed. A real-time clock should be used to produce interrupts at regular intervals; its interrupt service routine should increment a variable TIME in memory. A keyboard or similar input device should be used for button hits, producing an interrupt each time that the button is hit. A variable LHIT can be used to keep track of the time of the latest button hit. A CRT or other display output device should be used to print a message indicating the elapsed time after each time that the button is hit. The message should be formatted as a string and printed under interrupt control as in Table 11–1. *Note:* A single button hit that occurs while the message is being printed must not be lost. If two or more hits occur during this time, the second and successive ones may be lost. *Further note:* If a real-time clock is not available, then one can be simulated by a main program loop that busy-waits for approximately one millisecond (as determined by instruction exection times) and then increments TIME. The time lost servicing interrupts is negligible for the purposes of this exercise.

11.3   Modify the above program so that the button can be hit several times while a message is being printed, without losing information. In order to do this, provide a queue for elapsed time values. Each time that the button is hit, the elapsed time value should be put into the queue. There are two possible programming approaches for getting data out of the queue and printing it: (1) (Simple) The main program continuously checks to see if the output routine is idle; whenever output is idle, main checks the queue for a value to print; (2) (More difficult) The main program after initialization has just one instruction, SELF JMP SELF; the output routines and the pushbutton routines are treated as two separate processes communicating through a queue; output sleeps if the current message has been printed and the queue is empty; pushbutton wakes up output whenever it puts a value into a previously empty queue. In either approach, you should study and comment on the possibility of critical sections when the routines access the common queue data structure. Use a long message (say, 70 characters) and a slow output device (say, 30 characters per second) to test your program's behavior for multiple hits.

11.4   Write reentrant interrupt display output routines similar to those in Table 11–1 that can be shared among several identical display devices. When called, each routine should be passed in register Y the base address of a "configuration table" that contains information unique to each display device: (a) the address of the DSPCS register; (b) BUFPNT; (c) SBUSY.

11.5 Modify the polling routines in Table 11–4 so that the polling table contains *three* 16-bit numbers for each device. The third number would normally be the base address of a software "configuration table," such as the one used in the previous exercise. The polling routines should load this third number into the Y register before jumping to the specified interrupt service routine.

11.6 Describe how a deadlock could occur between the MainLoop and LineOut processes in Table 11–7.

11.7 Translate the ReverseLines program in Table 11–7 into an assembly language program for your favorite processor. Explain how you implement the WAKEUP and SLEEP primitives, and indicate where you disable interrupts to guard critical sections.

11.8 Write a service routine for the SWI3 instruction on the 6809 that assumes that the SWI3 is followed by a 1-byte code that designates a particular operating system utility routine to be called. The service routine should "fudge" the saved PC on the stack so that the utility routine can return using an RTI, and then use the 1-byte code as an index into a table of utility routine starting addresses.

11.9 Rewrite the DMA input program in Table 11–5 to use double buffering, so that the contents of the I/O buffer are copied into the work buffer upon the completion of each DMA operation.

11.10 Rewrite the DMA input program in Table 11–5 to use double buffering, so that the roles of the I/O buffer and the work buffer are swapped upon the completion of each DMA operation. Be sure to show how the main program selects the proper buffer to access.

11.11 Translate the processes in Table 11–7 into assembly language subroutines and a main program for your favorite processor. Use a coroutine-like mechanism for saving process resumption addresses. Provide a simple operating system that does something interesting when MainLoop is asleep (for example, flashing the lights on the front panel if your computer has one).

11.12 Which is a more stringent requirement for a subroutine, recursion or reentrancy? In other words, answer these two questions: (1) Are all recursive subroutines guaranteed to run without error if reentered by another process? (2) Are all reentrant subroutines guaranteed to run without error if they call themselves? Use examples to illustrate your answers.

11.13 Suppose that the statement WAKEUP LineOut near the end of the MainLoop process in Table 11–7 merely schedules LineOut to be executed soon, but does not necessarily cause it to be run immediately. Instead, MainLoop can keep running for a while. What potential problems does this introduce and how can they be solved?

11.14 Suppose a queue module were developed that dequeues items by shifting down all of the items in a memory buffer, as suggested in Exercise 3.13. How does this affect the reentrant behavior discussed in footnote 2?

11.15 Suppose we use the input and output routines in Table 11–10 with a CRT terminal. Since we cannot prevent a user from typing too fast, in the ISVC routine we may cause inputs to be lost if we disable interrupts. Show how to replace the code at IQFUL with code that warns the user of the impending disaster by ringing the bell at the terminal. Consider and explain your solution carefully, because it is easy to design an incorrect solution with deadlocks and other problems.

11.16 Modify the INTSOFF and INTSON subroutines in Table 11–11 so that INTSOFF examines the I bit in CC to determine whether or not interrupts should be turned on when INTSON is next encountered. Is INTCNT still needed?

11.17 Write a program that plays Life as described in Exercises 7.5 and 10.16, using interrupt-driven I/O. The program should contain three processes:

- *Input process:* Accepts hexadecimal characters (0–9, A–F) typed at an ASCII keyboard. The input process converts each digit into a binary number from 0 to 15 and places the number in an input queue.

- *Output process:* Removes characters from an output queue and prints them on a CRT screen.

- *Main program process:* Initializes Life array, queues, and I/O routines, and then looks for work in the input queue. Each time it finds a number in the input queue, it computes this number of generations of Life and then calls DISPLAY to display the current generation. DISPLAY outputs individual characters by placing them in the output queue.

When the output queue becomes full, DISPLAY must wait for characters to be sent to the CRT before putting more in the queue. For maximum efficiency, the output queue should have room for at least one screen full of characters. The input queue should have room for only five characters. If a character is typed and the input queue is full, the program should discard the character and place a "BEL" character in the output queue to warn the user that an input has been lost. Comment on the presence or absence of potential deadlock situations in your program.

12

PROGRAM DEVELOPMENT

Novice programmers are often preoccupied with what initially seems to be the most difficult aspect of writing programs: translating ideas into a programming language, or *coding*. However, this activity is only one stage in a complete programming project, which has at least seven definable components:

- Requirements analysis
- Specification
- Design
- Documentation
- Coding
- Testing and debugging
- Maintenance

The first six stages above take place during the traditional "development cycle" of a programming project. Figure 12–1 shows that coding is just a small part of the development cycle. But even more significant is a breakdown of programming effort expended over the entire lifetime of a large program. As shown in Figure 12–2, once a large program is in operation, maintaining it may actually require more effort than the original development cycle. The

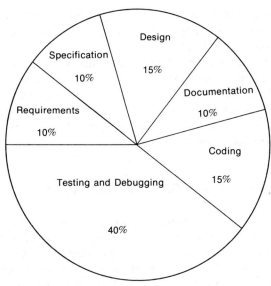

FIGURE 12-1 Development effort for a typical program.

high cost of program maintenance underscores the need for an effective development cycle to reduce or simplify maintenance requirements.

In this chapter we make some general comments on the stages of program development, and give particulars as they apply to assembly language

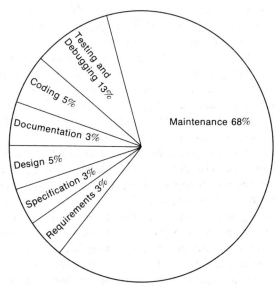

FIGURE 12-2 Total programming effort for a large program.

programming. A complete discussion of applicable "software engineering" techniques is beyond the scope of this text, but a large body of literature exists on the subject (see References).

At this point, you may not be too interested in the problems of medium-to-large programming projects because most of the programs you've encountered so far might be classified as "toy programs." The purpose of this chapter is to give you an appreciation of "real-world" programming problems and practices to encourage you to form good programming habits now, before you are forced to learn them the hard way!

12.1 THE STAGES OF PROGRAM DEVELOPMENT

Requirements analysis, present in some form in all problem-solving activities, defines the requirements for an acceptable solution to the problem. Most programmers don't get involved in this stage, because it usually takes place at a management level and involves issues such as general approach (should a computer be used at all?), staffing and other resources (will this project effectively utilize the talents of existing personnel?), project costs (can we afford to solve this problem?), and schedules (will the solution be ready soon enough to be useful?).

The inputs and outputs of a program and their relationship are defined by an *external specification*. For example, the specification for a text editor defines the format of the text files and it lists all of the editing commands and the effects of each. However, an external specification does not contain a description of *how* the program achieves these effects; this is part of design.

The structure of a program is defined during the *design* stage, remembering that "programs equal algorithms plus data structures." The design stage often decomposes the problem by outlining a solution in terms of a set of cooperating high-level program *modules*. This approach requires additional design and *internal* specification, since each module and its interaction with the others must be specified, and then the internal structure of each module must be designed. Depending on the module's complexity, additional decomposition into submodules might also take place.

Most *documentation* should be created during the specification and design stages. Concise yet complete documentation is needed to communicate specifications and design concepts among the current implementors and future users and maintainers of a program. To a lesser extent, documentation is needed in the coding stage to explain the details of program coding.

In the *coding* stage, the design is translated into a programming language for a specific computer system. When coding begins, design usually stops, which is a good argument for not starting coding prematurely. Several studies have shown that design errors are more common than coding errors, so that a good design is essential to project success. Also, one is much more likely to reduce the size of a program or enhance its performance by design improvements in algorithms and data structures than by coding tricks or local optimizations.

The word *debugging* usually suggests an activity in which the obvious errors in a program are eliminated so that the program runs without "blowing up." *Testing* refers to a more refined activity that verifies not only that the program runs, but also that it meets its external specifications. Testing requires a test plan, basically a set of input patterns and expected responses for verifying the behavior and operating limits of the program. Quite often the test plan is given as part of the original specification to ensure that the tests are not biased in a way that would obscure the errors in a known design.

Large programs require *maintenance* after they have been put into operation in the field for two reasons. First, there are usually errors that are not detected during the testing stage. Obviously, increased effort during the testing stage can reduce this maintenance requirement. Second, and almost inevitable, is that users of a system will call for changes and enhancements after the system has been put into operation. The cost of this maintenance is strongly influenced by the specification, design, and documentation of a program; therefore maintenance must be considered early in the development cycle.

12.2 SPECIFICATION AND DESIGN

The external specification of a program comes directly from the results of requirements analysis, while internal specifications come later. During the development cycle, some "looping" between specification and design often occurs as shown in Figure 12–3. This looping may be required when attempts to design the program reveal ambiguities, contradictions, or other deficiencies in the external specification. But most of the looping occurs because of the "top-down" approach that is used in problem solving. When the solution to an original external specification is designed as a collection of cooperating modules, each module and its interfaces with its partners must be documented by internal specifications. Then the workings of each module must be designed. The whole process may be repeated many times as modules at each level are designed as collections of lower-level modules.

12.2.1 Program Structure

The partitioning of a program into modules can be illustrated and documented in a *hierarchy chart* that shows the relationships among modules. For example, consider the following external specification:

> Write a program that multiplies pairs of 16-bit two's-complement integers to produce 32-bit results. The computer's input device

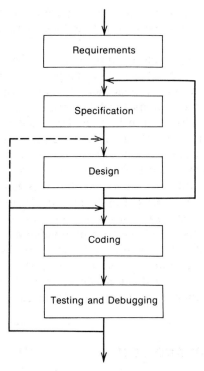

FIGURE 12-3   The program development cycle.

consists of 16 toggle switches and a pushbutton; for each input number, the user enters a binary number using the switches and then pushes the pushbutton. The output device consists of 16 lights. After completing the multiplication, the program uses the lights to display the multiplier, multiplicand, high-order product, and low-order product, each for ten seconds. The lights are turned off for one second after each number is displayed. The multiplication process is repeated until a pair of zeroes is entered.

Even this very simple program can be decomposed into a number of cooperating modules, as shown in Figure 12-4. The main program performs multiplication and calls three different subroutines for support:

- INSW: reads a 16-bit number from the switches.
- OUTDSP: displays a 16-bit number in the lights.
- DELAYN: delays for a specified number of seconds.

Top-down design breaks a program into smaller chunks that can be handled separately. Once we have specified the interfaces between MAIN and

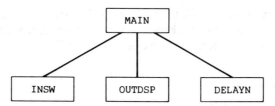

FIGURE 12-4 Preliminary hierarchy chart for multiplication program.

INSW, OUTDSP, and DELAYN, we can carry out their detailed design and coding more or less independently. We need not be concerned with *how* a particular module performs its function, only that it *does* perform it.

12.2.2 Detailed Module Design

Once the basic structure of a program and its data structures have been determined, the detailed design of algorithms and data structures may be started. At this stage it is convenient to outline algorithms using an informal block-structured language that allows English descriptions of actions. For example, the initial design of the multiplication program might be outlined as shown in Table 12-1. The pseudo-code shows the main program and defines the functions of its three supporting modules. Of course, we might not need so

TABLE 12-1 Initial design of multiplication program.

```
PROGRAM Multiply;
VAR X, Y -- input numbers (each a 16-bit 2's-comp integer)
   PH, PL -- high-order and low-order product
      (PH and PL form a 32-bit 2's-complement integer)
FUNCTION INSW : word;
   This function reads a 16-bit word from the input switches
   and returns the 16-bit value to the caller.
PROCEDURE OUTDSP (num : word);
   This procedure displays a 16-bit word in the lights.
PROCEDURE DELAYN (N : unsigned integer);
   This procedure delays for N seconds, where N is a 16-bit
   value interpreted as an unsigned integer (0 <= N <= 65535).
   (Reminder: Don't forget to check for N=0.)
BEGIN  Main program
   Read X and Y from the switches.
   WHILE (X<>0) OR (Y<>0) DO
      BEGIN
         Compute the double-length product PH,PL.
         Display X, Y, PH, and PL with appropriate delays.
         Read X and Y from the switches.
      END;
END.
```

much preliminary design work to develop such a simple program. However, our purpose is to illustrate techniques that can be easily applied to larger programs, and so we continue the example.

12.2.3 Design Iterations

After doing an initial design, we may determine that further decomposition is needed. For example, we may discover a sequence of steps that occurs often enough to warrant the definition of a new procedure:

```
PROCEDURE DISPLAY (num : word);
  This procedure displays a number in the lights with
  the delays required by the specification, that is:
    BEGIN  OUTDSP(num); DELAYN(10); OUTDSP(0); DELAYN(1)   END;
```

In addition, we may discover that our computer does not have a multiplication instruction and so we will have to use a 16×16-bit multiplication subroutine from a program library. We may also find that there is no hardware timer so that we will have to use "busy-waiting" to produce delays. Therefore, we will write a subroutine DLY1S that busy-waits for one second, and design DELAYN to delay N seconds by calling DLY1S N times. These changes result in the program structure shown in Figure 12–5. At this point we can also refine the design, so that the main program body reads as follows:

```
BEGIN  Main program
  X := INSW; Y := INSW;   (Read X and Y)
  WHILE (X<>0) OR (Y<>0) DO
    BEGIN
      PH,PL := X*Y;  (Call MULT16 for double-length product)
      DISPLAY(X); DISPLAY(Y);   (Display X and Y)
      DISPLAY(PH); DISPLAY(PL);   (Display product)
      X := INSW; Y := INSW;  (Read X and Y)
    END;
END.
```

Some design problems may not show up until coding or even testing, requiring another iteration of design and specification, as shown by the dotted line in Figure 12–3. For example, we may find that due to pushbutton "contact bounce," the INSW subroutine must wait ten milliseconds before reading an input number from the switches. Therefore we provide another subroutine DLY10M to delay for ten milliseconds. At the same time we may find it convenient to obtain a one-second delay in DLY1S by calling DLY10M 100 times, yielding the final program structure shown in Figure 12–6.

Large hierarchy charts may be partitioned according to the structure of the underlying modules themselves. The top level diagram shows the relationship among high-level modules whose internal structures are defined in lower-level diagrams. This reflects block structure in Pascal and the principle of "top-down" program development in any language.

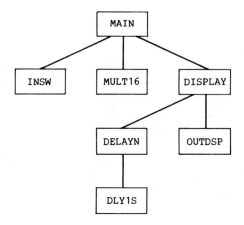

FIGURE 12–5 A second hierarchy chart for multiplication program.

12.2.4 Data Structures

So far we have shown the relationships among a main program and its subroutines, but data structures are also part of a program. Whenever a data structure is shared by two or more subroutines, it is important to specify exactly which subroutines may access the data structure and how. In a hierarchy chart, a "data module" may be shown as another module with dotted lines to the subroutines that may access it. Using this technique, Figure 12–7 shows the structure of a solution to the timer problem in Exercise 11.3.

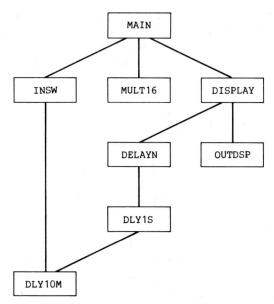

FIGURE 12–6 Final hierarchy chart for multiplication program.

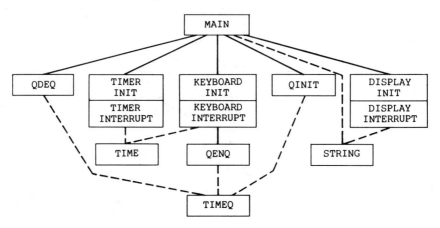

FIGURE 12-7   Hierarchy chart for the timer problem in Exercise 11.3.

Hierarchy charts and high-level descriptions of algorithms and data structures help a programmer to keep track of program structure during design, but the module specifications must be spelled out in much more detail in the program's documentation. In the next section we describe exactly what information is required and how it can be formatted in a "prologue" for each module.

12.3 DOCUMENTATION

Documentation should not be generated at one fixed time during the program development cycle. Instead, documentation should be generated as appropriate throughout the project. Your only documentation experience so far may be writing comments for high-level and assembly language code, but the most important program documentation is generated long before the coding stage, during specification and design.

In industry it is a growing practice to make all programs *self-documenting*, so that all documentation, including specifications and design, is contained in the same text file as the source code itself. Writing self-documenting code has several advantages over keeping separate handwritten or typed documentation:

- It is easier to relate the documentation to the code.

- Efficient procedures can be instituted for maintaining all code and documentation on a development computer system.

- When the design (or code) is changed, it is convenient to make the appropriate documentation changes (otherwise there is a tendency for documentation to lag design).

- During revisions and maintenance, if the source code is available then all the documentation is guaranteed to be available too (not lost in a paper shuffle).

The main disadvantage of self-documenting code is that it increases the size of the text files that the development computer system must handle. Including back-up files, a development system may need 200 to 1000 bytes or more of disk storage for every byte of object code that is developed.[1] Thus, developing a 50 Kbyte application program for a microprocessor may require a minicomputer or midicomputer with a 50 Mbyte file system.

12.3.1   Prologues

The external specification for a complete program is generated by requirements analysis. As the program design evolves, internal specifications must be generated for individual modules. All of these specifications may be documented by *prologues* for each module. Prologues are part of the source code text file for each module, thus creating self-documenting code.

A program contains both program modules and data modules. *Program modules* contain subroutines and local data structures. Separate *data modules* are required only for data structures that are shared among several program modules.

12.3.2   Program Module Prologues

Figure 12–8 shows the structure of the text file for a program module that contains a number of subroutines. The module begins with a brief overview of its overall function. Then the global and local data structures that are used by the subroutines are defined, and local data structures declared. (If a data structure is used by only one subroutine, it may appear with that subroutine instead.) A data structure is *local* to a program module if it is accessed only by the module and its submodules, otherwise it is *global*. Finally, the module contains a prologue and source code for each subroutine.

---

[1]For example, consider the queue module in Table 9–18. It generates about 60 bytes of code and with its modest documentation the text contains about 4800 ASCII characters, a storage factor of 80 to 1. If we had drawn pretty boxes around the prologues, as is done by some programmers, the figure would be 100 to 1 or higher. Adding to this the storage for hierarchy charts, memos, and notes and double the figure for backups, we get a minimum factor of 300 to 1. To this must be added the storage for object modules and temporary files created during assembly, editing, and formatting. If multiple copies or generations of programs are kept in the file system by different programmers, the storage factor quickly reaches 1000 to 1 or higher. Obviously a powerful development system is required to effectively manage all of the files associated with a large programming project.

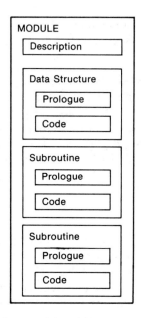

FIGURE 12–8 Structure of a program module's text file.

Examples of program modules with prologues were given in Tables 9–18 and 10–4. The module overview and definition of data structures do not follow a rigid format, but they must be present. Notice in both examples that it is possible to draw figures for data structures as part of the definition; this is easy to do with modern screen-oriented text editors. The prologue for each subroutine should contain the following information:

- *Name and short description:* the name of the subroutine and a 1-line description of what it does.

- *Description:* a longer description of the subroutine, if needed. Areas worth mentioning include: purpose, assumptions about operating environment, functions performed and algorithms used, and expected ranges of inputs and outputs.

- *Inputs:* the input parameters of the subroutine and how they are passed.

- *Outputs:* the output parameters of the subroutine and how they are passed. Input and output parameters should be given descriptive names even if they are passed in registers.

- *Global data:* definitions of any global data structures that are accessed (except for those already defined in the module prologue).

- *Local data:* definitions and declarations of all local data structures (except for those already defined in the module prologue).[2]

- *Functions:* a description of how the inputs of the subroutine are used to produce outputs, and any dependence or side effects on local and global data.

- *Registers affected (assembly language prologues only):* a description of which processor registers are modified by the subroutine (if missing, assume all registers are changed, except that output parameters will be passed as specified).

- *Typical calling sequence:* example code for calling the subroutine.

- *Notes:* operating restrictions, tricks, and any other information a programmer may need to understand, fix, or enhance the subroutine.

12.3.3 Data Module Prologues

Separate data modules may be required for data structures that are accessed by two or more program modules. Figure 12–7 showed such an example. Another example is the text buffer in a text editor program. It must be accessed by input, output, and editing modules; the hierarchy chart is shown in Figure 12–9.

Prologues for data modules should give a precise definition of the data structures, including graphics or an easily-understood pseudo-language to illustrate table layouts and pointers. Tables 9–18 and 10–4 illustrated the use of graphics for defining data structures.

In practice, separate data modules are often undesirable. Instead, a global data structure is "hidden" under a set of subroutines that access and manipulate the data structure. For example, consider the symbol table for an assembler. The assembler program must perform a number of different operations on the symbol table, such as inserting new symbols, looking up old ones, and sorting the symbol table. If the symbol table is defined as a global data structure, then the main program must know the table's structure in order to manipulate it.

A better program organization is shown in Figure 12–10. Here a module called SYMBOL ROUTINES contains the symbol table and several submodules that perform the required functions. Since the main program accesses the symbol table only through this module, it is possible to change the organiza-

---

[2]In defining local data, you usually need not be concerned with temporaries, but you must certainly define all variables and data structures whose values must be preserved between successive calls of the subroutine. For example, in Table 11–1 SBUSY is a global variable accessed by both the main program and interrupt routines; BUFPNT is a local variable whose value must be preserved between successive calls of the interrupt routines.

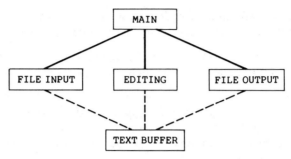

FIGURE 12-9 Hierarchy chart for a text editor.

tion of the symbol table (e.g., from contiguous table to linked list) without requiring any changes in the main program. SYMBOL ROUTINES hides the details of the symbol table's structure from the main program.

12.3.4 Ownership of Global Data Structures

A data structure is "owned" by the module in which it is declared (i.e., in which memory is allocated for it). The data is local to the declaring module, and global to lower-level modules. Thus, a low-level program module may have no local data structures, but its subroutines still must manipulate global data structures declared at a higher level. An example is the queue module in Table 9-18. It doesn't own any queues itself, but it can manipulate queues having the defined structure.

The definition of a global data structure should appear not only in the module that owns it, but also in every module that uses it. However, it is tedious to retype long data structure definitions for every module. Worse, it is impossible to ensure consistency when a definition appears in many different places. To eliminate these problems, sophisticated program development systems provide "Include" processing. In such a system, each global data structure is defined in a separate text file. The programmer may simply type

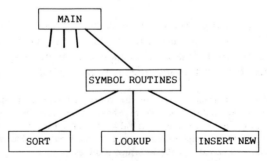

FIGURE 12-10 Partial hierarchy chart for an assembler.

"#include *filename*" (or something similar) in each prologue that is to include the data structure's definition. The "Include" processor automatically inserts the text from the specified file. Thus, any changes in the definition of a data structure are automatically propagated to all the prologues that use it. However, it is still the programmer's responsibility to make any required coding changes.

12.3.5 Documenting Code

In their excellent little book, *The Elements of Programming Style,* Kernighan and Plauger give sound advice for documenting code in a high-level language:

> The best documentation for a computer program is a clean structure. It also helps if the code is well formatted, with good mnemonic identifiers and labels (if any are needed), and a smattering of enlightening comments. Flowcharts and program descriptions are of secondary importance; the only reliable documentation of a computer program is the code itself. The reason is simple — whenever there are multiple representations of a program, the chance for discrepancy exists. If the code is in error, artistic flowcharts and detailed comments are to no avail. Only by reading the code can the programmer know for sure what the program does.

It is more difficult to follow this advice when coding in assembly language. In fact, the main purpose of comments in assembly language code is to relate the code to a higher-level description of what's going on.

Two different styles of documenting assembly language code have been used in this book. The first (and most popular) style is to use English language sentences and phrases to document individual statements or small groups of statements. You should not feel obliged to comment every line when you use this style. You should assume that anyone who reads your program understands the effects of each instruction in the programming language. Avoid comments like

```
      ADDA   #1            Add 1 to A.
```

A more descriptive comment might be

```
      ADDA   #1            Increment the iteration count.
```

If the reason for incrementing A is completely obvious, then there should be no comment at all. According to Kernighan and Plauger, "Anything that contributes no new information, but merely echoes code, is superfluous."

The second style is to use statements in a high-level language to document groups of assembly language statements. Any readable language or pseudo-language may be used; we've used Pascal (with occasional liberties) in Tables 7–3, 7–5, and 8–4. Good assembly language programmers formulate their initial designs using such a language anyway. This style of documentation simply retains the original design, explicitly showing the correspondence between the high-level formulation and the resulting assembly language code. The emphasis is not on syntactic correctness of the high-level description, but on readability and accuracy in describing what the assembly language program does.

12.4 CODING

12.4.1 Coding Rules

Coding is probably the best understood aspect of programming; in fact, coding a well-designed program is a fairly mechanical operation. The most important thing to know about coding is that good code must be built upon good design. A programmer cannot expect to make significant improvements in program performance by clever coding — the best improvements are made in design.

In *The Elements of Programming Style*, Kernighan and Plauger discuss the merits and pitfalls of dozens of programs, from which they compile a list of rules of programming style. Many of these rules are especially applicable to coding:

- Write clearly — don't be too clever.
- Say what you mean, simply and directly.
- Let the machine do the dirty work.
- Write first in an easy-to-understand pseudo-language; then translate into whatever language you have to use.
- Don't stop with your first draft.
- Choose a data representation that makes the program simple.
- Don't patch bad code — rewrite it.
- Make sure input cannot violate the limits of the program.
- Identify bad input; recover if possible.
- Make sure all variables are initialized before use.
- Watch out for off-by-one errors.
- Take care to branch the right way on equality.
- Make sure your program "does nothing" gracefully.

- Make it right before you make it faster.

- Make it clear before you make it faster.

- Keep it right when you make it faster.

- Don't diddle code to make it faster — find a better algorithm.

- Make sure comments and code agree.

- Don't just echo the code with comments — make every comment count.

- Don't comment bad code — rewrite it.

- Use variable names that mean something.

- Use statement labels that mean something.

The examples in Kernighan and Plauger's book clearly demonstrate the validity of these rules. All of the assembly language and Pascal programs in this book have been coded with these rules in mind, although there are undoubtedly a few violations (*exercise*: find some of them).

The most important rules are the ones that advise you to keep things simple and avoid tricky code. Having said this, we must now face reality — most programmers love to write tricky code. After all, it makes the job more interesting, it gives programmers an ego boost to show how clever they are, and in many cases it even provides job security (no one else can maintain the code!).

There *are* legitimate uses for tricky code. Occasionally it is necessary to squeeze the last drop of performance out of a program or squeeze the last possible byte of code into a computer's memory. Such needs may stem from anything from poor planning and design to simple economics — a potential cost savings in 100,000 copies of a computer system or program can pay for a lot of extra development work and still leave a profit. Therefore, the next subsection will describe a number of coding "tricks," pointing out their pitfalls as appropriate. However, we remind you that good design techniques can improve a program's potential performance long before coding has begun.[3]

12.4.2 Coding Tricks

The purpose of most coding tricks is to produce faster programs. Since a typical program spends most of its time executing loops, speeding up critical loops can improve a program's performance more than any other coding changes. In short loops, the speed improvement obtained by eliminating just a

---

[3]Design and coding techniques are discussed in the references at the end of this chapter. Apparently the difference between tricks and techniques is that tricks aren't normally dignified in textbooks (except this one!).

few instructions can be substantial. We shall discuss several methods for speeding up loops:

- Eliminating unnecessary instructions.

- Optimizing register usage within loops.

- Moving unconditional branches to outside the loop.

- Exploiting special cases (dangerous).

- Moving instructions with invariant results to outside the loop.

- Collapsing multiple conditional tests into one.

If a programmer mechanically translates a high-level language statement into assembly language, there will often be unnecessary instructions. For example, consider the following IF statement, which computes the maximum of two integers i and j:

```
IF i>j THEN max := i ELSE max := j;
```

This statement may be written in assembly language according to an equivalent primitive sequence as suggested in Section 2.8:

```
        LDA     I
        CMPA    J
        BGT     LABELA
        LDA     J
        STA     MAX
        BRA     LABELB
LABELA  LDA     I
        STA     MAX
LABELB  ...
```

However, a shorter and faster sequence can be written which is just as easy, perhaps easier, to understand:

```
        LDA     I
        CMPA    J
        BGT     LABELA
        LDA     J
LABELA  STA     MAX
```

Another general technique is to optimize the use of registers within loops. Since instructions that operate on registers are generally shorter and faster than ones that operate on memory, the most-frequently used variables and constants should be kept in registers during loops.

Unconditional branches that occur within loops can often be moved to outside the loop, reducing the number of instructions in the loop. For exam-

ple, look at the loop in Table 7–7, and then read the recoded version of it
below:

```
SCOREI  LDX   HEAD              Point to first list item.
        BRA   LOOPIN            Jump into loop.
SCLOOP  CLRA                    Initialization value.
        STA   SCORE1(X)         Clear the three exam scores.
        STA   SCORE2(X)
        STA   SCORE3(X)
        LDX   LINK(X)           Get address of next item.
LOOPIN  CMPX  #NULL             End of list?
        BNE   SCLOOP            Continue if not.
        RTS                     Done, return.
```

The general idea here is to structure the loop so that the unconditional branch
back to the beginning of the loop is replaced by a conditional branch that we
needed somewhere in the loop anyway.

The loop above contains two more areas for improvement. The first
takes advantage of a fortuitous combination of instructions and data. The
CMPX #NULL instruction is redundant because NULL is defined to be 0; the Z bit
will already be set if X was just loaded with 0. Therefore we can rewrite the
program as shown below:

```
SCOREI  LDX   HEAD              Point to first list item.
        BRA   LOOPIN            Jump into loop.
SCLOOP  CLRA                    Initialization value.
        STA   SCORE1(X)         Clear the three exam scores.
        STA   SCORE2(X)
        STA   SCORE3(X)
        LDX   LINK(X)           Get address of next item.
LOOPIN  BNE   SCLOOP            Continue if not end of list.
        RTS                     Done, return.
```

However, we'll soon see that this method is dangerous; it is *not* recommended.

The second improvement is to move instructions with invariant results
to outside the loop. Such instructions are often assignments of a constant
value to a variable; the assignment needs to be done only once before entering
the loop, not over and over as the loop is executed. In our example, CLRA
needs to be executed only once:

```
SCOREI  LDX   HEAD              Point to first list item.
        CLRA                    Initialization value.
        BRA   LOOPIN            Jump into loop.
SCLOOP  STA   SCORE1(X)         Clear the three exam scores.
        STA   SCORE2(X)
        STA   SCORE3(X)
        LDX   LINK(X)           Get address of next item.
LOOPIN  BNE   SCLOOP            Continue if not end of list.
        RTS                     Done, return.
```

Unfortunately, in all our cleverness we've just blown it, because CLRA sets Z to 1 for the BNE test. The problem occurs because of our careless exploitation of a special case.

Even if we fix the bug by swapping the CLRA and LDX HEAD instructions, our use of a special case still allows problems in the future. If someone decides to change the definition of NULL, for example from 0 to −1, the program fails — the CMPX instruction is needed again. Even worse, it is not evident from the code and documentation that the value of NULL matters. ("Make it clear before you make it faster.")

Perhaps the most clever method for speeding up a loop is to collapse multiple conditional tests into one. For example, consider the following subroutine that searches a buffer for a character:

```
*          Find the first occurrence in BUFFER of a character
*          passed in A.  Return with Z=1 if character not found,
*          or with Z=0 and X pointing to character if found.
SEARCH  LDX    #BUFFER       Point to start of buffer.
SLOOP   CMPA   (X)+          Match?
        BEQ    OUT           Exit if match found.
        CMPX   #BUFEND       At end?
        BNE    SLOOP         No, look some more.
        RTS                  No match, return with Z=1.
OUT     ADDX   #-1           Adjust X to point to matched character.
        CLRZ                 Set Z:=0 for match.
        RTS                  Done, return.
BUFFER  RMB    1000          Reserve 1000-byte buffer.
BUFEND  EQU    *             Define address just past buffer.
```

It appears that we have done the best coding that we possibly can, even using auto-increment addressing to save an instruction inside the loop. Both conditional tests inside the loop seem necessary — one to find the character and one to stop the loop if the character isn't found. However, we can eliminate one of the tests by ensuring that we will *always* find the character, deciding outside the loop whether we found the character inside the buffer or just past the buffer's end. In this example we can double the speed of the loop:

```
SEARCH  LDX    #BUFFER       Point to start of buffer.
        STA    EXTRA         Store character to stop us for sure.
SLOOP   CMPA   (X)+          Match?
        BNE    SLOOP         No, continue.
        ADDX   #-1           Yes, point to matched character.
        CMPX   #EXTRA        Stopped at end of buffer?
        RTS                  Return, Z=0 if match, Z=1 if no match.
BUFFER  RMB    1000          Reserve 1000-byte buffer.
EXTRA   RMB    1             Extra byte for termination.
```

Many high-level language compilers automatically perform code optimizations such as eliminating redundant instructions and removing invariant

computations from loops. ("Let the machine do the dirty work.") A programmer's best advice for coding in both high-level and assembly languages is
to "make it right before you make it faster."

12.5 TESTING AND DEBUGGING

The purpose of testing and debugging is to make a program meet its
specifications. *Testing* is an activity that detects the existence of errors in a
program. *Debugging* finds the causes of detected errors and then repairs
them. As shown in the pie chart in Figure 12-1, testing and debugging form the
largest single component in the program development process.

12.5.1 Development Approach

Even after starting with a good design, many novice programmers have
a haphazard approach to the remainder of program development. They code
the entire program and then run it the first time with their fingers crossed.
Every programmer should have the joy of seeing a large program perform
perfectly on its first run, but for most this is a once-in-a-lifetime experience.
More often, a program with such a daring first test either does nothing or
"blows up."

A more sensible method for developing a large program is code, test,
and debug it in small chunks. One of two approaches may be used:

- *Bottom-up development.* The lowest-level modules are coded, tested,
  and debugged first. These modules, which are now known to be working, may be employed in developing higher-level modules. For example,
  in developing the multiplication program in Section 12.2, a programmer
  could code and test the INSW, OUTSW, and DELAYN subroutines before
  coding the main program. However, a simple "throwaway" main program must be written to test each subroutine.

- *Top-down development.* The highest-level modules are coded, tested,
  and debugged first. In order to test them, the lower-level modules which
  have not yet been coded must be replaced by "stubs" that match their
  input/output specifications but with much less functionality. For example, in developing the multiplication program, a programmer could test
  the main program's input, output, and control, but use a stub for multiplication. The stub would return the values of X and Y in PH, PL instead
  of actually computing the product X·Y.

There are advantages and disadvantages to both approaches. In
bottom-up development, fundamental errors in the design of top-level modules may not be caught until late in the project. In top-down development,

problems with program size or performance may not become apparent until critical low-level modules are developed. Both approaches require additional code to be written for testing. In practice, it is often best to use a combination of the two approaches, developing both high-level and critical low-level modules first, and using stubs for less critical modules to be developed later.

In large programming projects the need to partition the testing and debugging problem is well recognized. About half of the total testing and debugging effort is devoted to ensuring that individual modules meet their internal specifications; this activity is sometimes called "unit testing." The remaining effort is spent on "system integration and test," in which the modules are linked together and the external specifications of the program are checked.

12.5.2 Testing

Testing detects the presence of bugs, while debugging locates known bugs and eliminates them. Debugging and testing a program or module usually requires several iterations. Each round of debugging allows the programmer to test for more subtle bugs.

The first tests that are applied to a program may be simple ones, because most programs contain obvious bugs at the outset. An example of a simple test is, "If I give the program an input, does it produce an output, any output at all?" Once we get the program to produce *some* output, we can check whether or not we get the *correct* output under all circumstances.

The next group of tests should ensure that the program behaves properly for typical inputs and boundary conditions. Ideally the "typical inputs" and expected behavior should be defined in the program's original specification, so that the programmer cannot subconsciously avoid cases that aren't handled properly by the actual design and code. A good prologue defines a module's behavior well enough that the prologue itself provides the list of test inputs.

Boundary conditions should be tested from both sides. First the program must produce correct outputs for inputs just inside the allowed range. But it may also need to detect the presence of inputs outside the allowed range. Even if it doesn't detect bad inputs, the program should at least behave reasonably when it receives them.

12.5.3 Debugging

Finding a bug in a program requires the same common-sense approach as any other kind of troubleshooting. By applying a succession of tests, a programmer may determine in what areas the bug might be and in what areas it cannot be, eventually narrowing the area of search until the bug is found. The logic of debugging is the same as the logic of program design — breaking a problem into smaller and smaller pieces until it is solved. The main question is, "What tools can be used to break the problem into smaller pieces?"

The most effective debugging tools are created during design and coding. A program should be designed and coded *defensively*. The range of inputs should be checked and the occurrence of "impossible" cases should be flagged rather than ignored. Quite often the erroneous values produced by bugs will be caught by these checks before they have propagated too far, making bug detection trivial and isolation simple.

In addition, a programmer can provide facilities for tracing the program's execution, printing the program's state at key points, and allowing the program to be initialized, started, and stopped in the middle. It may seem inefficient to write a lot of extra code that will eventually be thrown away, but it can lead to substantial savings in debugging time. In fact, up to half of a good programmer's code may be "throwaway" code written for debugging purposes only.

In many high-level language programming systems and in most assembly language programming systems, many of the facilities mentioned above can be obtained without writing any extra code. An *on-line debugger* is an interactive system program for debugging a user's assembly language program; it provides a number of useful facilities:

- *Single-stepping*. The user program may be executed one instruction at a time, with control returning to the debugger after each step.

- *Running*. The user program may be started at an arbitrary address and run at full speed.

- *Running with breakpoints*. The user may specify a list of addresses such that control is returned to the debugger whenever an instruction is executed at one of these addresses.

- *Memory examining and changing*. The contents of memory may be examined and altered.

- *Register examining and changing*. The last values that the processor registers had during program execution may be examined and altered.

- *Symbolic references*. Some debuggers, called *symbolic debuggers*, keep a copy of the assembler symbol table so the user can specify memory addresses by assembly-time symbols instead of by absolute numbers.

Debuggers are usually found only on program development systems. A small, dedicated microcomputer system in a cash register or automobile does not have or need a debugger. A debugger is needed only during the development of the application programs, not during system operation.

Dedicated systems are usually developed with the aid of an *in-circuit emulator*. The in-circuit emulator replaces the dedicated system's microprocessor with a plug and cable to a development system. The development system has more memory, peripherals, and programs, so that the application programs and debugger can run there during development.

Using a debugger and an accurate assembly listing, you can very quickly debug a program, even one with no built-in debugging facilities. The algorithm for a typical debugging session might go something like this:

(1) Run the program with a set of test inputs and observe the effects of the bug(s).

(2) Make an educated guess of where the bug is located (e.g., main program, multiplication subroutine, output subroutine, etc.). Check the assembly listing — if you suddenly see the bug staring you in the face, you're done. Otherwise, set a breakpoint just before the program enters the suspected area. If the suspected area is large, set the breakpoint somewhere near the middle.

(3) Run the program again. If the breakpoint is not reached, the bug obviously occurs earlier in the program; remove the breakpoint and return to step 2.

(4) Otherwise, if the breakpoint is reached, examine processor registers, stack, and important variables and subroutine parameters to see if they have the correct values. If the bug has already occurred, once again remove the breakpoint and return to step 2.

(5) Otherwise, if the bug has not yet occurred, single-step the program, observing whether branches are taken in the expected direction and also observing the states of registers and memory at key points. If the bug pops out, you're done. Otherwise, if this gets too confusing or the bug remains hidden, return to step 1 or 2.

Once you locate a bug, you can fix it. However, Kernighan and Plauger have stated a wise rule: "Don't stop at one bug." When you locate one bug, you should always suspect that there are others lurking nearby, and you should check the nearby code carefully. Also, you must be very careful not to introduce new bugs when fixing the old ones.

Sometimes there is a long turnaround time for editing, assembling, and reloading a program, so that it's important to catch as many bugs as possible in each debugging session. When small bugs are found, it is often possible to test a different area of the program or to "patch" one or two instructions, so you can continue debugging. If the patch involves deleting instructions, you can replace them with NOPs. If the fix requires instructions to be added, you can overwrite an instruction with a subroutine jump to a patch in an unused area of memory; the patch contains the overwritten instruction, the instructions to be added, and a return. You must carefully observe instruction lengths in this kind of patching (e.g., a 1-byte CLRA cannot be overwritten by a 3-byte JSR PATCH).

Experience has demonstrated the existence of some common bugs for beginning assembly language programmers:

- Failure to initialize SP at the beginning of the program.

- Putting data in line with instructions. You must keep data separate from the code to be executed (see Section 6.1.3).

- Altering constants. Anything declared with an FCB or FCW pseudo-operation must not be altered.

- Incorrect use of assembly-time and run-time constants. The following examples show possible ways to try to load A with the ASCII code for "J".

```
        ORG   1234H
LETJ    EQU   4AH        Defines symbol LETJ to be the same as 4AH.
ZLETJ   FCB   4AH        Stores 4AH at memory address 1234H.
        ...
        LDA   LETJ       Incorrect, loads A with MEM[4AH].
        LDA   #ZLETJ     Incorrect, loads A with low byte of 1234H.
        LDA   #LETJ      Correct.
        LDA   ZLETJ      Correct.
```

- Incorrect manipulation of the stack pointer. If your program jumps off into never-never land, it is probably a result of executing an RTS at the end of a subroutine that pushed more items onto the stack than it popped, or vice versa. Beware of constructs like the following:

```
SUBR    PSHS A          Save A-register.
        ...
        BEQ  DONE        Exit on special case.
        ...              Else continue.
        PULS A           Restore A-register.
DONE    RTS              Return to caller.
```

- In the same vein, note that subroutines must always return via RTS, not by a jump directly to some address in the main program.

- Improper use of the ORG pseudo-operation. Occasionally a programmer ORG's for data and then re-ORG's at a convenient, higher address for instructions, without leaving enough room for the data just declared. This doesn't cause any assembler errors but it will cause run-time errors.

- Improper base for constants. Forgetting the "H" or other prefix or suffix for hexadecimal or other constants is an innocent error that can have strange effects.

- Incorrect format of assembler expressions. Operand expressions may sometimes yield unexpected results without creating assembler errors. For example, the statement EBASE EQU BASE-2*FIRST may yield a value of (BASE-2)*FIRST or BASE-(2*FIRST) depending on whether or not operators have equal precedence. The statement CON EQU 3 + 5 will yield the value 3 if the assembler interprets the space after "3" as beginning the comment field. Be on the look out for values in the "Contents" column of the assembler listing that don't match up with what was apparently specified in the "Operand" column.

We close this section with some useful rules for debugging:

- Program defensively.

- Don't stop with one bug.

- Record all bugs as they are observed.

- Record all patches as they are created.

12.6 MAINTENANCE

Students and other novice programmers are seldom faced with the prospect of maintaining their programs. A student's programs are rarely used by anyone else. At best, they may be passed down to friends who take the course in the next semester, in the hope that the friends will benefit in some way (sound suspicious?). In the "real" world, however, programs are written for and used by customers who expect a certain degree of performance. Throughout the lifetime of any nontrivial program, lurking bugs will pop up, and at the same time customers will request new features and improvements. Thus, the program's code and even its specification and design may undergo frequent change.

In section 12.3 we indicated that a large, sophisticated computer system is needed to develop a large program and its documentation. Program maintenance requires an even larger and more sophisticated development system. Administrative programs are needed to send customers new software releases, or at least to inform them of their opportunities to purchase the latest version. Mechanisms are needed to keep track of the various program fixes and enhancements, especially since after a short time different customers will be using different versions of the program. A complete discussion of program maintenance strategies is well beyond the scope of this chapter, and so we leave you now to consult the References.

REFERENCES

The best source of practical advice on program design, documentation, coding, and debugging is *The Elements of Programming Style* by Brian W. Kernighan and P. J. Plauger [McGraw-Hill, 1978 (second edition)]. Pascal programmers can also benefit from the "style clinics" scattered throughout *An Introduction to Programming and Problem Solving with Pascal* by Schneider, Weingart, and Perlman [Wiley, 1978].

A number of good books have been published on the specific subject of software engineering. The classic is *The Mythical Man-Month* by F. P. Brooks [Addison-Wesley, 1975]. This short, entertaining, and easy-to-read book is a collection of thought-provoking essays on the nature and management of computer programming projects, and is required reading for anyone who participates in the development of large programs. In it, Brooks gives specific advice for program specification, design, documentation, coding, testing, and debugging, and he discusses the general problems of large program management.

Another useful book is *Principles of Software Engineering and Design* by Zelkowitz, Shaw, and Gannon [Prentice-Hall, 1979]. The central thesis of this book is prominently displayed on its front cover, which we've adapted here as Figure 12–2. A less recent but still interesting book for programmers and managers alike is *The Psychology of Computer Programming* by Gerald M. Weinberg [Van Nostrand Reinhold, 1971]. It investigates the actual behavior and thought processes of programmers as they carry out their daily activities, and relates them to the stages of program development.

EXERCISES

12.1   Design the program specified in Exercise 10.14. Your design should include a hierarchy chart, an outline of the code for all program modules except the queue module, and definitions of all data structures.

12.2   Write a prologue for the DIVIDE subroutine in Table 9–14.

12.3   Write a prologue for the polling subroutines in Table 11–4.

12.4   Recode the program in Table 7–3 so that all of the unconditional branches that now appear inside loops are moved to outside the loops.

12.5   Recode the list initialization loop in Section 12.4.2 so that a CMPX NULL instruction is not used if NULL=0, but the loop still works correctly if NULL<>0. (*Hint:* Use conditional assembly.)

12.6   Show what additional comments should be included if a programmer changes the tenth line in the QENQ subroutine in Table 9–18 to read as follows:

```
*        CLRZ                   Set Z:=0 since not full.
```

12.7   A comparison instruction usually has three possible outcomes: less than, equal, or greater than. Quite often only two of these outcomes are of interest, the third being "impossible." For example, in a loop that decrements a counter from some positive value and terminates when the counter reaches zero, the counter should never be negative. Nevertheless, defensive programming requires that BLE DONE rather than BEQ DONE be used to test for termination, to limit the effects of a bug that somehow makes the counter negative (otherwise the program could enter a very long or endless loop). Find at least four different Pascal or assembly language programs in this book in which this principle was followed. Also find at least four programs in which this principle was violated and show how to fix them.

13

DEC PDP-11
AND LSI-11

The PDP-11 was the first minicomputer architecture specifically designed to support an evolving family of computers spanning a range of price and performance. Thus the PDP-11/20, introduced in 1970, was just the first in a long series of compatible minicomputers and microcomputers manufactured by Digital Equipment Corporation (DEC). Members of the family include: PDP-11/34, PDP-11/40 and PDP-11/70, high-performance minicomputers supporting large timesharing systems such as UNIX; PDP-11/03 and PDP-11/04, low-end minicomputers for dedicated applications; LSI-11/23, a single-board computer module for custom systems; and the PDP-11/23, a packaged microcomputer that uses the LSI-11/23.

One measure of the success of a product or idea is how much it is copied. The PDP-11 family introduced (or in a few cases popularized) many features of contemporary minicomputers and microcomputers: memory-mapped I/O; NZVC condition codes; dedicated stack pointer SP for subroutine and interrupt calls; short relative conditional branches; auto-increment, auto-decrement, and immediate addressing modes; multi-level interrupt systems; software interrupts; byte-addressable memories. Because the PDP-11 architecture embodies so many important minicomputer and microcomputer features, it is an important machine to study even if you don't expect to be using one soon.

13.1   BASIC ORGANIZATION

13.1.1   Computer Structure

The basic structure of a PDP-11 computer is shown in Figure 13–1. The processor communicates with memory and peripherals using a single bus called the Unibus. This bus contains a 16-bit data bus, an 18-bit address bus, and various control signals.[1] Only 16 bits of the address bus are used in a basic processor without a memory management unit, since the program counter and instructions contain only 16-bit addresses. Each address specifies one of 2^{16} (64K) 8-bit bytes, arranged with the lower address assigned to the low-order byte of a word as shown in Figure 5-1(b).

The PDP-11 has no I/O instructions, and there are no Unibus control signals to distinguish between memory and I/O operations. Instead, the upper 8K bytes of the memory address space are reserved for memory-mapped I/O interfaces. The PDP-11 processor and Unibus support a multi-level, vectored, priority interrupt system.

13.1.2   Processor Programming Model

The PDP-11 processor is a fine example of a general register machine. As shown in Figure 13–2, the processor state consists of a 16-bit processor status word (PSW) and eight 16-bit general registers R0 through R7. Included in the PSW are the four standard condition code (CC) bits NZVC, a 1-bit flag T used in on-line debuggers, a 3-bit interrupt priority mask (PRI), and eight other bits[2]. The program counter (PC) is one of the general registers, R7. This means that the PC may be used as a source, destination, or address register for any operation, providing a novel means of obtaining some standard addressing modes, as we'll see later. Another one of the general registers also has a special use: R6 is used as a stack pointer (SP) for pushing and popping return addresses on subroutine and interrupt calls and returns.

13.1.3   Instruction Formats

The major instruction formats of the PDP-11 are shown in Figure 13–3. The fields labeled src and dst specify operands using addressing modes described in Section 13.3. The PDP-11 has a very regular instruction set in the sense that instructions with src and dst fields may specify addressing modes without restrictions. The instruction set is also very regular in the sense that

---

[1]LSI-11 systems use the Q-bus, which is somewhat different from the Unibus logically, mechanically, and electrically, but identical as far as a programmer is concerned.

[2]The meanings of the eight high-order PSW bits depend on the PDP-11 model.

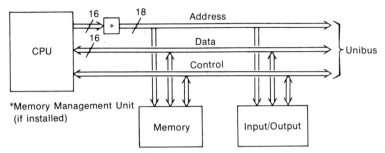

FIGURE 13-1 PDP-11 computer block diagram.

almost every instruction that operates on words can also operate on bytes, as specified by a bit in the opcode field.

As suggested by Figure 13–3, all basic PDP-11 instructions are one word long. For some addressing modes, one word of additional addressing information is appended to the instruction. Thus, an instruction with both src and dst fields may contain up to two words of addressing information, and PDP-11 instruction lengths may vary from one to three words.

13.2 ASSEMBLY LANGUAGE

Standard PDP-11 assembly language uses a free format as defined in Section 6.1. It does not rely on spaces to delimit label and comment fields. Instead, a label is followed by a colon, and a comment is preceded by a semicolon. Thus, all of the following are valid lines of assembly code:

```
START:MOV X,Y;These two lines are really tight.
SUB IND,COUNT
;                       The rest of these lines are more typical.
NEXT:    ADD    Z , Y      ;It's nice to make comments line up
         MOV    Y,X        ;...and other fields, too.
; *** Sometimes we use a whole line for an important message ***
```

15		8 7	5 4 3 2 1 0	
		PRI	T N Z V C	PSW

	R0
	R1
	R2
	R3
	R4
	R5
	R6 (SP)
	R7 (PC)

FIGURE 13-2 Programming model for the PDP-11.

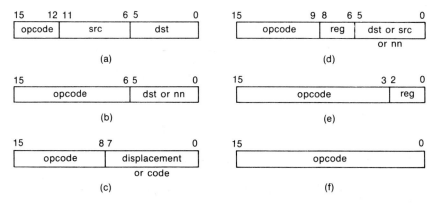

FIGURE 13–3 Major PDP-11 instruction formats: (a) double operand; (b) single operand and JMP; (c) branch and trap; (d) JSR, XOR, and fixed-point arithmetic; (e) RTS; (f) no operand.

Other important features of the assembly language are summarized below:

- Integer constants are assumed to be in octal, unless followed by a period for decimal.

- An equal sign is used instead of EQU or SET in symbol equations; the value of a symbol may be assigned more than once (as with SET).

- Register numbers are distinguished from memory addresses by preceding them with a percent sign, usually in symbol assignments at the beginning of the program (e.g., SP=%6).

- The program location counter (PLC) is denoted by a period; it may appear on the left-hand side as well as the right-hand side of an "=" symbol assignment.

- There is no ORG directive; instead, a statement like ".=1000" sets the starting value of the PLC.

- One-byte ASCII constants are denoted by preceding an ASCII character with a single quote; for example, 'A yields the value 101_8. Two-byte ASCII constants are denoted by double quotes; for example, "AC yields the value $101_8 + 256 \cdot 103_8 = 020701_8$. Notice that the first character (A) is stored in the least-significant byte.

- Directive names begin with a period. Important directives are summarized in Table 13–1.

The next section will give assembly language notation for PDP-11 operand addressing modes; relative addressing is the default. Table 13–2 illustrates some of the features of PDP-11 assembly language.

TABLE 13–1 PDP-11 assembly language directives.

Name	Example	Effect
.WORD	WT: .WORD 17,-789.,CAT	Store constant values into successive memory words.
.BYTE	BT: .BYTE 17,99.,'A	Store constant values into successive memory bytes.
.ASCII	AT: .ASCII /ABCDEFG/	Store ASCII values of characters into successive memory bytes.
.BLKW	BF: .BLKW 10.	Reserve a number of words of memory. BLKW N has the same effect as .=.+2·N
=	BE = BF+10.	Equate symbol with 16-bit expression.
.EVEN	.EVEN	Forces the PLC to an even value (i.e., increments it if it is odd). Useful after .BYTE and .ASCII.
.END	.END START	Indicates end of assembly and gives an optional starting address.

TABLE 13–2 PDP-11 assembly language program.

```
                        ;Sample program.
        .=2000          ;Starts at address 2000 octal.
R0     =      %0        ;Register definitions.
R1     =      %1
SP     =      %6
PC     =      %7
COUNT  =      10.       ;Iteration count.
;
START:  MOV   INIT,SUM;    sum := initialValue;
        CLR   R0
        MOV   TBADDR,R1;   i:=1  count
LOOP:   ADD   (R1),SUM;     sum := sum + table[i];
        ADD   #2,R1
        INC   R0
        CMP   R0,#COUNT
        BLT   LOOP
        HALT
;
SUM:    .=.+2           ;1-word variable.
INIT:   .WORD 17.       ;Initial value.
TBADDR: .WORD TABLE     ;Starting address of table.
TABLE:  .BLKW COUNT     ;Reserve COUNT words for table.
        .END  START
```

13.3 ADDRESSING

The PDP-11 memory is byte-addressable, and many instructions specify one-byte operands. Most instructions access two bytes as a unit — the word. A word has an even address and consists of two bytes arranged as shown in Figure 5–1(b). If an instruction that requires a 1-word operand tries to access an odd address, an error trap occurs. This restriction is made for reasons of efficiency — the PDP-11 memory is physically organized as an array of 16-bit words, so that it is impossible to access in one memory cycle a 2-byte quantity that is split across a word boundary.

13.3.1 Basic Addressing Modes

Both single and double operand instructions may have operands in memory; the PDP-11 is a two-address machine. An operand is specified by a 6-bit field in the instruction, consisting of a 3-bit register number and a 3-bit addressing mode designator, as shown in Figure 13–4. The reg field specifies one of the eight general registers and mode specifies how that register is used to obtain the operand. Mode 0 uses the register itself as the operand; modes 1–7 compute the effective address of an operand in memory, as summarized below.

(0) *Register.* The operand is reg itself; there is no effective address in memory.

(1) *Register Indirect.* The effective address of the operand is taken from reg.

(2) *Auto-increment.* The effective address of the operand is taken from reg and then reg is incremented by the length of the operand (1 or 2).

(3) *Auto-increment Indirect.* An indirect address is taken from reg and then reg is incremented by 2. The effective address is taken from the contents of memory at the indirect address.

(4) *Auto-decrement.* The reg is decremented by the length of the operand (1 or 2) and then the effective address of the operand is taken from reg.

(5) *Auto-decrement Indirect.* The reg is decremented by 2 and then an indirect address is taken from reg. The effective address is taken from the contents of memory at the indirect address.

(6) *Indexed.* Register reg and the next word in the instruction stream are added to form the effective address, and the PC is bumped to the next

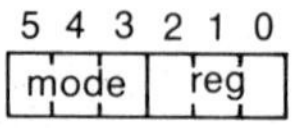

```
5 4 3 2 1 0
┌────┬────┐
│mode│ reg│
└────┴────┘
```

FIGURE 13–4 PDP-11 operand specification.

word in the instruction stream. Unless reg=PC, the contents of reg are not disturbed.

(7) *Indexed Indirect.* Register reg and the next word in the instruction stream are added to form an indirect address. The effective address is taken from the contents of memory at the indirect address.

The manufacturer's literature uses the word "deferred" instead of "indirect" when describing modes 1, 3, 5, and 7.

Modes 2 through 5 above increment or decrement register reg by one or two. Thus, they may be used to step forwards or backwards through tables of bytes or words without extra instructions to update address pointers. Auto-increment and auto-decrement modes also allow any register to be used as a pointer into a stack with standard characteristics:

- The stack pointer always points directly at the top stack item.

- The stack grows by decrementing the stack pointer.

With these conventions, a store instruction using auto-decrement mode pushes an item onto the stack, while load auto-increment pops an item. Thus, any register except PC can be conveniently used as a stack pointer in a program. After we discuss PDP-11 operation types, we shall see how appropriate combinations of addressing modes and operations allow the PDP-11 to be used as a stack machine.

The PDP-11 hardware reserves register R6 a system stack pointer SP, which it uses for interrupt and subroutine calls and returns. Because of the PDP-11's restriction that words have even addresses, it is difficult to store words and bytes in the same stack. For this reason, the processor forces an entire word to be pushed or popped in byte operations that auto-increment or auto-decrement SP.

13.3.2 PC Addressing Modes

At first glance, it may appear that some important addressing modes are missing in the PDP-11, such as immediate, absolute, and PC relative. However, when reg is PC, these modes are obtained as special cases of the basic modes:

(2) *Auto-increment PC (Immediate).* The effective address is the value of PC, that is, the operand is the next word in the instruction stream. The PC is incremented by 2, bumping it past the operand to the next word. (To keep PC even, it is incremented by 2 even if the operand is a byte.)

(3) *Auto-increment PC Indirect (Absolute).* The effective address is taken from the next word in the instruction stream and the PC is incremented by 2.

(6) *PC-indexed (Relative)*. The next word in the instruction stream is read and temporarily saved; PC is incremented by two. Then the saved value and the new PC are added to form the effective address.

(7) *PC-indexed Indirect (Relative Indirect)*. The next word in the instruction stream and the new PC are added to form an indirect address. The effective address is taken from the contents of memory at the indirect address.

13.3.3 Addressing Mode Summary

PDP-11 addressing modes and assembly language notation are summarized in Table 13–3. The fourth column of the table shows the value that is stored in the second or third word of the instruction for modes that require additional information.

13.3.4 Pascal Simulation of Addressing Modes

The PDP-11's addressing modes may also be defined by the Pascal simulation in Table 13–4. The function RMW in the simulation reads two bytes into a word and detects attempts to read a word at an odd address. Although it shows the correct effect on the processor state, RMW does not emulate an exact sequence of hardware operations. A typical PDP-11 computer has a 16-bit data path between the processor and memory, so that a full word may be read in one step instead of two.

TABLE 13–3 PDP-11 addressing modes.

mode	reg	Notation	Next Word	Name
0	0–7	R	not used	Register
1	0–7	(R) or @R	not used	Register indirect
2	0–7	(R) +	not used	Auto-increment
3	0–7	@ (R) +	not used	Auto-increment indirect
4	0–7	– (R)	not used	Auto-decrement
5	0–7	@– (R)	not used	Auto-decrement indirect
6	0–7	EXPR(R)	EXPR	Indexed
7	0–7	@EXPR (R)	EXPR	Indexed indirect
2	7	#EXPR	EXPR	Immediate
3	7	@#EXPR	EXPR	Absolute
6	7	EXPR	EXPR–PLC–2	Relative
7	7	@EXPR	EXPR–PLC–2	Relative Indirect

Notes: R = register number; EXPR = expression. PLC is the address of the offset word, not the first word of the instruction.

TABLE 13-4 Simulation of PDP-11 addressing modes.

```
PROGRAM PDP11 (input,output);
CONST PC = 7; SP = 6;
TYPE word = ARRAY [15::0] OF bit;
  byte = ARRAY [7::0] OF bit;
  address = 0..65535;
VAR R : ARRAY [0..7] OF word; {General registers}
  MEM : ARRAY [address] OF byte; {Main memory}
  EAR,PSW : word;  byteInstr,addrError : boolean;

FUNCTION RMW(addr : address) : word; {Read a memory word}
  BEGIN
    IF addr MOD 2 = 1 THEN BEGIN addrError := true; RMW := 0 END
    ELSE BEGIN
        addrError := false;
        RMW[7::0] := MEM[addr]; RMW[15::8] := MEM[addr+1];
      END;
  END;

PROCEDURE CalcEAR (opSpec : ARRAY [5::0] OF bit);
  VAR mode, reg : 0..7;
  BEGIN
    mode := opSpec[5::3]; reg := opSpec[2::0];
    CASE mode OF
      0: {register} ; {EAR not used}
      1: {register indirect} EAR := R[reg];
      2: {auto-increment}
        BEGIN EAR := R[reg];
          IF byteInstr AND reg<>PC AND reg<>SP THEN
            R[reg] := R[reg]+1 ELSE R[reg] := R[reg]+2;
        END;
      3: {auto-increment indirect}
        BEGIN EAR := RMW(R[reg]); R[reg] := R[reg]+2 END;
      4: {auto-decrement}
        BEGIN IF byteInstr AND reg<>PC AND reg<>SP THEN
            R[reg] := R[reg]-1 ELSE R[reg] := R[reg]-2;
          EAR := R[reg];
        END;
      5: {auto-decrement indirect}
        BEGIN R[reg] := R[reg]-2; EAR := RMW(R[reg]) END;
      6: {indexed}
        BEGIN EAR := RMW(R[PC]); R[PC] := R[PC]+2;
          EAR := EAR+R[reg];
        END;
      7: {indexed indirect}
        BEGIN EAR := RMW(R[PC]); R[PC] := R[PC]+2;
          EAR := RMW(EAR+R[reg]);
        END;
    END;
  END;
...
END.
```

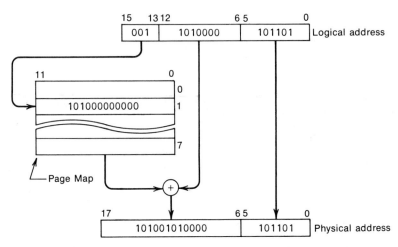

FIGURE 13-5 Mapping of 16-bit logical addresses into 18-bit physical addresses in the PDP-11.

13.3.5 Memory Mapping and Management

A memory management unit is available on some PDP-11s to map a 16-bit logical address into an 18-bit or 22-bit physical address, depending on the model. The PDP-11/34, PDP-11/40, and LSI-11/23 use the 18-bit mapping technique shown in Figure 13–5. The map has eight rows, selected by the three high-order bits of the logical address. Therefore, the logical address space is divided into eight 8K-byte pages. Mapping is accomplished by adding the logical address supplied by the processor to an 18-bit base address in the selected map entry. The 6 low-order bits of the base address are always assumed to be zero, so that each map entry actually specifies only the 12 high-order bits of the base address. Each map entry also contains control and status bits giving information such as the length of the page (in case less than 8K bytes are being used) and read/write protection status. The mapping registers appear in the I/O address space, and may be manipulated like other I/O registers.

PDP-11 models with memory management also have user and supervisor operating modes to support operating systems as described in Section 7.5.2. In addition, there are separate stack pointers and memory maps for user programs and the operating system (or "kernel"). Fields in the PSW indicate the current operating mode and which memory map is being used. Interrupts and traps always activate the kernel map, and push information onto the kernel stack. Special instructions allow data to be transferred between the user and kernel address spaces.

13.4 OPERATION TYPES

We shall classify PDP-11 instructions into five types: double operand, single operand, program control, miscellaneous, and extended.

13.4.1 Double Operand

PDP-11 double operand instructions, listed in Table 13–5, specify both a source (src) and a destination (dst) for the operation. The operation order in standard PDP-11 assembly language is left to right, for example, MOV src TO dst. Most operations may be performed on either words or bytes. Byte operations on registers access only the low-order byte, except for MOVB src,reg, which copies the byte src into the low-order byte of reg and extends its sign into the high-order byte. All operations set, clear, or hold condition code bits NZVC according to the result of the operation, usually as described in Chapter 8; refer to a PDP-11 processor handbook for the exact rules.

The MOV(B) instruction is the workhorse of the PDP-11 instruction set, accounting for 32% of all the opcodes counted in one study of typical PDP-11 programs. With appropriate addressing modes one or both operands of MOV may be in memory. Thus MOV performs the functions of both LD and ST found in other architectures, and it performs PUSH and POP when used with auto-decrement and auto-increment addressing. As an added bonus, it allows memory-to-memory data moves without intermediate storage in a register.

The ADD, SUB, BIS(B), BIC(B), and XOR instructions combine src and dst operands and store the result in dst. BIS (Bit Set) is just another name for logical OR, while BIC (Bit Clear) performs the logical AND of dst and the *complement* of src. XOR was an addition to the original PDP-11/20 instruction set, which accounts for its restricted format: it allows only a register as source operand. The CMP(B) and BIT(B) instructions compare two operands without modifying them, and set the condition codes according to the result.

TABLE 13–5 PDP-11 double operand instructions.

Mnemonic	Operands	Format	Description
MOV(B)	src,dst	a	Copy src to dst
ADD	src,dst	a	Add src word to dst
SUB	src,dst	a	Subtract src word from dst
CMP(B)	src,dst	a	Set NZVC according to src minus dst
BIS(B)	src,dst	a	Set corresponding 1 bits of src in dst
BIC(B)	src,dst	a	Clear corresponding 1 bits of src in dst
BIT(B)	src,dst	a	Set NZVC according to src AND dst
XOR	reg,dst	b	Exclusive OR reg into dst

Notes: The notation (B) indicates an instruction that exists for both bytes and words. For example, MOV moves a word, MOVB a byte.
src and dst are each given by a 6-bit operand specification.
reg is a 3-bit register number.

13.4.2   Single Operand

PDP-11 single operand instructions are listed in Table 13–6. Like the double-operand instructions, they all set the condition codes according to their results. Most of the operations are self-explanatory. The shift and rotate instructions operate in the usual way, and all store the lost bit into C. Although SWAB may look like a byte instruction, it swaps the bytes of a word. SXT loads a destination word with all zeroes or all ones depending on whether N is 0 or 1.

13.4.3   Program Control

Program control instructions of the PDP-11 are listed in Table 13–7. The most commonly used of these instructions are the conditional and unconditional branches, 20% of all the instructions counted in the study mentioned earlier. As indicated in Figure 13–3(c), a branch instruction has an 8-bit opcode and an 8-bit signed displacement. If the branch is taken, the displacement is multiplied by two and added to the PC to obtain the address of the next instruction. When this addition takes place, the processor has already incremented PC to point to the next instruction. Thus, a displacement of -1, not 0, causes an instruction to branch to itself.

The PDP-11 has 14 different conditional branches and one unconditional branch, precisely the branches that were defined and explained in Section 8.6. There is a slight difference in mnemonics: the 6809's BRA, BHS, and BLS are called BR, BHIS, and BLOS in the PDP-11.

TABLE 13–6   PDP-11 single operand instructions.

Mnemonic	Operand	Format	Description
CLR(B)	dst	b	Clear dst
COM(B)	dst	b	Complement dst (ones' complement)
INC(B)	dst	b	Increment dst by 1
DEC(B)	dst	b	Decrement dst by 1
NEG(B)	dst	b	Negate dst (two's complement)
TST(B)	dst	b	Set NZVC according to value of dst
ASR(B)	dst	b	Arithmetic shift right dst
ASL(B)	dst	b	Arithmetic shift left dst
ROR(B)	dst	b	Rotate dst right with C
ROL(B)	dst	b	Rotate dst left with C
ADC(B)	dst	b	Add C to dst
SBC(B)	dst	b	Subtract C from dst
SWAB	dst	b	Swap bytes of dst word
SXT	dst	b	Extend sign (N) into dst word

Notes: The notation (B) indicates an instruction that exists for both bytes and words. For example, CLR clears a word, CLRB a byte.
dst is given by a 6-bit operand specification.

TABLE 13-7 PDP-11 program control instructions.

Mnemonic	Operands	Format	Description
BR	rel8	c	Unconditional branch
Bcc	rel8	c	Conditional branch
JMP	dst	d	Jump to effective address of dst
JSR	reg,dst	d	Jump to subroutine
RTS	reg	e	Return from subroutine
MARK	nn	b	Strange stack clean-up
SOB	reg,nn	d	Subtract one and branch if not zero
EMT	code	c	Emulator trap
TRAP	code	c	User trap
BPT		f	Breakpoint trap
IOT		f	Input/output trap
RTI		f	Return from interrupt, allow trace
RTT		f	Return from interrupt, inhibit trace

Notes: rel8 = a target address within 128 words of the instruction.
cc = one of the conditions listed in Table 8–3;
nn = 6-bit unsigned integer; dst = 6-bit operand specification;
reg = 3-bit register number; code = arbitrary 8-bit value.

Other PDP-11 program control instructions are shown in the second part of Table 13–7. JMP and JSR both jump to the effective address specified by dst (register mode is not allowed). Before jumping, JSR reg,dst sets up a subroutine linkage as follows:

(1) Calculate and save the effective address of dst in an internal processor register TMP.

(2) Push the contents of reg onto the stack using SP.

(3) Save the current PC in reg.

(4) Load PC with the saved address from TMP.

A subroutine return is made by RTS reg; the same value of reg must be used in the call and the return. The effect of RTS is:

(1) Load PC with the contents of reg.

(2) Pop the value at the top of the stack into reg.

Figure 13–6 shows the effect of executing JSR R5,SUBR. The old value of R5 is pushed onto the stack and the return address is saved in R5. The subroutine must preserve the value of R5 so that a return can be effected by an RTS R5 instruction; this loads PC with the return address and restores the old value of R5. Nested subroutine calls should also use JSR R5,dst to automatically preserve the value of R5 on the stack.

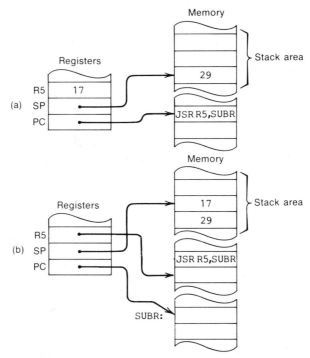

FIGURE 13–6 Effect of JSR R5,SUBR: (a) before; (b) after.

The primary use of JSR and RTS with reg equal to R0 through R5 is in subroutines with in-line parameter areas. In this case, reg will point to the parameter area after the call, and the parameters may be accessed by auto-increment or indexed addressing using reg. However, a much more popular subroutine calling convention is obtained when reg=PC. In this case, the effect of JSR is to simply push the return address (current PC) onto the stack, and the effect of RTS is to pop the return address back into PC, without affecting R0 through R5. Parameters may then be passed in the registers, on the stack, or using any other convention the programmer can think of.

The MARK nn instruction pops nn words off the stack and then does the equivalent of an RTS R5, part of a strange PDP-11 subroutine calling and returning convention that isn't very widely used (so we won't go into it!). SOB is a useful loop control primitive. After subtracting 1 from the designated register, it branches backwards 0 to 63 words (nn) if the register value is nonzero. The remaining instructions in Table 13–7 are explained later in connection with PDP-11 interrupt handling methods.

13.4.4 Miscellaneous

A few miscellaneous instructions are given in Table 13–8. Individual condition code bits in the PSW are cleared and set by CLC, CLV, . . ., SEN,

TABLE 13–8 PDP-11 miscellaneous instructions.

Mnemonic	Operand	Format	Description
NOP		f	No operation
CL(C,V,N,Z)		f	Clear CC bit(s)
SE(C,V,N,Z)		f	Set CC bit(s)
RESET		f	Reset Unibus
HALT		f	Halt the processor
WAIT		f	Wait for interrupt

Notes: The instructions on CC may be combined to either set or clear multiple bits in one instruction. For example, CLC|CLZ is a single 16-bit instruction that clears both C and Z.

SEZ. HALT stops the processor, leaving the PC pointing at the next instruction that would have been executed. Manual intervention is required to restart the processor. RESET causes a reset pulse to be generated on the Unibus; the effect of this pulse is device dependent.

WAIT temporarily suspends instruction fetching, resuming processing when any interrupt is received. After the interrupt service routine, instruction execution is resumed at the instruction following the WAIT. Executing a WAIT is more desirable than using a busy-wait loop in some situations; WAIT frees up the Unibus for DMA operations that would otherwise have to compete with the CPU for the bus as the CPU fetches the busy-wait instructions.

We still haven't encountered an instruction to read and write the entire PSW. A special instruction is avoided in many PDP-11 models, where the PSW may be accessed as memory location 177776_8. In LSI-11 models, it is accessed by MFPS dst (Move from PSW) and MTPS src (Move to PSW).

13.4.5 Extended

There are two main types of extended instructions in various PDP-11 models — addressing and arithmetic. The extended addressing instructions are used to move data between different address spaces in models with memory management units such as PDP-11/70s and LSI-11/23s. Extended arithmetic instructions provide fixed-point and floating-point arithmetic. They are now standard on most PDP-11 models, but they are optional or unavailable on older models. Details on the floating-point instructions can be found in the appropriate processor handbook — they are not the same in all models.

The fixed-point arithmetic instructions are listed in Table 13–9. The MUL instruction computes a double word product of two signed words and stores the result in reg,reg+1 if reg is even-numbered (high-order word in reg). If reg is odd, only the low-order word of the product is stored. In either case, C is set if the product takes more than one word to represent, held at its previous value otherwise. The V-bit is cleared (overflow is impossible), and N and Z are set according to the double-word product value.

TABLE 13-9 Fixed-point arithmetic instructions.

Mnemonic	Operands	Format	Description
MUL	src,reg	d	Multiply reg by src
DIV	src,reg	d	Divide reg by src
ASH	src,reg	d	Arithmetic shift reg according to src
ASHC	src,reg	d	Shift double reg according to src

DIV requires that reg be even and divides a signed src into the signed double word in reg,reg+1. The quotient appears in reg and the remainder in reg+1. The V-bit is set on overflow (zero divisor or quotient too big); C is set on divide-by-0. N and Z are set according to the quotient. The remainder has the same sign as the dividend.

The ASH instruction arithmetically shifts reg a number of times specified by the src operand, whose low-order six bits are interpreted as a two's-complement number in the range -32 to +31. Negative denotes a left shift, positive a right shift. ASHC does the same with a double register, reg, reg+1 if reg is even; else it *rotates* reg |src| bits right.

13.4.6 The PDP-11 as a Stack Machine

The PDP-11 can simulate most of the operations of the hypothetical H11 stack machine (Section 5.4) with single instructions, as shown in Table 13–10. The table uses the PDP-11's R6 to simulate the H11 stack pointer, and R5 for the H11 index register X. The data manipulating instructions could be adapted to work on bytes as well as words, leaving it to the programmer to always keep track of whether the top of stack contains a byte or a word. However, for byte operations one of the registers R0 through R5 must be used as the stack pointer, because the hardware forbids auto-incrementing or auto-decrementing R6 by only 1.

13.5 SAMPLE PROGRAMS

The simple multiplication program that we showed for the 6809 in Table 5–4 becomes even simpler when translated into PDP-11 assembly language, as shown in Table 13–11. Here we have taken advantage of the PDP-11's general-register architecture by using a register for each of the variables. This eliminates two pairs of load and store instructions in the program's main loop, since operations can be performed directly on the appropriate registers. The program could be further optimized using the PDP-11's SOB instruction as shown in Table 13–12.

The program also illustrates the PDP-11's double-operand addressing capabilities. Without changing any instructions in the program body, we can

TABLE 13-10 PDP-11 equivalents of stack instructions.

H11 Instruction	PDP-11 Instruction(s)	Description
PUSH addr	MOV @#addr,-(R6)	Push MEMW[addr] onto stack
PUSH #data	MOV #data,-(R6)	Push data onto stack
PUSH offset(X)	MOV offset(R5),-(R6)	Push MEMW[X+offset] onto stack
PUSHT	MOV (R6),-(R6)	Push TOS onto stack
PUSHS	MOV 2(R6),-(R6)	Push SOS onto stack
PUSHX	MOV R5,-(R6)	Push X onto stack
POP addr	MOV (R6)+,@#addr	Pop TOS, store into MEMW[addr]
POP offset(X)	MOV (R6)+,offset(R5)	Pop TOS, store into MEMW[X+offset]
CLR	CLR (R6)	Clear TOS
COM	COM (R6)	Ones' complement bits of TOS
NEG	NEG (R6)	Negate TOS (two's complement)
SWAB	SWAB (R6)	Swap bytes of TOS
ADD	ADD (R6)+,(R6)	Pop TOS, add to new TOS
AND	COM (R6)	Pop TOS, logical AND to new TOS
	BIC (R6)+,(R6)	
CMP	CMP (R6)+,(R6)	Pop TOS, compare with new TOS
MUL	MOV (R6)+,R1	Pop TOS,SOS, push TOS·SOS
	MUL (R6)+,R1	(1-word result, ignore overflow)
	MOV R1,-(R6)	
LD r,#data	MOV #data,r	Load r with data
LD r,addr	MOV @#addr,r	Load r with MEMW[addr]
LDXS	MOV R6,R5	Load X with a copy of SP
ST r,addr	MOV r,@#addr	Store r into MEMw[addr]
ADD r,#offset	ADD #offset,r	Add offset to r
VAL	MOV @(R6)+,-(R6)	Replace TOS with MEMW[TOS]
STOW	MOV (R6)+,@(R6)+	Store TOS into MEMW[SOS], pop both
BNE offset	BNE offset	Branch if Z=0
BEQ offset	BEQ offset	Branch if Z=1
BRA offset	BR offset	Branch always
JMP addr	JMP addr	Jump to addr
JSR addr	JSR PC,addr	Jump to subroutine at addr
RTS	RTS PC	Return from subroutine
NOP	NOP	No operation

Notes: r = SP or X
H11 SP = PDP-11 R6; H11 X = PDP-11 R5.
PDP-11 R1 is used as scratchpad for MUL.

eliminate the register definitions in Table 13–11 and instead declare all the variables to be in memory:

```
MPY:    .BLKW  1          ;Multiplier.
MCND:   .BLKW  1          ;Multiplicand.
PROD:   .BLKW  1          ;Product.
CNT:    .BLKW  1          ;Loop counter.
```

TABLE 13-11 Multiplication by repeated addition.

```
;         Enter with multiplier and multiplicand in R0, R1.
;         Exit with product in R2.
MPY     =      %0              ;Multiplier.
MCND    =      %1              ;Multiplicand.
PROD    =      %2              ;Product.
CNT     =      %3              ;Loop counter.
        .=25100                ;Program origin.
START:  CLR    PROD            ;Set PROD to 0.
        MOV    MPY,CNT         ;Do loop MPY times.
LOOP:   TST    CNT             ;Done if CNT = 0.
        BEQ    OUT
        DEC    CNT             ;Else decrement CNT.
        ADD    MCND,PROD       ;Add MCND to PROD.
        BR     LOOP            ;Repeat the loop again.
OUT:    JMP    10000           ;Go to operating system restart address.
        .END   START
```

The optimized program in Table 13-12 can have variables in memory too; only CNT must be in a register.

Keeping variables in registers results in programs that are shorter and faster. For example, consider the instruction ADD MCND,PROD. If the variables are kept in registers, the ADD instruction is one word long and only one memory reference is needed to fetch and execute it. If the variables are kept in memory, the instruction is three words long. Three memory references are needed just to fetch the instruction, and three more are needed to read the two operands and write the result. Since the execution times of most instructions are limited by memory access times, the register-oriented instructions are much faster. However, the choice of whether to keep variables in registers or in memory depends not only on program size and speed, but also on program complexity; see Section 12.4.

Table 13-13 illustrates auto-increment and byte addressing in the PDP-11. The program declares an array of five bytes, and uses the CLRB instruction to initialize each component. The address of the next component, kept in R0, is a 16-bit quantity even though the components themselves are bytes. Since auto-increment addressing is used with a byte instruction, the processor increments R0 by one at each step, not two.

TABLE 13-12 Body of optimized multiplication program.

```
START:  CLR    PROD            ;Set PROD to 0.
        MOV    MPY,CNT         ;Do loop MPY times.
        BEQ    OUT             ;Done if multiplier is 0.
LOOP:   ADD    MCND,PROD       ;Add MCND to PROD.
        SOB    CNT,LOOP        ;Repeat loop until CNT=0.
OUT:    JMP    10000           ;Go to operating system restart address.
```

TABLE 13-13 Initializing an array of bytes.

```
R0       =       %0
         .=30000              ;Program origin.
INIT:    MOV     #Q,R0        ;Address of first component.
ILOOP:   CLRB    (R0)+        ;Clear component and bump to next.
         CMP     R0,#Q+5      ;Past last component?
         BNE     ILOOP        ;If not, go do some more.
         JMP     10000        ;Go to operating system.
         .=30400              ;New origin for array.
Q:       .=.+5                ;Reserve 5 bytes for array.
         .END    INIT
```

PDP-11 subroutines are introduced in Table 13-14. The main program initializes SP to point just past the end of a 7-word stack buffer. Successive pushes, such as subroutine calls, decrement SP, so a maximum of seven words may be stored in the stack.

The program also shows the use of the stack for temporary storage. In WCNT1S it is necessary to save the 1-count of the low-order byte before calling BCNT1S the second time. Instead of using a register or an explicit variable in memory, the program pushes the 1-count onto the stack. Later the program pops the saved 1-count, adding it to the high-order 1-count. A subroutine may mix return addresses and data in the stack as long as it performs an equal number of pushes and pops between the entry and return. It is especially important to balance the number of pushes and pops inside loops, lest the stack systematically grow (or shrink) with each iteration.

The BCNT1S subroutine once again illustrates auto-increment and byte addressing. Addresses are 16-bit quantities (R2, #MASKE), but the BITB instruction manipulates 8-bit quantities (MEM[R2] and low-order byte of R0). Notice also how BITB is used to logically compare two operands without disturbing either.

A program that uses two stacks to sort a sequence of input numbers is shown in Table 13-15. Similar to the 6809 program in Table 7-3, this program shows the correspondence between Pascal statements and corresponding PDP-11 assembly language code. The operation of the Pascal program was explained and illustrated in Section 3.3. The power of PDP-11 double-operand addressing is best illustrated by popping a word from one stack and pushing it into another with a single 1-word instruction such as MOV (SPL)+,-(SPH). Without procedures, three or four Pascal statements are needed to do the same thing.

Besides declaring its own two stacks using R0 (SPL) and R1 (SPH) as stack pointers, the program in Table 13-15 assumes that the operating system has already initialized R6 to point into a return address stack. It further assumes that the operating system has called it by executing a JSR PC,SORT instruction, so that it may return by executing RTS PC. If a program

TABLE 13–14   Program that uses subroutines to count the number of "1" bits in a word.

```
RO      =       %0
R1      =       %1
R2      =       %2
SP      =       %6
PC      =       %7
SYSRET  =       10000           ;Operating system restart address.
        .=20000                 ;Program origin.
STK:    .BLKW   7               ;Space for 7 return addresses.
STKE    =       .               ;Initialization address for SP.
TWORD:  .WORD   55451           ;Test-word to count 1s.
;
MAIN:   MOV     #STKE,SP        ;Initialize stack pointer.
        MOV     TWORD,RO        ;Get test word.
        JSR     PC,WCNT1S       ;Count number of 1s in it.
        JMP     SYSRET          ;Go to operating system.
;
;       Count the number of '1' bits in a word.
;       Enter with word in RO, exit with count in R1.
WCNT1S: JSR     PC,BCNT1S       ;Count 1s in low-order byte.
        MOV     R1,-(SP)        ;Save '1' count on stack.
        SWAB    RO              ;Count 1s in high-order byte.
        JSR     PC,BCNT1S
        ADD     (SP)+,R1        ;Add low-order count to high-order.
        RTS     PC              ;Done, return.
;
;       Count number of '1' bits in a byte. Enter with byte in
;       low-order RO, exit with RO undisturbed and count in R1.
BCNT1S: CLR     R1              ;Initialize '1' count.
        MOV     #MASKS,R2       ;Point to 1-bit masks.
BLOOP:  BITB    RO,(R2)+        ;Got a '1'?
        BEQ     BNO1            ;Skip if none.
        INC     R1              ;Otherwise increment '1' count.
BNO1:   CMP     R2,#MASKE       ;Past last mask?
        BNE     BLOOP           ;Continue if not.
        RTS     PC              ;Else return.
;       Define 1-bit masks to test bits of byte.
MASKS:  .BYTE   200,100,40,20,10,4,2,1
MASKE   =       .
        .END    MAIN
```

reinitializes SP to point to its own stack area (as did the program in Table 13–14), it loses any return address on the operating system's stack and therefore must return by an absolute jump or a software interrupt.

PDP-11 indexed addressing is illustrated in Table 13–16, a program that finds prime numbers using the sieve of Eratosthenes. Like the 6809 version in Table 7–5, the PDP-11 program declares an array of bytes with each compo-

TABLE 13–15 Sorting subroutine for the PDP-11.

```
;                               PROCEDURE StackSort; {Based on Table 3-6}
MAXLEN  =       200.;           CONST maxLen = 200;
SIZE    =       201.;             stackSize = 201;
MINNUM  =       -9999.;           minNum = -9999;
MAXNUM  =       9999.;            maxNum = 9999;
SPL     =       %0;             VAR spL,spH: address; {Stack pointers
SPH     =       %1;                            for stackL and stackH}
INNUM   =       %2;                 inNum, {Input number}
NNUMS   =       %3;                 nNums  {Number of inputs}
PC      =       %7;                     : integer; {16-bit 2's comp}
STACKL: .BLKW   SIZE;               stackL, stackH :
STKEL   =       .-2;                  ARRAY [1..stackSize] OF integer;
STACKH: .BLKW   SIZE;
STKEH   =       .-2;
;                               BEGIN
SORT:   MOV     #STKEL,SPL;       spL := MemAddress(stackL[stackSize]);
        MOV     #STKEH,SPH;       spH := MemAddress(stackH[stackSize]);
        MOV     #MINNUM-1,@SPL;   MEM[spL] := minNum-1;
        MOV     #MAXNUM+1,@SPH;   MEM[spH] := maxNum+1;
        MOV     #1,NNUMS;         nNums := 1;
        JSR     PC,WRMSG1;        writeln('Input sequence: ');
        JSR     PC,READ;          read(inNum);
WHILE1: CMP     INNUM,#MINNUM;      WHILE inNum>=minNum
        BLT     WHILE4;
        CMP     INNUM,#MAXNUM;           AND inNum<=maxNum DO
        BGT     WHILE4;              BEGIN
WHILE2: CMP     INNUM,@SPL;          WHILE inNum < MEM[spL] DO
        BGE     WHILE3;                {Top of stackL --> stackH.}
        MOV     (SPL)+,-(SPH);         PushH(PopL);
        BR      WHILE2;
WHILE3: CMP     INNUM,@SPH;          WHILE inNum > MEM[spH] DO
        BLE     OUT3;                  {Top of stackH --> stackL.}
        MOV     (SPH)+,-(SPL);         PushL(PopH);
        BR      WHILE3;
OUT3:   MOV     INNUM,-(SPL);        PushL(inNum);
        JSR     PC,WRNUM;            write(inNum);
        INC     NNUMS;               nNums := nNums + 1;
IF1:    CMP     NNUMS,#MAXLEN;         IF nNums <= maxLen THEN
        BGT     ELSE1;
THEN1:  JSR     PC,READ;               read(inNum)
        BR      IFEND1;              ELSE BEGIN
ELSE1:  JSR     PC,WRMSG2;             writeln('***Too many inputs');
        MOV     #MINNUM-1,INNUM;       inNum := minNum - 1;
IFEND1: BR      WHILE1;              END;
;                               END; {Inputs are now sorted.}
WHILE4: CMP     SPL,#STKEL;       WHILE spL <>
        BEQ     OUT4;                MemAddress(stackL[stackSize]) DO
        MOV     (SPL)+,-(SPH);       {Move everything into stackH.}
        BR      WHILE4;            PushH(PopL);
OUT4:   JSR     PC,WRMSG3;        writeln; write('Sorted sequence: ');
```

TABLE 13–15 (continued)

```
WHILE5: CMP    SPH,#STKEH;      WHILE spH <>
        BEQ    OUT5;                MemAddress[stackH[stackSize]) DO
        MOV    (SPH)+,INNUM;    {Print contents of stackH.}
        JSR    PC,WRNUM;        write(PopH);
        BR     WHILE5;
OUT5:   RTS    PC;              {Return to caller.}
        END    SORT;            END;
```

TABLE 13–16 Program to find primes using an array and indexed addressing.

```
;                               PROCEDURE FindPrimes;
NPRIME  =       1000.;          CONST nPrime = 1000;
PLIMIT  =       32.;              pLimit = 32;
PRIME:  .=.+NPRIME-1;           VAR prime:ARRAY [2..nPrime] OF boolean;
        .EVEN;
I       =       %0;             {reg} I, J : word;
J       =       %1;
PC      =       %7;             BEGIN
FNDPRM: MOV     #2,I;           FOR I := 2 TO nPrime DO
SETEM:  MOVB    #1,PRIME-2(I);      {Set the entire array true.}
        INC     I;                 prime[I] := true;
        CMP     I,#NPRIME;
        BLE     SETEM;
        MOV     #2,J;           J := 2; {First known prime.}
MARKEM: ;                       REPEAT {Check integers 2 to pLimit.}
        TSTB    PRIME-2(J);       IF prime[J] THEN
        BEQ     NOTPRM;             BEGIN
        MOV     J,I;                I := 2 * J;
        ASL     I;
CLRLUP: CLRB    PRIME-2(I);         REPEAT {Mark multiples of J.}
        ADD     J,I;                  prime[I] := false; I := I+J;
        CMP     I,#NPRIME;          UNTIL I > nPrime;
        BLE     CLRLUP;             END;
NOTPRM: INC     J;                J := J+1;
        CMP     J,#PLIMIT;      UNTIL J > pLimit;
        BLE     MARKEM;
        JSR     PC,WRMSG1;      write('Primes between 2 and ');
        MOV     #NPRIME,I;      I := nPrime;
        JSR     PC,PRINTI;      writeln(I); {Print the number in I.}
        MOV     #2,I;           FOR I := 2 TO nPrime DO
PRTLUP: TSTB    PRIME-2(I);       {Print all the primes.}
        BEQ     NEXTP;            IF prime[I] THEN
        JSR     PC,PRINTI;          writeln(I);
NEXTP:  INC     I;
        CMP     I,#NPRIME;
        BLE     PRTLUP;
        RTS     PC;             {All done, return to caller.}
        .END    FNDPRM;         END;
```

nent corresponding to a number between 2 and 1000. By marking off multiples of known primes, it eliminates nonprimes until only primes remain.

It is interesting that this PDP-11 program contains only two fewer instructions than the corresponding 6809 program, in contrast with some of the other programs that we've examined. Since PDP-11 instructions are generally longer than the 6809's, the PDP-11 program occupies 88 bytes, compared to the 6809's 71 bytes. Apparently, the advantages of general registers and double-operand addressing do not come into play in a program that can be efficiently coded with all variables in a small number of registers. In fact, the PDP-11's flexibility is a disadvantage in this case, creating longer instructions and hence a longer program.

A stack-oriented parameter-passing convention was illustrated in Figure 9–4; a PDP-11 subroutine that uses this convention is shown in Table 13–17. A main program that calls DIVIDE is shown in Table 13–18. Initially the stack has the state shown in Figure 13–7(a). The main program pushes the input parameters onto the stack in the order shown in Figure 13–7(b), and then calls DIVIDE. The first three instructions of DIVIDE set up the stack frame pointer FP and push one local variable, CNT, leaving the stack as shown in Figure 13–7(c). The last four instructions clean up the stack and return to the calling program with only the output parameters on the stack, as shown in Figure 13–7(d).

Parameters and local variables are accessed within the DIVIDE subroutine by based addressing using fixed offsets from FP. PDP-11 single- and double-operand instructions and addressing modes allow all operations to be performed directly on variables in the stack frame; no processor registers are used as accumulators. Thus, the subroutine returns with the registers in exactly the same state as when it was entered. However, the speed of the program could be improved by keeping LODVND, HIDVND, DVSR, and CNT in registers during the division loop.

A set of queue manipulation subroutines for the PDP-11 is given in Table 13–19. Like the 6809 version in Table 9–18, this code is self-documenting, and so we leave you to read it.

13.6 INPUT/OUTPUT, INTERRUPTS, AND TRAPS

13.6.1 Input/Output

The PDP-11 introduced the concept of memory-mapped I/O. It has no I/O instructions; all devices are controlled by interface registers that are read and written as locations in the address space. Depending on device complexity, different interfaces have different numbers of registers and assign different functions and meanings to their bits.

TABLE 13-17   Unsigned division subroutine that passes parameters on a stack.

```
FP       =      %5              ;Stack frame pointer.
SP       =      %6
PC       =      %7
;               The offsets below define positions of parameters and local
;               variables in the stack relative to the frame pointer (FP).
CNT      =      -2              ;Loop counter.
OLDFP    =      0               ;Old value of frame pointer.
RETADR   =      2               ;Return address.
DVSR     =      4               ;1-word divisor (input).
HIDVND   =      6               ;High-order word of dividend (input).
LODVND   =      8.              ;Low-order word of dividend (input).
REM      =      10.             ;1-word remainder (output).
QUOT     =      12.             ;1-word quotient (output).
STATUS   =      14.             ;0 ==> OK, <>0 ==> overflow (output).
;
DIVIDE:  MOV    FP,-(SP)        ;Push old frame pointer onto stack.
         MOV    SP,FP           ;Copy SP into FP for new frame pointer.
         MOV    #16.,-(SP)      ;Push initial count.
         CLR    STATUS(FP)      ;Initial status OK.
         CMP    HIDVND(FP),DVSR(FP)  ;Will quotient fit in 1 word?
         BLO    DIVLUP          ;Branch if it will.
         INC    STATUS(FP)      ;Else report overflow.
         BR     CLNSTK
DIVLUP:  ASL    LODVND(FP)      ;Left shift dividend with LSB:=0.
         ROL    HIDVND(FP)      ;A carry here from MSB means
         BCS    QUOT1           ;   high DVND definitely > DVSR.
         CMP    HIDVND(FP),DVSR(FP)  ;Compare high DVND with DVSR.
         BLO    QUOTOK          ;Quotient bit = 0 if lower.
QUOT1:   INC    LODVND(FP)      ;Else set quotient bit to 1.
         SUB    DVSR(FP),HIDVND(FP)  ;And update high DVND.
QUOTOK:  DEC    CNT(FP)         ;Decrement iteration count.
         BGT    DIVLUP          ;Continue until done.
         MOV    HIDVND(FP),REM(FP)   ;Store remainder.
         MOV    LODVND(FP),QUOT(FP)  ;Store quotient.
CLNSTK:  MOV    RETADR(FP),LODVND(FP) ;Save return addr lower in stack.
         MOV    OLDFP(FP),FP    ;Restore old frame pointer.
         ADD    #LODVND-CNT,SP  ;Remove garbage except LODVND,
         RTS    PC              ;   which contains return address.
```

As an example, Figure 13–8 shows the interface registers for a typical read/write, character-oriented I/O device, such as a teleprinter, CRT terminal, or papertape reader/punch. The physical device consists of two independent logical devices, a "receiver" and a "transmitter", each of which uses two interface registers. In a typical PDP-11 installation, the system terminal keyboard is assigned addresses 177560_8 and 177562_8, and its screen or printer is assigned 177564_8 and 177566_8. Each bit of each register is classified as read-only, write-only, read/write, or unassigned, as explained in Section 10.3.1.

TABLE 13–18 Program that calls stack-oriented DIVIDE.

```
;         Compute PDIVQ := P DIV Q; PMODQ := P MOD Q;
;         where all are 1-word variables in memory.
DIVPQ:    ADD     #-6,SP      ;Reserve space for output parameters.
          MOV     P,-(SP)     ;Push low-order dividend.
          CLR     -(SP)       ;Push high-order dividend = 0.
          MOV     Q,-(SP)     ;Push divisor.
          JSR     PC,DIVIDE   ;Do the division.
          MOV     (SP)+,PMODQ ;Pop remainder and store.
          MOV     (SP)+,PDIVQ ;Pop quotient and store.
          TST     (SP)+       ;Test status.
          BNE     DIVOVF      ;Branch on overflow.
          ...
P:        .BLKW   1           ;Storage for P, Q, PDIVQ, PMODQ
Q:        .BLKW   1           ;   (all 1-word variables).
PDIVQ:    .BLKW   1
PMODQ:    .BLKW   1
```

Three bits control the receiver section of the interface. Writing a 1 in the ENB bit clears RDY in preparation for receiving a character. This also starts motion in the case of a papertape reader or other mechanical device. When a character is received, the interface sets RDY to 1. The character may then be read from the receiver data register RDATA; reading RDATA clears RDY as a side effect. The IEN bit enables the interface to interrupt the processor whenever a character is received. Precisely stated, the interface requests interrupt service from the processor whenever both RDY and IEN are 1.

Only two bits control the transmitter section of the interface. Writing a value in the transmitter data register XDATA automatically starts sending the

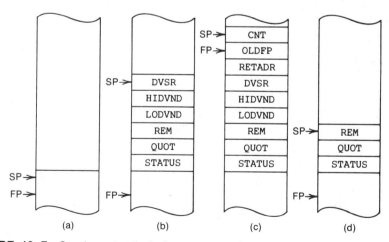

FIGURE 13–7 Stack contents during DIVPQ program: (a) at start; (b) just before calling DIVIDE; (c) after first three instructions of DIVIDE; (d) on return.

TABLE 13-19 Queue manipulation subroutines for the PDP-11.

```
; QUEUE MODULE
;
; This module contains three subroutines for manipulating queues
; of 16-bit words. A queue is defined by a queue descriptor table
; and a block of storage, as shown below.
;
;                                             QUEUE STORAGE BLOCK
;         --------------------               --------------------
; QDTBL | QHEAD  (word)   |  -------->|      (word)      |
;       |------------------|   |       |------------------|
;       | QTAIL  (word)   |   |       |                  |
;       |------------------|   |       |  o  o  o  o     |
;       | QSTRT  (word)   |----       |                  |
;       |------------------|           |------------------|
;       | QEND   (word)   |---------->|      (word)      |
;         --------------------               --------------------
;
; Offsets in descriptor table:
;
QHEAD   =       0
QTAIL   =       2
QSTRT   =       4
QEND    =       6
;
; In this table, the last two words are constants, initialized at
; load time, that give the starting and ending addresses of the block
; of storage (buffer) reserved for the queue itself. The first and
; second words are reserved to store the queue head and tail (absolute
; memory addresses), and are manipulated by the subroutines.
;
; If a program defines several queues, it allocates a separate queue
; descriptor table and storage block for each one.  For example, the
; statements below define a 5-word queue Q1 and a 100-word queue Q2:
;
;Q1BLK:  .BLKW   5           ;Storage block for Q1.
;Q1END  =        .-2         ;Last location in Q1 storage block.
;Q1DT:  .BLKW   2            ;Q1 descriptor table -- QHEAD and QTAIL.
;       .WORD   Q1BLK,Q1END  ;                      QSTRT and QEND.
;Q2BLK:  .BLKW   100.        ;Storage block for Q2.
;Q2END  =        .-2         ;Last location in Q2 storage block.
;Q2DT:  .BLKW   2            ;Q2 descriptor table -- QHEAD and QTAIL.
;       .WORD   Q2BLK,Q2END  ;                      QSTRT and QEND.
;
; Subroutines are provided to initialize a queue (QINIT), enqueue
; a word (QENQ), and dequeue a word (QDEQ).  Each subroutine must
; be passed the address of the descriptor table for the queue
; to be manipulated.
;
```

TABLE 13-19 (continued)

```
; SUBROUTINE QINIT -- Initialize a queue to be empty.
;
; INPUTS
;   #QDTBL -- The address of the queue descriptor table for the
;             queue to be initialized, passed in register R0.
; OUTPUTS, GLOBAL DATA, LOCAL DATA -- None
; FUNCTIONS
;   (1) Initialize the queue to empty by setting QHEAD and QTAIL
;       in QDTBL equal to the first address in the queue buffer.
; REGISTERS AFFECTED -- CC
;
; TYPICAL CALLING SEQUENCE
;       MOV     #Q1DT,R0
;       JSR     PC,QINIT
;
QINIT:  MOV     QSTRT(R0),QHEAD(R0)  ;Put buffer starting address
        MOV     QSTRT(R0),QTAIL(R0)  ;  into QHEAD and QTAIL.
        RTS     PC                   ;Done, return.
;
; SUBROUTINE QENQ -- Enqueue one word into a queue.
;
; INPUTS
;   #QDTBL -- The address of the queue descriptor table for the
;             queue to be manipulated, passed in register R0.
;   QDATA  -- The word to be enqueued, passed in register R1.
; OUTPUTS
;   QFULL  -- 1 if the queue is already full, else 0;
;             passed in condition bit Z.
; GLOBAL DATA, LOCAL DATA -- None.
; FUNCTIONS
;   (1) If the queue described by QDTBL is full, set QFULL to 1.
;   (2) If the queue is not full, enqueue QDATA and set QFULL to 0.
; REGISTERS AFFECTED -- R2,CC
;
; TYPICAL CALLING SEQUENCE
;       MOV     #Q1DT,R0          ;Enqueue AWORD.
;       MOV     AWORD,R1
;       JSR     PC,QENQ
;       BEQ     OVFL              ;Branch if queue is full.
;
QENQ:   MOV     QTAIL(R0),R2      ;Get queue tail.
        ADD     #2,R2             ;Bump to next free location.
        CMP     R2,QEND(R0)       ;Wrap-around?
        BLOS    QENQ1
        MOV     QSTRT(R0),R2      ;Reinitialize on wrap-around.
QENQ1:  CMP     R2,QHEAD(R0)      ;Queue already full?
        BEQ     QENQ2             ;Return with Z=1 if full.
        MOV     R1,@QTAIL(R0)     ;Else store QDATA.
        MOV     R2,QTAIL(R0)      ;Update tail.
        CLZ                       ;Set Z:=0 since not full.
QENQ2:  RTS     PC                ;Return.
```

TABLE 13-19   (continued)

```
; SUBROUTINE QDEQ -- Dequeue one word from a queue.
;
; INPUTS
;    #QDTBL -- The address of the queue descriptor table for the
;              queue to be manipulated, passed in register R0.
; OUTPUTS
;    QEMPTY -- 1 if the queue is empty, else 0; passed in
;              condition bit Z.
;    QDATA  -- The word dequeued, passed in register R1.
; GLOBAL DATA, LOCAL DATA -- None.
; FUNCTIONS
;    (1) If the queue described by QDTBL is empty, set QEMPTY to 1.
;    (2) If the queue isn't empty, dequeue QDATA and set QEMPTY to 0.
; REGISTERS AFFECTED -- R1, CC
;
; TYPICAL CALLING SEQUENCE
;         MOV     #Q1DT,R0        ;Dequeue a word into AWORD.
;         JSR     PC,QDEQ
;         BEQ     UNDFL           ;Branch if queue is empty.
;         MOV     R1,AWORD
;
QDEQ:     CMP     QHEAD(R0),QTAIL(R0) ;Queue empty?
          BEQ     QDEQ2           ;Return with Z=1 if empty.
          MOV     @QHEAD(R0),R1   ;Read QDATA word from queue.
          ADD     #2,QHEAD(R0)    ;Bump head to next item in queue.
          CMP     QHEAD(R0),QEND(R0)   ;Wrap-around?
          BLOS    QDEQ1
          MOV     QSTRT(R0),QHEAD(R0)  ;Reinitialize head on wrap-around.
QDEQ1:    CLZ                     ;Set Z:=0 since not empty.
QDEQ2:    RTS     PC              ;Return.
```

data to the device and clears the RDY bit. The interface sets RDY to 1 as soon as XDATA can accept another character (even though in some cases the character may not yet have been fully transmitted or physically printed). Like the receiver, the transmitter section interrupts whenever both RDY and IEN are 1.

Table 13-20 shows a subroutine that reads and echos a character using busy-wait I/O with the interface described above. The subroutine is called by JSR PC,RCVIN and it returns with the character in R0. It begins by initializing the receiver and then it waits for a character. After receiving the character, it busy-waits for the transmitter until XDATA is emptied of any previous character; then it echos the received character and returns immediately.[3] Note that any of the MOV instructions could be changed to MOVB.

---

[3]Normally relative addressing is used to obtain position-independent programs. But in Table 13-20, absolute addressing yields position independence because the interface registers are at fixed locations in memory.

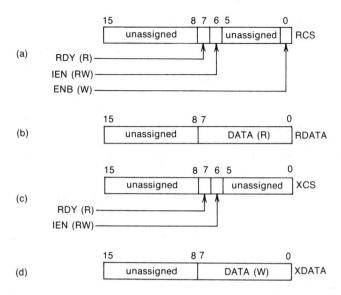

FIGURE 13-8 PDP-11 interface registers: (a) receiver control/status; (b) receiver data; (c) transmitter control/status; (d) transmitter data.

One advantage of memory-mapped I/O is that all of the addressing modes as well as opcodes may be used to specify I/O interface registers. This makes it very easy to write I/O handlers that can be shared by many devices. For example, in a system with several terminals, the subroutine in Table 13–20 can be modified to work with an interface at any address by having the calling program pass the address of the receiver control/status register in R1, as shown in Table 13–21.

TABLE 13-20 PDP-11 input and echo subroutine.

```
RCS     =       177560          ;Receiver control and status.
RDATA   =       177562          ;Received data.
XCS     =       177564          ;Transmitter control and status.
XDATA   =       177566          ;Transmit data.
;
RCVIN:  MOV     #1,@#RCS         ;Initiate read, interrupts off.
RCVWT:  TSTB    @#RCS            ;Reader RDY=1?
        BPL     RCVWT            ;No, busy wait.
        MOV     @#RDATA,R0       ;Yes, read character.
        BIC     #177400,R0       ;Mask off possible garbage.
XMTWT:  TSTB    @#XCS            ;Transmitter RDY=1?
        BPL     XMTWT            ;No, wait for previous character.
        CLR     @#XCS            ;Make sure transmitter interrupts off.
        MOV     R0,@#XDATA       ;Echo new character
        RTS     PC               ;   and return to calling program.
```

TABLE 13–21 PDP-11 shared input and echo subroutine.

```
RCS     =    0                ;Receiver control and status.
RDATA   =    2                ;Received data.
XCS     =    4                ;Transmitter control and status.
XDATA   =    6                ;Transmit data.
;
RCVIN:  MOV    #1,RCS(R1)      ;Initiate read, interrupts off.
RCVWT:  TSTB   RCS(R1)         ;Reader RDY=1?
        BPL    RCVWT           ;No, busy wait.
        MOV    RDATA(R1),R0    ;Yes, read character.
        BIC    #177400,R0      ;Mask off possible garbage.
XMTWT:  TSTB   XCS(R1)         ;Transmitter RDY=1?
        BPL    XMTWT           ;No, wait for previous character.
        CLR    XCS(R1)         ;Make sure transmitter interrupts off.
        MOV    R0,XDATA(R1)    ;Echo new character
        RTS    PC              ;  and return to calling program.
```

13.6.2 Interrupts

The PDP-11 has a multi-level, vectored, priority interrupt system. Each device may be physically connected to one of four priority levels, called BR4, BR5, BR6, and BR7; BR stands for "bus request". The highest priority level is BR7; the LSI-11 has only one level, BR4. Within each level, devices are "daisy-chained" so the one closest to the processor on the bus has the highest priority. For an interrupt to be serviced, the device priority level (BR number) must be higher than the processor priority set in PSW bits 7–5. Thus, setting the processor priority to 7 effectively disables the interrupt system.

In general, all of the following conditions must be met for an interface to successfully interrupt the processor:

(1) The IEN bit on the interface must be set to 1.

(2) The interface must have experienced an interrupt-generating condition (e.g., RDY=1 on the terminal interface, block transfer complete or read error on a disk interface).

(3) No interface with a higher BR number may be trying to interrupt.

(4) No interface closer to the processor with the same BR number may be trying to interrupt.

(5) The processor priority (PSW bits 7–5) must be strictly less than the BR number.

When the processor accepts an interrupt request, the interrupting interface identifies itself by placing a unique address on the Unibus (or Q-bus). This address points to an "interrupt vector", two words of memory containing the starting address of the interrupt service routine and a new PSW. The bottom 400_8 bytes of memory in the PDP-11 address space are reserved in two-word blocks for interrupt vectors (i.e., octal addresses 0, 4, 10, 14, 20, . . ., 370, 374). In a typical installation, the interrupt vector for the system terminal keyboard is at address 60_8, and the vector for the screen or printer is at 64_8.

After an interrupt is accepted, the processor pushes the current PSW into the stack, followed by the current PC. Then it fetches a new value for PC from the first word of the interrupt vector, and a new PSW from the second. Besides new values of the condition codes, the new PSW contains a new value for the processor priority. This value should be greater than or equal to the hardware priority of the interrupting device, to prevent the device from re-interrupting its own service routine if it is very fast.

The RTI instruction is used to return from an interrupt service routine. It pops the top word in the stack into the PC, and the next word into the PSW. The RTT instruction operates the same as RTI, except for its handling of the trace trap as explained in Section 13.6.3. User programs should always use RTI.

A program that uses interrupts to print strings of characters is shown in Table 13–22. A string is a sequence of ASCII characters stored one per byte and terminated by NUL (a zero byte). The CRT output initialization routine CRTOUT accepts a pointer to a string to be printed. The variable CRTBSY indicates whether a previous string is still being printed, so that a new operation is not started until the previous one is completed. The initialization routine CRTOUT prints the first character and the remaining characters are printed by the interrupt service routine CRTINT. Notice that CRTINT does not have to save any processor registers, because all of its operations can be performed directly on memory by appropriate double-operand instructions and addressing modes. In complicated interrupt service routines, it is usually more efficient to save registers on the stack, use them during the service routine, and then restore them before executing RTI.

13.6.3 Traps

The PDP-11 has several trap instructions which appeared in Table 13-7. Executing a trap instruction has the same effect as an interrupt — the current PSW and PC are pushed onto the stack and a new PSW and PC are taken from a vector in memory. As shown in Table 13–23, each of the different trap instructions has a different preassigned trap vector address. Except for the vector addresses, all of the trap instructions have the same effect, but their names indicate software applications intended by the original machine designers.

The TRAP and EMT instructions have an 8-bit opcode in the high-order byte, while the low-order byte is not decoded at all by the hardware. Therefore, the programmer may place an arbitrary 8-bit code into the low-order

TABLE 13–22   Interrupt-driven CRT output.

```
        .=64                    ;CRT interrupt vector address.
CVECT:  .WORD   CRTINT,200      ;CPU priority = 4.
        .=4000
;       Define addresses of CRT interface registers.
CRTCSR  =       177564          ;CRT control and status register.
CRTDTR  =       177566          ;CRT data register.
;
;       Global and local variables.
CRTBSY: .BLKW   1               ;Nonzero when string is being displayed.
BPNT:   .BLKW   1               ;Pointer to character being displayed.
;
;       CRT output initialization, pointer to string passed in R0.
;
CRTOUT: TST     CRTBSY          ;Still printing previous string?
        BNE     CRTOUT          ;Yes, wait for it.
        INC     CRTBSY          ;Else mark CRT busy for new string.
        MOV     R0,BPNT         ;Save pointer to string.
        MOVB    @R0,@#CRTDTR    ;Print first character.
        MOV     #100,@#CRTCSR   ;Turn on CRT interrupts
        RTS     PC              ; and return.
;
;       CRT output interrupt handler
;
CRTINT: INC     BPNT            ;Get pointer to next character.
        TSTB    @BPNT           ;Is it NUL (0)?
        BEQ     CDONE           ;We're done if it is.
        MOVB    @BPNT,@#CRTDTR  ;Otherwise print the character
        RTI                     ; and return.
CDONE:  CLR     CRTBSY          ;CRT is no longer busy.
        CLR     @#CRTCSR        ;Turn off CRT interrupts
        RTI                     ; and return.
;
;       Typical main program
MAIN:   MOV     #770,SP         ;Initialize stack pointer.
        CLR     CRTBSY          ;Mark CRT not busy.
        CLR     @#177776        ;Set processor priority to 0.
LOOP:   ...                     ;Do some computation.
        ...
        MOV     #MSG1,R0        ;Get address of first message
        JSR PC,CRTOUT           ; and print it.
        ...                     ;Do some more computation.
        MOV     #MSG2,R0        ;Get address of second message
        JSR PC,CRTOUT           ; and print it.
        JMP     LOOP            ;Do it all again.
;
MSG1:   .ASCII 'This is a rather unimaginative message.'
        .BYTE   15,12,0         ;Carriage return, line feed, NUL.
MSG2:   .ASCII 'But this one is even worse.'
        .BYTE   15,12,0         ;Carriage return, line feed, NUL.
        .END    MAIN
```

TABLE 13-23   PDP-11 trap vector addresses.

Address (octal)	Purpose
000	Reserved
004	Bus errors
010	Illegal and reserved instructions
014	BPT and trace trap
020	IOT
024	Power fail
030	EMT
034	TRAP

byte, to be decoded by the trap handler. The EMT (emulator trap) instruction is used by DEC operating systems for various system calls, while TRAP is generally reserved for the user. Table 13-24 shows a handler for the TRAP instruction which performs one of 256 possible actions depending on the code specified in the instruction. This effectively allows the user to have 256 different one-word subroutine calls. The other two trap instructions, BPT and IOT are fully-encoded 16-bit instructions.

The PDP-11 processor also traps on various unusual conditions shown in Table 13-23. For example, a trap is taken through location 4 on any attempt to access nonexistent memory or a word at an odd address.

The BPT instruction traps through location 14, allowing the on-line debugger to insert breakpoints by substituting BPT for user instructions. The "trace trap" is also used by on-line debuggers. If an instruction sets the T-bit in the PSW, a trap through location 14 will take place after the execution of the *next* instruction. This allows the debugger to single-step a user program. For example, assume that the CPU is executing the debugger and the current PC and PSW for a user program are stored at the top of stack. Then we can execute one instruction of the user program as follows:

(1) Set the T-bit in the copy of the user PSW in the stack to 1.

(2) Execute an RTT. This returns control to the user program and pops the user PSW, setting the real T-bit to 1.

(3) One instruction of the user program is executed, and then the trace trap is sprung, returning control to the debugger.

Notice that we specified an RTT instruction above instead of RTI. The RTI instruction is an exception to the general trace rule: if an RTI instruction sets the T bit, then the trace trap occurs immediately. This allows RTIs in user programs to be traced. RTT, on the other hand, allows one instruction of the user program to be executed before the trace trap is sprung.

TABLE 13-24 Handler for TRAP instruction.

```
        .=34
TVECT:  .WORD   THNDL,340       ;TRAP vector.
        .=5000
;       TRAP handler
THNDL:  MOV     R5,-(SP)        ;Save caller's registers on stack.
        MOV     R4,-(SP)
        MOV     R3,-(SP)
        MOV     R2,-(SP)
        MOV     R1,-(SP)
        MOV     R0,-(SP)
        MOV     12.(SP),R0      ;Get address of instruction after TRAP.
        MOV     -(R0),R0        ;Fetch the TRAP instruction.
        BIC     #177400,R0      ;Get its low-order byte.
        ASL     R0              ;Make it a word offset
        JMP     @TRAPTB(R0)     ;   and jump through table.
;
;       Table of trap routine starting addresses.
TRAPTB: .WORD   T0,T1,T2,...,T255
;
;       Format of typical trap routine.
T0:     ...                     ;Do some computation.
        ...                     ;Parameters in caller's registers may
        ...                     ;   be accessed by offsets from SP
        ...                     ;   (e.g., 10.(SP) = user R5).
        JMP     TRAPEX          ;Go to common trap exit code.
        ...
TRAPEX: MOV     (SP)+,R0        ;Restore caller's registers.
        MOV     (SP)+,R1
        MOV     (SP)+,R2
        MOV     (SP)+,R3
        MOV     (SP)+,R4
        MOV     (SP)+,R5
        RTI                     ;Return to calling program.
```

In rare situations, several traps and interrupts may become pending simultaneously. For example, suppose an instruction sets the T bit, the next creates an addressing error, and at the same time an interrupt request appears. Each PDP-11 model has a fixed set of priorities for handling such cases, as detailed in the model's processor handbook.

REFERENCES

The PDP-11 was first described in "A New Architecture for Minicomputers — The DEC PDP-11" by C. G. Bell et al. [*AFIPS SJCC Conf. Proc.*, Vol. 36, 1970, pp. 657–675]. This article and several original chapters on the PDP-11 architecture appear in *Computer Engineering* by Bell, Mudge, and McNamara [Digital Press, 1978]. The study of PDP-11 instruction frequencies that we mentioned in Section 13.4 appears in a Ph.D. thesis, "Analysis and Performance of Computer Instruction Sets," by Leonard J. Shustek [Stanford University, 1978, available from University Microfilms, Ann Arbor, MI].

DEC publishes "processor handbooks" for all of the different PDP-11 and LSI-11 models; these are generally available from local DEC sales offices. A number of programming textbooks are oriented towards the PDP-11, including *Introduction to Computer Organization and Data Structures: PDP-11 edition*, by H. S. Stone and D. P. Siewiorek [McGraw-Hill, 1975] and *Minicomputer Systems* by R. H. Eckhouse and L. R. Morris [Prentice-Hall, 1979 (second edition)].

DEC's successor to the PDP-11 architecture, called the VAX-11, extends the PDP-11 architecture in many ways. For example, the maximum address size supported by a VAX-11 CPU is 32 bits instead of 16, and the CPU has sixteen 32-bit registers instead of eight 16-bit registers. DEC introduced the first VAX-11 model in 1978; it is described in Chapter 17 of *Computer Engineering*, "VAX-11/780: A Virtual Address Extension to the DEC PDP-11 Family" by William D. Strecker.

We mentioned at the beginning of this chapter that many microcomputers have borrowed ideas from the PDP-11. The Motorola 6809, described in Chapter 17 of this book, borrows the most. In fact, the 6809 may be viewed as an 8-bit accumulator-based PDP-11.

EXERCISES

13.1   Assuming that each memory access (read or write) takes one microsecond, compare the size and execution time of the memory and register versions of the multiplication program in Table 13–11.

13.2   Assuming that each memory access takes one microsecond, compare the size and execution time of the multiplication programs in Tables 13–11 and 13–12.

13.3   Write a PDP-11 subroutine that adds two 48-bit unsigned integers P and Q, stored in memory words P2,P1,P0 and Q2,Q1,Q0, respectively. The sum should be stored in memory locations S2,S1,S0. When the subroutine returns, C should be set to 1 if the true sum is greater than $2^{48}-1$, else to 0.

13.4   Translate one of the multiplication or division algorithms in Table 4–6, 7, or 10 into an assembly language program for the PDP-11.

13.5   Show how to use auto-increment instead of indexed addressing in the "clear loop" and the "print loop" in Table 13–16.

13.6   Modify the DIVIDE program in Table 13–17 so that the frame pointer is not needed (i.e., SP is used for all stack references).

13.7   Rewrite the DIVIDE program in Table 13–17 using registers to improve the speed of the division loop. What is the effect on the program's length?

13.8   Modify the queue module in Table 13–19 to manipulate queues of bytes.

13.9   Rewrite the QENQ subroutine in Table 13–19 so that R2 is no longer needed for temporary storage (use the stack).

13.10   Rewrite the DIVIDE subroutine in Table 13–17 and the main program in Table 13–18 using a stack-oriented subroutine calling convention that uses the MARK instruction for stack clean up. The convention is explained along with the MARK instruction in PDP-11 processor handbooks. Comment on advantages and disadvantages of this approach.

13.11   Explain how two PDP-11 coroutines can use the instruction JSR PC,@ (SP) + to call each other.

13.12   Rewrite the recursive NIM subroutines in Table 9–19 for the PDP-11. Write a main program that analyzes the game for all combinations of values of NHEAP from 2 to 25 and NTAKE from 2 to 6.

13.13   Write a PDP-11 keyboard input and display output module similar to the 6809 module in Table 10–4.

13.14   Write a complete Pascal simulation of the PDP-11.

14

MOTOROLA 68000

The Motorola 68000 is the most recently announced of the microprocessor architectures in this book. In keeping with the general microprocessor trend of "newer is better," the 68000 has a larger register set, a larger address space, more addressing modes, and in some respects a more capable and consistent instruction set than any other microprocessor in this book.[1]

The 68000 architecture includes sixteen 32-bit general registers and a consistent set of condition bits, a large memory address space (2^{24} bytes or more), provisions for memory mapping and management, user and supervisor modes of operation, 16-bit multiply and divide instructions, and a 7-level vectored, priority interrupt system.

The name "68000" is a generic that refers to a CPU architecture that Motorola has defined and is probably still refining. The "MC68000" is an integrated circuit introduced in 1979 that contains a subset of the entire 68000 architecture. In this chapter we describe only the architectural features that are present in the MC68000 integrated circuit.

Since the MC68000 contains a CPU only, a system hardware designer must add memory and I/O to form a complete computer. In 1980, MC68000-based computers were being developed by Cromemco, Motorola, Zenith, and others.

---

[1]However, see the discussions in Section 14.4.5 and Chapter 15 References.

14.1 BASIC ORGANIZATION

The 68000 architecture borrows many features from the PDP-11, including addressing modes, instruction types, and memory-mapped I/O. Since the Motorola 6809 and the hypothetical H6809 are also based on the PDP-11, the architecture of the H6809 serves as a good starting point for understanding the 68000. Therefore, we assume that you have already read about the H6809 in Section 5.2.

14.1.1 Computer Structure

The basic structure of an MC68000-based computer is shown in Figure 14–1. The CPU communicates with memory and I/O using a single Memory and I/O Bus. Since the 68000 architecture does not contain any I/O instructions, memory-mapped I/O is required.

The MC68000 Memory and I/O Bus contains a 24-bit address bus, and so it can access up to 2^{24} (16M) bytes of memory. The 68000 architecture allows for 32 address bits internally, and future 68000 CPUs may have all 32 address bits available externally to access 2^{32} bytes of memory.

The MC68000 external data bus and internal data paths are 16 bits wide, and the CPU may fetch and process two bytes at a time from memory. However, any 68000 CPU regardless of data bus size is properly called a 32-bit machine according to the definition given in Section 5.5, because the largest operand handled by a majority of 68000 data operations is 32 bits wide. In fact, future 68000 CPUs may have 32-bit internal data paths and external data bus.

The 68000 processor contains a 7-level, vectored, priority interrupt system. Interrupt vectors are stored in the first 1024 bytes of memory.

14.1.2 Processor Programming Model

The processor state of the 68000 is shown in Figure 14–2. The 68000 processor is a general register machine with a twist: the general registers are divided into two sets. There are eight "data registers" D0–D7 and eight "ad-

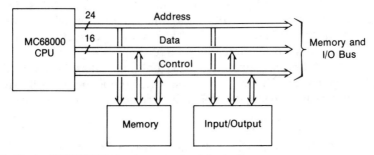

FIGURE 14–1 MC68000-based computer block diagram.

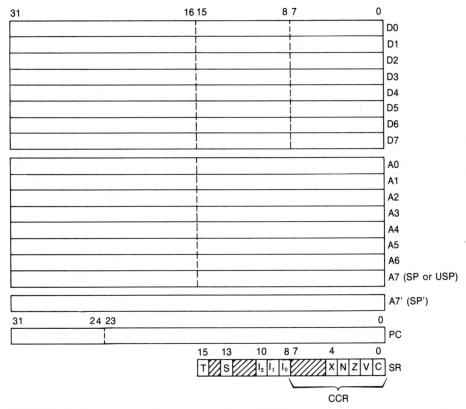

FIGURE 14-2 Programming model of the 68000.

dress registers" A0–A7. The data registers may be used in all data manipulation operations on bytes, words, and long words. Byte and word operations use the low-order byte or word of the register.

The address registers are used primarily to hold operand addresses in various addressing modes; most data manipulation operations cannot be performed on address registers. The CPU automatically uses A7 as a stack pointer (SP) for subroutine and interrupt calls and returns. Any of the sixteen general registers may contain an index value in the indexed addressing modes.

Thus, the architects of the 68000 have designed a register set with "data registers" intended for data manipulation and "address registers" intended for addresses. In a sense, this is a generalization of the 6809 architecture, in which the accumulators (A, B) are intended for data and the "index" registers (X, Y, U, S) are intended for addresses.

The 68000 contains a 32-bit Program Counter (PC). However, only the low-order 24 bits of PC or any other address are placed on the external address bus when memory is accessed. Therefore, we shall refer to addresses in the 68000 as 24-bit quantities. Although future 68000 chips *may* have 32-bit addresses, until the future chips are produced the architects always have the option of "stealing" a few of the high-order bits for other purposes.

The 68000 has a 16-bit Status Register (SR). The low-order byte of SR contains the condition bits and may be accessed as an 8-bit unit called the "Condition Code Register" (CCR). The CCR contains the four standard condition flags C (carry), V (overflow), Z (zero), and N (negative). There is also an "Extend" bit X that is set to the same value as C in certain arithmetic operations but left unchanged by data movement operations, facilitating multiprecision arithmetic.

The high-order byte of SR contains "processor control" bits. Setting the Trace bit T to 1 causes a trap to occur after the next instruction is executed, a useful primitive for on-line debuggers. The three interrupt mask bits (I_2, I_1, I_0) set the interrupt priority of the CPU to a value from 0 to 7, so that only interrupts of higher priority may be accepted. Setting the Supervisor bit S to 1 places the CPU in supervisor state; otherwise the CPU is in user state.

Supervisor state is important in the design of multi-user operating systems employing memory mapping and management, as discussed in Section 7.5. Certain 68000 instructions are "privileged" and can be executed only in supervisor state. Also, there are actually two stack pointers, A7 and A7'. The CPU always uses A7 in user state and A7' in supervisor state.

14.1.3 Instruction Formats

Typical 68000 instructions have an opcode and an addressing mode designator encoded in one word, and up to four successive words may contain additional addressing information. Several different formats are used for the first word of different instructions, as required by different operations and addressing modes. For example, six different formats are shown in Figure 14–3, and there are many other formats as well.

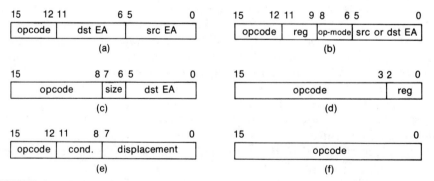

FIGURE 14-3 Format of the first word of typical 68000 instructions: (a) MOVE; (b) other double-operand; (c) single-operand; (d) single-register-operand; (e) branch; (f) inherent addressing.

Most 68000 data manipulation instructions can operate on bytes, words, or long words. The operand size is encoded as part of the opcode in MOVE instructions [Figure 14–3(a)], and in the size or op-mode field in other instructions [Figure 14–3(b,c)].

Instructions that reference memory contain a 6-bit "effective-address" (EA) field that specifies the location of the operand; MOVE contains two such fields. In all these instructions, the EA field can specify one of several addressing modes as discussed in Section 14.3; some addressing modes append one or two words of additional information to the instruction.

Rather than give all the details of instruction encoding, we shall concentrate on the effects and assembly language format of various 68000 operations and addressing modes. Readers interested in the detailed instruction encodings may find them in the manufacturer's literature.

14.2 ASSEMBLY LANGUAGE

Motorola's standard assembly language for the 68000 has the same basic format as the H6809 assembly language defined in Section 6.1. However, some of the conventions of Motorola's language are different from the H6809's:

- The maximum label length is 30 characters (!) instead of 8.

- Hexadecimal constants are denoted by a prefix of "$" instead of a suffix of "H".

- A character constant is denoted by a string of characters surrounded by single quotes, as in Pascal ('Here''s a string'). The character constant generates a sequence of bytes containing the corresponding ASCII characters, with the leftmost character at the lowest address. The assembler pads additional bytes with $00 if necessary, but rejects any string that contains more bytes than allowed by the operation in which it appears.

- Many 68000 instructions operate on bytes, words, or long words. In assembly language, a suffix of ".B", ".W", or ".L" on the opcode mnemonic indicates the size. If the suffix is missing, a word operation (.W) is assumed as the default.

Most of Motorola's 68000 assembler directives have names different from the H6809's; important directives are summarized in Table 14–1. Before storing constants or reserving storage, a DC or DS directive automatically forces the PLC to an even value if its size is "word" or "long word".

Motorola's standard 68000 assembler can produce absolute or relocatable code. The ORG and ORG.L directives indicate the beginning of a section of

TABLE 14-1 Motorola 68000 assembly language directives.

Name	Examples	Effect
ORG	ORG $4000	Set short absolute program origin.
ORG.L	ORG.L $C08000	Set long absolute program origin.
RORG	RORG 0	Set relative program origin.
EQU	CR EQU $0D	Equate symbol with 32-bit value.
SET	CT SET CT+1	Like EQU, but allows redefinition.
DC.B	CB DC.B 17,$EF,-1 ST DC.B 'ABCDEFG'	Store constant values into successive memory bytes.
DC.W or DC	CW DC.W $E800,DOG KW DC -1000,PUP+5	Store constant values into successive memory words.
DC.L	CL DC.L $ABCDE800 LC DC.L CAT,KIT-10	Store constant values into successive long words.
DS.B	BT DS.B 12	Reserve memory bytes.
DS.W or DS	WT DS.W 6 AY DS LAST-FIRST+1	Reserve memory words.
DS.L	LT DS.L 3	Reserve memory long words.
END	END	Indicate end of assembly.
MACRO	M1 MACRO FP1,FP2	Begin macro definition.
ENDM	ENDM	End macro definition.

absolute code. The choice between the two directives affects only the way in which the assembler handles certain forward references, as explained in Section 14.3.3.

The RORG directive indicates the beginning of a section of relocatable code (which Motorola calls "relative"). In fact, the default is to produce relocatable code — the assembler behaves as if RORG 0 is the first statement of the program. The distinction between absolute and relocatable quantities is very important in 68000 assembly language programs. As we'll see in the next section, the assembler automatically selects among different addressing modes according to whether an address expression is absolute or relocatable.

In the 68000 assembler, as in most relocatable assemblers, symbols that appear in the label field of an instruction are defined to be absolute if an ORG statement has occurred most recently, and relocatable if RORG has occurred most recently. The type of an expression is determined by the types of its components and operations, according to the rules given in Section 6.4.1 (also see Exercise 6.6).

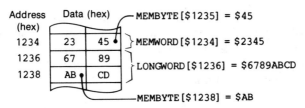

FIGURE 14–4 Memory addressing in the 68000.

14.3 ADDRESSING

The 68000 memory is byte addressable, and most instructions can specify operands that are one, two, or four bytes long. As shown in Figure 14–4, two-byte (word) and four-byte (long-word) operands always start at even addresses, and the bytes are assembled with the more significant bytes in the lower-numbered memory locations. An attempt to access a word or long word at an odd address causes an "Address Error" trap.

Typical 68000 single- and double-operand instructions may have one of their operands in memory; the MOVE instruction may have both operands in memory. An operand is specified by a 6-bit EA field in the instruction, consisting of a 3-bit addressing mode designator and a 3-bit register number, as shown in Figure 14–5.

The addressing modes of the 68000 are modeled after the PDP-11's. However, the encoding used in the 68000 is much more clever because it allows access to 16 general registers and 12 addressing modes with only 3-bit mode and register-number fields (8 combinations each). In conjunction with the reg field, the eight mode combinations are used as follows:

0   reg specifies a data register (D0–D7) that contains the operand.

1   reg specifies an address register (A0–A7) that contains the operand.

2–6 reg specifies an address register that is used to compute the effective address of an operand in memory.

7   reg specifies one of five addressing modes that do not use the general registers (e.g., immediate, absolute); three combinations are left over for future expansion.

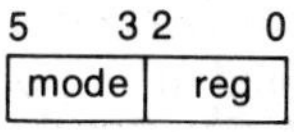

```
    5    3 2    0
   ┌──────┬──────┐
   │ mode │ reg  │
   └──────┴──────┘
```

FIGURE 14–5 68000 operand effective-address specification (mode and reg are reversed in the dst EA field of the MOVE instruction).

The 68000 has a "consistent" instruction set because any instruction that specifies an operand in memory may do so using any addressing mode that makes sense (but see Section 14.4.5 for the definition of "makes sense"). Individual addressing modes are summarized in Table 14–2 and discussed in detail in subsequent subsections.

14.3.1 Register Direct

In *register-direct addressing*, the operand is contained in one of the data registers D0–D7 or in one of the address registers A0–A7. Long-word operations on registers use the entire register. As suggested by the dotted lines in Figure 14–2, word operations use the 16 low-order bits of the register and byte operations use the 8 low-order bits.

Byte and word operations on data registers do not use or affect the higher-order bits of the register. In fact, the high-order bits of a data register cannot be read or written at all by word or byte instructions, except by a byte or word sign-extending instruction (EXT) and a word-swapping instruction (SWAP). Thus, to change only the high-order byte of a register, a program must store the entire 32-bit register into memory, change the appropriate byte in memory, and then reload the 32-bit register from memory. Compare this with the register addressing schemes of the Z8000 (Section 15.1.2) and the 8086 (Section 18.1.2).

Byte operations are not allowed on the address registers, but word operations are allowed. When used as a destination operand, the entire 32-bit contents of an address register is affected regardless of operation size. If the operation size is "word," then the source operand is sign-extended to 32 bits before being used. Thus, the instruction MOVE.W #$1234,A0 sets A0 to $00001234, while MOVE.W #$8234,A0 sets A0 to $FFFF8234.

14.3.2 Immediate

In *immediate addressing*, an operand is stored in one or two words following the first word of the instruction. This mode cannot be used for an operand that might be altered by the instruction, because it would require the instruction itself to be altered.

Depending on the size of the operation, an immediate operand may be one, two, or four bytes long. One-byte immediate operands are contained in the low-order byte of a word following the instruction; the high-order byte is wasted. Two- and four-byte immediate operands fit nicely into one or two words following the instruction. The assembler determines the immediate operand size from the size of the operation.

A few instructions have short ("quick") immediate operands contained in their first and only word. The ADDQ and SUBQ instructions each contain a 3-bit immediate operand, while MOVEQ contains an 8-bit immediate operand.

14.3.3 Absolute

In *absolute addressing*, the instruction contains or implies the 24-bit absolute memory address of the operand. The 68000 has two distinct absolute addressing modes. In *absolute long* addressing, the second and third words of

TABLE 14–2 Addressing modes and assembly language notation for the 68000.

Mode	Notation	Operand
Data-register direct	`Dn`	`Dn`
Address-register direct	`An`	`An`
Immediate	`#data`	`data`
Absolute long	`addr24`	`MEM[addr24]`
Absolute short	`addr16`	`MEM[addr16]`
Address-register indirect	`(An)`	`MEM[An]`
Auto-increment (by 1, 2 or 4)	`(An)+`	`MEM[An]`, then `An := An + operand size`
Auto-decrement (by 1, 2, or 4)	`-(An)`	`An := An - operand size,` then `MEM[An]`
Based	`offset16(An)`	`MEM[An+offset16]`
Based indexed (short)	`offset8(An,Xn)`	`MEM[An+XnLow+offset8]`
Based indexed (long)	`offset8(An,Xn.L)`	`MEM[An+Xn+offset8]`
Relative	`raddr16`	`MEM[raddr16]`
Relative indexed (short)	`raddr8(Xn)`	`MEM[XnLow+raddr8]`
Relative indexed (long)	`raddr8(Xn.L)`	`MEM[Xn+raddr8]`

Notes: `Dn` denotes a data register: `D0–D7`.

`An` denotes an address register: `A0–A7` or `SP` (same as `A7`).

`data` is an 8-, 16-, or 32-bit value as appropriate for the size of the operation.

`MEM[x]` is the 8-, 16-, or 32-bit value beginning at memory address *x*, as appropriate for the size of the operation.

`addr24` is a 24-bit absolute memory address.

`addr16` is an absolute address in the bottom 32K or top 32K of the 16M-byte address space. The instruction contains a 16-bit value that is sign-extended to 24 bits to obtain the absolute address of the operand.

`Xn` denotes an index register: `D0–D7`, `A0–A7`, or `SP` (same as `A7`).

`XnLow` denotes the 24-bit value obtained by sign-extending the contents of the 16 low-order bits of index register `Xn`.

`offset8` and `offset16` are 8- and 16-bit values, respectively, that are sign-extended to 24 bits before being used in the effective address calculation.

`raddr8` and `raddr16` are relocatable addresses that are within 128 and 32,768 bytes, respectively, of the instruction. The instruction contains an 8- or 16-bit displacement that is sign-extended to 24 bits when the instruction is executed and then added to the `PC` to obtain the effective address of the operand.

The assembler chooses among absolute long, absolute short, and relative modes according to the type of the address expression, even though the notation for all three modes is the same. In the same way, the assembler chooses between based mode and relative indexed mode.

the instruction contain a full 24-bit memory address, as shown in Figure 14–6(a).

In *absolute short* addressing, a 24-bit address is derived from a 16-bit value in the second word of the instruction, as shown in Figure 14–6(b). The MSB of the 16-bit value is extended to create a 24-bit number, yielding an absolute address in either the bottom 32K (MSB=0) or the top 32K (MSB=1) of the 16M-byte address space. This allows part of the address space to be accessed by shorter instructions.

Motorola's standard assembly language for the 68000 has no special notation for distinguishing between short and long absolute addressing; the assembler must choose between the two modes. If an absolute address expression is fully defined during Pass 1 of the assembly, the assembler chooses short or long mode according to whether or not the expression can be represented in 16 bits. If an address expression contains a forward reference, then the assembler chooses absolute short or long mode according to whether an ORG or ORG.L directive has occurred most recently.

The selection of long or short absolute addressing is independent of the size of an instruction's operand. Regardless of the operand's size — byte, word, or long word — the instruction contains the address of the most significant byte of the operand (see Figure 14–4).

14.3.4 Address-Register Indirect

In *address-register indirect addressing*, the specified address register (An) contains the 24-bit address of the operand. This mode is used when the address of the operand must be computed at run time.

14.3.5 Auto-Increment and Auto-Decrement

In *auto-increment addressing*, the specified address register (An) contains the 24-bit address of the operand. After using the address, the CPU

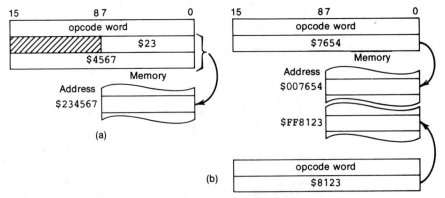

FIGURE 14–6 68000 instructions using absolute addressing: (a) long; (b) short.

increments the address register by 1, 2, or 4 according to the operand size — byte, word, or long word. In *auto-decrement addressing*, the CPU *decrements* the address register by the operand size *before* using the address contained there. In both cases, if An is A7 (SP) and the operand size is "byte," the CPU uses an increment of 2 to keep the stack pointer aligned on a word boundary; the high-order byte of the word is used. Auto-increment and auto-decrement addressing may be used to step through arrays, lists, and other data structures and to manipulate stacks as described in Section 7.2.5.

14.3.6 Based

In 68000 *based addressing*, a 16-bit offset in the instruction is added to the specified address register to form the effective address of the operand; the contents of the register are not disturbed. The offset is treated as a signed number; its sign is extended to make a 24-bit two's-complement number before adding to the address register. Thus, an offset is in the range -32768 through $+32767$.

Based addressing allows access to components of linked lists and other data structures when the offset to a particular component is known at assembly time, but the base address of the data structure must be computed at run time. Based addressing was explained in Section 7.3.3; examples for the 68000 will be given in Tables 14–14 and 14–16.

14.3.7 Indexed

The 68000 does not have a simple indexed addressing mode. However, the based mode discussed above is equivalent to indexed mode in small 68000 systems with 64K or fewer bytes of memory; since only 16 address bits are needed, the 16-bit value contained in the based-addressing instruction could be used as a base address instead of an offset. In larger systems, indexed addressing must be achieved with based indexed mode as discussed below.

14.3.8 Based Indexed

As explained in Section 7.3.4, *based indexed addressing* forms an effective address by combining a base address and an index value, both of which are contained in registers. In the 68000, this mode is embellished further; the instruction contains an 8-bit signed offset value (-128 to $+127$) that is also added in the effective-address computation. Only an address register A0–A7 may contain the base address, while the index value may be contained in any of the 16 general registers (hereafter called "index registers").

Based indexed addressing allows both the base address of a data structure and an offset into it to be computed at run time. One application of this addressing mode is in a subroutine that manipulates an array whose base address is passed as a parameter.

In the 68000, even an array whose base address is known at assembly time must be accessed by based indexed addressing, since there is no simple indexed mode. To access such an array, a program must load an address register with the array's base address and then use based indexed addressing. This is not a serious programming inconvenience since the 68000 has so many address registers available. Furthermore, once the base register has been set up, the rest of the program occupies less memory because based indexed instructions do not have to contain a 24-bit base address.

The 68000 has two varieties of based indexed addressing, in which either a 16-bit or a 24-bit index value may be used. Although all of the index registers are 32 bits long, an instruction with based-indexed addressing may use either the low-order 24 bits or the low-order 16 bits of the index register. If the low-order 16 bits are used, this value is sign-extended to 24 bits before being used in the effective-address computation.

The short-index variety of based indexed addressing improves the size and speed of programs that deal with small data structures, ones with indices between -32768 and $+32767$. Such "short" index values may be stored and manipulated as words instead of long words. In fact, standard 68000 assembly language uses short-index mode as the default; as shown in Table 14–2, a suffix of ".L" is needed to specify the long-offset mode. An example program using based indexed addressing will be presented in Table 14–13.

14.3.9 Relative

The 68000's relative addressing mode uses a 16-bit displacement which is sign-extended to 24 bits and added to the current PC to obtain the effective address of the operand. This allows constant data and jump targets to be accessed relative to the current program position.

The 68000 does not allow relative mode to specify an operand that might be altered, for example, the destination of a MOVE instruction. The architects of the 68000 intended for a program to stand by itself as a "read-only" unit; a program should not be modified by its own instructions. Therefore, alterable variables should not be accessed by relative addressing. If position-independent variable access is needed, based addressing should be used; the base registers may be changed whenever the program and its variables are moved in memory.

Motorola's standard assembly language for the 68000 does not have any special notation for distinguishing between relative and absolute addressing modes. Instead, the assembler automatically selects relative addressing when the operand is a relative expression. The assembler can distinguish between absolute and relative (relocatable) expressions as explained in Sections 14.2 and 6.4.1.

If a 68000 assembly language program specifies a relative operand in an instruction that may alter the operand, then the assembler produces an error message. Otherwise the assembler computes the required displacement as the difference between the given address expression (raddr16) and the address following the instruction. If the displacement can be expressed in 16 bits, the assembler assembles the instruction; otherwise it produces an "out-of-range" error message.

In addition to being one of the modes that may be specified by the EA field of an instruction, relative addressing is also used inherently in conditional branch instructions.

14.3.10 Relative Indexed

Relative indexed addressing in the 68000 works just like based indexed addressing, except that the PC is used as the base register. This mode allows a program to access a nearby table of read-only data or jump targets. An 8-bit displacement (raddr8) gives the distance to the table from the current instruction, and an index register contains an additional offset to a particular item in the table. As in relative mode, operands accessed by relative indexed addressing are considered to be unalterable. As in based indexed addressing, either a long or a short index may be used.

There is no special assembly language notation to distinguish between relative indexed and based addressing. If an assembly language statement contains a relative expression followed by an index register name in parentheses, the assembler automatically selects relative indexed mode. The assembler computes the required displacement from the current instruction to the specified relative address, and it produces an error message if the displacement cannot be expressed in 8 bits or if the operation is one that alters its operand.

14.4 OPERATIONS

We shall classify 68000 instructions into four types: memory reference, special memory reference, register reference, and program control.

14.4.1 Memory Reference

Instructions that can have operands of any size and can use all or almost all addressing modes are listed in Table 14–3. The MOVE instruction is the most flexible, since it can move any general register, an immediate datum, or an operand in memory to any general register or memory location.

Instructions in the second group of the table are almost as flexible as MOVE. For example, ADD can add a register to a memory location or add the contents of a memory location to a register. However, these instructions cannot perform memory-to-memory operations, such as adding the contents of one memory location to another.

TABLE 14–3 68000 memory reference instructions.

Mnemonic	Operands	Size	Notes	Description
MOVE	src,dst	B,W,L	1	Copy src to dst
ADD	src,dst	B,W,L	2,3	Add src to dst
SUB	src,dst	B,W,L	2,3	Subtract src from dst
CMP	src,dst	B,W,L	2	Set CCR according to dst−src
AND	src,dst	B,W,L	2,4	AND src to dst
OR	src,dst	B,W,L	2,4	OR src to dst
EOR	src,dst	B,W,L	4,5	Exclusive OR src to dst
CLR	dst	B,W,L	4	Clear dst
NEG	dst	B,W,L	4	Negate dst (two's complement)
NEGX	dst	B,W,L	4	Negate dst and subtract X
NOT	dst	B,W,L	4	Complement bits of dst
TST	dst	B,W,L	4	Set CCR according to dst

Notes: Each instruction may operate on bytes, words, or long words, as specified by a suffix of .B, .W, or .L on the mnemonic. If no suffix is given, a default of .W is used.

In general, src may use any addressing mode from Section 14.3, and dst may use any mode except immediate, relative, or relative indexed. However, src and dst may not be address registers if the operation size is "byte."

Additional notes:

1) The entire instruction may be encoded in one word if dst is a data register, the size is "long," and src is an immediate operand in the range −128 through +127. The assembler uses this short encoding for MOVE whenever possible. However, the mnemonics MOVEQ and MOVEI force the assembler to choose the "quick" and normal immediate encodings, respectively.

2) Memory-to-memory operations are not possible: if src is not a data register or an immediate operand then dst must be a register.

3) The entire instruction may be encoded in one word if src is an immediate operand in the range +1 through +8. The assembler uses this short encoding for ADD and SUB whenever possible. However, the mnemonics ADDQ, SUBQ and ADDI, SUBI force the assembler to choose the "quick" and normal immediate encodings, respectively.

4) src and dst may not be address registers.

5) src must be a data register or an immediate operand.

Instructions in the last group in the table are less flexible because they cannot be applied to the address registers. AND and OR, however, still have the advantage of being able to operate memory-to-register or register-to-memory.

All 68000 double-operand instructions are performed in left-to-right order, for example, ADD src TO dst and SUB src FROM dst.

All of the operations performed by instructions in Table 14–3 are fairly standard, with the exception of NEGX. This instruction subtracts its operand and current value of the X condition bit from 0, stores the result, and sets C and X to 1 if a borrow was generated. This is a useful primitive for negating multiprecision two's-complement numbers.

All of the instructions in Table 14–3 set, clear, or hold condition code bits XNZVC according to the result of the operation, roughly as described in Chapter 8; refer to a 68000 user's manual or reference summary card for the exact rules.

14.4.2 Special Memory Reference

We classify the instructions shown in Table 14–4 as "special" memory reference instructions because they do not allow all addressing modes or operand sizes. As you can see from the table, there are a large number of size and addressing mode variations. In the paragraphs below, we'll try to make some sense out of them.

The first group in the table contains data movement instructions. The LEA and PEA instructions may be used to compute the effective address of a VAR-type parameter at run time, using any memory addressing mode except auto-increment or auto-decrement. The MOVEP instruction is used in conjunction with certain peripheral devices as discussed in Section 14.6.1.

The MOVEM instructions load or store multiple registers in memory. The second word of MOVEM contains one bit for each general register, so that any combination of the 16 general registers may be specified to be moved. Depending on the instruction's size suffix (.W or .L), either the low-order word or the entire 32-bit long-word of each register is moved. In most cases, MOVEM moves to or from a block of memory beginning at the effective address of the src or dst operand. However, the registers may be pushed onto or popped from a stack by specifying auto-decrement addressing for dst or auto-increment for src, respectively.

The second group in Table 14–4 contains primitives for multiprecision binary arithmetic on bytes, words, and long words, and multiprecision BCD arithmetic on packed-BCD bytes. All of these instructions use the X condition bit to hold the carry or borrow between operations; X has the desirable property that it is not affected by data movement, comparison, and loop control instructions. The addition and subtraction instructions may access both operands in data registers or they may access both operands in memory by auto-decrement addressing. The memory addressing method is appropriate because multiprecision operands are typically stored with the more significant digits at the lower-numbered addresses, but the least significant digits are processed first (refer to Sections 8.9 and 8.11). Notice that the 68000 does not require "decimal adjust" instructions or condition bits, because it has add, subtract, and negate instructions that process packed-BCD numbers directly.

Instructions in the third group of Table 14–4 multiply and divide 16-bit numbers in both signed and unsigned formats. MULS and MULU multiply the 16 low-order bits of a data register by a 16-bit operand and leave a 32-bit result in the register. DIVS and DIVU divide a 32-bit data register by a 16-bit operand, leaving a 16-bit quotient in the low-order word of the register and a 16-bit remainder in the high-order word. An attempt to divide by zero causes a trap.

Bit-manipulation instructions comprise the fourth group in Table 14–4. These instructions can set, clear, complement, or simply test the value of a bit in a data register or memory byte. The bit number may be specified "statically" as an immediate value in the instruction, or "dynamically" in a

TABLE 14-4 68000 special memory reference instructions.

Mnemonic	Operands	Size	Notes	Description
LEA	src,An	L	1	Load An with eff. addr. of src
PEA	src	L	1	Push eff. addr. of src using SP
MOVEP	Dn,dst	W,L	2	Store peripheral data
MOVEP	src,Dn	W,L	2	Load peripheral data
MOVEM	regs,dst	W,L	3,4	Store multiple registers
MOVEM	src,regs	W,L	1,3,5	Load multiple registers
ADDX	src,dst	B,W,L	6	Add src and X to dst
SUBX	src,dst	B,W,L	6	Subtract src and X from dst
ABCD	src,dst	B	6	Add BCD src and X to dst
SBCD	src,dst	B	6	Subtract BCD src and X from dst
NBCD	dst	B	7	Negate BCD dst and subtract X
MULS	src,Dn	W	7	Signed multiply Dn by src
MULU	src,Dn	W	7	Unigned multiply Dn by src
DIVS	src,Dn	W	7	Signed divide Dn by src
DIVU	src,Dn	W	7	Unigned divide Dn by src
BSET	bnum,dst	B,L	7,8	Test and set bit bnum of dst
BCLR	bnum,dst	B,L	7,8	Test and clear bit bnum of dst
BCHG	bnum,dst	B,L	7,8	Test and change bit bnum of dst
BTST	bnum,src	B,L	7,8	Test bit bnum of src
CMPM	src,dst	B,W,L	9	Set CCR according to dst−src
CHK	src,Dn	W	7	Check for Dn between 0 and src
TAS	dst	B	7	Test dst and set its MSB to 1
SWAP	Dn	L		Swap 16-bit halves of Dn
EXT	Dn	W,L		Extend sign of byte or word
EXG	Xn,Xm	L		Exchange two 32-bit registers

Notes: If an instruction operates only on one operand size, no size suffix is required or allowed on the mnemonic. If an instruction operates on two or more operand sizes, an appropriate size suffix may be attached to the mnemonic; the default size is "word."

In general, src may use any addressing mode from Section 14.3, and dst may use any mode except immediate, relative, or relative indexed.

Additional notes:

1) src may use only absolute, address-register indirect, based, based indexed, relative, and relative indexed modes.

2) src or dst may only use based mode.

3) regs is a list of general registers; ranges are denoted by dashes (D2–D5), and multiple names and ranges are separated by slashes (A2/D2–D5/SP/D0). The order of the registers in the assembly language instruction is irrelevant; registers are moved in an order predetermined by the CPU hardware.

4) dst may only use absolute, address-register indirect, auto-decrement, based, and based indexed modes.

5) src may also use auto-increment mode.

6) src and dst must either both be data registers, or both use auto-decrement mode.

7) src and dst may not be address registers.

8) bnum may specify a data register (e.g., D0) for dynamic bit addressing, or an immediate bit number (e.g., #5) for static bit addressing. If src or dst is a data register, then the size must be "long" and the range of bnum is 0 to 31. Otherwise the size must be "byte" and the range of bnum is 0 to 7.

9) src and dst must both use auto-increment mode.

register. All instructions test the specified bit before performing their operation and set Z to 1 if the bit was 0, and to 0 if the bit was 1.

A few miscellaneous memory reference instructions appear in the fifth group in the table. CMPM is a version of CMP in which both operands are accessed by auto-increment addressing, a useful primitive for comparing strings (compare with the explicit string comparison instructions of the Z8000, Section 15.4.5). The CHK instruction compares the 16-bit signed value in a data register against 0 and an upper bound, and causes a trap if the value is outside of this range. This instruction may be used to quickly check that an array index is within bounds; a trap and its overhead occur only on indexing errors. The TAS instruction tests a memory byte and then sets the byte's MSB to 1, a useful primitive for synchronization and resource management in multi-programming and multiprocessing systems.[2]

The last group in the table contains instructions that operate only on registers. SWAP exchanges the two 16-bit halves of a data register. We have classified SWAP as a "long-word" instruction because it sets the condition bits according to the 32-bit result. EXT.W extends the sign of a data register's low-order byte into its next higher byte. EXT.L extends the sign of a data register's low-order word into its high-order word. The EXG instruction exchanges the contents of any two general registers.

14.4.3 Shifts and Rotates

The 68000 has a comprehensive set of shift and rotation instructions, shown in Table 14–5. The various shifts and rotates operate as described in Section 8.8. If the shifted operand is a register, then a byte, word, or entire long word may be shifted. A shift count of 1 to 8 may be specified statically in the instruction, or a shift count of 0 to 63 may be specified dynamically in a register. If the shifted operand is in memory, then the operand size must be "word" and a shift count of 1 is used.

The 68000 shift instructions set the condition bits in a very reasonable and consistent manner that is worth discussing. At the end of a shift operation, both the X bit and the C bit are loaded with the last bit shifted out of the operand. The Z and N bits are loaded according to the value of the result. The V bit is set if an ASL caused the sign of the operand to change; otherwise it is cleared. If a shift count of 0 was specified, the operand and X are not changed,

---

[2]TAS dst is not quite the same as BSET #7,dst. Both instructions require the CPU to read memory byte dst, test its value, and then rewrite the memory byte with a 1 in the MSB. However, TAS must be used if two or more CPUs share the same main memory. During TAS, the CPU "locks" the memory bus so that no other CPUs can access memory until both the read and the write cycles of TAS have been completed. This prevents two CPUs from simultaneously reading dst and both finding the MSB is 0 before one sets it to 1. If this happened, the CPUs could gain simultaneous access to a shared resource.

TABLE 14–5   68000 shift and rotate instructions.

Mnemonic	Operands	Size	Notes	Description
ASL	cntdst	B,W,L		Arithmetic shift left
ASR	cntdst	B,W,L		Arithmetic shift right
LSL	cntdst	B,W,L		Logical shift left
LSR	cntdst	B,W,L		Logical shift right
ROL	cntdst	B,W,L		Rotate left
ROR	cntdst	B,W,L		Rotate right
ROXL	cntdst	B,W,L		Rotate left with X
ROXR	cntdst	B,W,L		Rotate right with X

Notes: Each instruction may operate on bytes, words, or long words, as specified by a suffix of .B, .W, or .L on the mnemonic. If no suffix is given, a default of .W is assumed. There are three different formats for "cntdst" in each instruction:

Dm,Dn   Data register Dn is shifted by the amount specified in the six low-order bits of data register Dm.

#cnt,Dn   Data register Dn is shifted by cnt positions, where cnt ranges from 1 to 8.

dst   The memory word at location dst is shifted by one position. Any memory addressing mode except immediate, relative, or relative indexed may be used. However, the only allowed operand size is "word."

but Z and N are loaded according to the result, V is cleared, and C is loaded with the current value of X.

Since the X bit is not changed during data movement operations, it is used to hold the "carry" between iterations of loops that perform multiprecision operations. The "rotate with extend" instructions use the X bit as the carry input. Note that X is updated after each step of a multibit "rotate with extend" instruction; executing ROXR #5,D0 yields the same result as executing ROXR #1,D0 five times in a row.

14.4.4   Program Control

The 68000's program control instructions are listed in Table 14–6. The JMP and JSR instructions jump to a specified address. Before jumping, JSR pushes a 24-bit return address onto the stack using A7 as the stack pointer (SP). The return address occupies two words on the stack; the most significant byte is not used. As in other processors, the 68000's SP points directly at the top stack item, and the stack grows by decrementing SP.

The RTS instruction returns from a subroutine by popping the return address off the stack. RTR pops a word off the stack and loads its low-order byte into CCR; then it pops a return address from the stack just like RTS. This is useful in subroutines that save the status of their caller.

Stack-oriented subroutine parameter passing conventions are simplified by the LINK and UNLK instructions, which allow any address register An to be

TABLE 14–6   68000 program control instructions.

Mnemonic	Operands	Size	Notes	Description
JMP	addr	U	1	Jump to addr
JSR	addr	U	1	Jump to subroutine at addr
RTS		U		Return from subroutine
RTR		U		Pop CCR, then return
LINK	An,#disp	U	2	Create subroutine linkage
UNLK	An	U		Clean up subroutine linkage
BRA	addr16	U	3	Branch to addr16
BSR	addr16	U	3	Branch to subroutine at addr16
Bcc	addr16	U	3,4	Branch to addr16 if cc is true
DBcc	Dn,addr16	W	3,4	Conditional loop primitive
Scc	dst	B	4,5	Set dst according to cc
MOVE	src,CCR	W	6,7	Copy src to CCR
MOVE	SR,dst	W	5	Copy SR to dst
OR.B	#data,CCR	B	8	OR data to CCR
AND.B	#data,CCR	B	8	AND data to CCR
EOR.B	#data,CCR	B	8	Exclusive OR data to CCR
MOVE	src,SR	W	6,9	Copy src to SR
OR	#data,SR	W	8,9	OR data to SR
AND	#data,SR	W	8,9	AND data to SR
EOR	#data,SR	W	8,9	Exclusive OR data to SR
MOVE	An,USP	L	9	Copy An to user SP
MOVE	USP,An	L	9	Copy user SP to An
RTE		U	9	Return from exception
STOP	#data	U	8,9	Load SR with data, halt CPU
RESET		U	9	Reset external devices
NOP		U		No operation
TRAP	vector	U	10	Cause a trap using vector
TRAPV		U		Cause a trap if V=1

Notes: Size suffixes are not used with these instructions except as shown. Unsized instructions
are denoted by "U".

Additional notes:

1) addr specifies the effective address of the jump target using any memory addressing
mode except immediate, auto-increment, or auto-decrement.
2) disp ranges from -32768 to $+32767$.
3) addr16 is a target address within 32K bytes of the instruction.
4) cc may denote any of the conditions listed in Table 8–3.
5) dst may use any addressing mode except address-register direct, immediate, relative,
or relative indexed.
6) src may use any addressing mode except address-register direct.
7) CCR is loaded with the low-order byte of src.
8) data is an immediate operand appropriate for the operation size.
9) Privileged instruction, executable only in supervisor state.
10) vector ranges from 0 to 15.

used as a stack frame pointer FP. The LINK An,#disp instruction performs three operations:

(1) It pushes the old FP (current 32-bit value of An) onto the stack.

(2) It creates a new FP by loading An with the updated SP.

(3) It reserves space on the stack for local variables by adding disp (usually negative) to SP.

The UNLK An instruction undoes the effects of LINK:

(1) It loads SP with the contents of An, thereby deallocating the stack space that was occupied by local variables.

(2) It pops a 32-bit word from the stack and loads it into An, thereby restoring the old FP.

We'll give an example program using LINK and UNLK in Table 14–14.

The BRA and BSR instructions branch to nearby addresses using a special form of relative addressing. A "short" branch instruction is one word long and contains an 8-bit offset that specifies a target address within -128 to -1 or $+1$ to $+127$ bytes of the word following the instruction. A "long" branch instruction contains an 8-bit offset of 0, and a second word contains a 16-bit offset (-32768 to $+32767$ bytes). Given the target address (addr16) for a particular branch instruction, the assembler computes the required offset and decides whether to use the long or short format. If the addr16 expression contains a forward reference, then the assembler uses a long offset. In any case, a suffix of ".S" may be used on the branch mnemonic to force a short offset.

The second group in Table 14–6 contains conditional instructions. The 68000 has 14 distinct conditional branches (Bcc addr16), with the same mnemonics and conditions as the 6809's, as discussed in Section 8.6. The conditional branches contain an 8- or 16-bit offset and use the same relative addressing mode as BRA and BSR.

The DBcc Dn,addr16 instruction is a powerful loop control primitive with three parameters: a termination condition cc, a counter register Dn, and an address addr16. The instruction performs the following operations:

(1) The condition bit combination specified by cc is tested. cc may be any of the standard branch conditions from Table 8–3, or T (always true) or F (always false). If the condition is true, then DBcc terminates and control passes to the next sequential instruction.

(2) If the tested condition was false, then the low-order word of data register Dn is decremented by 1.

(3) If the result of decrementing the low-order word of Dn was -1, then DBcc terminates and control passes to the next sequential instruction.

Otherwise, a relative branch to address addr16 is taken by adding a 16-bit signed offset in the instruction to the current value of the PC.

Thus, the DBcc instruction may be used to create a loop that terminates on either a specified condition or the exhaustion of an iteration count. An example program using DBEQ will be shown in Table 14–11.

The Scc dst instruction tests the same cc conditions as DBcc. It sets the specified dst byte to $FF if the condition is true; otherwise it sets dst to $00. This instruction is typically used to set a boolean variable according to the result of an expression evaluation, where true and false are encoded as $FF and $00 respectively.

The third group of instructions in Table 14–6 explicitly manipulate the condition bits (CCR) and the status register (SR). A user program may load the CCR or read the entire SR with an appropriate MOVE instruction. Individual bits or groups of bits in the CCR may be set, cleared, or changed by appropriate OR, AND, and EOR instructions.

The fourth group contains "privileged" instructions, which may be executed only in supervisor state. The first four instructions may affect the CPU control bits in the high-order byte of the SR as well as the CCR. The next two instructions give a supervisor program access to the user program's stack pointer. RTE returns control to a program after an interrupt or trap as discussed in Section 14.6.2. STOP loads SR with an immediate value and halts the CPU until an external interrupt or reset input pulse occurs. The RESET instruction sends a reset output pulse to external devices; the effect of a reset pulse is device-dependent.

The last group of instructions in Table 14–6 contains NOP, which does nothing in its inimitable fashion, and two trap instructions that call an operating system or executive as explained in Section 14.6.3.

14.4.5 Regularity and Consistency

Despite the fact that the 68000's instruction set has been touted as being very "regular," the foregoing subsections show that it is far from perfect. In fact, in every computer design the goal of instruction set regularity is at odds with the goal of encoding a powerful set of instructions with a minimal number of bits. Many computers have 16-bit instuction words; once this design parameter is fixed, the designers are limited to an "instruction space" of just 65,536 16-bit combinations.

The flexibility of an instruction is roughly proportional to the amount of instruction space devoted to it. For example, MOVE is the most flexible 68000 instruction, and it uses 12,288 combinations[3] for its three size variations and all its addressing modes. On the other hand, the less flexible EOR uses 1,792

---

[3]Three opcodes in the format of Figure 14–3(a), each with 4096 addressing mode combinations.

combinations[4], and PEA uses only 64 combinations[5]. A completely flexible memory-to-memory version of EOR would have taken 12,288 combinations, while a version of PEA that allowed any register to be used as a stack pointer would have taken 512. Clearly in these and many other cases, the 68000 architects' desire for instruction set "regularity" was outweighed by the limited number of combinations available in the instruction word.

Although the 68000 instruction set is not perfectly regular, it is at least "consistent" in the sense that most of its irregularities are consistent with the machine architects' philosophy, the underlying set of concepts that they used to make design decisions. The 68000's irregularities "make sense" if you agree with the architects' philosophy. Here are some examples:

- Since MOVE is the most frequently used instruction, it should be the most flexible.

- Although there is not enough room for memory-to-memory versions of other instructions, studies have shown that memory-to-register, register-to-memory, and immediate-to-memory versions of double operand instructions satisfy the requirements of a large majority of program applications.

- Since address registers are supposed to hold addresses, there is no need for instructions to manipulate byte quantities in address registers.

- Even though the proper "holes" exist in the instruction set, data manipulation operations such as NEG, BSET, and SWAP should not be allowed on address registers, just to discourage programmers from using address registers to hold data.

- Relative addressing should be forbidden for operands that may be altered; a program should not modify locations in its own memory area. Allowing modifications of program memory destroys program "purity" and could complicate the design of instruction caches and pipelines (e.g., what happens if the program modifies an instruction that has already been pre-fetched?).

- The multiprecision addition and subtraction primitives should use autodecrement addressing, since arithmetic proceeds from least significant digit to most significant, and numbers are typically stored with less significant digits at higher-numbered addresses.

Still, some irregularities can be rationalized only by someone intimately familiar with the machine's design. Some examples in the 68000[6]:

---

[4]One opcode but only three of the eight possible op-mode combinations in the format of Figure 14–3(b), plus one opcode in the format of Figure 14–3(c).

[5]One opcode but only one of the four possible size combinations in the format of Figure 14–3(c).

[6]Rationalizations are based on the author's discussions and correspondence with two of the 68000's architects, Skip Stritter and John Zolnowsky.

- The CMP instruction performs its subtraction in the opposite order from most other machines; the sequence CMP P,Q; BLT LAB branches if Q<P. The 68000's architects opted for "internal consistency" so that SUB and CMP perform the same subtraction. Faced with the same dilemma 10 years earlier, the architects of the PDP-11 let CMP perform the reverse subtraction so that the above instruction sequence has the "natural" interpretation, branching if P<Q.

- The CHK instruction works only on short (16-bit) indices.

- The DBcc instruction only allows a short (16-bit) count. There were only enough opcode combinations available for one version. Since the 68000 has only 16-bit internal data paths, a long-word version would take longer to execute. The architects reasoned that on the rare occasions that a large count was needed, it would be more efficient to use the present version of DBcc and maintain the high-order word of the count outside the inner loop.

- CHK, CLR, TST, and arithmetic shift instructions do not work on address registers, complicating their use as index registers. There were simply not enough opcode combinations available to easily provide these instructions.

- AND and OR work both register-to-memory and memory-to-register, but EOR works only register-to-memory. There were not enough opcode combinations available for the memory-to-register version. Ironically, based on instruction-frequency studies, even a register-to-register version of EOR would have been sufficient.

- The bit manipulation instructions operate on long words in registers, but on bytes in memory. Long-word operations are obviously needed on registers, while byte operations on memory facilitate manipulation of bit strings and byte-oriented peripheral interfaces. There were not enough opcodes available for other options.

- The rotate and shift instructions can shift a byte, word, or long word in a register by 1 to 8 bits statically or 0 to 63 bits dynamically, but can shift only words in memory and by only 1 bit. The architects used the available opcode combinations as best they could.

- Motorola classifies the size of the SWAP instruction as "word," since it is generally used to gain access to the high-order word of a register after a multiply or divide instruction. However, SWAP sets the condition bits according to the long-word result, probably an oversight in the design.

- There is no SWAP instruction that swaps the bytes in a word. However, the bytes in a word may be swapped by ROL.W #8,Dn.

After all these comments, the 68000 architecture may not seem very consistent. However, when we closely examine the other architectures in this book, we find that the 68000 has one of the more well-planned and consistent architectures. The 68000's consistency is exceeded only by that of the PDP-11, a less powerful machine; and its power is rivaled only by the Z8000, whose consistency is no better. If there were a performance measure called the "consistency-power product," the 68000 would fare well.

14.5 SAMPLE PROGRAMS

The simple unsigned multiplication program that we showed for the 6809 in Table 5–4 becomes even simpler when translated into 68000 assembly language, as shown in Table 14–7. Here we have taken advantage of the 68000's general-register architecture by using a register for each of the variables and for the loop count. All of the data manipulation operations deal with long-word quantities, so that the multiplier, multiplicand, and product may all be up to 32 bits long. However, the program does not check for products that take more than 32 bits to express (see Exercise 14.3). The loop structure of the program could be optimized by using the 68000's DBF instruction in place of SUB and BEQ; however, see Exercise 14.2.

Table 14–8 illustrates auto-increment and byte addressing using an address register. The program declares an array of five bytes, and uses the CLR.B instruction to initialize each component. Since the size of the CLR instruction is "byte," at each step the processor increments A0 by one, not two or four.

The program in Table 14–8 was coded for a 68000 system with more than 64K bytes of memory, and so the address kept in A0 was assumed to be a 24-bit quantity. In a system with 64K or fewer bytes of memory, some improvement in program size and speed could be obtained by treating addresses as 16-bit quantities. As shown in Table 14–9, the size of the MOVE and CMP instructions may be changed to "word;" each instruction is one word shorter and executes somewhat faster.

TABLE 14–7 Multiplication by repeated addition.

```
*         Multiplication subroutine works for any two 32-bit unsigned
*         numbers whose product can be expressed in only 32 bits.
*         Enter with multiplier and multiplicand in D0, D1.
*         Exit with product in D2.
          ORG     $1000          Program origin.
START     CLR.L   D2             Set product to 0.
          MOVE.L  D0,D3          D3 holds loop count (multiplier).
LOOP      BEQ     OUT            Done if D3 is down to zero.
          ADD.L   D1,D2          Else add multiplicand to product.
          SUB.L   #1,D3          Decrement loop count...
          BRA     LOOP           ...and check for termination again.
OUT       JMP     $F800          Operating system restart address.
          END
```

TABLE 14–8 Initializing an array of bytes in the 68000.

```
        ORG     $20000          Absolute program origin.
INIT    MOVE.L  #Q,A0           Address of first component.
ILOOP   CLR.B   (A0)+           Clear component and bump to next.
        CMP.L   #Q+5,A0         Past last component?
        BNE     ILOOP           If not, go do some more.
        JMP     $FFF800         Operating system restart address.
*
Q       DS.B    5               Reserve 5 bytes for array.
        END
```

Subroutines in the 68000 are introduced in Table 14–10. The main program initializes SP to point just past the end of a 28-byte stack buffer. Successive pushes, such as subroutine calls, decrement SP, so a maximum of seven long words may be stored in the stack.

In LCNT1S and WCNT1S it is necessary to save the contents of D1 before processing the high-order half of the input number. A subroutine may use the return-address stack for temporary storage as long as it pops as much data as it pushed before returning. Note that even though the subroutines push and pop bytes, the 68000 hardware forces an increment or decrement of two to keep SP aligned on a word boundary.

Both LCNT1S and WCNT1S must swap the halves of their input number in order to count ones in two steps. As shown in LCNT1S, the two 16-bit halves of a data register may be swapped by the SWAP instruction. However, there is no corresponding instruction to swap bytes in the low-order word. Therefore, the program uses a memory location to save the low-order word of D0; then it reads back the high-order byte. It is also possible to use the stack to swap bytes:

```
        MOVE.W  D0,-(SP)        Save the low-order word.
        MOVE.B  (SP)+,D0        Get high-order byte (tricky).
```

This instruction sequence takes advantage of the way that the 68000 maintains word alignment in the SP stack: byte operations access the high-order byte but push or pop an entire word.

TABLE 14–9 Initializing an array of bytes in a 68000 system with 64K bytes of memory or less.

```
        ORG     $2000           Absolute program origin.
INIT    MOVE.W  #Q,A0           Address of first component.
ILOOP   CLR.B   (A0)+           Clear component and bump to next.
        CMP.W   #Q+5,A0         Past last component?
        BNE     ILOOP           If not, go do some more.
        JMP     $F800           Operating system restart address.
*
Q       DS.B    5               Reserve 5 bytes for array.
        END
```

TABLE 14–10   Program that uses subroutines to count the number of "1" bits in a word.

```
          ORG     $20000          Program origin.
*
SYSRET    EQU     $FF800          Operating system restart address.
STK       DS.L    7               Space for 7 return addresses.
STKE      EQU     *               Initialization address for SP.
TLWORD    DC.L    $13579BDF       Test long-word to count 1s.
TEMPD     DS.W    1               Temporary word for byte swapping.
*
MAIN      MOVE.L  #STKE,SP        Initialize stack pointer.
          MOVE.L  TLWORD,D0       Get test long-word.
          JSR     LCNT1S          Count number of 1s in it.
          JMP     SYSRET          Go to operating system.
*
*         Count the number of '1' bits in a long word. Enter with
*         long word in D0, exit with count in low-order byte of D1.
*         The subroutine splits the long word in D0 into two words,
*         and calls WCNT1S to count the number of 1s in each word.
*
LCNT1S    JSR     WCNT1S          Count 1s in low-order word.
          MOVE.B  D1,-(SP)        Save '1' count on stack.
          SWAP    D0              Count 1s in high-order word.
          JSR     PC,WCNT1S
          ADD.B   (SP)+,D1        Add low-order count to high-order.
          RTS                     Done, return.
*
*         Count number of '1' bits in a word. Enter with word in D0,
*         exit with D0 undisturbed and count in low-order byte of D1.
*         The subroutine splits the word in D0 into two bytes, and
*         calls BCNT1S to count the number of 1s in each byte.
*
WCNT1S    MOVE.W  D0,D2           Use D2 to pass bytes to BCNT1S.
          JSR     BCNT1S          Count 1s in low-order byte.
          MOVE.B  D1,-(SP)        Save '1' count on stack.
          MOVE.W  D0,TEMPD        Use memory to swap bytes.
          MOVE.B  TEMPD,D0        Get high-order byte.
          JSR     PC,WCNT1S       Count 1s in high-order byte.
          ADD.B   (SP)+,D1        Add low-order count to high-order.
          RTS                     Done, return.
*
*         Count number of '1' bits in a byte. Enter with byte in
*         low-order D2, exit with D2 destroyed and count in D1.
*
BCNT1S    CLR.B   D1              Initialize '1' count.
          MOVEQ   #7,D3           Initialize bit number.
BLOOP     BTST    D3,D2           Test bit D3 of input number.
          BEQ     BNEXT
          ADD.B   #1,D1           Update count if bit set.
BNEXT     SUB.B   #1,D3           Get next bit number.
          BGE     BLOOP           Done?
          RTS                     Yes, return.
          END
```

The BCNT1S subroutine counts the number of ones in a byte, a natural application of the 68000's bit manipulation instructions. Register D3 holds the number of the bit to be tested by the dynamic bit-test instruction. The two instructions at BNEXT are a natural place to substitute the DBcc instruction, with a condition of "false":

```
BNEXT    DBF    D3,BLOOP      Get next bit #, branch if <> -1.
```

An application for DBcc with a nontrivial condition is shown in Table 14–11. In this example, combining two conditional tests into one instruction speeds up the subroutine significantly. Since DBcc allows only a one-word count, the maximum buffer size in this example is limited to 64K bytes.

A subroutine that uses two stacks to sort a sequence of input numbers is shown in Table 14–12. Similar to the 6809 subroutine in Table 7–3, this subroutine shows the correspondence between Pascal statements and corresponding 68000 assembly language code. The operation of the Pascal program was explained and illustrated in Section 3.3.

Besides declaring its own two stacks using A0 and A1 as stack pointers, SORT assumes that its caller has already initialized A7 to point into a return address stack. SORT calls other subroutines to print various messages and to read or print a number in D0.

As shown, SORT sorts a sequence of input words. However, it has been carefully written to be easily modifiable to work with bytes or long words. All that is required is to change the definitions of MINNUM and MAXNUM and change all instructions with a suffix of ".W" to ".B" or ".L" for bytes or long words. Not all 68000 programs can be so easily modified to work with different data sizes.

The SORT subroutine may also be easily modified for a different memory size; as shown, it uses long addresses. To improve the size and speed of the program in a system with 16-bit addresses, all ".L" suffixes should be changed to ".W". As before, the example program was carefully written to

TABLE 14–11 String search subroutine.

```
*        Find the first occurrence in BUFFER of a character passed
*        in D0.  Return with Z=0 if character not found, or with
*        Z=1 and A0 pointing just past character if found.
*
SEARCH   MOVE.W #BUFSIZ,D1    Get size of buffer.
         MOVE.L #BUFFER,A0    Point to start of buffer.
         BRA    IN            Check for BUFSIZ=0.
SLOOP    CMP.B  (A0)+,D0      Got a match?
IN       DBEQ   D1,SLOOP      Fall through on match or D1=-1.
         RTS                  Return, Z=1 if character found.
*
BUFSIZ   EQU    1000          Declare size of buffer (must be <64K).
BUFFER   DS.B   BUFSIZ        Reserve storage for buffer.
```

TABLE 14-12 Sorting subroutine for the 68000.

```
*                                    PROGRAM StackSort;  {Based on Table 3-6}
MAXLEN  EQU   200                    CONST maxLen = 200;
SIZE    EQU   201                       stackSize = 201;
MINNUM  EQU   -9999                     minNum = -9999;
MAXNUM  EQU   9999                      maxNum = 9999;
*       Register allocation
*       A0                           VAR spL, spH : address;  {Stack
*       A1                               pointers for stackL and stackH}
*       D0                               inNum,  {Input number}
*       D1                               nNums  {Number of inputs} : integer;
STACKL  DS.W  SIZE-1                     stackL, stackH :
STKEL   DS.W  1                          ARRAY [1..stackSize] OF integer;
STACKH  DS.W  SIZE-1                                {16-bit integers}
STKEH   DS.W  1
*                                    BEGIN
SORT    MOVE.L #STKEL,A0                spL := MemAddress(stackL[stackSize]);
        MOVE.L #STKEH,A1                spH := MemAddress(stackH[stackSize]);
        MOVE.W #MINNUM-1,(A0)           MEM[spL] := minNum-1;
        MOVE.W #MAXNUM+1,(A1)           MEM[spH] := maxNum+1;
        MOVEQ  #1,D1                    nNums := 1;
        JSR    WRMSG1                   writeln('Input sequence: ');
        JSR    READ                     read(inNum); {Returns inNum in D0}
WHILE1  CMP.W  #MINNUM,D0             WHILE inNum>=minNum
        BLT    WHILE4
        CMP.W  #MAXNUM,D0                   AND inNum<=maxNum DO
        BGT    WHILE4                   BEGIN
WHILE2  CMP.W  (A0),D0                    WHILE inNum < MEM[spL] DO
        BGE    WHILE3                       {Top of stackL --> stackH.}
        MOVE.W (A0)+,-(A1)                  PushH(PopL);
        BRA    WHILE2
WHILE3  CMP.W  (A1),D0                    WHILE inNum > MEM[spH] DO
        BLE    OUT3                         {Top of stackH --> stackL.}
        MOVE.W (A1)+,-(A0)                  PushL(PopH);
        BRA    WHILE3
OUT3    MOV    D0,-(A0)                   PushL(inNum);
        JSR    WRNUM                      write(inNum);
        ADDQ   #1,D0                      nNums := nNums + 1;
IF1     CMP.L  #MAXLEN,D1                 IF nNums <= maxLen THEN
        BGT    ELSE1
THEN1   JSR    READ                         read(inNum)
        BRA    IFEND1                     ELSE BEGIN
ELSE1   JSR    WRMSG2                        writeln('***Too many inputs');
        MOVE.W #MINNUM-1,D0                  inNum := minNum - 1;
IFEND1  BRA    WHILE1                     END;
*                                      END; {Inputs are now sorted.}
WHILE4  CMP.L  #STKEL,A0              WHILE spL <>
        BEQ    OUT4                       MemAddress(stackL[stackSize]) DO
        MOVE.W (A0)+,-(A1)             {Move everything into stackH.}
        BRA    WHILE4                   PushH(PopL);
OUT4    JSR    WRMSG3                 writeln; write('Sorted sequence: ');
```

TABLE 14–12   (continued)

```
WHILE5   CMP.L   #STKEH,A1        WHILE spH <>
         BEQ     OUT5                MemAddress(stackH[stackSize]) DO
         MOVE.W  (A1)+,D0            {Print contents of stackH.}
         JSR     WRNUM               write(PopH);
         BRA     WHILE5
OUT5     RTS                      {Return to caller.}
         END                   END;
```

make the change look easy. Notice that address size and data size selections are made independently.

Indexed addressing in the 68000 is illustrated in Table 14–13, a subroutine that finds prime numbers using the sieve of Eratosthenes. Like the 6809 version in Table 7–5, the 68000 program declares an array of bytes with each component corresponding to a number between 2 and 1000. By marking off multiples of known primes, it eliminates nonprimes until only primes remain.

The FNDPRM subroutine begins by loading address register A0 with the effective base address of the PRIME array. This is necessary so that the rest of the program can use based indexed addressing to access components of the array. The code assumes that long (24-bit) memory addresses are needed; in a small (16-bit address) system, the MOVE.L instruction would be changed to MOVE.W. The use of based indexed addressing makes the rest of the program independent of the address size.

As shown, FNDPRM assumes that the array has fewer than 64K components, so that the short based indexed addressing mode is used. However, the program may be modified to use larger arrays: the suffix ".L" should be attached to the index register number in all of the instructions that use based indexed addressing, and the suffix ".W" should be changed to ".L" elsewhere. As in previous examples, the program was carefully written to make the change simple. The selections of index size here and base address size discussed earlier are independent, except that it makes little sense to have large indices in a system with only 64K bytes of memory.

A stack-oriented parameter-passing convention was illustrated in Figure 9–4; a 68000 DIVIDE subroutine that uses this convention is shown in Table 14–14. A main program that calls DIVIDE is shown in Table 14–15. Initially the stack has the state shown in Figure 14–7(a). The main program pushes the input parameters onto the stack in the order shown in Figure 14–7(b), and then calls DIVIDE. The LINK instruction in DIVIDE saves the old frame pointer (A6), sets up a new frame pointer, and reserves space on the stack for a local variable, thus leaving the stack as shown in Figure 14–7(c).

At the end of DIVIDE, the UNLK instruction deallocates local storage on the stack and restores the old frame pointer. In spite of UNLK's efficiency,

TABLE 14–13 68000 version of the Sieve of Eratosthenes.

```
*                                    PROCEDURE FindPrimes;
NPRIME   EQU     1000                CONST nPrime = 1000;
PLIMIT   EQU     32                    pLimit = 32;
PRIME    DS.B    NPRIME-1            VAR prime: ARRAY [2..nPrime] OF boolean;
         DS.L    0                      {Force PLC to word boundary.}
*        Register allocation
*        A0      Holds effective base address of PRIME array.
*        D1,D2   Indices into PRIME array.
*                                    BEGIN
FNDPRM   MOVE.L  #PRIME-2,A0
         MOVEQ   #2,D1               FOR D1 := 2 TO nPrime DO
SETEM    MOVE.B  #1,0(A0,D1)           {Set the entire array true.}
         ADDQ    #1,D1                 prime[D1] := true;
         CMP.W   D1,#NPRIME
         BLE     SETEM
         MOVEQ   #2,D2               D2 := 2; {First known prime.}
*                                    REPEAT {Check integers 2 to pLimit.}
MARKEM   TST.B   0(A0,D2)              IF prime[D2] THEN
         BEQ     NOTPRM                  BEGIN
         MOVE    D2,D1                     D1 := 2 * D2;
         ASL.W   #1,D1                     REPEAT {Mark multiples of D2.}
CLRLUP   CLR.B   0(A0,D1)                    prime[D1] := false;
         ADD.W   D2,D1                       D1 := D1+D2;
         CMP.W   #NPRIME,D1                UNTIL D1 > nPrime;
         BLE     CLRLUP                  END;
NOTPRM   ADDQ    #1,D2                 D2 := D2+1;
         CMP.W   #PLIMIT,D2          UNTIL D2 > pLimit;
         BLE     MARKEM
         JSR     WRMSG1              write('Primes between 2 and ');
         MOVE.W  #NPRIME,D1          D1 := nPrime;
         JSR     PRINTD1             writeln(D1); {Print the number in D1.}
         MOVE.W  #2,D1               FOR D1 := 2 TO nPrime DO
PRTLUP   TST.B   0(A0,D1)              {Print all the primes.}
         BEQ     NEXTP                 IF prime[D1] THEN
         JSR     PRINTD1                 writeln(D1);
NEXTP    ADDQ    #1,D1
         CMP.W   #NPRIME,D1
         BLE     PRTLUP
         RTS                         {All done, return to caller.}
         END                         END;
```

three instructions are still needed to return to the calling program and leave only output parameters on the stack as shown in Figure 14–7(d). Like most other processors in this book, the 68000 would benefit from an RTS n instruction that adds n to SP after popping the return address.

A set of queue manipulation subroutines for the 68000 is given in Table 14–16. The subroutines operate on queues of words in a 68000 system with full 24-bit addresses. They may be easily modified for queues of bytes or long words, and the queue descriptor table format and the subroutines may be optimized for 68000 systems with short (16-bit) addresses. Like the 6809 version in Table 9–18, the code is self-documenting, and so we leave you to read it at your leisure.

TABLE 14–14 A subroutine that passes parameters on a stack.

```
*           Unsigned divide subroutine. Divides a quad word by a long
*           word, producing long-word quotient and remainder. Registers:
*           D0     High-order dividend during subroutine execution.
*           D1     Low-order dividend during subroutine execution.
*           A6     Stack frame pointer.
*           The offsets below define positions of parameters and local
*           variables in the stack relative to the frame pointer (A6).
CNT     EQU    -2            Loop counter.
OLDFP   EQU    0             Old value of frame pointer.
RETADR  EQU    4             Return address.
DVSR    EQU    8             Long-word divisor (input).
HIDVND  EQU    12            High-order long-word of dividend (input).
LODVND  EQU    16            Low-order long-word of dividend (input).
REM     EQU    20            Long-word remainder (output).
QUOT    EQU    24            Long-word quotient (output).
STATUS  EQU    28            0 ==> OK, <>0 ==> overflow (output).
*
DIVIDE  LINK   A6,#-2        Push old A6 and reserve 2 bytes.
        MOVE.W #32,CNT(A6)   Push initial count.
        CLR.W  STATUS(A6)    Initial status OK.
        MOVE.L HIDVND(A6),D0 Keep high dividend and
        MOVE.L LODVND(A6),D1   low dividend in registers.
        CMP.L  DVSR(A6),D0   Will quotient fit in 1 word?
        BLO    DIVLUP        Branch if it will.
        ADDQ   #1,STATUS(A6) Else report overflow.
        BRA    CLNSTK
DIVLUP  LSL.L  #1,D1         Left shift dividend with LSB:=0.
        ROXL.L #1,D0         A carry here from MSB means
        BCS    QUOT1            high DVND definitely > DVSR.
        CMP.L  DVSR(A6),D0   Compare high DVND with DVSR.
        BLO    QUOTOK        Quotient bit = 0 if lower.
QUOT1   ADDQ   #1,D1         Else set quotient bit to 1.
        SUB.L  DVSR(A6),D0   And update high DVND.
QUOTOK  SUBQ   #1,CNT(A6)    Decrement iteration count.
        BGT    DIVLUP        Continue until done.
        MOVE.L D0,REM(A6)    Store remainder.
        MOVE.L D1,QUOT(A6)   Store quotient.
CLNSTK  UNLK   A6            Clean up locals and restore A6.
        MOVE.L (SP)+,8(SP)   Save return address lower in stack.
        ADD.L  #8,A7         Clean up input parameters.
        RTS                  Return.
```

TABLE 14–15   Program that calls stack-oriented DIVIDE.

```
*           Compute PDIVQ := P DIV Q; PMODQ := P MOD Q;
*           where all are long-word variables in memory.
DIVPQ       ADD.L   #-10,SP      Reserve space for output parameters.
            MOVE.L  P,-(SP)      Push low-order dividend.
            CLR.L   -(SP)        Push high-order dividend = 0.
            MOVE.L  Q,-(SP)      Push divisor.
            JSR     DIVIDE       Do the division.
            MOVE.L  (SP)+,PMODQ  Pop remainder and store.
            MOVE.L  (SP)+,PDIVQ  Pop quotient and store.
            TST.W   (SP)+        Test status.
            BNE     DIVOVF       Branch on overflow.
            ...
P           DS.L    1            Storage for P, Q, PDIVQ, PMODQ
Q           DS.L    1               (all long-word variables).
PDIVQ       DS.L    1
PMODQ       DS.L    1
```

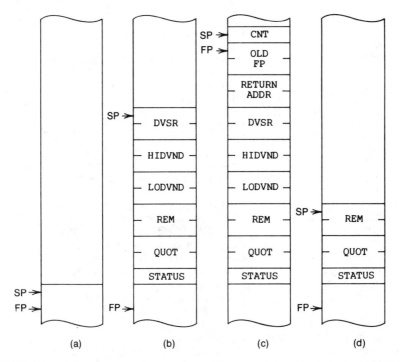

FIGURE 14–7   Stack contents during DIVPQ program: (a) at start; (b) just before calling DIVIDE; (c) after LINK A6,#-2; (d) on return.

TABLE 14-16 Queue manipulation subroutines for the 68000.

```
* QUEUE MODULE
*
* This module contains three subroutines for manipulating queues
* of 16-bit words. A queue is defined by a queue descriptor table
* and a block of storage, as shown below.
*
*                                           QUEUE STORAGE BLOCK
*        --------------------          -------------
* QDTBL | QHEAD (long word) |  -------->|   (word)  |
*       |-------------------|  |        |-----------|
*       | QTAIL (long word) |  |        |           |
*       |-------------------|  |        |   o o o   |
*       | QSTRT (long word) |----        |           |
*       |-------------------|           |-----------|
*       | QEND  (long word) |---------->|   (word)  |
*        --------------------           -------------
*
* Offsets in descriptor table:
*
QHEAD   EQU    0
QTAIL   EQU    4
QSTRT   EQU    8
QEND    EQU    12
*
* In this table, QSTRT and QEND are long-word constants, initialized
* at load time, that give the starting and ending addresses of the
* memory buffer reserved for the queue itself.  QHEAD and QTAIL are
* are long words reserved to store the queue head and tail (absolute
* memory addresses), and are manipulated by the subroutines.
*
* If a program defines several queues, it allocates a separate queue
* descriptor table and storage block for each one.  For example, the
* statements below define a 5-word queue Q1 and a 100-word queue Q2:
*
*Q1BLK  DS.W   5              Storage block for Q1.
*Q1END  EQU    *-2            Last location in Q1 storage block.
*Q1DT   DS.L   2              Q1 descriptor table -- QHEAD and QTAIL.
*       DC.L   Q1BLK,Q1END               QSTRT and QEND.
*Q2BLK  DS.W   100            Storage block for Q2.
*Q2END  EQU    *-2            Last location in Q2 storage block.
*Q2DT   DS.L   2              Q2 descriptor table -- QHEAD and QTAIL.
*       DC.L   Q2BLK,Q2END               QSTRT and QEND.
*
* Subroutines are provided to initialize a queue (QINIT), enqueue
* a word (QENQ), and dequeue a word (QDEQ).  Each subroutine must
* be passed the address of the descriptor table for the queue
* to be manipulated.
*
```

TABLE 14-16   (continued)

```
* SUBROUTINE QINIT -- Initialize a queue to be empty.
*
* INPUTS
*    #QDTBL -- The address of the queue descriptor table for the
*              queue to be initialized, passed in register A0.
* OUTPUTS, GLOBAL DATA, LOCAL DATA -- None
* FUNCTIONS
*    (1) Initialize the queue to empty by setting QHEAD and QTAIL
*        in QDTBL equal to the first address in the queue buffer.
* REGISTERS AFFECTED -- CCR
*
* TYPICAL CALLING SEQUENCE
*        MOVE.L  #Q1DT,A0
*        JSR     QINIT
*
QINIT   MOVE.L  QSTRT(A0),-(SP)  Put buffer starting address
        MOVE.L  (SP),QHEAD(A0)      into QHEAD and QTAIL.
        MOVE.L  (SP)+,QTAIL(A0)
        RTS                      Done, return.
*
* SUBROUTINE QENQ -- Enqueue one word into a queue.
*
* INPUTS
*    #QDTBL -- The address of the queue descriptor table for the
*              queue to be manipulated, passed in register A0.
*    QDATA  -- The word to be enqueued, passed in register D0.
* OUTPUTS
*    QFULL  -- 1 if the queue is already full, else 0;
*              passed in condition bit Z.
* GLOBAL DATA, LOCAL DATA -- None
* FUNCTIONS
*    (1) If the queue described by QDTBL is full, set QFULL to 1.
*    (2) If the queue is not full, enqueue QDATA and set QFULL to 0.
* REGISTERS AFFECTED -- CCR
*
* TYPICAL CALLING SEQUENCE
*        MOVE.L  #Q1DT,A0        Enqueue AWORD.
*        MOVE.W  AWORD,D0
*        JSR     QENQ
*        BEQ     OVFL            Branch if queue is full.
*
QENQ    MOVE.L  A1,-(SP)         Save A1.
        MOVE.L  QTAIL(A0),A1     Get queue tail.
        MOVE.W  D0,(A1)+         Store QDATA at tail (no harm if full).
        CMP.L   QEND(A0),A1      A1 points to next free location.
        BLS     QENQ1            Wrap-around?
        MOVE.L  QSTRT(R0),A1     Reinitialize on wrap-around.
QENQ1   CMP.L   QHEAD(A0),A1     Queue already full?
        BEQ     QENQ2            Return with Z=1 if full.
        MOVE.L  A1,QTAIL(A0)     Else update tail.
        AND.B   #$FB,CCR         Set Z:=0 since not full.
QENQ2   MOVEM.L (SP)+,A1         Restore A1 (CCR not affected).
        RTS                      Return.
```

TABLE 14-16   (continued)

```
* SUBROUTINE QDEQ -- Dequeue one word from a queue.
*
* INPUTS
*    #QDTBL -- The address of the queue descriptor table for the
*              queue to be manipulated, passed in register A0.
* OUTPUTS
*    QEMPTY -- 1 if the queue is empty, else 0; passed in
*              condition bit Z.
*    QDATA  -- The word dequeued, passed in register D0.
* GLOBAL DATA, LOCAL DATA -- None.
* FUNCTIONS
*    (1) If the queue described by QDTBL is empty, set QEMPTY to 1.
*    (2) If the queue isn't empty, dequeue QDATA and set QEMPTY to 0.
* REGISTERS AFFECTED -- D0, CCR
*
* TYPICAL CALLING SEQUENCE
*         MOVE.L  #Q1DT,A0        Dequeue a word into AWORD.
*         JSR     QDEQ
*         BEQ     UNDFL           Branch if queue is empty.
*         MOVE.W  D0,AWORD
*
QDEQ      MOVE.L  A1,-(SP)        Save A1.
          MOVE.L  QHEAD(A0),A1    Get copy of head.
          CMP.L   QTAIL(R0),A1    Queue empty?
          BEQ     QDEQ2           Return with Z=1 if empty.
          MOVE.W  (A1)+,D0        Read QDATA word from queue.
          CMP.L   QEND(A0),A1     A1 points to next queue item.
          BLS     QENQ1           Wrap-around?
          MOVE.L  QSTRT(R0),A1    Reinitialize head on wrap-around.
QDEQ1     MOVE.L  A1,QHEAD(A0)    Update real head in memory.
          AND.B   #$FB,CCR        Set Z:=0 since not empty.
QDEQ2     MOVEM.L (SP)+,A1        Restore A1 (CCR not affected).
          RTS                     Return.
```

14.6 INPUT/OUTPUT, INTERRUPTS, AND TRAPS

14.6.1 Input/Output

Like the 6809, the 68000 uses memory-mapped I/O. Similar to the examples in Chapters 10 and 11, I/O devices connected to a 68000 are controlled by interface registers that are read and written as locations in the memory address space.

Most computers communicate with terminals using the asynchronous serial I/O protocol described in Appendix C. The Motorola 6850 Asynchronous Communications Interface Adapter (ACIA) is an LSI interface circuit that may be used in a 68000 system to send and receive data in this serial format. A CPU controls the ACIA through two input ports and two output ports whose characteristics are described in Appendix C.3. A system has one ACIA for each serial I/O link, usually at least one for the "system console." The port addresses of ACIAs and other devices are system-dependent.

A hypothetical 68000 system could have console ACIA ports at the addresses shown in Table 14–17. These addresses are in the top 32K bytes of the address space, so that the ports may be accessed by short absolute addressing. Also notice that the port addresses differ by 2 instead of 1. This occurs because the 6850 and many other LSI peripheral circuits were originally designed for microprocessors with an 8-bit data bus. Such a circuit can be connected to only one byte of the 68000's 16-bit data bus. Depending on how it is connected, the circuit can respond to even addresses or odd addresses but not both.

Assuming that a 6850 ACIA exists at the addresses given in Table 14–17, Table 14–18 shows a subroutine CINIT that initializes the ACIA and a subroutine CRTIN that reads and echoes one character each time it is called. By referring to the ACIA description in Appendix C.3, you can see how the subroutines initialize the ACIA and then perform busy-wait I/O. The equated symbols in the first three lines of the program may be modified for different ACIA port addresses or mode requirements.

The 68000's MOVEP instruction was specifically included to facilitate access to peripheral circuits whose I/O programming models contain blocks of bytes at either successive even addresses or successive odd addresses. Circuits that fall into this category include Motorola's 68120 Intelligent Peripheral Controller and Zilog's 8010 Memory Management Unit. The instruction MOVEP.L Dn,offset16(Am) splits up the long word in a data register into four bytes and deposits the bytes into every second memory byte beginning at an address specified by based addressing. An example of MOVEP's use is shown in Table 14–19.

14.6.2 Interrupts

The 68000 CPU supports a seven-level, vectored priority interrupt system. It has three input lines, IPL2–0, to which external hardware must apply a 3-bit number giving the current interrupt priority level (IPL). The external hardware resolves multiple interrupt requests to arrive at the current IPL. An

TABLE 14–17 Console ACIA addresses in a hypothetical 68000 system.

Port Name	Type	Address
Control	Output	$FFF000
Status	Input	$FFF000
Transmitter Data	Output	$FFF002
Receiver Data	Input	$FFF002

TABLE 14–18 ACIA initialization and input/echo subroutines for the 68000.

```
CRTCS    EQU     $FFF000         Console ACIA control and status.
CRTDTA   EQU     $FFF002         Console ACIA xmt and rcv data.
CMODE    EQU     $11             ACIA mode control:  8 data bits,
*                                no parity, 2 stop bits, RTS active,
*                                divide-by-16 clock, no interrupts.
CRESET   EQU     $03             ACIA mode control reset.
RCVRDY   EQU     0               Receiver ready bit # in ACIA status port.
XMTRDY   EQU     1               Transmitter ready bit #.
*
CINIT    MOVE.B  #CRESET,CRTCS   Initialize console ACIA by
         MOVE.B  #CMODE,CRTCS      sending master reset and mode.
         RTS
*
CRTIN    BTST.B  #RCVRDY,CRTCS   Check for character.
         BEQ     CRTIN           Busy wait if buffer empty.
         MOVE.B  CRTDTA,D0       Read the character.
CRTWT    BTST.B  #XMTRDY,CRTCS   Can we echo the character now?
         BEQ     CRTWT           No, wait for previous character.
         MOVE.B  D0,CRTDTA       OK, echo the received character
         RTS                       and return to calling program.
```

IPL of 0 indicates that no interrupt is pending, while values of 1 to 7 indicate that at least one interrupt is pending.

Like other CPUs, the 68000 checks for and accepts interrupts only between instructions. It compares the IPL with the current "processor priority" contained in SR bits 10–8. If the IPL is greater than the processor priority, then the CPU acknowledges the interrupt and initiates interrupt processing. Otherwise the CPU continues program execution. IPL values 1 through 6 give rise to "normal" interrupts with level 6 having the highest priority. IPL values 0 and 7 are special:

TABLE 14–19 68000 code for moving a table from memory to a peripheral.

```
*        This code reads a table of 4*N bytes beginning at memory
*        address MEMTBL and deposits them in 4*N alternating bytes
*        beginning at address PERIPH and ending at PERIPH + 8*N - 2.
*
         MOVE.W  #N,D0           Get word count.
         MOVE.L  #MEMTBL,A0      Set up address of table.
         MOVE.L  #PERIPH,A1      Set up address of peripheral.
         BRA     IN              Check for N=0.
TLOOP    MOVE.L  (A0)+,D1        Get word from table.
         MOVEP.L D1,0(A1)        Transfer to peripheral.
         ADD.L   #8,A1           Get next peripheral address.
IN       DBF     D0,TLOOP        Done with N long words?
         ...                     Fall through when done.
```

- An IPL of 0 can never be greater than the processor priority and is therefore used to indicate that no interrupt is pending.

- An IPL of 7 is acknowledged even if the processor priority is 7. Therefore interrupt level 7 is "non-maskable."

The conditions for which a device generates an interrupt request depend on the device, but typically the interrupt enable bit in the device interface must be "on" and some kind of event must have occurred at the device. In a 68000 system, external hardware sorts out interrupt requests from all the devices and applies the number of the highest-priority request to the CPU's IPL input. If IPL is 7 or if it is greater than the CPU priority, the request is acknowledged; otherwise the request remains pending.

Once the 68000 CPU has decided to acknowledge an interrupt request, it performs several steps:

(1) The CPU makes an internal copy of SR.

(2) The CPU sets the processor priority in SR equal to IPL to prevent further interrupts at the same or lower levels.

(3) The CPU enters supervisor state by setting the S bit in SR to 1.

(4) The CPU clears the T bit in SR to inhibit tracing.

(5) The CPU pushes PC onto the stack. Then it pushes its internal copy of the old SR onto the stack. Since the CPU is in supervisor state, these operations use the supervisor stack pointer (A7').

(6) The CPU gives the device interface an opportunity to identify itself: the device may place an 8-bit "interrupt vector" on the data bus. The same external hardware that resolved among multiple interrupt requests to generate IPL must also decide which interface gets to put its interrupt vector on the data bus.

(7) The CPU uses the 8-bit interrupt vector as an index into a table of 256 long words beginning at memory address 0. For example, if the interrupt vector is n, then the CPU reads the long word beginning at memory address $4 \cdot n$. Each long word in the table should contain the starting address of an interrupt service routine.

(8) The CPU jumps to the interrupt service routine, using the starting address that it fetched from the vector table.

Although there are 256 possible interrupt vectors, the 68000 CPU uses the first 64 for traps and other CPU functions; I/O devices generally use the last 192 vectors. We should also point out that "lazy" devices need not supply an interrupt vector. Instead, they may activate a signal that instructs the CPU to use vector number $24+n$, where n is the IPL of the interrupt request. This "autovector" feature may be used in small systems to provide seven vectored interrupts with very little external hardware for priority arbitration. The choice of whether a device uses the autovector feature or supplies its own vector belongs to the system hardware designer.[7]

A program that uses interrupts to print strings of characters is shown in Table 14–20. The program assumes that a Motorola 6850 ACIA is attached to

TABLE 14–20 Interrupt-driven CRT output.

```
*          Define addresses and bit patterns for CRT ACIA.
CRTCS    EQU   $FFF000        ACIA control and status port.
CRTDTA   EQU   $FFF002        ACIA XMT and RCV data ports.
CRTVECT  EQU   25             ACIA interrupts -- level 1 autotor.
CRESET   EQU   $03            ACIA control pattern for reset.
CMODE    EQU   $11            Basic ACIA operating mode.
CINTON   EQU   $20            ACIA XMT interrupt enable bit.
CINTOFF  EQU   $00            ACIA interrupts disabled.
*
         ORG   $2000
*          Global and local variables.
CRTBSY   DS.B  1              Nonzero when string is being displayed.
BPNT     DS.L  1              Pointer to next character to display.
*
*          Messages printed by main program.
MSG1     DC.B  'This line is terminated by CR and LF',$0D,$0A,0
MSG2     DC.B  'This one is has two line feeds',$0D,$0A,0A,0
         DS.W  0              Force PLC to even value.
*
*          CRT output initialization, pointer to string passed in A0.
CRTOUT   TST.B  CRTBSY        Still busy with previous string?
         BNE    CRTOUT        Yes, wait for completion.
         MOVE.B #1,CRTBSY     Mark CRT busy for new string.
         MOVE.B #CMODE+CINTOFF,CRTS  Set ACIA mode, ints off.
         MOVE.B (A0)+,CRTDTA  Send first character to ACIA.
         MOVE.L A0,BPNT       Save pointer to next character.
         MOVE.B #CMODE+CINTON,CRTCS  Enable ACIA XMT ints.
         RTS                  Done, return.
*
*          CRT output interrupt handler.
CRTINT   MOVEM.L D0/A0,-(SP)  Save working registers.
         MOVE.L BPNT,A0       Get pointer to next character.
         MOVE.B (A0)+,D0      Fetch the character, is it NUL (0)?
         BEQ    CDONE         We're done if it is.
         MOVE.L A0,BPNT       Else save updated pointer,
         MOVE.B D0,CRTDTA        print the character,
CRTRET   MOVEM.L (SP)+,D0/A0     restore registers,
         RTE                    and return.
CDONE    MOVE.B #CMODE+CINTOFF,CRTCS   Disable ACIA interrupts.
         CLR.B  CRTBSY        CRT is no longer busy.
         BRA    CRTRET        Restore registers and return.
```

---

[7]The designer of a 68000-controlled fuel-injected carburetor would probably use autovectors.

TABLE 14–20 (continued)

```
*         Main program, runs entirely in supervisor state.
MAIN      MOVE.L #$1FFFF,SP    Initialize stack pointer.
          CLR.B  CRTBSY        Mark CRT not busy.
          MOVE.L #CRTINT,4*CRTVECT   Init. interrupt vector table.
          MOVE.B #CRESET,CRTCS Reset CRT ACIA, no interrupts.
          MOVE.W #$2000,SR     Supervisor state, CPU priority = 0.
LOOP      ...                  Do some computation.
          MOVE.L #MSG1,A0      Get address of first message
          JSR    CRTOUT            and print it.
          ...                  Do some more computation.
          MOVE.L #MSG2,A0      Get address of second message
          JSR    CRTOUT            and print it.
          BRA    LOOP          Do it all again.
          END
```

the 68000 at memory addresses \$FFF000 and \$FFF002, requests interrupts at
IPL 1, uses the autovector feature, and is being used for output only. The
string-printing subroutines assume that a string is a sequence of ASCII
characters stored one per byte and terminated by NUL (a zero byte).

The entire program in Table 14–20 is assumed to run in supervisor state
so that it has access to all the privileged instructions, in particular, RTE and
MOVE to SR. The main program initializes the vector table with the starting
address of the CRT output interrupt service routine and resets the ACIA.

The CRT output initialization routine CRTOUT accepts a pointer to a
string to be printed. The variable CRTBSY indicates whether a previous string
is still being printed, so that a new operation is not started until the previous
one is completed. CRTOUT sets up the ACIA operating mode, prints the first
character, enables the ACIA to interrupt after the character has been printed,
and returns to the main program.

Remaining characters are printed by the interrupt service routine
CRTINT. Before entering CRTINT, the CPU pushes only PC and SR onto the
supervisor stack, so it is up to CRTINT to save and restore any other registers
that it uses. Thus A0 and D0 are pushed onto the supervisor stack at the
beginning of CRTINT and popped at the end. The RTE instruction pops SR and
PC from the stack, effecting a return to the interrupted program.

14.6.3 Traps

A trap in the 68000 causes the same kind of processing as an interrupt:
the CPU changes to supervisor state, pushes PC and SR, and jumps to a
service routine whose starting address is read from the interrupt vector table.
The 68000 recognizes a large number of traps from various sources; their vector
numbers and names are as follows:

2   Bus error: a nonexistent memory or protection error detected by an external memory management unit.

3   Address error: attempting to access a word or long word at an odd address.

4   Illegal instruction: attempting to execute an instruction with an illegal combination of opcode and addressing mode.

5   Zero divide: attempting to divide by zero.

6,7   Conditional trap instruction: executing CHK or TRAPV and satisfying the conditions for a trap.

8   Privilege violation: attempting to execute a privileged instruction in user state. This trap allows an operating system to gain control if a user program attempts to thwart it.

9   Trace: completing the execution of an instruction when the T bit was 1 at the beginning of the instruction. This feature may be used by a debugger to single-step a program as follows. The debugger executes an RTE to the user program such that the SR value restored from the stack has the T bit set. The CPU then executes one instruction of the user program and returns control to the debugger via the trace trap.

10,11   Unimplemented instruction: attempting to execute an instruction with a high-order nibble of 1010 or 1111. These opcodes will be used in future 68000 processors for additional instructions such as floating-point arithmetic and string manipulation. Current users may write service routines to emulate these unimplemented instructions.

32–47   Unconditional trap instruction: executing TRAP vector, where vector ranges from 0 to 15. These instructions are typically used to call various operating system utilities.

The designers of the 68000 have reserved vectors 0 through 63 for system use, leaving 64 through 255 for I/O devices. Besides the traps listed above, the system vectors include the autovectors (25–31), a spurious interrupt vector (24), and a reset vector (0,1). The remaining system vectors are unassigned and reserved for future use.

The reset condition is handled differently from interrupts and traps. When a reset signal is applied to the 68000, the CPU comes up in supervisor state with processor priority 7. No assumptions are made about the validity of the processor registers, and so the CPU does not save the old PC and SR. Instead, it immediately loads the supervisor SP with a value fetched from vector table entry 0, and loads the PC with a value fetched from vector table entry 1. Then it begins instruction execution at the address contained in PC.

Motorola classifies interrupts, traps, and reset as "exceptions." The 68000 handles more exceptions than any other processor in this book.

REFERENCES

The architects of the 68000 described their processor in "A Microprocessor Architecture for a Changing World" [by Skip Stritter and Tom Gunter, in *Computer*, Vol. 12, No. 2]. Although the title may sound a bit sociological, the article is a good technical discussion of the 68000 system architecture and the philosophy behind it. The MC68000 integrated circuit itself is a microprogrammed processor; its internal structure is described in "Design and Implementation of System Features for the MC68000" by John Zolnowsky and Nick Tredennick [*Proc. Compcon Fall 1979*] and in "Microprogrammed Implementation of a Single Chip Microprocessor" by Stritter and Tredennick [*Proc. 11th Ann. Microprogramming Workshop*, Nov. 1978].

Of course Motorola publishes quite a bit of technical information on the 68000, including *MC68000 16-bit Microprocessor User's Manual* [second edition, Jan. 1980] which describes only the processor features, and *MC68000 Cross Macro Assembler Reference Manual* [third edition, Sept. 1979] which describes the assembly language that we've used in this chapter. Motorola also publishes a handy *MC68000 Reference Summary*; call it a "pocket reference card" if you have a large pocket.

EXERCISES

14.1   About how long does the multiplication program in Table 14–7 take to execute in the worst case? Show how to speed up the worst-case performance by several orders of magnitude, still performing multiplication by repeated addition.

14.2   A programmer recoded the multiplication program in Table 14–7 as shown below and found that it sometimes gave incorrect results. Explain.

```
START   CLR.L   D2          Set product to 0.
        MOVE.L  D0,D3       Set up iteration count for DBF.
        BRA     IN          Go do it.
LOOP    ADD.L   D1,D2       Add multiplicand to product.
IN      DBF     D3,LOOP     Decrement multiplier and repeat.
OUT     JMP     $F800       Return to operating system.
```

14.3   Rewrite the multiplication program in Table 14–7 so that it produces a quad word result and gives the correct result for all input numbers.

14.4   Is the DBT instruction good for anything?

14.5   Rewrite the FNDPRM subroutine in Table 14–13 to find primes among the first 8000 integers, still using only a 1000-byte array. This is an excellent application of the 68000's dynamic bit manipulation instructions.

14.6   Write an unsigned multiplication subroutine that takes two long words and produces a quad-word result, using MULU as a primitive. Use a stack-oriented parameter-passing convention, and write a prologue for the subroutine that shows inputs, outputs, registers affected, and a typical calling sequence.

14.7   Modify the queue module in Table 14–16 to run more efficiently in a 68000 system with only 16-bit addresses. Be sure to show documentation as well as coding changes.

14.8   Write a 68000 subroutine that adds two 56-bit numbers P and Q and produces a 56-bit sum S, where each number is stored in seven sequential memory bytes.

14.9   Write a 68000 subroutine that adds two BCD numbers P and Q and produces a sum S, where each number contains eight digits and a sign digit in 10's-complement representation. The numbers are stored in memory, but you are to define the exact format.

14.10   Devise a coroutine calling convention for the 68000 in which each coroutine has its own stack.

14.11   Recode Table 14–14 without the benefit of MOVEP. Compare the size and execution time of the two approaches.

14.12   Compare the efficiency of the 68000's MOVEP instruction with the Z8000's block I/O instructions.

14.13   Write a keyboard input and display output module for the 68000, similar to the 6809 module in Table 10–4.

14.14   Setting and clearing the ACIA transmitter interrupt bit in Table 14–20 seems like a natural application of the 68000's bit manipulation instructions. Why can't these instructions be used?

14.15   Write a complete Pascal simulation of the 68000.

15

ZILOG Z8000

The Zilog Z8000 was the first single-chip microprocessor to support many features previously found only in larger minicomputers and maxicomputers. These features include sixteen 16-bit general registers, a large memory address space (2^{23} bytes or more), provisions for memory mapping and management, user and supervisor modes of operation, string manipulation instructions, multiprecision multiply and divide instructions, and instructions and hardware to support multiprogramming and multiprocessing.

A Z8000 integrated circuit contains a CPU only; the system designer must add external memory and I/O to form a complete computer. Z8000-based computers include Zilog's ZSCAN emulation system and the Onyx C8002 computer.

Actually, "Z8000" is a generic name that refers to two different integrated circuits that can access different amounts of main memory. The Z8001 is the larger of the two; it provides 23 address lines to access a maximum memory size of 8 megabytes. The Z8002 provides only 16 address lines, allowing a maximum memory size of 64 kilobytes.

Much of the discussion in this chapter applies to both the Z8001 and the Z8002, and so we use the generic designation "Z8000." Most of our specific programming examples are written for the Z8002. However, we also point out differences between the Z8001 and Z8002 as appropriate.

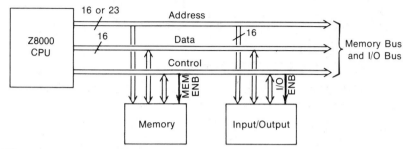

FIGURE 15-1 Z8000-based computer block diagram.

15.1 BASIC ORGANIZATION

A hypothetical processor called the H8000 was described in Section 5.3. The H8000 has a subset of the registers and instructions of the Z8002. In what follows we assume that you have already read Section 5.3.

15.1.1 Computer Structure

The basic structure of a Z8000-based computer is shown in Figure 15-1. The Z8000 processor architecture supports isolated I/O, so that at least logically there could be separate buses for I/O and for memory. However, in the Z8001 and Z8002 integrated circuits, the I/O bus and the memory bus both share the same pins. The processor generates bus control signals to indicate whether a particular transaction using the shared pins is for an I/O interface or for memory.[1]

The data buses in both the Z8001 and Z8002 are 16 bits wide, so that a 16-bit word may be transferred in one bus cycle. In the Z8002, the address bus is also 16 bits wide, supporting an address space of 64K 8-bit bytes. In the Z8001, the address bus is 23 bits wide, supporting an address space of 8M 8-bit bytes.

In both the Z8001 and the Z8002, I/O transactions use a 16-bit address, so that a Z8000 processor may access up to 64K bytes of I/O interface registers (ports) in addition to the main memory. The Z8000 processor contains a

---

[1]The bus control signals also indicate whether the CPU is in user or supervisor mode and indicate the type of memory access — code, data, or stack. In principle a Z8000 system could be designed with six separate main memories, for executable code, working data, and pushdown stack for both the user and the supervisor. Hence the Z8001 is sometimes said to address "up to 48 megabytes" (six times 8 megabytes) and the Z8002 "up to 384 kilobytes." However, in most systems there is just a single main memory (8 megabytes or 64 kilobytes maximum) that is accessed regardless of the type of memory access. The signals that indicate the type of access are typically used by a memory management unit to enforce access rules.

multi-level, vectored, priority interrupt system. Interrupt vectors are found in an area of memory called the "Program Status Area."

15.1.2   Processor Programming Model

The Z8000 processor is a 16-bit general register machine. The processor state of the Z8001 and Z8002 is shown in Figure 15–2. The Z8001 increases the size of certain registers to accommodate its larger address space, as indicated by dashed lines in the figure and as described in Section 15.3.1.

The Z8000 has sixteen 16-bit general registers R0 through R15. Registers R0–R7 may be accessed as sixteen 8-bit registers RH0–RL7 for byte operations. Register R15 is used as a stack pointer to push and pop return addresses during subroutine and interrupt calls and returns.

The Z8000's "Processor Status" consists of a 16-bit program counter (PC) and a 16-bit Flag and Control Word (FCW). There is also a 16-bit Program Status Area Pointer (PSAP) that designates the base address of a "Program Status Area" that contains the interrupt vectors.

The FCW contains four "standard" condition flags called C (carry), Z (zero), S (sign), and P/V (parity/overflow). For BCD operations there are also a half-carry flag (H) and a decimal adjust flag (D). Note that the P/V bit is not standard since it is sometimes set according to two's-complement overflow, sometimes set according to the result's parity (even or odd number of ones), and sometimes left undefined. Therefore, signed conditional branches may give unexpected and unwanted results, especially after the TEST instruction.

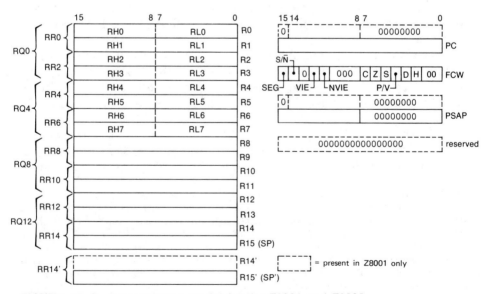

FIGURE 15–2 Programming model for the Z8001 and Z8002.

A number of bits in the FCW are classified as "processor control" bits. As discussed in Section 15.3.1, setting the SEG bit to 1 forces the Z8001 CPU to use segmented addressing; otherwise nonsegmented addressing is used. When set to 1, the VIE and NVIE bits enable the CPU to accept vectored and nonvectored interrupts, respectively. Setting the S/$\overline{N}$ bit to 1 places the CPU in system (supervisor) mode; otherwise the CPU is in normal (user) mode.

Certain instructions are "privileged" and can be executed only in system mode. All I/O instructions and most CPU control instructions are privileged. Also, the Z8000 CPU actually contains two different stack pointers, R15 and R15'. The CPU always uses R15 in normal mode and R15' in system mode. System mode is important in the design of multi-user operating systems employing memory mapping and management, as discussed in Section 7.5.

15.1.3 Instruction Formats

Z8000 instructions have an opcode and an addressing mode designator encoded in one word, and successive words are used to contain additional addressing information as required. Several different formats are used for the first words of different instructions, as required by different operations and addressing modes. For example, six different formats were shown in Figure 5–9, and there are other formats as well.

Many Z8000 instructions can operate on either words or bytes, depending on the contents of a W/B bit in the instruction (formats 1, 2, and 5 in Figure 5–9). Some instructions can also operate on 32-bit "long words;" the long-word version usually has an opcode encoding completely different from the word/byte version.

Rather than give all the details of instruction encoding, we shall concentrate on the effects and assembly language format of various Z8000 operations and addressing modes. In most cases it is sufficient to know that a basic instruction is one word long, and that one or two additional words are appended as required for address information and immediate data. Readers interested in the detailed instruction encodings may find them in the manufacturer's literature.

15.2 ASSEMBLY LANGUAGE

Zilog's standard assembly language for the Z8000 is a structured assembly language called PLZ/ASM. The structuring features of PLZ/ASM have much the same purpose as those of SAL, a structured assembly language described in Section 6.6. The syntax of SAL is derived from Pascal, but the syntax of PLZ/ASM is much different, being derived from PL/I, PL/M, and Zilog's own PL/Z. Readers interested in the structuring features can find a complete description in Zilog's *Z8000 PLZ/ASM Assembly Language Programming Manual*.

There are a number of other assembly languages that have been defined for the Z8000, including Advanced Micro Devices' MACRO8000 and the one used in Onyx's C8002 system, and cross assemblers that run on PDP-11s and other systems. The basic syntax, notations, and pseudo-operations of these assemblers vary widely. Since no one of these assembly languages is used in a majority of Z8000 systems, we shall continue to use the simple assembly language that we defined for the H8000 in Section 5.3. We simply extend it to include all of Zilog's standard opcode mnemonics and addressing mode notations.

15.3 ADDRESSING

Most Z8000 instructions specify operands in the general registers or in memory. Depending on the type of instruction, an operand may be a byte, a word, or a long word. (There are also instructions, described in Section 15.4, that operate on bits, BCD digits, byte strings, and word strings.) Instructions that manipulate bytes treat registers R0–R7 as a set of sixteen 8-bit registers, RH0–RH7 and RL0–RL7 as shown in Figure 15–2. Furthermore, some instructions treat registers R0–R15 as a set of eight 32-bit registers RR0–RR14 or four 64-bit registers RQ0–RQ12 for manipulating long words or quad words (the lower-numbered register contains the most significant part).

Bytes in memory are assembled into words and long words with the lower-numbered bytes on the left, as shown in Figure 15–3. (There are no instructions that access quad words in memory.) Data is fetched from memory a word at a time, and for reasons of processor efficiency, words and long words must be aligned on word boundaries. That is, the high-order byte of a word or long word must begin at an even address as shown in the figure. The address of a word or long word is the address of its high-order byte.

The Z8000 has a somewhat "irregular" instruction set since not all instructions that specify operands in memory may do so using all addressing modes that make sense. You may think that a 16-bit instruction has enough bits to encode all the desired combinations. However, after we take away eight bits to specify two registers in a double-operand instruction, and one bit to specify operand size, the remaining seven bits cannot encode all possible

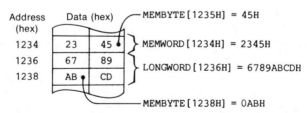

FIGURE 15–3 Addressing bytes, words, and long words in the Z8000's memory.

combinations of operations and addressing modes. Thus, the designers of the Z8000 had to leave out some operation/addressing-mode combinations.

To sort out the instruction set a bit, in Section 15.4 we shall classify as "Memory Reference Instructions" all instructions that can access operands using any of the following addressing modes: Register, Immediate (where applicable), Absolute, Register Indirect, and Indexed. Other instructions that reference operands in memory will be classified as "Special Memory Reference Instructions." Table 15–1 summarizes the Z8000's addressing modes and the assembly language notation for each mode.

15.3.1 Z8001 vs. Z8002

Memory addresses in the Z8001 are 23 bits long, while addresses in the Z8002 are only 16 bits long. The Z8001's addressing scheme is called *seg-*

TABLE 15–1 Addressing modes and assembly language notation of the Z8000.

Mode	Notation	Next Word(s)	Operand
Register	R	none	R
Immediate	#n	n	n
Absolute	addr	addr	MEM[addr]
Register indirect	@RR	none	MEM[RR]
Indexed	addr(RI)	addr	MEM[addr+RI]
Based	RR(#disp)	disp	MEM[RR+disp]
Based indexed	RR(RI)	RI	MEM[RR+RI]
Relative	addr	addr-PLC	MEM[addr]

Notes: R denotes a byte, word, or long-word register as appropriate for the instruction in which register addressing is used.

RR denotes a register that contains an address, R1–R15 in nonsegmented mode, RR2–RR14 in segmented mode.

RI denotes an index register, R1–R15 in either segmented or nonsegmented mode.

n denotes an expression yielding a byte, word, or long word value as appropriate for the instruction in which immediate addressing is used.

addr denotes an address expression yielding a 16-bit value in nonsegmented mode, or a 7-bit segment number and 16-bit offset in segmented mode.

disp denotes an expression yielding a 16-bit displacement value in either segmented or nonsegmented mode.

MEM[x] denotes the memory byte, word, or long word starting at address x, as appropriate for the instruction.

PLC denotes the address of the word following the instruction.

In based and indexed addressing in segmented mode, address addition is performed only on the 16-bit offset part, with no carry into the segment number part.

In relative addressing in segmented mode, the operand address must be in the same segment as the instruction.

The assembler distinguishes relative addressing from absolute by the opcode mnemonic (e.g., LDR addr vs. LD addr).

mented mode, while the Z8002's is called *nonsegmented mode*. The Z8001 can be forced to operate in the Z8002's nonsegmented mode by clearing bit 15 of the FCW.

In the subsections that follow, we shall give a description of each addressing mode as it is used in nonsegmented mode (Z8002, 16-bit addresses). In the last paragraph of each subsection, we describe any differences in the addressing mode's behavior in segmented mode (Z8001, 23-bit addresses). Thus, if you're not interested in the Z8001's segmented mode, don't read the last paragraph of any of the following subsections, or the rest of this one!

The address space of the Z8001 is partitioned into 128 segments of 64K bytes each, a total of 2^{23} bytes. A 23-bit address in the Z8001 may be stored in a register pair, such as RR2 as shown in Figure 15–4(a). A 7-bit segment number is specified in the even-numbered register, and a 16-bit offset is specified in the odd-numbered register. The shaded bits in the even-numbered register are not used. The processor forms a 23-bit operand address by concatenating the segment number and the offset.

A 23-bit address may also be stored in memory as part of an instruction. In this case, the format in Figure 15–4(b) or (c) is used. In Figure 15–4(b), the segment number and offset are stored in two successive memory words; this is called *long offset format*. This format looks the same as the one used with register pairs, except that the MSB of the first word is set to 1. Once again, the processor forms a 23-bit address by concatenating the segment number and the offset.

In Figure 15–4(c) the segment number and a short 8-bit offset are stored in a single memory word with the MSB set to 0; this is called *short offset format*. In this case, the processor forms a 23-bit address by concatenating the segment number, eight 0s, and the 8-bit offset. Thus, the first 256 bytes in a segment may be addressed in short offset format.

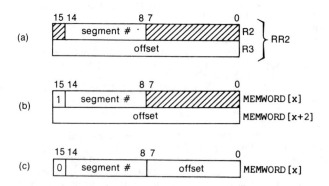

FIGURE 15–4 Format of 23-bit addresses in segmented mode: (a) stored in a register pair; (b) with long offset, two words in an instruction; (c) with short offset for the first 256 addresses in a segment, one word in an instruction.

Z8001 instructions that require an absolute address may store the address in either long or short offset format. When the processor executes the instruction, it determines whether the long or short format has been used by examining the MSB of the first (and possibly only) address word.

Since a Z8001 address consists of a segment number and an offset, a Z8001 assembler must keep track of both parts of the address when assigning address values to symbols in the symbol table. A special notation must be provided if a programmer wishes to explicitly define an address. For example, in PLZ/ASM the notation <<*segment*>>*offset* in an expression denotes an address in segment number *segment*, with offset value *offset*.

A typical assembler for the Z8001 will automatically use short offset format for an absolute address if the offset part is known to be less than 256 during Pass 1 of the assembly. Provisions are also made for forcing either short offset or long offset format regardless of the value of the offset part.

The Z8001's address computations in based, indexed, relative, and auto-increment/decrement addressing affect only the offset part of an address, so that the segment number of the effective address is never modified. Therefore, a data structure with more than 64K bytes cannot always be accessed directly. For example, it is impossible to directly access items in a million-component array using Z8000 indexed addressing. In exchange for this programming inconvenience, the designers of the Z8000 obtained certain hardware efficiencies and helped ensure Z8001/Z8002 compatibility.

The programming model of the Z8001 differs slightly from that of the Z8002 as shown in Figure 15–2 because of the Z8001's longer addresses. In the Z8001, the PC and PSAP are both two words long, in the format of Figure 15–4(a) with the shaded bits set to 0. The normal and system stack pointers are also two words long, RR14 and RR14'. The "Program Status" of the Z8001 is a total of four words long: two-word PC, one-word FCW and one word of all 0s reserved for future use.

The MSB of the FCW is called "SEG"; a 1 in this bit position forces the CPU to operate in segmented mode, and a 0 forces nonsegmented mode. In the Z8002, this bit is always 0. A Z8001 program can set SEG to either value, and thus emulate the Z8002's addressing modes by setting SEG to 0.

15.3.2   Register

In *register addressing*, the operand is contained in one of the processor's sixteen general registers. Depending on the size of the operand, it may be contained in one of the regular 16-bit registers (R0–R15), or in one of the different-sized "pseudo" registers (RL0–RL7, RH0–RH7 for bytes; RR0, RR2, . . ., RR14 for long words). Typical instructions specify one or two registers using one or two 4-bit fields in the instruction, as in Figure 15–5(a).

Register addressing is the same in segmented or nonsegmented mode.

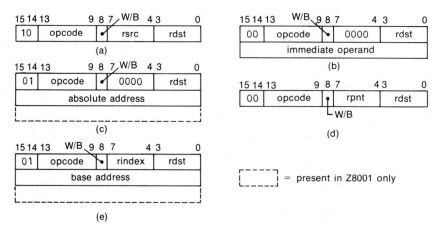

FIGURE 15–5 Typical encodings of memory reference instructions with different addressing modes: (a) register; (b) immediate; (c) absolute; (d) register indirect; (e) indexed.

15.3.3 Immediate

In *immediate addressing*, the instruction contains the operand. In the Z8000, immediate addressing may be used by any memory reference instruction for which it makes sense. Instructions for which it does *not* make sense include jump, call, and single-operand instructions.

Depending on the operation, an immediate operand may be one, two, or four bytes long. One-byte immediate operands are usually stored in the high-order byte of the second word of the instruction, wasting the low-order byte (although some assemblers may replicate the immediate value in the low-order byte). Two-byte (word) immediate operands fit nicely into the second word of the instruction as shown in Figure 15–5(b), and four-byte (long-word) immediate operands occupy the second and third words of the instruction.

Immediate addressing is the same in segmented or nonsegmented mode.

15.3.4 Absolute

In *absolute addressing* (which Zilog calls *direct*), the instruction contains the 16-bit absolute memory address of the operand. Absolute addressing may be used with any memory reference instruction. A typical instruction with absolute addressing is two words long — one word for the opcode and one word for the absolute memory address, as shown in Figure 15–5(c).

The instruction LDB RL2, 2000H loads 8-bit register RL2 with the 8-bit value stored at memory address 2000H. On the other hand, the instruction LD R2, 2000H must load the entire 16-bit register R2. In this case, 2000H is considered to be the address of the high-order byte of a word. Thus, RH2 is loaded with a byte from memory address 2000H and RL2 is loaded with a byte from address 2001H. Both the LDB and LD instructions contain a 16-bit address, but the W/B bit in the instruction tells the CPU whether it must load a byte or a word starting at that memory address.

In segmented mode, absolute addresses are one or two words long, encoded in short or long offset format. Thus a typical instruction using absolute addressing is two words long if it accesses an operand in the first 256 bytes of a segment, three words long otherwise.

15.3.5 Register Indirect

In *register indirect addressing*, a specified register contains the 16-bit effective address of the operand. Any general register except R0 may be specified (i.e., R1–R15 may be used). Register indirect addressing is available with all memory reference instructions.

Referring to the instruction formats and addressing mode encodings shown in Figure 15–5(b) and (d), we see that the processor interprets register indirect addressing with R0 as a special case. In this case, the processor does not use R0 or register indirect addressing at all; instead it takes the operand from the next one or two words of the instruction, using immediate addressing as described in Section 15.3.3.

Note that the assembler takes care of creating the proper instruction encoding when immediate or register indirect addressing is specified. If a program attempts to specify register indirect addressing using R0, as in the instruction LD R2,@R0, the assembler will give an error message.

In segmented mode, addresses are two words long and so the instruction must specify which of the eight register pairs (RR0, RR2, . . ., RR14) contains the operand address. In this case, specifying RR0 yields absolute addressing.

15.3.6 Indexed

In Z8000 *indexed addressing*, any of the general registers except R0 may be used as an index register. The effective address of the operand is formed by adding a 16-bit displacement in the specified register and a 16-bit base address contained in the instruction. The contents of the register are not changed. This allows access to arrays and other data structures when the base address is known at assembly time, but the index of the particular element to be accessed must be computed at run time. In the Z8000, indexed addressing is available with all memory reference instructions.

Referring to the instruction formats and addressing mode encodings shown in Figure 15–5(c) and (e), we see that the processor interprets indexed addressing with R0 as a special case. In this case, the processor does not use R0 or indexed addressing at all; instead it takes the operand address from the second word of the instruction, using absolute addressing as described in Section 15.3.4.

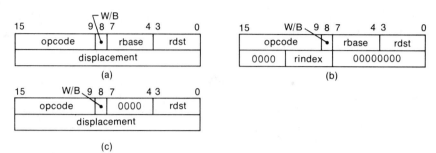

FIGURE 15–6   Typical encodings of memory reference instructions with special addressing modes: (a) based; (b) based indexed; (c) relative with 16-bit displacement.

A base address in segmented mode is contained in one or two words, depending on whether short or long offset format is used. Thus an instruction that uses indexed addressing is two or three words long. The displacement is still contained in a single 16-bit register, any one except R0. This 16-bit displacement is added to the 16-bit offset part of the base address, *with no carry into the segment number part*. Therefore, an attempt to access data beyond the end of a 64K-byte segment simply "wraps around" to the beginning of the segment. If desired, the 16-bit displacement could be considered to be a signed number; a displacement of 0FFFFH (−1) yields an effective address one less than the base address, in the same segment.

15.3.7   Based

In Z8000 *based addressing*, any of the general registers except R0 may be used as a base register. The effective address of the operand is formed by adding a base address in the specified register and a 16-bit displacement contained in the instruction. This allows access to list items and other data structures when the offset to a particular item is known at assembly time, but the base address of the data structure must be computed at run time. In the Z8000, based addressing is only available with Load (LD, LDB, LDL) and Load address (LDA) instructions; a typical instruction encoding is shown in Figure 15–6(a).

In nonsegmented mode, based addressing is logically equivalent to indexed addressing because base addresses and displacements are the same length, 16 bits. Thus the instructions LD R5, 1234 (R2) (indexed addressing) and LD R5, R2 (#1234) (based addressing) have different encodings, but they perform the same action.

In segmented mode, a base address is 23 bits long and must therefore be contained in a register pair in the format of Figure 15–4(a). Any register pair except RR0 may be specified. When the 16-bit displacement in the instruction and the 16-bit offset part of the base address are added, there is *no carry into the segment number part*. Therefore, the effective address always remains within the segment specified in the high-order word of the base address. Note that LD R5,<<3>>1234(R2) (indexed addressing) has a different effect from LD R5,RR2(#1234) (based addressing).

15.3.8 Based Indexed

Based indexed addressing forms an effective address by adding a base address and a displacement, both of which are contained in registers. This allows both the base address of a data structure and a displacement to one of its components to be computed at run time. In the Z8000, based indexed addressing is only available with Load and Load address instructions; a typical encoding is shown in Figure 15-6(b).

In nonsegmented mode, both base address and displacement are 16 bits long and either may be contained in any single-word register except R0.

In segmented mode, a base address is 23 bits long and therefore must be contained in a register pair in the format of Figure 15-4(a).

15.3.9 Relative

In Z8000 *relative addressing*, the operand address is relative to the address of the current instruction. The effective address is computed as the sum of the PC and a displacement contained in the instruction. The PC value used is the address of the word *following* the current instruction.

Relative addressing in the Z8000 is used only by the Jump relative (JR), Call relative (CALR), Decrement and jump if not zero (DJNZ), Load relative (LDR), and Load address relative (LDAR) instructions. The LDR and LDAR instructions are two words long and contain a 16-bit displacement, as shown in Figure 15-6(c). The JR, CALR, and DJNZ instructions are one word long and contain shorter displacement values. In the assembly language notation for all of these instructions, the programmer specifies the desired operand address, and the assembler figures out the proper displacement value to put in the instruction.

In segmented mode, relative displacements are still only 16-bit values. The effective address is the sum of the displacement in the instruction and the offset part (low-order 16 bits) of the PC, *with no carry into the segment number part*. Thus, relative addressing always references an operand within the current segment.

15.4 OPERATIONS

We shall classify Z8000 instructions into six types: memory reference, special memory reference, register reference, program control, string manipulation, and input/output. The I/O instructions are discussed in Section 15.6.

15.4.1 Memory Reference

The Z8000's memory reference instructions are listed in Table 15–2. Each memory reference instruction has one operand (`src` or `dst`) that may be contained either in a register or in a memory location specified by immediate, absolute, register indirect, or indexed addressing. Z8000 assembly language specifies operands in "assignment" order; for example, "LD `reg,src`" may be read "`reg:=src`".

All Z8000 memory reference instructions can operate on 16-bit words;

TABLE 15–2   Z8000 memory reference instructions.

Mnemonic	Operands	Description
LD(B,L)	reg,src	Load reg with src
LD(B,L)	dst,reg	Load dst with reg
LD(B,L)	dst,#data	Load dst with immediate data
EX(B)	reg,src	Exchange reg with src
POP(L)	dst,@reg	Pop into dst, using reg as SP
PUSH(L)	@reg,src	Push src, using reg as SP
ADD(B,L)	reg,src	Add src to reg
SUB(B,L)	reg,src	Subtract src from reg
CP(B,L)	reg,src	Compare reg with src (reg−src)
CP(B,L)	dst,#data	Compare dst with immediate data
AND(B,L)	reg,src	Logical AND src to reg
OR(B,L)	reg,src	Logical OR src to reg
XOR(B,L)	reg,src	Logical XOR src to reg
DIV(L)	reg,src	Divide reg,reg+1 by src
MULT(L)	reg,src	Multiply reg+1 by src
TEST(B,L)	dst	Test dst (dst OR 0)
CLR(B)	dst	Set dst to 0
COM(B)	dst	Complement bits of dst
NEG(B)	dst	Negate dst
INC(B)	dst{,#n}	Increment dst by n
DEC(B)	dst{,#n}	Decrement dst by n
SET(B)	dst,#b	Set bit b of dst
RES(B)	dst,#b	Reset bit b of dst
BIT(B)	dst,#b	Test bit b of dst
TSET(B)	dst	Test MSB of dst, set dst to all 1s

Notes: Each instruction operates on 16-bit words. The notation (B) or (L) indicates an instruction that works on bytes or long words as well. For example, TEST tests a word, TESTB a byte, and TESTL a long word.

In general, a src or dst operand may be specified by register, immediate, absolute, register indirect, or indexed addressing. However, immediate mode is not allowed with LD immediate, EX, POP, CP immediate, or any instruction in the last group (TEST through TSET).

reg may be any byte, word, or long word register, according to the size of the operation.

data is an immediate value appropriate to the size of the operation.

n is an integer from 1 to 16; the assembler uses a default of 1 if the optional ",#n" is missing.

b is a bit number from 0 (LSB) to 15 (MSB).

there are also versions that work on bytes or long words or both as indicated in the table. Most Z8000 instructions set, clear, or hold the condition flags according to the result of the operation, as described in Chapter 8. Refer to a Z8000 assembly language programming manual for detailed flag settings.

The first group of instructions in Table 15–2 are for data movement (LD through PUSH). Data movement instructions in the Z8000 do *not* affect the condition flags.

Z8000 assembly language uses the same mnemonic, LD, for instructions that load from and store into memory, but the machine language actually uses several different opcode encodings for "load" instructions. The assembler must deduce from the operand expression which opcode and addressing mode to use. Note that LD may store an immediate operand directly into memory without first loading it into a register. This is the longest Z8000 instruction, five words when used with a long-word immediate operand and absolute addressing in segmented mode.

The PUSH and POP instructions allow any general register to be used as a stack pointer. Although useful for saving and restoring data and passing parameters, this facility is less general than the PDP-11's, which can perform arithmetic operations such as addition and subtraction on the stack.

Instructions in the second group (ADD through MULT) combine a source operand (src) with an operand in a register (reg) and store a result, if any, in the register. The CP instruction simply compares the operands by subtraction and sets the condition flags accordingly, without storing a result. Note that CP may compare an operand in memory with an immediate value without using a register. The DIV and MULT instructions operate on signed, two's-complement integers; refer to a Z8000 manual for details.

Instructions in the last group in Table 15–2 operate on a single operand (dst) in a register or memory. Most of the operations are self-explanatory. The INC and DEC instructions allow an operand to be incremented or decremented by a small value (1 to 16) contained in the instruction. The TEST instruction sets the condition bits according to the result obtained by ORing its operand with all 0s; TEST should never be followed by a conditional branch that depends on the value of C or P/V.

The SET, RES, and BIT instructions allow a single bit in the destination operand to be set to 1, reset to 0, or tested (Z is set to 1 if the bit is 0). The number of the bit to be tested is contained in the instruction. Another set of bit-manipulation instructions, presented in Section 15.4.3, has both the bit number and the destination in registers. The TSET instruction tests its operand (S is set equal to the MSB) and then sets the operand to all 1s. This is a useful synchronization primitive in interrupt and multiprogramming environments.

15.4.2 Special Memory Reference

Special memory reference instructions may only be used with certain addressing modes, as listed in Table 15–3. Only the LD and LDA instructions

TABLE 15–3   Z8000 special memory reference instructions.

Mnemonic	Operands	Modes	Description
LD(B,L)	reg,src	ba,bx	Load reg with src
LD(B,L)	dst,reg	ba,bx	Load dst with reg
LDR(B,L)	reg,src	rel	Load reg with src
LDR(B,L)	dst,reg	rel	Load dst with reg
LDA	areg,src	a,x,ba,bx	Load areg with address of src
LDAR	areg,src	rel	Load areg with address of src
LDK	r,#k		Load r with k
LDM	r,src,#n	a,ri,x	Load r through r+n−1 from src
LDM	dst,r,#n	a,ri,x	Load dst with r through r+n−1

Notes: src or dst may be specified in any of the addressing modes indicated: ba = based; bx = based indexed; a = absolute; ri = register indirect; x = indexed; rel = relative.
reg may be any byte, word, or long-word register, according to the size of the operation.
areg is a word register in nonsegmented mode, a long-word register in segmented mode.
k is an integer from 0 to 15.
n is an integer from 1 to 16.
r is a word register.

use based and based indexed addressing. There is also a load instruction (LDR) that uses relative addressing.

The LDA instruction loads a register with the effective address of an operand, as computed at run-time. This is useful for passing the addresses of VAR-type parameters to subroutines.

The LDK instruction loads a word register with a small constant, from 0 to 15; the twelve high-order bits of the register are set to 0. The LDM instruction may be used to save and restore multiple registers in memory. Beginning with register r, n registers are saved (or restored) in a block of memory beginning at the address specified by dst (or src). This is useful for saving and restoring the processor state in interrupt service routines.

15.4.3   Register Reference

Register reference instructions only operate on registers; they are listed in Table 15–4. The first group in the table contains miscellaneous arithmetic instructions. The second group contains bit manipulation instructions in which the bit number is specified at run time in a register. The third group contains various rotations and shifts. In the "dynamic" shifts (SDA and SDL), the number of bits by which to shift is also specified at run time in a register. The rotates and shifts generally operate as described in Section 8.8; refer to a Z8000 manual for details.

15.4.4   Program Control

The Z8000's program control instructions are shown in Table 15–5. The first six instructions in the table are the most important. JP and JR jump to the

TABLE 15–4   Z8000 register reference instructions.

Mnemonic	Operands	Description
ADC(B)	reg,src	Add src and C to reg
SBC(B)	reg,src	Subtract src and C from reg
EXTS(B,L)	reg	Extend sign of low-order half of reg
DAB	rb	Decimal adjust byte in rb
SET(B)	reg,r	Set bit of reg specified by r
RES(B)	reg,r	Reset bit of reg specified by r
BIT(B)	reg,r	Test bit of reg specified by r
RL(B)	reg{,#t}	Rotate reg left t bits
RR(B)	reg{,#t}	Rotate reg right t bits
RLC(B)	reg{,#t}	Rotate reg left t bits with carry
RRC(B)	reg{,#t}	Rotate reg right t bits with carry
RLDB	rc,rb	Rotate BCD digits in rb left with rc
RRDB	rc,rb	Rotate BCD digits in rb right with rc
SLL(B,L)	reg{,#s}	Logical shift reg left s bits
SRL(B,L)	reg{,#s}	Logical shift reg right s bits
SDL(B,L)	reg,r	Logical shift reg as specified by r
SLA(B,L)	reg{,#s}	Arithmetic shift reg left s bits
SRA(B,L)	reg{,#s}	Arithmetic shift reg right s bits
SDA(B,L)	reg,r	Arithmetic shift reg as specified by r

Notes: reg may be any byte, word, or long-word register, according to the size of the operation.
rb and rc are byte registers.
r is a word register. In SET, RES, and BIT the register contains a bit number from 0 to 15.
In SDA and SDL, it contains a shift count, -8 to $+8$ for byte shifts, -16 to $+16$ for
word shifts, or -32 to $+32$ for long-word shifts. Positive values denote left shifts,
negative values denote right shifts, and a value of 0 denotes no shift.
s is an integer from 0 to 8, 16, or 32 for byte, word, or long-word shifts, respectively.
The assembler uses a default of 1 if the optional ",#s" is missing.
t is 1 or 2; the assembler uses a default of 1 if the optional ",#t" is missing.

effective address specified by dst only if a specified condition cc is true. The
allowable conditions are precisely the ones that were described in Section 8.6,
but Zilog's mnemonics for the conditions are different, as shown in Table
15–6. The JR instruction contains an 8-bit signed displacement that is multiplied by two and added to the PC if the specified condition cc is true. Thus
the range of conditional jumps is about 128 words forwards or backwards
from the JR instruction.

The CALL and CALR instructions unconditionally call a subroutine at the
destination address, pushing a return address onto the stack pointed to by R15
(or RR14 in segmented mode). The CALR instruction contains a 12-bit signed
displacement that is multiplied by two and added to the PC; thus the target
range is about 2048 words forwards or backwards. The RET instruction exits a
subroutine called by CALL or CALR if a specified condition cc is true.

The DJNZ and DBJNZ instructions subtract one from a specified register
and jump to a destination address if the register has become zero. The displacement is treated as an 7-bit unsigned (nonnegative) number that is multi-

TABLE 15–5 Z8000 program control instructions.

Mnemonic	Operands	Modes	Description
JP	cc,dst	a,x,ri	Jump to dst if cc true
JR	cc,dst	rel	Jump to dst if cc true
CALL	dst	a,x,ri	Call subroutine at dst
CALR	dst	rel	Call subroutine at dst
RET	cc		Return from subroutine if cc true
D(B)JNZ	reg,dst	rel	Decrement reg, jump to dst if reg<>0
LDCTLB	FLAGS,reg		Load low byte of FCW from reg
LDCTLB	reg,FLAGS		Load reg from low byte of FCW
RESFLG	flags		Reset condition flags
SETFLG	flags		Set condition flags
COMFLG	flags		Complement condition flags
TCC	cc,reg		Set LSB of reg if cc is true
SC	#code		System call
NOP			No operation
IRET			Return from interrupt
DI	int		Disable interrupts
EI	int		Enable interrupts
HALT			Halt
LDCTL	ctrl,reg		Load control register from reg
LDCTL	reg,ctrl		Load reg from control register
LDPS	src	a,x,ri	Load Program Status (FCW and PC)
MBIT			Test multi-micro bit
MREQ			Multi-micro request
MRES			Multi-micro reset
MSET			Multi-micro set

Notes: reg may be any byte, word, or long-word register according to the size of the operation.
dst denotes a destination address specified by one of the following addressing modes:
a = absolute; x = indexed; ri = register indirect; rel = relative.
cc is a standard Z8000 condition code chosen from the next table.
code is an arbitrary 8-bit number.
flags denotes any combination of C, Z, S, P, and V, separated by commas.
int denotes VIE or NVIE or VIE,NVIE.
ctrl denotes a control register, such as FCW or PSAP.
Instructions in the last group may be executed only in system mode.

plied by two and subtracted from the PC if the register has become zero. Thus, the instruction may jump up to 127 words backwards.

Instructions in the second group in Table 15–5 manipulate the condition flags. The LDCTLB instruction transfers the low-order byte of the FCW, which contains the flags, to or from any byte register. The next three instructions allow the programmer to set, clear, or complement one or more of the condition flags. The last instruction does not affect the flags, but simply tests their values to see if a specified condition cc is true. If the condition is true, then the LSB of the specified register is set to 1, otherwise the register is unchanged. This instruction is useful in high-level language statements that must evaluate a boolean expression; a result of true may be encoded as 1 and false as 0 in the LSB of a register.

The SC instruction returns control to an operating system or executive as explained in Section 11.3.2. The user may specify an arbitrary 8-bit number as part of the instruction, to select one of 256 different operating system services. NOP does nothing of course.

Instructions in the last group in Table 15–5 are used for interrupt servicing and CPU control. Executing these instructions can do fairly nasty things to the CPU, such as halting it or changing the operating mode, and so the Z8000 CPU only allows these instructions to be executed in system mode. We'll see some of these instructions again when we discuss interrupts in Section 15.6.2.

15.4.5 String Manipulatíon

Although the Z8000 does not have auto-increment and auto-decrement addressing modes for its memory reference instructions, it does have a number of special-purpose instructions for processing blocks or strings of data. These instructions are described in Table 15–7. There are only five basic

TABLE 15–6 Z8000 branch conditions.

Type	Mnemonic	Branch If	Condition
Single Bit			
	(blank)	Always	true
	C	Carry	C = 1
	NC	No carry	C = 0
	MI	Minus	S = 1
	PL	Plus	S = 0
	Z	Zero	Z = 1
	NZ	Not zero	Z = 0
	EQ	Equal	Z = 1
	NE	Not equal	Z = 0
	OV	Overflow	P/V = 1
	NOV	No overflow	P/V = 0
	PE	Parity even	P/V = 1
	PO	Parity odd	P/V = 0
Signed			
	LT	Less than	S XOR P/V = 1
	GE	Greater than or equal	S XOR P/V = 0
	LE	Less than or equal	(S XOR P/V) OR Z = 1
	GT	Greater than	(S XOR P/V) OR Z = 0
Unsigned			
	ULT	Unsigned less than	C = 1
	UGE	Unsigned greater than or equal	C = 0
	ULE	Unsigned less than or equal	C OR Z = 1
	UGT	Unsigned greater than	C OR Z = 0

instructions, but there are three options for each one. The instruction can (a) operate on bytes or words, (b) use auto-increment or auto-decrement addressing, and (c) operate only once or a number of times. Since the options can be selected independently, there are eight versions of each basic instruction. A few examples of program applications for the string manipulation instructions will be given in the next section.

15.5 SAMPLE PROGRAMS

Several sample programs for the H8000 were presented in Section 5.3; these programs are also good examples for the Z8000. Additional sample

TABLE 15-7 Z8000 block and string manipulation instructions.

Mnemonic	Operands	Description
CP(DI)(R)(B)	reg,@rsrc,rcnt,cc	Compare reg with components of string (reg-MEM[rsrc])
CPS(DI)(R)(B)	@rdst,@rsrc,rcnt,cc	Compare components of two strings (MEM[rdst]-MEM[rsrc])
LD(DI)(R)(B)	@rdst,@rsrc,rcnt	Copy components of string (block move) (MEM[rdst] := MEM[rsrc])
TR(DI)(R)B	@rdst,@rsrc1,rcnt	Translate components of string (MEMB[rdst] := MEMB[rsrc1+MEMB[rdst]])
TRT(DI)(R)B	@rsrc,@rsrc1,rcnt	Translate and test components of string (RH1 := MEMB[rsrc1+MEM[rsrc]])

Notes: The notation (B) indicates that the instruction operates on either bytes or words, depending on whether or not a B is present at the end of the instruction mnemonic.
reg is a byte or word register, according to the size of the operation.
MEM[x] denotes a byte or word starting at memory address x, according to the size of the operation.
MEMB[x] denotes a byte at memory address x.
rdst, rsrc, and rsrc1 are word registers in nonsegmented mode, long-word registers in segmented mode.
The notation (DI) indicates that the instruction mnemonic must contain either D or I, indicating auto-decrement or auto-increment addressing, respectively. Accordingly, the instruction increments or decrements rsrc and/or rdst by the size of the operation (1 for bytes, 2 for words) *after* the operation. Note that rsrc1 is never modified.
rcnt is a word register that is decremented after each operation. After an operation that decrements rcnt to zero the P/V register is set to 1, else P/V is set to 0.
In CP and CPS, the two operands are subtracted without storing the result (e.g., reg-MEM[rsrc]). The Z flag is set to 1 if this subtraction would normally result in the condition flag setting specified by cc; otherwise Z is cleared.
In TRT, the Z flag is set to 1 if zero is loaded into RH1; otherwise Z is cleared.
The notation (R) indicates that the processor should or should not automatically repeat the instruction, depending on whether or not the optional R is present in the instruction mnemonic. If the R is absent, the operation is performed once. If the R is present, the operation is repeated until it sets rcnt to zero, or RH1 to a nonzero value (TRT only), or Z to 1 (CP, CPS only).

programs are presented in this section. These programs are written for the
Z8002 or the Z8001 in nonsegmented mode.

A program that uses two stacks to sort a sequence of input numbers is
shown in Table 15–8. This is a direct translation of the 6809 program that was
given in Table 7–3. The program shows the correspondence between Pascal
statements and corresponding Z8000 assembly language code. Input/output
subroutines are assumed to have been defined elsewhere. The subroutine
READ reads a 16-bit number and returns it in R5. Subroutine WRNUM prints a
16-bit number passed to it in R5. The WRMSG subroutines print various messages.

Besides declaring its own two stacks using R2 (SPL) and R3 (SPH) as
stack pointers, the program in Table 15–8 assumes that the operating system
has already initialized R15 to point into a return address stack. It further
assumes that the operating system has called it by executing a CALL SORT
instruction, so that it may return by simply executing RET.

The Z8000 can handle long-word data as easily as word data in many
programs. For example, the program in Table 15–8 can be modified to handle
double-word inputs as shown in Table 15–9. All that has been done is to
change the definitions of some constants and variables, change the register
allocation to make INNUM a register pair, and change the instructions that deal
with input numbers to their long-word counterparts. Lines that were changed
are marked with exclamation points.

Modifying the program for byte data is not as easy, because there are no
PUSHB or POPB instructions. In fact, examination of the Z8000 instructions in
Tables 15-2 and 4 shows that the only instructions we can really count on are
the word instructions.

The program in Table 15–8 could also be modified to work in segmented
mode. In this case, only instructions that depend on the size of addresses
must be modified. Therefore SPL and SPH must be defined to be long-word
registers, and the instructions that load them must be changed accordingly:

```
        ...
SPL     EQU     RR2             VAR spL, spH : address;
SPH     EQU     RR4                 {Stack pointers for stackL, stackH}
NNUMS   EQU     R6              nNums, {Number of inputs}
INNUM   EQU     R7              inNum  {Input number}    : integer;
        ...
SORT    LDL     SPL,#STKEL      spL := MemAddress(stackL[stackSize]);
        LDL     SPH,#STKEH      spH := MemAddress(stackH[stackSize]);
        ...
```

Z8000 indexed addressing is illustrated in Table 15–10, a program that
finds prime numbers using the sieve of Eratosthenes. Like the 6809 version in
Table 7–5, the Z8000 program declares an array of bytes with each component
corresponding to a number between 2 and 1000. By marking off multiples of
known primes, it eliminates nonprimes until only primes remain.

TABLE 15–8   Sorting subroutine that uses stacks.

```
*                             PROCEDURE StackSort; {Based on Table 3-6}
MAXLEN   EQU    500            CONST maxLen = 500;
SIZE     EQU    501              stackSize = 501;
MINNUM   EQU    -9999            minNum = -9999;
MAXNUM   EQU    9999             maxNum = 9999;
SPL      EQU    R2             VAR spL, spH : address;
SPH      EQU    R3               {Stack pointers for stackL, stackH}
NNUMS    EQU    R4               nNums, {Number of inputs}
INNUM    EQU    R5               inNum {Input number}    : integer;
STACKL   RMB    2*SIZE           stackL, stackH :
STKEL    EQU    *-2                ARRAY [1..stackSize] OF integer;
STACKH   RMB    2*SIZE             {16-bit integers}
STKEH    EQU    *-2
*                             BEGIN
SORT     LD     SPL,#STKEL       spL := MemAddress(stackL[stackSize]);
         LD     SPH,#STKEH       spH := MemAddress(stackH[stackSize]);
         LD     @SPL,#MINNUM-1   MEM[spL] := minNum-1;
         LD     @SPH,#MAXNUM+1   MEM[spH] := maxNum+1;
         LDK    NNUMS,#1         nNums := 1;
         CALL   WRMSG1           writeln('Input sequence: ');
         CALL   READ             read(inNum);
WHILE1   CP     INNUM,#MINNUM    WHILE inNum>=minNum
         JR     LT,WHILE4
         CP     INNUM,#MAXNUM        AND inNum<=maxNum DO
         JR     GT,WHILE4         BEGIN
WHILE2   CP     INNUM,@SPL          WHILE inNum < MEM[spL] DO
         JR     GE,WHILE3            {Top of stackL --> stackH.}
         POP    R0,@SPL             PushH(PopL);
         PUSH   @SPH,R0
         JR     WHILE2
WHILE3   CP     INNUM,@SPH          WHILE inNum > MEM[spH] DO
         JR     LE,OUT3              {Top of stackH --> stackL.}
         POP    R0,@SPH             PushL(PopH);
         PUSH   @SPL,R0
         JR     WHILE3
OUT3     PUSH   @SPL,INNUM          PushL(inNum);
         CALL   WRNUM              write(inNum);
         INC    NNUMS,#1           nNums := nNums + 1;
IF1      CP     NNUMS,#MAXLEN      IF nNums <= maxLen THEN
         JR     GT,ELSE1
THEN1    CALL   READ                 read(inNum)
         JR     IFEND1             ELSE BEGIN
ELSE1    CALL   WRMSG2                 writeln('***Too many inputs');
         LD     INNUM,#MINNUM-1        inNum := minNum - 1;
IFEND1   JR     WHILE1             END;
*                               END; {Inputs are now sorted.}
WHILE4   CP     SPL,#STKEL       WHILE spL <>
         JR     EQ,OUT4            MemAddress(stackL[stackSize]) DO
         POP    R0,@SPL            {Move everything into stackH.}
         PUSH   @SPH,R0            PushH(PopL);
         JR     WHILE4
```

TABLE 15-8 (continued)

```
OUT4    CALL   WRMSG3              writeln; write('Sorted sequence: ');
WHILE5  CP     SPH,#STKEH          WHILE spH <>
        JR     EQ,OUT5                MemAddress(stackH[stackSize]) DO
        POP    INNUM,@SPH          {Print contents of stackH.}
        CALL   WRNUM                 write(PopH);
        JR     WHILE5
OUT5    RET                        {Return to operating system.}
        END    SORT                END;
```

TABLE 15-9 Sorting subroutine for long integers.

```
*                                  PROCEDURE StackSort; {Based on Table 3-6}
MAXLEN  EQU    500                 CONST maxLen = 500;
SIZE    EQU    501                    stackSize = 501;
!MINNUM EQU    -9999999               minNum = -9999999;
!MAXNUM EQU    9999999                maxNum = 9999999;
SPL     EQU    R2                  VAR spL, spH : address;
SPH     EQU    R3                     {Stack pointers for stackL, stackH}
NNUMS   EQU    R4                     nNums, {Number of inputs} : integer
!INNUM  EQU    RR6                    inNum {Input number} : longInteger;
!STACKL RMB    4*SIZE                 stackL, stackH :
!STKEL  EQU    *-4                       ARRAY [1..stackSize] OF longInteger;
!STACKH RMB    4*SIZE                    {32-bit long-integers}
!STKEH  EQU    *-4
*                                  BEGIN
SORT    LD     SPL,#STKEL             spL := MemAddress(stackL[stackSize]);
        LD     SPH,#STKEH            spH := MemAddress(stackH[stackSize]);
!       LDL    @SPL,#MINNUM-1        MEM[spL] := minNum-1;
!       LDL    @SPH,#MAXNUM+1        MEM[spH] := maxNum+1;
        LDK    NNUMS,#1             nNums := 1;
        CALL   WRMSG1              writeln('Input sequence: ');
        CALL   READ                read(inNum);
!WHILE1 CPL    INNUM,#MINNUM       WHILE inNum>=minNum
        JR     LT,WHILE4                AND inNum<=maxNum DO
!       CPL    INNUM,#MAXNUM
        JR     GT,WHILE4
!WHILE2 CPL    INNUM,@SPL             BEGIN
        JR     GE,WHILE3              WHILE inNum < MEM[spL] DO
!       POPL   RR0,@SPL                 {Top of stackL --> stackH.}
!       PUSHL  @SPH,RR0                 PushH(PopL);
        JR     WHILE2
!WHILE3 CPL    INNUM,@SPH             WHILE inNum > MEM[spH] DO
        JR     LE,OUT3                  {Top of stackH --> stackL.}
!       POPL   RR0,@SPH                 PushL(PopH);
!       PUSHL  @SPL,RR0
        JR     WHILE3
```

TABLE 15-9 (continued)

```
!OUT3    PUSHL  @SPL,INNUM           PushL(inNum);
         CALL   WRNUM               write(inNum);
         INC    NNUMS,#1            nNums := nNums + 1;
IF1      CP     NNUMS,#MAXLEN       IF nNums <= maxLen THEN
         JR     GT,ELSE1
THEN1    CALL   READ                  read(inNum)
         JR     IFEND1              ELSE BEGIN
ELSE1    CALL   WRMSG2                 writeln('***Too many inputs');
!        LDL    INNUM,#MINNUM-1       inNum := minNum - 1;
IFEND1   JR     WHILE1              END;
*                                 END; {Inputs are now sorted.}
WHILE4   CP     SPL,#STKEL        WHILE spL <>
         JR     EQ,OUT4              MemAddress(stackL[stackSize]) DO
         POP    R0,@SPL             {Move everything into stackH.}
         PUSH   @SPH,R0             PushH(PopL);
         JR     WHILE4
OUT4     CALL   WRMSG3             writeln; write('Sorted sequence: ');
WHILE5   CP     SPH,#STKEH        WHILE spH <>
         JR     EQ,OUT5              MemAddress(stackH[stackSize]) DO
!        POPL   INNUM,@SPH          {Print contents of stackH.}
         CALL   WRNUM               write(PopH);
         JR     WHILE5
OUT5     RET                       {Return to operating system.}
         END    SORT             END;
```

A stack-oriented parameter-passing convention was illustrated in Figure 9–4; a Z8000 subroutine that uses this convention is shown in Table 15–11. Much of this code could be rewritten to be more efficient, but the existing code better illustrates calling conventions and Z8000 instructions. For example, the code at CLNSTK could be rewritten:

```
CLNSTK  LD    R0,RETADR(FP)    Save return addr lower in stack.
        LD    LODVND(FP),R0
```

However, the original code shows the use of indexed addressing with PUSH and POP, and also shows the advantage of a separate FP for constant offsets even when SP is changing.

A main program that calls DIVIDE is shown in Table 15–12. This program operates the same as the PDP-11 DIVPQ program shown in Table 13–18, and the stack has the same states as those shown in Figure 13–7 on p. 421.

A set of queue manipulation subroutines for the Z8000 are given in Table 15–13. Like the 6809 version in Table 9–18, this code is self-documenting, and so we leave you to read it.

To illustrate the Z8000's string manipulation instructions, we consider a subroutine to search for the first occurrence of a character in a buffer, coded without the string manipulation instructions as shown in Table 15–14. The body of this subroutine may be optimized using the CPIRB instruction as shown below:

```
SEARCH  LD    R1,#BUFFER      Point to start of buffer.
        LD    R2,#1000        Buffer size.
        CPIRB RL0,@R1,R2,EQ   Search for match.
*       R1 now points just past matched char and Z=1 if found.
        RET                   Return.
```

The subroutine is obviously shorter, and it is much faster too. According to published instruction speeds for the Z8001 and Z8002 CPU chips, the execu-

TABLE 15–10 Subroutine to find primes using an array and indexed addressing.

```
*                               PROCEDURE FindPrimes;
NPRIME  EQU   1000              CONST nPrime = 1000;
PLIMIT  EQU   32                  pLimit = 32;
PRIME   RMB   NPRIME-1          VAR prime:ARRAY [2..nPrime] OF boolean;
*                                 {reg} R1, R2 : integer;
        ORG   ((*+1)/2)*2       BEGIN  {Force PLC even.)
FNDPRM  LDK   R1,#2               FOR R1 := 2 TO nPrime DO
SETEM   LDB   PRIME-2(R1),#1        {Set the entire array true.}
        INC   R1,#1                 prime[R1] := true;
        CP    R1,#NPRIME
        JR    LE,SETEM
        LDK   R2,#2             R2 := 2; {First known prime.}
*                               REPEAT {Check integers 2 to pLimit.}
MARKEM  TESTB PRIME-2(R2)         IF prime[R2] THEN
        JR    Z,NOTPRM             BEGIN
        LD    R1,R2                  R1 := 2 * R2;
        ADD   R1,R2                  REPEAT {Mark multiples of R2.}
CLRLUP  CLRB  PRIME-2(R1)            prime[R1] := false;
        ADD   R1,R2                  R1 := R1 + R2;
        CP    R1,#NPRIME           UNTIL R1 > nPrime;
        JR    LE,CLRLUP            END;
NOTPRM  INC   R2,#1               R2 := R2+1;
        CP    R2,#PLIMIT        UNTIL R2 > pLimit;
        JR    LE,MARKEM
        CALL  WRMSG1            write('Primes between 2 and ');
        LD    R1,#NPRIME        R1 := nPrime;
        CALL  PRINTR1           writeln(R1); {Print the value in R1.}
        LDK   R1,#2             FOR R1 := 2 TO nPrime DO
PRTLUP  TESTB PRIME-2(R1)         {Print all the primes.}
        JR    Z,NEXTP             IF prime[R1] THEN
        CALL  PRINTR1               writeln(R1);
NEXTP   INC   R1,#1
        CP    R1,#NPRIME
        JR    LE,PRTLUP
        RET                     {All done, return to caller.}
        END   FNDPRM           END.
```

TABLE 15-11   Unsigned division subroutine that passes parameters on a stack.

```
SP       EQU    R15                    System stack pointer.
FP       EQU    R14                    Stack frame pointer.
LODIV    EQU    R1                     Holds low dividend during iterations.
HIDIV    EQU    R0                     Holds high dividend during iterations.
*
*        The offsets below define positions of parameters and local
*        variables in the stack relative to the frame pointer (FP).
CNT      EQU    -2                     Loop counter.
OLDFP    EQU    0                      Old value of frame pointer.
RETADR   EQU    2                      Return address.
DVSR     EQU    4                      1-word divisor (input).
HIDVND   EQU    6                      High-order word of dividend (input).
LODVND   EQU    8                      Low-order word of dividend (input).
REM      EQU    10                     1-word remainder (output).
QUOT     EQU    12                     1-word quotient (output).
STATUS   EQU    14                     0 ==> OK, <>0 ==> overflow (output).
*
DIVIDE   PUSH   @SP,FP                 Push old frame pointer onto stack.
         LD     FP,SP                  Copy SP into FP for new frame pointer.
         PUSH   @SP,#16                Push initial count.
         CLR    STATUS(FP)             Initial status OK.
         LD     HIDIV,HIDVND(FP)       Put high DVND in a register.
         CP     HIDIV,DVSR(FP)         Will quotient fit in 1 word?
         JR     ULT,DIVVY              Branch if it will.
         INC    STATUS(FP),#1          Else report overflow.
         JR     CLNSTK
DIVVY    LD     LODIV,LODVND(FP)       Put low DVND in a register.
DIVLUP   SLL    LODIV,#1               Left shift dividend with LSB:=0.
         RLC    HIDIV,#1               A carry here from MSB means
         JR     C,QUOT1                  high DVND definitely > DVSR.
         CP     HIDIV,DVSR(FP)         Compare high DVND with DVSR.
         JR     ULT,QUOTOK             Quotient bit = 0 if lower.
QUOT1    INC    LODIV,#1               Else set quotient bit to 1.
         SUB    HIDIV,DVSR(FP)         And update high DVND.
QUOTOK   DEC    CNT(FP),#1             Decrement iteration count.
         JR     GT,DIVLUP              Continue until done.
         LD     REM(FP),HIDIV          Store remainder.
         LD     QUOT(FP),LODIV         Store quotient.
CLNSTK   PUSH   @SP,RETADR(FP)         Save return addr lower in stack.
         POP    LODVND(FP),@SP
         LD     FP,OLDFP(FP)           Restore old frame pointer.
         INC    SP,#LODVND-CNT         Remove garbage except LODVND,
         RET                             which contains return address.
```

tion time of the original subroutine is approximately $26+29n$ clock cycles, where n is the number of items searched before a match is found. On the other hand, the execution time of optimized version is only $24+9n$ clock cycles, about three times faster.

TABLE 15-12 Program that calls stack-oriented DIVIDE.

```
*          Compute PDIVQ := P DIV Q; PMODQ := P MOD Q;
*          where all are 1-word variables in memory.
DIVPQ     DEC    SP,#6            Reserve space for output parameters.
          PUSH   @SP,P            Push low-order dividend.
          PUSH   @SP,#0           Push high-order dividend = 0.
          PUSH   @SP,Q            Push divisor.
          CALL   DIVIDE           Do the division.
          POP    PMODQ,@SP        Pop remainder and store.
          POP    PDIVQ,@SP        Pop quotient and store.
          POP    R0,@SP           Get status.
          TEST   R0               Test it.
          JR     NZ,DIVOVF        Branch on overflow.
          ...
P         RMB    2                Storage for P, Q, PDIVQ, PMODQ
Q         RMB    2                   (all 1-word variables).
PDIVQ     RMB    2
PMODQ     RMB    2
```

TABLE 15-13 Queue manipulation subroutines for the Z8000.

```
* QUEUE MODULE
*
* This module contains three subroutines for manipulating queues
* of 16-bit words. A queue is defined by a queue descriptor table
* and a block of storage, as shown below.
*
*                                            QUEUE STORAGE BLOCK
*         ---------------------              ---------------------
* QDTBL  |       QHEAD         |  -------->|                     |
*        |---------------------|    |      |---------------------|
*        |       QTAIL         |    |      |                     |
*        |---------------------|    |      |                     |
*        |       QSTRT         |----       |        o o o        |
*        |---------------------|           |---------------------|
*        |       QEND          |---------->|                     |
*         ---------------------             ---------------------
*
* Offsets in descriptor table:
*
QHEAD     EQU    0
QTAIL     EQU    2
QSTRT     EQU    4
QEND      EQU    6
*
* In this table, the last two words are constants, initialized at
* load time, that give the starting and ending addresses of the block
* of storage (buffer) reserved for the queue itself. The first and
* second words are reserved to store the queue head and tail (absolute
* memory addresses), and are manipulated by the subroutines.
*
```

TABLE 15-13 (continued)

```
* If a program defines several queues, it allocates a separate queue
* descriptor table and storage block for each one.  For example, the
* statements below define a 100-word queue Q1 and a 5-word queue Q2:
*
*Q1BLK  RMW   100              Storage block for Q1.
*Q1END  EQU   *-2              Last location in Q1 storage block.
*Q1DT   RMW   2                Q1 descriptor table -- QHEAD and QTAIL.
*       FCW   Q1BLK,Q1END                      QSTRT and QEND.
*Q2BLK  RMW   5                Storage block for Q2.
*Q2END  EQU   *-2              Last location in Q2 storage block.
*Q2DT   RMW   2                Q2 descriptor table -- QHEAD and QTAIL.
*       FCW   Q2BLK,Q2END                      QSTRT and QEND.
*
* Subroutines are provided to initialize a queue (QINIT), enqueue
* a word (QENQ), and dequeue a word (QDEQ).  Each subroutine must
* be passed the address of the descriptor table for the queue
* to be manipulated.
*
* SUBROUTINE QINIT -- Initialize a queue to be empty.
*
* INPUTS
*    #QDTBL -- The address of the queue descriptor table for the
*              queue to be initialized, passed in register R1.
* OUTPUTS, GLOBAL DATA, LOCAL DATA -- None
* FUNCTIONS
*    (1) Initialize the queue to empty by setting QHEAD and QTAIL
*        in QDTBL equal to the first address in the queue buffer.
* REGISTERS AFFECTED -- R0, FLAGS
*
* TYPICAL CALLING SEQUENCE
*        LD    R1,#Q1DT
*        CALL  QINIT
*
QINIT   LD    R0,QSTRT(R1)     Put buffer starting address
        LD    QHEAD(R1),R0        into QHEAD and QTAIL.
        LD    QTAIL(R1),R0
        RET                    Done, return.
*
* SUBROUTINE QENQ -- Enqueue one word into a queue.
*
* INPUTS
*    #QDTBL -- The address of the queue descriptor table for the
*              queue to be manipulated, passed in register R1.
*    QDATA  -- The word to be enqueued, passed in register R0.
* OUTPUTS
*    QFULL  -- 1 if the queue is already full, else 0;
*              passed in condition flag Z.
* GLOBAL DATA, LOCAL DATA -- None.
* FUNCTIONS
*    (1) If the queue described by QDTBL is full, set QFULL to 1.
*    (2) If the queue is not full, enqueue QDATA and set QFULL to 0.
```

TABLE 15-13   (continued)

```
* REGISTERS AFFECTED -- R2, FLAGS
*
* TYPICAL CALLING SEQUENCE
*         LD    R1,#Q1DT          Enqueue AWORD.
*         LD    R0,AWORD
*         CALL  QENQ
*         JR    Z,OVFL            Branch if queue is full.
*
QENQ      LD    R2,QTAIL(R1)      Get queue tail.
          LD    @R2,R0            Store QDATA at tail (no harm if full).
          INC   R2,#2             Bump to next free location.
          CP    R2,QEND(R1)       Wrap-around?
          JR    ULE,QENQ1
          LD    R2,QSTRT(R1)      Reinitialize on wrap-around.
QENQ1     CP    R2,QHEAD(R1)      Queue already full?
          JR    EQ,QENQ2          Return with Z=1 if full.
          LD    QTAIL(R1),R2      Update tail, Z=0 still.
QENQ2     RET                     Return.
*
* SUBROUTINE QDEQ -- Dequeue one word from a queue.
*
* INPUTS
*   #QDTBL -- The address of the queue descriptor table for the
*             queue to be manipulated, passed in register R1.
* OUTPUTS
*   QEMPTY -- 1 if the queue is empty, else 0; passed in
*             condition flag Z.
*   QDATA  -- The word dequeued, passed in register R0.
* GLOBAL DATA, LOCAL DATA -- None.
* FUNCTIONS
*   (1) If the queue described by QDTBL is empty, set QEMPTY to 1.
*   (2) If the queue isn't empty, dequeue QDATA and set QEMPTY to 0.
* REGISTERS AFFECTED -- R0, R2, FLAGS
*
* TYPICAL CALLING SEQUENCE
*         LD    R1,#Q1DT          Dequeue a word into AWORD.
*         CALL  QDEQ
*         JR    Z,UNDFL           Branch if queue is empty.
*         LD    AWORD,R0
*
QDEQ      LD    R2,QHEAD(R1)      Get copy of head.
          CP    R2,QTAIL(R1)      Queue empty?
          JR    EQ,QDEQ2          Return with Z=1 if empty.
          LD    R0,@R2            Read QDATA word from queue.
          INC   R2,#2             Bump copy head to next item in queue.
          CP    R2,QEND(R1)       Wrap-around?
          JR    ULE,QDEQ1
          LD    R2,QSTRT(R1)      Reinitialize copy head on wrap-around.
QDEQ1     LD    QHEAD(R1),R2      Update real head in memory.
          RESFLG Z                Z:=0 since not empty.
QDEQ2     RET                     Return.
```

TABLE 15-14 String search subroutine.

```
*              Find the first occurrence in BUFFER of a character
*              passed in RL0.  Return with Z=0 if character not found,
*              or with Z=1 and R1 pointing to the character if found.
*
SEARCH   LD      R1,#BUFFER       Point to start of buffer.
SLOOP    CPB     RL0,@R1          Match?
         JR      EQ,OUT           Exit with Z=1 if match found.
         INC     R1,#1            Bump to next character.
         CP      R1,#BUFEND       At end?
         JR      NE,SLOOP         No, look some more.
         RESFLG Z                 Not found, set Z to 0.
OUT      RET                      Return.
*
BUFFER   RMB     1000             Reserve 1000-byte buffer.
BUFEND   EQU     *                Address just past end of buffer.
```

The program in Table 15–8 may also be modified to make use of the string instructions. For example, the WHILE2, WHILE3, and WHILE4 loops move a block of data from one stack to another, suggesting an application for the CP(DI)R and LD(DI)R instructions. However, the way that the stacks are defined, a transfer between stacks requires one stack pointer to be incremented while the other is decremented, which neither LDIR nor LDDR can do. Therefore, to make use of these instructions we must redefine the stacks as shown in Figure 15–7. Now stackL grows towards increasing memory locations, so that block transfers between the stacks move both pointers in the same direction. The WHILE3 loop may now be recoded as shown below:

```
WHILE3   CLR     R0               Allow up to 65536 repetitions of CPIR.
         LD      R1,SPH           Pointer to stackH for CPIR.
         CPIR    INNUM,@R1,R0,LE  Search until
*                                   stackH entry <= innum found.
         NEG     R0               Compute number of stackH entries
         DEC     R0,#1              that were > innum.
         JR      EQ,OUT3          Done if none.
         INC     SPL,#1           Else move them to stackL.
         LDIR    @SPL,@SPH,R0
         DEC     SPL,#1
OUT3     ...
```

This code is longer than the original, but for large moves it is somewhat faster. Its total execution time is $57+18n$ clock cycles, where n is the number of stack entries moved. The WHILE3 loop in Table 15–8, on the other hand, takes $13+36n$ cycles.

The preceding examples show that string instructions may give speed improvements over explicit program loops, but not necessarily huge ones. The gains are less impressive considering that, with techniques described in

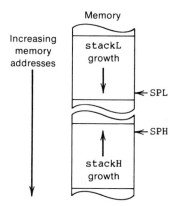

FIGURE 15–7 Modified stack structure for sorting program.

Section 12.4.2 and without string instructions, the program in Table 15–14 may be optimized to take only $35+16n$ cycles, and the WHILE3 loop in Table 15–8 may be optimized to take only $19+30n$ cycles.

Thus, the string manipulation instructions may yield a speed increase of less than 2 to 1. The capabilities of the string manipulation instructions often do not exactly match the requirements of a data structure or algorithm, and so compromises in program design, coding, or clarity may be needed to achieve even a moderate speed increase. A programmer should not bend over backwards to use these seemingly powerful instructions; they are best used in the limited number of applications that precisely match their capabilities.

15.6 INPUT/OUTPUT, INTERRUPTS, AND TRAPS

15.6.1 Input/Output

The Z8000 uses isolated I/O; it can access 2^{16} bytes of input ports and output ports in an address space separate from the memory address space. Like memory bytes, port bytes may be assembled into words with the even-numbered byte on the left, as shown in Figure 5–1(c). Instructions that access the I/O ports are listed in Table 15–15.

The two most important I/O instructions are INB and OUTB, which transfer data between a byte register and an 8-bit I/O port. A sample I/O program using INB and OUTB was discussed in Section 10.2.1. There are also word versions of the instructions, IN and OUT, which transfer data between a word register and a 16-bit I/O port. (In 1980, most commercially available I/O interface ICs contained 8-bit ports as opposed to 16-bit ports.)

Each of the four I/O instructions mentioned above may be used in either of two "port addressing" modes. In *absolute* mode, the instruction contains a 16-bit absolute port number, as shown in Figure 10–5. In *register indirect*

TABLE 15–15   Z8000 I/O instructions.

Mnemonic	Operands	Description
IN(B)	reg,port	Load reg from input port
OUT(B)	port,reg	Load output port from reg
IN(DI)(R)(B)	@rdst,@rp,rcnt	Load memory block from input port
OUT(DI)(R)(B)	@rp,@rsrc,rcnt	Load output port with memory block
SIN(B)	reg,port	Load reg from special input port
SOUT(B)	port,reg	Load special output port from reg
SIN(DI)(R)(B)	@rdst,@rp,rcnt	Load memory block from special input port
SOUT(DI)(R)(B)	@rp,@rsrc,rcnt	Load special output port with memory block

Notes: The notation (B) indicates that the instruction operates on either bytes or words, depending on whether or not a B appears at the end of the instruction mnemonic.

reg is a byte or word register, according to the size of the operation.

port denotes either an absolute 16-bit port number (e.g., 1234H), or a word register that contains a port number (e.g., @R2).

rp is a word register that contains a port number.

rsrc and rdst are word registers in nonsegmented mode, long-word registers in segmented mode.

The notation (DI) indicates that the instruction mnemonic must contain either D or I, indicating auto-decrement or auto-increment addressing, respectively. Accordingly, the instruction increments or decrements rsrc or rdst by the size of the operation *after* the operation (1 for bytes, 2 for words).

rcnt is a word register that is decremented after each operation. After an operation that decrements rcnt to zero, the P/V flag is set to 1, else P/V is set to 0.

The notation (R) indicates that the processor should or should not automatically repeat the instruction, depending on whether or not the optional R is present in the instruction mnemonic. If the R is absent, the operation is performed once. If the R is present, the operation is repeated until it sets rcnt to zero.

The "OUT" and "SOUT" instruction mnemonics are shortened to "OT" and "SOT" if both the DI and R options are used (e.g., "OUTDB", but "OTDRB" and "SOTIRB"). Apparently Zilog wanted to keep all mnemonic lengths six characters or less while still retaining some consistency.

I/O instructions may be executed only in the system mode of operation.

mode, the instruction specifies a word register that contains the 16-bit port number. This mode is required in shared I/O drivers (Section 10.4.2) and other I/O routines in which the address of an I/O port is not established until run time.

The Z8000 also has a unique set of block I/O instructions that allow a block of memory to be loaded from or transferred to a single I/O port. These instructions are useful for dealing with devices such as disks and tapes that store blocks of data.

For example, suppose a Z8000 system contains a disk interface with the programming model shown in Figure 15–8. (Notice that a particular interface may have a mix of byte and word ports, strictly according to the whims of the system hardware designer.) The disk control and status port (DSKCS) contains a read/write (R/W) bit to indicate whether a particular transaction should read

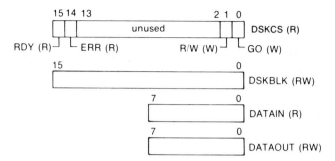

FIGURE 15-8   Disk interface in Z8000 system.

or write the disk, and a GO bit to begin the transaction. The transaction will read or write 256 bytes of data from or to the disk block whose number has been placed in the DSKBLK port. During read operations, the RDY bit in DSKCS indicates that the interface has just placed an input byte in the DATAIN port and the processor should read it; reading the byte clears RDY. During write operations, RDY indicates that the processor should place an output byte in the DATAOUT port, which the interface will write to the disk; placing a byte in DATAOUT clears RDY. If the processor fails to read or write bytes fast enough to keep up with the rotational speed of the disk, both the ERR and RDY bits in DSKCS are set to 1, and they remain set until the next GO command.

Without the block I/O instructions, a program to read 256 bytes of data from the disk could be written as shown in Table 15-16. The program reads bytes one at a time from the DATAIN port, using the RDY bit in DCS to determine when each byte is available.

Using block I/O instructions, the I/O part of the program could be re-written as shown in Table 15-17. The WAITIN loop in the original program synchronized itself with the speed of the disk by busy-waiting on the RDY bit. The new program has no such busy-wait loop. Instead, the system hardware designer has connected the RDY signal from the disk interface to a "WAIT" input of the Z8000 CPU circuit, so that the processor will automatically wait between iterations of the INIRB instruction until the disk interface is ready for another transfer.

The new program is somewhat shorter than the original, and it is also much faster. According to published Z8000 instruction timings, the WAITIN loop in Table 15-16 requires a minimum of 61 clock cycles per iteration. The INIRB instruction, on the other hand, requires only 10 clock cycles per iteration. While both the WAITIN loop and the INIRB instruction can synchronize with very slow devices, INIRB can synchronize with devices that produce inputs up to six times faster than the WAITIN loop's maximum speed. In a typical Z8000 system with a 250 nanosecond clock period, this means that the WAITIN loop can only read from disks that produce input bytes one per 15.25

TABLE 15–16 Disk input program without block I/O instructions.

```
*                              Addresses of disk I/O ports.
DSKCS    EQU    0100H          Control and status port (word).
DSKBLK   EQU    0102H          Disk block number port (word).
DATAIN   EQU    0104H          Input data during reads (byte).
DATAOUT  EQU    0105H          Output data during writes (byte).
*
BLOCKN   RMW    1              Program variable -- disk block number.
DSKBUF   RMB    256            Buffer for one disk block.
DSKBUFE  EQU    *              Address just past end of buffer.
*
DISKIO   ...                   Begin program.
         ...                   Process one block per iteration.
LOOP     ...                   Determine block number, put in BLOCKN.
         ...                   Now ready to get a block from the disk.
         LD     R0,BLOCKN      Get block number.
         OUT    DSKBLK,R0      Send to block number port.
         LD     R1,#DSKBUF     Point to beginning of memory buffer.
         LD     R0,#0003H      Set control port for read and go.
         OUT    DSKCS,R0
WAITIN   IN     R0,DSKCS       Check ready bit.
         TEST   R0             Check ready bit.
         JR     PL,WAITIN      Busy-wait if not ready.
         INB    RL0,DATAIN     Otherwise, read data byte.
         LDB    @R1,RL0        Store input byte into memory.
         INC    R1,#1          Bump buffer pointer.
         CP     R1,#DSKBUFE    Done 256 bytes?
         JR     ULT,WAITIN     No, wait for another byte.
         SLL    R0,#1          Check error bit (still in R0).
         JR     MI,DERROR      Go handle error if any.
         ...                   Now process the buffer...
         JR     LOOP           ...and go do some more.
DERROR   ...                   Handle disk errors.
```

TABLE 15–17 Disk input program using block I/O instructions.

```
         ...                   Now ready to get a block from the disk.
         LD     R0,BLOCKN      Get block number.
         OUT    DSKBLK,R0      Send to block number port.
         LD     R3,#256        Number of bytes to read.
         LD     R2,#DATAIN     Address of byte input port.
         LD     R1,#DSKBUF     Point to beginning of memory buffer.
         LD     R0,#0003H      Set control port for read and go.
         OUT    DSKCS,R0
         INIRB  @R1,@R2,R3     Read 256 bytes.
         IN     R0,DSKCS       Check error bit.
         SLL    R0,#1
         JR     MI,DERROR      Go handle error if any.
         ...
```

microseconds or slower, while INIRB can read from a disk that produces input bytes as fast as one per 2.5 microseconds. In many applications, the block I/O instructions can be used instead of the direct memory access (DMA) hardware that is normally required to handle fast block-I/O devices.

The second half of Table 15–15 contains "special" I/O instructions. These instructions operate exactly the same as their counterparts in the first half of the table, except that they use a different set of lines in the Memory and I/O Bus for transferring data. This facilitates transfers to and from a Memory Management Unit that does not have access to the data bus lines used by normal I/O transfers.

15.6.2 Interrupts

The Z8000 CPU contains a three-level, vectored priority interrupt system with three interrupt request lines, one for each level. In order of decreasing priority, the levels are NMI (non-maskable interrupt), VI (vectored interrupt), and NVI (non-vectored interrupt). Within each level, a system hardware designer may provide additional interrupt lines and priority by means of external hardware.

An NMI request is accepted as soon as it is received by the CPU. A VI or NVI request is accepted only if the corresponding enable bit (VIE or NVIE) in the FCW is 1. Of course, for any interrupt to be accepted, a device must first generate an interrupt request on one of the Z8000 interrupt request lines. The conditions for generating an interrupt request are device-dependent, but typically the device interrupt must be enabled and some kind of event must have occurred at the device. Thus, at least three conditions are needed for the Z8000 to accept an interrupt:

(1) The interrupt enable bit (e.g., IEN) on the device interface must be equal to 1.

(2) The corresponding enable bit (for VI and NVI) in the CPU's FCW must be equal to 1.

(3) The interface must have experienced an interrupt-generating event (e.g., character received from keyboard, ready to send character to screen, disk block transfer complete, etc.).

When an interrupt is accepted, the CPU automatically switches to system mode and pushes onto the system stack the current program status (FCW and PC) and a 1-word identifier indicating the source of the interrupt. Then it loads the FCW and PC with new values from an "interrupt vector" found in the Program Status Area, thus transferring control to an interrupt service routine. The interrupt service routine eventually returns control to the interrupted program by executing an IRET instruction, which pops the old FCW and PC from the system stack.

The arrangement of interrupt vectors in the Z8000's Program Status Area is shown in Table 15–18. In the Z8002 and the Z8001 in nonsegmented mode, the PC and FCW are each one word long, so an interrupt vector is two words long. In the Z8001 in segmented mode, the PC is two words long and there is an additional reserved word associated with the FCW, so an interrupt vector is four words long. In any case, the PSAP contains the base address of the table of vectors, and the CPU fetches an interrupt vector using an offset that depends on the interrupt (or trap) being serviced.

For non-maskable and non-vectored interrupts, the CPU fetches the corresponding FCW and PC from the Program Status Area and executes the interrupt service routine at the address indicated by the new PC. If the system has multiple devices connected to the same interrupt request line (NMI or NVI), then it is up to the service routine to determine which device has interrupted on a particular occasion.

For vectored interrupts, the CPU allows the interrupting device to place an 8-bit number on the data bus to identify itself. If two or more devices can make a request on VI simultaneously, external hardware must determine priority, that is, determine which device is allowed to place its identifier on the data bus. All vectored interrupts cause the CPU to fetch the same FCW from the Program Status Area. However, the CPU uses the 8-bit identifier supplied by the device as an index into a table of 256 new PC values, a different one for each vectored interrupt. Thus each device may have a different interrupt service routine that is automatically selected by the hardware.

The Z8000's VI and NVI inputs are level-sensitive, so that the CPU will accept an interrupt whenever an interrupt request signal is present and the corresponding enable bit in the FCW is 1. Therefore the programmer must

TABLE 15–18 Z8000 interrupt and trap vectors.

Offset	Contents	Interrupt or Trap
0	FCW,PC	Reserved
4	FCW,PC	Unimplemented-instruction trap
8	FCW,PC	Privileged-instruction trap
12	FCW,PC	System Call instruction
16	FCW,PC	Segmentation trap
20	FCW,PC	Non-maskable interrupt
24	FCW,PC	Non-vectored interrupt
28	FCW	Vectored interrupts (all)
30	PC	Vectored interrupt 0
32	PC	Vectored interrupt 1
34	PC	Vectored interrupt 2
. . .	PC	. . .
540	PC	Vectored interrupt 255

Notes: Offsets are shown for the Z8002; all offsets are doubled in the Z8001 in segmented mode.

ensure that the corresponding enable bit (VIE or NVIE) in the new FCW is 0, to prevent the interrupt service routine from being continuously re-interrupted by the same condition. Once the service routine has removed the condition that caused the interrupt, it may set the enable bit to 1 to allow interrupts from other devices on the same level. Alternatively, it may leave the enable bit at 0, so that no further interrupts will be accepted at the current level until the service routine exits using the IRET instruction.

Since an NMI request cannot be disabled, a different scheme must be used to keep the NMI service routine from being continuously interrupted by the same condition. Therefore, the NMI input is edge-sensitive. The Z8000 CPU sets an internal NMI request flip-flop when the NMI line makes an inactive-to-active transition, and resets it when the NMI service routine is entered. Therefore, the interrupt system can accept a second NMI request only after the condition causing the first NMI request has been removed and a second inactive-to-active transition has occurred on the NMI input.

A program that uses interrupts to print strings of characters is shown in Table 15–19. The program assumes that a Motorola 6850 ACIA (Appendix C.3) is attached to the Z8000 as I/O ports 100H and 101H. It further assumes that a string is a sequence of ASCII characters stored one per byte and terminated by NUL (a zero byte).

The entire program in Table 15–19 is assumed to run in system mode so that it has access to the system stack pointer and to all the privileged instructions, such as LDCTL and I/O instructions. The main program in Table 15–19 allocates the space for the program status area and initializes the control registers.

The CRT output initialization routine CRTOUT accepts a pointer to a string to be printed. The variable CRTBSY indicates whether a previous string is still being printed, so that a new operation is not started until the previous one is completed. CRTOUT prints the first character, enables the ACIA to interrupt after the character has been printed, and returns to the main program.

Remaining characters are printed by the interrupt service routine CRTINT. Before entering CRTINT, the CPU pushes only the FCW, the PC, and an interrupt identifier onto the system stack, so it is up to CRTINT to save and restore any general registers that it needs. Thus R1 is saved on the system stack at the beginning of CRTINT.

Notice the use of LD @R15,R1 instead of PUSH at the beginning of CRTINT. This overwrites the interrupt identifier that the CPU pushed onto the stack when it accepted the interrupt; the identifier is generally not needed to determine the source of a vectored interrupt. If additional registers were needed in CRTINT, they would be pushed onto the system stack at the beginning of CRTINT, and popped before the return.

A few words should be said about the interruptibility of Z8000 programs. In general, a CPU should accept interrupts only between instructions. How-

TABLE 15–19   Interrupt-driven CRT output.

```
*         Define addresses and bit patterns for CRT ACIA.
CRTCS    EQU    100H              ACIA control and status port.
CRTDATA  EQU    101H              ACIA XMT and RCV data ports.
CRTVECT  EQU    2                 ACIA interrupt vector number.
CRESET   EQU    03H               ACIA control pattern for reset.
CMODE    EQU    11H               Basic ACIA operating mode.
CINTON   EQU    20H               ACIA XMT interrupt enable bit.
CINTOFF  EQU    00H               ACIA interrupts disabled.
*
         ORG    1000H             PSA must start on 256-byte boundary.
PSA      RMW    271               Program status area.
*
*         Global and local variables.
CRTBSY   RMW    1                 Nonzero when string is being displayed.
BPNT     RMW    1                 Pointer to character being displayed.
*
*         Messages printed by main program.
MSG1     FCC    'Debugging always takes longer than expected...'
         FCB    0DH,0AH,0         Carriage return, line feed, NUL.
MSG2     FCC    '...even when this rule is taken into account.'
         FCB    0DH,0AH,0         Carriage return, line feed, NUL.
         ORG    ((*+1)/2)*2       Force PLC to a word boundary.
*
*         CRT output initialization, pointer to string passed in R1.
CRTOUT   TEST   CRTBSY            Still busy with previous string?
         JR     NE,CRTOUT         Yes, wait for completion.
         INC    CRTBSY,#1         Mark CRT busy for new string.
         LD     BPNT,R1           Save pointer to string.
         LDB    RL0,#CMODE+CINTOFF    Set ACIA operating mode,
         OUTB   CRTCS,RL0                 XMT interrupts off.
         LDB    RL0,@R1           Get first character.
         OUTB   CRTDATA,RL0       Send it to ACIA.
         LDB    RL0,#CMODE+CINTON   Enable ACIA XMT interrupts.
         OUTB   CRTCS,RL0
         RET                      Done, return.
*
*         CRT output interrupt handler.
CRTINT   LD     @R15,R1           Save R1 (overwriting identifier).
         LD     R1,BPNT           Get pointer to character just printed.
         INC    R1,#1             Point to next character.
         LD     BPNT,R1           Save updated pointer.
         LDB    RL1,@R1           Fetch the character.
         TESTB  RL1               Is it NUL (0)?
         JR     EQ,CDONE          We're done if it is.
         OUTB   CRTDATA,RL1       Otherwise print the character,
CRTRET   POP    R1,@R15              restore R1,
         IRET                        and return.
CDONE    LDB    RL1,#CMODE+CINTOFF   Disable ACIA interrupts.
         OUTB   CRTCS,RL1
         CLR    CRTBSY            CRT is no longer busy.
         JR     CRTRET            Restore R1 and return.
```

TABLE 15-19 (continued)

```
*           Main program, runs entirely in system mode.
MAIN        LD      R15,#0FFF0H        Initialize stack pointer.
            CLR     CRTBSY             Mark CRT not busy.
            LD      PSA+28,#4000H      FCW for vectored interrupts -- non-seg,
*                                      system mode, vectored interrupts off.
            LD      PSA+30+2*CRTVECT,#CRTINT    Starting PC for CRT
            LD      R0,#PSA                     interrupt service routine.
            LDCTL   PSAP,R0            Set up PSAP to point to PSA.
            LDB     RL0,#CRESET        Reset CRT ACIA, no interrupts.
            OUTB    CRTCS,RL0
            EI      VI                 Enable vectored interrupts.
LOOP        ...                        Do some computation.
            LD      R1,#MSG1           Get address of first message
            CALR    CRTOUT                and print it.
            ...                        Do some more computation.
            LD      R1,#MSG2           Get address of second message
            CALR    CRTOUT                and print it.
            JR      LOOP               Do it all again.
            END     MAIN
```

ever, the Z8000's repetitive string manipulation instructions can have long execution times when they process long strings of data. The long "interrupt latency" that would be created by waiting for the completion of these instructions is unacceptable in some applications. Therefore the Z8000 CPU accepts interrupts between iterations of repetitive instructions. Because the repetition counts and memory pointers for a repetitive instruction are stored in general registers, the CPU can continue the instruction after the interrupt has been serviced. There are no errors or loss of information as long as the interrupt service routine does not disturb the register values.

For the same reasons, the repetitive block I/O instructions are also interruptible. In this case, however, the block I/O device may not be able to tolerate the delay caused by the interrupt service routine, and data may be lost. One approach for dealing with the situation is to simply disable interrupts while performing block I/O. If this is unacceptable, another approach is to allow interrupts, and to check for timing errors at the end of the block I/O operation as in Table 15–17. When an error is detected, the block I/O operation can be retried one or more times, perhaps with interrupts disabled if the first few retries fail.

15.6.3 Traps

The Z8000 has four interrupt vectors for exceptional conditions and the System Call instruction:

- *Unimplemented Instruction.* A trap occurs if the processor attempts to execute an instruction with an illegal opcode.

- *Privileged Instruction.* A trap occurs if the processor attempts to execute an I/O or other privileged instruction in normal (non-system) mode.

- *System Call Instruction.* A trap occurs if the processor executes an SC instruction.

- *Segmentation Trap.* A trap occurs if the Memory Management Unit (if installed) detects a memory protection violation.

A trap has the same effect as an interrupt — the CPU changes to system mode, the current FCW and PC and an identifier are pushed onto the system stack, and a new FCW and PC are loaded from the Program Status Area as dictated by Table 15–18.

Since the low-order byte of the SC instruction is not decoded by the CPU, a programmer may place an arbitrary 8-bit code there to be decoded by the service routine for SC. The service routine is always executed in system mode, and so SC provides a convenient way for a user program to call the operating system and request an operating system service. The CPU pushes the SC instruction itself onto the system stack as the interrupt "identifier," so that the service routine can easily read and decode the low-order byte to determine which service is being requested.

REFERENCES

The Z8000 processor architecture borrows some ideas from the IBM System/370 and some from the PDP-11. A few rough spots in the architecture, such as the P/V flag, can be traced directly to Zilog's desire for the Z8000 to easily emulate their Z80, which was in turn designed to be compatible with the original Intel 8080 microprocessor. A description of the philosophy and trade-offs that went into the Z8000's architecture may be found in "Architecture of a New Microprocessor" by Bernard Peuto [*Computer*, Vol. 12, No. 2, Feb. 1979].

The *Z8000 PLZ/ASM Assembly Language Programming Manual* published by Zilog [Cupertino, CA 95014] contains an architectural overview of the Z8000, as well as detailed descriptions of instructions, condition flags settings, and assembly language notations. Advanced Micro Devices, a second source for Z8000-family devices, also publishes a complete description of the architecture and instructions in a conveniently-sized book, *AmZ8001/2 Processor Instruction Set* [Sunnyvale, CA 94086].

Computer engineers are often asked, "Which microprocessor is better, *X* or *Y*?" An experienced computer engineer will answer, "It depends on the application." As a case in point, comparisons between the Motorola 68000 and the Z8000 were rampant at the time this book was written. The choice of a microprocessor for an application is a very complicated process that depends on many architectural and non-architectural issues. Comparing just a few aspects of the 68000 and Z8000 architectures, one would find that the 68000 has a larger register set, a larger unsegmented address space, more addressing modes, and better BCD arithmetic instructions, while the Z8000 has a better register addressing scheme, better memory management support, and block I/O and 32-bit multiply and divide instructions that the 68000 lacks. Even when architectural trade-offs are clear, non-architectural issues may be more important; see "How to choose a microcomputer" by J. Wakerly [*Computer*, Vol. 12, No. 2, February 1979, p. 24].

EXERCISES

15.1   Compare the size in bytes of the Z8000 sorting program in Table 15–8 with that of the 6809 version in Table 7–3. To what do you attribute the difference? In what ways is the Z8000 program more capable?

15.2   Modify the Z8000 sorting program in Table 15–8 so that it sorts byte values between −99 and +99 instead of words and uses stacks of bytes. Comment on any difficulties that you encounter.

15.3   Indicate what changes must be made to the primes program in Table 15–10 to run on the Z8001 in segmented mode. What is the difference in lengths (in bytes) between the segmented and nonsegmented versions?

15.4   Indicate what changes must be made to the division subroutine in Table 15–11 to run on the Z8001 in segmented mode.

15.5   Indicate what changes must be made to the queue module in Table 15–13 to run on the Z8001 in segmented mode.

15.6   Write a Z8000 subroutine that adds two 48-bit unsigned integers P and Q, stored in memory words P2,P1,P0 and Q2,Q1,Q0, respectively. The sum should be stored in memory locations S2,S1,S0. When the subroutine returns, C should be set to 1 if the true sum is greater than $2^{48}-1$, else to 0.

15.7   Write a faster version of the 16-bit unsigned division program in Table 15–11 that uses the DIVL instruction.

15.8   Rewrite the recursive NIM subroutines in Table 9–19 for the Z8000. Write a main program that analyzes the game for all combinations of values of NHEAP from 2 to 25 and NTAKE from 2 to 6.

15.9   Write a Z8000 keyboard input and display output module similar to the 6809 module in Table 10–4.

15.10 Write a sequence of instructions that saves registers R0–R14 on the system stack using the LDM instruction instead of 15 PUSHes. Then write an instruction sequence that restores the registers, also using LDM.

15.11 Write a *subroutine* that saves registers R0–R14 on the system stack as using the LDM instruction instead of 15 PUSHes. Then write a subroutine that restores the registers, also using LDM. (*Hint:* Watch out for the return address on the stack.)

15.12 Write a complete Pascal simulation of the Z8000.

16

TEXAS INSTRUMENTS 9900

The Texas Instruments TMS9900, introduced in 1976, was the first widely-used single-chip 16-bit microprocessor. The architecture of the TMS9900 evolved from the 900-series of minicomputers designed by Texas Instruments (TI) in the late 1960s. A TMS9900-like architecture is used in TI's 990 family of minicomputers, as well as in the TMS9940, a single-chip microcomputer. We'll use the name "9900" as a generic to refer to the CPU architecture shared by all of these computers.

The 9900 architecture is interesting to study because many of its features are different from those of any other processor in this book. For example, the 9900 CPU does not have an accumulator, general registers, or even a stack pointer, so it does not fall into any of the CPU categories introduced in Chapter 5. You'll have to keep reading to find out how the 9900 gets any computation done at all!

Since the TMS9900 integrated circuit contains a CPU only, a system hardware designer must add memory and I/O to form a complete computer. Computers that contain a 9900-type CPU circuit include the TI 990/4 micro-computer and 99/4 home computer.

16.1 BASIC ORGANIZATION

16.1.1 Computer Structure

The basic structure of a TMS9900-based computer is shown in Figure 16–1. The CPU uses a Memory Bus to access memory and a separate I/O Bus to communicate with I/O interfaces. Of course, a system hardware designer can always provide memory-mapped I/O interfaces as well.

The 9900 Memory Bus contains a 16-bit address bus, and so it can access up to 2^{16} (64K) bytes of memory. The TMS9900 data bus is 16 bits wide, and the CPU accesses two memory bytes at a time. TI also makes TMS9980 and TMS 9995 CPU circuits that have a 9900 architecture but only an 8-bit wide data bus; in this case memory is accessed a byte at a time. Any 9900 CPU regardless of data bus width is properly called a 16-bit machine according to the definition given in Section 5.5, because the largest operand handled by a majority of 9900 data operations is 16 bits wide.

The 9900 CPU contains a novel I/O system for accessing 4K individually addressable input bits and output bits. I/O instructions access I/O bits in fields of 1 to 16 bits. The CPU also contains a 16-level, vectored, priority interrupt system.

16.1.2 Processor Programming Model

The processor state of the 9900 is very minimal, as shown in Figure 16–2(a). A 16-bit Program Counter (PC) points to the next instruction to be executed, a 16-bit Workspace Pointer (WP) points to the start of a 16-word "workspace" area in memory, and a 16-bit Status Register (ST) contains condition bits and interrupt priority.

Despite its small processor state, the 9900 may be programmed much like a general-register machine. As indicated by Figure 16–2(b), WP points to a block of 16 "workspace registers" R0–R15 in memory. Instructions may address the workspace registers using short, 4-bit fields; the CPU calculates an actual memory address relative to the current value of WP. Like general registers, the 9900's workspace registers may be accessed more efficiently

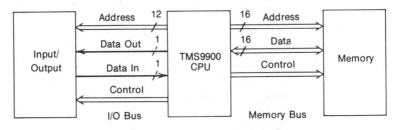

FIGURE 16–1 TMS9900-based computer block diagram.

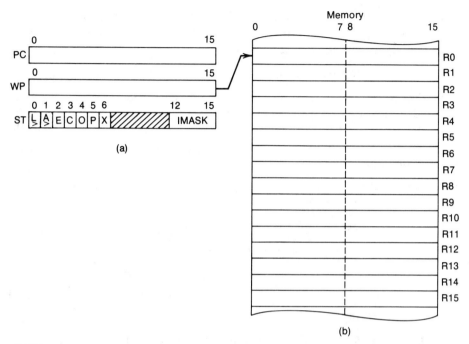

FIGURE 16–2 Programming model of the 9900: (a) processor registers; (b) workspace registers. TI's documentation numbers the bits in a word from left to right as shown.

than arbitrary memory locations; also like general registers, they may contain operand addresses in various addressing modes as well as data.

Once a program has initialized WP to point to an appropriate block of memory, it can make use of the workspace registers just as if they were general registers. The 9900's main difference from a true general register machine is in speed; since the workspace registers are in memory, they take longer to access than on-chip registers. This speed penalty is partially offset in applications that use frequent interrupts; as discussed in Section 16.6.2, context switching may be performed by simple manipulations of WP. Also, the speed penalty may be overcome in future 9900-type circuits by means of an on-chip "cache" memory that stores the workspace registers.

The condition bits in ST are set or cleared according to the results of most data manipulation instructions. However, they are somewhat different from the "standard" condition bits introduced in Section 8.2, and so we give their general meanings below:

- L> (Logical Greater Than). Set if the true result of an operation is greater than zero, interpreting operands as unsigned integers; else cleared.

- A> (Arithmetic Greater Than). Set if the true result of an operation is greater than zero, interpreting operands as signed integers in the two's-complement system; else cleared.

- E (Equal). Set if the result of an operation is zero; else cleared.

- C (Carry). During arithmetic operations, set if a carry out of the MSB occurs; else cleared. During shift operations, loaded with the last bit shifted out of the operand. (Note that other machines load C with the borrow during subtraction operations — the borrow is the complement of the carry.)

- O (Overflow). Set if an arithmetic operation causes two's-complement overflow; else cleared.

- P (Parity). Set if the result has an odd number of 1s; else cleared.

- X (XOP). Set when the XOP instruction is executed.

- IMASK (Interrupt Mask). Contains current CPU priority.

16.1.3   Instruction Formats

Typical 9900 instructions have an opcode and one or two addressing mode designators encoded in one word. One or two successive words may be used to contain additional addressing information. Several different formats are used for the first word of different instructions, as required by different operations and addressing modes. For example, six different formats are shown in Figure 16–3. Detailed instruction encodings may be found in the manufacturer's literature.

Most 9900 data manipulation instructions operate on words, but a few double-operand instructions can operate on bytes as well. These instructions use the format of Figure 16–3(a) and indicate the operand size by a "B" bit.

Instructions that reference memory contain a 6-bit "effective-address" (EA) field that specifies the location of the operand; memory-to-memory instructions contain two such fields. In all these instructions, an EA field can specify one of several addressing modes as discussed in Section 16.3.

16.2   ASSEMBLY LANGUAGE

TI's standard assembly language for the 9900 has the same basic line format as the H6809 assembly language defined in Section 6.1. At this point, however, the similarity with H6809 and most other assembly languages ends. A peek at the example programs later in this chapter makes some differences immediately evident:

- Most of the assembler directives have different names.

- Hexadecimal constants are denoted by a prefix of ">" instead of by a suffix of "H".

- The program location counter (PLC) is denoted by "$" instead of "*".

- Register indirect addressing is denoted by a prefix of "*" instead of "@".

- Absolute addressing is denoted by a prefix of "@" instead of no prefix.

Important features of TI's 9900 assembly language are summarized in Table 16–1; addressing mode notations are summarized in the next section.

16.3 ADDRESSING

The 9900 memory is byte addressable, with the bytes arranged to form words as shown in Figure 5–1(c). However, the 9900's documentation numbers the bits in a byte from left to right, just the opposite of the convention used by all the other machines in this book.

Most 9900 instructions operate on words, which begin at even addresses; a few instructions operate on bytes, which may have any address. Word instructions ignore the LSB of the address; a word instruction that specifies an odd address accesses the word containing the specified odd byte.

Typical 9900 instructions may have one or two operands in memory. An operand is specified by a 6-bit EA field in the instruction, consisting of a 2-bit addressing mode designator T and a 4-bit workspace register number R, as shown in Figure 16–4. The four combinations of the T field actually provide five different addressing modes, since R=0 is treated as a special case in one of the combinations.

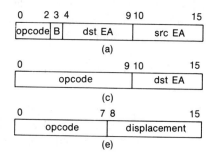

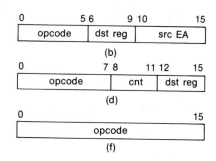

FIGURE 16–3 Format of the first word of typical 9900 instructions: (a) memory-to-memory; (b) memory-to-register; (c) single-operand; (d) shifts; (e) branch; (f) inherent addressing.

TABLE 16–1 TI 9900 assembly language summary.

Feature	Example	Description
*	* HI KIDS!	Begin comment line.
EQU	TEN EQU 10	Equate symbol with 16-bit value.
>	SIXTY EQU >3C	Hex specifier.
$	HERE EQU $	PLC specifier.
'chr'	ASCA EQU 'A'	Use value of ACSII character.
AORG	AORG >4000	Set absolute origin.
RORG	RORG 0	Set relocatable origin.
BYTE	CB BYTE 17,>F9,−1 CC BYTE 'C','C'	Store constant values into successive memory bytes.
DATA	CW DATA −789,>E800 KW DATA PUP,PUP+2	Store constant values into successive memory words.
TEXT	ST TEXT 'ABCDEFG' NM TEXT 'BAT'	Store ASCII values of characters into successive memory bytes.
BSS	TB BSS 10	Reserve a number of bytes of memory.
EVEN	EVEN	Add 1 to PLC if it is odd.
DEF	DEF PTIME	Define entry symbol.
REF	REF HOUR,MINUTE	Define external symbol.
END	END START	Indicate end of assembly, optionally give starting-execution address.
OPTION	OPTION XREF	Select assembly options (see TI documentation).

The 9900 instruction set is fairly regular in the sense that any instruction that contains an EA field can use any addressing mode encoding without restrictions (compare with the 68000 in Chapter 14). Individual addressing modes are summarized in Table 16–2 and discussed in detail below.

16.3.1 Register Direct

In *register-direct addressing*, the operand is contained in one of the workspace registers R0–R15. When the instruction is executed, the CPU computes the memory address of the register as the sum of WP and twice the register number.

Byte operations on registers use the 8 high-order bits of the register and do not affect the low-order bits.

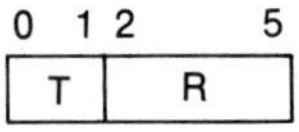

```
0  1 2      5
┌──┬─────────┐
│ T│    R    │
└──┴─────────┘
```

FIGURE 16-4 9900 operand effective-address specification.

16.3.2 Immediate

In *immediate addressing*, an operand is stored in the second word of the instruction. Unfortunately, this important addressing mode cannot be specified by the EA field of an instruction. Instead, immediate addressing is used inherently by a limited number of "immediate register" instructions, such as LI R,data, which loads register R with an immediate value data.

16.3.3 Absolute

In *absolute addressing*, the instruction contains the 16-bit absolute memory address of the operand. TI's 9900 assembly language is a little unusual in that it requires a prefix of "@" on an address expression to denote absolute addressing. Most other assembly languages use a similar prefix to indicate indirect addressing. However, novice assembly language programmers may find TI's notation to be a helpful reminder that, in assembly language, a symbol such as COUNT usually stands for a memory address, not the value of a variable. Therefore, it is natural to read the statement "MOV @COUNT,R0" as "*Move* the word stored *at* address COUNT to R0."

TABLE 16-2 Addressing modes and assembly language notation for the 9900.

Mode	T	R	Notation	Operand
Register direct	0	0–15	R	WR
Immediate			data	data
Absolute	2	0	@addr	MEM[addr]
Register indirect	1	0–15	*R	MEM[WR]
Auto-increment (by 1 or 2)	3	0–15	*R+	MEM[WR] , then WR := WR + operand size
Based or indexed	2	1–15	addr(R)	MEM[addr+WR]

Notes: R denotes a workspace register, denoted either by a reserved identifier R0 through R15 or by an expression yielding a result in the range 0 to 15.

WR is the content of workspace register R, i.e., MEM[WP+2*R].

addr and data are 16-bit values.

MEM[x] is the 8- or 16-bit value beginning at memory address x, as appropriate for the size of the operation.

Immediate addressing cannot be specified by the EA field, but is available inherently in certain instructions.

16.3.4   Register Indirect

In *register indirect addressing*, the specified workspace register contains the 16-bit address of the operand. This mode is used when the address of the operand must be computed at run time.

16.3.5   Auto-Increment

In *auto-increment addressing*, the specified workspace register contains the 16-bit address of the operand. After using the address, the CPU increments the register by 1 or 2 according to the size of the operand — byte or word. Auto-increment addressing may be used to step through arrays, lists, and other data structures as described in Section 7.2.5. Unfortunately, the 9900 does not have auto-decrement addressing, so stack manipulations are inconvenient.

16.3.6   Based or Indexed

In 9900 *based addressing*, the effective address of the operand is formed by adding a 16-bit offset in the instruction and a 16-bit base address in a specified workspace register; the contents of the register are not disturbed. Since base addresses and offsets are the same length, this mode may also be considered to be *indexed addressing*, depending on the application. Applications of based and indexed addressing are discussed in Sections 7.3.2 and 7.3.3.

Based or indexed addressing is not allowed using R0 as the base or index register. As shown in Table 16–2, the combination of mode 2 with R0 is used to denote absolute addressing mode.

16.4   OPERATIONS

We shall classify 9900 instructions into five types: memory-to-memory, memory-to-register, single-operand, program control, and input/output. The I/O instructions will be introduced in Section 16.6.

16.4.1   Memory-to-Memory

Instructions that have the format of Figure 16–3(a) are listed in Table 16–3. Since each instruction has two EA fields, either operand may be in memory or in a register. Thus, register-to-register and register-to/from-memory as well as memory-to-memory variations are possible.

Each instruction in Table 16–3 can operate on either words or bytes as specified by a "B" bit in the instruction; byte operations on registers access only the high-order byte. All of the instructions affect the L>, A>, and E

TABLE 16-3 9900 memory-to-memory instructions.

Mnemonic	Operands	Description
MOV(B)	src,dst	Copy src to dst
A(B)	src,dst	Add src to dst
C(B)	src,dst	Compare src and dst
S(B)	src,dst	Subtract src from dst
SOC(B)	src,dst	Set corresponding 1 bits of src in dst
SZC(B)	src,dst	Clear corresponding 1 bits of src in dst

Notes: The notation (B) indicates that the instruction exists for both bytes and words. For
example, MOV moves a word, MOVB a byte.
src and dst are each given by a 6-bit EA specification.

condition bits. The addition and subtraction instructions also affect C and O,
and the byte versions of all the instructions affect P.

The operations performed by instructions in Table 16–3 are fairly standard. SOC (Set Ones Corresponding) is just another name for logical OR,
while SZC (Set Zeroes Corresponding) performs the logical AND of dst
and the complement of src.

Since both the src and dst operands have their own EA field, memory-
to-memory and register-to-memory operations are possible, in addition to the
more commonly used memory-to-register and register-to-register operations.
Still, the src and dst fields do not provide an immediate addressing mode for
these or any other 9900 instructions. However, the next subsection will show
instructions that specify immediate operands inherently and operate on registers only.

16.4.2 Memory-to-Register

The instructions shown in Table 16–4 combine a source operand with an
operand in a register and leave a result, if any, in the register. Instructions in
the first group allow only immediate addressing for the source operand. These
are immediate-to-register versions of the instructions in Table 16–3: LI serves
for MOV; CI for C; ORI for SOC; ANDI for SZC; and AI for both A and S.

Some inconsistencies in 9900 assembly language are apparent in Table
16–4. Instructions in the first group have the format OP dst,src, while instructions in the second group and in Table 16–3 have the format OP src,dst.

Instructions in the second group of Table 16–4 specify the source
operand using a 6-bit EA field; thus the source operand may use any of the
addressing modes from Section 16.3 except immediate. The XOR instruction
operates in the usual way. MPY performs an unsigned multiplication of a 16-bit
register by a 16-bit operand and produces a 32-bit result. It stores the high-
order word of the result in the original register, and the low-order word in the
next register. DIV performs an unsigned division of a 32-bit dividend in a

TABLE 16–4   9900 memory-to-register instructions.

Mnemonic	Operands	Description
LI	R,data16	Load R with data16
AI	R,data16	Add data16 to R
CI	R,data16	Compare data16 and R
ANDI	R,data16	AND data16 to R
ORI	R,data16	OR data16 to R
XOR	src,R	Exclusive OR src to R
MPY	src,R	Unsigned multiply src times R
DIV	src,R	Unsigned divide R,R+1 by src
COC	src,R	Does R have 1s everywhere src has 1s?
CZC	src,R	Does R have 0s everywhere src has 1s?

Notes: R denotes a workspace register, R0–R15.
        src denotes an operand in memory using a 6-bit EA specification.
        data16 is a 16-bit immediate value.

register and its successor by a 16-bit divisor. It leaves the 16-bit quotient in the specified register, and the 16-bit remainder in the successor register. If the divisor is less than or equal to the high-order word of the dividend, no division is performed and the O bit is set.

The COC (Compare Ones Corresponding) and CZC (Compare Zeroes Corresponding) instructions have unusual names, but they perform standard logical operations. COC src,R sets the E bit if R has a 1 bit in at least every position that src has a 1 bit; otherwise it clears the E bit. This is equivalent to performing the logical operation (src AND (NOT R)) and setting E if the result is zero. CZC src,R checks R for 0s in positions that src has 1s, equivalent to performing (src AND R) and setting E if the result is zero.

16.4.3 Single Operand

Instructions with only one operand in a register or memory are listed in Table 16–5. Instructions in the first group manipulate a 16-bit operand using any of the addressing modes from Section 16.3 except immediate. An operand in a register or memory may be cleared, set to all ones, ones'-complemented ("inverted"), negated, negated if negative ("abs'ed"), incremented or decremented by one or two, or have its bytes swapped. Wheww!

The 9900 also has an "execute" (X) instruction which allows a program to fetch and execute an instruction stored in a designated memory location or even in a register, and then continue program execution at the instruction following X instruction. Although an "execute" instruction allows some very clever programming tricks, its use is frowned upon in modern software design. A program should not execute "data" as instructions.

TABLE 16-5 9900 single-operand instructions.

Mnemonic	Operands	Description
CLR	dst	Clear dst
SETO	dst	Set dst to all 1s
INV	dst	Complement bits of dst
NEG	dst	Negate dst (two's complement)
ABS	dst	Negate dst if negative
INC	dst	Add one to dst
INCT	dst	Add two to dst
DEC	dst	Subtract one from dst
DECT	dst	Subtract two from dst
SWPB	dst	Swap bytes of dst
X	dst	Execute instruction stored in dst
SLA	R,cnt	Shift left arithmetic R by cnt
SRA	R,cnt	Shift right arithmetic R by cnt
SRC	R,cnt	Shift right circular R by cnt
SRL	R,cnt	Shift right logical R by cnt

Notes: dst denotes an operand in memory using a 6-bit EA specification.
R denotes a workspace register, R0–R15.
cnt denotes the shift count. A cnt of 1 to 15 is a static shift count stored in the
instruction. A cnt of 0 indicates that a dynamic shift count is contained in the four
low-order bits of R0 (where a value of 0 denotes a count of 16).

The 9900's shift and rotate instructions operate on registers, basically as described in Section 8.8. Each instruction may contain a static shift count from 1 to 15, or it may specify that a dynamic shift count of 1 to 16 is contained in register R0. All of the shifts set the L>, A>, and E condition bits according to their result's value; all load the C bit with the last bit shifted out of the word. SLA sets O if the MSB of the operand changes at any time during the shift. SRC is a right circular shift (rotation) without C. Although there is no left circular shift instruction, the operation "SLC R,cnt" can be approximated by SRC R,16-cnt.

16.4.4 Program Control

The 9900's program control instructions are listed in Table 16–6. The first thing you may notice in this table is that TI's nomenclature for jumps and branches is the opposite of what we adopted in Section 8.6. The B (Branch) instruction jumps to a memory address using any addressing mode, while JMP (Jump) branches to a nearby address using relative addressing.

Much more significant than TI's nomenclature is the way in which the 9900 calls subroutines — the 9900 is the only processor in this book that does not have a return address stack. Instead, the BL (Branch and Link) instruc-

TABLE 16-6   9900 program control instructions.

Mnemonic	Operands	Description
B	dst	Jump to dst
BL	dst	Jump to subroutine at dst
JMP	addr8	Unconditionally branch to addr8
Jcc	addr8	Branch to addr8 if cc is true
BLWP	dst	Save CPU state, jump to subroutine
RTWP		Return and restore CPU state
XOP	src,data4	Deposit src address in R12, then trap
LWPI	data16	Load WP with data16
STWP	R	Store WP into R
LIMI	data4	Load IMASK with data4
STST	R	Store ST into R

Notes: src and dst denote operands using a 6-bit EA specification.
addr8 is a target address within 128 words of the instruction.
R denotes a workspace register, R0–R15.
data16 and data4 denote 16- and 4-bit immediate operands.

tion saves the return address in workspace register R11. A subroutine may return control to its caller by a jump instruction using register indirect addressing on R11, that is, B *R11.

Since return addresses are stored in a dedicated register, a subroutine called by BL cannot call a second, nested subroutine using BL without first saving the contents of R11 somewhere. The simplest approach is to save the return address in a dedicated memory location associated with the subroutine. A more general solution that allows reentrancy and recursion is to push the return address onto a stack, simply emulating the return-address stacking mechanism found in most other processors.

Unlike all other machines in this book, the 9900 allows a B or BL instruction to specify a target address using the register-direct addressing mode. This works because the effective address of a register is a legitimate memory address. However, this facility should not be used in practice. Tricky programmers must resist the temptation to write programs that jump to dynamically created instructions sequences in the registers!

The 9900's relative branch instructions, JMP and Jcc, are one word long and contain an 8-bit displacement that specifies a target address within -127 to $+128$ words of the address following the instruction. The conditional branch, Jcc, allows one of twelve different conditions to be specified as shown in Table 16–7. The set is not complete, since the complements of JNO, JOP, JLT, and JGT are not included in the 9900 instruction set.

Besides BL, the 9900 offers a novel subroutine-calling instruction, BLWP (Branch and Load Workspace Pointer), that saves the entire context of the caller. As shown in Figure 16–5, the effective address of BLWP is not the

TABLE 16–7 Conditional branch instructions in the 9900.

Type	Mnemonic	Jump	Condition
Single Bit			
	JOC addr8	On Carry	C = 1
	JNC addr8	No Carry	C = 0
	JNO addr8	No Overflow	O = 0
	JOP addr8	Odd Parity	P = 1
	JEQ addr8	Equal	E = 1
	JNE addr8	Not Equal	E = 0
Signed			
	JLT addr8	Less Than	(A> = 0) AND (E = 0)
	JGT addr8	Greater Than	A> = 1
Unsigned			
	JL addr8	Low	(L> = 0) AND (E = 0)
	JLE addr8	Low or Equal	(L> = 0) OR (E = 1)
	JH addr8	High	(L> = 1) AND (E = 0)
	JHE addr8	High or Equal	(L> = 1) OR (E = 1)

subroutine address itself, but the address of a two-word "context vector." The first word of the context vector points to a new set of workspace registers, and the second word contains the starting address of the subroutine. Before jumping to the subroutine, BLWP loads WP with the pointer to the new workspace, and then saves the old CPU state (WP, PC, and ST) in R13–R15 in the new workspace.

Because it saves three registers instead of one, BLWP takes longer to execute than BL. However, BLWP still offers a distinct advantage by creating sixteen new workspace registers, of which thirteen are available for the subroutine's immediate use. The RTWP instruction returns from a subroutine called by BLWP, by loading ST, PC, and WP from the registers. The last step, loading WP, restores the previous set of workspace registers.

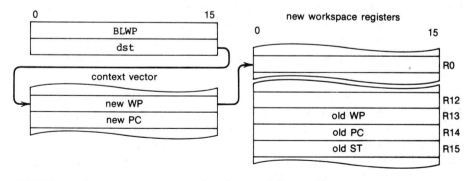

FIGURE 16–5 Memory organization for BLWP instruction.

Subroutines called by BLWP may be nested if each subroutine uses a different block of memory for its workspace registers. In Section 16.5, we'll describe a strategy in which new workspaces are allocated on a pushdown stack.

Because BLWP saves the processor state and workspace registers, it is the appropriate instruction for calling interrupt service routines. Therefore, the 9900 services an interrupt by automatically executing a BLWP using a predetermined context vector address, as explained in Section 16.6.2.

The XOP (Extended Operation) instruction executes a BLWP using one of 16 predetermined context-vector addresses, as specified by a 4-bit operand data4 (address $= 40_{16}+4\cdot$data4). It also computes the address of a specified operand (src) and deposits this address in the new R11. Thus, XOP can pass to a subroutine a parameter or the base address of a parameter area. XOP is primarily used to call operating system utilities or user-defined utilities such as floating-point routines.

The last group in Table 16–6 contains housekeeping instructions for WP and ST. Notice that LWPI uses immediate data. If WP must be loaded with a variable, then it must be done in conjunction with a jump using BLWP.

16.5 SAMPLE PROGRAMS

The simple multiplication program that we showed for the 6809 in Table 5–4 is recoded in 9900 assembly language as shown in Table 16–8. This program uses the memory-to-memory instruction capabilities of the 9900. Unlike most other processors in this book, the "@" prefix on various operands specifies absolute addressing, not indirect.

Most 9900 programs must use workspace registers, not only for efficiency, but also to utilize instructions that require registers (e.g., shifts and subroutine jumps). The multiplication program may be recoded using workspace registers as shown in Table 16–9. To begin, the program initializes WP to gain access to 16 workspace registers. The program's inputs and outputs happen to be stored in memory locations that become workspace registers when WP is loaded. Thus, the data manipulation instructions in the program are all short, 1-word instructions that specify operands using register-direct addressing. This version of the program runs faster and occupies less memory than the original version.

Table 16–10 illustrates auto-increment and byte addressing in the 9900. The program declares an array of five bytes, and uses the MOVB instruction to initialize each component. The address of the next component, kept in R1, is a 16-bit quantity even though the components themselves are bytes. Since auto-increment addressing is used with a byte instruction, the processor increments R1 by one at each step.

TABLE 16–8 Multiplication by repeated addition.

```
*          Enter with multiplier and multiplicand in memory words
*          >2000 and >2002. Exit with product in memory word >2004.
*
           AORG    >2000           Program origin.
MPY        BSS     2               Multiplier.
MCND       BSS     2               Multiplicand.
PROD       BSS     2               Product.
CNT        BSS     2               Loop counter.
*
START      CLR     @PROD           Set PROD to 0.
           MOV     @MPY,@CNT       Do loop MPY times.
           JEQ     OUT             Done if MPY = 0.
LOOP       A       @MCND,@PROD     Add MCND to PROD.
           DEC     @CNT            Decrement CNT.
           JNE     LOOP            Repeat until CNT = 0.
OUT        B       @>F000          Go to operating system restart address.
           END     START
```

Subroutines in the 9900 are introduced in Table 16–11. The main program sets up R0 with a pointer to a list of words and calls a subroutine TCNT1S that counts the number of "1" bits in all the words in the list. TCNT1S fetches words from the list and calls a subroutine WCNT1S to count ones in each word. WCNT1S uses a table of 1-bit masks and a loop to check each bit position of its input word.

TABLE 16–9 Multiplication program using workspace registers.

```
*          Enter with multiplier and multiplicand in memory words
*          >2000 and >2002. Exit with product in memory word >2004.
*
           AORG    >2000           Program origin.
WRKSPC     BSS     32              Reserve 16 words for registers.
MPY        EQU     0               Multiplier register.
MCND       EQU     1               Multiplicand register.
PROD       EQU     2               Product register.
CNT        EQU     3               Loop counter register.
*
START      LWPI    WRKSPC          Set up WP to point to register area.
           CLR     PROD            PROD = R2 = MEM[WP+4] = MEM[>2004] := 0
           MOV     MPY,CNT         Do loop MPY times.
           JEQ     OUT             Done if MPY = 0.
LOOP       A       MCND,PROD       Add MCND to PROD.
           DEC     CNT             Decrement CNT.
           JNE     LOOP            Repeat until CNT = 0.
OUT        B       @>F000          Go to operating system restart address.
           END     START
```

TABLE 16–10   Initializing an array of bytes.

```
        AORG   >2000        Program origin.
WRKSPC  BSS    32           Reserve 16 words for registers.
Q       BSS    5            Reserve 5 bytes for array.
        EVEN                Force PLC even for program.
IVAL    EQU    17           Initial value for array components.
*
INIT    LWPI   WRKSPC       Set up WP to point to register area.
        LI     R0,IVAL      Load initial value for components.
        SWPB   R0           MOVB will use high-order byte of R0.
        LI     R1,Q         Load address of first component.
ILOOP   MOVB   R0,*R1+      Initialize component and bump to next.
        CI     R1,Q+5       Past last component?
        JNE    ILOOP        If not, go do some more.
        B      @F000        Go to operating system restart address.
        END    INIT
```

You may recall that the 6809 version of the ones-counting program, presented in Table 5–10, broke input words into bytes and then counted ones in a byte. It is difficult to code the 9900 to use this algorithm. In this example and in many other areas the 9900 is not a very good machine for processing bytes, because it does not have a complete set of byte manipulation instructions.

Since it calls another subroutine, the TCNT1S subroutine in Table 16–11 must save the contents of R11 somewhere before it calls WCNT1S. In this example we have used a processor register, R10, to save R11. When there are more levels of subroutine nesting, a different register must be used at each level. After a few levels of nesting we may run out of available registers. At this point an alternative is to store the return address in a dedicated memory location associated with each subroutine. For example, the return address could be stored just before the subroutine entry point as shown below:

```
        BSS    2            Reserve storage for return address.
TCNT1S  MOV    R11,@$-2     Save return address.
        ...
TDONE   MOV    @TCNT1S-2,R11 Get return address.
        B      *R11         Jump to it.
```

However, this convention does not support reentrancy and recursion, since the return address is destroyed if the subroutine is re-entered before returning. Also, the convention of using the word before the subroutine entry point cannot be used if subroutines are stored in read-only memory.

By dedicating a processor register for use as a stack pointer, a programmer can use a stack to save return addresses. For example, we can use R10 as a pointer to the top of a stack of words that grows towards lower-numbered memory locations, similar to the hardware-supported stacks in

TABLE 16-11 Program that uses subroutines to count the number of "1" bits in a list of words terminated by an all-zero word.

```
        AORG   >2000              Program origin.
WRKSPC  BSS    32                 Reserve 16 words for registers.
LIST    DATA   >37BE,>1234,>D0AC,0    Test-list to count 1s.
*
MAIN    LWPI   WRKSPC             Set up WP to point to register area.
        LI     R0,LIST            Get address of test list.
        BL     @TCNT1S            Count number of 1s in it.
        B      @>F000             Go to operating system.
*
*       Count the number of '1' bits in a list of words. Enter
*       with pointer to list in R0; list is terminated by a
*       zero word. Exit with total 1-count in R1.
TCNT1S  MOV    R11,R10            Save return address.
        CLR    R1                 Initialize 1s-count.
WLOOP   MOV    *R0+,R2            Get next word from list.
        JEQ    TDONE              Zero signifies end of list.
        BL     @WCNT1S            Else count 1s in R2.
        A      R3,R1              Add new count to old.
        JMP    WLOOP              Continue with next list entry.
TDONE   B      *R10               Return.
*
*       Count number of '1' bits in a word. Enter with word in R2;
*       exit with count in R3 and R0-R2, R5-R15 undisturbed.
WCNT1S  CLR    R3                 Initialize '1' count.
        LI     R4,MASKS           Point to 1-bit masks.
BLOOP   COC    *R4+,R2            Got a '1'?
        JNE    NO1                Skip if none.
        INC    R3                 Otherwise increment '1' count.
NO1     CI     R4,MASKE           Past last mask?
        JNE    BLOOP              Continue if not.
        B      *R11               Else return.
*       Define 1-bit masks to test bits of word.
MASKS   DATA   >8000,>4000,>2000,>1000,>800,>400
        DATA   >200,>100,>80,>40,>20,>10,8,4,2,1
MASKE   EQU    $
        END    MAIN
```

other processors in this book. We can initialize the stack at the beginning of a program with the following code:

```
STACK   BSS    100                Reserve storage for stack.
STACKE  EQU    $                  Stack pointer initialization address.
SP      EQU    10                 Use R10 for stack pointer.
WRKSPC  BSS    32                 Reserve storage for workspace registers.
*
MAIN    LWPI   WRKSPC             Set up WP to point to workspace.
        LI     SP,STACKE          Initialize stack to empty.
        ...
```

At the beginning of each subroutine called by BL, we can then use the following code to push the return address:

```
SUBR    DECT    SP              Reserve a word on the stack.
        MOV     R11,*SP         Save return address.
        ...
```

At the end of the subroutine, we can return as follows:

```
        ...
RETURN  MOV     *SP+,R11        Pop return address.
        B       *R11            Jump to it.
```

The stack may also be used for storing temporary data and for passing parameters, as shown in Section 16.5. The stack convention allows reentrancy and recursion in 9900 subroutines. In a subroutine that does not call any other subroutines, the return address still may be left in R11 for the duration.

Indexed addressing in the 9900 is illustrated in Table 16–12, a program that finds prime numbers using the sieve of Eratosthenes. Like the 6809 version in Table 7–5, the 9900 program declares an array of bytes in which each component corresponds to a number between 2 and 1000. By marking off multiples of known primes, it eliminates nonprimes until only primes remain.

A stack-oriented parameter-passing convention was illustrated in Figure 9–4; 9900 subroutines may use the same convention. For example, the 6809 DIVIDE subroutine in Table 9–16 has been mechanically translated into a 9900 version in Table 16–13. The return address is saved on the stack using the convention presented earlier in this section, and parameters are passed on the return-address stack. A main program that calls DIVIDE could be developed from Table 9–17 in a similar way. Both the subroutine and main program use the stack layout shown in Figure 13–7 on p. 421.

Although it is straightforward, the subroutine-calling convention described above is inefficient. In order to access data on the stack, an instruction must contain a 16-bit offset to the desired datum. Therefore, instructions that access input parameters and local variables will be two or three words long. An alternative is to create a new workspace on the stack, so that a small number of input parameters and local variables can be efficiently accessed as workspace registers.

The new parameter-passing convention is illustrated in Figure 16–6. The workspace registers are actually stored in a block of 16 words on the stack as shown in Figure 16–6(a); R10 is still used as the stack pointer. In order to call a subroutine, a program first allocates at the top of the stack 16 words that will become the new workspace. It then places the input parameters and a copy of SP into the future workspace registers as shown in Figure 16–6(b) and calls the subroutine using an appropriate BLWP instruction. This gives the

TABLE 16-12   Subroutine to find primes using an array and indexed addressing.

```
*                                          PROCEDURE FindPrimes (input,output);
NPRIME   =      1000                        CONST nPrime = 1000;
PLIMIT   =      32                            pLimit = 32;
PRIME    BSS    NPRIME-1                     VAR prime:ARRAY [2..nPrime] OF boolean;
         EVEN                                  {Force PLC even for program.}
I        EQU    1                            {reg} I, J : word; {Indices into PRIME.}
J        EQU    2
FNDPRM   MOV    R11,R10                      BEGIN  {Save return address in R10.}
         LI     I,2                            FOR I := 2 TO nPrime DO
         SETO   R0                               {00 = false, FF = true}
SETEM    MOVB   R0,PRIME-2(I)                     {Set the entire array true.}
         INC    I                                prime[I] := true;
         CI     I,NPRIME
         JLE    SETEM
         LI     J,2                          J := 2; {First known prime.}
*                                          REPEAT {Check integers 2 to pLimit.}
MARKEM   MOVB   PRIME-2(J),R0                  IF prime[J] THEN
         JEQ    NOTPRM                            BEGIN
         MOV    J,I                                 I := 2 * J;
         SLA    I,1
         CLR    R0
CLRLUP   MOVB   R0,PRIME-2(I)                        REPEAT {Mark multiples of J.}
         A      J,I                                    prime[I] := false; I := I+J;
         CI     I,NPRIME                            UNTIL I > nPrime;
         JLE    CLRLUP                            END;
NOTPRM   INC    J                            J := J+1;
         CI     J,PLIMIT                     UNTIL J > pLimit;
         JLE    MARKEM
         BL     @WRMSG1                      write('Primes between 2 and ');
         LI     I,NPRIME                     I := nPrime;
         BL     @PRINTI                      writeln(I); {Print the number in I.}
         LI     I,2                          FOR I := 2 TO nPrime DO
PRTLUP   MOVB   PRIME-2(I),R0                  {Print all the primes.}
         JEQ    NEXTP                          IF prime[I] THEN
         BL     @PRINTI                          writeln(I);
NEXTP    INC    I
         CI     I,NPRIME
         JLE    PRTLUP
         B      *R10                         {All done, return to caller.}
         END    FNDPRM                     END;
```

subroutine access to the input parameters and local variables as workspace registers as shown in Figure 16–6(c). Output parameters are accessed in the old workspace relative to SP, and are available as registers upon return as shown in Figure 16–6(d).

In the convention of Figure 16–6, the input parameters and local variables of a called subroutine and the output parameters of nested subroutines

TABLE 16–13 Unsigned division subroutine that passes parameters on a stack.

```
HIDIV    EQU    1              Registers to hold high dividend and
LODIV    EQU    2                 low dividend during iterations.
FP       EQU    9              Frame pointer register.
SP       EQU    10             Stack pointer register.
*        The offsets below define positions of parameters and local
*        variables in the stack relative to the frame pointer (FP).
CNT      EQU    -2             Loop counter.
OLDFP    EQU    0              Old value of frame pointer.
RETADR   EQU    2              Return address.
DVSR     EQU    4              1-word divisor (input).
HIDVND   EQU    6              High-order word of dividend (input).
LODVND   EQU    8              Low-order word of dividend (input).
REM      EQU    10             1-word remainder (output).
QUOT     EQU    12             1-word quotient (output).
STATUS   EQU    14             0 ==> OK, <>0 ==> overflow (output).
*
DIVIDE   AI     SP,-4          Make room for ret. addr. and old FP.
         MOV    R11,2(SP)      Save return address on stack.
         MOV    FP,*SP         Save old frame pointer on stack.
         MOV    SP,FP          Copy SP into FP for new frame pointer.
         LI     R0,16          Push initial count onto stack.
         DECT   SP
         MOV    R0,*SP
         CLR    STATUS(FP)     Mark initial status OK.
         MOV    HIDVND(FP),HIDIV  Put high DVND in a register.
         MOV    LODVND(FP),LODIV  Put high DVND in a register.
         C      HIDIV,DVSR(FP) Will quotient fit in 1 word?
         JL     DIVLUP         Branch if it will.
         INC    STATUS(FP)     Else report overflow.
         JMP    CLNSTK
DIVLUP   SLA    LODIV,1        Left shift dividend with LSB:=0.
         JOC    CARRY1         Now a mess because no ROLC.
CARRY0   SLA    HIDIV,1        A carry here
         JMP    CHKCY
CARRY1   SLA    HIDIV,1          or here from MSB means
         ORI    HIDIV,1          {C not affected}
CHKCY    JOC    QUOT1            high DVND definitely > DVSR.
         C      HIDIV,DVSR(FP)   Compare high DVND with DVSR.
         JL     QUOTOK         Quotient bit = 0 if lower.
QUOT1    INC    LODIV          Else set quotient bit to 1.
         S      DVSR(FP),HIDIV And update high DVND.
QUOTOK   DEC    CNT(FP)        Decrement iteration count.
         JGT    DIVLUP         Continue until done.
         MOV    HIDIV,REM(FP)  Store remainder.
         MOV    LODIV,QUOT(FP)  Store quotient.
CLNSTK   MOV    RETADR(FP),R11 Save return address in R11.
         MOV    OLDFP(FP),FP   Restore old frame pointer.
         AI     SP,REM-CNT     Remove input parameters and locals.
         B      *R11           Return.
```

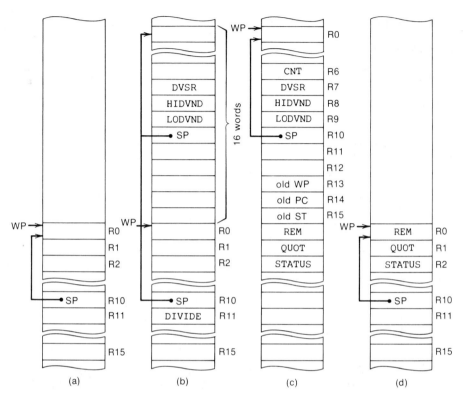

FIGURE 16–6 Parameter-passing convention with workspace registers stored on the stack: (a) normal state of stack; (b) setup with 16 new workspace registers allocated and input parameters loaded, just before calling subroutine SUBR via BLWP R10; (c) after entering subroutine, input parameters and local variables available as registers in new workspace; (d) after return, output parameters available as registers in old workspace.

that it calls may occupy a total of ten words (R0 through R9). The convention may be extended for subroutines with more parameters, but then some parameters and local variables will not be accessible as workspace registers. For example, output parameters could be stored on the stack between the old workspace and the new workspace, instead of in the first few registers of the old workspace. In a more general case, a frame pointer would be needed as well as the stack pointer. Specifications for extensions, as well as code for the convention of Figure 16–6, are left as exercises for the reader.

Queue manipulation subroutines for the 9900 are given in Table 16–14. Like the 6809 version in Table 9–18, this code is self-documenting, and so we leave you to read it.

TABLE 16–14 Queue manipulation subroutines for the 9900.

```
* QUEUE MODULE
*
* This module contains three subroutines for manipulating queues
* of 16-bit words. A queue is defined by a queue descriptor table
* and a block of storage, as shown below.
*
*                                             QUEUE STORAGE BLOCK
*         --------------------               --------------------
* QDTBL |    QHEAD (word)    |  -------->|        (word)        |
*       |-------------------|     |      |--------------------|
*       |    QTAIL (word)    |     |      |                    |
*       |-------------------|     |      |   o   o   o   o    |
*       |    QSTRT (word)    |----         |                    |
*       |-------------------|            |--------------------|
*       |    QEND  (word)    |----------->|        (word)        |
*         --------------------               --------------------
*
* Offsets in descriptor table:
*
QHEAD   EQU    0
QTAIL   EQU    2
QSTRT   EQU    4
QEND    EQU    6
*
* In this table, the last two words are constants, initialized at
* load time, that give the starting and ending addresses of the block
* of storage (buffer) reserved for the queue itself. The first and
* second words are reserved to store the head and tail (absolute
* memory addresses), and are manipulated by the subroutines.
*
* If a program defines several queues, it allocates a separate queue
* descriptor table and storage block for each one.  For example, the
* statements below define a 100-word queue Q1 and a 5-word queue Q2:
*
*Q1BLK  BSS    200             Storage block for Q1.
*Q1END  EQU    $-2             Last location in Q1 storage block.
*Q1DT   BSS    4               Q1 descriptor table -- QHEAD and QTAIL.
*       DATA   Q1BLK,Q1END                  QSTRT and QEND.
*Q2BLK  BSS    10              Storage block for Q2.
*Q2END  EQU    $-2             Last location in Q2 storage block.
*Q2DT   BSS    4               Q2 descriptor table -- QHEAD and QTAIL.
*       DATA   Q2BLK,Q2END                  QSTRT and QEND.
*
* Subroutines are provided to initialize a queue (QINIT), enqueue
* a word (QENQ), and dequeue a word (QDEQ).  Each subroutine must
* be passed the address of the descriptor table for the queue
* to be manipulated.
*
```

TABLE 16–14 (continued)

```
* SUBROUTINE QINIT -- Initialize a queue to be empty.
*
* INPUTS
*   QDTBL --  The address of the queue descriptor table for the
*             queue to be initialized, passed in register R1.
* OUTPUTS, GLOBAL DATA, LOCAL DATA -- None
* FUNCTIONS
*    (1) Initialize the queue to empty by setting QHEAD and QTAIL
*        in QDTBL equal to the first address in the queue buffer.
* REGISTERS AFFECTED -- ST
*
* TYPICAL CALLING SEQUENCE
*         LI    R1,Q1DT
*         BL    @QINIT
*
QINIT  MOV   QSTRT(R1),QHEAD(R1)  Put buffer starting address
       MOV   QSTRT(R1),QTAIL(R1)    into QHEAD and QTAIL.
       B     @R11           Done, return.
*
* SUBROUTINE QENQ -- Enqueue one word into a queue.
*
* INPUTS
*   QDTBL --  The address of the queue descriptor table for the
*             queue to be manipulated, passed in register R1.
*   QDATA  -- The word to be enqueued, passed in register R0.
* OUTPUTS
*   QFULL  -- 1 if the queue is already full, else 0;
*             passed in condition bit E.
* GLOBAL DATA, LOCAL DATA -- None.
* FUNCTIONS
*    (1) If the queue described by QDTBL is full, set QFULL to 1.
*    (2) If the queue is not full, enqueue QDATA and set QFULL to 0.
* REGISTERS AFFECTED -- R2, ST
*
* TYPICAL CALLING SEQUENCE
*         LI    R1,Q1DT        Enqueue AWORD.
*         MOV   @AWORD,R0
*         BL    @QENQ
*         JEQ   OVFL           Branch if queue is full.
*
QENQ   MOV   QTAIL(R1),R2   Get queue tail.
       MOV   R0,*R2+        Store QDATA at tail (no harm if full).
       C     R2,QEND(R1)    R2 points to next free word in queue.
       JLE   QENQ1          Wrap-around?
       MOV   QSTRT(R1),R2   Reinitialize on wrap-around.
QENQ1  C     R2,QHEAD(R1)   Queue already full?
       JEQ   QENQ2          Return with E=1 if full.
       MOV   R2,QTAIL(R1)   Else update tail, return with E=0.
       LI    R2,1           Dummy operation to clear E.
QENQ2  B     *R11           Return.
```

TABLE 16-14   (continued)

```
* SUBROUTINE QDEQ -- Dequeue one word from a queue.
*
* INPUTS
*   QDTBL --   The address of the queue descriptor table for the
*              queue to be manipulated, passed in register R1.
* OUTPUTS
*   QEMPTY -- 1 if the queue is empty, else 0; passed in
*              condition bit E.
*   QDATA  -- The word dequeued, passed in register R0.
* GLOBAL DATA, LOCAL DATA -- None.
* FUNCTIONS
*   (1) If the queue described by QDTBL is empty, set QEMPTY to 1.
*   (2) If the queue isn't empty, dequeue QDATA and set QEMPTY to 0.
* REGISTERS AFFECTED -- R0, R2, ST
*
* TYPICAL CALLING SEQUENCE
*        LI     R1,Q1DT       Dequeue a word into AWORD.
*        BL     @QDEQ
*        JEQ    UNDFL         Branch if queue is empty.
*        MOV    R0,@AWORD
*
QDEQ     MOV    QHEAD(R1),R2  Get copy of head.
         C      R2,QTAIL(R1)  Queue empty?
         JEQ    QDEQ2         Return with E=1 if empty.
         MOV    *R2+,R0       Read QDATA word from queue.
         C      R2,QEND(R1)   R2 points to next queue item.
         JLE    QDEQ1         Wrap-around?
         MOV    QSTRT(R1),R2  Reinitialize head on wrap-around.
QDEQ1    MOV    R2,QHEAD(R1)  Update real head in memory.
         LI     R2,1          Set E:=0 since not empty.
QDEQ2    B      *R11          Return.
```

16.6 INPUT/OUTPUT, INTERRUPTS, AND TRAPS

16.6.1 Input/Output

Like all other microprocessors, the 9900 can support memory-mapped I/O using appropriate interfaces. In fact, 9900 systems must use memory-mapped I/O to communicate with most commercially available LSI peripheral circuits. In addition, the 9900 contains a novel serial I/O interfacing arrangement called the "communications register unit" (CRU). The CRU may be used with 9900-family LSI peripheral circuits as well as with custom-designed interface circuits.

The CRU supports an array of 4K individually addressable 1-bit input ports and output ports. As shown in Figure 16-1, the CRU communicates with the ports using one line for input, one line for output, twelve lines to specify a bit address, and a few lines to control read and write commands.

Instructions that access the I/O ports are listed in the first part of Table 16–15. All I/O instructions access I/O ports using a form of based addressing in which R12, the "CRU base register," contains the 12-bit address of a 1-bit CRU port. The first three instructions in Table 16–15 each contain an 8-bit signed displacement so that CRU ports "nearby" the current CRU base address may be accessed. SBO and SBZ access an output port, allowing a selected bit to be set or cleared. TB accesses an input port, setting the E status bit equal to the contents of the selected input bit.

The LDCR and STCR instructions allow up to 16 sequentially numbered bits to be accessed as a unit. The CRU base address points to the first CRU bit to be transferred, and successive CRU bits are used to complete the transfer. The src or dst operand may specify an effective address using any of the normal addressing modes — register direct and indirect, absolute, auto-increment, and based or indexed; the instruction accesses the src or dst bits beginning with the least significant bit position.

With LDCR and STCR, byte and word transfers between the CPU and an I/O port take place serially, one bit at a time. Therefore, a programmer must pay close attention to the order in which I/O control bits are accessed using these instructions. For example, the "GO" bit for an operation should not be set before various mode bits for the operation have been initialized.

TABLE 16–15　9900 input/output and processor control instructions.

Mnemonic	Operands	Description
SBO	disp	Set selected CRU output bit to 1
SBZ	disp	Set selected CRU output bit to 0
TB	disp	Set E equal to selected CRU input bit
STCR	dst,n	Store n CRU input bits into dst
LDCR	src,n	Load n CRU output bits from src
IDLE		Stop until interrupt, load, or reset occurs
RESET		System dependent
CKOF		System dependent
CKON		System dependent
LREX		System dependent

Notes:　All CRU bit addresses are computed relative to a 12-bit "CRU base address" contained in bits 3 through 14 of the "CRU base register" R12.

disp is an 8-bit displacement in the range −128 through +127 that is added to the CRU base address to form the bit number of the operand. The contents of the CRU base register are not affected.

src and dst are each given by a 6-bit EA specification.

n specifies the number of bits to be transferred, 1 to 16 (encoded in the instruction as 1–15, 0). The bits are transferred one at a time, least significant bit first, beginning at the CRU base address. If n is between 1 and 8, the operand is considered to be a byte for the purposes of the src or dst effective address computation, otherwise the operand is considered to be a word.

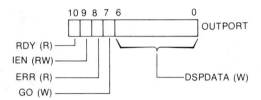

FIGURE 16–7 Programming model for a character output device connected to the 9900 CRU.

To illustrate the CRU instructions, let us define a character output device similar to the one described in Section 10.3.3, whose programming model was shown in Figure 10–12. The port bits shown in Figure 10–12 could be accessed as 11 CRU bits addressed as shown in Figure 16–7. The bit numbers shown in the figure are actually offsets to be added to the CRU base address of the device. For this example we'll assume that the base address is >AD0. Notice that CRU bits are numbered from right to left. This is appropriate, even though CPU and memory bits are numbered backwards, because the LDCR and STCR instructions transfer bits beginning with the least significant.

A subroutine that prints a character using this interface is shown in Table 16–16. Since the base address of the device interface is kept in a register, it is straightforward to rewrite this routine as a shared I/O driver for several identical devices connected to a 9900 CPU.

The last group of instructions in Table 16–15 contains IDLE, which stops the CPU until an external event occurs. It also includes four instructions which have no effect on the 9900 processor but which may be decoded by external hardware to perform system-dependent functions.

TABLE 16–16 Subroutine to display a character using the interface of Figure 16–7.

```
OUTPORT EQU    >AD0           Base address of CRU bits.
DSPDATA EQU    0              Offset to first output data bit.
GO      EQU    7              Offset to GO bit.
ERR     EQU    8              Offset to error bit.
IEN     EQU    9              Offset to interrupt enable bit.
RDY     EQU    10             Offset to ready bit.
*
*       Display a character passed in high byte of R0.
CHROUT  LI     R12,OUTPORT    Set up CRU base register.
WTOUT   TB     RDY            Device ready?
        JNE    WTOUT          Busy-wait if not equal to 1.
        LDCR   R0,7           Transfer ASCII char to output port.
        SBZ    IEN            Be sure interrupts are off.
        SBO    GO             Start next operation.
        B      *R11           Return to caller.
```

16.6.2 Interrupts

The 9900 CPU contains a 16-level, vectored, priority interrupt system. The levels are numbered from 0 (highest priority) to 15 (lowest priority). The TMS9900 CPU circuit has a 4-bit "interrupt level" input to which external hardware applies the level number of the highest-priority interrupt request, and an INTREQ input by which the external hardware indicates that a level number has been applied.

Like other CPUs, the 9900 accepts an interrupt request only between the execution of individual instructions. Furthermore, the level number of the request must be less than or equal to the current CPU priority number contained in ST bits 12–15 (IMASK field). Thus, all interrupts except level 0 may be disabled by setting IMASK to 0. Level 0 is reserved for the hardware reset function, and the remaining levels are used by I/O devices. Within each level, a system hardware designer may provide additional interrupt lines and priority by means of external hardware. The conditions for the 9900 to accept an interrupt are summarized below:

(1) A device interface must have experienced an interrupt-generating event (e.g., character received from keyboard, ready to send character to screen, disk block transfer complete, etc.).

(2) The interrupt enable bit (e.g., IEN) on the device interface must be equal to 1.

(3) The level number at which the interrupt was requested must be less than or equal to the current CPU priority number in IMASK.

(4) The CPU must have just finished the execution of an instruction.

When an interrupt is accepted, the CPU automatically executes a BLWP instruction using a context vector from a predetermined address. As shown in Table 16–17, the first 64 bytes of memory are reserved to hold context vectors for interrupt service routines. Following the standard convention used by BLWP, the first word of each 4-byte entry contains a new value for WP, and the second word contains the starting execution address for the interrupt subroutine. BLWP automatically saves the old context (WP, PC, and ST) in registers R13–R15 in the new workspace.

Besides the "reset" interrupt level, the TMS9900 CPU circuit has a LOAD input that causes a non-maskable interrupt using a context vector in high memory. This input is intended to be used to transfer control to debuggers or other software stored in read-only memory after a "cold start."

A program that uses interrupts to print strings of characters is shown in Table 16–18. This program uses the hypothetical character output device whose programming model was shown in Figure 16–7. The program assumes that a string is a sequence of ASCII characters stored one per byte and terminated by NUL (a zero byte).

TABLE 16–17 9900 interrupt and trap vectors.

Address	Interrupt or Trap
>0000	Interrupt level 0 (reset)
>0004	Interrupt level 1
>0008	Interrupt level 2
. . .	. . .
>0038	Interrupt level 14
>003C	Interrupt level 15
>0040	XOP src,0 instruction
>0044	XOP src,1 instruction
>0048	XOP src,2 instruction
. . .	. . .
>0078	XOP src,14 instruction
>007C	XOP src,15 instruction
>FFFC	LOAD function

TABLE 16–18 Interrupt-driven character output for the 9900.

```
*          Define addresses and bit positions for display interface.
OUTPORT EQU    >AD0            Base address of CRU bits.
DSPDATA EQU    0               Offset to first output data bit.
GO      EQU    7               Offset to GO bit.
ERR     EQU    8               Offset to error bit.
IEN     EQU    9               Offset to interrupt enable bit.
RDY     EQU    10              Offset to ready bit.
*
DSPVCT  EQU    >10             Interrupt vector number (level 4).
*
WORKSP  BSS    32              Workspace main program.
*
DSPWRK  BSS    32              Workspace for DSPINT.
DSPR12  EQU    DSPWRK+24       R12's address in DSPINT workspace.
*
*          Global and local variables.
DSPBSY  BSS    2               Nonzero when string is being displayed.
BPNT    EQU    DSPWRK+2        Pointer to next character to display,
RBPNT   EQU    1                 == R1 in interrupt routine workspace.
*
*          Messages printed by main program.
MSG1    TEXT   'Debugging always takes longer than expected...'
        BYTE   >0D,>0A,0       Carriage return, line feed, NUL.
MSG2    TEXT   '...even when this rule is taken into account.'
        BYTE   >0D,>0A,0       Carriage return, line feed, NUL.
        EVEN                   Force PLC to a word boundary.
*
```

TABLE 16–18 (continued)

```
*          Display initialization, pointer to string passed in R1.
DSPOUT LI    R12,OUTPORT  Set up CRU base register.
WTOUT  MOV   DSPBSY,R0    Busy with previous string?
       JNE   WTOUT        Yes, wait for it.
       SETO  DSPBSY       Mark display busy for new string.
       LDCR  *R1+,7       Send first character to output port.
       MOV   R1,BPNT      Save pointer to next char and
       MOV   R12,DSPR12     CRU base reg in DSPINT's workspace.
       SBO   GO           Start output operation.
       SBO   IEN          Enable display interrupts.
       B     *R11         Done, return.
*
*          Display output interrupt handler.
DSPINT LDCR  *RBPNT+,7    Get character, is it NUL (0)?
       JEQ   DSPDUN       We're done if it is.
       SBO   GO           Else start output operation
       RTWP               and return.
DSPDUN SBZ   IEN          Disable output device interrupts.
       CLR   DSPBSY       Display is no longer busy.
       RTWP               Return.
*
*          Main program.
MAIN   LWPI  WORKSP       Initialize workspace pointer.
       CLR   DSPBSY       Mark display not busy.
       LI    R0,DSPWRK    Initialize context vector for
       MOV   R0,DSPVCT      display interrupt service routine.
       LI    R0,DSPINT
       MOV   R0,DSPVCT+2
       LI    R12,OUTPORT  Set up CRU base register.
       SBZ   IEN          Make sure display interrupts off.
       LIMI  4            Enable CPU level 4 interrupts.
LOOP   ...                Do some computation.
       LI    R1,MSG1      Get address of first message
       BL    DSPOUT         and print it.
       ...                Do some more computation.
       LI    R1,MSG2      Get address of second message
       BL    DSPOUT         and print it.
       B     LOOP         Do it all again.
       END   MAIN
```

The display output initialization routine DSPOUT accepts a pointer to a string to be printed. The variable DSPBSY indicates whether a previous string is still being printed, so that a new operation is not started until the previous one is completed. DSPOUT prints the first character, enables the display interface to interrupt after the character has been printed, and returns to the main program.

Remaining characters are printed by the interrupt service routine DSPINT. Since a new context is established by the BLWP instruction inherent in interrupt servicing, DSPINT does not have to save any registers; it begins with its own context. In fact, the global variable BPNT is actually stored as part of DSPINT's workspace, so that it is accessed very efficiently as a register. Likewise, the CRU base register R12 in DSPINT's workspace is initialized just once in DSPOUT, saving time in DSPINT.

16.6.3 Traps

The 9900 has a trap-type instruction, XOP src,n, that transfers control to one of sixteen different trap handlers by executing a BLWP using one of the context vectors listed in Table 16–17. In addition, XOP computes the effective address of a src operand and deposits this address in register R11 of the new workspace. Thus, XOP can pass the address of a parameter or the base address of a parameter area to the trap handler.

Typical uses of XOP are to call floating-point routines and operating system utilities. The caller needs only to know a "trap number" for the desired routine, not the absolute address at which the routine starts. This facilitates relocation and independence of the utilities.

REFERENCES

The basic 9900 architecture is old, having evolved from the Texas Instruments 900 family of minicomputers. The 9900 single-chip microprocessor architecture was first described in "16-bit Microprocessor Performs Like a Minicomputer," by A. Lofthus and D. Ogden [*Electronics*, Vol. 49, No. 12, May 20, 1976, pp. 99–105].

Texas Instruments publishes quite a bit of technical information on various 9900-family components, for example the *TMS9900 Microprocessor Data Manual*. TI also publishes documentation on 9900-based computer systems and software development tools, such as *Model 990 Computer Assembly Language Programmer's Guide* and a handy *Model 990 Computer Programming Card*.

EXERCISES

16.1   Rewrite the multiplication program in Table 16–9 so that it produces a double word result and gives the correct result for all input numbers.

16.2   Write a 9900 subroutine that adds two 8-digit unsigned BCD numbers P and Q and produces a sum S. The numbers are stored in memory, but you are to define the exact format. Since the 9900 does not have BCD arithmetic or decimal adjust instructions, use table look-up to find the sum of two BCD digits.

16.3   Modify the program in Table 16–10 so that the run-time swap of R0's bytes is not needed.

16.4   Write a program for the 9900 that sorts bytes using the same algorithm as the 6809 program in Table 7–3. Comment on any difficulties that you encounter.

16.5   Rewrite the FNDPRM subroutine in Table 16–13 to find primes among the first 8000 integers, still using only a 1000-byte array.

16.6   In the 9900 there is no SLL R,cnt instruction. Can another instruction substitute?

16.7   In the 9900 there is no SLC R,cnt instruction. Is the instruction SRC R,16-cnt equivalent?

16.8   Write an unsigned multiplication subroutine that takes two long words and produces a quad-word result, using MPY as a primitive. Use a stack-oriented parameter-passing convention, and write a prologue for the subroutine that shows inputs, outputs, registers affected, and a typical calling sequence.

16.9   Write a DIVIDE subroutine and calling program that use the parameter passing convention illustrated in Figure 16–6.

16.10   Devise a parameter-passing convention for the 9900 in which the workspace registers are stored on the stack, and in which both input and output parameters are always accessible by both the subroutine and its caller as workspace registers. (*Hint:* You may find it useful to reverse the direction of stack growth in memory.)

16.11   Modify the queue module in Table 16–14 to manipulate queues of bytes.

16.12   Under what circumstances can the LI R2,1 instructions in the queue module in Table 16–14 be eliminated?

16.13   Rewrite the recursive NIM subroutines in Table 9–19 for the 9900. Write a main program that analyzes the game for all combinations of values of NHEAP from 2 to 25 and NTAKE from 2 to 6.

16.14   Devise a coroutine calling convention for the 9900 in which each coroutine has its own set of workspace registers.

16.15   Describe the possible ill effects of reversing the order of the instructions SBO GO and SBO IEN in the DSPOUT subroutine in Table 16–18.

16.16   Write a keyboard input and display output module for the 9900, similar to the 6809 module in Table 10–4.

16.17   Write a complete Pascal simulation of the 9900.

17

MOTOROLA 6809

The Motorola 6800 was one of the most popular processors of the "micro-processor revolution" of the 1970s. The 6800 has two 8-bit accumulators, condition bits, and 16-bit index register, stack pointer, and program counter. The 6809 is Motorola's successor to the 6800; it extends the original 6800 architecture by including more registers, instructions, and addressing modes.

The 6809 integrated circuit contains a CPU only; a system designer must add external memory and I/O to get a complete computer. A number of "turnkey" systems which use the 6809 CPU are available from different man-ufacturers. These include Motorola's EXORciser II development system, the Tandy TRS-80 Color Computer, and the Southwest Technical Products S/09.

There are a few intermediate members of the "6800" family besides the original 6800 and the advanced 6809. The 6801 has the same registers and instructions as the 6800 plus several additional instructions. The 6802 is in-tended for microcontroller applications; it has the 6800 registers and instruc-tion set plus 128 bytes of on-chip read/write memory. The 6805 is also in-tended for microcontroller applications; it has 6800-type instructions but only one accumulator, plus it has extensive bit-manipulation instructions. In this chapter we shall focus only on the 6809; other family members are easily understood by anyone familiar with the 6809.

17.1 BASIC ORGANIZATION

17.1.1 Computer Structure

The basic structure of a 6809-based computer is shown in Figure 17–1. Like the hypothetical H6809 processor that we introduced in Chapter 5, the real 6809 communicates with memory and peripherals using a single memory and I/O bus. This bus contains an 8-bit data bus, a 16-bit address bus, and various control signals, so that the maximum memory size is 2^{16} (64K) bytes. A system designer always has the option of using a memory mapping unit such as the Motorola 6829 to increase the amount of physical memory that can be connected to the CPU, but programs cannot access more than 64K bytes at one time.

The 6809 has no I/O instructions, and so it must use memory-mapped I/O. The system designer must allocate a portion of the total memory address space for I/O interface registers. Usually addresses in the upper regions of the address space are used. The 6809 processor supports a three-level vectored priority interrupt system. Additional sublevels and vectors may be provided within each level by external hardware, a system-dependent characteristic.

17.1.2 Processor Programming Model

The hypothetical H6809 processor has only a subset of the real 6809's registers and instructions. The complete programming model of the real 6809 is shown in Figure 17–2. There are two 8-bit accumulators (A and B), two 16-bit index registers (X and Y), two 16-bit stack pointers (S and U), a 16-bit program counter (PC), an 8-bit direct-page register (DP), and a set of 8 condition bits (CC). Some instructions manipulate the two accumulators A and B as a single 16-bit unit called D (using A as the most significant byte).

Comparing with the H6809, the real 6809's additional accumulator, index register, and stack pointer provide added programming flexibility. The use of DPR in the 6809 is explained in Section 17.3.

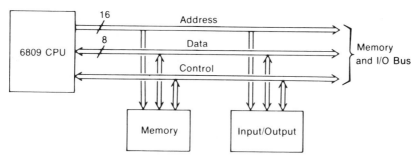

FIGURE 17–1 Structure of a computer that uses the 6809 processor chip.

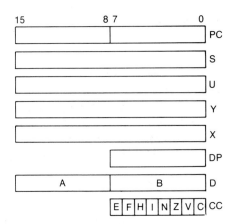

FIGURE 17–2 Programming model for the 6809.

Of the two stack pointers, S is the "system" stack pointer; it is automatically used by the processor for pushing and popping registers during subroutine and interrupt calls and returns. The other, U, is a "user" stack pointer — the programmer can use it to create another stack. The processor has instructions for pushing and popping registers in either stack. Also, all addressing modes that use the index registers (X and Y) can use either stack pointer (S or U) as well. Thus U may be conveniently used as a third index register.

17.1.3 Instruction Formats

A typical 6809 instruction specifies an *operation* (add, subtract, increment, test, etc.) and one of several basic *addressing modes* (inherent, immediate, absolute, or indexed). This combination of operation and addressing mode is encoded in the instruction's *opcode*.

Most 6809 instructions have an 8-bit opcode. However, the designers of the 6809 found that they needed more than 256 distinct opcodes to encode all of the desired operation/addressing mode combinations. Rather than reduce the number of instructions, the designers encoded some instructions using 16-bit (2-byte) opcodes. In these instructions the first byte is 10H or 11H, and the second byte specifies the exact instruction. Thus, a total of 254 8-bit opcodes and 512 16-bit opcodes are available. This encoding scheme easily accommodates the 268 distinct opcodes of the original 6809, and leaves plenty of spare opcode space for new instructions in future versions of the 6809. The particular encoding that the designers chose also simplified the circuit design of the 6809 processor chip.

Up to three additional bytes are used with some addressing modes to contain addressing information. With a 2-byte opcode, this yields instructions that are up to five bytes long.

17.2 ASSEMBLY LANGUAGE

Motorola's standard assembly language for the 6809 has the same basic format as the H6809 assembly language defined in Section 6.1. However, two of the conventions of Motorola's language are different from the H6809's:

- Hexadecimal constants may be denoted by a prefix of "$" as well as by a suffix of "H".

- The maximum label length is 6 characters instead of 8.

Also, some of Motorola's 6809 assembler directives have different names, and the RMW directive does not exist at all. Important Motorola assembler directives are summarized in Table 17–1.

As detailed in the next section, some of Motorola's addressing mode notations for the 6809 are different from those presented in Chapters 5 and 7 for the H6809. Also, some of the H6809 instructions that we used in various programs in Chapters 5 through 12 have different machine and/or assembly language encodings in the real 6809. All of the differences between the H6809

TABLE 17–1 Motorola 6809 assembly language directives.

Name	Example	Effect
ORG	ORG $4000	Set starting address of program.
EQU	CR EQU $0D	Equate symbol with 16-bit value.
FCB	CB FCB 17,$F9,−1	Store constant values into successive memory bytes.
FDB	CW FDB −789,$E800,CAT	Store constant values into successive memory words.
FCC	ST FCC /ABCDEFG/	Store ASCII values of characters into successive memory bytes.
RMB	TB RMB 10	Reserve memory bytes.
END	END START	Indicate end of assembly and give an optional starting address.
OPT	OPT ABS,S,W	Select assembly options (see Motorola assembler manual).

and the real 6809 are summarized in Table 17–2. We shall use standard Motorola assembly language for all 6809 programs in this chapter.

17.3 ADDRESSING

Many 6809 instructions use *inherent* addressing, in which the location of the operand is specified in the instruction opcode itself. The operand of such an instruction is generally a processor register. For example, the INCA in-

TABLE 17–2 Comparison of H6809 and Motorola 6809 features.

Assembler conventions	H6809	Motorola 6809
Hexidecimal specifier	H (suffix)	$ (prefix)
Maximum label length	8	6
Form constant word	FCW	FDB
Reserve memory words	RMW *n*	RMB 2*n*
Relocatable origin	RORG	See 6809 refs.
External reference	EXT	XREF
External definition	ENT	XDEF
Begin macro	MACRO	MACR
End IF statement	ENDIF	ENDC
Local label in macro	.label	Nonexistent

Addressing modes	H6809	Motorola 6809
Register indirect	@RR	,RR
Absolute indirect	@expr	[expr]
Auto-increment	(RR)+	,RR+ or ,RR++
Auto-decrement	-(RR)	,-RR or ,--RR
Relative	expr(PCR)	expr,PCR
Based or indexed	expr(RR)	expr,RR
Based indexed	R1(RR)	R1,RR

Instructions	H6809	Motorola 6809
Add to X	ADDX #expr	LEAX expr,X
Add to X	ADDX addr	PSHS X
		LDX addr
		LEAX [,S++]
Add to Y	ADDY #expr	LEAY expr,Y
Add to S	ADDS #expr	LEAS expr,S
Clear Z	CLRZ	ANDCC #$FB
Set Z	SETZ	ORCC #$04
Clear I	CLRI	ANDCC #$EF
Set I	SETI	ORCC #$10
Hardware Reset	PC:=0	PC:=MEMW[$FFFE]

struction (opcode $4C) increments accumulator A, while INCB (opcode $5C) increments accumulator B.

Other 6809 instructions specify operands in memory. The 6809 memory is byte-addressable, and most instructions specify one-byte operands. Some instructions access two bytes as a unit — the word. In the 6809, a word may start at an even or odd address and occupies two consecutive bytes. The most significant byte of a word is stored in the lower-numbered address. These concepts are illustrated in Figure 17–3.

The 6809 has a very "regular" instruction set because any instruction that specifies an operand in memory may do so using *any* addressing mode that makes sense. Thus, the addressing modes in this section may be used with just about any operation that specifies an operand in memory. Table 17–3 summarizes the 6809's addressing modes and assembly language notation for each mode.

17.3.1   Immediate

In *immediate addressing*, the instruction contains the operand. This is the only 6809 addressing mode that cannot be used with all memory operations, since it makes no sense with instructions that test a value (the test outcome would always be the same) or store a result (the result would have to be stored in the instruction). Thus, immediate mode can be used with Load and Add, but not with Store, Test, Increment, Rotate, and so on.

Depending on the operation, an immediate operand may be one or two bytes long. For example, the instruction LDA #$15 loads A with an 8-bit operand $15. As shown in Figure 17–4(a), the instruction is two bytes long. In Figure 17–4(b), the 3-byte instruction LDX #$1234 loads X with a 16-bit operand $1234. In both cases, an assembly language program denotes an immediate operand using the prefix "#"; the assembler deduces from the opcode (e.g. LDA or LDX) whether an 8-bit or 16-bit immediate operand is required. Thus, the assembly language instruction LDX #1 generates the 3-byte machine instruction shown in Figure 17–4(c).

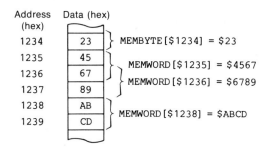

FIGURE 17–3   Memory addressing in the 6809.

TABLE 17–3 6809 addressing modes and assembly language notation.

Mode	Notation	Next Byte(s)	Operand
Immediate	`#n`	`n[lo]` or `n[hi],n[lo]`	`n`
Absolute	`n` or `>n`	`n[hi],n[lo]`	`MEM[n]`
Direct-page	`n` or `<n`	`n[lo]`	`MEM[n[lo]+256·DPR]`
Register indirect	`,RR`	`PB`	`MEM[RR]`
Based or indexed (16-bit offset)	`n,RR` or `>n,RR`	`PB,n[hi],n[lo]`	`MEM[n+RR]`
Based (8-bit offset)	`n,RR` or `<n,RR`	`PB,n[lo]`	`MEM[xtnd(n[lo])+RR]`
Based (5-bit offset)	`n,RR`	`PB`	`MEM[xtnd(n[so])+RR]`
Based indexed (16-bit offset)	`D,RR`	`PB`	`MEM[D+RR]`
Based indexed (8-bit offset)	`A,RR` or `B,RR`	`PB`	`MEM[xtnd(A)+RR]` or `MEM[xtnd(B)+RR]`
Relative (16-bit disp.)	`n,PCR` or `>n,PCR`	`PB,(n-PLC)[hi],(n-PLC)[lo]`	`MEM[n]`
Relative (8-bit disp.)	`n,PCR` or `<n,PCR`	`PB,(n-PLC)[lo]`	`MEM[n]`
Auto-increment (by 1 or 2)	`,RR+` or `,RR++`	`PB`	`MEM[RR]`, then `RR := RR + 1 or 2`
Auto-decrement (by 1 or 2)	`,-RR` or `,--RR`	`PB`	`RR := RR - 1 or 2`, then `MEM[RR]`

Notes: n denotes the 16-bit two's-complement value of an expression.

`MEM[x]` denotes the memory byte or word starting at address x, as appropriate for the instruction.

RR denotes an address register, X, Y, S, or U.

PB denotes the indexed addressing postbyte.

PLC denotes the address of the byte following the instruction.

`n[lo]` denotes the low-order byte of n; `n[hi]` denotes the high-order byte; `n[so]` denotes bits 4 to 0.

`xtnd(x)` sign-extends x to a 16-bit two's-complement value.

In based and relative modes, the assembler attempts to use the smallest possible offset or displacement size, unless the prefix > or < is used, which forces a 16-bit or 8-bit value, respectively.

17.3.2 Absolute

In *absolute addressing* (which Motorola calls *extended*), the instruction contains the 16-bit absolute memory address of the operand. As shown in Figure 17–5, a typical instruction using absolute addressing is three bytes long — one byte for the opcode and two bytes for the address.

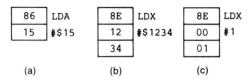

FIGURE 17–4 Immediate addressing: (a) 8-bit operand; (b,c) 16-bit operands.

The instruction LDA $2000 loads accumulator A with the 8-bit contents of memory location $2000. On the other hand, the instruction LDX $2000 must load register X with a 16-bit quantity. In this case, $2000 is considered to be the address of the first byte of a word. Thus, the high-order byte of X is loaded with MEM[$2000] and the low-order byte of X is loaded with MEM[$2001]. Both instructions LDA $2000 and LDX $2000 contain a 16-bit address, but the CPU deduces from the opcode whether it must load a byte or a word starting at that memory address.

17.3.3 Direct Page

Direct-page addressing partitions the 6809's 64K-byte address space into 256 pages of 256 bytes each, as was shown in Figure 7–7(a). Thus, a 16-bit address may be partitioned into an 8-bit *page number* and an 8-bit *page address* within the page, as shown in Figure 7–7(b).

The 6809 has a direct page register, DP, that a program may load with an 8-bit *direct page number*. When an opcode specifies direct-page addressing, a full 16-bit address is obtained by concatenating the contents of DP with an 8-bit page address in the instruction, as shown in Figure 7–7(e).

Operands in the direct page may be accessed by short instructions that contain only an 8-bit page address instead of a full 16-bit absolute address. By storing frequently-used variables in the direct page, a programmer can significantly reduce the size of a program (and improve its speed, too). Since the programmer specifies the direct page number in a register, different programs or subroutines can use different regions of memory for the direct page; however, some overhead is required to manage DP.

An assembly language program may indicate direct-page addressing using the prefix "<" before an address expression. The assembler places the 8

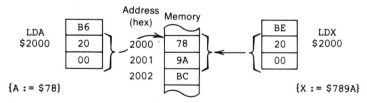

FIGURE 17–5 Typical 6809 instructions using absolute addressing.

TABLE 17–4 Excerpt from a program that uses direct-page addressing.

PLC	CONTENTS	LABEL	OPCODE	OPERAND	COMMENTS
			ORG	$3000	Begin direct-page
3000	??	POINT	RMB	2	variables and
3002	0D	CARRET	FCB	$0D	constants.
3003	??	CHAR	RMB	1	
3004			...		
			ORG	$3100	Begin program.
3100	86 30	START	LDA	#$30	Direct-page number.
3102	1F 8B		TFR	A,DP	Load DP with page number.
3104	96 02		LDA	<CARRET	Get terminator.
3106	97 03		STA	<CHAR	Save character.
3108	8E 1800		LDX	#$1800	Initialize pointer.
310B	9F 00		STX	<POINT	
310D			...		

low-order bits of the expression in the instruction, and assumes that the programmer has already set up the direct-page register to the proper value. This technique is illustrated in Table 17–4. If the programmer had not indicated direct-page addressing where applicable, the program would have longer instructions, as shown in Table 17–5.

In the simple example above, direct-page addressing actually made the program fragment longer than the corresponding program with absolute addressing. In a complete program, the overhead of setting up DP (two instructions, four bytes) would be amortized over a much larger number of direct page references.

If the assembler could predict the run-time value of DP, it could automatically select direct-page mode where applicable. However, the assembler is not smart enough to do this. Instead, the programmer may tell the assembler what value DP will have at run time, using an internal assembler variable called the direct page pseudo register (DPPR).

TABLE 17–5 The same program without direct-page addressing.

PLC	CONTENTS	LABEL	OPCODE	OPERAND	COMMENTS
			ORG	$3000	Begin variables
3000	??	POINT	RMB	2	and constants.
3002	0D	CARRET	FCB	$0D	
3003	??	CHAR	RMB	1	
3004			...		
			ORG	$3100	Begin program.
3100	B6 3002	START	LDA	CARRET	Get carriage return.
3103	B7 3003		STA	CHAR	Save character.
3106	8E 1800		LDX	#$1800	Initialize pointer.
3109	BF 3000		STX	POINT	
310C			...		

In assembly language, the SETDP pseudo-operation is used to change the value of DPPR. Corresponding to each run-time change of DP, the programmer must insert a SETDP pseudo-operation to tell the assembler the proper value for DPPR. Then the assembler can automatically select direct-page addressing for all instructions that access operands in the direct page, according to DPPR. This is shown in Table 17–6. Even though the "<" prefix is gone, the assembler automatically selects direct-page addressing whenever the high-order byte of an address matches the current value of DPPR. For example, "STA CHAR" generates a two-byte instruction the first time it appears. However, the second appearance of "STA CHAR" generates a three-byte instruction, since CHAR's page ($30) is no longer the direct page.

The assembler initializes DPPR to zero when assembly begins, because the 6809 processor initializes DP to zero whenever it is reset. Thereafter it is the programmer's responsibility to maintain the proper values of DPPR in the assembly language program and DP in the run-time program.

The programmer can always force the assembler to use 16-bit absolute addressing, even when direct-page addressing is applicable, by placing the prefix ">" before an address expression. Likewise the programmer can force direct-page addressing, even when it seems inapplicable, with the "<" prefix.

TABLE 17–6 Direct-page addressing with direct-page pseudo register.

PLC	CONTENTS	LABEL	OPCODE	OPERAND	COMMENTS
			ORG	$2E00	Begin one direct page.
2E00	??	VAR1	RMB	1	
2E01	??	VAR2	RMB	1	
2E02			...		
			ORG	$3000	Begin another direct page.
3000	??	POINT	RMB	2	
3002	0D	CARRET	FCB	$0D	
3003	??	CHAR	RMB	1	
3004			...		
			ORG	$3100	Begin program.
3100	86 30	START	LDA	#$30	Direct-page number.
3102	1F 8B		TFR	A,DP	Load DP with page number.
3104			SETDP	$30	Tell assembler about it.
3104	96 02		LDA	CARRET	Get carriage return.
3106	97 03		STA	CHAR	Save character.
3108	8E 1800		LDX	#$1800	Initialize pointer.
310B	9F 00		STX	POINT	
310D	86 2E		LDA	#$2E	New direct-page number.
310F	1F 8B		TFR	A,DP	Load DP with page number.
3111			SETDP	$2E	Tell assembler about it.
3111	86 11		LDA	#17	Get initial value.
3113	97 00		STA	VAR1	Initialize variables.
3115	97 01		STA	VAR2	
3117	B7 3003		STA	CHAR	
311A			...		

When no prefix is used, the assembler chooses either absolute or direct-page addressing. For direct-page addressing to be chosen, the high-order byte of the address expression must match the value of DP during *pass 1* of the assembly. If the expression contains a forward reference, the assembler assumes that it will necessitate 16-bit absolute addressing.

17.3.4 "Indexed" Addressing Modes

Motorola's "indexed addressing" for the 6809 is actually a family of addressing modes. When an instruction opcode specifies indexed addressing, the opcode is followed by another byte, called an *indexed addressing post-byte*, that specifies exactly which "indexed" mode is to be used. In some modes, the postbyte itself is followed by one or two additional bytes of addressing information.

Figure 17–6 shows the layout of the indexed addressing postbyte. A 2-bit field in the postbyte usually specifies one of four address registers that may be used in an addressing computation — X, Y, S, or U. If the MSB of the postbyte is 0, then the mode is based addressing with a 5-bit offset in the low-order bits. If the MSB is 1, then the mode is specified by the 4 low-order bits and a 1-bit field selects an extra level of indirection. The individual "indexed" addressing modes are described in detail in the remaining subsections.

17.3.5 Register Indirect

In register indirect mode, the specified address register (RR) contains the address of the operand. For historical reasons, Motorola's standard assembly language notation for indexed and indirect modes is a little strange, as shown in Table 17–3. In general, Motorola's 6809 assembly language uses a comma ",X" where other assembly languages use an at-sign "@X" or parentheses " (X) ". Thus, the Motorola instruction LDA ,X is the same as the hypothetical H6809 instruction LDA @X. In this chapter, we use Motorola's standard notation for all addressing modes.

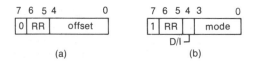

(a)   (b)

FIGURE 17–6 Indexed addressing postbyte for: (a) based addressing with 5-bit offset; (b) other modes.

17.3.6 Based and Indexed

In 6809 *based* and *indexed* modes, a constant offset in the instruction is added to the specified address register to form the effective address of the operand; the contents of the register are not disturbed. The postbyte can call for a 5-, 8-, or 16-bit offset. As shown in Figure 17–6, a 5-bit offset is encoded as part of the postbyte itself. An 8-bit offset is placed in a byte following the postbyte, while a 16-bit offset is placed in two bytes following the postbyte.

The short offsets are treated as signed numbers; their signs are extended to make a 16-bit two's-complement number before adding to the address register. Thus a 5-bit offset is between −16 and +15, and an 8-bit offset is between −128 and +127. The 16-bit offsets may be viewed as either signed or unsigned numbers, since a 16-bit addition gives the same 16-bit result in either case — think about it. According to the definitions of based and indexed addressing in Section 7.3, the 5- and 8-bit offsets yield based addressing, while the 16-bit offset yields based or indexed addressing according to the application.

The 5-bit offset mode is very useful, since it allows efficient access of operands in small tables and in stack frames using short, 2-byte instructions (1-byte opcode plus postbyte). In most programs, these short instructions are used much more often than the longest 6809 instructions, which are five bytes long (2-byte opcode plus postbyte plus 2-byte offset).

The assembly language notation for 6809 based and indexed modes was shown in Table 17–3. The prefixes "<" and ">" may be used to force 8-bit and 16-bit offsets respectively. If no prefix is given, the assembler automatically selects the shortest offset mode that works with the given expression. Thus, if the value of the offset expression is 0, register indirect mode is selected; otherwise if it is between −16 and +15, 5-bit offset mode is selected; otherwise if it is between −128 and +127, 8-bit offset mode is selected; otherwise 16-bit offset mode is selected. As with direct-page addressing, the value of the expression should be known during pass 1 of the assembly; otherwise the assembler must select a worst-case default of a 16-bit offset mode to avoid phasing errors.

17.3.7 Based Indexed

As explained in Section 7.3.4, *based indexed addressing* forms an effective address by combining a base address and an index value, both of which are contained in registers. In the 6809, any of the address registers X, Y, U, or S may contain the base address, while the index value may be contained in A or B (8 bits) or D (16 bits).

As shown in Table 17–3, assembly language programs specify based indexed addressing by using one of the reserved identifiers A, B, or D as the offset for based addressing.

17.3.8   Auto-Increment and Auto-Decrement

Auto-increment and auto-decrement addressing may be used to step through arrays, lists, and other data structures and to manipulate stacks as described in Section 7.2.5. The 6809 supports these addressing modes for both byte and word operands. But unlike the PDP-11, which deduces the operand size from the opcode, the 6809 requires the programmer to explicitly indicate the operand size, as shown in Table 17–3. Thus, the following instruction sequence initializes a table of bytes to contain 12_{16}:

```
        LDA    #$12
        LDX    #TABBEG      Starting address of table.
ILOOP   STA    ,X+          Initialize table entry.
        CMPX   #TABEND      Past end?
        BLO    ILOOP        Repeat until all entries done.
```

On the other hand, the following sequence initializes a table of words (recall that D is the concatenation of A and B):

```
        LDD    #$1234
        LDX    #TABBEG      Starting address of table.
ILOOP   STD    ,X++         Initialize table entry.
        CMPX   #TABEND      Past end?
        BLO    ILOOP        Repeat until all entries done.
```

What initial values would the table contain if the instruction STD ,X+ were mistakenly used above?

17.3.9   Relative

The 6809 provides relative addressing modes with both 8-bit and 16-bit displacements, in which the (sign-extended) displacement is added to the current PC to obtain the effective address of the operand. The 8-bit displacement mode allows efficient access to data nearby the current instruction, while both modes allow data references to be coded in a position-independent manner, as explained in Section 7.4.

In Motorola's 6809 assembly language the suffix ",PCR" denotes relative addressing, as shown in Table 17–3. The assembler computes the required displacement as the difference between the given address expression (n) and the address following the instruction. As with the direct-page and based and indexed modes, the assembler automatically selects the shortest possible relative mode according to the information that it has during pass 1 of the assembly. The prefixes ">" and "<" force use of the mode with the "greater" and "lesser" number of displacement bits, respectively.

Relative addressing is often used in jump-type instructions. For the 6809, a programmer could write "JMP <target,PCR" to jump to a target address within 127 bytes of the JMP instruction. However, this is a 3-byte

instruction (JMP opcode plus postbyte plus 8-bit displacement). The programmer would be better off using the BRA (branch) instruction, which has an 8-bit opcode and 8-bit displacement, and uses relative addressing inherently. Likewise, for a long jump (>127 bytes distant), the programmer could write "JMP >target,PCR" (four bytes long) or "LBRA target" ("long branch," three bytes long, not a saloon).

Relative addressing is also useful for looking up information in tables in a position-independent manner. For example, suppose the programmer created a 256-byte table N1S[0..255], where N1S[i] contains the number of ones in the binary representation of i:

```
N1S     FCB     0,1,1,2,...     256-byte table.
I       RMB     1               Variable i.
```

The following code loads A with the number of ones in I:

```
        LDB     I               Load X with value of i.
        CLRA
        TFR     D,X
        LDA     N1S,X           Get value of N1S[X].
```

An alternate version of the code is shown below:

```
        LDB     I               Get value of i.
        LEAX    N1S             Get base address of table.
        LDA     B,X             Get value of N1S[i].
```

However, neither version is position-independent, since both contain instructions that fix the absolute addresses of I and N1S at assembly time. A position-independent version may be coded as shown below.

```
        LDB     I,PCR           Get value of i.
        LEAX    N1S,PCR         Get base address of table.
        LDA     B,X             Get value of N1S[i].
```

In the new code, the first two instructions contain *offsets* to I and N1S; absolute addresses are computed at run time by adding the PC and the offsets.

17.3.10 Indirect

Most of the "indexed" addressing modes can specify an additional level of indirection by setting the direct/indirect bit in the postbyte to 1. In assembly language, indirect addressing is indicated by a pair of square brackets surrounding the usual address and mode expression (except that the prefixes ">" and "<" should appear before the brackets if used).

When indirect addressing is used, an indirect address is calculated in the same way as the effective address in the nonindirect mode. The memory word starting at the indirect address is then fetched and used as the effective address of the operand. In the case of based and indexed addressing, the mode would therefore be classified as "pre-indexed" indirect.

The 6809 does not support indirection with auto-increment-by-1 and auto-decrement-by-1 modes, since a sane program should use an increment of two when stepping through a table of indirect addresses. Also, indirect addressing with the 5-bit offset mode is not provided, since the direct/indirect bit has been used as the sign of the offset; the 8-bit offset mode must be used instead.

Recall that the 6809 provides absolute addressing as a non-"indexed" mode (2-byte absolute address, no postbyte). *Absolute indirect* is provided as one of the indirect "indexed" modes (postbyte of 10011111, plus 2-byte absolute address).

For examples of indirect addressing, consider the following instruction sequences, coded without and with indirect addressing.

```
INSTRUCTIONS     WITH INDIRECT    COMMENTS

LDX HEAD         LDA [HEAD]       Get first item in queue.
LDA ,X

LDX 10,S         LEAX [10,S]      Get address of VAR-type
                                      parameter from stack.

LDX 10,S         LDA [10,S]       Get value of VAR-type
LDA ,X                                parameter from stack.

LDX ,X           JMP [,X]         Jump to address in jump
JMP ,X                                table, pointed to by X.

RTS              JMP [,S++]       Return from subroutine.
```

17.4 OPERATIONS

We shall classify 6809 instructions into three types: memory reference, program control, and miscellaneous.

17.4.1 Memory Reference

Instructions that have an operand in memory are listed in Table 17–7. As you can see from the pattern in the table, only the most important operations may be performed on all registers; less important instructions have decreasing flexibility. In particular, all operations may be performed on the 8-bit accumulators and 8-bit memory operands, but only operations considered essential for address manipulations may be performed on the index registers. Depending on your point of view, you might consider the 6809 instruction set to be either regular or irregular in this respect.

TABLE 17-7   6809 memory reference instructions.

Mnemonic	Operand	Description
LDabdxyus	mem	Load register from memory
STabdxyus	mem-imm	Store register into memory
CMPabdxyus	mem	Compare register with memory
ADDabd	mem	Add memory to accumulator
SUBabd	mem	Subtract memory from accumulator
ADCab	mem	Add with carry memory to accumulator
SBCab	mem	Subtract with carry memory from accumulator
ANDab	mem	AND memory to accumulator
ORab	mem	OR memory to accumulator
EORab	mem	EXCLUSIVE OR memory to accumulator
BITab	mem	Bit test memory with accumulator
CLR	mem-imm+acc	Clear operand
TST	mem-imm+acc	Test operand and set condition bits
NEG	mem-imm+acc	Negate operand
COM	mem-imm+acc	Ones'-complement operand
INC	mem-imm+acc	Increment operand
DEC	mem-imm+acc	Decrement operand
ROL	mem-imm+acc	Rotate operand left with C
ROR	mem-imm+acc	Rotate operand right with C
LSR	mem-imm+acc	Logical shift operand right
LSL/ASL	mem-imm+acc	Logical/arithmetic shift operand left
ASR	mem-imm+acc	Arithmetic shift operand right
LEAxyus	indexed	Load register with effective address

Notes: abdxyus denotes A, B, D, X, Y, U, or S; ab denotes A or B; and so on.
mem denotes any memory addressing mode; imm denotes immediate mode only; acc denotes accumulator A or B; indexed denotes "indexed" modes only. For accumulator addressing, some 6809 assemblers require the A or B to be appended to the mnemonic, rather than appear separately in the operand field.

The first part of the table (LD through BIT) shows instructions that have two operands, one in memory and the other in a CPU register. There are only three operations that may be performed on any accumulator or index register—load, store and compare. Addition and subtraction may be performed on accumulator A or B or on the double length pseudo-accumulator D, which is the concatenation of A and B. The other arithmetic and logical operations may only be performed on accumulators A and B.

The second part of the table shows single-operand instructions that may be performed on operands in memory or in accumulator A or B. The shift and rotate instructions operate in the usual way and store the lost bit into C.

The last instruction in the table, LEA (load effective address), loads an address register with the effective address of an operand specified by an "indexed" addressing mode. This instruction is useful for passing the addresses of VAR-type parameters to subroutines; an example will be given in the next section. LEA also provides a means of adding constants or accumulator values to the address registers, for example:

```
LEAX   NUM,X        Add the constant value NUM to X,
                    that is, ADDX #NUM.
LEAY   A,Y          Add the contents of accumulator A to Y.
```

In general, an instruction may use any memory addressing mode for which the instruction makes sense. All instructions except LEA set, clear, or hold condition code bits HNZVC according to the result of the operation, roughly as described in Chapter 8; refer to a 6809 processor handbook or pocket reference card for the exact rules.

17.4.2 Program Control

The 6809's program control instructions are shown in Table 17–8. The JMP and JSR instructions provide unconditional jumps as explained in Section 5.2. JMP and JSR may use any memory addressing mode except immediate; control is transferred to the effective address specified by the addressing mode.

The JSR instruction saves the return address on a stack pointed to by the S register; RTS pops the return address from the same stack. The BSR instruction is a short form of JSR that uses relative addressing with an 8-bit

TABLE 17–8 6809 program control instructions.

Mnemonic	Operand	Description
JMP	mem–imm	Unconditional jump
JSR	mem–imm	Jump to subroutine
RTS		Return from subroutine
BSR	rel8	Branch to subroutine
BRA	rel8	Unconditional branch
Bcc	rel8	Conditional branch
LBSR	rel16	Long branch to subroutine
LBRA	rel16	Long unconditional branch
LBcc	rel16	Long conditional branch
ANDCC	imm	AND immediate to CC
ORCC	imm	OR immediate to CC
CWAI	imm	AND immediate to CC and wait for interrupt
RTI		Return from interrupt
SWIn		Software interrupt
SYNC		Synchronize with interrupt

Notes: mem denotes any memory addressing mode; imm denotes immediate mode only; rel8 denotes relative mode with an 8-bit displacement; rel16 denotes relative mode with a 16-bit displacement;
SWIn denotes SWI, SWI2, or SWI3.
cc denotes any of the conditions listed in Table 8–3.

two's-complement displacement. This two-byte instruction allows a program to call a nearby subroutine, and it is a byte shorter than JSR using absolute addressing.

The BRA and 14 different conditional branch (Bcc) instructions also use relative addressing with an 8-bit displacement and are two bytes long. The conditional branches are precisely the ones listed in Section 8.6. When a branch is taken, the displacement is added to the PC to obtain the address of the next instruction. When this addition takes place, the processor has already incremented PC to point to the next instruction. Thus, a displacement of -2, not 0, causes the instruction to branch to itself.

The long branch instructions (LBSR, LBRA, LBcc) are like their shorter counterparts, except that they give a 16-bit displacement for relative addressing. Thus, they may specify target addresses anywhere in the 64K-byte address space of the 6809.

The long conditional branches certainly fill a need for reaching distant targets, allowing us to write

```
        LBGE    FAR
NEXT    ...
```

instead of

```
        BLT     NEXT
        JMP     FAR
NEXT    ...
```

On the other hand, LBRA and LBSR seem to invade an area already covered by JMP and JSR with 16-bit absolute addressing. The main use of LBRA and LBSR is to create position-independent programs; position-independence is maintained because the target address is specified relative to PC. The same effect could be achieved by JMP and JSR using one of the "indexed" modes — PC-relative with 16-bit displacement — but the LBRA and LBSR instructions are one byte shorter and faster.

The ANDCC and ORCC instructions allow a program to clear or set the condition bits. Refering to the layout of the condition bits in Figure 17–2, we can see that ANDCC #$F3 clears N and Z, while ORCC #$11 sets I and C.

The remaining instructions in Table 17–8, RTI, SWIn, SYNC, and CWAI, will be discussed in connection with input/output and interrupts.

17.4.3 Miscellaneous

Several commonly needed operations are provided by the 6809's miscellaneous instructions, shown in Table 17–9. NOP does nothing in its usual, inimitable fashion. None of the instructions in the first part of the table affect the condition bits.

TABLE 17–9   6809 miscellaneous instructions.

Mnemonic	Operands	Description
NOP		No operation
TFR	reg1,reg2	Transfer reg1 to reg2
EXG	reg1,reg2	Exchange reg1 and reg2
PSHus	reglist	Push registers onto stack
PULus	reglist	Pull (pop) registers from stack
ABX		Unsigned add B to X
DAA		Decimal adjust accumulator A
SEX		Sign extend B into A
MUL		Unsigned multiply A·B, result in A,B

Notes: us denotes U or S.
reg1 and reg2 may be freely chosen from A, B, DPR, and CC, or from D, X, Y, U, S, and PC (reg1 and reg2 must be the same size).
reglist contains zero or more of the register names PC, U (in PSHS) or S (in PSHU) , Y, X, DPR, B, A, and CC.

The TFR and EXG instructions allow the contents of any register to be transferred to or exchanged with a like-sized register. Both of these instructions have a one-byte opcode followed by another byte with reg1 and reg2 specified in the two 4-bit halves.

The PSH and PUL instructions allow registers to be pushed onto or popped from a stack using either the U or S stack pointer. The instruction opcode byte is followed by another byte that contains one bit position for each register in the list PC, U or S, Y, X, DPR, B, A, and CC. If the bit is 1, then the register is pushed or popped, otherwise it is not; thus zero to eight registers may be pushed or popped by a single two-byte instruction. The pushing order is governed by the order of the above register list, regardless of the order in which the registers appear in an assembly language statement. Thus, the instruction PSHS A,PC,B pushes PC, then B, and then A onto the S stack. Registers are popped in the opposite order from pushing.

Like the PDP-11's stack, a 6809 stack grows towards decreasing memory locations, and the stack pointer points directly to the top item in the stack. When a 16-bit quantity is pushed, the low-order byte is pushed first, so that the resulting two bytes in the stack "read" in the correct order, according to Figure 17–3.

It is up to the programmer to initialize U and S before using PSH or PUL. Also recall that the S stack is also used by subroutine and interrupt calls and returns.

The ABX instruction, one byte long, adds B to X as an 8-bit unsigned integer. Almost the same thing can be accomplished by a two-byte instruction LEAX B,X (which sign-extends B). Since ABX is "irregular" (e.g., there is no

AAX or ABY) you probably won't remember it, so you might as well forget it! The 6809's designers included ABX for compatibility with the 6801.

The DAA instruction adjusts accumulator A after a BCD operation as described in Section 8.11. An 8-bit two's-complement number in B may be sign-extended to a 16-bit two's-complement number in A,B (D) using SEX. The MUL instruction multiplies two 8-bit unsigned numbers in A and B and leaves the 16-bit unsigned result in A,B. This instruction is useful for computing offsets in arrays whose components are more than one byte long, and as a primitive in subroutines for multiplication of larger quantities (e.g., see Section 8.10).

17.5 SAMPLE PROGRAMS

All of the program examples for the H6809 that appear throughout Part 2 apply to the real 6809, with the appropriate assembly language and instruction translations in Table 17–2. A few additional examples are given in this section.

The LEA (Load effective address) instruction is useful for passing the addresses of VAR-type parameters to subroutines. For example, consider the Pascal program shown in Table 17–10. The Swap procedure could be coded in 6809 assembly language as shown in Table 17–11 using a stack-oriented parameter-passing convention. The main program passes the SWAP subroutine the addresses of two parameters, CAT and AY1[INDEX]. For the first parameter, X is loaded with the address of variable CAT using immediate addressing. For the second parameter, LEAX AY1-1,X loads X with the address of array element AY1[X]. Without LEAX, the instructions could be coded as follows:

```
LDD     #AY1-1          Get effective base address of AY1.
ADDD    INDEX           Add index.
PSHS    D               Pass address of AY1[index] to subroutine.
```

TABLE 17–10 Pascal program that uses VAR-type parameters.

```
PROGRAM VarParms (input,output);
VAR cat : byte; index : 1..300; AY1 : ARRAY [1..300] OF byte;
PROCEDURE Swap(VAR v1,v2 : byte);
  VAR temp : byte;
    BEGIN temp := v1; v1 := v2; v2 := temp END;

BEGIN {Main Program}
  ... Swap(cat,AY1[index]); ...
END.
```

TABLE 17-11 Assembly language program using VAR-type parameters.

```
*                           Define offsets to parameters from SP.
RETADR  EQU     0           Offset to return address (top of stack).
AV1     EQU     2           Offset to address of V1.
AV2     EQU     4           Offset to address of V2.
*
SWAP    LDA     [AV1,S]     A-reg gets V1.
        LDB     [AV2,S]     B-reg gets V2.
        STB     [AV1,S]     Store in opposite order.
        STA     [AV2,S]
        LDX     RETADR,S    Get return address.
        LEAS    6,S         Remove return address and parameters
        JMP     0,X             from stack and return.
*
MAIN    ...                 Main program.
        ...
        LDX     INDEX       Get address of AY1[INDEX]
        LEAX    AY1-1,X
        PSHS    X               and pass to subroutine.
        LDX     #CAT        Get address of CAT
        PSHS    X               and pass to subroutine.
        JSR     SWAP        Swap CAT and AY1[INDEX].
        ...
CAT     RMB     1           Variable storage.
INDEX   RMB     2
AY1     RMB     300
```

Suppose that we wanted to make the above program position independent, so that it may be executed in different memory locations without reassembly. No changes are needed in the SWAP subroutine because it uses only registers and variables whose addresses are passed to it at run time. However, the main program must be recoded to compute addresses in a position-independent manner. The new main program code is shown below.

```
        LEAX    CAT,PCR     Get address of CAT
        PSHS    X               and pass to subroutine.
        LEAX    AY1-1,PCR   Get effective base address of AY1.
        LDD     INDEX,PCR
        LEAX    D,X         Add INDEX and pass address
        PSHS    X               of AY1[INDEX] to subroutine.
        LBSR    SWAP        Swap CAT and AY1[INDEX].
```

All of the variable references and even the subroutine jump now use PC-relative addressing. Computing the address of AY1[INDEX] is tricky, because three quantities must be added — the PC, a fixed offset from PC to the effective base address of the array, and an index into the array.

As you can see, writing position-independent code for the 6809 takes more than just writing ",PCR" after each memory reference instruction. Even the code above (and most 6809 position-independent code) is only statically position independent. The program fails if it is dynamically moved after the parameter addresses are computed but before SWAP is executed.

17.6 INPUT/OUTPUT, INTERRUPTS, AND TRAPS

17.6.1 Input/Output

Like the hypothetical H6809, the 6809 uses memory-mapped I/O. As shown in the examples in Chapters 10 and 11, I/O devices connected to a 6809 are controlled by interface registers that are read and written as locations in the address space.

Most computers communicate with terminals using the asynchronous serial I/O protocol described in Appendix C. The Motorola 6850 Asynchronous Communications Interface Adapter (ACIA) is an LSI interface circuit used in many 6809 systems to send and receive data in this serial format. A CPU controls the ACIA through two input ports and two output ports whose characteristics are described in Appendix C.3. A system has one ACIA for each serial I/O link, usually at least one for the "system console." The port addresses of these ACIAs are system-dependent. Table 17–12 shows the port addresses for the console ACIA in the Motorola EXORciser II system.

Assuming that a 6850 ACIA exists at the above port addresses, Table 17–13 shows a subroutine CINIT that initializes the ACIA and a subroutine CRTIN that reads and echoes one character each time it is called. By referring to the ACIA description in Appendix C.3, you can see how the subroutines intialize the ACIA and then perform busy-wait I/O. The equated symbols in the first four lines of the program may be modified for different ACIA port addresses or mode requirements.

17.6.2 Interrupts

The 6809 interrupt system works exactly as described in Section 11.1, using interrupt vectors listed in Table 11–2. The 6809 also uses an "interrupt

TABLE 17–12 Console ACIA addresses in Motorola EXORciser II.

Port Name	Type	Address
Control	Output	$FCF4
Status	Input	$FCF4
Transmitter Data	Output	$FCF5
Receiver Data	Input	$FCF5

TABLE 17-13 ACIA initialization and input/echo subroutines for the 6809.

```
CRTCS   EQU     $FCF4           Console ACIA control and status.
CRTDTA  EQU     $FCF5           Console ACIA xmt and rcv data.
CRESET  EQU     $03             ACIA mode control reset.
CMODE   EQU     $11             ACIA mode control:  8 data bits,
*                               no parity, 2 stop bits, RTS active,
*                               divide-by-16 clock, no interrupts.
*
CINIT   LDA     #CRESET         Initialize console ACIA
        STA     CRTCS               by sending master reset...
        LDA     #CMODE              ...and setting proper mode.
        STA     CRTCS
        RTS
*
CRTIN   LDA     CRTCS           Check for character.
        RORA                    Receiver data register full?
        BCC     CRTIN           No, busy wait.
        LDA     CRTDTA          Yes, read the character.
CRTWT   LDB     CRTCS           Can we echo the character now?
        RORB                    Must wait for transmitter buffer empty.
        RORB
        BCC     CRTWT           No, wait for previous character.
        STA     CRTDTA          OK, echo the received character
        RTS                         and return to calling program.
```

vector" when an external reset signal is applied to the 6809, typically when power is first applied to the system. In this case, however, it simply loads the PC with the word found at memory address $FFFE. It does not save any registers onto the stack since S may have an arbitrary value.

Two special 6809 instructions are used with interrupts. SYNC suspends instruction fetching and execution until an interrupt request is received on the IRQ, FIRQ, or NMI input. When an interrupt request is finally received, what happens next depends on whether or not that interrupt is masked in CC. If the interrupt is not masked, then processor executes an interrupt service routine in the usual way and then returns control to the instruction following SYNC. If the interrupt is masked, then the service routine is not executed, but execution proceeds immediately with the instruction following SYNC. This allows the processor to wait for or synchronize with external events without incurring the overhead of interrupt processing.

The CWAI instruction ANDs an immediate byte with CC; this operation may clear one or both interrupt mask bits. Then it pushes the entire CPU state onto the stack and waits for an interrupt to occur. When an unmasked interrupt finally does occur, the processor state will already have been stacked, and so the interrupt service routine will be entered and executed more quickly. Note that if the interrupt request occurs on FIRQ, the proper value of E will be set in CC on the stack so that the entire CPU state will be popped by RTI on the return.

As shown in Appendix C.3, the Motorola 6850 ACIA may be programmed to make an interrupt request after completing each input or output operation. The interrupt request output of the ACIA may be connected to one of the 6809 interrupt request inputs. This connection is system-dependent, but typically an ACIA would be connected to the IRQ input.

A user may write an interrupt service routine similar to Table 11–1 to service interrupts from the ACIA, making appropriate changes to the initialization and interrupt service routines for the particular layout of control and status bits in the 6850 ACIA. If both input and output interrupts are enabled, then the service routine must check both the transmitter and receiver "ready" bits to determine which side of the ACIA caused the interrupt. If there are other devices that can request interrupts on IRQ as well, then a more general interrupt polling routine must be written, such as the one shown in Table 11–4 (also see Exercise 17.8).

The 6809 does not have an explicit "test and set" instruction for mutual exclusion and synchronization among multiple processes, but the ASR instruction may be adapted to perform this function in a single-processor environment (see Exercise 17.9).

17.6.3 Traps

The 6809 processor does not trap on abnormal conditions such as illegal instructions, but it does have three explicit trap-type instructions. These are the software interrupt instructions (SWI, SWI2, and SWI3) described in Section 11.3.2.

REFERENCES

The 6809 was first described in "A Microprocessor for the Revolution: The 6809," a three-part series by Terry Ritter and Joel Boney that appeared in *Byte* [January, February, March, 1979 (Vol. 4, No. 1,2,3)]. Motorola publishes a programming reference manual for the 6809, a pocket-sized instruction reference card, and various application notes. The *68 Micro Journal* (Hixson, TN 37343) is a monthly magazine devoted exclusively to 6800-family hardware, programming, and systems.

EXERCISES

17.1   What is a "phasing error"?

17.2   Explain any difference in instruction effect, size, or speed between the 6809's register indirect addressing mode and the based mode with a 5-bit offset of 0.

17.3 There are a number of instruction pairs in the 6809 that have exactly the same effect (e.g., LBRA expr and JMP expr,PCR) or almost the same effect (e.g., LDX expr and LEAX [expr], the second instruction does not affect the condition bits). Find five other such pairs; pairs obtained by simply changing a register name (e.g. LDY and LEAY from above) are not allowed. For each pair, either indicate that the instructions have exactly the same effect or explain their differences.

17.4 Table 17–2 indicates that the 6809 instruction LEAX addr,X is equivalent to the H6809 instruction ADDX #addr. Why is the 6809 instruction LEAX [addr,X] not equivalent to the H6809 instruction ADDX addr?

17.5 Suppose we tried to write a 6809 assembler that could automatically select between BRA and LBRA instructions according to the distance of the target address from the instruction. What problems occur when the target address expression contains a forward reference? How many passes does the assembler need to resolve forward references?

17.6 In Table 17–11, why didn't we use LEAX CAT instead of LDX #CAT?

17.7 Rewrite the program in Table 7–5 to use position-independent code.

17.8 Modify the polling routine in Table 11–4 so that different interfaces may have their ready bits in different positions in the control and status registers.

17.9 Show how to use the 6809's ASR instruction on a memory location to perform a locking function equivalent to the TSET instruction described in Section 11.5.8.

17.10 Write a complete Pascal simulation of the 6809.

18

INTEL 8086

The roots of the Intel 8086 microprocessor go back to the first single-chip microprocessors, the Intel 4004 and 8008. The events leading to the 8086 have been rather blasphemously summarized by one of the 8086's architects:[1]

In the beginning Intel created the 4004 and the 8008. And these processors were without enough memory and throughput. And Intel said, "Let there be an 8080," and there was an 8080 and Intel saw that it was good. . .

And Intel said, "Let a new-generation processor serve the midrange market. And let there be true 16-bit facilities in the midrange. And let there be one megabyte of memory and efficient interruptible byte-string instructions and full decimal arithmetic." And Intel saw the collection of all of these things, that it was good, and Intel called it the 8086. . .

And Intel saw everything that he [sic] had made and, behold, it was good.

[1]S. P. Morse, in "Intel Microprocessors — 8008 to 8086" by S. P. Morse, B. W. Ravenel, S. Mazor, and W. B. Pohlman, in *Computer*, Vol. 13, No. 10, October 1980, p. 46.

The Intel 8088 is a 16-bit microprocessor with the same instruction set and internal architecture as the 8086. The only difference between the two circuits is in their external Memory Buses — the 8086 accesses two memory bytes at a time, while the 8088 accesses only one byte at a time. We'll use the name "8086" as a generic to refer to the architecture shared by both circuits.

The 8086 architecture was derived from the very popular 8080 for a good reason — to ensure a measure of software compatibility and thereby preserve the industry's large investment in 8080 software. Although 8080 machine language programs cannot be run directly on an 8086, it is fairly straightforward to translate an 8080 assembly language program into an equivalent program for the 8086. In fact, Intel has a program, CONV-86, that does this automatically.

An 8086 integrated circuit contains a CPU only; the system designer must add external memory and I/O to form a complete computer. 8086-based computers include the Convergent Technologies 1000 Series computers and the Intel SBC 86/12A Single Board Computer.

18.1 BASIC ORGANIZATION

18.1.1 Computer Structure

The basic structure of an 8086-based computer is shown in Figure 18–1. The 8086 processor architecture supports isolated I/O, so that at least logically there could be separate buses for I/O and for memory. However, in the 8086 and 8088 integrated circuits, the I/O bus and the memory bus both share the same pins. The processor generates bus control signals to indicate whether a particular transaction using the shared pins is for an I/O interface or for memory.

As indicated in Figure 18–1, the data part of the 8086 Memory Bus is 16 bits wide, so that a 16-bit word may be transferred in one bus cycle. In the 8088, the data bus is only 8 bits wide, and so all data transfers take place a

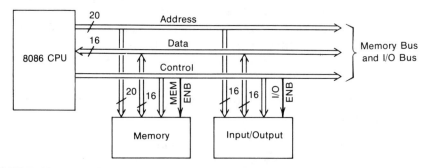

FIGURE 18–1 8086-based computer block diagram.

byte at a time. The 8086 and 8088 circuits are identical in almost every other respect. For example, both processors use an internal "instruction queue" to assemble memory words or bytes into instructions of the required length. In the remainder of this chapter, we shall use the designation "8086" to refer to both 8086 and 8088 CPUs.

The 8086 address bus is 20 bits wide, so that up to one megabyte of memory may be addressed. However, most instructions deal with 16-bit addresses, and an on-chip memory-mapping unit translates 16-bit addresses into 20-bit addresses as explained in Section 18.3.10.

Input/output operations in the 8086 use a 16-bit address, so that the CPU may access up to 64K bytes of I/O interface registers (ports) in addition to the main memory. Of course, memory-mapped I/O may also be used at the discretion of the system hardware designer.

The 8086 processor contains a two-level, vectored, priority interrupt system. Interrupt vectors are contained in the bottom 1K bytes of memory.

18.1.2 Processor Programming Model

The processor state of the 8086 contains a total of fourteen 16-bit registers, as shown in Figure 18–2. Intel calls eight registers, AX through DI, "general registers" because they contain data and addresses during computations. However, these registers are fairly specialized, and the 8086 is hardly a general-register machine in the traditional sense of the word. In a strict taxonomy, the 8086 is more closely related to extended accumulator-based architecures such as the Motorola 6809 (Chapter 17). In fact, the 8086's registers were designed to be a compatible superset of the registers of the Intel 8080, an older accumulator-based machine.

Four of the 8086's general registers, AX through DX, are "data registers" primarily intended to hold data. Most 8086 data manipulation instructions can operate on either bytes or words; byte-manipulation instructions can access either half of a data register, for example, AH or AL.

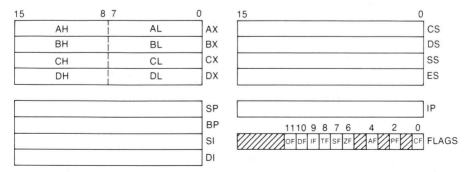

FIGURE 18–2 Programming model of the 8086.

The other four general registers, SP through DI, are "address registers" intended to hold 16-bit addresses. Register SP is used as a stack pointer to push and pop return addresses during subroutine and interrupt calls and returns. Like the stacks in other processors in this book, the 8086 stack grows towards decreasing memory locations and SP points directly at the top stack item.

Address registers BP, SI, and DI may be used as base or index registers in various addressing modes as explained in Section 18.3. Just to confuse things, data register BX can also be used as a base or index register (actually, this feature was included for 8080 compatibility).

Besides distinguishing between data registers and address registers, the 8086 CPU performs certain operations using only one or two specific registers, reinforcing our claim that the registers are not really "general." Special-purpose uses of the registers are outlined in Table 18–1.

At this point it should be apparent that the 8086 has the most irregular register structure of any processor in this book, requiring a programmer or compiler to allocate and keep track of specific registers for specific coding tasks. On the other hand, the implicit use of registers with certain operations and addressing modes allows instructions to be encoded with a smaller number of bits than would be needed for completely general register-selection. Faced with a trade-off between assembly language programming effort and program size and execution time, the 8086's designers chose to optimize the latter.

TABLE 18–1   Special-purpose functions of 8086 "general" registers.

Register	Description	Special Function
AX	Accumulator	Word multiply, divide, and I/O; optimized
AL	Accumulator (low byte)	Byte multiply, divide, and I/O; translate; decimal arithmetic; optimized
AH	Accumulator (high byte)	Byte multiply and divide
BX	Base	Base register; translate
CX	Count	String operations; loops
CL	Count (low byte)	Dynamic shifts and rotates
DX	Data	Word multiply and divide; indirect I/O
SP	Stack Pointer	Stack operations
BP	Base Pointer	Base register
SI	Source Index	String source; index register
DI	Destination Index	String destination; index register

Although an 8086 circuit contains a 20-bit memory address bus that connects to physical memory, the CPU manipulates "logical addresses" consisting of a 16-bit "segment base address" and a 16-bit "segment offset." Logical addresses in the CPU are translated into 20-bit "physical addresses" for the address bus by an on-chip memory mapping unit.

Most 8086 instructions deal only with the 16-bit "segment offset" part of a logical address; the segment base address is assumed to be contained in one of four "segment registers," CS through ES in Figure 18–2. After a 16-bit segment offset has been derived from the instruction and general registers using traditional addressing modes, the offset is added to the contents of a segment register to form a 20-bit physical address using rules given in Section 18.3.10. In systems that use 64K or fewer bytes of memory, the segment registers may be initialized to zero and then ignored, since zero plus a 16-bit offset yields a 16-bit address.

In one sense, the 8086's support of memory mapping goes beyond that of processors such as the Z8000 and the 68000: the 8086's memory mapping scheme is defined as part of the processor architecture and the mapping circuits are contained in the same integrated circuit as the CPU. On the other hand, the 8086 lacks two essential ingredients for employing memory management in a multiprogramming system: segment length registers and a privileged mode of operation.

Strangely, the 8086 does not have a program counter (PC). However, it does have a 16-bit instruction pointer IP which, except for its name, is just like the PC found in every other processor. Intel gives no reason why the name has been changed, except perhaps to protect the innocent.

The 8086's condition bits and processor control bits are grouped together in a 16-bit register called FLAGS that may be pushed onto or popped from the stack as a single unit. FLAGS contains four "standard" condition bits called CF (carry flag), ZF (zero flag), SF (sign flag), and OF (overflow flag). There is also an auxiliary carry flag AF that is set to the carry or borrow between nibbles during decimal addition and subtraction operations. The even-parity flag PF is set to 1 if a result has an even number of 1s.

Three bits in FLAGS are classified as "processor control" bits. Setting the direction flag DF to 1 causes string-manipulation instructions to use auto-decrement addressing; otherwise they use auto-increment addressing. Setting the interrupt flag IF allows the processor to accept interrupt requests on its INTR input. Setting the trace flag TF causes the processor to generate a trace trap after each instruction is executed, allowing on-line debuggers to single-step programs.

The arrangement of bits in FLAGS is unusual since not all of the condition bits are grouped together; compare with the "system byte" and "user byte" arrangements of the PDP-11, 68000, and Z8000. However, in the present arrangement the low-order byte of FLAGS is compatible with the 8-bit

PSW of the older 8080; the control and condition bits in the high-order byte of FLAGS did not exist in the 8080 processor.

18.1.3 Instruction Formats

Basic instruction lengths in the 8086 vary from one to six bytes. The opcode is always contained in the first byte of the instruction, and successive bytes, if any, contain addressing information. In addition, one or more "instruction prefix" bytes may be placed before the opcode byte of any basic instruction to override certain default operation modes; the prefixes allowed in various situations will be discussed later as appropriate.

The 8086 has many different instruction formats; a few are shown in Figure 18–3. In formats (b), (c), and (e), one or two additional bytes may be appended to the postbyte field for certain addressing modes, yielding the maximum instruction length of six bytes in format (b). Most 8086 instructions can operate on either words or bytes, as designated by a w bit in the opcode byte (w=1 for words).

Instruction encodings will be discussed as appropriate in the sections on 8086 addressing modes and operations. However, we concentrate mainly on the effects and assembly language format of various 8086 operations and

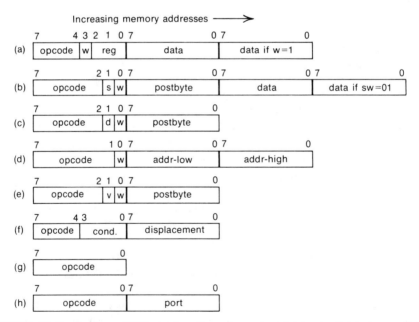

FIGURE 18–3 A few 8086 instruction formats: (a) immediate to register; (b) immediate to register or memory; (c) memory to or from register; (d) absolute short format; (e) shifts and rotates; (f) conditional branches; (g) inherent addressing; (h) input/output with fixed port.

addressing modes. Readers interested in all the details of instruction encodings may find them in the manufacturer's literature.

18.2 ASSEMBLY LANGUAGE

Intel's standard assembly language for the 8086, called ASM-86, is very unusual, complex, and sophisticated. In a small space we can only touch on the philosophy and basic features of the language, and so you must read Intel's literature to find all of the features of ASM-86 that are used in large programs.

In a typical assembler, the symbol table contains a list of symbols and a value for each symbol. In ASM-86, a symbol can have a 16-bit value. However, ASM-86 implements an unusual concept for assembly languages, namely, that symbols may have other attributes besides value, including *type* and *segment name*. We'll discuss the uses of these attributes shortly.

The basic line format of ASM-86 is simple enough, containing label, opcode, operand, and comments, similar to the "free-format" assembly language discussed at the end of Section 6.1.1. Comments start with semicolons, and labels of executable instructions are followed by colons. However, labels in directive statements are not followed by a colon. Hexadecimal numbers are denoted by a suffix of H.

Important ASM-86 assembler directives are listed in Table 18–2. The EQU directive defines a new symbol as in other assembly languages, except that it gives to the new symbol *all* of the attributes of its operand expression. The DB, DW, and DD directives define byte, word, and double word data. ASM-86 is unique in that these same statements are used to declare constant data (initialized at load time) and variable storage (uninitialized): an operand of "?" denotes a variable, that is, an uninitialized byte, word, or double word. Multiple operands are separated by commas. Any operand, including "?", may be repeated n times by enclosing it in parentheses and then preceding the parenthesized expression with "n DUP". The remaining directives in Table 18–2 will be introduced in sample programs in Section 18.5.

Each symbol in an ASM-86 program has an associated *type*. Most symbols have one of the following types:

- BYTE PTR. The value of the symbol is the 16-bit segment offset (i.e., address in segment) of a 1-byte variable in memory.

- WORD PTR. The value of the symbol is the 16-bit segment offset of a 1-word variable in memory.

- DWORD PTR. The value of the symbol is the 16-bit segment offset of a 2-word variable in memory.

TABLE 18–2 ASM-86 assembly language directives.

Name	Examples	Effect
EQU	CR EQU 0DH	Equate symbol with operand.
DB	CB DB 17,0EFH,-1,CR VB DB ? ST DB 'ABCDEFG'	Define 1-byte data. Memory may or may not be initialized.
DW	CW DW 8800H,OFFSET CB TW DW 10 DUP (?)	Define 1-word data. Memory may or may not be initialized.
DD	CD DD 456789ABH TD DD ?	Define 2-word data. Memory may or may not be initialized.
SEGMENT	SEG0 SEGMENT	Begin logical segment.
ENDS	SEG0 ENDS	End logical segment.
ASSUME	ASSUME CS:SEG0	Tell assembler expected run-time contents of segment register(s)
ORG	ORG 4000H	Set program origin within logical segment.
PROC	GO PROC NEAR	Begin procedure definition.
ENDP	GO ENDP	End procedure definition.
EXTRN	EXTRN OS:FAR	Define external symbol.
END	END START	Indicate end of assembly.

- NEAR PTR. The value of the symbol is the 16-bit segment offset of an instruction that may be referenced by an intrasegment jump or call instruction.

- FAR PTR. The value of the symbol is the 16-bit segment offset of an instruction that can be referenced only by an intersegment jump or call instruction.

- NUMBER. The value of the symbol is an arbitrary 16-bit number. The programmer has assigned a symbolic label to the number simply for convenience.

Any symbol of one of the first five types also has an associated *segment name*. ASM-86 provides a few more types, not discussed here, to facilitate program relocation and linking.

In many cases, "typing" allows the assembler to "figure out" the programmer's intentions without specific directions. For example, the 8086 has an "INC" instruction that increments a byte or word in memory. The assembler determines whether the assembly language instruction

```
INC    JET              ;Add one to variable JET.
```

should increment a byte or a word at memory location JET according to the type of symbol JET — BYTE PTR or WORD PTR. Other assembly languages would use different opcodes for byte and word operations (e.g., INCB and INC in the Z8000).

Typing also allows the assembler to check the consistency of a programmer's statements. For example, the statement INC WELL is an error if the type of WELL is anything but BYTE PTR or WORD PTR. As another example, the statement

```
      MOV    AL,QUICK       ;Move Al, quick.
```

is an error if "QUICK" has type WORD PTR, since this is an attempt to load a byte register with a memory word.

Despite its benefits, some programmers may find typing a disadvantage because of the structure it imposes. For example, suppose you declared a 1-word variable,

```
CATS    DW     ?                ;Counts cats in Kate's kitchen.
```

and for some reason you wanted to read the first byte of the word. If you wrote

```
      MOV    AL,CATS        ;Move all cats.
```

then you would get an error message for trying to load a byte register with a word value. Therefore, ASM-86 provides special operators, listed in Table 18–3, that convert symbols and expressions from one type to another. The correct code for the above example is

```
      MOV    AL, BYTE PTR CATS ;Move all bright pewter cats.
```

Typing and the absence of opcode size suffixes sometimes create ambiguity. For example, the statement

```
      INC    [BX]            ;Add one to byte pointed to by BX.
```

may be intended to increment a byte, but ASM-86 has no way of determining whether BX points to a byte or word (it doesn't read comments!). In such cases, the programmer must explicitly inform the assembler of the operand's intended type using one of the special operators:

```
      INC    BYTE PTR [BX]  ;Add one to byte pointed to by BX.
```

The program location counter (PLC) in ASM-86 has a 16-bit offset value and an associated segment name (as defined by the SEGMENT directive). When PLC is used in an expression, a type must be associated with it as well. Therefore, the PLC may be specified by the reserved symbol THIS followed by

TABLE 18-3 ASM-86 special operators.

Operator	Converts From	To	Comments
OFFSET	Any PTR	NUMBER	16-bit segment offset
SEG	Any PTR	NUMBER	16-bit segment base address
SIZE	Any data PTR	NUMBER	# of bytes allocated for data
LENGTH	Any data PTR	NUMBER	# of bytes, words, or d-words
BYTE PTR	Any PTR or NUMBER	BYTE PTR	Segment name (if any) preserved
WORD PTR	Any PTR or NUMBER	WORD PTR	Segment name (if any) preserved
DWORD PTR	Any PTR or NUMBER	DWORD PTR	Segment name (if any) preserved
NEAR PTR	Any PTR or NUMBER	NEAR PTR	Segment name (if any) preserved
FAR PTR	Any PTR or NUMBER	FAR PTR	Segment name (if any) preserved

a type designator: BYTE, WORD, DWORD, NEAR, or FAR. Thus, you might define the address just past the end of a table of 20 data words as follows:

```
TABLE    DW     20 DUP (?)
TEND     EQU    THIS WORD
```

At this point we can introduce the concepts of relocation and linking that are embodied in the 8086 memory-mapping scheme and in ASM-86 and related program development tools. We assume that you are familiar with the general concepts of relocation and linking discussed in Section 6.4.

The 8086's designers intended for programs to be broken into well-defined modules for code, data, and stack. Each module may be stored in a separate "logical segment" that is accessed through an appropriate segment register. The exact physical address used by a logical segment is unimportant as long as the segment registers are maintained properly. Therefore, the binding of each logical segment to a physical base address may be deferred until all of the logical segments (relocatable object modules) of the program are brought together at load time.

In an 8086 program development system, individual assembly language program modules are assembled by ASM-86, which produces relocatable object modules. The PLM-86 high-level language for the 8086 also produces relocatable object modules. Both types of modules may be linked together by the LINK-86 link editor, which produces a single relocatable object module in which external references have been resolved. The logical segments in a single relocatable object module may be bound to physical addresses using the LOC-86 relocater, which produces an absolute object module.

18.3 ADDRESSING

Most 8086 instructions specify operands in the general registers or in memory. Depending on the type of instruction, an operand may be a byte or a

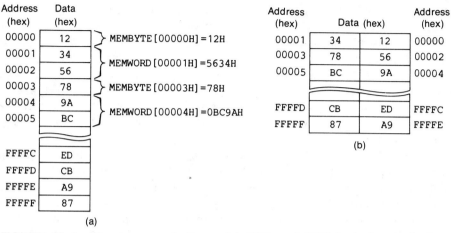

FIGURE 18–4 Memory organizations: (a) 8086 and 8088 logical organization, and 8088 physical organization; (b) 8086 physical organization.

word. (There are also instructions, described in Section 18.4, that operate on BCD digits, byte strings, and word strings.) Typical word instructions can access any of the general registers AX–DI in Figure 18–2. Byte instructions treat registers AX–DX as a set of eight 8-bit registers AH–DL as shown in Figure 18–2, and cannot access registers SP–DI. In either case, a 3-bit field in the instruction is used to encode the register number.

The 8086's memory is logically organized as a contiguous list of bytes, as shown in Figure 18–4(a). Bytes in memory are assembled into words with the lower-numbered byte in the least significant position. When we write an instruction from left to right, as in Figure 18–5, word values come out backwards; in fact, 8086 co-architect S. P. Morse has observed that this arrangement could be called "backwords" storage! The DEC PDP-11 also has "backwords" storage.

Unlike other 16-bit processors, the 8086 architecture does not require memory words to start at even addresses; instructions may specify words starting at even or odd addresses.

The memory of the 8088 circuit is physically as well as logically organized as a list of bytes as shown in Figure 18–4(a). However, the memory of an 8086 circuit is physically organized as a list of words as shown in Figure

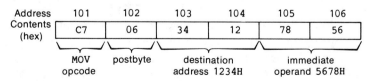

FIGURE 18–5 Layout of 2-byte values in a typical 8086 instruction.

18–4(b). The 8086 processor may access a word in one memory cycle if the word starts at an even address (i.e., if the word is *aligned* on a word boundary). If an instruction specifies a word at an odd address, then the CPU must access two memory words and extract the appropriate bytes from each. Although alignment operations are done without explicit program intervention, programs that access aligned words can run faster than ones that access unaligned words. In particular, programs that keep the stack pointer SP aligned on a word boundary can run faster than ones that push and pop individual bytes.

Basic 8086 instructions and addressing modes specify 16-bit segment offsets. After a 16-bit segment offset has been computed, it is combined with a segment register to produce a 20-bit physical address. In the next nine subsections we'll describe the traditional addressing modes by which the 8086 generates 16-bit segment offsets; these modes are summarized in Table 18–4. We'll call the 16-bit segment offset computed by an addressing mode an *effective address* for compatibility with traditional addressing-mode parlance. In the last subsection we'll describe how 20-bit physical addresses are generated.

18.3.1 Postbyte Addressing Modes

Some 8086 instructions specify their operand addressing modes in the opcode byte, for example, in formats (a) and (d) in Figure 18–3. Other formats, such as (b), (c), and (e), contain an *addressing-mode postbyte*. The postbyte can specify one or two operands and has the layout shown in Figure 18–6.

The postbyte always specifies one operand using the mod and r/m fields. If the 2-bit mod field contains 11_2, then the operand is a register and the 3-bit r/m field contains the register number. Otherwise, mod and r/m are decoded together to yield one of the memory addressing modes we discuss later: absolute, register indirect, based, indexed, or based indexed. If the selected mode requires additional addressing information, the information is contained in one or two bytes immediately following the postbyte.

The use of the reg field depends on whether the instruction requires the postbyte to specify one or two operands. Instructions such as ADD dst,reg [format (c)] require two operands. In this case, the second operand is always a register whose number is contained in the reg field of the postbyte.

On the other hand, instructions such as ROL dst [format (e)] require only one operand. In this case, the postbyte's reg field is not needed for operand selection. The reg field is used instead with the opcode byte to specify an operation. For example, the instructions ROL dst and ROR dst both have the same opcode byte followed by a postbyte; however, ROL's postbyte reg field is 000_2 while ROR's is 001_2. This encoding scheme is similar to the Z8000's (Figure 5–9), in which four bits specify a register number in double-operand instructions but specify an auxiliary opcode in single-operand instructions.

```
7  65 4 32 1 0
┌───┬─────┬─────┐
│mod│ reg │ r/m │
└───┴─────┴─────┘
```

FIGURE 18–6 Layout of the addressing-mode postbyte.

TABLE 18–4 Addressing modes and assembly language notation for the 8086.

Mode	Notation	Operand
Register	reg	reg
Immediate	n	n
Absolute	addr16	MEM[addr16]
Register indirect	[rireg]	MEM[rireg]
Based (8-bit disp.)	[bireg].disp8 or [bireg+disp8]	MEM[bireg+disp8]
Based or Indexed (16-bit disp.)	[bireg].disp16 or addr16[bireg] or [bireg+disp16] or [addr16+bireg]	MEM[bireg+disp16] or MEM[addr16+bireg]
Based indexed (no disp.)	[breg][ireg] or [breg+ireg]	MEM[breg+ireg]
Based indexed (8-bit disp.)	[breg].disp8[ireg] or [breg+disp8+ireg]	MEM[breg+disp8+ireg]
Based indexed (16-bit disp.)	[breg].disp16[ireg] or [breg+disp16+ireg]	MEM[breg+disp16+ireg]

Notes: reg denotes a general register, AX–DI in word instructions, or AH–DL in byte instructions.

reg denotes BX, SI, or DI.

bireg denotes BX, BP, SI, or DI.

breg denotes BX or BP.

ireg denotes SI or DI.

n denotes an expression of type NUMBER yielding a byte or word value as appropriate for the instruction.

MEM[x] denotes the memory byte or word starting at physical address x+segbase, where segbase is the segment's starting physical address implied by one of the segment registers as described in Section 18.3.10. If all of the segment registers contain 0, then segbase is always 0.

addr16 denotes an expression of some PTR type yielding a logical address in a segment that is currently accessible though one of the segment registers, according to the most recent ASSUME statements. The 16-bit offset part of the logical address is used in the instruction, and a segment override prefix is generated if necessary.

disp8 denotes an expression of type NUMBER yielding an 8-bit displacement value (-128 through $+127$). disp16 denotes an expression yielding a 16-bit NUMBER (-32768 through $+32767$). The assembler chooses the shortest possible displacement based on the value of the expression.

The assembler distinguishes between absolute and immediate addressing modes according to the type of the operand expression: absolute for PTR types, immediate for the NUMBER type.

18.3.2 Register

In *register addressing*, the operand is contained in one of the general registers. In the 8086, register addressing may be specified in the opcode byte as in Figure 18–3(a), or as a postbyte addressing mode as explained earlier. In double-operand instructions, two registers may be specified.

A register number is contained in a 3-bit field. In word instructions (w=1), a register number specifies one of the 16-bit registers, AX–DI in Figure 18–2. In byte instructions (w=0), a register number specifies one of the 8-bit registers, AH–DL.

18.3.3 Immediate

In *immediate addressing*, the instruction contains the operand. In the 8086, immediate addressing is designated by a particular opcode combination, and is available for most double-operand instructions. Immediate instructions contain an addressing-mode postbyte, so that immediate-to-memory as well as immediate-to-register operations are possible. Instructions for which immediate addressing is *not* available include segment register loads and PUSH.

In a byte instruction (w=0), an immediate operand is one byte long and appears at the end of the instruction [data in formats (a) and (b) in Figure 18–3]. In a word instruction (w=1), the immediate operand is usually two bytes long [format (a)]. However, some word instructions can have 1-byte immediate operands as designated by an s bit [format (b)]. If s is 1 then a 1-byte immediate value in the instruction is sign-extended to 16 bits before being used in a word operation. This allows arbitrary word operands and small immediate values between −128 and +127 to be added, subtracted, or compared using only one immediate byte instead of two.

18.3.4 Absolute

In *absolute addressing* (which Intel calls *direct*), the instruction contains the 16-bit effective address of the operand. Absolute addressing is a postbyte addressing-mode; the 16-bit address immediately follows the postbyte, low-order byte first.

There is also a *long absolute* addressing mode in which the instruction contains a 16-bit segment base address as well as a 16-bit offset (effective address), allowing the program to directly access any logical memory address. However, this mode is available only with jump and call instructions, and not with general data manipulation instructions. As we'll see in sample programs, the lack of long absolute addressing is sometimes very inconvenient.

18.3.5 Register Indirect

In *register indirect addressing*, a specified register contains the 16-bit effective address of the operand. This is another mode that may be specified by the addressing-mode postbyte.

The 8086 contains four "base registers": BX, BP, SI, and DI. However, register indirect mode is only available with three of the base registers: BX, SI, and DI. Register indirect addressing with BP must be simulated using based addressing with a displacement of 0.

Register SP, though classified as an "address register," is not one of the base registers. The 8086's designers intended for references to data on the stack to use BP as a stack frame pointer. Notice that the top of stack can be accessed no more efficiently than the middle, because register indirect addressing is not available with BP or SP.

18.3.6   Based

Based addressing allows access to list items and other data structures when the offset to a particular item is known at assembly time, but the base address of the data structure must be computed at run time. Based addressing is a postbyte addressing mode in the 8086. Any of four registers — BX, BP, SI, or DI — may be used as a base register. The effective address of the operand is formed by adding the 16-bit address in the specified base register and an 8- or 16-bit displacement contained in the instruction. The displacement byte(s) immediately follow the addressing-mode postbyte.

In the 8-bit displacement mode, the displacement byte is treated as a signed number in the range −128 through +127. In assembly language programs, the assembler automatically determines whether a long or short displacement should be used when based addressing is specified.

ASM-86 assembly language allows two different notations for based addressing. The first, [bireg].disp, is similar to the notation used for record structures in Pascal. The second, [bireg+disp], explicitly reminds us of the run-time addition that takes place in based addressing.

18.3.7   Indexed

The 8086 does not have a separate indexed addressing mode. However, based mode with a 16-bit displacement is logically equivalent to indexed mode. In this case, the instruction contains a 16-bit base address, and the "base register" contains an index value.

Although any of the 8086's four "base registers" may be used in based and indexed modes, the designers of the 8086 intended for BX and BP to be used as base registers and for SI and DI to be used as index registers. Compliance with the designer's wishes is motivated by the implicit use of the base and index registers in certain instructions and by defaults in the memory mapping unit described in Section 18.3.10.

While indexed and based addressing modes have the same encoding in 8086 machine language, ASM-86 assembly language provides separate notations for them. The notation for indexed mode, addr16[bireg], is similar to notations used in high-level languages and other assembly languages.

18.3.8 Based Indexed

Based indexed addressing forms an effective address by adding a base address and a displacement, both of which are contained in registers. This allows both the base address of a data structure and a displacement to one of its components to be computed at run time. Based indexed addressing is a postbyte addressing mode in the 8086. Either BX or BP may be used as the base register, and either SI or DI may be used as the index register. Thus, there are four different combinations of registers that may be used in based indexed addressing.

The 8086 embellishes based indexed mode by allowing the instruction to contain an optional 8- or 16-bit displacement that is also added in the effective-address computation. An 8-bit displacement is treated as a signed number in the range -128 through $+127$. In assembly language programs, the assembler determines from the operand expression whether to use an 8-bit or 16-bit displacement or no displacement. The displacement bytes, if any, follow the postbyte in the assembled instruction.

18.3.9 Relative

In the 8086, *relative addressing* is used only in jump, call, conditional branch, and loop control instructions. The effective address is computed as the sum of the IP and an 8- or 16-bit signed displacement contained in the instruction. The IP value used is the address of the byte following the current instruction.

18.3.10 Memory Mapping

The memory mapping unit in the 8086 derives 20-bit physical addresses from logical addresses consisting of a 16-bit segment base address and a 16-bit segment offset. At any time, logical addresses may be translated into physical addresses in any of four different 64K-byte "segments" of physical memory. The four segments are named according to their intended uses: code, data, stack, and extra. Each of the four 16-bit "segment registers" — CS, DS, SS, and ES in Figure 18–2 — contains a 16-bit segment base address which implies the starting 20-bit physical address of a 64K-byte segment.

The "effective addresses" produced by the addressing modes in previous subsections are actually 16-bit segment offsets. As shown in Figure 18–7(a), a 20-bit physical address is obtained by adding the segment offset to a shifted segment base address. Shifting the segment base address left by four bits yields a 20-bit segment starting address, so that segments start on 16-byte boundaries. The addition of the 16-bit segment offset and the 20-bit segment starting address yields a 20-bit physical address; carries beyond the 20th bit are ignored.

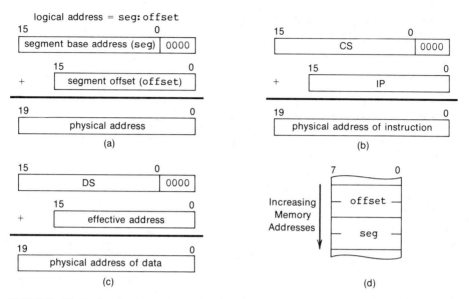

FIGURE 18–7 Logical-to-physical address translation in the 8086: (a) general computation; (b) instruction fetch; (c) variable references; (d) `seg:offset` format in memory.

Since there are four different segment registers, a particular one must be selected to provide the segment base address for each logical-to-physical address translation. Instead of explicitly selecting segment registers by 2-bit fields in instructions, the 8086 hardware selects a default segment according to the purpose of each memory reference.

Segment defaults are listed in Table 18–5. Instruction bytes are always fetched from the segment indicated by CS, the "Code Segment" register. As shown in Figure 18–7(b), IP contains the 16-bit segment offset for the instruction byte, and is added to the shifted CS to obtain the 20-bit physical address of the instruction byte. Likewise, stack operations always read and write bytes in the "Stack Segment" indicated by SS.

Most data manipulation operations access variables in the "Data Segment" indicated by DS. As shown in Figure 18–7(c), the effective address obtained from the traditional addressing mode computation is combined with DS to yield the physical address.

Subroutine parameters and other data on the stack must be accessed in the stack segment; thus operands accessed with BP as a base register use SS as the segment register. String operations use DS as the segment register for source operands and ES for destination operands; the use of different segment registers allows efficient intersegment block transfers.

Data manipulation instructions can override the segment defaults with "segment override prefix" bytes. The override prefix immediately precedes

TABLE 18–5 Default segment registers for memory reference types.

Reference Type	Segment Register	Alternates	Offset
Instruction fetch	CS (Code Segment)	None	IP
Stack operation	SS (Stack Segment)	None	SP
Variable (except below)	DS (Data Segment)	CS,ES,SS	Effective address
BP used as base register	SS (Stack Segment)	CS,ES,DS	Effective address
String source	DS (Data Segment)	CS,ES,SS	SI
String destination	ES (Extra Segment)	None	DI

the opcode byte in the instruction stream and instructs the processor to use a particular segment to access variables, instead of the default. Regardless of the override prefix, all instruction-fetch, stack, and string-destination references use the default segments.

For example, the instruction "MOV AL, BYTE PTR 100" loads AL from memory location 100 in the data segment; the corresponding machine instruction is four bytes long (opcode byte, addressing-mode postbyte, and 2-byte absolute address). The instruction "MOV AL, ES:BYTE PTR 100" loads AL from memory location 100 in the extra segment; the machine instruction is five bytes long (override prefix followed by the original 4-byte instruction). In both cases, all instruction bytes are fetched from the code segment.

Using the four segment registers, a program may access four disjoint 64K-byte regions of physical memory at any time. However, nothing prevents segments from being partially or fully overlapped. Figure 18–8 shows a case in which the code segment is totally disjoint from the others, but the data and extra segments are identical and partially overlap the stack segment.

Although the 8086 segment size is 64K bytes, most programs can use smaller segments. A program may use only part of a 64K-byte segment, say the first or last n bytes, according to some software convention. For example, a program might intend to use only the non-overlapping portion of the stack segment shown in Figure 18–8. However, since the 8086 does not have any "segment length" registers, the unused $64K-n$ bytes of physical memory in a segment are not protected from inadvertent reading or writing by program errors.

A few 8086 instructions, such as intersegment jumps and calls, specify absolute physical addresses. Such addresses occupy a double word in memory and contain a 16-bit offset and a 16-bit segment base address as shown in Figure 18–7(d). A 20-bit physical address is computed at run time by shifting the segment base address and adding the offset in the usual manner shown in Figure 18–7(a).

A major flaw in the 8086 architecture is the difficulty in dealing with 20-bit physical addresses at run time, for example, comparing two physical addresses. Many different logical addresses can yield the same physical ad-

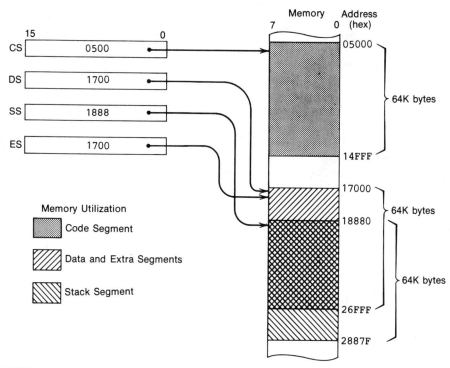

FIGURE 18–8 A possible segment allocation.

dress. For example, physical address 12345H may be produced by a seg:offset of 1000H:2345H or 1234H:0005H or any of 4094 other seg:offset pairs. Therefore, it is insufficient to simply compare the seg and offset parts of logical addresses. Instead, the 20-bit physical addresses produced by the logical addresses must be compared.

Unfortunately, the 8086 has no instruction that directly compares the physical addresses produced by a pair of logical addresses. Likewise, it has no "load effective *physical* address" instruction; such an instruction would have to compute a 20-bit physical address from a logical address and deposit it in a pair of registers. Instead, a program that needs to compare physical addresses must use an explicit sequence of instructions to convert logical addresses to physical addresses. For example, in Intel's PLM/86 high-level language, a programmer might declare a logical-address "pointer variable" using the statement

```
DECLARE LIST$HEAD POINTER;
```

and check for the end of a linked list with the statement

```
IF LIST$HEAD = 0 THEN RETURN;
```

Since LIST$HEAD is a logical address, the compiled machine code must compute the resulting 20-bit physical address and compare it with 0. Intel's PLM/86 compiler, version 1.1, generates a 44-byte sequence of 21 machine instructions for the IF test in the above statement!

18.4 OPERATIONS

We shall classify 8086 instructions into six types: data movement, arithmetic, logic and shifts, program control, string manipulation, and input/output. Input/output instructions will be discussed in Section 18.6.

18.4.1 Data Movement

The 8086's data movement instructions are listed in Table 18–6. Typical instructions have one operand (src or dst) specified by an addressing-mode postbyte; such operands may use register, absolute, register indirect, based, indexed, or based indexed addressing. None of the 8086 data movement instructions affect the condition flags, except for two instructions that explicitly load FLAGS.

Although many 8086 instructions can operate on either bytes or words, 8086 assembly language mnemonics do not contain size suffixes. Instead, the assembler associates a size attribute with each symbol so that the operand size for an instruction can be deduced from the attributes of symbols in the operand expression.

As shown in the first part of Table 18–6, the 8086 has a fairly powerful "MOV" instruction. A MOV instruction in the format of Figure 18–3(c) specifies one general-register operand and another general-register or memory operand (r/m) using an addressing mode postbyte. A "w" bit specifies whether a word or byte is to be moved, and an "d" bit specifies the direction of transfer. Thus, r/m-to-register and register-to-r/m MOVs are possible. Notice that the assembly language operand order (dst,src) of 8086 MOV and other double-operand instructions is the reverse of the order used in PDP-11, 68000, and 9900 assembly languages (src,dst).

Another MOV format [Figure 18–3(b)] allows immediate-to-r/m MOVs. There are also MOV instructions for transferring data to or from the segment registers. However, notice that there is no "move immediate to segment register" instruction; this omission in the 8086 instruction set is inconvenient because segment registers often must be loaded with constant values (see sample programs). The XCHG instruction swaps the contents of a general register and another general register or memory location.

The PUSH and POP instructions in the 8086 implicitly use the stack pointed to by SP. Like other stacks in this book, the 8086 stack grows towards decreasing memory locations and SP points directly at the top stack

TABLE 18-6 8086 data movement instructions.

Mnemonic	Operands	Size	Description
MOV	dst,src	B,W	Copy src to dst
MOV	dst,data	B,W	Load dst with immediate data
MOV	dst,sreg	W	Load dst with sreg
MOV	sreg,src	W	Load sreg with src
XCHG	dst,reg	B,W	Exchange dst with reg
PUSH	src	W	Push src onto stack
PUSH	sreg	W	Push sreg onto stack
PUSHF		W	Push FLAGS onto stack
POP	dst	W	Pop stack into dst
POP	sreg	W	Pop stack into sreg
POPF		W	Pop stack into FLAGS
LAHF		B	Load AH with low byte of FLAGS
SAHF		B	Store AH into low byte of FLAGS
XLAT		B	Load AL with MEM[BX+AL]
LEA	reg,src	W	Load reg with effective address of src
LDS	reg,src	D	Load DS and reg with double-word src
LES	reg,src	D	Load ES and reg with double-word src

Notes: Instructions operate on bytes (B), words (W), or double words (D). When two operand sizes are allowed, the assembler determines the proper size according to the type of the operand expression.

reg may be any word register AX–DI in word operations, or any byte register AH–DL in byte operations.

sreg may be any segment register, CS–ES.

In general, a src or dst operand is specified by an addressing-mode postbyte and therefore may use register, absolute, register indirect, based, indexed, or based indexed addressing. However, register mode is not allowed with LEA, LDS, and LES. Also, in the MOV instruction there is only one addressing-mode postbyte for src and dst. Therefore, either src or dst must be a register.

MOV instructions that have AX or AL as one of the operands and an absolute memory address as the other have an optimized encoding with no addressing-mode postbyte [Figure 18–3(d)].

data indicates an immediate operand (an expression of type NUMBER) appropriate to the size of the operation.

item. As indicated in the second part of Table 18–6, a general register, segment register, memory operand, or FLAGS may be pushed onto the stack; and the word at the top of the stack may be popped into a register, memory word, or FLAGS. Notice that there is no "push immediate" instruction; a constant value to be pushed must first be loaded into a register.

The third part of Table 18–6 contains several miscellaneous data movement instructions. LAHF and SAHF transfer the low-order byte of FLAGS to and from AH; these instructions were included for compatibility with similar instructions in the 8080. The XLAT instruction replaces AL with a byte from a 256-byte translation table pointed to by BX.

LEA loads a general register with the effective address of a `src` operand using any postbyte addressing mode except register. The value loaded is the 16-bit offset part of the operand's logical address, not the physical address.

The LDS and LES instructions load a general register and a segment register DS or ES with a 4-byte logical address found in memory in the format of Figure 18–7(d). This allows a segment register and base register to be initialized to a logical address in one step. For example, DS:BX may be initialized to 2000H: 7FFFH as shown below:

```
MYSEG   DD      2000H:7FFFH    ;Store logical address value.
        ...
        LDS     BX, MYSEG      ;Load DS:BX with logical address.
```

There should be a corresponding instruction to load SP and SS in one step, but there isn't. To initialize SP and SS to the logical address above, two instructions must be executed:

```
        MOV     SS, WORD PTR MYSEG+2    ;SS := segment base address.
        MOV     SP, WORD PTR MYSEG      ;SP := segment offset.
```

A problem is that if an interrupt occurs between the execution of the two MOV instructions, then SS:SP will be in an inconsistent state and the interrupt handler will store data in the wrong place in memory. The 8086's designers discovered this problem and modified the CPU circuit so that interrupts cannot take place immediately after a MOV instruction that stores a value into SS.

18.4.2 Arithmetic

Arithmetic instructions of the 8086 are listed in Table 18–7. All of these instructions set the condition flags according to their result, roughly as described in Chapter 8; refer to an 8086 user's manual for detailed flag settings.

Instructions in the first part of Table 18–7 have a comprehensive and consistent set of formats. For double-operand instructions, there are r/m-to-register, register-to-r/m, and immediate-to-r/m formats available. We observed earlier that the 8086's "general" register set is very irregular with respect to addressing modes and special-purpose instructions. However, the present example and others show that the 8086's basic instructions have a very regular set of formats available.

Most 8086 arithmetic instructions can operate on bytes or words. There is a complete set of add, add with carry, subtract, and subtract with borrow instructions (CF=1 indicates a borrow). The CMP instruction performs the same operation as SUB except that it does not store the result. The three single-operand instructions allow a general register or memory operand to be incremented, decremented, or negated.

Instructions in the second group in Table 18–7 allow signed and unsigned multiplication and division of bytes and words. Multiply and divide

TABLE 18–7 8086 arithmetic instructions.

Mnemonic	Operands	Size	Description
ADD	dst,src	B,W	Add src to dst
ADD	dst,data	B,W	Add immediate data to dst
ADC	dst,src	B,W	Add with carry src to dst
ADC	dst,data	B,W	Add with carry immediate data to dst
SUB	dst,src	B,W	Subtract src from dst
SUB	dst,data	B,W	Subtract immediate data from dst
SBB	dst,src	B,W	Subtract with borrow src from dst
SBB	dst,data	B,W	Subtract with borrow immediate data from dst
CMP	dst,src	B,W	Compare dst with src (dst−src)
CMP	dst,data	B,W	Compare dst with immediate data (dst−data)
INC	dst	B,W	Add 1 to dst
DEC	dst	B,W	Subtract 1 from dst
NEG	dst	B,W	Negate dst (two's complement)
MUL	src	B,W	Unsigned multiply AL or AX by src
IMUL	src	B,W	Signed multiply AL or AX by src
DIV	src	B,W	Unsigned divide {DX,}AX by src
IDIV	src	B,W	Signed divide {DX,}AX by src
CBW		B	Convert byte in AL to word in AX
CWD		W	Convert word in AX to double word in DX,AX
DAA		B	Decimal adjust AL for add
DAS		B	Decimal adjust AL for subtract
AAA		B	ASCII adjust AL for add
AAS		B	ASCII adjust AL for subtract
AAM		B	ASCII adjust AX for multiply
AAD		B	ASCII adjust AL for divide

Notes: Instructions operate on bytes (B) or words (W). When two operand sizes are allowed, the assembler determines the proper size according to the type of the operand expression.

In general, a src or dst operand is specified by an addressing-mode postbyte and therefore may use register, absolute, register indirect, based, indexed, or based indexed addressing. However, in instructions with both src and dst operands there is only one addressing-mode postbyte. Therefore, either src or dst must be a register.

data indicates an immediate operand (an expression of type NUMBER) appropriate to the size of the operation.

operations on bytes use AX as a double-length accumulator: MUL and IMUL multiply AL by an 8-bit src, leaving the 16-bit product in AX; DIV and IDIV divide AX by an 8-bit src, leaving 8-bit quotient in AL and 8-bit remainder in AH. Multiply and divide operations on words use DX:AX in an analogous manner: DX holds a 16-bit multiplier, remainder, or high-order word of a 32-bit product or dividend; AX holds a 16-bit multiplier, quotient, or low-order word of a 32-bit product or dividend. Two instructions orginally named SEX[2] are

[2]Stephen P. Morse, *The 8086 Primer*, Hayden, 1980, p. 52.

consistent with IMUL and IDIV: CBW sign-extends the byte in AL into a word in
AX, and CWD sign-extends the word in AX into a double word in DX:AX.

Instructions in the last group of Table 18–7 support arithmetic on decimal numbers in one of two formats. Standard packed-BCD arithmetic (Sections 4.10 and 8.11) is supported by DAA and DAS. The remaining four instructions support "unpacked" BCD format. This format stores one BCD digit per
byte; the low-order nibble contains the BCD digit and the high-order nibble is
irrelevant. One common unpacked format is "ASCII" format, in which the
high-order nibble is always 0011. Thus, each byte contains the ASCII code for
a BCD digit. Methods of performing unpacked BCD arithmetic in the 8086 are
discussed in some of the references at the end of this chapter.

18.4.3   Logic and Shifts

As shown in the first part of Table 18–8, the 8086 logical instructions
have the same format flexibility as the arithmetic instructions. All of the

TABLE 18–8   8086 logical and shift instructions.

Mnemonic	Operands	Size	Description
AND	dst,src	B,W	Logical AND src to dst
AND	dst,data	B,W	Logical AND immediate data to dst
OR	dst,src	B,W	Logical OR src to dst
OR	dst,data	B,W	Logical OR immediate data to dst
XOR	dst,src	B,W	Logical Exclusive OR src to dst
XOR	dst,data	B,W	Logical Exclusive OR immediate data to dst
TEST	dst,src	B,W	Set FLAGS according to src AND dst
TEST	dst,data	B,W	Set FLAGS according to immediate data AND dst
NOT	dst	B,W	Invert bits of dst (ones' complement)
SHR	dst,cnt	B,W	Logical shift dst right cnt bits
SHL/SAL	dst,cnt	B,W	Logical/arithmetic shift dst left cnt bits
SAR	dst,cnt	B,W	Arithmetic shift dst right cnt bits
ROL	dst,cnt	B,W	Rotate dst left cnt bits
ROR	dst,cnt	B,W	Rotate dst right cnt bits
RCL	dst,cnt	B,W	Rotate dst left with CF cnt bits
RCR	dst,cnt	B,W	Rotate dst right with CF cnt bits

Notes: Instructions operate on bytes (B) or words (W). The assembler determines the proper
size according to the type of the operand expression.

In general, a src or dst operand is specified by an addressing-mode postbyte and
therefore may use register, absolute, register indirect, based, indexed, or based
indexed addressing. However, in instructions with both src and dst operands there
is only one addressing-mode postbyte. Therefore, either src or dst must be a
register.

data indicates an immediate operand (an expression of type NUMBER) appropriate to the
size of the operation.

cnt is either "1", specifying a shift count of 1, or "CL", specifying that the shift count is
contained in register CL.

"standard" logical instructions — AND, OR, XOR, NOT, and AND-TEST — are provided. However, the 8086 lacks the static and dynamic bit manipulation instructions found on two other advanced microprocessors, the 68000 and the Z8000.

The 8086 contains a complete set of static and dynamic shift and rotate instructions that operate like the generics described in Section 8.8. These instructions have a "v" bit [Figure 18–3(e)] that indicates whether the shift count is 1 (v=0) or a variable contained in register CL (v=1).

18.4.4 Program Control

The 8086's program control instructions are shown in Table 18–9. The first six instructions handle jumps, subroutine calls, and subroutine returns both within a segment (intrasegment or NEAR) and between segments (intersegment or FAR). Several opcodes are associated with each mnemonic; the assembler picks the proper one according to the type of the operand expression. For example, there are four possible interpretations of the assembly language instruction JMP expr, according to the type of expr:

(1) expr has type NEAR PTR, so that expr denotes an instruction address in the current segment. The assembler generates opcode E9H for a NEAR direct jump with long offset. The opcode is followed by two bytes containing a signed number in the range -32768 through $+32767$ that is added to IP when the instruction is executed. If the target address is within 128 bytes of the JMP instruction, the assembler may instead generate opcode EBH for a NEAR direct jump with short offset. In this case the opcode is followed by one byte containing a signed number in the range -128 through $+127$ that is added to IP when the instruction is executed. In either case, the value of IP used is the address of the byte following the instruction.

(2) expr has type FAR PTR, so that expr denotes an instruction address in a different segment. The assembler generates opcode EAH for a FAR direct jump. The opcode is followed by two words. The first word is loaded into IP and the second word is loaded into CS when the instruction is executed.

(3) expr has type WORD PTR, so that expr specifies a single-word operand using any of the 8086's postbyte addressing modes. The assembler generates an opcode of FFH followed by an addressing-mode postbyte with a reg field of 100_2 for a NEAR indirect jump. The operand word specified by the postbyte is loaded into IP when the instruction is executed.

(4) expr has type DWORD PTR, so that expr specifies a double-word operand using any of the 8086's postbyte addressing modes except register mode.

TABLE 18-9 8086 program control instructions.

Mnemonic	Operands	Description
JMP	addr	Jump to address addr
JMP	src	Jump to address contained in src
CALL	addr	Call subroutine at address addr
CALL	src	Call subroutine at address contained in src
RET		Return from subroutine
RET	n	Return from subroutine, add n to SP
Jcc	addr8	Conditional branch to address addr8
LOOP	addr8	Decrement CX, jump to addr8 if CX<>0
LOOPE/ LOOPZ	addr8	Decrement CX, jump to addr8 if CX<>0 and ZF=1
LOOPNE/ LOOPNZ	addr8	Decrement CX, jump to addr8 if CX<>0 and ZF=0
JCXZ	addr8	Jump to addr8 if CX=0
CLC		Clear carry (CF:=0)
CMC		Complement carry (CF:=1−CF)
STC		Set carry (CF:=1)
CLD		Clear direction (DF:=0)
STD		Set direction (DF:=1)
CLI		Clear interrupt-enable (IF:=0)
STI		Set interrupt-enable (IF:=1)
HLT		Halt and wait for reset or interrupt
WAIT		Wait for external event
ESC	opc,srce	Fetch opc and srce for external processor
NOP		No operation

Notes: addr is a target address in the current segment or a different segment.
  src is a word or double-word operand that contains the target address in the current segment or in a different segment, respectively.
  n is a 16-bit number added to SP after the return address is popped.
  cc is a standard 8086 condition code chosen from the next table.
  addr8 is a target address in the current segment within 128 bytes of the instruction.
  opc is a 6-bit opcode for an external processor. srce is a source operand for the external processor, specified by a standard addressing-mode postbyte.

The assembler generates an opcode of FFH followed by an addressing-mode postbyte with a reg field of 101_2 for a FAR indirect jump. The first word of the operand specified by the postbyte is loaded into IP and the second word is loaded into CS when the instruction is executed.

Wheww! It is fortunate that the assembler can sort out all the cases. Also, notice that the "indirect" jumps do not jump to their operand address; rather they load IP and possibly CS with values found at the operand address. In a FAR indirect jump, the double-word operand contains seg:offset in the standard format shown in Figure 18-7(d).

The CALL instruction has the same options and effects as JMP, except that it pushes a return address onto the stack before jumping. In a NEAR CALL, only IP is pushed. In a FAR CALL, first CS and then IP is pushed; this pushing order produces on the stack the standard seg: offset format shown in Figure 18–7(d).

The RET instruction returns from a subroutine by popping a return address from the stack. Since a return address may be one or two words long, two different RET opcodes are needed. A NEAR RET pops a word into IP, while a FAR RET pops one word into IP, and then a second word into CS. The assembler determines which RET opcode to use according to how the subroutine was declared — PROC NEAR or PROC FAR, with PROC NEAR being the default. As with parameter-passing conventions, it is up to the programmer to ensure that a subroutine and its callers agree on which call and return instructions will be used.

The RET n instruction returns from a subroutine and adds n to SP after popping the return address. This instruction is very useful for cleaning up input parameters in stack-oriented parameter-passing conventions. As with RET, there are NEAR and FAR forms of RET n that the assembler chooses as appropriate.

The 8086 has sixteen distinct conditional branch instructions of the form Jcc addr8. The branches add a displacement of -128 to $+127$ to IP if a specified condition is true. The allowable conditions include all of the standard ones described in Section 8.6 plus parity, but Intel's mnemonics for the conditions are different, as shown in Table 18–10.

The four instructions in the third group of Table 18–9 are useful loop-control primitives. If CX contains a number X, then the LOOP instruction may be placed at the end of a loop to execute the loop X times. The LOOPZ and LOOPNZ instructions keep an iteration count in the same way and also allow the loop to be terminated early by a zero or nonzero result. The JCXZ instruction may be placed just before a loop controlled by CX in order to skip it completely if CX is already zero.

None of the program control instructions described so far affect FLAGS. The fourth group of Table 18–9 contains instructions whose sole purpose is to manipulate individual bits in FLAGS; their operations are self-explanatory.

A few miscellaneous instructions are listed in the last group in Table 18–9. HLT suspends processing until a reset or interrupt signal is received. WAIT suspends processing until a signal is received on the 8086's TEST input line, allowing the processor to synchronize with an external event without requiring an interrupt. ESC is used to fetch an opcode and operand for an external "co-processor" such as the Intel 8087 Numeric Processor. NOP needs no explanation.

18.4.5 String Manipulation

Although the 8086 does not have auto-increment and auto-decrement addressing modes for its memory reference instructions, it does have a number of special-purpose instructions for processing blocks or strings of

TABLE 18–10 8086 branch conditions.

Type	Mnemonic	Branch If	Condition
Single Bit			
	C	Carry	CF = 1
	NC	Not Carry	CF = 0
	S	Sign	SF = 1
	NS	Not Sign	SF = 0
	E / Z	Equal / Zero	ZF = 1
	NE / NZ	Not Equal / Not Zero	ZF = 0
	O	Overflow	OF = 1
	NO	No Overflow	OF = 0
	P / PE	Parity / Parity Even	PF = 1
	NP / PO	No Parity / Parity Odd	PF = 0
Signed			
	L / NGE	Less / Not Greater nor Equal	SF XOR OF = 1
	GE / NL	Greater or Equal / Not Less	SF XOR OF = 0
	LE / NG	Less or Equal / Not Greater	(SF XOR OF) OR ZF = 1
	G / NLE	Greater / Not Less nor Equal	(SF XOR OF) OR ZF = 0
Unsigned			
	B / NAE	Below / Not Above nor Equal	CF = 1
	AE / NB	Above or Equal / Not Below	CF = 0
	BE / NA	Below or Equal / Not Above	CF OR ZF = 1
	A / NBE	Above / Not Below nor Equal	CF OR ZF = 0

data. These instructions are described in Table 18–11. The string instructions are only one byte long, and implicitly use index registers SI and DI to point to the source string and the destination string, respectively. Destination strings are always accessed in the extra segment, via ES. By default, source strings are accessed in the data segment, via DS; however a segment override prefix may be used to access source strings in a different segment.

At run time, string instructions use either auto-increment or auto-decrement addressing on SI and DI depending on the value of the DF flag. Each instruction may operate on either byte strings or word strings according to a w bit in the instruction. ASM-86 determines the proper size at assembly time according to the attributes of dummy src and dst operands.

A "repeat" prefix may be used on any string instruction to efficiently process a string in one instruction with the CPU maintaining a loop count in CX. A few examples of program applications for the string manipulation instructions will be given at the end of the next section.

18.5 SAMPLE PROGRAMS

The simple unsigned multiplication program that we showed for the 6809 in Table 5–4 is recoded for the 8086 in Table 18–12. In this and the next example, we ignore the 8086's segment registers and memory mapping sys-

TABLE 18–11 8086 block and string manipulation instructions.

Mnemonic	Operands	Size	Description

MOVS
MOVSB/
  MOVSW
	dst,src	B,W
		B
		W
			Copy src string element to dst
			Alternate mnemonics for MOVS
			  (size explicit, no dst or src used)

CMPS	dst,src	B,W	Set FLAGS according to dst-src
SCAS	dst	B,W	Set FLAGS according to A-dst
LODS	src	B,W	Load A with src
STOS	dst	B,W	Store A into dst
REP	minstr		Repeat minstr while CX<>0 WHILE CX<>0 DO BEGIN CX:=CX-1; minstr END

REPE/
  REPZ
	cinstr		Repeat cinstr while equal/zero and CX<>0
			WHILE CX<>0 DO BEGIN CX:=CX-1;
			      cinstr; IF ZF=0 THEN EXIT END

REPNE/
  REPNZ
	cinstr		Repeat cinstr while unequal/nonzero and CX<>0
			WHILE CX<>0 DO BEGIN CX:=CX-1;
			      cinstr; IF ZF=1 THEN EXIT END

Notes: String operations may be performed on byte strings or word strings, depending on a w bit in the instruction's opcode byte.

A denotes AL in byte-string operations, AX in word-string operations.

The CPU implicitly uses ES:DI as a pointer to a destination string and DS:SI as a pointer to a source string (register indirect addressing). It is up to the programmer to ensure that DI, SI, ES, and DS have the proper values at run time.

dst and src denote the source and destination operands in assembly language string instructions. However, the string instructions are only one byte long, and have no operand fields corresponding to src and dst. Nevertheless, the ASM-86 examines the attributes of the dst and src operands to determine the size of the string operation (byte or word), and whether a segment override prefix is needed for the src operand (the dst operand *must* be in the extra segment). Typically, dst and src are symbols corresponding to the base addresses of destination and source string buffers, respectively.

Each string instruction automatically updates DI and/or SI after each dst and/or src string element is processed. The registers are updated by either incrementing or decrementing, depending on the run-time value of DF in FLAGS (DF=1 for decrementing). Incrementing and decrementing are by 1 or by 2 depending on whether byte strings or word strings are being processed.

minstr denotes a MOVS, MOVSB, MOVSW, or STOS instruction. cinstr denotes a CMPS or SCAS instruction. One of the "repeat" prefixes may be placed before a string instruction to cause it to repeat a number of times under CPU control, as governed by the Pascal algorithms shown. Note that if CX is 0 initially, then instr is skipped. Otherwise, the instruction is repeated until CX has been decremented to zero or a termination condition on ZF has been reached.

tem; this simplification can only be used in 8086 systems with 64K or fewer bytes of physical memory. The SEGMENT directive tells the assembler that the program contains one segment (SEG0) starting AT physical address 0000H. It also initializes the program location counter (PLC) to 0, so that assembly

TABLE 18–12   Multiplication by repeated addition.

```
SEG0    SEGMENT AT 0000H
        ASSUME CS:SEG0, DS:SEG0, SS:SEG0, ES:SEG0
;
        ORG     200H            ;Program origin within segment.
;
;       Multiplication program works for any two 16-bit unsigned
;       numbers whose product can be expressed in only 16 bits.
;       Enter with multiplier and multiplicand in BX, DX.  Exit
;       with BX and DX undisturbed, CX bombed, and product in AX.
;
START:  MOV     AX,0            ;Set AX to 0 (initial product).
        MOV     CX,BX           ;CX holds loop count (multiplier).
        JCXZ    OUT             ;Already done if loop count zero.
MLOOP:  ADD     AX,DX           ;Else add multiplicand to product.
        DEC     CX              ;Decrement loop count...
        JNZ     MLOOP           ;...and check for termination again.
OUT:    JMP     OPSYS           ;Go to operating system.
;
OPSYS   EQU     NEAR PTR 1000H  ;Define OS address in current segment.
;
SEG0    ENDS
        END     START
```

begins at offset 0 in the current segment. Within a segment, an ORG statement may be used to set the PLC to another value as shown. Thus, within a segment we can use ORG statements to locate code and data just as we did with the H6809 and other processors.

The program tells the assembler to ASSUME that all segment registers will contain the base address of SEG0 (0000H) when the program runs. Later we'll show programs that may use multiple segments and more memory.

How do the segment registers get set to zero in the first place? When power is applied to the 8086, and whenever the 8086 is reset, the CPU automatically sets CS to FFFFH and IP to 0000H. Therefore, the first instruction will be fetched from physical memory address FFFF0H. Most 8086 systems are configured with read-only memory (ROM) at this address, so that the ROM may contain a FAR JMP to the actual starting address of a start-up program. Since the FAR JMP specifies new values for both CS and IP, the system designer can choose any new value for CS, including zero. At reset the CPU also automatically sets the other segment registers to zero, where they will remain unless explicitly changed.

In Table 18–12, the multiplication program itself is straightforward and uses a loop to generate a product by repeated addition. The program could be optimized by replacing the DEC and JNZ instructions with the LOOP instruction, which performs the equivalent operations. Of course, the biggest optimization could be obtained by replacing the whole loop with the 8086 MUL instruction, but then it would be an even less interesting example!

Table 18–13 is a program that declares and initializes an array of bytes and illustrates some unusual aspects of ASM-86 assembly language. The first executable instruction uses immediate addressing to load BX with the starting address of the array. Since there are no addressing mode notations to distinguish between absolute and immediate addressing, ASM-86 must examine the types of its operands to determine the addressing mode. It uses immediate addressing if the source operand is a NUMBER, and absolute addressing if the source operand is a BYTE PTR or WORD PTR. For example, if we were to write

```
INIT:   MOV    BX,Q           ;Address of first component.
```

then ASM-86 would find that the operand Q is of type BYTE PTR; it would therefore assume that we are trying to load BX with the memory byte at address Q (absolute addressing). This is why the OFFSET operator is necessary. Given an expression expr of any PTR type, "OFFSET expr" returns a 16-bit NUMBER equal to the offset part of expr. Therefore, the instruction

```
INIT:   MOV    BX,OFFSET Q    ;Address of first component.
```

uses immediate addressing, because its operand has type NUMBER. A "word" rather than a "byte" move is used because BX is a word register. If we wrote

```
INIT:   MOV    BL,OFFSET Q    ;Low byte of component address.
```

then we would get a "move byte immediate" instruction because BL is a byte register; the immediate value would be the low-order byte of the offset part of address Q. With immediate addressing in general, the assembler determines the operand size from the size of the destination operand.

In the second instruction in Table 18–13, the source operand 0 is clearly a NUMBER for immediate addressing, but another special ASM-86 operator is needed just the same. In this case, if we simply wrote

```
ILOOP:  MOV    [BX],0         ;Clear component.
```

then the size of the destination operand would be ambiguous, because BX may point to either a byte or a word using register indirect addressing. The BYTE PTR operator informs the assembler that the destination operand is a byte, and so a "move byte immediate" instruction is assembled.

ASM-86 can make sense out of arithmetic expressions in operands in most cases. For example, in the CMP instruction in Table 18–13, the symbol Q has type BYTE PTR and therefore Q+5 is assumed to be a BYTE PTR as well. Then OFFSET Q+5 is a NUMBER, and the instruction

```
        CMP    BX,OFFSET Q+5 ;Past last component?
```

uses immediate addressing to compare the value of BX with the offset part of the logical address five bytes past the start of array Q.

TABLE 18-13   Initializing an array of bytes in the 8086.

```
SEG0     SEGMENT AT 0000H
         ASSUME CS:SEG0, DS:SEG0, SS:SEG0, ES:SEG0
;
         ORG     200H             ;Program origin within segment.
INIT:    MOV     BX,OFFSET Q      ;Address of first array component.
ILOOP:   MOV     BYTE PTR [BX],0 ;Clear component.
         INC     BX               ;Bump to next component.
         CMP     BX,OFFSET Q+5 ;Past last component?
         JNE     ILOOP            ;If not, go do some more.
         JMP     NEAR PTR 1000H  ;Go to operating system.
;
Q        DB      5 DUP (?)        ;Reserve 5 bytes for array.
;
SEG0     ENDS
         END     INIT
```

The next two programs in this section use multiple segments and illustrate some of the concepts of relocation and linking that are embodied in the
8086 memory-mapping scheme and in ASM-86 and related program development tools. In Table 18-14, we have recoded the array initialization program
using separate segments for code and data, CSEG and DSEG.

The sixth line of the program tells the assembler to ASSUME that when
the program is run, CS will have been loaded with the proper segment base
address for the segment named CSEG and DS will have been loaded with the

TABLE 18-14   A program with separate segments for code and data.

```
DSEG     SEGMENT              ;Define data segment.
Q        DB      5 DUP (?)    ;Reserve 5 bytes for array.
DSEG     ENDS
;
CSEG     SEGMENT              ;Define code segment.
         ASSUME CS:CSEG, DS:DSEG
;
INIT:    MOV     AX,DSEG      ;Initialize segment register.
         MOV     DS,AX
         MOV     BX,OFFSET Q  ;Address of first component.
ILOOP:   MOV     BYTE PTR [BX],0 ;Clear component.
         INC     BX           ;Bump to next component.
         CMP     BX,OFFSET Q+5 ;Past last component?
         JNE     ILOOP        ;If not, go do some more.
         JMP     OPSYS        ;Go to operating system.
;
         EXTRN   OPSYS:FAR    ;Label OPSYS is defined elsewhere.
;
CSEG     ENDS
         END     INIT
```

base address of DSEG. Two new instructions have been added at INIT to initialize DS to the proper base address for the data segment; note the lack of immediate addressing for segment register loading <groan>. CS need not be initialized since it is loaded by the instruction that jumps to INIT in the first place.

This example uses the linking and relocation facilities of ASM-86 in conjunction with LINK-86 and LOC-86. The operating system restart address OPSYS is defined as an "external" instruction address in another segment; its value will be supplied when the INIT module is linked with other modules using LINK-86. Also, the starting physical addresses of CSEG and DSEG are not tied down, as SEG0 was tied down by the "AT" clause in the original program. Instead, LOC-86 performs the final binding of logical segments CSEG and DSEG to physical memory addresses, and it patches all instructions and other locations that are to contain the now-known segment base addresses (e.g., MOV AX,DSEG and JMP OPSYS in Table 18–14).

Subroutines in the 8086 are introduced in Table 18–15. This program counts the number of "1" bits in a word. The main program initializes the segment registers and SP, loads AX with a test word, and then calls WCNT1S to count 1s in AX. The WCNT1S subroutine performs its task by calling BCNT1S twice to count 1s in the high and low bytes of AX.

Four separate segments are used in Table 18–15: STACK for the return-address stack; MAIND for main program data; MAINC for main program code; and CNTSEG for code for both subroutines. A small data table (MASKS) is also included in CNTSEG; it is reasonable to put this data in the code segment because it is "read-only."

Appropriate segment register initializations are made in MAIN. After initialization, the only segment register changes are the ones made to CS by FAR CALL and RET instructions.

A number of ASM-86 conventions are shown for the first time in Table 18–15. One pseudo-operation, DW, is used to define data words in memory whether the locations are to be initialized or not. Thus, the statement

```
TWORD   DW      1357H        ;Test word to count 1s.
```

defines a memory word whose contents will be initialized to 1357H at load time, similar to the FCW statement in the H6809 and H8000. On the other hand, the statement

```
        DW      32 DUP (?)   ;Reserve space for stack buffer.
```

reserves 32 memory words that will not be initialized at load time, similar to RMW in the H6809 and H8000. The statement

```
STKE    EQU     THIS WORD    ;Define initialization address for SP.
```

defines STKE as a symbol whose value is the current PLC and whose type is "WORD PTR".

Each subroutine in Table 18–15 is preceded by a "PROC" pseudo-operation to inform the assembler whether the subroutine will be called by a NEAR or FAR CALL. Since WCNT1S is declared by PROC FAR, the assembler uses the FAR format for the CALL WCNT1S instruction in MAIN and for the RET instruction in WCNT1S. The FAR declaration and format are appropriate because MAIN and WCNT1S are in different segments. On the other hand, WCNT1S

TABLE 18–15 Program that uses subroutines to count the number of "1" bits in a word.

```
STACK     SEGMENT              ;Stack segment for entire program.
          DW      32 DUP (?)   ;Reserve space for stack buffer.
STKE      EQU     THIS WORD    ;Define initialization address for SP.
STACK     ENDS
;
MAIND     SEGMENT              ;Data segment for main program.
TWORD     DW      1357H        ;Test word to count 1s.
MAIND     ENDS
;
MAINC     SEGMENT              ;Code segment for main program.
          ASSUME CS:MAINC, DS:MAIND, SS:STACK, ES:MAIND
MAIN:     MOV     AX, STACK    ;Initialize stack segment register.
          MOV     SS, AX
          MOV     SP, OFFSET STKE ;Initialize stack pointer.
          MOV     AX, MAIND    ;Initialize data segment register.
          MOV     DS, AX
          MOV     ES, AX       ;Initialize extra segment register.
          MOV     AX, TWORD    ;Get test word.
          CALL    WCNT1S       ;Count number of 1s in it.
          JMP     OPSYS        ;Go to operating system.
          EXTRN   OPSYS:FAR    ;Operating system restart address.
MAINC     ENDS                 ;End main program.
;
CNTSEG    SEGMENT              ;Define code segment for subroutines.
          ASSUME CS:CNTSEG     ;CS will have new value here.
WCNT1S    PROC    FAR
;         Count the number of '1' bits in a word. Enter with word in
;         AX, exit with count in AX.  WCNT1S splits AX into two bytes,
;         and calls BCNT1S to count the number of 1s in each byte.
;
          CALL    BCNT1S       ;Count 1s in AL, leave count in CX.
          PUSH    CX           ;Save '1' count on stack.
          MOV     AL, AH       ;Count 1s in AH.
          CALL    BCNT1S
          POP     AX           ;Get low-order count.
          ADD     AX, CX       ;Add high-order count.
          RET                  ;Done, return.
WCNT1S    ENDP
```

TABLE **18**–15 (continued)

```
BCNT1S   PROC    NEAR
;        Count number of '1' bits in a byte. Enter with byte in AL,
;        exit with count in CX.
;
         MOV     CX, 0            ;Initialize '1' count.
         MOV     SI, 0            ;Index of first mask in table.
BLOOP:   TEST    AL, MASKS[SI]    ;Test a bit of AL.
         JZ      BNEXT            ;Skip if bit is zero.
         INC     CX               ;Update count if bit set.
BNEXT:   INC     SI               ;Point to next mask.
         CMP     SI, 8            ;Past last mask?
         JNE     BLOOP            ;No, continue?
         RET                      ;Yes, return.
;
MASKS    DB      80H,40H,20H,10H,8,4,2,1
BCNT1S   ENDP
CNTSEG   ENDS
         END     MAIN
```

and BCNT1S are in the same segment, and so BCNT1S may be declared by
PROC NEAR. In this case, the assembler uses the NEAR format for the
CALL BCNT1S instruction in WCNT1S and for the RET instruction in BCNT1S.
When NEAR CALL and RET instructions are executed, CS is neither saved on
the stack nor restored, because the subroutine is in the same segment as its
caller.

Subroutine BCNT1S checks the bits of AL using indexed addressing to
compare AL against each element of a table of eight 1-bit masks. The subroutine could also be recoded to use register indirect addressing instead of
indexed, as shown below:

```
         MOV     CX,0             ;Initialize '1' count.
         MOV     SI, OFFSET MASKS ;Address of first mask in table.
BLOOP:   TEST    AL, [SI]         ;Test a bit of AL.
         JZ      BNEXT            ;Skip if bit is zero.
         INC     CX               ;Update count if bit set.
BNEXT:   INC     SI               ;Point to next mask.
         CMP     SI, OFFSET MASKS+8  ;Past last mask?
         JNE     BLOOP            ;No, continue?
         RET                      ;Yes, return.
```

Although the change appears straightforward, it contains a subtle bug. Register indirect addressing with SI normally uses DS as the default segment register. However, in the above code SI contains an offset in the *code* segment,
and so segment register CS should be used. The assembler is not smart
enough to figure out what segment the programmer expects SI to be pointing
into at run time, and therefore it generates a TEST instruction that uses the

default segment register DS. To access the desired segment, we must recode the instruction as follows:

```
BLOOP:  TEST   AL, CS:[SI]   ;Test a bit of AL.
```

The "CS:" tells the assembler to generate a segment override prefix so that segment register CS is used instead of the default DS. So why didn't we have to use a prefix in the original code? In the original statement

```
BLOOP:  TEST   AL, MASKS[SI] ;Test a bit of AL.
```

the base address MASKS is explicitly mentioned. In this case, the assembler can determine that segment name of MASKS is "CNTSEG". Since DS has been ASSUMEd to contain MAIND, address MASKS is not accessible through the default segment register DS. However, CS has been ASSUMEd to contain CNTSEG, and therefore MASKS should be accessible using the CS segment override prefix. The assembler automatically generates the override prefix for the TEST instruction. This example shows why ASSUME statements are needed — they help the assembler make "intelligent" decisions.

Another example of indexed addressing in the 8086 is given in Table 18–16, a program that finds prime numbers using the sieve of Eratosthenes. Like the 6809 version in Table 7–5, the 8086 program declares an array of bytes with each component corresponding to a number between 2 and 1000. By marking off multiples of known primes, it eliminates nonprimes until only primes remain. For simplicity in this example, we have omitted details of segment register setups; as shown, code and data will be in the same segment.

A stack-oriented parameter-passing convention was illustrated in Figure 9–4; an 8086 subroutine that uses this convention is shown in Table 18–17. Much of this code could be rewritten to be more efficient, for example, by using the 8086 DIV instruction instead of a loop. However, the existing code better illustrates calling conventions and 8086 instructions.

In the JMP instruction just before label DIVVY:, the special operator SHORT informs the assembler that the label CLNSTK is within 128 bytes of the JMP instruction. Since CLNSTK is a forward reference, the assembler has no other way of learning its distance during pass 1 of the assembly. The SHORT operator forces the assembler to generate the short, 8-bit-offset form of the JMP instruction, instead of the 16-bit-offset form that the assembler would have to assume is needed otherwise.

A main program that calls DIVIDE is shown in Table 18–18. This program operates the same as the PDP-11 DIVPQ program shown in Table 13–18, and the stack has the same states as those shown in Figure 13–7 on p. 421.

A set of queue manipulation subroutines for the 8086 is given in Table 18–19. Like the 6809 version in Table 9–18, this code is self-documenting. However, as in most 8086 programs, the fine points of segment utilization need some explanation.

TABLE 18-16   Subroutine to find primes using an array and indexed addressing.

```
;                               PROCEDURE FindPrimes;
NPRIME    EQU   1000;           CONST nPrime = 1000;
PLIMIT    EQU   32;               pLimit = 32;
;                               VAR prime:ARRAY [2..nPrime] OF boolean;
PRIME     DB    NPRIME-1 DUP (?);     {reg} SI, DI : integer;
FNDPRM    PROC  NEAR;           BEGIN
          MOV   DI,2;             FOR DI := 2 TO nPrime DO
SETEM:    MOV   PRIME-2[DI],1;    {Set the entire array true.}
          INC   DI;               prime[DI] := true;
          CMP   DI,NPRIME;
          JLE   SETEM;
          MOV   SI,2;             SI := 2; {First known prime.}
;                                 REPEAT {Check integers 2 to pLimit.}
MARKEM:   CMP   PRIME-2[SI],0;    IF prime[SI] THEN
          JEQ   NOTPRM;             BEGIN
          MOV   DI,SI;               DI := 2 * SI;
          ADD   DI,SI;               REPEAT {Mark multiples of SI.}
CLRLUP:   MOV   PRIME-2[DI],0;        prime[DI] := false;
          ADD   DI,SI;               DI := DI + SI;
          CMP   DI,NPRIME;          UNTIL DI > nPrime;
          JLE   CLRLUP;            END;
NOTPRM:   INC   SI;                SI := SI+1;
          CMP   SI,PLIMIT;        UNTIL SI > pLimit;
          JLE   MARKEM;
          CALL  WRMSG1;           write('Primes between 2 and ');
          MOV   SI,NPRIME;        SI := nPrime;
          CALL  PRINTSI;          writeln(SI); {Print the value in SI.}
          MOV   SI,2;             FOR SI := 2 TO nPrime DO
PRTLUP:   CMP   PRIME-2[SI],0;    {Print all the primes.}
          JZ    NEXTP;            IF prime[SI] THEN
          CALL  PRINTSI;            writeln(SI);
NEXTP:    INC   SI;
          CMP   SI,NPRIME;
          JLE   PRTLUP;
          RET;                    {All done, return to caller.}
FNDPRM    ENDP;                  END;
```

The offsets that define the queue descriptor table (QHEAD, QTAIL, etc.) have type NUMBER and are therefore not associated with any segment as far as the assembler is concerned. Instructions such as MOV SI, [BX] .QHEAD use the default segment register DS, and so the queue descriptor table is accessed in whatever segment DS happens to be pointing to. Therefore, the queue subroutine calling conventions insist that DS contain the segment base address for the queue descriptor table.

Now suppose we wanted to redefine the queue subroutines so that ES instead of DS contains the segment base address for the queue descriptor table. We could recode a typical calling sequence as follows:

```
;        MOV    AX, SEG Q1DT  ;Set up ES with segment #
;        MOV    ES, AX        ;  of queue descriptor table.
;        MOV    BX, OFFSET Q1DT ;Set up BX with offset.
;        CALL   QINIT           ;Initialize descriptor table.
```

However, in the queue subroutines the assembler has no way of knowing that ES holds the segment base address unless we use explicit segment override prefixes. Thus, we must recode QINIT as follows:

TABLE 18–17 Unsigned division subroutine that passes parameters on a stack.

```
;        The statements below define positions of parameters and local
;        variables in the stack relative to the frame pointer (BP).
CNT      EQU    -2              ;Loop counter.
OLDBP    EQU    0               ;Old value of frame pointer.
RETADR   EQU    2               ;Return address.
DVSR     EQU    4               ;1-word divisor (input).
HIDVND   EQU    6               ;High-order word of dividend (input).
LODVND   EQU    8               ;Low-order word of dividend (input).
REM      EQU    10              ;1-word remainder (output).
QUOT     EQU    12              ;1-word quotient (output).
STATUS   EQU    14              ;0 ==> OK, <>0 ==> overflow (output).
;
DIVIDE   PROC   NEAR            ;Unsigned division subroutine.
         PUSH   BP              ;Push old frame pointer onto stack.
         MOV    BP, SP          ;Copy SP into BP for new frame pointer.
         SUB    SP, 2           ;Allocate local variable space.
         MOV    [BP].CNT, 16    ;Initialize loop count.
         MOV    [BP].STATUS, 0  ;Initial status OK.
         MOV    AX, [BP].HIDVND ;Put high DVND in a register.
         CMP    AX, [BP].DVSR   ;Will quotient fit in 1 word?
         JB     DIVVY           ;Branch if it will.
         INC    [BP].STATUS     ;Else report overflow.
         JMP    SHORT CLNSTK
DIVVY:   MOV    BX, [BP].LODVND ;Put low DVND in a register.
DIVLUP:  SAL    BX, 1           ;Left shift dividend with LSB:=0.
         RCL    AX, 1           ;A carry here from MSB means
         JC     QUOT1           ;  high DVND definitely > DVSR.
         CMP    AX, [BP].DVSR   ;Compare high DVND with DVSR.
         JB     QUOTOK          ;Quotient bit = 0 if lower.
QUOT1:   INC    BX              ;Else set quotient bit to 1.
         SUB    AX, [BP].DVSR   ;And update high DVND.
QUOTOK:  DEC    [BP].CNT        ;Decrement iteration count.
         JG     DIVLUP          ;Continue until done.
         MOV    [BP].REM, AX    ;Store remainder.
         MOV    [BP].QUOT, BX   ;Store quotient.
CLNSTK:  MOV    SP, BP          ;Remove local variables.
         POP    BP              ;Restore old frame pointer.
         RET    6               ;Discard input parameters and return.
DIVIDE   ENDP
```

```
QINIT    PROC    FAR
         MOV     AX, ES:[BX].QSTRT ;Put buffer starting address
         MOV     ES:[BX].QHEAD, AX ;  into QHEAD and QTAIL.
         MOV     ES:[BX].QTAIL, AX
         RET                       ;Done, return.
QINIT    ENDP
```

Another note on coding is also in order. At the end of QDEQ, ZF must be cleared. Since the 8086 does not have a single instruction to set or clear ZF, we push the current value of FLAGS when ZF is known to be 0, and pop this desired value later. Without this trick, it would have taken several more instructions to explicitly clear ZF without affecting other registers (see Exercise 18.3).

To illustrate the 8086's block and string manipulation instructions, we consider the prime-number program in Table 18–16. The first five executable instructions of the program initialize an array of memory bytes. These instructions could be replaced with a repeated STOS instruction as follows:

```
FNDPRM   PROC    NEAR
         MOV     AX, SEG PRIME ;Point ES:DI to start of buffer.
         MOV     ES, AX
         MOV     DI, OFFSET PRIME
         MOV     CX, LENGTH PRIME  ;Set up total number of array bytes.
         MOV     AL, 1             ;Set up initialization value.
         CLD                       ;Set up DF for auto-increment.
   REP   STOS    ES:PRIME          ;Initialize the entire array.
```

TABLE 18–18 Program that calls stack-oriented DIVIDE.

```
;          Compute PDIVQ := P DIV Q; PMODQ := P MOD Q;
;          where all are 1-word variables in memory.
DIVPQ:     SUB     SP, 6            ;Reserve space for output parameters.
           PUSH    P                ;Push low-order dividend.
           MOV     AX, 0            ;Push high-order dividend = 0.
           PUSH    AX               ; (No push immediate instruction.)
           PUSH    Q                ;Push divisor.
           CALL    DIVIDE           ;Do the division.
           POP     PMODQ            ;Pop remainder and store.
           POP     PDIVQ            ;Pop quotient and store.
           POP     AX               ;Get status.
           CMP     AX, 0            ;Test it.
           JNE     DIVOVF           ;Branch on overflow.
           ...
P          DW      ?                ;Storage for P, Q, PDIVQ, PMODQ
Q          DW      ?                ;    (all 1-word variables).
PDIVQ      DW      ?
PMODQ      DW      ?
```

TABLE 18-19   Queue manipulation subroutines for the 8086.

```
; QUEUE MODULE
;
; This module contains three subroutines for manipulating queues
; of 16-bit words. A queue is defined by a queue descriptor table
; and a block of storage, as shown below.
;
;                                             QUEUE STORAGE BLOCK
;         --------------------         --------------------
; QDTBL |    QHEAD (word)    | -------->|      (word)      |
;       |------------------|    |       |------------------|
;       |    QTAIL (word)   |    |       |                  |
;       |------------------|    |       |    o  o  o  o     |
;       |    QSTRT (word)   |----       |                  |
;       |------------------|            |------------------|
;       |    QEND  (word)   |----------->|      (word)      |
;         --------------------         --------------------
;
QHEAD   EQU    0               ;Define offsets in descriptor table.
QTAIL   EQU    2
QSTRT   EQU    4
QEND    EQU    6
;
; In this table, the last two words are constants, initialized at
; load time, that give the starting and ending addresses of the block
; of storage (buffer) reserved for the queue itself. The first and
; second words are reserved to store the queue head and tail (absolute
; memory addresses), and are manipulated by the subroutines.  The
; queue descriptor table and the queue storage block must be in the
; same segment.
;
; If a program defines several queues, it allocates a separate queue
; descriptor table and storage block for each one.  Different queues
; may be in different segments. The statements below define a 100-word
; queue Q1 and a 5-word queue Q2:
;
;Q1BLK  DW     100 DUP (?)   ;Storage block for Q1.
;Q1END  EQU    (THIS WORD)-2 ;Last location in Q1 storage block.
;Q1DT   DW     ?, ?, OFFSET Q1BLK, OFFSET Q1END ;Q1 descriptor table.
;
;Q2BLK  DW     5 DUP (?)     ;Storage block for Q2.
;Q2END  EQU    (THIS WORD)-2 ;Last location in Q2 storage block.
;Q2DT   DW     ?, ?, OFFSET Q2BLK, OFFSET Q2END ;Q2 descriptor table.
;
; Subroutines are provided to initialize a queue (QINIT), enqueue
; a word (QENQ), and dequeue a word (QDEQ).  On entry, each
; subroutine assumes that DS contains the segment base address
; for the queue's segment, and BX contains the segment offset for
; for the descriptor table of the queue.
;
```

TABLE 18–19 (continued)

```
QCODE     SEGMENT
          ASSUME CS:QCODE
;
; SUBROUTINE QINIT -- Initialize a queue to be empty.
;
; INPUTS
;   QDTBL -- The address of the queue descriptor table for the
;            queue to be initialized, passed in registers DS:BX.
; OUTPUTS, GLOBAL DATA, LOCAL DATA -- None
; FUNCTIONS
;   (1) Initialize the queue to empty by setting QHEAD and QTAIL
;       in QDTBL equal to the first address in the queue buffer.
; REGISTERS AFFECTED -- AX
;
; TYPICAL CALLING SEQUENCE
;         MOV    AX, SEG Q1DT   ;Set up DS with segment #
;         MOV    DS, AX         ; of queue descriptor table.
;         MOV    BX, OFFSET Q1DT ;Set up BX with offset.
;         CALL   QINIT          ;Initialize descriptor table.
;
QINIT     PROC   FAR
          MOV    AX,[BX].QSTRT  ;Put buffer starting address
          MOV    [BX].QHEAD,AX  ; into QHEAD and QTAIL.
          MOV    [BX].QTAIL,AX
          RET                   ;Done, return.
QINIT     ENDP
;
; SUBROUTINE QENQ -- Enqueue one word into a queue.
;
; INPUTS
;   QDTBL -- The address of the queue descriptor table for the
;            queue to be manipulated, passed in registers DS:BX.
;   QDATA -- The word to be enqueued, passed in register AX.
; OUTPUTS
;   QFULL -- 1 if the queue is already full, else 0;
;            passed in condition flag ZF.
; GLOBAL DATA, LOCAL DATA -- None.
; FUNCTIONS
;   (1) If the queue described by QDTBL is full, set QFULL to 1.
;   (2) If the queue is not full, enqueue QDATA and set QFULL to 0.
; REGISTERS AFFECTED -- SI, FLAGS
;
; TYPICAL CALLING SEQUENCE
;         MOV    AX, SEG Q1DT   ;Set up DS with segment #
;         MOV    DS, AX         ; of queue descriptor table.
;         MOV    BX, OFFSET Q1DT ;Set up BX with offset.
;         MOV    AX, AWORD      ;Enqueue AWORD.
;         CALL   QENQ
;         JZ     OVFL           ;Branch if queue is full.
```

TABLE 18-19 (continued)

```
QENQ      PROC    FAR
          MOV     SI,[BX].QTAIL   ;Get queue tail.
          MOV     [SI],AX         ;Store QDATA at tail (no harm if full).
          ADD     SI,2            ;Bump to next free location.
          CMP     SI,[BX].QEND    ;Wrap-around?
          JBE     QENQ1
          MOV     SI,[BX].QSTRT   ;Reinitialize on wrap-around.
QENQ1:    CMP     SI,[BX].QHEAD   ;Queue already full?
          JEQ     QENQ2           ;Return with ZF=1 if full.
          MOV     [BX].QTAIL,SI   ;Update tail, ZF=0 still.
QENQ2:    RET                     ;Return.
QENQ      ENDP
;
; SUBROUTINE QDEQ -- Dequeue one word from a queue.
;
; INPUTS
;   QDTBL -- The address of the queue descriptor table for the
;            queue to be manipulated, passed in registers DS:BX.
; OUTPUTS
;   QEMPTY-- 1 if the queue is empty, else 0; passed in
;            condition flag ZF.
;   QDATA -- The word dequeued, passed in register AX.
; GLOBAL DATA, LOCAL DATA -- None.
; FUNCTIONS
;   (1) If the queue described by QDTBL is empty, set QEMPTY to 1.
;   (2) If the queue isn't empty, dequeue QDATA and set QEMPTY to 0.
; REGISTERS AFFECTED -- AX, SI, FLAGS
;
; TYPICAL CALLING SEQUENCE
;         MOV     AX, SEG Q1DT    ;Set up DS with segment #
;         MOV     DS, AX          ;   of queue descriptor table.
;         MOV     BX, OFFSET Q1DT ;Set up BX with offset.
;         CALL    QDEQ            ;Dequeue a word into AWORD.
;         JZ      UNDFL           ;Branch if queue was empty.
;         MOV     AWORD,AX
;
QDEQ      PROC    FAR
          MOV     SI,[BX].QHEAD   ;Get copy of head.
          CMP     SI,[BX].QTAIL   ;Queue empty?
          JEQ     QDEQ2           ;Return with ZF=1 if empty.
          PUSHF                   ;Else save ZF=0 on stack.
          MOV     AX,[SI]         ;Read QDATA word from queue.
          ADD     SI,2            ;Bump copy head to next item in queue.
          CMP     SI,[BX].QEND    ;Wrap-around?
          JBE     QDEQ1
          MOV     SI,[BX].QSTRT   ;Reinitialize copy head on wrap-around.
QDEQ1:    MOV     [BX].QHEAD,SI   ;Update real head in memory.
          POPF                    ;Restore ZF=0 since queue not empty.
QDEQ2:    RET                     ;Return.
QDEQ      ENDP
QCODE     ENDS
```

Although some overhead is required to set up the registers, the hardware-repeated STOS instruction is much faster than the original software loop. Note that the operand of STOS merely serves to inform the assembler of the element size and segment of the destination string.

Next, we consider a subroutine to search for the first occurrence of a character in a buffer, coded without the string manipulation instructions as shown in Table 18–20. The subroutine may be optimized by replacing the code beginning at SLOOP: with the following:

```
SLOOP:    CLD                    ;Clear DF for auto-increment.
          MOV    CX,LENGTH BUFFER ;Set up length of BUFFER.
   REPNE SCAS    BUFFER          ;Search for match.
;         DI now points just past matched char and ZF=1 if found.
          RET                    ;Return.
```

The optimized code is obviously shorter, and it is much faster too. As in the previous example, the operand of SCAS serves merely to inform the assembler of the element size and segment of the destination string.

A subroutine that uses the CMPS instruction is shown in Table 18–21. A calling program wants to know if a desired string occurs anywhere in BUFFER, and so it passes the base address and length of the desired string to the

TABLE 18–20 Character search subroutine for the 8086.

```
;         Find the first occurrence in BUFFER of a character
;         passed in AL.  Return with ZF=0 if character not found,
;         or with ZF=1 and DI pointing to the character if found.
;
ZCODE     SEGMENT
          ASSUME CS: ZCODE, ES: ZDATA
SEARCH    PROC   FAR
          MOV    BX, SEG BUFFER  ;Point ES:DI to start of buffer.
          MOV    ES, BX
          MOV    DI, OFFSET BUFFER
SLOOP:    CMP    AL, ES:[DI]     ;Match?
          JEQ    OUT             ;Exit with ZF=1 if match found.
          INC    DI              ;Bump to next character.
          CMP    DI, OFFSET BUFEND ;At end?
          JNE    SLOOP           ;No, look some more.
          MOV    AH, 0           ;Not found, set ZF to 0.
          SAHF
OUT:      RET                    ;Return.
SEARCH    ENDP
ZCODE     ENDS
;
ZDATA     SEGMENT
BUFFER    DB     1000 DUP (?)    ;Reserve 1000-byte buffer.
BUFEND    EQU    THIS BYTE       ;Address just past end of buffer.
ZDATA     ENDS
```

TABLE 18–21   String search subroutine for the 8086.

```
;          Find the first occurrence in BUFFER of a specified string.
;          The base address of the string is passed in DS: BX, and the
;          length of the string is passed in DX. Return with ZF=0 if
;          string not found, or with ZF=1 and ES: DI pointing to the
;          first character of the string in BUFFER if found.
;
ZCODE    SEGMENT
         ASSUME CS: ZCODE, ES: ZDATA, DS: ZSRC
STSRCH   PROC    FAR
         MOV     AX, SEG BUFFER   ;Point ES: DI to start of buffer.
         MOV     ES, AX
         MOV     DI, OFFSET BUFFER
         MOV     AX, OFFSET BUFEND ;Compute last possible starting
         SUB     AX, DX           ; address in BUFFER for a match.
         CLD                      ;Clear DF for auto-increment.
         JMP     SHORT CHKLST     ;Make sure string not too long.
CHKSTR:  MOV     SI, BX           ;Get starting address of string.
         MOV     CX, DX           ;Get length of string.
         PUSH    DI               ;Save current starting point in BUFFER.
   REPE  CMPS    BUFFER, STRING   ;Check for a match.
         POP     DI               ;Restore starting point (ZF unaffected).
         JEQ     FNDIT            ;Got a match, return with ZF=1.
         INC     DI               ;Try starting with next byte in BUFFER.
CHKLST:  CMP     DI, AX           ;Still possible to get a match?
         JBE     CHKSTR           ;Yes, try some more.
NOTFND:                           ;No, return with ZF=0 (from JBE).
FNDIT:   RET
STSRCH   ENDP
ZCODE    ENDS
;
ZDATA    SEGMENT
BUFFER   DB      1000 DUP (?)     ;Reserve 1000-byte buffer.
BUFEND   EQU     THIS BYTE
ZDATA    ENDS
;
ZSRC     SEGMENT                  ;Dummy segment for source string.
STRING   DB      ?
ZSRC     ENDS
```

subroutine STSRCH. Beginning with the first byte in BUFFER, the STSRCH subroutine checks each possible starting address in BUFFER to see if a copy of the desired string begins there. A method for speeding up STSRCH is suggested in Exercise 18.10.

A possible calling program is shown in Table 18–22. The "ES: " prefix on the operand of STOS is redundant since STOS always uses ES for its destination operand. However, ES: has another function besides generating a segment override prefix if one is required. It tells ASM-86 to omit its usual comparison of the operand's segment number with the value that is currently

ASSUMEd to be in ES, if any; the programmer guarantees that ES contains the proper segment number, regardless of what the assembler may think.

18.6 INPUT/OUTPUT, INTERRUPTS, AND TRAPS

18.6.1 Input/Output

The 8086 uses isolated I/O; it can access 2^{16} bytes of input ports and output ports in an address space separate from the memory address space. Like memory, I/O ports may be accessed one or two bytes at a time. Instructions that access the I/O ports are listed in the first part of Table 18–23.

Unlike most other aspects of the 8086, the I/O organization and I/O instructions are exceedingly simple. All I/O transfers in the 8086 use the accumulator AX (word I/O) or its low-order byte AL (byte I/O). The assembler determines the size of the operation according to whether the programmer has written AX or AL in the assembly language instruction.

The IN instruction transfers a byte or word from a specified port to the accumulator; OUT transfers from accumulator to the port. A small port-address, between 0 and 255, may be specified as an 8-bit immediate value in an I/O instruction. Thus, ports with small addresses may be accessed more efficiently than other ports. Any port address, between 0 and 65535, may be specified using register indirect addressing with DX. Besides allowing larger port addresses, this mode is useful in shared I/O drivers where the port number must be computed at run time.

Noninterrupt I/O programming practices for the 8086 faithfully follow the general principles that we presented in Chapter 10.

TABLE 18–22 A program fragment that eliminates MONEY.

```
ZCALLER SEGMENT
WANTED  DB     'MONEY'          ;Desired string.
;
        ASSUME CS:ZCALLER
START:  MOV    AX, SEG WANTED   ;Set up logical address of
        MOV    DS, AX           ;   WANTED string in DS:BX.
        MOV    BX, OFFSET WANTED
        MOV    DX, LENGTH WANTED ;Load DX with length (5).
        CALL   STSRCH           ;Look for string.
        JNE    TOOBAD           ;Jump if not found.
FOUND:                          ;ES:DI points to 'MONEY' in BUFFER.
        MOV    CX, LENGTH WANTED ;Length of 'MONEY'.
        MOV    AL, ' '          ;Load AL with ASCII space.
  REP   STOS   ES:BUFFER        ;Replace 'MONEY' with spaces.
TOOBAD: ...
;
ZCALLER ENDS
```

TABLE 18–23   8086 I/O, interrupt, and trap instructions.

Mnemonic	Operands	Size	Description
IN	accum,port	B,W	Load accum from input port
IN	accum,DX	B,W	Load accum from input port specified by DX
OUT	port,accum	B,W	Load output port from accum
OUT	DX,accum	B,W	Load output port specified by DX from accum
IRET			Return from interrupt
LOCK			Bus lock prefix
INT	3		Trap using vector 3 (breakpoint trap)
INTO			Trap using vector 4 (overflow trap)
INT	v		Trap using vector v

Notes: accum is AL or AX according to the size of the operation, byte or word.
port denotes an 8-bit port number, between 0 and 255.
v denotes an 8-bit interrupt vector number, between 0 and 255.

18.6.2   Interrupts

The 8086 CPU contains a two-level, vectored priority interrupt system with two interrupt request lines, one for each level. The higher priority level is NMI (non-maskable interrupt) and the lower is INTR (vectored interrupt). Within each level, a system hardware designer may provide additional interrupt lines and priority by means of external hardware.

Interrupts in the 8086 are usually accepted between the executions of individual instructions. An NMI request is generally accepted immediately after the current instruction is executed. An INTR request is accepted only if the IF (interrupt flag) bit in FLAGS is 1. Of course, for any interrupt to be accepted, a device must first generate an interrupt request on the NMI or INTR input line. The conditions for generating an interrupt request are device-dependent, but typically the interrupt enable bit in the device interface must be "on" and an I/O event must have occurred at the device. Thus, three conditions are needed for the 8086 to accept an interrupt:

(1)   For INTR, the IF bit in FLAGS must be equal to 1.

(2)   The interrupt enable bit in the device interface must be "on."

(3)   The interface must have experienced an interrupt-generating event (e.g., character received from keyboard, ready to send character to screen, disk block transfer complete, etc.).

When an interrupt is accepted, the CPU automatically pushes the current values of FLAGS, CS, and IP onto the stack, in the order just given. Then it clears the IF and TF bits in FLAGS to prevent any more vectored interrupts or trace traps from occurring. Finally it loads CS and IP with new values from an "interrupt vector" found in memory, thereby transferring control to an interrupt service routine. The interrupt service routine eventually returns control to the interrupted program by executing an IRET instruction, which restores the old IP, CS, and FLAGS from the stack.

The 8086 allocates the first 1024 bytes of physical memory for a table of interrupt vectors, as shown in Table 18–24. Each vector is four bytes long, containing new values for IP and CS in the format of Figure 18–7(d).

For NMI interrupts and for traps, the CPU fetches the corresponding IP and CS from the vector table and executes the interrupt service routine at the address indicated by the new CS and IP. If the system has multiple devices connected to the NMI request line, then it is up to the service routine to determine which device has interrupted on each occasion.

For INTR interrupts, the CPU allows the interrupting device to place an 8-bit number on the data bus to identify itself. If two or more devices can make a request on INTR simultaneously, external hardware must determine priority, that is, determine which device may place its identifier on the data bus. Then the CPU uses the 8-bit identifier supplied by the device as an index into the vector table. The identifier, which should be between 32 and 255, is multiplied by 4 to obtain the address of the interrupt vector. Thus, each device connected to INTR may have a different interrupt service routine that is automatically selected by the hardware.

The 8086's INTR input is level-sensitive, so that the CPU will accept an interrupt whenever an interrupt request signal is present and the IF bit in FLAGS is 1. The CPU automatically clears IF upon accepting an INTR request to prevent the interrupt service routine from being continuously re-interrupted by the same condition. Once the service routine has removed the condition that caused the interrupt, it may set IF to 1 to allow INTR interrupts from other devices. Alternatively, it may leave IF at 0, so that no further INTR interrupts will be accepted until the service routine exits using the IRET instruction.

Since an NMI request cannot be disabled, a different scheme must be used to keep the NMI service routine from being continuously interrupted by

TABLE 18–24   8086 interrupt and trap vectors.

Vector Number	Physical Address (hex)	Interrupt or Trap
0	00000	Divide error trap
1	00004	Single-step (trace) trap
2	00008	NMI interrupt
3	0000C	Breakpoint trap (INT 3 instruction)
4	00010	Overflow trap (INTO instruction)
5–31	00014–0007C	Reserved for Intel products
32–255	00080–003FC	User vectored interrupts

the same condition. Therefore, the NMI input is edge-sensitive. The 8086 CPU accepts an NMI request only when it detects an inactive-to-active transition on the NMI input line. Therefore, the CPU can accept a second NMI request only after the condition causing the first NMI request has been removed and a second inactive-to-active transition has occurred on the NMI input.

A set of subroutines for displaying strings of characters using interrupt I/O is shown in Table 18–25. The subroutines assume that a Motorola 6850 ACIA (Appendix C.3) is attached to the 8086 as I/O ports 40H and 41H. They further assumes that a string is a sequence of ASCII characters stored one per byte and terminated by NUL (a zero byte).

A main program that calls the display subroutines is shown in Table 18–26. The main program sets up the stack pointer and segment registers and then calls INITCRT to reset the ACIA hardware and initialize the ACIA interrupt vector and software busy-flag (CRTBSY). In its main processing loop, the main program passes a pointer to the CRT output routine CRTOUT each time it wants to display a string. The variable CRTBSY indicates whether or not a previous string is still being displayed, so that a new operation is not started until the previous one is completed. CRTOUT prints the first character of a new string, enables the ACIA to interrupt after the character has been printed, and then returns to the main program.

Remaining characters are printed by the interrupt service routine CRTINT. Before entering CRTINT, the CPU pushes only FLAGS, CS, and IP onto the stack, so it is up to CRTINT to save and restore any registers that it needs. Thus AX, BX, DS, and ES are saved on the stack at the beginning of CRTINT and restored at the end.

Some of the code in this example shows the weaknesses of the 8086 as compared with other advanced microprocessors such as the Z8000 and the 68000. Since there are no "load multiple" and "store multiple" instructions, individual pushes and pops are needed for register saving and restoring.

Especially troublesome is the lack of an absolute addressing mode that allows the segment as well as the offset to be specified in the instruction. For example, in INITCRT we need to set CRTBSY to 0. It would be nice to have an instruction "MOV IODATA: CRTBSY,0" that contains a two-word logical address (IODATA: CRTBSY) and performs the desired operation in one step. Instead, we must load the segment number into a segment register and then use an instruction such as"MOV DS: CRTBSY,0". If the contents of registers are not to be disturbed, then the old values of DS must be saved and restored.

The problem above is exacerbated by the lack of immediate addressing with segment register MOVs, so that it takes two instructions to load DS in the first place. In addition, AX must be now saved and restored too. You might wonder, why not PUSH IODATA and then POP DS to avoid destroying AX? Sorry, immediate addressing is not allowed with PUSH either!

We should now say a few words about the interruptibility of 8086 programs. Although interrupts normally occur between the execution of individ-

TABLE 18-25 Interrupt-driven CRT output subroutines for the 8086.

```
;           Define addresses and bit patterns for CRT ACIA.
CRTCS    EQU      40H            ;ACIA control and status port.
CRTDATA  EQU      41H            ;ACIA XMT and RCV data ports.
CRTVECT  EQU      WORD PTR 34    ;ACIA interrupt vector number.
CRESET   EQU      03H            ;ACIA control pattern for reset.
CMODE    EQU      11H            ;Basic ACIA operating mode.
CINTON   EQU      20H            ;ACIA XMT interrupt enable bit.
CINTOFF  EQU      00H            ;ACIA XMT interrupts disabled.
;
IODATA   SEGMENT                 ;Local variables.
CRTBSY   DB       ?              ;Nonzero when string is being displayed.
BPNT     DD       ?              ;seg:offset for char being displayed.
IODATA   ENDS
;
IOCODE   SEGMENT
         ASSUME CS:IOCODE, DS: IODATA
;
INITCRT  PROC     FAR            ;Initialization procedure for CRT.
         PUSH     DS             ;Save caller's DS.
         PUSH     AX             ;Save caller's AX.
         MOV      AX,IODATA      ;Set up DS to access I/O data.
         MOV      DS,AX
         MOV      AL,CRESET      ;Reset CRT ACIA, no interrupts.
         OUT      CRTCS,AL
         MOV      CRTBSY,0       ;Mark CRT not busy.
         MOV      AX,0           ;Initialize DS to get at
         MOV      DS,AX          ; vector table in low memory.
         MOV      DS:CRTVECT,OFFSET CRTINT   ;Initialize CRT
         MOV      DS:CRTVECT+2,SEG CRTINT    ; interrupt vector.
POPRET:  POP      AX             ;Restore caller's AX.
         POP      DS             ;Restore caller's DS.
         RET                     ;Done.
INITCRT  ENDP
;
;           CRT output routine, pointer to string passed in ES:BX.
CRTOUT   PROC     FAR
         PUSH     DS             ;Save caller's DS.
         PUSH     AX             ;Save caller's AX.
         MOV      AX,IODATA      ;Set up DS to access IODATA.
         MOV      DS,AX
WTOUT:   CMP      CRTBSY,1       ;Still busy with previous string?
         JEQ      WTOUT          ;Yes, wait for completion.
         MOV      CRTBSY,1       ;Mark CRT busy for new string.
         MOV      WORD PTR BPNT,BX   ;Save pointer to new string.
         MOV      WORD PTR BPNT+2,ES
         MOV      AL,CMODE+CINTOFF   ;Set ACIA operating mode,
         OUT      CRTCS,AL           ;  XMT interrupts off.
         MOV      AL,ES:[BX]     ;Get first character.
         OUT      CRTDATA,AL     ;Send it to ACIA.
         MOV      AL,CMODE+CINTON ;Enable ACIA XMT interrupts.
         OUT      CRTCS,AL
         JMP      POPRET         ;Restore caller's AX and DS and return.
CRTOUT   ENDP
```

TABLE 18–25   (continued)

```
;          CRT output interrupt handler.
CRTINT: PUSH    AX                ;Save some working registers.
        PUSH    BX
        PUSH    DS
        PUSH    ES
        MOV     AX,IODATA         ;Set up DS to access I/O data.
        MOV     DS,AX
        LES     BX,BPNT           ;ES:BX points to char just displayed.
        INC     BX                ;Point to next character.
        MOV     WORD PTR BPNT,BX  ;Save updated pointer.
        MOV     AL,ES:[BX]        ;Fetch the character.
        CMP     AL,0              ;Is it NUL (0)?
        JEQ     CDONE             ;We're done if it is.
        OUT     CRTDATA,AL        ;Otherwise display the character,
CRTRET: POP     ES                ;   restore registers,
        POP     DS
        POP     BX
        POP     AX
        IRET                      ;   and return.
;
CDONE:  MOV     AL,CMODE+CINTOFF  ;Disable ACIA interrupts.
        OUT     CRTCS,AL
        MOV     CRTBSY,0          ;Mark CRT no longer busy.
        JMP     CRTRET            ;Restore registers and return.
IOCODE  ENDS
```

ual 8086 instructions, they may also occur in the middle of a repeated string instruction. In this case, the address of the REP prefix of the string instruction is saved on the stack, so that the string instruction starts repeating itself again when the interrupt service routine returns control to it. The instruction resumes properly because its progress is reflected in SI, DI, CX, and FLAGS, which presumably are not altered by the interrupt service routine.

The 8086 also has a DMA facility that allows other devices to access its memory between the individual bus cycles of an instruction, temporarily suspending the instruction in execution. As discussed in Section 11.4, DMA is used by some I/O devices to transfer blocks of data without processor intervention. DMA may also be used in multiprocessor systems to allow several CPUs to share the same memory.

The LOCK prefix may be placed before any 8086 instruction to forbid DMA access during the execution of that instruction. This allows the programmer to create an "atomic" instruction that executes with the guarantee that no other processor can read or write memory during its execution. LOCK may be used to create a test-and-set primitive for the purposes discussed in Section 11.5.8 as follows:

```
CHECK:  MOV    AL,0FFH       ;Get old value of SEMAPH
  LOCK  XCHG   AL,SEMAPH     ;   and set new value to FF.
        CMP    AL,0          ;Is resource available?
        JNE    CHECK         ;No, wait for someone to clear SEMAPH.
        ...                  ;Yes, use resource.
DONE:   MOV    SEMAPH,0      ;Release resource for others.
```

18.6.3 Traps

The 8086 has four interrupt vectors for exceptional conditions and the trap instructions:

- *Divide Error*. A trap occurs if the quotient produced by a DIV or IDIV instruction is larger than the specified destination.

TABLE 18-26 Main program that uses interrupt output routines.

```
ZDATA    SEGMENT               ;Messages printed by main program.
MSG1     DB     'Correct programs are difficult to write when...'
         DB     0DH,0AH,0      ;Carriage return, line feed, NUL.
MSG1PNT DD      MSG1           ;Stores seg:offset of MSG1.
;
MSG2     DB     '...simple operations require many instructions.'
         DB     0DH,0AH,0      ;Carriage return, line feed, NUL.
MSG2PNT DD      MSG2           ;Stores seg:offset of MSG2.
ZDATA    ENDS
;
ZSTACK   SEGMENT               ;Define stack segment.
         DW     32
STACKE   EQU    OFFSET (THIS WORD)
ZSTACK   ENDS
;
ZMAIN    SEGMENT               ;Main program
         ASSUME CS:ZMAIN, SS:ZSTACK, DS:ZDATA
MAIN:    MOV    AX,ZSTACK      ;Initialize stack pointer.
         MOV    SS,AX
         MOV    SP,STACKE
         MOV    AX,ZDATA       ;Initialize DS.
         MOV    DS,AX
         CALL   INITCRT        ;Initialize CRT software and hardware.
         STI                   ;Enable INTR interrupts.
LOOP:    ...                   ;Do some computation.
         LES    BX,MSG1PNT     ;Get pointer to first message
         CALL   CRTOUT         ;  and print it.
         ...                   ;Do some more computation.
         LES    BX,MSG2PNT     ;Get pointer to second message
         CALL   CRTOUT         ;  and print it.
         JMP    LOOP           ;Do it all again.
ZMAIN    ENDS
         END    MAIN
```

- *Trace Trap*. A trap occurs after the execution of each instruction for which the TF bit was 1 at the beginning of the instruction.

- *Breakpoint Trap*. A trap occurs if the processor executes an INT 3 instruction.

- *Overflow Trap*. A trap occurs if the processor executes an INTO instruction when OF in FLAGS is 1.

A trap has the same effect as an interrupt: the CPU pushes the current FLAGS, CS and IP onto the stack, and a new CS and IP are loaded from the an interrupt vector as specified in Table 18–24.

In on-line debuggers, the trace trap is used to single-step programs, and the INT 3 instruction (one byte long) is used in the place of executable instructions to create breakpoints. The divide error trap and the INTO instruction are used to detect arithmetic errors. The 8086 also has a general trap instruction, INT v, which causes a trap using interrupt vector v. The 8-bit value of v is contained in the second byte of the instruction.

REFERENCES

The 8086 processor architecture evolved from the 8080, which evolved from the 8008, which Intel originally developed as a custom chip according to the specifications of one of its customers in about 1970. The history of this evolution has been traced in "Intel Microprocessors — 8008 to 8086," by Morse, Ravenel, Mazor, and Pohlman [*Computer*, Vol. 13, No. 10, October 1980]. A discussion of the 8086 in particular appeared in "The Intel 8086 Microprocessor: A 16-bit Evolution of the 8080," by Morse, Pohlman, and Ravenel [*Computer*, Vol. 11, No. 6, June 1978].

A very readable introduction to 8086 hardware and software can be found in *The 8086 Primer* by Stephen P. Morse [Hayden, 1980]. An example of a large 8086 program can be found in "An 8088 Processor for the S-100 Bus, Part 3," by T. W. Cantrell [*Byte*, Vol. 5, No. 11, November 1980]; this article presents complete specifications and code for a ROM-based system monitor and debugger for the 8086.

Naturally, Intel publishes plenty of technical information on the 8086, including *The 8086 Family User's Manual* and *MCS-86 Assembly Language Reference Manual*. The 8086 family contains other components besides the 8086 and 8088. Most noteworthy are the 8087, a "co-processor" for floating-point computations, and the 8089, an "I/O processor" that manages DMA operations and executes complex I/O programs independently of the main CPU.

EXERCISES

18.1   Write an 8086 subroutine that sets the contents of a memory byte at logical address seg:offset to zero, assuming that the values of seg and offset are known at assembly time. Sounds like absolute addressing — easy? Your subroutine must make no assumptions about the contents of the segment registers and it may not disturb the contents of any processor register.

18.2   Write an 8086 subroutine that sets ZF according to whether or not DS:BX and ES:DX point to the same physical memory address. Your subroutine may not disturb the contents of any processor register.

18.3   Write an 8086 subroutine that sets ZF to 0 without affecting any other condition bits or processor registers.

18.4   The alternative to having a DF bit in the 8086 is to have separate string manipulation instructions for auto-increment and auto-decrement. How many opcodes does having DF save?

18.5   Write an 8086 subroutine that adds two 24-bit unsigned integers P and Q, stored in memory bytes P2,P1,P0 and Q2,Q1,Q0, respectively. The sum should be stored in memory locations S2,S1,S0. When the subroutine returns, CF should be set to 1 if the true sum is greater than $2^{48}-1$, else to 0.

18.6   Rewrite the sorting program of Table 7–3 for the 8086.

18.7   Rewrite the sorting program of Table 7–3 for the 8086, using string manipulation instructions to improve the speed of the program wherever possible. (*Hint:* Reverse the order of one of the stacks as suggested in Figure 15–7.)

18.8   Show the statements needed in Table 18–16 for the FNDPRM procedure and the PRIME array to occupy different segments.

18.9   Rewrite the queue module of Table 18–19 to manipulate queues of bytes. As much as possible, make the new code independent of queue element size, byte or word.

18.10   Show how to speed up the string search subroutine in Table 18–21 by using the SCAS instruction to look for occurrences of the first character of the specified string in BUFFER, and then using CMPS to check for a complete match.

18.11   Rewrite the recursive NIM subroutines in Table 9–19 for the 8086. Write a main program that analyzes the game for all combinations of values of NHEAP from 2 to 25 and NTAKE from 2 to 6.

18.12   Write an 8086 keyboard input and display output module similar to the 6809 module in Table 10–4.

18.13   Write a complete Pascal simulation of the 8086.

19

INTEL MCS-48 FAMILY

The Intel MCS-48 family contains single-chip microcomputers and related support chips. Included are ten different microcomputer chips sharing a common instruction set, but with differing amounts of on-chip Read-Only Memory (ROM), Read/Write Memory (RWM), and Input/Output (I/O).

The family also includes several "expander" chips to provide an MCS-48 computer with up to 4K bytes of program ROM, 256 or more bytes of external RWM, and as many I/O bits as a designer would ever need. Software rather than hardware considerations tend to limit the usefulness of expanded MCS-48 system configurations. Because of its limited addressing capability and primitive instruction set, the MCS-48 family is best suited for low-end microcontroller applications requiring small assembly language programs (no more than 4K bytes), a small amount of storage for variables (a few 256 byte pages), and a small, simple I/O capability.

Since an MCS-48 computer is a microcontroller, it is usually buried deep inside a product and its general-purpose computing potential is hidden. In fact, there are no MCS-48-based general-purpose computer systems. By its very nature, an MCS-48 computer cannot support the development of its own programs, and so MCS-48 programs are always created using a larger development system.

In 1980, Intel announced a successor to the MCS-48 family, called the MCS-51 family. The new family is an evolution of the MCS-48 architecture

TABLE 19–1   MCS-48 microcomputers.

Part #	Program Memory	Data Memory	I/O lines
8048	1K ROM[1]	64[2]	27
8748	1K EPROM[1]	64[2]	27
8035	none[1]	64[2]	27
8049	2K ROM[1]	128[2]	27
8749	2K EPROM[1]	128[2]	27
8039	none[1]	128[2]	27
8021	1K ROM	64	21
8022	2K ROM	64	23[3]
8041	1K ROM	64	18[4]
8741	1K EPROM	64	18[4]

Notes: (1) Expandable to 4K bytes with external chips.
          (2) Plus 256 bytes or more of external data memory with
               external chips.
          (3) Plus two 8-bit analog-to-digital converters.
          (4) Plus master system interface.

that supports a larger memory address space and has other improvements that we'll mention briefly as appropriate.

19.1   BASIC ORGANIZATION

19.1.1   Computer Structure

Figure 19–1 shows the basic structure of a typical MCS-48 microcomputer, and Table 19–1 lists the facilities available in each circuit in the family. The first member of the family was introduced in late 1976 — the 8048 with 1K bytes of on-chip ROM, 64 bytes of RWM, a timer/counter, and 27 I/O bits. Some MCS-48 expander chips are listed in Table 19–2. A detailed description of the entire family can be found in the *MCS-48 Family User's Manual* published by Intel.

Program memory and data memory in an MCS-48 computer are logically and physically separated. Regardless of the physical components used to con-

TABLE 19–2   MCS-48 expander chips.

Part #	Program Memory	Data Memory	I/O lines
8355	2K ROM	none	16
8755	2K EPROM	none	16
8155/56	none	256	22[1]
8243	none	none	16

Notes: (1) Plus timer/counter.

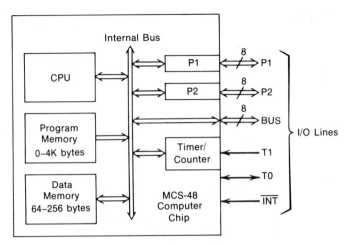

FIGURE 19–1   MCS-48 microcomputer structure.

struct it, the program memory in an MCS-48 computer is inherently read-only; there are no instructions to write into it. The maximum program address space supported by the architecture is 4K bytes, including external ROM. The architecture allows for a maximum of 256 bytes of on-chip (internal) read/write data memory. In addition to internal data memory, an MCS-48 processor directly supports 256 bytes of external data memory.

Most MCS-48 family members have 27 I/O pins, arranged as three 8-bit ports, two test inputs, and an interrupt input. Additional pins are provided for such functions as power-on reset, single-stepping, and memory and I/O expansion. One 8-bit port and part of a second are used to form a multiplexed address and data bus for I/O and memory expansion.

An MCS-48 processor has a single-level, vectored, priority interrupt system that accepts interrupts from two sources — the internal timer/counter and an external interrupt input pin. Interrupt calls and returns automatically push and pop the program counter and certain status flags using a stack in the internal data memory.

19.1.2   Processor Programming Model

The programming model of an MCS-48 processor is shown in Figure 19–2. The program counter PC is 12 bits long, but the high-order bit is not affected by counting. For example, if a non-jump instruction is fetched from address 7FFH, the next instruction will be fetched from address 000H. This has the effect of creating two 2K-byte program memory banks. Special instructions are needed to jump between memory banks, as explained later.

An MCS-48 CPU contains a single accumulator A in which arithmetic and logical operations take place. There are several 1-bit registers that can be

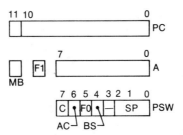

FIGURE 19–2 Programming model of MCS-48 processor.

manipulated by programs: C (carry), F0 and F1 (flags), BS (register bank select), and MB (program memory bank select). A 3-bit stack pointer (SP) points to a push-down stack in data memory; the stack contains return addresses during subroutine and interrupt calls. Most of the 1-bit registers and SP are grouped together as a unit called PSW that may be transferred to and from the accumulator.

19.1.3 Instruction Formats

Most MCS-48 instructions are only one byte long. Many instructions can access one of eight "working registers" contained in the data memory; the register number is contained in the first instruction byte along with the opcode. Instructions that specify an immediate operand or a memory address contain a second byte.

19.2 ASSEMBLY LANGUAGE

Intel's standard assembly language for MCS-48 processors has the same basic format as the "free-format" assembly language discussed at the end of Section 6.1.1; important characteristics are listed below.

- Labels (maximum length six characters) are followed by colons.

- Comments start with semicolons.

- The program location counter (PLC) is denoted by "$".

- Hexadecimal constants are denoted by a suffix of "H".

Important assembler directives are summarized in Table 19–3. Notice that the PLC and the assembler directives refer to *program* memory. Since there are no directives for managing data memory, a programmer typically reserves data memory locations by assigning specific locations to symbols using EQU. Alternatively, a programmer may write macros for this purpose along the lines suggested by the RESERV macro in Section 6.5.

TABLE 19–3   Intel MCS-48 assembly language directives.

Name	Examples		Effect
ORG		ORG 200H	Set origin for program storage.
EQU	CR	EQU 0DH	Equate symbol with 16-bit value.
SET	CT	SET CT+1	Like EQU, but allows redefinition.
DB	CB: ST:	DB 17,0EFH,−1 DB 'ABCDEFG'	Store constant values into successive program memory bytes.
DW	CW: KW:	DW 0E800H,DOG DW −1000,PUP+5	Store constant values into successive program memory words.
DS	BT:	DS 12	Reserve program memory bytes.
END		END START	Indicate end of assembly and give an optional starting address.
MACRO	M1	MACRO FP1,FP2	Begin macro definition.
ENDM		ENDM	End macro definition.
IF		IF CT LT 32	Conditionally assemble following lines.
ENDIF		ENDIF	End conditional assembly.

19.3   ADDRESSING

Since an MCS-48 computer has separate program and data memories, we treat them separately.

19.3.1   Program Memory

The MCS-48 architecture supports a maximum of 4K bytes of program memory, configured as shown in Figure 19–3. Although MCS-48 instructions manipulate only bytes, for programming convenience the DW assembler directive may be used to store a 2-byte word into program memory at load time, with the more significant byte at the lower numbered address.

A close look at program memory organization shows that the MCS-48 CPU was originally designed as a 2K-byte machine; the second 2K-byte capability was added as an afterthought. As we mentioned earlier, only the 11 low-order bits of PC are a counter, addressing a 2K-byte bank of program memory. Jump and subroutine call instructions likewise specify an 11-bit address. A 12th PC address bit is provided by an internal flag MB that can be set and cleared by two instructions (SEL MB1 and SEL MB0, respectively). Whenever a jump or subroutine call is executed, the 11 low-order bits of PC are loaded from the instruction, and the high-order bit is loaded from MB. Thus, a program can change program memory banks by changing the value of

MB and then executing a jump or call instruction. On subroutine calls and returns, a full 12-bit return address is pushed onto and popped from the stack.

There are some difficulties with this scheme. First, in a general sequence of subroutine calls in a 4K system, a program doesn't always know the current value of MB. For example, suppose a program MAIN in bank 0 calls SUBR0 in bank 0, which in turn may or may not call SUBR1 in bank 1. Depending on whether or not SUBR1 was called, MB could be 1 or 0 after the return from SUBR0. Thus, to be safe, a SEL MB0 instruction should be executed in MAIN after the return from SUBR0. A clever programmer may be able to avoid the extra instruction, but this may lead to mysterious bugs when the program is modified.

The second problem is that although MB is part of the processor state, there is no straightforward way of reading it. Consider this: an interrupt service routine must save and restore every bit of the processor state that it affects. If a service routine must set MB to a new value in order to do jumps and calls, how can it restore it? The MCS-48 CPU avoids this problem in hardware by ignoring MB and forcing the MSB of PC to 0 whenever an interrupt service routine is in progress. Thus, MB need not be modified by the service routine. However, this solution forces all interrupt service routines, and all subroutines called by them, to be in the bottom 2K bytes of memory.

Besides the 2K banks, program memory is also divided into 256-byte pages. Conditional jumps specify an 8-bit target address in the current page. This is less useful than an 8-bit signed offset from the current address, as we have seen in all other processors in this book. The program memory's page boundaries create a partitioning problem when many subroutines must be packed into the address space and split across page boundaries. The problem is severe because the pages are small, and therefore many boundary conditions must be satisfied.

The indirect jump instruction also uses an 8-bit target address in the current page. We'll see how this works when we discuss programming of CASE statements in an MCS-48 computer.

Although the MCS-48 program memory is mainly for storing programs, there are two addressing modes for getting read-only data from it:

- *Immediate Addressing.* An operand is contained in the second byte of the instruction.

- *Accumulator Indirect Addressing.* The accumulator is used as a pointer to an operand in either the current page or page 3 of program memory.

The successor to the MCS-48 architecture, the MCS-51 architecture, has a much improved addressing scheme for program memory. The address space contains 64K bytes, and unconditional jumps and calls may specify a full 16-bit target address. Conditional branches use relative addressing, like all the other machines in this book. A based indexed addressing mode may be used to access read-only look-up tables of any size stored anywhere in the program memory.

19.3.2 Data Memory

Most data manipulation operations in an MCS-48 computer use an on-chip read/write "internal data memory" containing up to 256 bytes of storage; see Figure 19–4. Most instructions that access data memory manipulate single bytes; however, the subroutine call and return instructions access 2-byte words. In data memory, words are stored with the more significant byte at the higher numbered address, the opposite of program memory.

Included in internal data memory are two sets of "working registers" of 8 bytes each, called register banks 0 and 1 (RB0 and RB1). A flag bit BS specifies which set of working registers should be accessed by instructions. If BS is 0, then the current register bank is the one in internal data memory locations 0–7; if BS is 1, then the current register bank is the one in locations

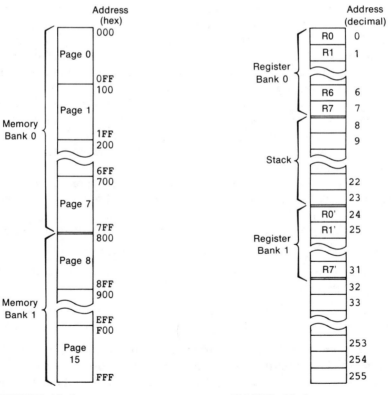

FIGURE 19–3
MCS-48 program memory.

FIGURE 19–4
MCS-48 internal data memory.

24–31. An additional 16 bytes (8–23) are reserved for a return address stack as described later.

The MCS-48 CPU has only two addressing modes for accessing internal data memory:

- *Internal Register Direct*. An operand is contained in a working register (R0–R7) in the current register bank, as specified by a 3-bit field in the instruction.

- *Internal Register Indirect*. Either R0 or R1 in the current register bank contains the address of an internal data memory byte that contains the operand.

The MCS-48 architecture also supports 256 bytes of external data memory, which reside on a separate chip and are accessed by indirect addressing:

- *External Register Indirect*. Either R0 or R1 in the current register bank contains the address of an external data memory byte that contains the operand.

Since R0 and R1 are 8-bit registers, the maximum amount of data memory supported by the MCS-48 architecture is 256 bytes internal plus 256 bytes external. However, bank switching via I/O bits can be used to address any desired amount of additional external data memory under program control. For example, four I/O port bits could be wired to select among 16 different 256-byte pages of external data memory. When such a technique is used, the page bits become part of the processor state and must be preserved by interrupt service routines.

Locations 8–23 of the internal data memory are reserved for a return address stack (8 entries, 2 bytes per entry). These locations are written by interrupt and subroutine calls, and read by interrupt and subroutine return instructions. The stack is arranged as a circular buffer, so that it wraps around on overflow or underflow. The stack is rather small, so an MCS-48 programmer must pay close attention to calling sequences. In particular, it may be necessary to enable interrupts only at the top level of the main program, to prevent stack overflow resulting from a complex interrupt service routine being activated with the stack already several levels deep.

There are no instructions to directly push or pop a byte. However, the stack can be rather inconveniently written or read by extracting the stack pointer field from the program status word (PSW), building the appropriate address, and using Internal Register Indirect mode.

The MCS-51 architecture, like the MCS-48 architecture, supports only 256 bytes of internal data memory. However, it has four 8-register banks instead of two, and the first 128 bytes of internal data memory may be accessed by internal register direct addressing. The MCS-51 stack, also stored in internal data memory, may theoretically be up to 256 bytes deep, and there are instructions for directly pushing or popping any register. The architecture also supports up to 64K bytes of external data memory accessible by indirect addressing.

19.4   OPERATIONS

19.4.1   Accumulator and Data Memory

An MCS-48 processor contains a single accumulator in which arithmetic and logical operations take place. There is a full set of move operations to and from the accumulator, as shown in the first part of Table 19–4.

Other operations on the MCS-48 accumulator are shown in the next two parts of Table 19–4. Double-operand instructions combine the accumulator and an operand specified by register, internal register indirect, or immediate addressing. A 1-bit carry flag C in the PSW is set or cleared according to the carry generated during addition and rotate-with-carry operations. Addition operations also set or clear an auxiliary carry flag AC according to the carry between nibbles; C and AC are used by the DA A instruction to correct the accumulator value when BCD digits are added.

Three single-operand instructions on internal data memory are given in last part of the table.

The MCS-51 CPU has 8-bit multiply and divide instructions that use an additional accumulator B. For most instructions in Table 19–4, the MCS-51 CPU also has a version that uses direct addressing to access an operand in any register, not just registers in the current register bank. The MCS-51 CPU also has a set of "boolean instructions" that allow individual bits of registers and I/O ports to be copied, combined, set, cleared, complemented, and tested.

19.4.2   Program Control and Miscellaneous Instructions

Instructions that can alter program flow are shown in Table 19–5. The JMP and CALL instructions contain an 11-bit address; the 12th bit is obtained from the MB flag as explained earlier. The CALL instruction pushes the current 12-bit PC and four flag bits (BS, F0, AC, and C) onto the stack and jumps to a subroutine; RET returns by popping PC from the stack without restoring the four flags; RETR returns and restores the flags.

Conditional jumps specify an 8-bit target address in the current page of program memory and test for a zero or nonzero accumulator, or for the state of individual bits. The C, F0, F1, and TF bits are internal flags, while T0, T1, and INT are external inputs. The JBb instructions test for a 1 in accumulator bit b; the range of b is 0 (LSB) to 7 (MSB). The DJNZ instruction decrements a register and then jumps if the register is nonzero, a useful primitive for loops. Notice that not all conditional jumps have a complemented version. Expres-

TABLE 19–4 MCS-48 instructions on accumulator and data memory.

Mnemonic	Operands	Description
MOV	A,src	Move src to A
MOV	r,A	Move A to register
MOV	@rp,A	Move A to internal data memory
MOV	@rp,#data	Move immediate data to internal data memory
MOV	r,#data	Move immediate data to register
XCH	A,r	Exchange register and A
XCH	A,@rp	Exchange internal data memory and A
XCHD	A,@rp	Exchange low nibbles of data memory and A
MOVX	A,@rp	Move external data memory to A
MOVX	@rp,A	Move A to external data memory
MOVP	A,@A	Move from current program page to A
MOVP3	A,@A	Move from program page 3 to A
MOV	A,PSW	Move PSW to A
MOV	PSW,A	Move A to PSW
ADD	A,src	Add src to A
ADDC	A,src	Add src to A with carry
ANL	A,src	AND src to A
ORL	A,src	OR src to A
XRL	A,src	EXCLUSIVE OR src to A
CLR	A	Clear A
CPL	A	Complement A
DA	A	Decimal adjust A
DEC	A	Decrement A
INC	A	Increment A
RL	A	Rotate A left
RLC	A	Rotate A left with carry
RR	A	Rotate A right
RRC	A	Rotate A right with carry
SWAP	A	Swap nibbles of A
DEC	r	Decrement register
INC	r	Increment register
INC	@rp	Increment internal data memory

Notes: r denotes R0–R7; rp denotes R0 or R1; data denotes an 8-bit immediate value.
src denotes an operand using any of three addressing modes: internal register direct (r), internal register indirect (@rp), or immediate (#data).

sion evaluation with the MCS-48 conditional jumps is inconvenient, since only the accumulator can be tested, and there is no arithmetic overflow flag (needed for signed comparisons).

Miscellaneous MCS-48 instructions are shown in Table 19–6; input/output and related operations are discussed in Section 19.6.

The MCS-51 CPU has jump and call instructions that specify a full 16-bit target address in program memory. It also has additional conditional jump instructions that can compare A with other registers, and compare arbitrary registers with immediate operands.

TABLE 19–5 MCS-48 program control instructions.

Mnemonic	Operands	Description
JMP	addr11	Unconditional jump
CALL	addr11	Subroutine call
RET		Subroutine return (12-bit address)
RETR		Return and restore status (12-bit address)
JMPP	@A	Indirect jump in current page
DJNZ	r,addr8	Decrement register, jump if not zero
JC	addr8	Jump if C=1
JNC	addr8	Jump if C=0
JZ	addr8	Jump if A=00000000
JNZ	addr8	Jump if A<>00000000
JT0	addr8	Jump if T0=1
JNT0	addr8	Jump if T0=0
JT1	addr8	Jump if T1=1
JNT1	addr8	Jump if T1=0
JF0	addr8	Jump if F0=1
JF1	addr8	Jump if F1=1
JTF	addr8	Jump if timer flag set
JNI	addr8	Jump if $\overline{\text{INT}}$=0
JBb	addr8	Jump if Accumulator bit b = 1

Notes: r denotes R0–R7.
addr8 is an address within the current 256-byte page of program memory.
addr11 is an address within the 2K-byte program memory bank selected by the current value of MB.

19.5 SAMPLE PROGRAMS

Assembly language programs for MCS-48 microcomputers tend to require more instructions than programs for the other more advanced microprocessors in this book, because of the limitations of the MCS-48 architecture. We shall illustrate some of these limitations by showing the MCS-48 assembly

TABLE 19–6 MCS-48 miscellaneous instructions.

Mnemonic	Operands	Description
CLR	C	Clear carry
CPL	C	Complement carry
CLR	F0	Clear flag 0
CPL	F0	Complement flag 0
CLR	F1	Clear flag 1
CPL	F1	Complement flag 1
SEL	RB0	Select register bank 0
SEL	RB1	Select register bank 1
SEL	MB0	Select memory bank 0
SEL	MB1	Select memory bank 1
NOP		No operation

language statements corresponding to high-level Pascal statements. Then we'll show how to manipulate simple data structures with MCS-48 programs. More complex programs are left as exercises for the reader.

Examples of Pascal assignment statements coded for an MCS-48 computer are given in Table 19–7. Variables R4 and Q are 8-bit unsigned numbers. While R4 is accessed as a register in the current memory bank, variables Q and FLAG are stored higher in data memory and can only be accessed by register indirect addressing. Thus, a variable such as Q in memory needs three instructions and two temporary registers (A and R0) to initialize it. If the temporary registers are needed in other operations, then additional instructions may be needed to save and restore them.

It should be apparent that the lack of an absolute addressing mode in the MCS-48 CPU creates unnecessary overhead. Most of the other processors in this book can load a memory location with an immediate value using just one instruction and no temporary registers (only the 6809 and 9900 require two instructions and one register). Absolute addressing was added to Intel's successor to the MCS-48 architecture, the MCS-51 architecture.

TABLE 19–7 MCS-48 coding of assignment statements.

```
Q       EQU    32           ;VAR R4,Q : 0..255 {unsigned integer};
FLAG    EQU    33             ;FLAG : boolean {0 = false; 1 = true};
;
;                           R4 := 5;
        MOV    R4,#5        ;Store 5 into R4.
;
;                           Q := R4;
        MOV    A,R4         ;Get value of R4.
        MOV    R0,#Q        ;Address of Q (not a working register).
        MOV    @R0,A        ;Store value into Q.
;
;                           R4 := R4-Q+5;
        MOV    R0,#Q        ;Address of Q.
        MOV    A,@R0        ;Get value of Q.
        CPL    A            ;Negate value of Q.
        INC    A
        ADD    A,R4         ;A gets -Q plus R4.
        ADD    A,#5         ;Add 5.
        MOV    R4,A         ;Store value.
;
;                           FLAG := R4>0;
        MOV    R1,#0        ;Set false initially.
        MOV    A,R4         ;Get value of R4.
        JB7    OUT1         ;Skip if negative...
        JZ     OUT1         ;...or if zero.
        INC    R1           ;Set FLAG true.
OUT1:   MOV    R0,#FLAG     ;Address of FLAG.
        MOV    A,R1
        MOV    @R0,A        ;Store value of FLAG.
```

All tests and arithmetic operations in the MCS-48 CPU take place in the single accumulator A. As shown in the third part of Table 19-7, subtraction is performed by negating the subtrahend (two instructions) and then adding. Unless the order of operations is optimized, this may require saving the current value of the accumulator before proceeding. Complicated signed arithmetic expression evaluation is rarely required in microcontroller applications, but simple addition and subtraction without overflow detection is often used, as shown in the example.

Several simple IF statements for an MCS-48 computer are coded in Table 19-8. The first two examples show simple comparisons of a signed integer variable with zero. The variable must be loaded into the accumulator for testing, and one or two conditional jump instructions may be needed depending on condition. The next example shows a comparison of two unsigned integer variables by subtraction. Comparison of signed integer variables would be more difficult, because the processor has neither signed conditional branches nor a two's-complement overflow flag.

A CASE statement can be programmed by making use of the JMPP instruction and a jump table, as shown in Table 19-9. Since JMPP only jumps in the current page, the jump table and all of the first-level jump targets must be in the same 256-byte page as the JMPP instruction itself. If there are many or long cases, a second level of jumps must be used to jump out of the current page as shown.

TABLE 19-8 Coding of IF statements for an MCS-48 computer.

```
;                              IF Q=0 THEN GOTO LABEL;
        MOV    R0,#Q           ;Address of Q.
        MOV    A,@R0           ;Accumulator needed to test value of Q.
        JZ     LABEL           ;Jump if A zero (only in current page).
;
;                              IF Q>0 THEN GOTO LABEL;
        MOV    R0,#Q           ;Address of Q.
        MOV    A,@R0           ;Accumulator needed to test value of Q.
        JB7    OUT             ;Continue if negative...
        JZ     OUT             ;...or zero.
        JMP    LABEL           ;Else jump (anywhere in memory bank).
OUT:    ...
;
;                              IF P<=Q THEN GOTO LABEL;
;                              {P and Q are UNSIGNED integers}
        MOV    A,P             ;Get value of P.
        CPL    A               ;Negate.
        INC    A
        MOV    R0,#Q           ;Address of Q.
        ADD    A,@R0           ;Now we have Q + (-P).
        JC     LABEL           ;Jump (in current page) if Q-P>=0.
        JZ     LABEL           ;Taken if P=Q=0.
```

TABLE 19-9 Coding of a CASE statement for an MCS-48 computer.

```
;                              CASE N OF
;                                 0: statementa;
;                                 1,3: statementb;
;                                 2,4: statementc;
;                                 5: statementd;
;                              END;
        ORG    PAGE*256
CASE:   MOV    R0,#N            ;Check for N in range.
        MOV    A,@R0
        ADD    A,#-6            ;A >= 6 will cause a carry.
        JC     ERROR           ;Go handle error.
OK:     MOV    A,@R0            ;Restore case number.
        ADD    A,#JTAB-(PAGE*256)    ;Offset of JTAB in page.
        JMPP   @A               ;Jump through table.
;       First-level jump table must be in the same page.
JTAB:   DB     JA-(256*PAGE)
        DB     JB-(256*PAGE)
        DB     JC-(256*PAGE)
        DB     JB-(256*PAGE)
        DB     JC-(256*PAGE)
        DB     JD-(256*PAGE)
;       Second-level jump table must still be in same page.
JA:     JMP    LA
JB:     JMP    LB
JC:     JMP    LC
JD:     JMP    LD
;
;       Statements below may be anywhere in memory bank.
;
LA:     ...                     ;  statementa
        JMP    OUT
LB:     ...                     ;  statementb
        JMP    OUT
LC:     ...                     ;  statementc
        JMP    OUT
LD:     ...                     ;  statementd
OUT:    ...
```

The MCS-48 CPU provides a subroutine calling instruction, CALL, that pushes the 12-bit return address and four high-order PSW bits onto the stack in the internal data memory. The RETR and RET instructions return from a subroutine, with and without restoring the PSW bits, respectively. The only real trick in using CALL is to avoid overflowing the stack, since the stack is only 16 bytes deep and can thus hold only 8 return addresses.

Subroutine parameters are most easily passed in the registers, since a typical subroutine has fewer than eight bytes of parameters. Of course, parameters may always be passed in dedicated data memory locations or in a parameter area shared by all subroutines. Passing parameters in the stack is impractical because of the stack's small size and the absence of instructions to push and pop a byte. Luckily, a parameter stack is not really needed in MCS-48 applications. Since the MCS-48 CPU has only a single-level interrupt system, reentrant subroutines do not normally occur; and simple microcontroller applications seldom benefit from recursive subroutines.

Data structures such as arrays may be stored in the MCS-48 data memory. For example, suppose we wished to reserve ten data memory locations for an array BUF[1..10] of ten 8-bit characters. Although Intel's standard assembly language has no equivalent of the H6809's RMB pseudo-operation, we could define a macro RESERV as in Section 6.5 to reserve space in data memory. Then the array could be declared as shown below:

```
        RESERV BUF,10        Reserve space for 10-byte array.
EBUF    EQU    BUF-1         Effective base address of BUF.
```

Since there is no indexed addressing mode in the MCS-48 CPU, array address polynomials must be evaluated by arithmetic operations in the accumulator. For example, we can read item J in the array BUF as follows:

```
        MOV    A,#EBUF       ;Get effective base address of array.
        ADD    A,Rj          ;Add index (assume J is in register Rj).
        MOV    R0,A          ;Use result as a pointer.
        MOV    A,@R0         ;Load A with BUF[J].
```

Table 19–10 gives an example of an MCS-48 subroutine for finding the index of the first array element that matches a given character. The assembly language program manipulates absolute addresses in the array rather than indices, in order to save the overhead of performing an index computation at each iteration. If a match is found, the absolute address of the matching item is converted into an index before returning.

Although the MCS-48 internal data memory is small, large data structures may be kept in external data memory. For example, a system could have 64K bytes of external data memory, consisting of 256 256-byte pages selected by the contents of output port P2. Since an 8-bit address is easiest to handle, it is best to limit the size of each data structure to 256 bytes in order to fit it entirely within one external data memory page.

For example, suppose we needed a pushdown stack capable of storing a few hundred bytes of data. The stack could be stored in one page of external data memory. Suppose that the first byte of the external data memory page contains the stack pointer, and the remaining 255 bytes are the stack buffer itself. Then the subroutines in Table 19–11 could be used to initialize the stack and to push and pop data. The callers of these subroutines must set up the bank switching bits if any (e.g., P2) to the proper external data memory page before each call. In this way, a separate stack could be kept in each external

TABLE 19–10 MCS-48 subroutine to search an array for a character.

```
;       Finds the index of the first component of array STRING
;       that matches MCHAR, returning 0 if no match is found.
;       MCHAR is passed in R7, result in A.
;
        RESERV STRING,20    ;Character array indexed 1 to 20.
;
MATCH:  MOV     R0,#STRING    ;Get address of first array item.
MAT1:   MOV     A,@R0         ;Get array item.
        XRL     A,R7          ;Compare with MCHAR.
        JZ      MAT2          ;Jump if match found.
        INC     R0            ;Bump pointer to next item.
        MOV     A,#STRING+20  ;Get address past end of array.
        XRL     A,R0          ;Past the end?
        JNZ     MAT1          ;No, keep looking.
        RET                   ;No match, return with A=0.
MAT2:   MOV     A,R0          ;Got match, compute index.
        ADD     A,#1-STRING
        RET                   ;Return with index in A.
```

data memory page, but all stacks could be manipulated by the same sub-routines. In a similar manner, the 6809 queue module of Table 9–18 could be redesigned and recoded to maintain queues in external data memory.

19.6 INPUT/OUTPUT AND INTERRUPTS

19.6.1 Input/Output

Most MCS-48 microcomputers have three 8-bit I/O ports, P1, P2, and BUS, as shown in Figure 19–1. Two of the ports (P1 and P2) have a "quasi-bidirectional" interfacing arrangement. Each I/O pin is both an open-drain output and an input with a high impedance pull-up to the logic 1 level. When a pin is used for output, the corresponding input buffer is unused except possibly for checking the output value. When an I/O pin is used for input, the corresponding output bit must be set to logic 1 so that the input device drives only the high impedance pull-up.

What quasi-bidirectional I/O means to a programmer is that input data on the port is logically ANDed with the current output. Ports P1 and P2 are set to all 1s at system reset, and the programmer must leave bits intended for inputs set at output value 1 at all times.

The BUS port has conventional 3-state outputs and can be used for 8 strobed inputs, 8 strobed outputs, or for adding external program or data memory.

MCS-48 I/O and related instructions are shown in Table 19–12. The first eight instructions affect P1, P2, or BUS. Included are logical operations that

TABLE 19–11   MCS-48 stack subroutines using external data memory.

```
;           Stack manipulation routines for external data memory.
;           SP is stored in location 0, points directly at top
;           stack item, and grows towards high memory locations.
;
;           Subroutine to initialize stack to empty.
SPINIT: CLR    A             ;Initial value for SP...
        MOV    R0,A          ;...and also the address of SP.
        MOVX   @R0,A         ;Remember, stack is in external data mem.
        RET                  ;Stack is now empty.
;
;           Subroutine to push the byte in R7.
PUSHR7: MOV    R0,#0         ;Address of SP.
        MOVX   A,@R0         ;Get value of SP.
        INC    A             ;Bump to next free location.
        JZ     OVFL          ;No push on overflow.
        MOVX   @R0,A         ;Else store updated SP...
        MOV    R0,A          ;...and put in R0 for use as pointer.
        MOV    A,R7          ;Transfer value of R7 to A for push.
        MOVX   @R0,A         ;Put value of R7 on stack.
OVFL:   RET                  ;Done.
;
;           Subroutine to pop a byte into A.
POPA:   CLR    A             ;Address of SP.
        MOV    R0,A
        MOVX   A,@R0         ;Get value of SP.
        JZ     UNDFL         ;Return with 0 in A on underflow.
        MOV    R1,A          ;Save value of SP for later.
        DEC    A             ;But first decrement SP value
        MOVX   @R0,A         ;   and save updated SP value.
        MOVX   A,@R1         ;Now get byte from stack.
UNDFL:  RET                  ;Done.
```

allow a program to set or clear any bit or group of bits using just one instruction. However, the bits to be set or cleared must be known at assembly time since the mask is an immediate value in program memory. If the mask value is not known until run time, then a copy of the output port value must be kept in data memory, combined with the mask by logical operations in the accumulator, and then loaded into the port. (In general, one cannot simply read P1 or P2 to get the old value of the output port, because of the quasi-bidirectional interface.)

A novel "expander port" arrangement allows four external 4-bit I/O ports (P4 through P7) to be added to an MCS-48 computer using a 5-wire interface. Table 19–12 shows four operations using these ports. For these ports, dynamic selection of logical mask bits is possible since the mask is in the accumulator.

Both the on-chip and expander I/O port instructions have the port number contained as an immediate value in the instruction; it is not possible to specify the port number dynamically in a register. This makes it impossible to write re-usable I/O handlers for identical devices on different ports of the MCS-48 computer or of the same expander chip. However, dynamic device selection is possible by means of memory-mapped I/O using external data memory instructions.

In addition to the I/O ports, an MCS-48 computer has three additional input pins (T0, T1, $\overline{\text{INT}}$) that can be tested by conditional jump instructions. All may be configured for other uses under program control: T0 as a clock output (ENT0 CLK); T1 as the input to the on-chip timer/counter (STRT CNT); and $\overline{\text{INT}}$ as the external interrupt input (EN I).

19.6.2 Interrupts

An MCS-48 CPU accepts interrupts from two sources — a level-sensitive input pin $\overline{\text{INT}}$ and the on-chip timer/counter. Interrupts from the two

TABLE 19–12   MCS-48 input/output instructions.

Mnemonic	Operands	Description
IN	A,p	Input port to A
OUTL	p,A	Output A to port
ANL	p,#data	AND immediate data to port
ORL	p,#data	OR immediate data to port
INS	A,BUS	Input BUS to A
OUTL	BUS,A	Output A to BUS
ANL	BUS,#data	AND immediate data to BUS
ORL	BUS,#data	OR immediate data to BUS
MOVD	A,ep	Input expander port to low nibble of A
MOVD	ep,A	Output low nibble of A to expander port
ANLD	ep,A	AND low nibble of A with expander port
ORLD	ep,A	OR low nibble of A with expander port
ENT0	CLK	Enable clock output on T0
MOV	A,T	Read Timer/Counter value
MOV	T,A	Initialize Timer/Counter value
STRT	T	Start Timer
STRT	CNT	Start Counter
STOP	TCNT	Stop Timer/Counter
EN	TCNTI	Enable Timer/Counter interrupts
DIS	TCNTI	Disable Timer/Counter interrupts
EN	I	Enable external interrupts
DIS	I	Disable external interrupts

data denotes an 8-bit immediate value;
p denotes an on-chip port P1 or P2;
ep denotes one of the expander ports P4–P7.

sources can be selectively enabled and disabled by EN and DIS instructions. However, the enabled/disabled state of an interrupt source cannot be read by the processor. Therefore, programs that need to disable interrupts and then return the interrupt system to its previous state must use software flags to keep track of the interrupt system state.

When the CPU accepts an interrupt request, it automatically executes a CALL to either location 3 (external interrupt) or 7 (timer/counter interrupt), and it sets an internal interrupt-in-progress flag (IIP). Recall that the CALL instruction pushes the current 12-bit PC and the four high-order bits of PSW onto the stack.

When set, IIP prevents additional interrupts from being accepted and forces jump and call instructions to remain within memory bank 0 regardless of the value of MB. Executing a RETR instruction returns control to the interrupted program and clears IIP, allowing further interrupts to be accepted.

Interrupt service routines must save and restore any register that they modify. In typical MCS-48 applications, register bank 1 is reserved for interrupt service routines. Therefore, the first action of an interrupt subroutine is to execute SEL RB1 and then save A in one of the registers. The high-order PSW bits are saved in the stack automatically by the interrupt CALL, but F1 must be saved separately if it is modified. As mentioned earlier, all instructions executed before returning from the interrupt (via RETR) must be in the bottom 2K bytes of memory, MB0.

REFERENCES

The MCS-48 architecture is described in the *MCS-48 Family User's Manual*, and MCS-48 assembly language is described in the *MCS-48 Assembly Language Manual*, both published by Intel. This chapter was adapted from "The Intel MCS-48 Microcomputer Family: A Critique," by John F. Wakerly [*Computer*, Vol. 12, No. 2, February 1979].

The MCS-51 architecture is described in Intel's *MCS-51 Family User's Manual*. A lucid introduction to the MCS-51 family appears in Intel Application Note AP-69, by John Wharton.

EXERCISES

19.1   Rewrite the multiplication program of Table 5–4 for an MCS-48 CPU.

19.2   Rewrite the 1s-counting program of Table 5–10 for an MCS-48 CPU.

19.3   Adapt the primes program of Table 7–5 for an MCS-48 CPU. Use a 256-byte array in external data memory to find primes between 2 and 2049 (i.e., allocate one bit per integer).

19.4   Adapt the stack sorting program of Table 7–3 for an MCS-48 CPU. Use two separate 256-byte "pages" of external data memory to store the two stacks. Assume that one page is selected by setting output port P2 to 00H, the other by setting P2 to 01H.

19.5   Write an MCS-48 subroutine that adds two BCD numbers P and Q and produces a sum S, where each number contains eight digits and a sign digit in 10's-complement representation. The numbers are stored in data memory, but you are to define the exact format.

19.6   Adapt the word queueing program of Table 8–4 for an MCS-48 CPU. Use a 256-byte array in external data memory for the queue buffer.

19.7   Adapt the queue module of Table 9–18 for an MCS-48 CPU. Assume that the head and tail pointers and a 254-byte buffer for each queue are stored in external data memory; it is up to the caller to switch to the appropriate external data memory bank before calling a queue module subroutine.

19.8   Repeat the previous exercise, but provide a 4-byte descriptor table for each queue and allow several small queues to share a bank of external data memory.

19.9   Repeat the previous exercise, except also allow large queues that occupy more than one bank of external data memory. Assume that up to 256 different external data memory banks may be selected according to the value placed in output port P2.

19.10 Adapt the recursive subroutines of Table 9–19 to analyze the game of NIM on an MCS-48 computer. Assume that you have one page of external data memory available to store a stack. (*Hint*: Save registers and return addresses on the external stack.)

19.11 Suppose that the MCS-48 CPU contained only one register bank, so that there are no SEL RBi instructions. How would this complicate interrupt handling and how could the problem be solved? Write code for an interrupt service routine to demonstrate your solution.

19.12 Write a complete Pascal simulation of an MCS-48 computer.

APPENDIX A

THE ASCII
CHARACTER CODE

A.1 ASCII ENCODING

The most commonly used character encoding in computers is ASCII (pronounced ass'-key), shown in Table A–1. The code contains the uppercase and lowercase alphabet, numerals, punctuation, and various nonprinting control characters that are sometimes used in serial communications links.

ASCII is a 7-bit code, so its characters are stored one per byte in most computers. The MSB of an ASCII byte is usually unused and set to zero. However, ASCII bytes received from a serial communication link may use the MSB as a parity bit or may have the MSB set to some arbitrary value. Therefore it is wise for a program to clear the MSB of a received ASCII byte before comparing it with other ASCII bytes.

Notice that the numeric and alphabetic codes are ordered, so that character sequences may be sorted lexicographically using numeric comparisons of the corresponding character codes. Also, there is a simple relationship between uppercase and lowercase letters, so that lowercase letters may be converted to uppercase by subtracting 0100000.

A.2 ASCII AND TERMINALS

A few words should be said about the relationship between the ASCII characters and the keyboards and screens of typical terminals. Typically each key transmits one of three or four possible ASCII codes, depending on

TABLE A–1 American Standard Code for Information Interchange (ASCII), Standard No. X3.4–1968 of the American National Standards Institute.

		$b_6 b_5 b_4$ (column)							
	row	000	001	010	011	100	101	110	111
$b_3 b_2 b_1 b_0$	(hex)	0	1	2	3	4	5	6	7
0000	0	NUL	DLE	SP	0	@	P	`	p
0001	1	SOH	DC1	!	1	A	Q	a	q
0010	2	STX	DC2	"	2	B	R	b	r
0011	3	ETX	DC3	#	3	C	S	c	s
0100	4	EOT	DC4	$	4	D	T	d	t
0101	5	ENQ	NAK	%	5	E	U	e	u
0110	6	ACK	SYN	&	6	F	V	f	v
0111	7	BEL	ETB	'	7	G	W	g	w
1000	8	BS	CAN	(	8	H	X	h	x
1001	9	HT	EM	)	9	I	Y	i	y
1010	A	LF	SUB	*	:	J	Z	j	z
1011	B	VT	ESC	+	;	K	[	k	{
1100	C	FF	FS	,	<	L	\	l	|
1101	D	CR	GS	–	=	M	]	m	}
1110	E	SO	RS	.	>	N	^	n	~
1111	F	SI	US	/	?	O	_	o	DEL

Control Codes

NUL	Null	DLE	Data link escape
SOH	Start of heading	DC1	Device control 1
STX	Start of text	DC2	Device control 2
ETX	End of text	DC3	Device control 3
EOT	End of transmission	DC4	Device control 4
ENQ	Enquiry	NAK	Negative acknowledge
ACK	Acknowledge	SYN	Synchronize
BEL	Bell	ETB	End transmitted block
BS	Backspace	CAN	Cancel
HT	Horizontal tab	EM	End of medium
LF	Line feed	SUB	Substitute
VT	Vertical tab	ESC	Escape
FF	Form feed	FS	File separator
CR	Carriage return	GS	Group separator
SO	Shift out	RS	Record separator
SI	Shift in	US	Unit separator
SP	Space	DEL	Delete or rubout

whether or not the SHIFT and CTRL keys on the keyboard are depressed at the same time as the key. Thus, typing L by itself transmits a lowercase L, binary code 1101100. Holding down SHIFT and typing L transmits an uppercase L, binary code 1001100. Holding down CTRL and typing L transmits binary code 0001100, regardless of the position of the SHIFT key on most keyboards.

In general, a control code in column 0 or 1 of Table A-1 is obtained by holding down the CTRL key and typing the character from the same relative position in column 4 or 5. Thus, holding down CTRL and typing C (i.e., typing CTRL-C) transmits the binary code 0000011, the ASCII control code named ETX. Many computer systems use these control codes as special system commands, for example, CTRL-C to return control to an executive, CTRL-O to suspend the current output, CTRL-U to cancel the current input line, and so on.

Note that the ESC key found on most terminals sends a particular ASCII code (0011011), while the CTRL key performs a mapping on other key codes as described above. The BREAK key places an abnormal condition on the serial data link, as described in Appendix C. In some systems this abnormal condition is detected and used as another system command, but it is not an ASCII character.

A typical CRT screen ignores most control codes that it receives, but there are five control codes to which all screens respond:

SP   Prints a blank space.

BS   Moves the cursor (current printing position) one space left.

CR   Moves the cursor to the beginning of the current line. Some terminals are configured to also move the cursor to the next line when CR is received.

LF   Moves the cursor down one line. Some terminals are configured to also move the cursor to the beginning of the line when LF is received.

BEL Produces an audible sound (usually a beep) at the terminal.

Some "smart" CRT screens respond to special "escape sequences," typically consisting of an ESC character followed by one or more additional characters. For example, a terminal might respond to ESC H by "homing" the cursor (moving it to the upper left-hand corner of the screen), and to ESC J by clearing all of the text from the current cursor position to the end of the screen. Different escape sequences are defined for different smart terminals.

APPENDIX B

EXTENDED PASCAL

The purpose of this appendix is to present extensions to standard Pascal that make it suitable as an instruction-set description and simulation language.

B.1 UNSIGNED INTEGERS

In standard Pascal, an unsigned integer is represented by a string of decimal digits. In extended Pascal, three other representations are allowed by placing a suffix at the end of a digit string:

- Unsigned Binary Integer, a string of binary digits followed by "b" or "B". Examples are 10011b, 00001011b, and 1111111001B, which correspond to decimal constants 19, 11, and 1017.

- Unsigned Octal Integer, a string of octal digits followed by "o", "O", "q", or "Q". Examples are 23o, 177777q, and 10001Q, which correspond to decimal constants 19, 65535, and 4097.

- Unsigned Hexadecimal Integer, a string of hexadecimal digits followed by "h" or "H". The digits a-f may be written in either upper or lower case. If the number begins with digits a-f, a leading 0 must be prefixed to distinguish it from an identifier. Examples are 13h, 0Beach, and 0ABC1H, which correspond to decimal constants 19, 48812, and 43969.

These forms may be used any place an unsigned integer is allowed, and they may be given symbolic names in the CONST declaration of a block.

B.2 BIT TYPE

Bytes and words in a computer are easily viewed as being arrays of bits. A bit could be represented in Pascal as a boolean variable. However, in order to improve the readability of programs involving bit arrays, we introduce a new predefined type bit which is a subrange of integer:

```
TYPE bit = 0..1;
```

B.3 BIT ARRAYS AND SUBARRAYS

Standard Pascal allows array types to be defined by specifying a component type and an index type. Individual array components or entire arrays of the same type may be manipulated, but subarrays larger than one component and smaller than all the components are not handled.

In manipulating bytes and words in a computer, it is often necessary to access a field of bits in a byte or word. Therefore, in extended Pascal we define a *subarray* of an array to be an ordered, contiguous subset of the array. For example, if we define an array

```
VAR Q : ARRAY [1::10] OF bit;
```

then the components Q[3],Q[4],Q[5] form a subarray containing three consecutive bits of Q. The components Q[3],Q[4],Q[6] do not form a subarray because they are not contiguous; and the components Q[9],Q[10],Q[11] do not because Q[11] does not exist. A valid subarray of an array of n bits can have from 1 to n bits.

For simplicity and efficiency, we only allow subarray operations on one-dimensional arrays of bits, whose type is declared in the following way:

BAtype = ARRAY [*BAspec*] OF bit

An array whose type is declared in this manner is called a *bit array*. The declaration is the same as a normal array type declaration, except that a bit-array specifier (*BAspec*) has the special form a::b where a and b are both integers. Alternatively, *BAspec* may be an identifier that has been equated to an a::b range in the CONST declaration. Examples are given below.

```
CONST bits4 = 3::0;
TYPE
  nibble = ARRAY [bits4] OF bit;
  byte = ARRAY [7::0] OF bit;
  word = ARRAY [15::0] OF bit;
  IBM370byte = ARRAY [0::7] OF bit;
VAR
  B,C,D : byte;
  Q,R : word;
```

Some computer documentation numbers the bits in a word from left to right, others from right to left; extended Pascal supports both conventions. Thus, the order of a and b used in a bit-array specifier in the array declaration affects later usage of the array. We consider a bit array V[a::b] to be stored horizontally with V[a] on the left and V[b] on the right, whether a>b or a<b. Thus, V[0] is the rightmost bit if V has type byte, the leftmost bit if V has type IBM370byte.

If aname is the name of a bit array, then we use aname[a::b] to denote a subarray of aname consisting of items a through b. Suppose a bit array V is declared:

```
VAR V : ARRAY [7::0] OF bit;
```

Then V[a::b] is a valid subarray of V if the elements of a::b are contained in 7::0 and are in the same order. For example, V[3::0] is a valid subarray but V[8::5] and V[0::2] are not.

The *length* of a subarray is |a−b|+1. The original array itself is considered to be a subarray; the array above may be referenced either as V or V[7::0] in expressions. Likewise, the ith component of an array is a subarray, and may be referenced either as V[i] or V[i::i]; either form may be treated as a variable of type bit. Since bit-array specifiers are defined by constants, the length of a bit-array or subarray is static; that is, it is known at compile time.

B.4   SIMPLE BIT-ARRAY ASSIGNMENT

Standard Pascal allows assignment statements involving structured variables of the same type and their components, for example:

```
C := D;
Q := R;
Q[1] := B[5];
R[15] := 0;
```

In extended Pascal, we allow equal-length bit arrays and subarrays to appear on either side of an assignment statement. For example, we could copy bits of one subarray into another by statements such as:

```
B[7::4]  := D[3::0];
D[3::0]  := Q[15::12];
R[10::7] := C[4::1];
Q[11::11] := B[3];
D[7::4]  := D[4::1];
R[12::5] := C;
D := Q[10::3];
```

Assignment of unequal-length subarrays is not allowed. The general form of the subarray assignment statements above is

```
var1[a1::b1] := var2[a2::b2];
```

where var1 and var2 are both arrays of bits, and $|a1-b1| = |a2-b2|$. The effect of the statement is to copy a subarray of one bit-array into an equal-length subarray of another, preserving the left-to-right order of the array components.

B.5   BIT-ARRAY EXPRESSIONS AND GENERAL ASSIGNMENT

When a bit-array specifier appears in an expression, the specified subarray is extracted from the bit array. At this point, the subarray's length and the left-to-right order of its components are known, but all information about its original position in the base array is discarded. Thus, if B is a byte variable with components $B[7]..B[0] = 1,1,0,1,0,1,0,1$, then the subarrays $B[6::4]$, $B[4::2]$, and $B[2::0]$ have exactly the same effect when they appear in expressions.

As described shortly, bit-array expressions can be constructed using concatenation and other functions that yield bit-array results. The general form of a bit-array assignment statement is

BAvar [*BAspec*] := *BAexpr*

The expression on the right-hand side of the assignment statement is characterized solely by the length of the result bit array. The statement is valid if the bit-array expression has the same length as the bit array specifier on the left-hand side.

B.6   CONCATENATION

Concatenation joins two bit-arrays to make a larger one, for example, joining two bytes to make a word. We shall use the symbol "|" as an infix operator (like +, *, DIV/, etc.) denoting concatenation. Some assignment statements using concatenation are shown below.

```
A := B[7::4] | C[3::0];
A[6::4] := Q[15] | B[3::2];
Q := B | C;
R[14::1] := A[4::0] | B[6::1] | A[7::5];
```

Concatenation produces a bit array whose length is the sum of the lengths of the concatenated bit arrays. It preserves the left-to-right order of bits within each bit array, and arranges the bit arrays in the result according to their left-to-right order in the concatenation expression. In the last example above, parentheses are not needed because the result is the same with any parenthesization.

B.7 STANDARD FUNCTIONS ON BIT ARRAYS

Standard functions are defined to allow arithmetic and logical operations on bit arrays and conversions to and from the standard type `integer`. The actual parameters of most of these functions are expressions yielding n-bit arrays,

```
TYPE bitarray = ARRAY [1::n] OF bit;
```

The choice of `1::n` for the range of the formal-parameter type is arbitrary except for its length n; `0::n-1` or `5::n+4` would serve just as well. Only the length of the bit-array expression is checked when its value is assigned to a formal parameter on the function call. In functions on two bit-arrays, both bit arrays must have the same length. Most functions yield results of the same bit-array size.

The functions defined below work on bit arrays with lengths from 1 to `maxbitlen`, an implementation-dependent constant that is 64 or greater. Functions on bit arrays of length 1 also work on variables of type `bit`. Another implementation-dependent constant is `maxintbits`, the number of bits in the binary representation of `maxint`.

We also define two global variables BC and BV of type `bit` that are modified as a side-effect of some bit-array functions. Since these variables are not explicitly mentioned in the function invocations, it is especially important to remember the side effects when working with bit-array functions.

```
FUNCTION Bint(x : bitarray) : integer;
```

This function converts a bit array into an unsigned integer in the range 0 to `maxint`. The rightmost bit has a weight of 2^0; weights increase as powers of two for bits to the left in the usual manner. A compile-time error is produced if the length of x is greater than `maxintbits`.

```
FUNCTION Bits(i,n : integer) : bitarray;
```

This function converts a nonnegative integer i into a bit array of length n in the obvious manner. If i is negative or requires more than n bits to represent, a run-time error is produced. The value of n must be a constant known at compile time.

```
FUNCTION Bcom(x : bitarray) : bitarray;
```

`Bcom` takes the bit-by-bit complement of the components of x and returns a bit array of the same length.

FUNCTION Bshl(x : bitarray; c : bit) : bitarray;

This function returns a bit array of the same length as x, with components of x shifted left by one position. The rightmost bit is set to the value c and the global variable BC is set to the value of the leftmost bit before the shift.

FUNCTION Bshr(x : bitarray; c : bit) : bitarray;

`Bshr` returns a bit array of the same length as x, with components shifted right by one position. The leftmost bit is set to the value c and the global variable BC is set to the value of the rightmost bit before the shift.

FUNCTION Band(x,y : bitarray) : bitarray;

This function computes the bit-by-bit logical AND of two bit-arrays x and y and returns a result of the same length.

FUNCTION Bor(x,y : bitarray) : bitarray;

`Bor` computes the bit-by-bit logical OR of two bit-arrays and returns a result of the same length.

FUNCTION Bxor(x,y : bitarray) : bitarray;

`Bxor` computes the bit-by-bit Exclusive OR of two bit-arrays and returns a result of the same length.

FUNCTION Badd(x,y : bitarray; c : bit) : bitarray;

`Badd` converts two bit-arrays x and y to unsigned integers according to the usual expansion formula; the resulting integers may be greater than maxint. It then adds x, y, and c, producing an n+1-bit sum. The n rightmost bits of the sum are returned as the result; the global variable BC is set to the value of the leftmost bit of the sum. The global variable BV is set to 1 if the leftmost bits of x and y are the same as each other but different from the leftmost bit of the result, to 0 otherwise (standard overflow bit in ones' or two's complement).

B.8 INFIX OPERATORS

The infix operator " | " for bit arrays has already been described. Two other infix operators that return bit-array results are "+" and "−". These operators compute the results x+y and x−y using standard two's-complement addition and subtraction according to the predefined functions Bplus and Bminus:

```
FUNCTION Bplus(x,y : bitarray) : bitarray;
  BEGIN Bplus := Badd(x,y,0) END;  {BC and BV are affected.}

FUNCTION Bminus(x,y : bitarray) : bitarray;
  BEGIN Bminus := Badd(x,Bcom(y),1) END;   {BC and BV are affected.}
```

The "+" and "–" signs may also be used as unary operators. The expressions "+x" and "–x" yield the results of Bplus(zero,x) and Bminus(zero,x), where zero denotes a bit array constant of n 0s.

Equal-length bit arrays may be compared using the standard infix relational operators (=, <>, >, <, >=, <=). For the purposes of the comparison they are interpreted as unsigned integers in the usual way, and a boolean result is returned. BC and BV are not affected.

B.9 BIT-ARRAY CONSTANTS

A bit array constant consists of a value part followed by a bit-array specification. The value part may be an unsigned binary, octal, decimal, or hexadecimal constant. The bit-array specification has the form [a::b], where a≥b.

The value part must evaluate to a nonnegative integer i less than or equal to maxint. It is converted into a bit array temp[maxintbits-1::0], by a call to Bits(i,maxintbits). Then the specified subarray is extracted from temp.

Some examples of bit-array constants are shown below.

```
CONST {bit array constants}
  zero8 = 0[7::0]; z4 = 0[3::0]
  minus1 = 11111111b[7::0]; fives = 0ffh[4::0];
VAR A,B : byte;
BEGIN
  A := 0[7::0];  A := 0h[7::0];  A := zero8;  A := z4 | 0b[6::3];
  B := 0FFFFH[15::8];  B := minus1;  B := fives | 7o[2::0];
  A[7::4] := 195[3::0];   A[7::4] := 11b[3::0];
```

The assignment statements grouped together on each line above have exactly the same effect. Notice also that bit-array constants may be named in the CONST declaration of a block.

B.10 BIT-ARRAY EXPRESSIONS

We may now give general rules governing the use of bit arrays and bit-array functions in expressions. Equal-length bit arrays may be combined in expressions using the infix operators + and –, yielding bit arrays of the same length. Bit arrays may be concatenated with | , which has precedence over + and – (like * in integer operations).

Function-calls yielding bit-array results may be used as operands in bit-array expressions. Procedures and functions requiring bit-array arguments may use any bit-array expressions that give results of the proper length.

B.11 AUTOMATIC TYPE CONVERSION

Automatic type conversion eliminates the need to explicitly convert integer variables and constants to bit arrays and vice versa in expressions and assignment statements. The rules apply to two kinds of assignment statements: explicit assignment of an expression value to a variable; and implicit assignment of an expression value to a formal parameter in a function or procedure call. The rules are as follows:

(1) If an expression contains both integer and bit-array variables and constants, all integers are converted via Bits to bit arrays with length equal to the largest bit array in the expression.

(2) If a bit-array expression is assigned to an integer variable, it is automatically converted to an integer value via Bint.

(3) If an integer expression is assigned to a bit-array variable, it is automatically converted to a bit array via Bits.

B.12 EXAMPLES

Examples of bit arrays are scattered throughout the text. The first examples appear in Chapter 4 in the discussion of multiplication and division algorithms. Examples employing bit arrays in the definition of computer instruction sets appear in Chapters 5 through 8.

APPENDIX C

SERIAL COMMUNICATION

Serial data links are most commonly used by computers to communicate with both local and remote terminals. *Serial* communication means that information transmitted from source to destination is carried over a single pathway. Within the immediate physical confines of a computer system, the use of serial links is most often motivated by cost considerations — serial links can reduce packaging and cabling cost and reduce the number and complexity of components for sending and receiving data. Outside the computer system, use of a serial communication link is often forced by the very nature of the available data transmission media — telephone lines and radio waves can only send one analog signal at a time.

In this appendix we shall describe the simple serial data links that are most often used by computers to communicate with local and remote terminals.

C.1 SERIAL DATA LINKS

A *simplex* serial data link transmits data in only one direction. A connection from a computer to a remote printer could be a simplex serial data link.

There are usually two serial data links between a computer and a terminal, one for transmission in each direction. This is called *full-duplex* operation and is illustrated in Figure C–1. Transmission in the two directions is independent and simultaneous. A typical terminal consists of a keyboard and a screen or hardcopy printing mechanism. Even though they may be packaged together, the keyboard and screen are logically independent devices. When a

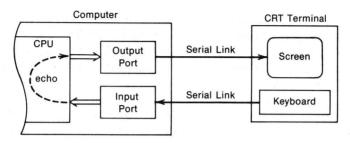

FIGURE C–1 Full-duplex serial communication link.

character is typed at the keyboard, it is not automatically printed. In most full-duplex systems, the computer must receive each character and *echo* it back to the terminal. A few full-duplex systems have terminals hard-wired to locally print all typed characters, saving the computer the overhead of echoing them. This mode of operation is sometimes called *echo-plex*. (The "half-duplex" option on most modern terminals is really echo-plex.)

Bidirectional communication can also be achieved with a single link as shown in Figure C–2, but only in one direction at a time. A special control sequence is needed to "turn the line around" whenever the direction of transmission is changed. This is called *half-duplex* operation. Local printing of typed characters is essential with half-duplex links, because of the high overhead that would be incurred if the computer had to turn the line around to echo each character. Most serial links in use today are full-duplex.

The rate of transmission of a data stream in bits per second (bps) is called the *bit rate*. This rate is sometimes mistakenly called the "baud rate." The bit rate and the baud rate are usually equal, but not always; the exact definition of baud rate must wait until we discuss modems. Serial transmission rates for typical computer terminals range from 75 to 19200 bps (19.2 Kbps). The reciprocal of the bit rate is called the *bit time* — the time that it takes to transmit one bit.

By far the most commonly used character encoding in minicomputer and microcomputer systems is ASCII, which represents each character by 7 bits

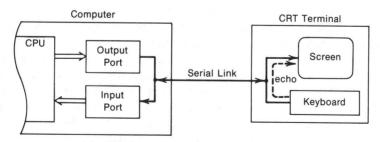

FIGURE C–2 Half-duplex serial communication link.

(see Appendix A). A character is transmitted over the link one bit at a time, with two to four control bits added to each character. Thus, 9 to 11 bits are required to transmit one character, and the typical bit transmission rates mentioned above yield about 8 to 2000 characters per second. A typical 24×80 CRT screen contains 1920 characters, so it can be completely filled in one second by a 19.2 Kbps data link.

Standard bit rates are 75, 110, 134.5, 150, 300, 600, 1200, 2400, 4800, 9600, and 19200 bps. The standard bit rates form a geometric progression, except for 110 bps, used by old-fashioned ASR-33 teleprinters and similar equipment, and 134.5 bps, used by some IBM printing terminals. Modern CRT terminals have switch-selectable bit rates up to a maximum of 9.6 or 19.2 Kbps.

Most often the same bit rate is used for both directions in a full-duplex serial communication link. This is especially true in communications between a computer and a local terminal, since data is carried over relatively inexpensive, short, high-bandwidth copper wires.

On the other hand, there is nothing to prevent different bit rates from being used in a so-called "split bit rate" arrangement. This is advantageous for connections to remote equipment connected by telephone lines or other expensive links with limited bandwidth. A human can type only so fast, even with a repeat key, and so a bit rate supporting more than 15 characters per second from a keyboard to the computer is wasteful. On the other hand, a computer can easily send data to a CRT continuously at rates of 100 characters per second or higher. Therefore, one popular split bit rate arrangement uses a 150 bps link from terminal to computer, but 1200 bps from computer to terminal.

A simple serial communication link uses the signals *mark* and *space* to encode the binary digits 1 and 0, respectively. The names mark and space are used instead of 1 and 0 to remind us that the physical values used to represent them depend on the type of physical link. In fact, each bit has several representations during its journey from source to destination, as shown by the example in Figure C–3.

Within a computer, 1s and 0s of a character are represented by a sequence of standard voltage levels for a particular logic family, say transistor-transistor logic (TTL). An interface in the computer converts TTL levels to another standard set of voltage levels prescribed by EIA (Electronic Industries Association) standard RS-232, and connects to a device called a modem.

A standard telephone link cannot transmit and receive absolute voltage levels, only sounds whose frequency components are between approximately 300 and 3000 Hz. Therefore the modem converts RS-232 voltage levels into tones that can be transmitted over a telephone line. For example, the modem could transmit a 1270 Hz tone whenever an RS-232 mark level is present, and 1070 Hz for an RS-232 space level. This modulation scheme is called

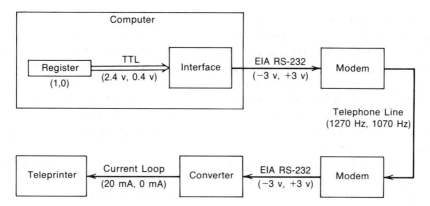

FIGURE C–3   Encodings of (mark,space) in a serial communication link.

frequency-shift keying (FSK). Another modem at the receiving end can detect FSK tones and convert them back into RS-232 levels.

In Figure C–3, the RS-232 levels at the receiving end are converted to a "current-loop" interface — a pair of wires in which a 20 milliampere (mA) current represents a mark and 0 mA represents a space. The resulting sequence of on/off currents controls the motion of a teleprinter's mechanical wheels and cams that finally print a character. Alternatively, the RS-232 levels could be connected to a typical CRT terminal which is designed to accept RS-232 levels directly.

Most serial communication links are full-duplex, so that Figure C–3 should really show another serial link in the reverse direction. However, another telephone line and pair of modems usually is not required for the reverse link. Most modems can provide a full-duplex link using a single telephone line. They do this by using a different pair of frequencies for communicating in the reverse direction, for example, 2225 Hz for a mark and 2025 Hz for a space. The choice of transmitting and receiving frequencies for the computer and terminal is predetermined by convention in any given system. The modem handles the links in both directions simultaneously; in fact the name "modem" stands for "modulator/demodulator."

The bit rate that can be reliably transmitted and received by a particular modem is limited. For example, suppose we tried to send data at 9600 bps using the FSK modulation scheme described above. Then one bit time would correspond to only about one-eighth of a sine wave period at a transmitting frequency of 1270 Hz. Such a tiny slice of a sine wave cannot be reliably detected at the receiving end after passing through the distortions of the telephone network.

Modulation and demodulation schemes more sophisticated than FSK are used in high bit-rate modems. It may seem paradoxical that it is indeed possible to send 9600 bits per second over a telephone link that has a bandwidth of only about 3000 Hz. Such high bit rates are achieved by modulation techniques in which each transmitted signal element has more than two values. For example, some 1200 bps modems use a modulation scheme that transmits only 600 signal elements per second, where each signal element can have one of four values, representing the four possible combinations of two bits.

The number of signal elements per second is called the *baud rate*. In low speed modems the bit rate and baud rate are usually equal; in high speed modems they usually are not.

Inexpensive, low-speed modems transmit and receive data at 300 to 1200 bits per second. When a terminal is connected directly to a computer without using a telephone link and modems, it is usually practical to use a much higher bit rate such as 9.6 or 19.2 Kbps.

C.2 ASYNCHRONOUS SERIAL COMMUNICATION FORMAT

The majority of serial communication links now in use are asynchronous links. *Asynchronous* means that the transmitter and receiver do not share a common clock, and no clock signal is sent with the data. So how does the receiver know when the data bits begin and end? We shall describe a simple algorithm that can be used if the transmitter and receiver agree on a standard bit rate and format.

The standard asynchronous serial bit format used by computers and terminals is shown in Figure C–4(a). When the transmitter is idle (no data being sent), the line is maintained in a continuous mark state. The transmitter may initiate a character at any time by sending a *start bit*, that is, by putting the line in the space state for exactly one bit time. It then transmits the data bits, least significant first, optionally followed by an even or odd parity bit.[1] Finally, it maintains the mark state for 1, 1.5, or 2 bit times — so-called *stop bits*.

The period of time from the beginning of the start bit to the end of the stop bits is called a *frame*. After the stop bits, the transmitter may immediately send a new start bit if it has another character to send. Otherwise, it may maintain the mark state as long as it is idle. A new start bit may be sent at any time, not necessarily an integral number of bit times since the last stop bit.

An old-fashioned teleprinter operating at 110 bps transmits a start bit, 7 ASCII data bits, an odd parity bit, and two stop bits, as shown in Figure C–4(b) for the character 0110101 (ASCII '5'). Since 11 bits are required to send each character, at 110 bps there are 10 characters per second.

---

[1] An even (odd) parity bit is chosen in such a way that the total number of 1s among the data bits and parity bit is even (odd).

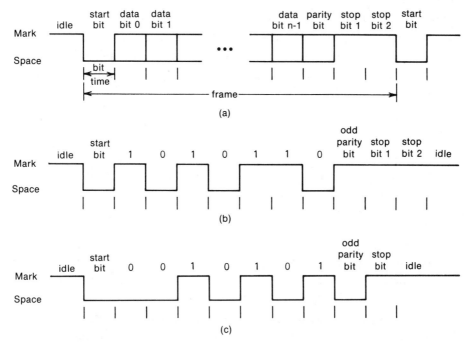

FIGURE C–4 Asynchronous serial data: (a) general bit format; (b) typical teleprinter format; (c) typical high-speed terminal format.

Terminals operating at 300 bps and higher usually transmit a start bit, 7 ASCII data bits, a parity bit, and one stop bit, as shown in Figure C–4(c) for the character 1010100 (ASCII 'T'). Since only 10 bits are needed for each character, at 300 bps there are 30 characters per second. The usage of the parity bit varies widely among different systems. There are three possibilities: even, odd, or no parity. These possibilities are compounded by the fact that most terminals and computers can send and receive an optional eighth data bit before the optional parity bit. There are four possibilities for the eighth bit: not transmitted, constant 1, constant 0, or useful data. The last case creates an additional 128 non-ASCII characters that may be transmitted between the terminal and computer for extended character sets or special functions.

In a serial communication link, the transmitter and receiver must agree upon all of the parameters of the bit format in Figure C–4(a), including a nominal bit time (or equivalently, bit rate). Since transmitter and receiver have different clocks, they will have slightly different bit times. The decoding procedure described below allows a difference of up to a few percent in the bit times.

For optimum immunity to signal distortion, noise, and clock inaccuracies, the receiver should sample each incoming bit in the middle of its bit time. This can be accomplished by the following procedure which samples the input signal at a frequency that is m times the bit rate; typical values of m are 8, 16, 32, and 64.

(1) *Start-bit detection*. Sample the input for a space. After the first detection of a space, be sure that the input remains in the space state for $(m/2)-1$ more sample times. If successful, we are now approximately at the middle of the start bit. Otherwise, we have detected a noise pulse and we should start again.

(2) *Data-bit sampling*. After m more sample times after start bit detection, read the first data bit from the input. Repeat a total of n times for n data bits, and repeat if necessary for the parity bit. Each bit will be sampled approximately in the middle of its bit time. Place the assembled character in a buffer for the processor or terminal to read.

(3) *Stop-bit detection*. After m more sample times, sample the input for the mark state (stop bit). Repeat if there are two stop bits. If the input is in the space state, set a "framing error" status flag along with the received character. Set a "character received" flag for the processor and return to step 1.

The leading edge of the start bit signals the beginning of a character, and the time of its occurrence provides a timing reference for sampling the data bits. The stop bits provide time for "clean-up" required between characters on older terminals, and also provide a degree of error detection. If the line is not in the mark state when a stop bit is expected, a *framing error* is said to occur. Framing errors occur most often when the receiver erroneously synchronizes on a space bit that is not the real start bit. Proper resynchronization can always be accomplished if the transmitter is idle (sending mark) for one frame or longer. Unfortunately, if synchronization is lost when the transmitter is sending at full speed, in general it will not be regained until an idle frame occurs.

When the line is continuously held in the space state for one frame or longer, a *break* is said to occur. The "BREAK" key on most keyboards actually holds the line in the space state for as long as the key is depressed. The serial interfaces on most computers have the capability of detecting break as a special condition. Many software systems then treat break as an extra, special-function character. However, break must be used cautiously in remote communication links, because most modems automatically disconnect from the telephone line if a break is held too long.

C.3   SERIAL I/O INTERFACE CIRCUITS

A computer must have a special I/O interface to transmit and receive data on a serial communication link. Many manufacturers of integrated circuits offer a complete asynchronous serial interface packaged as a single LSI circuit, called a Universal Asynchronous Receiver/Transmitter (UART), or some similar name.

C.3.1 Motorola 6850 ACIA

As an example of an LSI serial I/O interface circuit, we introduce the Motorola 6850, which Motorola calls an "Asynchronous Communications Interface Adapter" (ACIA). A block diagram of the ACIA is shown in Figure C–5. On one side, the ACIA can transmit data and receive data on an asynchronous, full-duplex serial link at speeds up to 19.2 Kbps or more. On the other side, the ACIA communicates with a CPU by means of two 8-bit input ports and two 8-bit output ports.

The I/O programming model of the ACIA is shown in Figure C–6. In a typical system configuration the STATUS input port and the CONTROL output port have the same address or port number (e.g., 0FCF4H for the console ACIA in the Motorola EXORcisor II development system for the 6809). Likewise, the RCV DATA input port and the XMT DATA output port have the same port number, usually one greater than the STATUS/CONTROL port number (e.g., 0FCF5H). Although other configurations are possible, the 6850's I/O bus signals are arranged so that the above configuration is the most convenient.

An example I/O program that uses the 6850 ACIA was given in Section 17.6 for the Motorola 6809. That program made use of some of the characteristics of the ACIA that are described in the following subsections.

C.3.2 Control Port

In order to use the ACIA to send and receive serial data, a program must first set up the operating mode of the ACIA. Sending a byte of 03H to

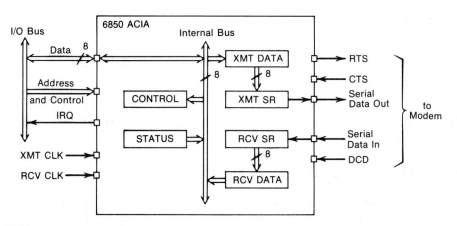

FIGURE C–5 Simplified block diagram of the Motorola 6850 ACIA.

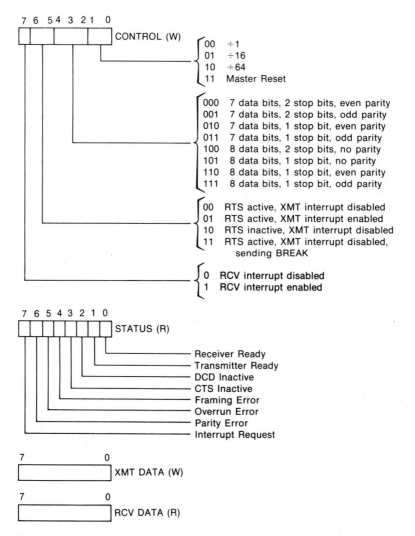

FIGURE C–6 I/O programming model of the Motorola 6850 ACIA.

the ACIA CONTROL port resets the ACIA, clearing out any previous operating mode and disabling the ACIA from sending or receiving data until a new mode is established. The new mode is established by sending an appropriate bit pattern to CONTROL, as detailed in Figure C–6 and explained below.

The transmitting and receiving bit rates of the ACIA are established by a combination of external clock inputs (XMT CLK and RCV CLK in Figure C–5) and a programmable divider ratio. The ACIA transmits serial data at a bit rate equal to the incoming XMT CLK frequency divided by 1, 16, or 64, according to the bit pattern loaded into bits 1–0 of CONTROL. On receiving, the ACIA uses the bit-sampling procedure described in the previous section. Here the sampling rate equals the RCV CLK frequency, and the number of samples per bit equals 1, 16, or 64 as determined by bits 1–0 of CONTROL. The same divider ratio is used for transmitting and receiving. In practice, only divider ratios of 16 and 64 are useful for receiving.

Usually the XMT CLK and RCV CLK inputs are both connected to the same clock source. For example, suppose they are both connected to a 153.6 KHz clock. Then a programmed divider ratio of 16 would allow the ACIA to transmit and receive at 9600 bps, while a ratio of 64 would allow it to operate at 2400 bps. To operate the ACIA at a different bit rate, the user would have to modify the hardware to connect the XMT CLK and RCV CLK inputs to a different frequency, for example, 19.2 KHz for 1200 or 300 bps (this can be done in many systems by a mechanical switch).

The ACIA may be configured to transmit and receive 7 or 8 data bits, an even, odd, or no parity bit, and 1 or 2 stop bits according to a 3-bit pattern loaded into bits 4–2 of CONTROL. The same format is used for both transmitting and receiving.

CONTROL port bits 6–5 control the ACIA's ability to request an interrupt after transmitting a character; they also turn the ACIA's RTS (Request to Send) output signal on or off. The ACIA will place an interrupt request on its IRQ output if the transmitter interrupt is enabled and the transmitter is ready to accept another character for transmission. The RTS signal is discussed later.

Setting bit 7 of CONTROL allows the ACIA to place an interrupt request on its IRQ output when the receiver has received a character and is ready for a program to read it from RCV DATA.

The IRQ output of the ACIA may be connected to an interrupt input of the CPU, typically to the IRQ input in 6809 systems. If both transmitter and receiver interrupts are enabled, then it is up to the interrupt service routine to figure out which section of the ACIA caused the interrupt request to be made.

Once the ACIA operating mode is established, it remains the same as long as the ACIA is not reset by sending CONTROL a pattern of 03H. Thus, the operating mode needs to be set up only at the beginning of a sequence of I/O operations; there is no need to reestablish the mode before each operation.

The CONTROL port is write-only; attempts to read from it do not return the last value written into it. Instead, they return the current value of the STATUS port, described later.

C.3.3 Transmitter Data Port

Once the ACIA operating mode has been established, the CPU may transmit characters to the serial data link through the ACIA's XMT DATA output port. Unlike the generalized output interface described in Section

10.3.3, the ACIA has no "XMT GO" bit; a new output operation is begun each time the CPU writes a character into XMT DATA.

As shown in Figure C–5, the transmitted data is double-buffered. Initially, after the ACIA is reset, both XMT DATA and XMT SR are empty. When the CPU writes the first transmitted character into XMT DATA, the ACIA immediately transfers the contents of XMT DATA into XMT SR, a shift register from which the character is shifted into the serial output line with the prescribed format and speed. Since XMT DATA is now empty, the CPU may immediately place a second character into XMT DATA. However, the ACIA will not transfer this second character into XMT SR until the first character has been fully transmitted, a format and speed dependent wait. In general, the CPU can determine when XMT DATA is empty only by checking the Transmitter Ready bit in the STATUS port.

C.3.4 Receiver Data Port

Unlike the generalized input interface described in Section 10.3.1, the ACIA has no "RCV GO" bit. Once the ACIA operating mode has been established in CONTROL, the ACIA immediately starts looking for input characters in the prescribed format.

Like transmitted data, received data is double buffered. Incoming serial data is assembled and its format is checked in the RCV SR shift register. Once a complete character has been assembled, it is transferred into RCV DATA, where the processor may read it at its leisure. In the meantime, RCV SR is available to assemble another incoming character. An "overrun" error occurs only if the processor fails to read the character presently in RCV DATA before a second character is completely assembled in RCV SR.

In general, the CPU can determine that a new character is present in RCV DATA by checking the Receiver Ready bit in STATUS. The ACIA sets Receiver Ready each time a new character appears in RCV DATA, and clears it each time the CPU reads RCV DATA.

C.3.5 Status Port

Input/output programs can test the bits in the ACIA's STATUS port to determine if operations have been completed and if any errors have occurred.

Bit 1 of STATUS is the Transmitter Ready bit. The ACIA sets this bit on reset and whenever XMT DATA is empty, indicating that the CPU may write XMT DATA with a character for the ACIA to transmit. The ACIA clears this bit when the CPU writes a new character into XMT DATA. (The bit is also forced to 0 if the CTS input is inactive. The CTS and DCD modem control inputs and status bits are discussed later.)

Likewise, bit 0 indicates Receiver Ready when set; RCV DATA now contains a new character that a program may read. This bit is cleared on reset and whenever the CPU reads RCV DATA. (The bit is also forced to 0 if the DCD input is inactive.)

Three possible receiving errors are indicated by bits 4–6 of STATUS. The Framing Error bit is set if a received character does not have the proper number of stop bits (i.e., if a space is detected in the serial input during the stop-bit time). Parity Error is set if the received serial input does not have the proper parity. Both of these bits are updated each time the ACIA puts a new received character into RCV DATA. An Overrun Error is set if one or more additional characters are received before the CPU reads the character presently in RCV DATA. This bit is cleared each time the CPU reads RCV DATA.

Bit 7 of STATUS is 1 if either the transmitter section or the receiver section of the ACIA has placed an interrupt request on the IRQ output. An interrupt request is made if the transmitter or receiver interrupt has been enabled and the corresponding Ready bit in STATUS is 1. (An interrupt request is also made if an active-to-inactive transition is detected on DCD.)

C.3.6   Modem Control Lines

In addition to the serial data input and output lines, the ACIA has three *modem control lines* that may be used to indicate or detect certain conditions when the ACIA is connected to a modem. The RTS (Request To Send) output from the ACIA to the modem is intended to indicate that the ACIA would like to send characters to the modem. If the modem has established a connection to another modem and it is in a state in which it can transmit characters, it responds to RTS by activating the CTS (Clear to Send) ACIA input signal.

The ACIA will not set the Transmitter Ready bit in STATUS while the CTS input signal is inactive. Thus, RTS and CTS form a "handshake" by which a modem or other device can prevent the ACIA from sending characters until it is ready for them. For example, the modem can prevent data transmission until a valid telephone connection has been established. The CTS bit in STATUS equals 1 whenever the CTS input signal is inactive.

The DCD (Data Carrier Detect) ACIA input signal is intended to be connected to a modem output signal that indicates that the modem has detected the presence of another modem capable of transmitting to it from the far end. The DCD bit in STATUS is set to 1 whenever the DCD input signal changes from active to inactive. This event causes an interrupt request to be placed on the ACIA's IRQ output. The DCD status bit is not cleared until the CPU reads STATUS and RCV DATA or resets the ACIA. This convention is useful in telephone links in which a program would like to detect a loss of the received signal, for example, if the far-end party hangs up.

When the ACIA is connected directly to a terminal without going through a modem, the dispositions of the modem control leads are system dependent. Quite often the CTS and DCD ACIA inputs are connected to be always active, and the RTS output is unused.

Many inexpensive printers and other devices may accept data at speeds as high as 19.2 Kbps (approximately 2000 characters per second), even though they can only physically process much lower data rates, say 100 characters per second. Such a printer accepts data at the higher speed and places it in an internal buffer until the buffer becomes full. It also has an output signal that indicates that the printer's input buffer is full. By connecting this signal to CTS, the user can automatically prevent the ACIA from transmitting additional characters until some of the previous characters have been physically printed and there is once again room in the buffer.

GENERAL INDEX

SPECIAL INDEXES

This is a set of indexes for Pascal and for each of the processors described in Chapter 5 and Part 3. Space limitations prevent us from indexing all of the machine instructions and pseudo-operations of every processor. "Generic" instructions similar to specific machine instructions may be found in the General Index. Complete lists of instructions for each processor are given in the text as the processors are introduced.

PASCAL

AND operator, 31
Arithmetic operators, 29–31
ARRAY declaration, 35, 54
Arrays, 53–59
Assignment statement, 19, 35–36

Badd function, 99–100, 231, 655
Band function, 231, 655
Bcom function, 101, 231, 654
Bint function, 654
Bit arrays, 651–657
Bits function, 654
BEGIN, 19, 26, 39
Block structure, 19–21
Block, 25–26, 263–264
Boolean expressions, 29, 31–32
boolean type, 29, 31–32, 34
Bor function, 231, 655
Bshl function, 100, 104, 246–247, 655
Bshr function, 98–100, 246–247, 655
Bxor function, 101, 231, 655

Capitalization of identifiers, 24
CASE statement, 35, 46–49
char type, 31
Character ordering, 34
Comment, 24
Compiler, 10, 19, 28, 32, 35, 45, 56, 62, 70, 264
Compound statement, 19–20, 26, 39–40

Concurrent Pascal, 366
Condition, 40
CONST definition, 27
Constants, 27–28, 30, 31
COROUTINE, pseudo-declaration, 290

Data structures, 32, 52–79
Declarations, 19, 24–29
DIV operator, 30, 31
DO, 42–44
DOWNTO, 43

ELSE, 40
Empty statement, 35, 40
END, 19, 26, 39
Enumerated types 32–34, 46
EXIT statement, 46, 77–78, 243
Expressions, 29–32, 267
Extended Pascal, 98–100, 121, 124, 132–134, 231, 650–657
  addition, 99–100, 655–656
  shifts, 98–100, 246–247, 655

false constant, 31
File handling, 19, 26
FOR statement, 19, 42–45
Forward references, 264, 286, 290
FUNCTION declaration, 29
Functions, 20–21, 24, 28, 267–268

Global items, 21, 264–265
GOTO statement 19, 27, 36, 43, 46, 77–78, 243

Identifiers, 23–24
IF statement, 40–42, 46

HYPOTHETICAL H6809

HYPOTHETICAL H8000

HYPOTHETICAL H11

DEC PDP-11 AND LSI-11

MOTOROLA 68000

MOTOROLA 6809

INTEL 8086

INTEL MCS-48 FAMILY